The Spanish Craze

꧁ THE ꧂

SPANISH
CRAZE

America's Fascination with the
Hispanic World, 1779–1939

RICHARD L. KAGAN

University of Nebraska Press ꧂ Lincoln

Portions of chapter 2 are adapted from ideas originally
expressed in "The Invention of Junípero Serra and the Spanish
Craze," in *The Worlds of Junípero Serra: Historical Contexts
and Cultural Representations*, ed. Steven W. Hackel (Oakland:
University California Press for the Huntington-usc Institute
and Huntington Library, 2017) and "Florida's Discovery of
Spain," in *La Florida: Five Hundred Years of Hispanic Presence*,
ed. Viviana Díaz Balsera and Rachel A. May (Gainesville:
University Press of Florida, 2014). Portions of chapter 4 are
adapted from ideas originally expressed in "The Spanish Craze
in the United States: Cultural Entitlement and the Appropriation
of Spain's Cultural Patrimony, ca. 1890–ca. 1930," *Revista
Complutense de Historia de América* 36 (2010): 37–58.

Library of Congress Cataloging-in-Publication Data
Names: Kagan, Richard L., 1943– author.
Title: The Spanish craze: America's fascination with the
Hispanic world, 1779–1939 / Richard L. Kagan.
Description: Lincoln: University of Nebraska Press, [2019] |
Includes bibliographical references and index.
Identifiers: LCCN 2018032362
ISBN 9781496207722 (cloth: alk. paper)
ISBN 9781496211132 (epub)
ISBN 9781496211149 (mobi)
ISBN 9781496211156 (pdf)
Subjects: LCSH: United States—Civilization—Spanish
influences. | United States—Civilization—Hispanic influences.
| Spain—Foreign public opinion, American—History. | United
States—Relations—Spain. | Spain—Relations—United States.
Classification: LCC E169.1 .K215 2019 | DDC 327.73046—dc23 LC
record available at https://lccn.loc.gov/2018032362

Set in Fournier MT Pro by Mikala R. Kolander.

For Jonathan Brown
colleague, mentor, friend

Contents

List of Illustrations ix

Acknowledgments xv

Introduction: The Spanish Fever 1

1. Rival Empires 27

2. Sturdy Spain 83

3. Sunny Spain 133

4. Hispanism, *Hispanismo*, and
   the Hispanic Society of America 169

5. Collectors and Collecting 231

6. "Castles in Spain Made Real" 305

7. The Spanish Blaze 371

   Conclusion: The "Back-and-
   Forth" Style 441

   Epilogue 461

   Notes 469

   Bibliography 525

   Index 573

Illustrations

MAPS

1. Map of Spain, 1900   5

2. Adams-Onís Treaty map of 1818   51

FIGURES

1. Anders Zorn, *Augustus Saint-Gaudens*, 1897   2

2. *La Carmencita*, 1894   7

3. Henry Adams, 1883   30

4. *His Excellency John Jay, President of Congress & Minister Plenipotentiary from Congress at Madrid*, 1783   38

5. Luis de Onís, ca. 1821   43

6. Pierre Soulé, minister to Spain, 1853   56

7. Charles Dana Gibson cartoon, "Come, Let's Forgive and Forget," 1898   67

8. Daniel H. Burnham and Lorado Taft, Columbus Memorial Fountain, 1912   84

9. William H. Prescott   94

10. Ponce de León celebration program, St. Augustine   102

11. Tertio-Millennial Celebration, Santa Fe, 1883   112

12. Cover page for an album of photographs, *The Home of Ramona*, 1888   119

13. John W. Combs, Father Serra monument, ca. 1897   122

14. Charles F. Lummis, 1897   124

15. Constantino Brumidi, *The Burial of Hernando de Soto*, ca. 1870–80   131

16. Washington Irving, ca. 1855–60   139

17. Title page illustration for *The Alhambra*, 1851 edition   149

18. J. Laurent and Company, interior of the gallery and west pavilion of the Court of the Lions, Alhambra, Granada, 1871   151

19. Title page, John L. Stoddard, *Red-Letter Days Abroad*, 1883   154

20. Thomas Eakins, "San Bernardo" Spanish sketchbook, 1870   156

21. Charles S. Reinhart, *A Mandurra Solo*   161

22. E. C. Potter, equestrian statue of De Soto, 1904   166

23. William H. Rau, *Spanish Students on the Streets of Seville*, 1904   166

24. Henry Wadsworth Longfellow, self-portrait en route from Málaga to Granada, 1828   171

25. *El Jaleo de Jeres (The New Cachucha), with Fanny Elssler*, playbill, 1840   180

26. Infanta Eulalia de Borbón, ca. 1893   185

27. Miguel de Unamuno with Federico de Onís and Licinio Perdigón, 1905   195

28. Archer Milton Huntington in Spain, 1892   205

29. Carolina "La Belle" Otero, ca. 1890   208

30. Charles W. Hawthorne, *Georgiana Goddard King*, 1905   224

31. Joaquín Sorolla exhibition, Hispanic Society of America, New York, 1909   226

32. Diego Velázquez and Workshop, *King Philip IV of Spain*, ca. 1626–28   232

33. Bartolomé de Murillo, *Vision of St. Anthony of Padua*, 1656   240

34. Robert Lamborn Collection, ca. 1890   255

35. El Greco (and Workshop?), *Crucifixion*, ca. 1610   257

36. Patio de la Fonda de Madrid, Seville   262

37. The Spanish Chapel, Fenway Court, Boston, ca. 1926   265

38. Vélez Blanco patio, ca. 1920   271

39. Joaquín Sorolla y Bastida, *¡Otra Margarita!*, 1892   276

40. Maricel de Mar, Sitges, Spain   278

41. Golden Room, Maricel, ca. 1915   279

42. Panoramic view of Hearst's Enchanted Hill, ca. 1930   289

43. William R. Hearst, Arthur Byne, and others in Toledo, Spain, ca. 1924   294

44. Cloister, Sacramenia monastery, Segovia, Spain, and reconstructed in Miami, Florida   296

45. Choir screen, Valladolid Cathedral, Spain, 1763   299

46. William Ward Watkin, architect, Administration

Building, Texas Tech University, 1924 311

47. Thomas W. Hastings, architect, Ponce de León Hotel, St. Augustine, 1887 313

48. Thomas Moran, *Ponce de León in Florida*, 1877–78 315

49. Stanford White, architect, Tower of Madison Square Garden, New York, 1890 319

50. Augustus Saint-Gaudens, *Diana*, Madison Square Garden, New York, 1890 320

51. A. Page Brown, architect, Ferry Building, San Francisco, 1906 323

52. A. Page Brown, architect, California State Building, Chicago, 1893 324

53. Arthur Benton and Myron Hunt, architects, Old Adobe, Glenwood–Mission Inn, Riverside, California, ca. 1920 327

54. John Galen Howard, architect, Electric Tower, Pan-American Exposition, Buffalo, New York, 1901 329

55. Bertram G. Goodhue, architect, California State Building, Panama-California Exposition, San Diego, 1915 334

56. William Mooser III (with J. Wilmer Hershey),

architect, Santa Barbara County Courthouse, Santa Barbara, California, 1929 338

57. Edward Eichenbaum, architect, Granada Theatre, Chicago, 1926 341

58. "Follow the Golden Galleon" promotional poster for Coral Gables, 1925 343

59. View of the Everglades Club from Lake Worth–Palm Beach, ca. 1928 346

60. Addison Mizner, architect, El Mirasol, Palm Beach, 1919 348

61. "The Barcelona," advertisement for a Montgomery Ward Wardway home, 1930 353

62. Palace of the Governors, Santa Fe, New Mexico, 1890 354

63. Palace of the Governors, Santa Fe, New Mexico, after 1911 354

64. Isaac H. Rapp, architect, Scottish Rite temple, Santa Fe, New Mexico, 1914 356

65. Warren & Wetmore, architects, Eagle's Nest, Centerport, Long Island, ca. 1926 359

66. "Shores of Seville" advertisement, *Brooklyn Daily Eagle*, 1926 361

67. Edward Buehler Delk, architect, Country Club Plaza, Kansas City, Missouri, 1930   363

68. Edwin H. Clark, Plaza del Lago, Wilmette, Illinois, 1927   364

69. D. Paul Witmer, architect, Castilian Court, Hershey Hotel, Hershey, Pennsylvania, 1934   366

70. Addison Mizner, architect, La Ronda, Bryn Mawr, Pennsylvania   368

71. *The Land of Joy* playbill, 1916   373

72. Raquel Meller, *Time* magazine, 1926   375

73. Movie poster for *Gypsy Blood*, starring Pola Negri, 1921   379

74. Charles F. Lummis, *Spanish Songs of Old California* songbook cover, 1923   383

75. Playbill for *Spanish Love* at Maxine Elliott's Theatre, New York, 1920   386

76. Sheet music for "In a Little Spanish Town," 1926   387

77. *Ramona* movie poster, 1928   391

78. *Don Q, Son of Zorro* movie poster, 1925   394

79. *Blood and Sand* movie poster, 1922   396

80. William Dean Howells, 1903   405

81. Gertrude Stein, ca. 1930   411

82. Playbill for the film *The Spanish Earth*, 1937   422

83. and 84. Postcard from Ernest Hemingway in Pamplona, Spain, to Gertrude Stein and Alice B. Toklas, 1924   436

85. Original book jacket, Ernest Hemingway, *Death in the Afternoon*, 1932   438

86. Rafael Doménech, *La Casa del Greco*, 1911   445

87. Patio of a house in the Barrio de Santa Cruz, Seville, ca. 1920   453

88. William Templeton Johnson, architect, former U.S. consulate, Seville, 1928   460

89. Medallions, former U.S. consulate, Seville   460

PLATES

Following page 300

1. William H. Powell, *Hernando de Soto Discovers the Mississippi River*, 1847

2. Samuel Colman, *Hill of the Alhambra*, 1865

3. John Singer Sargent, *El Jaleo*, 1881

4. Francisco de Zurbarán, *A Doctor of Law at Salamanca*, ca. 1635

5. Sir Gerald Kelly, *Henry C. Frick in the West Gallery*, 1925

6. George Washington Smith, Casa del Herrero, Montecito, California, 1925

7. Daniel Sayre Groesbeck, Spanish colonial history mural at the Santa Barbara County Courthouse, Santa Barbara, California, 1929

8. *Loves of Carmen* movie poster, 1927

Acknowledgments

Ten years ago, shortly after having presented a lecture on the collecting of Spanish Old Master art in the United States, I asked my friend and colleague Jonathan Brown a simple question: "Jonathan, do you think it's worth expanding my talk in a book?" Never one to mince words, Jonathan responded, "Go for it." For this reason—and there are many others I could add—I am dedicating this book to Jonathan, arguably the world's premier specialist in the art history of both Spain and its empire.

Jonathan apart, many others, far more than I can remember, have helped make this book possible. The list begins with the archivists and librarians at various institutions who assisted my research. In North America these institutions include the Art Institute of Chicago; Avery Library, Columbia University; Bancroft Library, University of California, Berkeley; Museum of Fine Arts, Boston; Braun Research Library, Los Angeles; Rhys Carpenter Library, Bryn Mawr College; Casa del Herrero, Montecito, California (where Robert Sweeney made a special trip to assist with my research); Charles Deering Library, Northwestern University; Deering Estate, Cutler, Florida; Four Arts Society, Palm Beach, Florida; Frick Art Reference Library, New York; Hispanic Society of America (there John O'Neill, Patrick Lenaghan, and the director, Mitchell Codding, deserve a special expression of thanks); Houghton Library, Harvard University; Kennedy Library, California Polytechnic State University; Library of Congress; Milton S. Eisenhower Library, Johns Hopkins University; Metropolitan Museum of Art, New York; Royal Ontario Museum, Toronto; the New-York Historical Society; Philadelphia Museum of Art; Rauner Library, Dartmouth College; Shelburne Museum, Shelburne, New Hampshire; Southwest Collection, Texas Tech University; Stirling Library, Yale University; Fray Angélico

Chávez History Library, Santa Fe, New Mexico; George A. Smathers Libraries, University of Florida; Special Collections, University of Miami Libraries; Van Pelt Library, University of Pennsylvania; Architectural and Design Collection, AD&A Museum, University of California, Santa Barbara; and West Palm Beach Historical Society, West Palm Beach, Florida. I am equally grateful for the assistance provided by the staff in various Spanish repositories. They include the Archivo General de la Administración in Alcalá de Henares, Barcelona's Casa de América, and in Madrid the Archivo de Ministerio de Asuntos Extranjeros (now part of Archivo Histórico Nacional), Archivo General de Palacio Real, Museo de Romanticismo, Museo del Prado, Museo Sorolla (especially its director, Consuelo Luca de Tena), and the Real Academia de la Historia.

I am equally indebted to numerous colleagues and friends who offered both assistance and encouragement as this project progressed. In Spain they include James Amelang, Patricia Fernández Lorenzo, Sylvia Hilton, Fernando Marías, José Antonio Montero, Benito Navarrete, Andrés Sánchez Padilla, Inmaculada Socías, and Ignacio Zuloaga and, in the United States, Daniela Bleichmar, Jesús Escobar, Steven Hackel, Michael Johnson, Susan Larson, Geoffrey Parker, Teófilo Ruiz, Louise Stein, Nicolás Wey Gómez, and David Van Zanten (who generously served as my tour guide to Spanish-style houses and shopping centers in Wilmette, Illinois). Rounding up illustrations for this volume was a far greater challenge than I had expected, and here I wish to acknowledge the invaluable assistance provided by Escardiel González, Ted Goldsborough of the Lower Merion (Pennsylvania) Historical Society, Thomas Hensle, Catherine Larkin, Rebecca Long, Benito Navarrete, John Pollack, Michael Seneca, Elizabeth Sudduth, and Tanya Tiffany, along with Andrea Gottschalk, who prepared the maps included in the introduction and chapter 1.

My thinking about the genesis and development of this volume has also been shaped by the many helpful comments and criticisms provided by various audiences who attended my talks and seminars relating to the "Spanish craze." I am afraid that the names of most of the individual questioners escape me, but the institutions and conference organizers that offered me an opportunity to speak about the subject include Brown University; California Institute of Technology; Getty Research

Institute; Johns Hopkins University; New York University's Institute of Fine Arts; Northwestern University; Texas Tech University; University of Barcelona; University of Miami; William & Mary University; University of California, San Diego (where Pamela Radcliffe rightly suggested that romanticism alone does not account for Spain's image in the United States); the Association of Spanish and Portuguese History, annual meeting in Ottawa, 2013; the College Art Association, annual meeting in 2015 (where I presented a paper on Charles Deering); and Yale University.

I am particularly grateful for the comments provided by the two initially anonymous readers—M. Elizabeth Boone and John M. Nieto-Phillips—who evaluated this manuscript for the University of Nebraska Press; my editor, Matthew Bokovoy, who helped shape this project almost from the inception; Heather Stauffer, who skillfully guided this volume through the early stages of the editorial process; Elizabeth Zaleski (in-house project editor); and Maureen Creamer Bemko (freelancer), my copyeditor and fact-checker extraordinaire.

Finally, my gratitude to my beloved wife and scholar-in-arms, Marianna Shreve Simpson, knows no bounds. Without her patience, editorial skills, and steadfast support this book could never have been completed. As for Roxy, our late lamented cat, may she posthumously accept my apologies for having regularly ignored her plaintive cries for attention over the many years *The Spanish Craze* took shape.

The Spanish Craze

Introduction

The Spanish Fever

The journey we took with its enthusiasms and experiences is
the one that has been written about so frequently and remarkably,
and on it we were promptly infected with what Sargent
has told me we would be taken by, namely the fever of Spain—
"La Fièvre Espagnole." —AUGUSTUS SAINT-GAUDENS,
Reminiscences, referring to his trip to Spain in 1899

The winter of 1899 was not an especially auspicious moment for any American tourist to visit Spain. Just a year earlier Americans and Spaniards had been shooting at and killing one another on Cuba's San Juan Hill. Fortunately that war ended in a matter of months, and in December 1898 the two countries signed a peace treaty en route to restoring the diplomatic relations that had been suspended at the start of the war the previous April. In the months that followed, relations between Madrid and Washington also improved to the point where regular steamship service, via Catalonia's Compañía Transatlántica, resumed between Barcelona, Cádiz, and New York.

Even so, resentments lingered. Spanish newspapers reporting on Central America and the ongoing insurrection against U.S. forces in the Philippines were quick to highlight "Agresión Yankee." Similarly, *Harper's Pictorial History of the War with Spain*, published in 1899, pointedly reminded readers about the "inner core of cruelty" that all Spaniards shared.[1]

None of this deterred America's most prominent sculptor, Augustus Saint-Gaudens, from visiting Spain in the fall of 1899. Two years

Fig. 1. During his visit to Spain, Augustus Saint-Gaudens followed an itinerary suggested by his friend, the painter John Singer Sargent. Anders Zorn, *Augustus Saint-Gaudens*, 1897, etching, 7½ × 5 ⅛ in. Gift of Herschel V. Jones, 1916, P.5.382, William M. Ladd Collection, Minneapolis Institute of Art. Photo: Minneapolis Institute of Art.

earlier, at the apogee of his career, Saint-Gaudens had embarked from New York with his family for an extended European stay. His immediate destination was Paris, where years earlier he had enrolled as a student in the famed École des Beaux-Arts. But Saint-Gaudens was especially keen on visiting Spain, a country that two of his artist friends, William Merritt Chase and John Singer Sargent, had long urged him to see. Sargent even supplied him with a detailed itinerary listing the cities and the important monuments and museums he could not afford to miss.[2]

The trip began in November, and as Saint-Gaudens later recalled, he was "traveling fast," although not fast enough to avoid lingering in a small mountain village in Aragon, to visit the El Escorial monastery, and to make stops at Burgos, Madrid, and Toledo before heading south to Andalucia. Once there he visited Muslim monuments in both Córdoba and Seville, and in Granada he even found the time to attend a bullfight. Most American travelers who witnessed a *corrida* reacted with a mixture of disgust and disdain, coupled with comments on the innate cruelty of the Spanish race. In contrast, when Saint-Gaudens reminisced about the event, he emphasized the artistry and dignity of the ritual unfolding before his eyes, together with the courage of everyone involved, including the bull.

The sculptor's positive reaction to Spain defies easy explanation. Other tourists who had visited the country generally found something to complain about—the quality of the food, the difficulty of travel, the lack of accommodations comparable in quality to those they encountered elsewhere in Europe. But in his *Reminiscences* Saint-Gaudens confessed that upon entering the country he was almost immediately stricken by the mysterious ailment known as "Spanish fever," which Sargent had previously warned him about. The malady was not to be found in any medical book, nor was it related to the killer "Spanish flu" that devastated so much of the world in the immediate aftermath of World War I. But its symptoms, among them a seemingly insatiable appetite for the art and culture of Spain, were real and occasionally morphed into *hispanophilia*, a related ailment, albeit one far more common in France and Great Britain than the United States. So it was that Saint-Gaudens, writing four years after his visit to Spain, freely admitted, "I have become insatiable about that fascinating land and my interest in it never flags."[3]

Saint-Gaudens was far from the only American to be affected by this unusual ailment. As this book will explain, the Spanish fever—I will also refer to it as a craze—morphed into an epidemic in the aftermath of the war of 1898, spreading rapidly across the vast expanse of the United States and infecting taste in numerous domains, especially in art and architecture but also in music, theater, cinema, and literature, along with fashion and, to a more limited degree, food. This fascination with Spain was virtually unprecedented. With the exception of popular music, in which the guitar and Spanish rhythms had long proved influential, throughout most of the nineteenth century the influence of Spanish culture in the United States was minimal at best. Well into the Gilded Age the chief markers of American taste and refinement, as Richard Bushman and Lawrence Levine have both observed, were customarily English or French. Italian culture had a place in both music and art, and during the 1880s, thanks in large part to Wagner, a German repertoire dominated opera in New York and other cities.[4]

Spain, by contrast, barely made a dent in America's elite culture, and Spanish, especially when compared to French, was rarely studied, let alone taught. At work here too were long-standing prejudices that belittled the value of Spanish culture. Archer Milton Huntington, future founder of New York's Hispanic Society of America, learned this lesson in 1891 after telling the prominent financier Morris Ketchum Jesup about his interest in Spain's literature and art. Jesup promptly rebuked the young man for wasting his time on a "dead and gone civilization."[5]

Jesup's criticism neatly summarized the attitude of most upper-crust Americans toward Spain and Spaniards alike, but change was under way. As Kristin Hoganson has observed, in the course of the Gilded Age a rapidly expanding economy, together with the growth of foreign trade, brought new interest in foreign cultures most Americans knew little about.[6] This new, more cosmopolitan spirit found different outlets, among them a growing demand for books and travelogues dealing with faraway lands, the formation of reading circles and travel clubs whose members embarked on imagined journeys abroad, together with attendance at

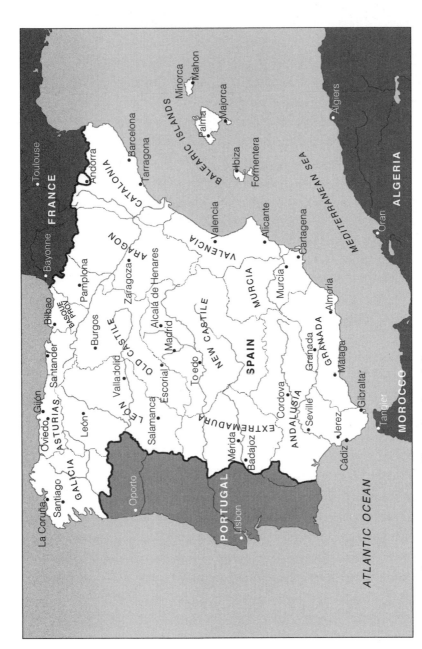

Map 1. Map of Spain, 1900. Prepared by Andrea Gottschalk.

illustrated travel lectures—those offered by John Stoddard in different cities are said to have attracted a public numbering in the millions. Stoddard's lectures did not necessarily focus solely on Spain—other topics included Germany and Russia, along with Egypt, China, and Japan—but his repertoire of talks often began with his "Travels in Sunny Spain."

Nor was Stoddard alone. Starting in the 1880s travel writers and their publishers provided readers with a steady stream of new books and articles touting the "romance" of Spain. Part of that romance was linked to Carmen, the gypsy featured in Bizet's famous opera, and also to La Carmencita, a Spanish flamenco dancer who, starting in 1890, delighted audiences in New York, Washington, Chicago, and other cities and whose whirls and kicks Thomas Alva Edison managed to capture in one of the first motion pictures ever filmed in the United States. Interest in Spain and its culture also derived from Chicago's immensely popular World's Columbian Exposition of 1893, which, in keeping with the four-hundredth anniversary of Columbus's momentous voyage, introduced millions of visitors to the historic links uniting Spain's history with that of the United States. Meanwhile the start of pan-Americanism, a movement emphasizing hemispheric unity, fomented new interest in the history and culture of Spanish-speaking countries south of the Rio Grande, especially Mexico. The tilt toward Spain momentarily ended with the onset of the Spanish-American War but resumed shortly thereafter. Within a few years the craze for Spain and its culture was hitting its stride.

Most infected were those regions—California, Texas, New Mexico, Florida—formerly subject to Spanish colonial rule. But early and quite serious flare-ups occurred in Chicago, New York, and other parts of the country where Spaniards had never made their presence felt. In contrast, New England, protected by its British traditions, remained relatively immune to the fever's spread, although, as we shall see, the region counted its share of victims as well.

The effects of the fever were not equally felt. As with all fevers, the ailment infected some individuals more than others. Especially hard hit were men of letters, one of the first being the Boston book dealer Obadiah Rich (1777–1850), a specialist in the early history of the Americas, an avid collector of rare Spanish books and manuscripts, and the first foreigner ever granted permission to do research in Spain's "secret" national archives at Simancas.[7]

Rich also shouldered part of the responsibility for passing the disease on to Washington Irving (1783–1859). The two met in Madrid during the winter of 1826. Irving had journeyed to the Spanish capital at the invitation of Alexander Hill Everett (1792–1847), a Boston man of letters who had been appointed U.S. minister to Spain in 1825. Everett was hoping to persuade Irving to translate some recently published documents relating to Christopher Columbus and to Spain's early discoveries in the New World, and he subsequently introduced him to Rich, then serving as the delegation's secretary. Irving's decision to travel to Spain was somewhat unusual. Apart from diplomats, consuls, and merchant seamen, few Americans ventured to Spain. The country's seemingly chronic political instability kept them away. So too did its reputation for being a country where travelers were likely to fall prey to bandits and thieves. But Irving was not one to be put off, in part because, living in Paris since 1824, he had already begun to learn Spanish. He therefore jumped at Everett's invitation, and in January 1826 he arrived in Madrid prepared to embark on the project Everett had proposed. But after having immersed himself in Rich's vast library of old Spanish books, he abandoned the translation project and decided instead to write a full-fledged biography of Columbus. Writing for the next two years at a breakneck pace, Irving published his path-

Fig. 2. *La Carmencita*, 1894. Carmencita was in New York for a music hall performance when Thomas Edison filmed her at his Black Maria Studio in New Jersey in 1894. She was the first woman Edison ever filmed. Courtesy Library of Congress.

breaking *The Life and Voyages of Christopher Columbus* in February 1828 and, just a year later, *A Chronicle of the Conquest of Granada* under the pen name of a fictitious Spanish monk, Fray Antonio Agapida. At this point Irving embarked on an extended journey to Andalucia in southern Spain, residing in Granada as well as Seville before finally departing for England during the fall of 1829.

It is not exactly clear when or where during the course of his three years in Spain Irving succumbed to the ailment Sargent later described, although it is likely to have occurred in March 1828, when, having left the high central plateau of Castile, he first caught a glimpse of the lush, rolling fields of Andalucia. The vista sparked this comment: "a country like a historic map—full of history and romance, where the Moors and Christians have fought." Upon reaching Granada and residing for a time within the precincts of that city's medieval Muslim fortress known as the Alhambra (meaning "red fort"), Irving wrote letters suggesting that his symptoms approximated those that Saint-Gaudens would later describe. "Granada," he explained, was not only "beautiful and picturesque" but a "city of Romantic history": "Every mountain in this country spreads before you a mass of history filled with places renowned for some wild and heroic event." Once in Seville, Irving's readiness to describe Andalucians as a "gallant and elegant" people suggests that the fever had advanced to a full-fledged bout of Hispanophilia that continued to influence his attitude toward both Spain and its people for the remainder of his life.[8]

Irving's sympathy for Spain was especially apparent in his book *The Alhambra: A Series of Tales and Sketches of the Moors and Spaniards*, an instant best seller following its initial publication in 1832. Those tales and sketches, typically Irving, offered a fictionalized view of both Spain and its people and in doing so added a bit of light to the then prevalent Anglo-American view of Spain as a dark, sinister, almost gothic country ruled by tyrannical monarchs and fanatical priests, and of Spaniards as a people synonymous with cruelty, rapaciousness, and greed. That image of the country is now integral to the "Black Legend," a term popularized in 1914 by the Spanish historian Julián Juderías to refer to anti-Catholic Protestant propaganda that began circulating during the age of religious wars. The propagandists, using Fray Bartolomé de Las Casas's polemical treatise *A Brief History of the Destruction of the Indies* (1552) as their principal source, managed to craft a wholly negative image of Spain that endured for centuries.[9] Edgar Allan Poe adroitly captured the essence of that legend in "The Pit and Pendulum" (1842), a terrifying short story that recounted the sufferings of a hapless prisoner in "the grasp of the Inquisition."[10] Irving, by contrast, served up the image of "Sunny Spain," representing it as a light-hearted, quasi-Oriental country that was charming, hospitable, and, most important, relentlessly romantic and picturesque. In other words, he pictured it as a must-see for any American with the wherewithal to travel abroad.

Sunny Spain was a land of castles, dashing caballeros, gypsy dancers, and hardy peasants garbed in traditional dress. The Sunny Spain idea proved infectious, and in this respect Irving's role in the spread of the Spanish fever was roughly analogous to that of Mary Mallon, aka Typhoid Mary, the Irish immigrant (wrongly) credited for triggering the lethal typhoid fever epidemic that ravaged New York in 1906. The Spanish fever was not nearly as dangerous as typhoid, but it did not take long before other writers, friends, and acquaintances of Irving came down with the disease. Among the first was Henry Wadsworth Longfellow (1807–82), who, following his visit to the country in 1827, penned a series of poems and plays touching on Spanish themes.

Other nineteenth-century writers who also embraced both Spain and its culture included George Ticknor (1791–1871), Harvard's first professor of modern languages and the author of a comprehensive survey of Spanish literature; Walt Whitman (1819–92), a self-confessed Columbus addict who highlighted the importance of what he termed the "Spanish element" in America's national character in an important essay published in 1883; Helen Hunt Jackson (1830–85), whose best-selling novel *Ramona*, first published in 1884 and still in print today, awakened new interest in the Spanish role in the history of California and other parts of the Southwest; and Charles F. Lummis (1859–1928), the so-called Apostle of the South West. Lummis's *Spanish Pioneers*, first printed in 1893, helped lay the foundation for the so-called White Legend, or the idea of Spain as the standard-bearer of civilization, religion, and progress in the New World.[11]

By this time a whole series of artists had caught the same fever that Saint-Gaudens was later to catch. The contagion for them stemmed partly from Irving but also from David Roberts (1796–1864), the Scottish Romantic artist whose widely published engravings of the Alhambra and Spain's other "Moorish" monuments did much to fan the growing artistic fascination with the "picturesque." These monuments also served to "orientalize" Spain, adding to the country's image as an exotic nation inhabited exclusively by picturesque types that ranged from bandits and bullfighters to flamenco dancers, gypsies, and noblemen stereotypically cast as dashing Don Juans. The prospect of painting such characters had special appeal for the New York artist Samuel Colman (1832–1920), who first journeyed to Spain in 1861 and whose picturesque images of Andalucia found a ready market in New York and other American cities. Hard on Colman's heels were other artists, especially those who had trained in Paris and were familiar with the work of Édouard Manet (1832–83), arguably the first modern painter influenced by the art and technique of Velázquez, the great Spanish master of the seventeenth century. Manet's passion for Velázquez subsequently passed undiminished to an entire generation of U.S. artists that included Thomas Eakins, John Singer Sargent, and William Merritt Chase, all of whom, especially Sargent and Chase, exhibited signs of the same fever that later infected Saint-Gaudens. Mary Cassatt (1844–1926) was yet another American artist with interest in Spain—she first ventured there in 1872—although she proved more resilient to the Hispanophilia that the *fièvre espagnole* was known to produce. That resilience, however, did not prevent Cassatt from developing a keen appreciation for Spanish art, especially pictures by El Greco and Goya. Starting around 1900, Cassatt also assumed the role of a dealer, actively promoting the work of these and other Spanish artists among her American friends and patrons.

As might be expected, the propaganda campaign that characterized the immediate run-up to the war of 1898 brought a sudden halt to Spain's growing appeal in the United States. But whereas that short conflict temporarily succeeded in slowing the fever's spread, it paradoxically created the conditions that sparked a renewed, even stronger, more virulent outbreak in the years that followed. Much in the same way that nineteenth-century Americans had previously embraced and romanticized the so-called "vanquished" or "vanishing Indian," they did the same with their newly defeated foe. A similar embrace had momentarily occurred in 1822, less than a year after Spain, in accordance with the Transcontinental Treaty of 1821, ceded Florida to the United States. It was then that the territory's first governor, William P. DuVal, informed Pres. James Monroe, "The Spanish inhabitants of this country are the *best* even among the most quiet and orderly of our own citizens."[12] More of this kind of thinking occurred after the war of 1898, when Spain, no longer a threat let alone a rival to American interests in the Caribbean, became a country and a culture the United States could freely embrace.

That embrace enabled the fever that first infected Irving, as well as artists such as Sargent and Chase, to spread to Saint-Gaudens and then a new generation of writers who rose to prominence in the early years of the twentieth century. To be sure, there were some, Henry James, for example, who proved impervious to the disease. In contrast, Edith Wharton, having visited Spain on several occasions prior to 1914, found the country both "soothing" and "exhilarating," and in one letter she announced that the mountain monastery of Monserrat was "by far the most romantically and improbably beautiful thing" she knew.[13] Then there was Gertrude Stein, a writer for whom Spain practically became a second home during the course of World War I. Stein is generally associated with Paris, but she herself admitted that the city of Ávila— birthplace of Saint Teresa—served as the inspiration for her *Tender Buttons* (1914), one of her best-known literary creations. In her autobiography Stein confessed that "I am impartial on every subject except that of Spain and Spaniards."[14]

Next in the long line of American authors to fall prey to the disease was John Dos Passos, who first exhibited symptoms of Hispanophilia during his initial visit to Spain in 1916. Waldo Frank came next, quickly followed by Ernest Hemingway. He succumbed to the fever—and he caught it in spades—in 1923 following his first visit to Pamplona to attend the bullfights associated with that city's raucous festival of San Fermín.

The Spanish fever, though initially confined to artistic and literary circles, also infected various members of America's moneyed elite. In the

Gilded Age wealthy Americans prided themselves on their cosmopolitan tastes, building for themselves sprawling mansions modeled on European buildings of Renaissance design. These were then stuffed—crammed is another term—with pictures, furniture, tapestries, and miscellaneous bric-a-brac from various countries, especially England, Italy, the Low Countries, and France. Artifacts from China and Japan also found a place in these mansions, and more than one carried their understanding of cosmopolitanism into Asia and the Middle East by including a Turkish corner, sometimes even an entire Turkish room, ornately outfitted in "neo-Moorish" or "Oriental" style with rugs, mosque lamps, brass tables, and divans.

Singularly absent in these sumptuous dwellings were objects illustrative of the arts of Spain. When it came to pictures, for example, Murillo's Madonnas enjoyed a certain cachet, but otherwise most art critics and connoisseurs had little positive to say about Spanish art. Many were openly hostile, suggesting that there was something of the "faggot"—a reference to the Inquisition's practice of ordering unrepentant heretics to be burned at the stake—inherent in the religious paintings of the Spanish school, and one, James Jackson Jarves (1818–88), openly admitted, "We need not look for the poetical or imaginative in Spanish art."[15]

By the opening of the twentieth century, such hostility had passed. Wealthy collectors in Boston, Chicago, Philadelphia, and New York were competing with one another to purchase choice examples of pictures by Spanish Old Master artists—providing they could afford them. Works by Mariano Fortuny (1838–74), Spain's first modern painter to achieve international prominence, were also in demand, but most of the responsibility for triggering what amounted to a vogue for modern Spanish painting belonged to Joaquín Sorolla y Bastida (1863–1923), Spain's heralded "painter of light." That vogue is best exemplified by the huge crowds—more than 160,000 visitors in less than two months— who clamored to see the exhibition of Sorolla's pictures organized by New York's recently opened Hispanic Society of America in 1909. The Sorolla exhibition met with equal success in Buffalo and Chicago, and such was this artist's reputation that he was summoned to Washington in order to paint the portrait of President Taft.

But painting alone could not satisfy the cravings the Spanish fever had seemingly produced. At one extreme it sparked Archer Milton Huntington's desire to create a new institution, the Hispanic Society of America, designed to showcase the arts and cultures of the Ibero-American world. Almost equally hard hit by the affliction was Charles Deering, a wealthy Chicago industrialist who invested in not just one but two castles in Spain and then furnished them with a collection of Spanish artifacts that rivaled the one Huntington was amassing in New York.

Otherwise, interest in things Spanish was less of an affliction than a fashion, a vogue expressed in various media, including architecture, furniture, music, and film. The trendsetters included Henry Flagler, the developer who, starting in 1887, introduced Spanish-themed hotels to Florida, greeting guests with *bienvenida*—the Spanish word for welcome—etched into their entranceways; the New York architect Stanford White, who, starting in 1890, created a fashion by modeling the tower of the new Madison Square Garden after the Giralda, the famed bell tower of the cathedral of Seville; and Arthur Page Brown, who, starting with the California State Building at the World's Columbian Exposition in Chicago in 1893, helped to create a new style of building inspired by the white stucco walls and red-tile roofs of old Spanish missions found in California and other parts of the Southwest. Various iterations of this new style of building, generally known as Spanish colonial or Spanish revival architecture, soon spread to other parts of the United States and in doing so sparked a new and growing demand for grillwork, tiles, and furniture imported from both Mexico and Spain. And when imports proved insufficient to meet this demand, a number of enterprising architects, starting with Addison Mizner in Florida, established workshops that churned out replicas of these and other items of Spanish design.

The demand for such objects reached its peak in the 1920s, the decade during which the Spanish fever morphed into something closer to a pandemic. Much of that demand was restricted to the wealthy, but in the course of the decade Spanish-themed architecture was "democratized" to the extent that the sales catalogs of mass marketers such as Montgomery Ward and Sears Roebuck advertised building kits for inexpensive Spanish homes. The idea here is that anyone, whether in Nebraska, New York, or North Carolina, could have a personal version of a castle in Spain.

Yet the vogue for Spanish art, music, and other aspects of Spanish culture had surfaced well before then. As early as 1916 Gertrude Stein, then on a protracted visit to the Spanish Mediterranean island of Palma de Mallorca, wrote to a friend in New York about a Spanish newspaper that had reported on "Spain's peaceful revenge for the Spanish war [and] How music dress painting and everything in Yankilandia, as they poetically call [the] Us is dominated by Spain." That article anticipated another, published the following year in the Madrid newspaper *ABC*, noting that New Yorkers were dressing like Spaniards, eating *cocido* (a typical Spanish stew) and *paella*, and quaffing "vino de jerez." "Everything Spanish," the reporter added, "was all the rage. . . . We discovered America, and this is the moment when Americans have discovered us."[16]

What the reporter failed to mention was the new and seemingly unstoppable rush to learn Spanish, a foreign language that most educated Americans had previously shunned in favor of either German or French. This newfound interest in Spanish was partly driven by the opening of the Panama Canal in 1914 and, along with it, the growing awareness that Spanish America offered new and promising markets still to be tapped. It also paralleled newly awakened interest in the Hispanic origins of America's Southwest. But whatever the exact reason, high schools across the country registered a growing demand for Spanish lessons while colleges and universities added new courses in the history and literature of both Spain and Spanish America. No surprise then that a number of contemporary Spanish authors caught the attention of some prominent American critics, especially William Dean Howells (1837–1920), the so-called dean of American letters. In an essay published in *Harper's New Monthly Magazine* in 1915 Howells went so far as to announce, "Take the Spanish, and you have first-class modern fiction, easily surpassing the fiction of that of any other people of our time, now that the Russians have ceased to lead."[17]

Among Howells's favorite modern Spanish writers was Vicente Blasco Ibáñez, a novelist who rose to international prominence about the time of World War I. His *Four Horsemen of the Apocalypse*, translated into English in 1918, quickly found its way onto the best-seller charts, and together with his *Blood and Sand* (1919), a paean to bullfighting, it was soon made into a motion picture as well. The success of these films heralded others featuring Spanish themes, so it was no accident that the first talkie ever produced in the United States—it dates from 1923—featured a short routine by the Spanish flamenco dancer Concha Piquer, who was just then starring in a revue on Broadway. The film's producer, the De Forest Phonofilm Company, clearly sought to cash in on Piquer's reputation and success.

In the end the Spanish fever, as with most bodily fevers, proved evanescent. It flared up, infecting different people and different parts of the country in varying ways until the end of the 1920s, when, for reasons that this study will later address, it had run its course. But this ailment was far from unique. Since its inception in 1776, if not before, the United States, in the process of formulating a national culture of its own, regularly looked abroad for inspiration. The result: a series of crazes, among which the Spanish craze was only one. Others include the vogue for prints, wallpaper, and rooms of Japanese design unleashed by Japan's exhibit at the Centennial Exposition in Philadelphia in 1876 and reenergized following the first performance of Puccini's *Madame Butterfly* at New York's Metropolitan Opera in 1906; a Dutch craze, partially triggered by New York's Hudson-Fulton Celebration exhibition of 1909, which found expression in both art and design; an Indian or Native American craze that surfaced toward the end of the nineteenth century, one facet of which entailed the collecting of native artifacts and their display in domestic "Indian corners"; an Egyptomania unleashed by the opening of King Tut's tomb in 1922 but whose origins can be traced back to Napoleon's ill-fated expedition to Egypt in 1798 or, even earlier, to the fascination of Renaissance scholars with Egyptian hieroglyphs; and finally a Mexican craze that surfaced during the late 1920s and blossomed in the 1930s in conjunction with the announcement of Pres. Franklin Roosevelt's Good Neighbor policy of 1933, manifested in the popularity of works by such Mexican artists as José Clemente Orozco and Diego Rivera, as well as in a craving for tacos and burritos.[18]

None of these crazes were exactly alike. The *Oxford English Dictionary* defines "craze" as an "insane or irrational fancy; a mania." "Craze" in the *OED* is also a synonym for a "rage," interpreted as a "vehement passion or desire," a definition roughly akin to Sargent's use of the term "fever" to describe the longings that his sculptor friend Saint-Gaudens was likely to experience after he crossed the border from France to Spain. Yet by emphasizing the irrational, almost serendipitous character of crazes, rages, and vogues, these definitions do not begin to explain the complex pathologies these phenomena ordinarily entail. To begin with, crazes are often linked to the changing dynamics of international politics and trade. The Japan craze, for example, can be directly related to the arrival of Commodore Matthew Perry's fleet in Tokyo harbor in 1853, followed by subsequent efforts on the part of the United States to promote commerce with a country that was industrializing rapidly following the Meiji restoration of 1868. Similarly, the Mexican craze was an offshoot of pan-Americanism, which began in the 1890s, along with growing U.S. involvement in the Mexican economy. It was also in tune with increased Mexican immigration to the United States. The Mexican craze, like most other crazes, also incorporated a commercial dimension and a wide range of actors—promoters, developers, vendors, and entrepreneurs—whose participation cannot be dismissed as an "insane or irrational fancy."

Another important facet of crazes, especially those entailing aesthetic and ideological borrowings across national frontiers, is the idea of cultural transfer. The textbook case is the Dutch craze, whose origins can be traced to the image of the United Provinces as a crucible of liberty, an idea popularized in the United States by John Lothrop Motley (1814–77), an author whose best-selling *Rise of the Dutch Republic* (1855) presented the revolt the Dutch began in 1566 against their tyrannical overlord, Philip II of Spain, as a model of "conspicuous resistance of historical and chartered liberty to foreign despotism."[19] That connection resonated with Dutch immigrants anxious to carve out a distinctive identity within the broad compass of American society, but for a time at least it increased the value—hence the craze—other Americans attached to various items—artworks, housing design, along with chocolate and cheese—associated with Netherlandish culture.

Motley's contributions to the Dutch craze highlight yet another, often forgotten aspect of this and other vogues: the role of scholarship, together with the participation of actors motivated by something other than irrational whims. Just as Egyptomania rested on the shoulders of skilled Egyptologists, the Indian craze drew inspiration from the pioneering fieldwork of Adolph Bandelier, Frank Hamilton Cushing, and other anthropologists interested in the folkways of various groups of Native Americans in New Mexico and other parts of the Southwest. The Spanish craze was no different. It depended on and actively involved various writers deeply committed to promoting the image of Spain in the United States. Some of these writers were committed Hispanists, scholars specializing in the study of Spanish language and literature. Others were historians keen on establishing connections between the history of Spain and that of the United States, and there were various Spanish American writers, such as Guadalupe Vallejo, interested in promoting the "Spanishness" of California's early history.[20] Still others were travel writers for whom Spain was less of a passion than a way to earn money through the sale of books.

A craze—how long does it last? The *OED* indicates that a craze is a "widespread, temporary fashion or enthusiasm." But how long is temporary? One year, two, perhaps five, even ten? What's interesting about the Spanish craze, especially when compared with other crazes that periodically swept across the United States, is that it proved exceptionally durable, stretching out across several decades. It also left a lasting imprint in several areas of American society before it finally ran out of steam. In the realm of politics, for example, it helped lay the foundations for the Good Neighbor policy and improvements in ties between the United States and its Spanish-speaking neighbors to the south. On the home front it fostered a more positive attitude toward the language and traditions of Hispanic culture within the boundaries of the United States, new recognition of the importance of the Spain's historic contribution in the development of the Southwest, and greater sympathy and respect for Americans of Hispanic background. Interestingly, outside Florida, California, and other parts of the Southwest these changes had relatively little to do with immigration and the concomitant importation of language, culture, and cuisine. Such importations did accompany the mass emigration of Italians and Jews from eastern Europe to the United States.

Immigrants from Spain were harder to find. According to official census statistics (and these may be wrong), between 1820 and 1900 only forty-two hundred Spaniards—or fewer than five hundred per year on average—arrived in the United States, whereas the 1900 census indicated that the total Spanish-born population was just over seven thousand, a figure that represented a minuscule fraction of the more than ten million foreign-born then in the country. The following decades—an era of massive emigration from Spain to various countries in the Americas, especially Argentina—brought more. The 1910 census registered slightly more than twenty-two thousand Spaniards in the United States, and by the early 1920s that figure was probably as high as eighty thousand, owing to the arrival of no fewer than fifty-two thousand Spaniards between 1917 and 1921. But these new arrivals ended up in a few specific enclaves: New York City, host to about six thousand Spaniards in 1908; the zinc factories in Spelter and other towns in Harrison County, West Virginia; Tampa, Florida, where a cluster of cigar factories employed what one report referred to as ten thousand *españoles*, the majority of whom were displaced Cubans; Louisiana, which had attracted émigré Spaniards since the nineteenth century; and, with its booming agricultural sector, California, the favored U.S. destination of Spanish immigrants in the wake of the war of 1898.[21]

The elasticity of the term "Spaniard" underscores yet another important facet of the Spanish craze, namely, that it was not exclusively Spanish in the peninsular sense of the term. Rather it intermingled with, and drew energy from, the customs and traditions from various parts of the Spanish-speaking world, primarily Cuba and Mexico, together with those of the Hispanic population—often referred to as "Spanish Americans" in the nineteenth century—residing in the American Southwest. But such subtleties were lost on most Americans, given the strength of prevailing racialist theories maintaining that the basic characteristics and traits of humans were predicated upon race. The world's population was consequently divided and often hierarchically arranged into a series of racial categories that included, among others, the Anglo-Saxon, the Oriental, the Latin, and so forth. Further subdivisions along national lines also occurred, but in general all Spanish speakers, regardless of nationality, were thought to stem from a single racial stock. For this reason Anglo Americans often confused Mexicans with Spaniards, frequently referring to them as "Spaniards of the Mexican type" and therefore fundamentally alike. Take Zorro, the fictional character created in 1919 by the pulp writer Johnston McCulley in 1919 and later played by Douglas Fairbanks Sr. in two wildly popular films, *The Mark of Zorro* (1920) and *Don Q, Son of Zorro* (1925). In the films as well as the book, Zorro, the Robin Hood of Spanish California, was a pure-blooded *hidalgo* or nobleman, albeit one who was interchangeably both Mexican and Spanish. Similarly, what was (and still is) known as Spanish revival architecture—a style popularized during the 1920s—was actually a blend of Spanish design elements with others, elaborately decorated doorways, for example, that are more properly defined as Spanish colonial or Mexican.[22]

I should also mention that when it came to architecture, the Spanish craze also harbored various elements connected with what is known as neo-Moorish architecture. Prominent among these was the use of colorful glazed tiles, layered and richly carved plaster, and elaborate geometrical designs inspired in large part by the Alhambra, the building most emblematic of Muslim Spain. In the mid-nineteenth century the neo-Moorish style was also associated with the Sephardic Jews of medieval Spain, a connection that helps to explain why the style made its inaugural U.S. appearance in the guise of Manhattan's Temple Emanu-El, a building designed by the versatile Czech-born architect Leopold Eidlitz and completed in 1868. Over time, however, the style's connections with the Alhambra, a building that Irving had used to conjure up images of the luxuries and leisured lifestyle of al-Andalus and more generally Spain itself, won out. It is no accident therefore that Spanish-themed architecture found favor among the builders and designers of upscale houses, retail centers, and resorts.

The Spanish fever, in short, manifested itself in differing places, in differing intensities, and in differing ways. Parts of its etiology and development have already been examined by specialists versed in the history of California, Florida, and the Southwest, but these regional approaches, though useful, have obscured the extent to which the fever affected the nation as a whole. This lacuna also exists because a comprehensive explanation of the phenomenon requires a detailed knowledge of the history of America together with that of Spain itself. I possess some of this knowledge, having devoted much of my professional career as a historian to the study of Spanish history and culture. But when it comes to American history, especially the years between 1890 and 1930, the era of U.S. history with which this study is principally concerned, I am not much more than a novice. On the other hand, I have long grappled with questions relating to the image of both Spain and Spanish America in the United States, and what follows here is an attempt to understand the varying ways in which the United States dealt with the cultures and peoples of the wider Hispanic world.

It begins, as it should, with politics, since the often turbulent relations between the two countries helped condition the frequently contradictory American attitudes toward both Spain and its culture. Chapter 1 offers a brief survey of the political relations between Spain and the United States, starting with John Adams's "accidental" visit to the country in 1779, subsequent U.S. efforts to acquire Spanish territories in North America, disputes over Spanish rule in Cuba and Puerto Rico, and the disruptions and misunderstandings that culminated in the Spanish-American War of 1898. This survey is not meant to be exhaustive, as the literature on this topic is already quite extensive. It focuses instead on a few key moments when the relations between the two countries were particularly tense and marked by mutual distrust and suspicion: the late eighteenth century, a time when the two countries were at odds over the Mississippi River; the debates over which of the two should control Florida and the often fractured negotiations leading up to the Transcontinental (Adams-Onís) Treaty of 1821; the middle years of the nineteenth century and the efforts of marauding bands of *filibusteros* to wrest the island of Cuba from Spanish control; and finally the post-1898 era, when the United States, in an effort to embrace its former imperial rival, embarked on a policy of "forgive and forget" and in doing so prepared the way for the Spanish craze.

As for the war of 1898, I will not dwell upon details of this well-studied conflict. More important for my purposes is the virulent anti-Spanish propaganda campaign that preceded it, much of it orchestrated by the editors of newspapers controlled by Joseph Pulitzer and William Randolph Hearst. As I shall argue here, however, the effects of that campaign were temporary and soon gave way to a more positive view of Spain and, more generally, the wider Hispanic world.

Politics, of course, is one thing, culture another, and when it came to Spain, even Hearst, arguably the most outspoken proponent of the war, was able to keep them apart. Otherwise it is difficult to explain the press magnate's deep and abiding interest in Spanish architecture, an interest that later expressed itself in the design and furnishings of the ostentatious mansion Hearst built for himself at San Simeon on the California hills overlooking the Pacific.

Such ambivalence was not limited to Hearst. Americans had long been of two minds about Spain. As they saw it, there were two Spains. One was negative and associated with the older, Protestant, Black Legend view: the Spain of the Inquisition, the Spain that expelled Jews from their beloved homeland, Sepharad, in 1492; the Spain of bloodthirsty conquistadors who slaughtered their way across the Americas; and the Spain that waged endless wars against Protestants on several fronts.

The flip side was the Spain of the White Legend, or what I call here Sturdy Spain: the Spain whose soldiers, missionaries, and settlers, far from decimating America's indigenous inhabitants, allegedly brought them the gifts of civilization, learning, and religion. Chapter 2 offers a survey of various American authors, beginning with the famed Boston historian William Hickling Prescott, who endeavored to create a positive image of Spain and to endow Florida, California, and other parts of the Southwest with a distinguished colonial history comparable to that of New England. This effort entailed the "invention" of a series of founding fathers—a "genealogy of virtue"—whose deeds matched those of the signatories of the Declaration of Independence. A key figure here was Father Junípero Serra, the eighteenth-century Franciscan who founded a string of missions along California's coast. These missions and their benevolent friars figured centrally in Helen Hunt Jackson's

Ramona, a novel whose sales were second only to those of *Uncle Tom's Cabin*, as well as in Lummis's *Spanish Pioneers*, another best seller that emphasized Spain's manifold contributions to the character and culture of United States. Today controversy surrounds the role of the missions in the history of California and other states, together with what Serra managed to achieve, but traces of the cultural bleach that Jackson, Lummis, and other like-minded authors used to whiten the Black Legend proved instrumental in building the foundation for the craze for Spain.

None of this would have happened, however, without Irving's "Sunny Spain"—the Spain of the fandango; the Spain of the bullring; the Spain of al-Andalus, envisioned as the era in which Jews, Christians, and Muslims lived in peaceful harmony; and the Spain whose economic backwardness enabled it to preserve customs, traditions, and folkloric types that the combined forces of industrialization and urbanization had elsewhere destroyed. For this reason Spain was considered authentic in ways that other, supposedly more advanced countries (the United States among them) were not.

Starting with the contributions of Irving, Longfellow, and other writers, both European and American, chapter 3 highlights the ingredients that rendered Sunny Spain so alluring. Of key importance here was the Alhambra, arguably the one Spanish monument that epitomized the Spanish picturesque. Equally important was the imaginary figure of Carmen, the fiery gypsy first featured in the 1845 short story by the French author Prosper Mérimée and later in the eponymous opera by Georges Bizet first performed in Paris in 1875, one whose legend rendered Seville a mandatory destination for travelers seeking to experience the "romance" of Spain.

Black Legend and White, Spain the torchbearer of civilization and religion, Spain romantic and picturesque—these different Spains underscore the contradictions in the attitudes of Hearst and other Americans toward the people and culture of Spain. These different Spains also help to explain the rapid shifts in the nation's policies toward Spain. This tension, between the dark, rather menacing Spain of the Black Legend and the sunny one associated with Irving, along with the sturdy one, is a leitmotif that runs though most American writing about Spain, from the eighteenth century almost to the present. For a moment, however, the stars of Sturdy Spain aligned with those of Sunny Spain, creating an astral conjunction that helped foster the Spanish craze.

Different aspects of this craze are addressed in several chapters. Chapter 4 focuses on scholarship, or what I will refer to as *hispanismo*, the study of Spain, its language, and its culture as well. Explored here are different aspects of hispanismo, including the explosive rise of Spanish-language study associated with the growing pan-American movement and the opening of the Panama Canal in 1914, as well as the role of Archer M. Huntington's newly formed Hispanic Society of America, with its attendant museum exclusively devoted to the art and culture of the "Spanish race." At the time the idea of orienting both a library and a museum along racial lines was virtually unprecedented, and while it made for an unusual if perhaps eccentric collection, it underscored Huntington's determination to promote both Spanish and Hispanic culture in the United States.

The Hispanic Society sets the stage for the Spanish craze in the world of art, the subject of chapter 5. My focus here is on the collecting of Spanish art and how the work of particular Spanish artists—El Greco and Velázquez, for example—proved instrumental in changing attitudes about the importance and originality of Spanish art. Those changes triggered what I see as a new and unprecedented demand among some of the country's most prominent collectors for pictures attributed to these two painters as well as Goya, Zurbarán, and other Spanish masters. Of crucial importance here were two women, Isabella Stewart Gardner, based in Boston, and Louisine Havemeyer, in New York. Though sometimes rivals, Isabella and Louisine were tastemakers in the best sense of the term, and as such they unleashed what amounted to a no-holds-barred competition—at least for those able to afford it—for choice examples of Spanish Old Master art.

Architecture—the first truly public face of the Spanish craze—follows in chapter 6. The starting points are three. The first is St. Augustine, Florida, where Flagler's magnificent Ponce de León Hotel, opened in 1887, established the linkage between Spanish-themed buildings and leisure, a concept that was shortly to spread across the whole of the United

States and express itself in the guise of a wide spectrum of buildings, both commercial and domestic. The second is New York, where Stanford White constructed his replica of the Giralda in 1890. Replicas of various European building styles—Romanesque, Gothic, Renaissance—were synonymous with the architecture of America's Gilded Age, but White was among the first to turn to Spain for inspiration. His decision to do so, moreover, sparked a series of copycat Giraldas in other cities, together with a raft of other buildings modeled loosely on the architecture of Spain's Renaissance. The rationale underscoring the popularity of this new style is complex, but as the historian Julian Hawthorne explained with specific reference to the Spanish-themed architecture at Buffalo's Pan-American Exposition of 1901, it was seen as a hybrid style, part Old World and part New, an admixture that, as one architect of that exposition put it, symbolized "our welcome to the genius of the Latins to mingle their strain with the genius of the Anglo-Saxon."[23]

Chicago is the location of the third starting point: the World's Columbian Exposition of 1893, specifically the California State Building that Arthur Page Brown designed in what came to be known as mission revival style. The pavilion's unadorned simplicity inspired the construction of other mission revival buildings in California and other parts of the Southwest. Starting in 1915 with the buildings by Bertram Grosvenor Goodhue for San Diego's Panama-California Exposition, this style morphed into a more ornamented Spanish colonial or Spanish revival architecture that quickly spread nationwide. "Dignity," "honesty," "sincerity"—such were the words contemporary architectural critics chose to characterize the Spanish revival style. These words mapped precisely onto those that the French traveler Alexis de Tocqueville, along with Mark Twain and other observers, had used to describe the American character in general. It was precisely this overlap in attributes, together with the contemporaneous idea that this Spanish-styled architecture was quintessentially "American" rather than "foreign," which accounts for its widespread popularity.

The linkage between Spain and America also helps to explain the vogue for Spanish-themed music and movies that started around the time of World War I. Chapter 7 introduces these aspects of the Spanish

craze—the New York music critic Carl Van Vechten called it a "blaze"—
together with Spain's appeal for established authors such as William
Dean Howells. It also explores Spain's ongoing attraction for a group of
younger, more avant-garde writers, including Gertrude Stein, John Dos
Passos, Waldo Frank, and Ernest Hemingway—an appeal that eventually eroded during the course of Spain's destructive civil war of 1936–39.

The concluding chapter deals with a related subject: the impact of
America's Spanish craze on Spain itself. There the country's first promoters of tourism, anxious to attract visitors from abroad, sought to give
Spain a decidedly more "Spanish" look by copying the Spanish revival
architecture they would likely have previously encountered in California
and the American Southwest. In the words of one Spanish writer, this
cultural interchange created an "estilo de ida y vuelta," that is, a "back
and forth" or "round-trip style." This chapter concludes with a discussion of the various factors that, starting around 1930, conspired to pre-
cipitate the end of the Spanish craze.

Finally, an epilogue surveys changes in Spain's image in the decades that
followed, coupled with some reflections on the status of that image today.

Rival Empires

Spain had immense influence over the United States; but it
was the influence of the whale over its captors—the charm of
a huge, helpless, and profitable victim. —HENRY ADAMS

In 1889 Henry Adams published the first part of his *History of the United
States during the Administrations of Thomas Jefferson and James Madison*. This history, which eventually encompassed nine volumes, is one
that the historian and critic Garry Wills described in 2005 as "the non-
fiction prose masterpiece of the nineteenth century in America." Wills
applauded Adams's history for its attention to matters of economic and
social history, its reliance on archival sources, the quality of the prose,
and especially the thesis crediting the Jeffersonians with the creation of
America's sense of national unity and purpose.[1]

What escaped Wills's attention but captured mine is the short section with the running head "Spanish Court," found in chapter XIII and
woven into the first volume of Adams's work. It is easy to skip over or
miss, as the chapter rather confusingly begins with Adams's somewhat
incongruous description of Napoleon as one of the most "picturesque"
figures in modern history. It then segues into a discussion centered on
the Spanish-American dispute over access to the Mississippi River, which
ran through Louisiana and other territories that belonged to Spain. The
United States was demanding that its citizens should have the freedom
to navigate the river as far south as New Orleans, but Spain's ruler,
King Charles IV (r. 1788–1808), refused to grant this concession on the
grounds it would only serve to encourage further westward American
expansion and thus pose a threat to Spanish Louisiana. The dispute was
partially settled in 1795 when the American minister, Thomas Pinckney,

and his Spanish counterpart, Manuel de Godoy, negotiated the Treaty of San Lorenzo (aka Pinckney's Treaty). This landmark agreement called for "a firm and inviolable Peace and sincere Friendship between His Catholic Majesty, his successors and subjects, and the United States and their Citizens without exception of persons or places." It also created the legal framework that would govern commerce between the two countries for a century to come. More to the point the treaty granted the United States shipping access to the Mississippi and the right to use New Orleans as a "port of deposit," and it put a temporary fix on yet another issue over which the two countries had been at odds—the boundary (along the thirty-first parallel) separating Georgia and the Spanish colony of Florida. Finally, the treaty obliged the two countries to respect each other's shipping so long as the vessels were not transporting contraband or involved in hostile actions of any sort.[2]

Adams's account of these negotiations is still worth reading today, as it draws extensively on contemporary sources as well as his own research in French and Spanish archives. It also offers an introduction to the subject of this chapter: Spain's troubled and occasionally turbulent relations with the United States during the course of the nineteenth century, culminating in the Spanish-American War of 1898. These conflicts centered on disputes over both territory and trade but also involved differences in political culture and the distance separating Spain's conservative monarchy from the democratic institutions of the United States. Religion was also a factor: the overwhelmingly Protestant United States, the self-styled champion of religious liberty, had little in common with Spain, which was overwhelmingly Catholic and hostile to the separation of church and state. Other differences arose from long-standing anti-Spanish prejudices connected with the Black Legend and the tendency of U.S. observers to cast Spain, its leaders, and its people in a decidedly negative light. Adams hinted at these prejudices in a series of fascinating but negative thumbnail biographies of Charles IV; his queen, María Luisa de Parma; and the other Spaniards with whom Pinckney had to deal. Adams dismisses the king as little more than amiable, fun-loving "nullity" while suggesting that María Luisa's character reflected the "rottenness" of the society of which she was part. As for Godoy, he was "the most contemptible of mortals" yet deserving of respect owing to his role in negotiating a treaty that served American interests.[3]

Adams used these same pages to outline what he perceived as the fundamental differences between Spain's national character and that of the United States. Today the idea that individual nations possess an inherited, racially determined character or spirit uniquely their own is largely dismissed, but it was dogma throughout most of the nineteenth century and much of the twentieth as well. It was also a subject, together with that of race as a causal factor in history, Adams had grappled with ever since his days as a professor of history at Harvard in the 1870s. "Of all historical problems," he once wrote, "the nature of national character is the most difficult and the most important."[4] It was difficult because Adams understood that regional differences tempered what were generally understood as "national traits," and it was important because Adams, together with most nineteenth-century historians, believed that national character was a dynamic historical force, one that determined a nation's trajectory, as well as what it could or could not achieve. In keeping with these ideas Adams wove "national traits" into the fabric of his history, among them his own country's "antipathy to war." Other characteristics he attributed to America included intelligence, rapidity, mildness, native energy, and boundless ambition.

Adams had less to say about Spain's national character other than suggesting that it aligned with the country's record of "despotism, bigotry, and corruption." He also hinted that Spaniards were far more timid than Americans, who, as he put it, were "persistent aggressors" out to expand their territories at the expense of Spain. It was easy therefore for Adams to suggest, "That the Spaniards should dread and hate the Americans was natural; for the American character was one which no Spaniard could like, as the Spanish character had qualities few Americans could understand." He then added that Spaniards were so different from Americans that between them "no permanent friendship could exist." The two, in short, were "natural enemies" and thus hard-wired imperial rivals whose interests would sooner or later lead them to war.[5]

Natural enemies? Exactly how and when Adams (1838–1918) arrived at this formulation is not entirely clear. Regrettably, his posthumously

Fig. 3. Henry Adams, 1883. Adams based parts of his *History of the United States* on research conducted in various Madrid archives and libraries in 1879. Photograph by Margaret Hooper Adams. Photo 50.52. Courtesy Massachusetts Historical Society.

published third-person autobiography, *The Education of Henry Adams*, provides few clues. Adams considered knowledge of Spanish as useful a "tool" as French, German, and mathematics. He could read the language, but his command of spoken Spanish was limited prior to his decision in 1879 to travel to Spain, accompanied by his wife, Clover, in order to conduct archival research related to his *History of the United States*. Their stay was short—only two months—but Adams engaged a Spanish tutor soon after his October arrival in Madrid. Within a matter of days he claimed to know only about "ten words of Spanish together with Clover" yet still managed to converse "fluently all day." A month later the couple's mastery of the language had improved to the point where Adams, visiting Granada, reported that he took tea at the home of the antiquarian Leopold Eguílaz, "talking fluid Spanish with the Señora, two padres of the holy Inquisition, and two pure Moors of the race of Boabdil; it was life of the fifteenth century with full local color."[6]

As this last comment suggests, Washington Irving's view of Spain as both romantic and picturesque, as expressed in his best-selling *Tales of the Alhambra*, seems to have colored Adams's impressions of the country right from the very start. Prior to traveling there he had already told a friend that "my hope is to pass Christmas in Granada, and making love to Señoritas in Seville and Cadiz. Perhaps we can make a party and bottle a little Andalusian sunshine for our old age. How would your wife like to try the quality of a December moon in the Alhambra?"[7]

Once in Madrid, however, Adams began to see things rather differently: "We have been a week on the territory of this proud race of Caballeros, and I entirely agree with those who think that a meaner territory may be widely sought and not found. As for Madrid, it is without exception the ugliest and most unredeemable capital I ever saw. . . . The hotels are bad; the streets vulgar, and the people simply faded Jews. . . . In short, if I were to draw a just conclusion from my impression, I should say that I think Spain a hole, and that I only want to get out of it." He then added, "In spite of everything, Spain does amuse me," although this particular observation probably had more to do with the weather ("a sun so glorious as the shadows are palpably black") and the Prado Museum ("Never did I dream of such Titians") than with the people ("good natured, dirty") he saw in the streets. A month later Adams had better things to say about Andalucia and especially Granada, which he judged "first-class."[8]

Adams's bittersweet reaction to Spain is striking but nothing out of the ordinary, as the remainder of this chapter explains. As for his contention that Spain was America's "natural enemy," that idea is not likely to have come from either Adams's negative impression of Madrid or his research on Jefferson and Madison. Jefferson understood that whoever controlled New Orleans—whether France, Spain, or Great Britain, a possibility Jefferson feared—constituted America's natural enemy, although "natural" here was predicated principally on the notion of rival territorial ambitions as opposed to hard-wired differences in national character. Indeed when it came to describing the Spanish, in 1801 Jefferson offered the opinion that "with respect to Spain, our disposition is sincerely amicable, and even affectionate," a quote that Adams even includes in his own book.[9]

The vocabulary Adams used to write about Spain was somewhat different. Although certain aspects of Spain amused him during the course of his visit there in 1879, his comments about Spanish "bigotry" and the "rottenness" of Spanish society suggest his overall view of the country aligned with that of the Black Legend. They also followed observations about Spain and Spaniards he is likely to have encountered in the Adams family archives. Both his great-grandfather, John Adams, and grand-father, John Quincy Adams, were instrumental in negotiating several treaties that orchestrated relations between Spain and the United States for almost one hundred years. In addition, both kept a diary during their one—and only—visit to Spain, in 1779, and it appears that Henry Adams had access to these diaries as early as 1859.

John Adams's diary was especially detailed and recounted what turned out to be an unexpected overland journey across northern Spain during the winter of 1779–80. Having been charged by the Continental Congress to negotiate an end to the war of independence and sign a treaty for commerce and friendship with Great Britain, Adams's intended destination was Paris, but the French frigate on which he, his twelve-year old son John Quincy, and the other members of his entourage had embarked in New York leaked so badly that its captain sought safety in the northwestern Spanish port of El Ferrol. After waiting there for another ship, Adams decided to travel overland, and for this purpose he hired coaches, horses, and a French-speaking guide. His route followed the famous pilgrimage route (or *camino*) of Santiago de Compostela, albeit in reverse, and six weeks passed before Adams reached Fuenter-rabía (also known by its Basque name, Hondarribia) and crossed the Bidasoa River into France. Given the season, it was a cold, slow, often difficult journey made worse by the poor condition of the roads and a series of flea-infested, poorly provisioned inns.

It is hard to know what Henry Adams took away from these diaries, but he would have learned that his great-grandfather was a curious traveler who commented at length on Spain's system of government, the workings of its law courts, the wealth and variety of its agricultural products, its commerce and trade. He would have also seen John Adams as something of an amateur ethnographer interested in the customs and living conditions of the peasants he encountered. A more surprising discovery, given that John Adams was a devout Congregationalist of

Puritan ancestry, might have been his great-grandfather's fascination with the artwork and other decorations of the Roman Catholic churches he visited. The senior statesman regretted his failure to visit the pilgrimage center of "Saint Iago de Compostella," but he recounted with pleasure his initial encounter with Spanish hot chocolate: "Breakfasted for the first time on Spanish Chocolate which fully answered the fame it had acquired in the World. Till that time I had no Idea that any thing that had the Appearance of Chocolate and bore that name could be so delicious and salubrious."[10]

Yet, in view of his own Protestant upbringing, Henry would not have missed John Adams's critical comments about Spanish ignorance and poverty and especially his readiness to attribute these and the country's other ills—the lack of industry, for example—to the shortcomings of monarchy and the malign influence of the Roman Catholic Church. Particularly striking in this regard was the following entry dated January 8, 1780: "Together Church, State and Nobility exhaust the Labour and Spirits of the People to such a degree, that I had no Idea of the Possibility of deeper Wretchedness. . . . Ignorance more than Wickedness has produced this deplorable State of Things, Ignorance of the true Policy which encourages Agriculture, Manufactures and Commerce. The Selfishness and Lazyness of Courtiers and Nobles, have no doubt been the Cause of this Ignorance: and the blind Superstition of the Church has cooperated with all the other causes and increased them."[11]

Reading further, Henry Adams would have encountered similar observations in the travel diary of John Quincy Adams, whose ideas about Spanish peasants echoed those of his father: "They are Lazy, dirty, Nasty, and in short I can compare them to nothing but a parcel of hogs." Yet the boy struck a somewhat more sympathetic note when he attributed the brutishness of the Spanish peasantry not to some kind of deep-seated character flaw but to the pernicious influence of the Roman Catholic Church. "Poor creatures," he wrote, "they are eaten up by their priests. Near three quarters of what they earn goes to the Priests and the other Quarter they must live [on] as they can. Thus is the whole of this Kingdom deceived and deluded by their Religion."[12]

At work here was a cluster of anti-Catholic prejudices that dated back to the sixteenth century and the age of European religious wars. Layered on top was a series of High Enlightenment beliefs, especially those that envisioned the Roman Church as the archenemy of scientific progress and economic advance. Echoes of the great eighteenth-century Scottish historian William Robertson can also be heard. John Adams had read Robertson's *Europe in the Age of Charles V* (1769) as early as 1773, and it appears that his understanding of the pernicious effects of feudalism and the inherited privileges of nobility derived from that influential work. He may also have had the opportunity to read parts of Robertson's *History of America* (1777) before arriving in Spain; it offered a lengthy discussion of the manner in which an unhappy combination of high taxes and poor management contributed to the general corruption and stagnation of Spain's New World colonies along with the "declension" of Spain itself. In addition to these ideas about the country's decline, Adams brought with him to Spain the idea that government ought to serve as a motor of economic development and social welfare, or what he, together with Jefferson and other members of the Continental Congress, would have understood as "Life, Liberty, and Happiness."

Coupling these ideas to the Black Legend, which depicted Spaniards as backward, bigoted, and cruel, and the criticisms of Spain contained in the two diaries, one can understand with relative ease how Henry Adams might have formulated the idea of Spain as a natural enemy of the United States. For his great-grandfather the United States epitomized freedom, progress, and change, and Spain meant just the opposite, an idea that John Quincy also embraced. It later passed to Henry, as well as to Henry's wife, Clover, who in a letter drafted in Madrid succinctly observed that Spaniards were all "tomorrow," that is, lazy and pro-crastinating, whereas Americans were quintessentially "today," that is, enterprising and ambitious.[13]

Years ago I grouped this formulation of America as Spain's polar opposite under the rubric "Prescott's paradigm," a reference to the manner in which the great Boston historian William Hickling Prescott envisioned Spain in his *History of the Reign of Ferdinand and Isabel* (1837) and later books on the Spanish conquests of both Mexico and Peru.[14] I did so partly to underscore the importance of Prescott's historical writings about Spain but also because he too had emphasized the differences separating a "backward" Spain from a progressive United States. It was perhaps a mistake; the apposition antedates Prescott, as the Adams family diaries clearly reveal. But whatever one calls it—and here I will continue to employ "Prescott's paradigm" for clarity's sake—the paradigm proved instrumental in shaping not only Henry Adams's notion of the United States as Spain's natural enemy but also, and far more important, as this chapter argues, U.S. policies toward Spain well before the start of the war of 1898.

The first overview of these policies can be found in French Ensor Chadwick's *Relations of the United States and Spain: Diplomacy*, published in 1909. A veteran naval officer and retired director of the U.S. Naval War College, Chadwick (1844–1929) set out to determine the causes, both long-term and short, of the Spanish-American War. He organized the history around a series of territorial disputes, starting with those centered on U.S. access to the Mississippi River during the 1780s and 1790s. Next came the wrangles over Florida leading up to the Transcontinental Treaty of 1821, the agreement that required Spain to cede Florida, together with the Oregon Country, to the United States. Subsequent chapters addressed the decades immediately preceding the American Civil War, when a series of disputes over tariffs and trade regularly sparked talk of war in Washington, New York, and Madrid. Cuba came next. Here Chadwick offered a detailed account of the insurrection that erupted on that island in 1895, Spain's brutal if unsuccessful efforts to snuff it out, the explosion aboard the battleship *Maine* in Havana harbor in February 1898, and the United States' unilateral declaration of war on Spain the following April, before he concluded the work with a detailed account of the conflict itself.

Chadwick's narrative of these developments is still worth reading today, leaving aside the importance he accorded to the issue of race. From his perspective the 1898 war represented "the final act in the struggle for supremacy between the Anglo-Saxons and men of the Latin race in North America, in which Philip [II of Spain], Elizabeth [I of England], Drake, Howard, Chatham, Vernon, Wolf, Montcalm, Washington had, all, a part. It was the end of a race struggle which had lasted all of three hundred years." The outcome of that struggle was furthermore entirely predictable, as it pitted the Americans—a "practical [people] . . . untrammeled by the conventions and conservatism attached to an old civilization"—against Spaniards temperamentally locked in the "grip of antiquity" and hampered by what he termed their "Moro-Iberian" heritage. Small wonder that Chadwick, whose views about Spain neatly align with Prescott's paradigm, rendered the "Spanish nation an enigma to the northern [read Anglo-Saxon] mind."[15]

More difficult to determine is the extent to which race-based think- ing of this kind figured in the actual formation of policy, whether in Washington or in Madrid. Stereotypes abounded, and for most of the nineteenth-century policy makers, both Spanish and American, had little understanding of what made the other tick. These stereotypes did not prevent individual representatives of the two countries from establishing close personal relations. George Washington, for example, befriended the wealthy Havana-based Spanish merchant and slave trader Juan de Miralles (1713–80). As Spain's first emissary to the United States, Miralles showered Washington with Spanish chocolate and other gifts and supplied material assistance for his troops in exchange for his support in persuad- ing the first Continental Congress to respect Spanish claims to Florida, a territory then under British control. Miralles even visited Washington at his camp in Morristown, and following the Spaniard's death in February 1780, Washington personally presided over the funeral of his friend.[16]

In general, however, the racial differences to which Chadwick referred created a gulf between Spain and the United States that few individual policy makers managed to overcome. An early demonstration of this kind of mutual miscomprehension occurred in 1780, when John Jay (1745–1829), acting as a representative of the first Continental Con- gress, journeyed to Madrid to negotiate a "treaty of commerce and friendship" that Benjamin Franklin had previously considered essential if the colonies were to secure independence. Jay's experiences during this mission were quite unique, but in other ways they set the tone for what Chadwick later described as a century of ill feeling between Spain and the United States.

Total Darkness, Violent Prejudices

As he prepared to embark from New York for Cádiz in December 1779, Jay carried with him instructions to secure Spain's formal recognition of the United States together with what Robert Livingston, soon to be appointed the rebel colonies' first secretary of foreign affairs, called a "treaty of commerce" that would "lay the foundation of a friendship, that will endure for ages."[17] Unfortunately for Jay, who was accompanied by his wife and several other family members, the possibility of laying that foundation floundered in the murky waters of the Mississippi. In an early demonstration of what later become known as "manifest destiny," the Continental Congress claimed that access to the river was the breakaway colonies' "natural" right, an interpretation that Spain's monarch, Charles III (r. 1759–88) and his ministers rejected out of hand. From their perspective, any concession offered to the Americans with respect to the Mississippi would serve to accelerate the encroachment of the so-called western adventurers into regions over which Spain had sovereignty.

Nor did Charles III see any need to cater to the Americans. They were weak, impoverished, and desperately in need of the kind of monetary aid and military support he had been supplying to their army, albeit informally, since 1777. Then there was the threat of contamination. The monarch feared, and quite legitimately so, that any kind of formal treaty with the rebellious British colonies would encourage similar independence movements in Mexico, Peru, and Spain's other American possessions. Better therefore to stall, keep Jay waiting, and see what the outcome of the war might bring. Spain in the late eighteenth century was no longer the superpower it had been in the era of Philip II (1556–1598), but compared to the thirteen colonies it was far from the "huge . . . helpless . . . whale" that Henry Adams later described in his history of Jefferson and Madison.[18] It was more like a lumbering giant, little inclined to surrender to Jay's demands.

It was thus no surprise that negotiations got off on the wrong foot. Jay was in a hurry. The king was not, but he was reluctant to grant Jay an audience. Jay's go-between was the foreign minister, Gaspar Melchor de

His Excellency JOHN JAY *President of Congress*
& Minister Plenipotentiary from Congress at Madrid.
Pub.d May 15.th 1783, by R. Wilkinson No. 58, Cornhill, London.

Fig. 4. *His Excellency John Jay, President of Congress & Minister Plenipotentiary from Congress at Madrid*, 1783. Engraving by Pierre Eugène du Simitière. Jay arrived in Madrid in 1780 hoping to secure the king of Spain's support for the American revolutionary cause. He met with only limited success. Courtesy the New York Public Library.

Jovellanos, Count of Floridablanca (1744–1811), a learned, one might say "enlightened" individual who maintained a regular correspondence with Thomas Jefferson. Communication was another stumbling block. Jay had no Spanish, the Count of Floridablanca no English, so the two spoke in French. Jay was persistent, and after getting nowhere after more than a year of fruitless negotiations with Floridablanca, with Franklin's help he managed to persuade the Continental Congress to relinquish its demand about free access to the Mississippi south of the thirty-first parallel. Still the king dithered, and in September 1781 Jay expressed his frustration in a letter to Floridablanca, impressing on the minister the importance and value of the treaty in question. "The eyes of America," he wrote, "and indeed of all Europe, are turned towards Spain. It is in the power of His Catholic Majesty to increase his friends and humble his enemies."[19]

Still nothing happened, so Jay spent two rather frustrating years in and around Madrid, muddling about and filling his days with garden walks (which he enjoyed), attending the occasional bullfight (which he did not), socializing with other members of the diplomatic community (mostly by speaking French), and learning about Spanish food (he especially enjoyed the grapes and was so impressed with the onions that he sent some seeds to Dr. John Bard in New York). He also groused about the high cost of living in Madrid, occasionally finding himself so short of funds that he was obliged to borrow money from Floridablanca. Another lender was Diego María de Gardoquí, a Basque merchant whose firm in Bilbao had been surreptitiously sending munitions and other supplies to Washington's army for several years and who was one of a handful of individuals from the Iberian Peninsula who earned Jay's respect.[20]

Adding to Jay's frustrations was a heavy dose of isolation, as well as associated feelings of cultural distance, problems he addresses in the following, rather poignant way:

> The people in this country are in almost total darkness about us. Scarce any American publications have reached them, nor are they informed of the most recent and important events in that country. . . . There are violent prejudices among them against us. Many of them have even serious doubts of our being civilized, and men-

tion a strange story of a ship driven into Virginia by distress, about thirty years ago, that was plundered by the inhabitants, and some of the crew killed in a manner and under circumstances which, if true, certainly indicate barbarity. The King and Ministry are warm, yet I have reason to believe that the bulk of the nation is cold, toward us; they appear to me to like the English, hate the French, and to have prejudices against us.[21]

In the end Jay never secured the agreement he sought, and just prior to leaving Madrid in May 1782 he poured out his frustrations in a lengthy letter to Robert Morris, governor of New York. He commented favorably on Spanish gardens and noted that some of the people he met had "praiseworthy qualities," but he criticized the country's "absolute government." That government, he wrote, "constrains every one to watch and respect their opinions and inclinations of their superiors in power. I confess that I find little here that resembles, and nothing that compensate[s] for, the free aid, the free conversation, the equal liberty, and the numerous blessings which God, and nature, and the laws of our making, have given and secured to our happier country."[22]

Three years later, after having succeeded Livingston as the U.S. secretary of foreign affairs, Jay renewed treaty negotiations with Diego María de Gardoquí, then residing in New York as Spain's newly appointed *encargado de negocios* (mission chief) to the now independent United States. Together the two worked out a compromise, albeit one that best served the interests of East Coast merchants eager to expand trade with Cuba. In exchange for full diplomatic recognition and free access to Havana and Spain's other Caribbean ports, Jay promised that the United States would surrender all claims to the Mississippi for a period of twenty-five years. The deal was practically done, but Congress, which had to consent to the treaty, put a stop to it, teaching both Gardoquí and Jay a valuable lesson in the differences between America's republican form of government and Spain's absolute monarchy, in which the king could sign off on a treaty with a quick stroke of his pen.

As it happened, the terms of the Jay-Gardoquí treaty, well suited to the business interests of merchants based in New York and other East

Coast ports, did not sit well with members of Congress from Kentucky and Tennessee as it made no provision for access to the Mississippi and the port of New Orleans. Put simply, sectionalism, a recurrent problem in American politics, reared its ugly head and went one step further when James Wilkinson, a prominent Kentuckian and leader of the so-called Spanish Conspiracy, advocated that Kentucky break with the United States, ally itself with Spain, and in doing so secure access to the Mississippi. In the end Congress rejected the treaty, bringing negotiations between the two countries to a virtual halt for more than a decade. Only in 1795, following further negotiations between Pinckney and Godoy, did the two countries agree to the Treaty of San Lorenzo, an alliance of commerce and friendship that Henry Adams was later to applaud. In the short term, however, the treaty did relatively little to improve relations between the two countries as disputes over issues of trade and tariffs continued, as did the particularly thorny matter of American access to the Mississippi and the port of New Orleans. For this reason the treaty did little to improve Spain's image in the United States. Its reputation remained wholly negative, as the description of Spaniards as "bigotted Catholics" prone to "the practice of every vice" and as members of "a poor, lazy, idle, dirty, ignorant race of almost semi-savages" in school texts of the era readily attest.[23]

"Things Here Are Going Badly for Us"

Fast forward now to 1809, the start of another key moment in Chadwick's century of diplomatic ill feeling. October of that year marked the arrival in Washington of the Castilian nobleman Luis de Onís (1762–1827), Spain's minister plenipotentiary to the United States. His primary mission was to defend Spain's sovereignty over West Florida; to arrange for either the cession, sale, or exchange of other Spanish territories in North America; and also to secure indemnities for the losses Spanish merchants had recently suffered at the hands of privateers based in U.S. ports. Onís had the additional responsibility of ensuring that the administration of Pres. James Madison would maintain its policy of neutrality and non-interference with respect to the rebellions that had recently erupted in Argentina, Mexico, Venezuela, and other parts of Spanish America. It did not take long, however, for Onís to discover that he had to contend with the president, Congress, and indeed an entire nation without much sympathy for, let alone much understanding of, the country whose interests he had come to defend and protect.

Troubles—or what Onís referred to as "vexations"—haunted the new minister's mission from the very moment he and his wife set foot in Washington in October 1809. In 1807, in conjunction with his efforts to gain control of Europe, Napoleon had persuaded Spain's reigning monarch, Charles IV, to station an army in Spain, ostensibly in preparation for an invasion of neighboring Portugal. Within less than a year, however, Napoleon had turned the tables on Charles, along with his son, Ferdinand VII, forced their abdication (and exile), and installed his own brother, Joseph Bonaparte, as the new king of Spain, albeit with little in the way of popular support. Armed uprisings soon erupted in Madrid and elsewhere, and by the fall of 1809 the opposition to Bonaparte had established a *junta suprema* (supreme council or committee) that represented itself as the country's legitimate government.[24]

That junta, rather than Bonaparte, was also responsible for Onís's appointment as Spain's official representative to Washington, and here is where the new minister's problems began. Although he had come with a letter from the U.S. consul in Cádiz that described the minister and his wife as "most friendly, unpretentious, and genuine," that letter was addressed to Thomas Jefferson, the former president, as opposed to Madison, who, rightly confused by Spain's complicated political situation, had yet to recognize the legitimacy of either the junta or Bonaparte.[25] He consequently refused to accept Onís's credentials as minister plenipotentiary, a decision that left the Spaniard in a diplomatic limbo lasting almost six years.[26]

Limbo, however, did not mean inaction, nor did it prevent Onís from acting as a private citizen on Spain's behalf and doing all he could to present his country in a favorable light. In 1812, for example, Onís, in recognition of what he called Thomas Jefferson's interest in the "happiness and prosperity of the Spanish nation," sent the former president a copy of the new constitution that the junta had recently proclaimed in Cádiz. In reply Jefferson lauded Spain for having taken a giant step

Fig. 5. Luis de Onís (1762–1827), ca. 1821. As Spain's representative in Washington, Onís negotiated the Transcontinental Treaty of 1819 with John Quincy Adams. That agreement led to the sale of East and West Florida to the United States in 1821. Courtesy Library of Congress.

toward "political happiness" in addition to branding Napoleon's invasion of the country as "the most unprecedented and unprincipled of the transactions of modern times."[27] Yet, if Onís thought that Jefferson might also become an advocate for Spain in the United States, he miscalculated in light of Jefferson's criticism of the failure of Spain's new constitution to grant freedom of worship to any religion other than Roman Catholicism.

Onís's response to Jefferson remains unknown, but he continued on his quest to defend Spain's interests in the Americas, deploying for this purpose a combination of words and deeds. The deeds began in the summer of 1810, when he arranged for a cargo of munitions and other supplies to be shipped to Venezuela to help the Spanish governor in Maracaibo do battle with rebels opposed to Spanish rule. As for words, Onís, using the pen name Verus, a third-century Roman gladiator who figured in one of Martial's poems, published a series of pamphlets critical of U.S. policy with respect to West Florida, then a region that stretched from Pensacola in Florida's panhandle to the east bank of the Mississippi River. Officially West Florida belonged to Spain, but the United States disputed that claim, arguing that it was part of the territory it acquired from France with the Louisiana Purchase of 1803.

In an effort to resolve this dispute, President Madison sent James Monroe on an "extraordinary" but also "temporary" mission to Madrid in May 1805. Monroe personally communicated his government's claims to West Florida to Charles IV and his ministers. But these claims went nowhere, at which point Madison altered the tenor of the negotiations by suggesting that the United States was prepared to purchase West Florida, a region he likened to a "barren tract" of "little importance" to Spain. Once again the king and his ministers would not listen. Monroe went away rebuffed.[28]

But whereas Presidents Jefferson and Madison attempted to secure West Florida through diplomatic means, others were prepared to act. In 1810 a group of armed Americans, whom Onís considered to be adventurers, seized the Spanish fort at Baton Rouge and proclaimed the independent Republic of Florida under a flag, the famed Bonnie Blue, later utilized by the Confederacy. At this juncture, acting on the grounds of self-defense, Madison ordered troops to the region, ousted the rebels, and replaced the Bonnie Blue with the Stars and Stripes, effectively annexing that stronghold at a moment when Spain, preoccupied by its own internal struggles, stood idly by, too weak and far too divided to protest.

Verus's response to this crisis was a pamphlet, printed in Philadelphia, that addressed the "forcible occupation" of West Florida by U.S. troops, calling it a "rash, unwarranted and ill-fated measure" launched by a "treacherous friend." Verus also presented a series of proofs rejecting all U.S. claims to West Florida. The pamphlet ended on a more diplomatic note by suggesting that Madison engage the "Spanish minister" then in the United States in "friendly negotiation" over the status of West Florida and also reaffirm his pledge of neutrality with respect to Spain's rebellious colonies in South America.[29]

Judging from various references to Verus in the periodical press, Onís's pamphlet circulated fairly widely, but whether Madison ever read it remains unknown. What is certain is that in February 1810 the president learned that Onís had floated a bizarre scheme designed to reduce the United States to a "state of Nullity." The scheme was this: Spain should ally itself with Great Britain and the two would then declare war on the United States with the idea of dividing it into "two or three republics." Spain, Onís suggested, could then ally itself with the "Republic of the North," the region that he perceived as the most prosperous of the new mini-states, while the others would soon "perish from Poverty and quarrels among themselves."[30] The plan was far-fetched, but as news of it leaked out, Onís's standing in Washington, together with that of Spain itself, seemingly took a turn for the worse as it provided Madison with the justification to press his claims to the whole of West Florida.

The issue became even more complex following the outbreak in 1812 of hostilities between Great Britain and the United States. This struggle gave rise to fears in Washington that the British, taking advantage of Spanish weakness, would transform West Florida into a base from which its forces could attack New Orleans. These fears were largely unfounded, but they provided the cover Gen. Andrew Jackson needed to launch a raid on the Spanish fort at Pensacola on the grounds that the authorities there were harboring British troops. Onís, residing in Philadelphia, reacted to news of these developments in a letter written to his son in which, in a gross understatement, he reported, "Things here are going badly for us" (Nuestras cosas aquí van mal). [31]

Those "things" would soon go from bad to worse. In 1815, following Napoleon's defeat at Waterloo and the restoration of the exiled Ferdinand VII to the Spanish throne, Madison finally agreed to recognize Onís as Spain's minister plenipotentiary and envoy extraordinary in the United States. Recognition, however, did little to end his administration's plans for the annexation of West Florida. Jackson had apparently received as early as 1813 orders for what James Monroe, now serving as Madison's secretary of state, termed the "possession" of that province. The issue became even more Machiavellian when in December 1814 Monroe wrote Jackson indicating that, if he had already or was about to invade the region, he should declare that he did so "for the sole purpose of freeing it from British violation."[32] Onís again responded in a series of letters sent to Monroe the following year. These demanded the "restoration" of West Florida to Spain and an end to tacit American support for what he called the "factious band of insurgents and incendiaries" responsible for a series of murderous attacks by "American volunteers" in Texas, then still part of the Viceroyalty of New Spain.[33]

Monroe's response to these criticisms was a pamphlet, *Message from the President of the United States*, that put forward the country's claims to West Florida in addition to reproducing the texts of the letters Onís had previously directed to him. The pamphlet defended the legitimacy of U.S. claims to the region in addition to asserting that the federal government was not in a position to prevent private citizens from providing aid to the insurgents in Texas. Monroe also turned the tables on Onís when he branded efforts of the Spanish navy to prevent U.S.-based vessels from supplying munitions to rebels in Mexico and its other American colonies as "unlawful seizure."[34]

Yet this pamphlet—the government's official response to Onís's demands—was decidedly diplomatic as compared to the one that Monroe formulated in private. Following his unsuccessful visit to Madrid in 1805, Monroe viewed Spaniards as "disrespectful, disingenuous, and unfriendly," an impression that his experiences with Onís seemingly reinforced. He therefore suggested that Madison should dissimulate and contrive policies expressly designed to put Spain on the defensive: "If we quarrel with Spain, the more guarded we are in every step we take, and the more we put her in the wrong, the better effect here and in Europe."[35]

To put Spain in the wrong, Monroe hatched several schemes designed to abet the American cause in Florida, both east and west. One was to create a pretext for the "breakup" of the small Spanish fort located on Amelia Island, in northeastern Florida, and he did so by representing the island as a smugglers' den, a haven for runaway slaves from Georgia, and a place responsible for "great injury" to the United States.[36] His next move was to instruct Jackson to find ways to persuade Americans to settle in Florida for the purpose of creating a demographic "preponderance" designed to encourage Spain to relinquish its hold on the region. In another letter to Jackson citing Spain's "pertinacious refusals to cede the Floridas to us," Monroe indicated that "if we engage in a war [over Florida], it is of greatest importance that our people be united, and with that view, that Spain commence it."[37]

How much Onís knew about these behind-the-scenes machinations is open to question, but he is likely to have read or at least caught wind of a damning article about Spain that appeared in an influential Boston periodical, the *North American Review*, in 1817. Entitled "The Trait of the Spanish Character," its anonymous author launched a short but pithy diatribe lambasting both the character and the culture Onís was so proud to represent: "In no civilized country of equal advantages and equal antiquity, have the interests of learning been so feebly supported as in Spain. . . . As a nation, the Spaniards are at present a full century behind every other nation of Europe in the arts of life, the refinements of society, and enlightened views of civil polity; and almost a millennium in the modes of education, and intellectual culture. It may be questioned whether they have taken a step in the right direction since the days of the Cid."[38]

Onís's response was to unleash Verus in yet another pamphlet: *Observations on the existing differences between the government of Spain and the United States*. Published in Philadelphia in 1817, the pamphlet took direct aim at American policies toward Spain and the people—Anglo-Americans, in his description—behind them. Policy came first. Verus labeled the actions of General Jackson in West Florida "public acts of aggression and violence" and the attacks on Spanish shipping by privateers operating out of American ports an "organized system of pillage and robbery" operating with the tacit consent of a government that was "insatiable in the acquisition of territory." He further contended that Washington's sympathy for the rebel cause in Spanish America was fundamentally misguided, owing to exaggerated reports about the "evils" of Spanish rule.[39]

Such observations aligned with Onís's previous pamphlets, and they were views to which he would return in other publications. What was new—and surely a sign of Onís's increasing exasperation with both Madison and Monroe—was Verus's criticism of the character of the "Anglo-American people." The list of their failings was surprisingly long, as it included "effrontery," "ostentatious confidence," "avarice and ambition," and an unbridled appetite for "gigantic projects." Yet another shortcoming was "presumptuous pride" and the readiness of Anglo-Americans to consider themselves "superior to the rest of mankind" and to "look upon every nation with disdain and contempt, admiring the

English only." To add one final dig, Verus criticized Anglo-Americans for their lack of culinary taste, noting that even in the wealthiest homes dinner consisted of little more than of "potatoes and cold salt meat, with a little butter."[40]

None of this could have sat well with either Madison or Monroe, let alone John Quincy Adams, Monroe's replacement as secretary of state and the individual with whom Onís eventually sat down to hash out a solution to Florida and other disputes. As noted earlier, Adams's boyhood experiences in Spain had not been especially positive, and he later derided the "procrastinating temperament and disposition of Spain."[41] While Adams publicly treated Onís with respect, in his diary he likened the Spanish diplomat to a "viper" and excoriated his "double dealing," "fraudulent declarations," and "shuffling equivocations." Later, in his memoirs, he also noted that Onís "has more of diplomatic *trickery* in his character than any other of the foreign Ministers now here."[42]

For his part Onís, apart from Adams, also had to contend with George Erving (1769–1850), the veteran American minister in Madrid who, in addition to having a Black-Legendish view of Spain as a "land ruled by priests," had little sympathy either for Verus's pamphlets or what he considered the Spanish government's ambivalent attitudes toward the United States."[43] Yet another adversary was Henry Clay, the fiery congressional representative from Kentucky who was soon to become President Monroe's secretary of war. In 1818, shortly after negotiations between Adams and Onís had begun, Clay stood up on the floor of the House of Representatives to denounce the "odious tyranny" Spain had imposed on its American possessions and to describe Spaniards as "blind and capricious men." In another speech Spain came off as an "aged" country with "enervated arms," one that posed little or no threat to the United States, a country Clay envisioned as "the centre of a system which would constitute the rallying point of human freedom against all the despotism of the Old World."[44]

Such ideas obviously factored into Verus's comments on the Anglo-American character, but they were by no means the only obstacles Onís encountered as his negotiations with Adams began. Far more threatening were what he later described as the "vexations of the populace." The character of these vexations is not entirely clear, but in a letter directed to Adams in February 1818 Onís complained that his Washington house had been "of late repeatedly insulted—windows broken, lamps before the house broken, and one night a dead fowl tied to the bell-rope at his door." These incidents, he added, constitute a "gross insult to his sovereign and the Spanish monarchy," but Onís, ever the diplomat, ended the letter on a more generous note with this comment: "I hoped it was nothing more than the tricks of some mischievous boys."[45]

These "tricks" aside, Onís also worried about the "disdain" (*desprecio*) with which he felt that the *americanos* were treating both him and his country. Nor could he quite understand why Clay represented "aged Spain" as little more than an obstacle in the path of the "American system." These fears appeared in another letter, dated November 1, 1818, in which he observed that "the system of the United States is to take advantage of our [Spain's] weakness, take control of the territories that [suit] their enormous ambition, and guarantee the emancipation of the Americas, something they do openly and in any way convenient to their Machiavellian conduct."[46]

These were dark thoughts, but Onís was a realist. In the course of his negotiations with Adams he came to the realization that Spain's time on the North American mainland was rapidly coming to an end. He consequently agreed to cede—he called it a "permutation"—Florida, both east and west, together with the Oregon Country, to the United States. His consolation came in the form of Adams's guarantee of Spanish sovereignty over Texas, a stronger legal framework for commerce between the two countries, and new assurances of friendship and peace.

First made public in February 1819, the draft of the Adams-Onís Treaty triggered outcries in both Washington and Madrid. The first to complain was Spain's great nemesis, Henry Clay, who was longing to acquire both Texas and Cuba for the United States. The senator denounced the treaty as an "avowed cession of territory from the United States to Spain"—a phrase best understood to mean a shameless giveaway that pandered solely to the interests of Spain. Other members of Congress asserted that Adams had been "bamboozled by the crafty Spaniard." Criticisms in Madrid were no less shrill, with some officials labeling it a "disgraceful treaty" and accusing Onís of selling out the country owing to his "partiality" toward the United States.[47]

Whatever their personal differences, Adams and Onís prevailed in the end. Ferdinand VII signed off on what became officially known as the Transcontinental Treaty in October 1820. President Monroe followed suit in February 1821 and in doing so reaffirmed the bonds of peace and friendship that the two countries had originally agreed to in 1795 and that perdured, less in theory than in practice, until 1898. For his part Adams, soon to be elected to the presidency, was proud of what the treaty had accomplished: "I considered the signature of this treaty as the most important event in my life. It was an event of magnitude in the history of my Union. . . . It promised well for my reputation in the public opinion."[48]

As for Onís, his first known reaction to the treaty can be found in a letter directed to his son in February 1819. In it he wrote, "I have done all that I could and I am sure that no one else would have been able to obtain any more."[49] Shortly thereafter Onís resigned his post in Washington and traveled to London and then Paris, where in June 1819 he again wrote to his son, expressing his fear that if King Ferdinand failed to ratify the treaty, it would not only trigger "the general hatred of the entire American people" but also become a sign of "Spain's bad faith" throughout Europe. He then explained that he was proud of having been able to hold on to Cuba, as he believed that the island, together with the Philippines, would well serve Spain in the decades to come: "With only these [two] places, Spain will be able to restore order in its finances; without them, any hope of such a restoration is irrevocably lost."[50]

Onís's ideas about the importance of Cuba to the Spanish economy proved prophetic. Throughout most of the nineteenth century the island's mineral and sugar riches served as the metropole's cash cow, generating fortunes for hundreds if not thousands of plantation owners and merchants, along with cushy offices for bureaucrats and soldiers alike. Onís's immediate concern, however, was to restore his reputation in Spain, which had taken a beating in Madrid, where he was thought to have sold his country's interests short. Toward this end he drafted a lengthy

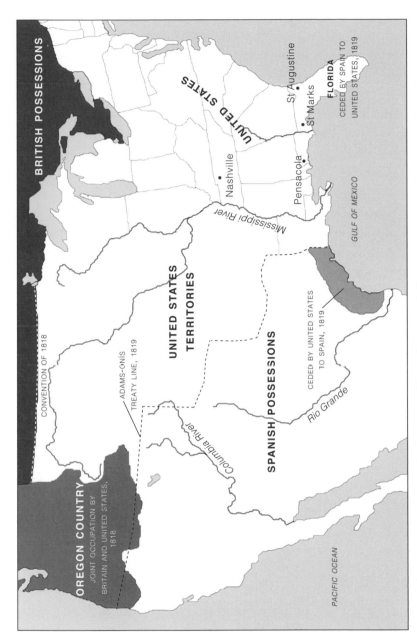

BRITISH POSSESSIONS

UNITED STATES

St Augustine

FLORIDA
CEDED BY SPAIN TO
UNITED STATES, 1819

St Marks

Nashville

Pensacola

GULF OF MEXICO

OREGON COUNTRY
JOINT OCCUPATION BY
BRITAIN AND UNITED STATES,
1818

CONVENTION OF 1818

UNITED STATES
TERRITORIES

ADAMS-ONÍS
TREATY LINE, 1819

Columbia River

Mississippi River

SPANISH POSSESSIONS

CEDED BY UNITED STATES
TO SPAIN, 1819

Rio Grande

PACIFIC OCEAN

Map 2. Adams-Onís Treaty map of 1818. Prepared by Andrea Gottschalk.

if somewhat confusing and at times contradictory *memoria* first published, in Spanish, in 1820 and in English translation the following year.[51]

The *memoria* in question was deemed contradictory because, as its translator, Dr. Tobias Watkins, co-founder of *The Portico*, an influential Baltimore periodical, knew, it combined "the weirdest slander" of American values and culture with "the most extravagant eulogy of our country." The slander Watkins referred to was a reprise of Verus's previous characterization of Anglo-Americans as a bunch of pompous, potato-eating, uncultured, and unprincipled sharks, and Onís's rationale for including it in the memoir was evidently to defend himself against the charge of having been far too "partial" toward the United States in his negotiations with Adams. As for the "eulogy," it took the form of a region-by-region account of American agriculture and manufacturing, together with a description of its unsurpassed shipbuilding industry and powerful navy. Here Onís's aim was to convey to other Spaniards an impression of the United States as a modern colossus against which Spain could hardly be expected to put up a decent fight. Rarely read today, Onís's account of the United States was far from accurate, and his translator in the notes to the text was keen on pointing out the author's errors and mistakes. But Onís's account of the country is important and stands witness to what one historian has aptly called Spain and America's "ambivalent embrace."[52]

Filibusteros

"There is no earthly reason why Spain and the United States of America should not be the best of friends in the world." So wrote James Johnston Pettigrew (1828–63), a state legislator from South Carolina, in *A Note on Spain and the Spaniards, in the Summer of 1859, with a Glance at Sardinia*, a book he privately published in Charleston in 1860.[53] The short print run—only three hundred copies—along with Pettigrew's use of the pen name "A Carolinian" instead of his own name suggests that the author knew the book would raise eyebrows, especially in the Carolinas and other parts of the South where prevailing attitudes about Spain and Spaniards approximated those Henry Adams would later articulate in his history of the United States.

Except for the immediate run-up to the 1898 war, the decade of the 1850s marked one of the most troubled moments in the history of Spain's already troubled relations with the United States. In previous decades the two countries had squabbled over Spain's territories in North America, but the flashpoint was now Cuba, in large part because the island figured in the increasingly cantankerous North-South debate over the future of slavery. Southern slaveholders and their supporters in Congress were set on annexation, imagining Cuba as another slave state and potentially one that would strengthen their position in the event that Kansas was admitted into the union as a free state.

Acting largely as front men for these southern interests, two presidents—James Polk and Franklin Pierce, Democrats both—offered to purchase Cuba in the wrongheaded belief that Spain's monarchy, confronting myriad domestic upheavals, was ready to sell. It was not. Nor did it help that these offers, often accompanied with the threat of war, were handled so poorly that they sparked little more than insult and resentment in Madrid. Compounding these resentments was the Spanish perception that the U.S. government was secretly supporting or simply turning a blind eye to the efforts of *filibusteros*—the term derived from an Old Dutch term for freebooters, or pirates—bent on launching armed expeditions to Cuba in the hope of fomenting a revolution designed to secure the island's independence from Spain.

The most famous of these filibusteros was Narciso López (1797–1851), a Venezuelan who had immigrated to the United States and settled in New Orleans, which was soon to become his main base of operations. López never received anything in the way of official support in Washington— Pres. Millard Fillmore, though a supporter of U.S. efforts to purchase Cuba, issued orders to prevent López from invading Cuba, but the filibustero had many supporters throughout the South. He was also able to raise funds and recruit "volunteers" for his expeditions in New York City, Baltimore, and other East Coast ports. The first of these expeditions, launched in 1849, resulted in failure, while a second one, organized during the summer of 1851, wound up as a kind of eerie prelude to the disastrous invasion attempt at the Bay of Pigs in 1961. Setting out with three well-equipped ships and six hundred well-armed soldiers, López landed on Cuba's north shore and briefly took control of the small town of Cárdenas before he and many of his men were captured and then promptly executed by Spanish military authorities.[54]

News of these executions prompted outrage on both sides of the Atlantic. In New Orleans a mob set fire to the residence of the local Spanish consul and looted a number of Spanish-owned coffeehouses and cigar shops. In Madrid the American minister, Daniel Barringer, was afraid that his official residence would suffer a similar attack. In New York a normally sober-headed lawyer, George Templeton Strong, having learned about the incident while reading a newspaper in the middle of his supper at Delmonico's, claimed that his initial response was "the instant assassination of a little whiskered monkey of a Spaniard who was innocently swallowing his chocolate at the next table." But Strong soon changed his mind about López and what other filibusteros were up to, noting in his diary that the "law of nations" justified the decision of the captain general of Cuba to execute "people taken red-handed in piracy."[55]

In Washington meanwhile, López's attack prompted the Spanish minister, Ángel Calderón de la Barca, to send Secretary of State James Buchanan a lengthy letter of protest that included a short history of U.S. designs on Cuba, a lecture on the extent to which filibustering expeditions symbolized the failure of the United States to abide by the terms of its existing peace treaty with Spain, and an urgent demand to bring the filibusteros and their supporters to justice.

Calderón's protests did not go very far. Despite official pronouncements to the contrary, neither Buchanan nor President Pierce had any interest in the Spanish worries about the filibusteros. Their view of the subject is best related to what Pettigrew labeled "Anglo-Saxonism," which he defined as the tendency of his compatriots to view Spaniards as a racially inferior people who merited little attention, let alone respect. Such ideas were not new, but Pettigrew connected them to the federal government's indifference to "pitiful filibustering," Washington's "lamentable ignorance" about Spain, and especially "the character of some of the men who are sent abroad to represent us in an official capacity."[56]

Pettigrew's observations were essentially correct. The Carolinian had the advantage of having traveled to Spain, not just once but twice. He was fairly proficient in Spanish and, in addition to having visited many of the country's monuments, had made a point of learning about its economy, political system, and other institutions, including the Catholic Church. The Spain described in his book was hardly a utopia. Pettigrew recognized the country's urgent need to end its bloody regional conflicts and to create a more harmonious and stable (read democratic) system of government. But as he was keen to improve Spain's relations with the United States, Pettigrew went out of his way to gather information about the history of the U.S. mission in Madrid.

That mission officially began in 1782, when William Carmichael (1739–95), a wealthy Marylander who had accompanied John Jay on his mission to Spain in 1779, stayed on to become the country's first permanent chargé d'affaires in Madrid (his Spanish counterpart was Diego María de Gardoquí, who had arrived in Philadelphia following Spain's recognition of the independence of the United States). Carmichael, who married a Spanish noblewoman and later helped to negotiate the Treaty of San Lorenzo, ranked among the most competent—and respected—of America's early diplomats in Madrid. Others who earned high marks included the intellectual Bostonian Alexander Hill Everett (serving 1825–29) and especially Washington Irving, who practically received a hero's welcome when he first presented his credentials at the Spanish court on the first of August 1842.

Compared to other U.S. ministers in Madrid, Irving, a Spanish speaker, entered into Spanish society with relative ease. He was also fortunate in that his diplomatic tenure in Madrid (1842–46) coincided with a moment when relations between Spain and the United States were remarkably free of crisis. But what really worked to bolster Irving's reputation in Madrid was his deep and abiding commitment to what he described at the start of his tenure as a "harassed, impoverished, depressed, yet proud-spirited and noble country."[57]

That commitment was notably lacking among the diplomats whom Pettigrew singled out for criticism. One was Romulus Saunders (1791–1867), the North Carolina Democrat whom President Polk appointed in 1846 as Irving's successor. Polk made a poor choice. Lacking Spanish as well as French, Saunders had difficulty communicating with the

Fig. 6. Pierre Soulé (1801–70), minister to Spain, 1853. Depicted here as a family man, Soulé was a short-tempered "red-hot Democrat" whose lack of either diplomatic skill or respect for Spain's government was the source of scandal during his time in Madrid (1853–55). Courtesy Library of Congress.

officials he met and partly for this reason made a total hash of Polk's effort to offer the Spanish government up to $100 million if it agreed to sell Cuba to the United States.[58]

Pettigrew was even more critical of Saunders's successor, Pierre Soulé (1801–70), arguably the most controversial—and least respected—of all U.S. ministers in Madrid prior to the war of 1898. A naturalized American citizen of French origin, Soulé had earned the reputation of being a "red-hot democrat" in the sense of being an outspoken supporter of slavery well before he arrived in Madrid.[59]

Together with James Buchanan and William Marcy, Soulé was a charter member of the Young America movement, a small, loosely organized but vigorous cabal of business leaders and politicians that emerged in the wake of the U.S.-Mexico War of 1846–48. The movement subscribed to the idea of "manifest destiny"—a term coined by one of the group's members, John L. O'Sullivan—and advocated the continuing territorial expansion of the United States, by force if necessary. So read its motto: "East by sunrise, West by sunset, North by the Arctic, . . . and South as far as we darn please."[60] "South" here really meant Cuba and Puerto Rico, islands that John Quincy Adams had previously considered "natural appendages to the North American continent" and of "transcendent importance to the political and commercial interests of our Union."[61]

But while Adams had advocated patience, warning that the time for annexation had not yet come, adherents of Young America were prepared to act. In 1849 O'Sullivan was among those who helped persuade President Polk to offer Spain up to $100 million for the purchase of Cuba, but when this offer was rebuffed he actively and openly raised money to help finance the expeditions of López and other filibusteros. In addition the Louisianan acquired a reputation for "bellicose discourse" when, in a speech delivered to the Senate in 1851, he argued that America's "lusty manhood" needed to expand beyond its "narrow confines." In another he pointedly suggested that "the Antilles flower . . . must be plucked from the crown of the old spanish wolf."[62]

Such talk, combined with Soulé's appointment as minister in Madrid, spelled no end of trouble for relations between Spain and the United

States. Calderón de la Barca labeled Soulé a "mortifying choice," his ministerial appointment nothing short of a "bad trick."[63] Criticism also appeared in the press, especially in New York and other northern cities. C. Edwards Lester, the New York correspondent for the *Times* of London, described Soulé as an integral part of the "filibuster system" and probably "the most obnoxious man that could have been chosen to represent us in Madrid."[64] The reaction of the Spanish press was much the same.

If Soulé's advance billing in Madrid was somewhat dicey, his reputation nosedived soon after his arrival there in October 1853. Starting with his youth in France, where he was arrested and imprisoned and from which he was later exiled for his opposition to the monarchy of Louis-Philippe, Soulé evinced little respect for royalty. Nor did he have any patience for the elaborate protocols surrounding the Spanish monarch, Queen Isabella. Before presenting his diplomatic credentials to the queen, he planned to lecture her about Spain's need to sell Cuba to the United States, although when it came to the actual meeting, he apparently refrained from doing so, much to his later regret.

This meeting was arguably the only occasion upon which Soulé displayed a bit of diplomatic finesse. As one observer put it, he lacked "prudence and tact," a comment possibly occasioned by Soulé's description of the Cortes, the nation's parliament: "such a body of political prostitutes and unprincipled knaves never before sat together in one room."[65] Soulé's first official dispatch, sent at the beginning of December 1853, contained similar language, as he referred derogatorily to the "blind stubbornness and the supercilious susceptibility" of the Spanish officials with whom he had to deal.[66]

What's clear is that Soulé's ideas about Spain approximated those of the filibusteros he had supported in previous years. He also believed that Spaniards, especially the ones he met in the foreign ministry in Madrid, had little respect for Americans: "There we are cordially hated. For we are looked upon as being any better than . . . barbarians," he informed the secretary of state.[67] On this issue Soulé was wrong. The main cause of Soulé's problem in Madrid was Soulé himself.

His first gaffe occurred within a few weeks of his arrival in Madrid, at a ball held at the residence of the French ambassador, the Marquis de

Turgot. After hearing what he understood as Turgot's criticism of his wife's low-cut dress, Soulé challenged the marquis to a duel with pistols that left the Frenchman with a nasty wound in his leg. The *New York Herald*, a newspaper known for its support of Cuban independence, proudly reported that "we wanted an ambassador [in Madrid], we have sent a matador." The press reaction was much the same in New Hampshire, where Concord's *State Capital Reporter* maintained that "the exhibition of a little American grit may do those lacqueys [*sic*] of despotism some good." In contrast Madrid's press transformed Soulé into a pariah. The duel also put him at odds with Horatio J. Perry, the long-serving (and much-respected—he had married a Spanish woman and spoke fluent Spanish) secretary of the American legation in Madrid, whose ideas about Spaniards were far more positive than those of Soulé.[68]

More trouble was on the way. In March 1854 news of the seizure of the USS *Black Warrior* by Spanish officials in Cuba trickled into Madrid. The *Black Warrior* was a coastal steamer that regularly stopped in Havana en route from Mobile to New York. On this occasion irregularities in its cargo manifest and, more menacingly, the possibility that it might be carrying supplies to the filibusteros raised suspicions among Havana's port authorities, who ordered the vessel's seizure and impounded both its cargo and crew. The incident, one of several such seizures occasioned by Spanish fears of filibusteros, was relatively minor and settled fairly quickly when the ship's agents, acknowledging malfeasance, agreed to pay a fine (later returned by the Spanish government).

Pro-expansionist interests in the United States, however, regarded the *Black Warrior*'s seizure as nothing short of a casus belli. One member of the House of Representatives argued for the suspension of America's treaty of neutrality with Spain while several newspapers, including the *Washington Daily Union* and the ever incendiary *New York Herald*, editorialized in support of war. Soulé labeled the incident an "outrage" and testily demanded that Spain immediately pay a hefty indemnity for the damages. Soulé's demands unfortunately came at a time when Spain's weak government, headed by a liberal minister, Gen. Bartolomé Espartero, was preoccupied with threats of rebellion among armed groups of Carlists in the Basque Country and other parts of northern Spain.

Nor did Soulé help matters by meddling personally in Spanish politics, apparently urging factions opposed to the government to rebel.

The foreign ministry's response to Soulé's actions was prevarication and delay, tactics that the Louisianan attributed to Spain's proverbial *mañana* attitude and that frustrated him enough to warn that the United States would resort to military action should the Spanish government fail to agree to his demands and to accede immediately to the sale of Cuba. He was also reported as having gone so far as to offer to pay Queen Isabella's personal debts if she would support such a sale. Such actions—a combination of what Spanish observers called "extravagant claims," "imaginary grievances," "stubborn promotions," and "turbulent spirit"—were said to have "astounded" Spanish officials and also to have exhausted what little remained of Soulé's "diplomatic prestige."[69]

But Soulé, though weakened, was tenacious. So too was William Marcy, the ardent expansionist who served as Pierce's secretary of state. During the summer of 1854 Marcy secretly instructed Soulé to draft a plan on how to secure Cuba for the United States. The following October Soulé traveled to Belgium, where he had arranged to meet with his fellow expansionists James Buchanan, then serving as the American minister in London, and John Y. Mason, head of the American legation in Paris. Together the trio signed the so-called Ostend Manifesto, a document that reflected Soulé's idea that Cuba belonged "naturally" to the United States and that its sale stood in the "highest and best interest of the Spanish people," as it would enable them to become "rich, powerful and contented."[70] It further stipulated that the United States was prepared to purchase the island for $130 million—$30 million more than what Polk had offered a few years earlier. But it also stipulated that should the Cortes refuse the offer, the United States would act unilaterally and take the island "without consent," or as one New York newspaper reported it, the United States was to approach Spain with "the purse in one hand, the sword in the other."[71]

In the end the Ostend Manifesto went nowhere. The Spanish government called it an "insult" inspired by Soulé's "spirit of hostility to Spain," while one prominent Madrid newspaper described it as a testament to Soulé's "clumsiness and lack of circumspection" (*torpeça y falta de circun-*

spección) and his ability to sow "discord" wherever he went.[72] The document also backfired in Washington, where it galvanized fears about the expansion of slavery and prompted renewed criticism of the expansionist-cum-annexationist policies of both Pierce and especially Marcy, who soon distanced himself from Soulé and policies the manifesto had proposed.

As for Soulé, the manifesto precipitated the end of what amounted to a failed diplomatic career. He submitted his resignation in December 1854, but before leaving Madrid he still had enough guile left to hatch one last-ditch scheme designed to force Spain to sell Cuba to the United States. It involved paying Perry to resign his office as the mission's secretary so as to create the impression that the United States was about to break diplomatic ties with Spain in preparation for war. Perry, however, refused to play ball with the outgoing minister and soon blew the whistle, publicly denouncing Soulé to the Spanish press as a "traitor to the interests of the United States."[73]

For his part Soulé, stubborn as ever, remained indignant, complaining openly about the "baseness and trickery of Spanish statesmanship." And just before leaving Spain for the United States, he wrote Marcy, "I long to be off from a Court where so little respect is paid to our country." Soulé also registered one final, embittered complaint to Lord Howden, the British ambassador, about the character and quality of the Spanish people.[74] Yet Soulé was by no means naïve. Just before saying goodbye to Madrid, he took the precaution of burning his private papers in a last-ditch effort to protect his reputation.

Soulé was clearly a diplomatic embarrassment, arguably the only U.S. minister in Madrid who managed, as Pettigrew correctly observed, to "arouse the hatred of the [Spanish] nation."[75] His immediate successors, Augustus C. Dodge (served 1855–60), a former Democratic senator from Iowa appointed by Franklin Pierce; Carl Schurz (served 1860–61), a Republican politico from Wisconsin appointed by Abraham Lincoln; and Gustav Koerner (served 1862–64), fared considerably better even though the first two shared some of Soulé's prejudices about the shortcomings of Spain's national character as well as his dim view of the quality of its politicians. Dodge, for example, described the deputies in the Spanish Cortes as "base, venal, and unworthy of names which they bear" in addition to bearing responsibility for what he regarded as the country's "lamentable condition." That, he added, "should serve as a beacon light to warn other nations how speedily and completely the most magnificent fabric of national greatness may crumble into ruins when undermined by the depravity and wickedness of those to whose its preservation has been connected." Like Soulé before him, Dodge was also keen on the annexation of Cuba—"Cuba will be ours," he once remarked—yet once in Madrid he quickly understood that Spain's government would never agree to its sale—he called it an "impossibility," also "unattainable," attributing the standoff mainly to "the stubborn and uncalculating character of the degenerate Spaniard." In contrast, Koerner proved far more conciliatory toward Spain's position on the island, noting that U.S. policy, having previously oscillated between "tempting offers of buying at almost any price" and "the use of intimidating and threatening language," had succeeded only in alienating the officials in Spain's foreign ministry.[76]

To be sure, American interest in securing the island was by no means dead, but the start of the U.S. Civil War in 1861 effectively halted efforts to do so; there were other, far more pressing issues on President Lincoln's agenda. In addition, Lincoln's Emancipation Proclamation in 1863 effectively ended the aspirations of southerners like Soulé who had envisioned the island as another slave state. Thus for a brief moment the United States took its eye off Cuba, although this did not mean that relations with Spain were totally harmonious during the course of Lincoln's presidency. Owing to past frictions between the two countries, Secretary of State William Henry Seward worried that Spain's government might recognize and offer material support to the Confederacy, although this never materialized, owing in part to some adroit diplomacy by Schurz and then Koerner. Seward also protested Spain's abortive attempt in 1862 to restore its lost sovereignty over the Caribbean island nation of Santo Domingo, but this mini-crisis ended almost as soon as it began.[77]

Shortly after the Civil War ended, Cuba was again in America's sights. In 1868 the start of an armed insurrection on the island (later to be called the Ten Years' War) attracted widespread attention in the United States.

The uprising, led in part by Cuba's large population of slaves, focused new attention on Spain's continuing presence in the Americas, as well as what many regarded as its misguided colonial policies, especially its refusal to follow the example of the United States and abolish slavery. As a result, many in Congress called on Pres. U. S. Grant to intervene in the conflict on humanitarian grounds. This the former general steadfastly refused to do even though he pointedly made reference to Cuba's "ruinous conflict" in his 1875 State of the Union of address.[78]

The one moment when Grant teetered on the edge of the intervention occurred in October 1873, after Spanish military authorities in Santiago de Cuba ordered the summary execution of eight American crew members aboard the USS *Virginius*, a filibustering vessel that was caught red-handed as it attempted to smuggle arms and munitions meant to aid the rebel cause. When news of the incident reached Washington, Grant was among the first to beat the drums of war. Another voice for armed intervention was Gen. Daniel Sickles (1819–1914), the Civil War hero Grant had appointed to be the U.S. minister in Madrid. Like Soulé before him, the imperious Sickles alienated most of the Spaniards he met, calling them a "vacillating people." His position on Cuba harked back to the era of Presidents Polk and Pierce—"if we want the island, we must go there and take it."[79] Fortunately the *Virginius* crisis—arguably the worst in Spanish-U.S. relations since that of the *Black Warrior* twenty years before—ended peacefully, owing to the timely intervention of Hamilton Fish, Grant's secretary of state. Fish was no friend of Spain, but he refused to succumb to what he called "sensationalist emotions" and insisted upon doing what was "honest and right."[80]

Taking advantage of the speed of transatlantic telegraphic communication, Fish recalled Sickles from Madrid and replaced him with Caleb Cushing, a seasoned diplomat with previous experience in Spain. Working in harmony with Agosto Ulloa, Spain's foreign minister, Fish negotiated a settlement in which Spain's government agreed to issue an official apology, punish the officers responsible for the killings, and pay a sizable cash indemnity. Upon signing this last agreement, Ulloa remarked that it promised to "draw closer the ties of friendship that bind Spain and the United States."[81]

Such optimism went too far. With the revolt still raging in Cuba, sentiment in the United States, and especially in Congress, was not about to swing very far in Spain's favor. Nor was President Grant particularly enamored with the policies of the Spanish government. The former general repeatedly used his annual State of the Union address to remind Spain that it needed to introduce the administrative reforms necessary to end the conflict in Cuba and to abolish slavery there as well as in Puerto Rico.

The peaceful settlement of the *Virginius* crisis did, however, allow for a slight thaw in relations between the two countries. The Spanish government, for example, readily accepted Grant's invitation to participate in the Centennial Exposition, which was to be held in Philadelphia in 1876. Although money was tight, Spain's commissioners set out to plan a good show, organizing several exhibits devoted to Spanish agriculture, industry, and art that were spread over several buildings. They also arranged for the construction of a national pavilion whose exhibits were expressly designed to improve commercial relations with what Spain's ministers called the "emporium of modern industry" and to "tighten the bonds between peoples . . . who ought to consider themselves brothers."[82]

The art exhibit in the Centennial Exposition's main building featured tapestries from Spain's royal collections together with photographs of prized objects in the famed armory in Madrid's royal palace—these photographs won a prize. Reaction to the paintings in the art exhibit was mixed. After having made note of the absence of works by Mariano Fortuny (1834–74), Spain's most illustrious contemporary artist and one whose picturesque renderings of Spanish life had already found their way into a number of U.S. collections, critics such as Edward Strahan, pseudonym of Earl Shinn (1837–86), fastened onto the pictures with religious themes. In doing so Strahan dredged up old Enlightenment-era prejudices with the observation that one "cause of the exclusively religious character which is stamped on the art of Spain was the all-powerful and all-pervading influence of the Inquisition, dwarfing and withering all invention, all thought that dared to express itself, except in the stereotyped forms permitted to a nation held in perpetual leading-strings."[83] But even Strahan responded favorably to the exhibition's history paintings, especially Dióscoro Puebla's *Landing of Columbus in America*, a picture reminiscent of the one by the American painter John Vanderlyn on display in the rotunda of the Capitol in Washington, along with its pendant, Antonio Gisbert's *Landing of the Puritans in America*. As for the exhibits in Spain's national building, these featured barrels of Spanish wine, crates of Cuban cigars, and a variety of ceramics, metalwork, handicrafts, and other goods meant to convey the image of Spain as a thriving nation with whom the United States could do business.

Whether these exhibits did very much to improve Spain's image in the United States is difficult to judge. More, it seems, was gained by King Alfonso XII's decision in 1876 to implement a new constitution that granted Spain's citizens a limited degree of religious liberty and guaranteed new freedoms to its press. That constitution failed to transform Spain into a democracy, but it represented an important step in that direction and was widely reported in newspapers across the United States. Further assistance came from General Grant, who at the close of his presidency in 1878 embarked on a grand tour of Europe and the Mediterranean that included a goodwill visit to Spain. Once there, Grant met with the king, as well as various officials in Madrid and Seville, but he spent most his time as a tourist, visiting not only Toledo and the Escorial but also the famed Muslim monuments in Córdoba and Granada. Upon leaving the country in December 1878, he recorded the following comment in his diary: "A most delightful trip it was, but with some discomforts of travel. Spain is generally a very poor country, with resources destroyed, but a better people than I expected to find. My impression is that the Spanish people would be industrious if they could find a reward for their labour, and that the Nation might become—again—prosperous."[84]

Few historians have paid much attention to Grant's visit to Spain, let alone his impressions of the people he met. But the significance of this visit—widely reported in both the Spanish and U.S. press—is far more important than the short entry in Grant's diary suggests. Grant was the most prominent American to travel to Spain since the visit of John Adams in 1779. In addition, his favorable impression of the country, excerpts of which were published the year after his return, paved the way for other American tourists interested in touring the Prado, the

Alhambra, and the country's other important monuments. Nor was there any inkling in the diary that Spain and the United States were necessarily the implacable "natural" enemies that Henry Adams would later suggest they were. For Grant, Spain was economically backward, but its people were basically "good." He also suggested that changes in Spain's fiscal policy—was he thinking of the tariffs that hampered the export of U.S. goods to Cuba?—could unleash Spain's potential for advancement. Such suggestions were timid, but together they augured for a closer, more amicable relationship between Spain and the United States. But for that to happen, a war—that of 1898 and one whose history I will not recount here in any detail—would first have to be fought.[85]

"Come, Let Us Forgive and Forget"

On August 11, 1898, representatives of both Spain and the United States signed a protocol ending the fighting in the war that had begun in April. On the very same day—one imagines that the protocol's ink was barely dry—*Life*, then a popular humor magazine edited in New York, published a double-page cartoon with the caption, "Come, let us forgive and forget."[86]

Drawn by the noted New York illustrator Charles Dana Gibson, the cartoon features a super-sized Columbia whose refined feminine features resemble one of the artist's famed Gibson girls. Dressed in a classical toga and a Phrygian cap—a symbol of liberty—embroidered with stars and stripes, Columbia is sitting by the seashore on a rock; in the distance a flotilla of vessels—presumably American warships—steam triumphantly by. Her extended right hand holds an olive branch, which she offers to a dark, sulking, diminutive Spaniard dressed as a matador, a metaphor for the cruelty of Spain's national pastime and, by extension, that of the Spanish people themselves. The matador looks warily toward Columbia while his contorted facial expression denotes shame, possibly embarrassment, probably both, as he reflects upon Spain's disastrous defeat in a war that ended triumphantly for the United States.

Gibson's cartoon has been used to highlight the role that racism and racial stereotypes played in the Spanish-American War.[87] Cartoons in Spanish newspapers at the time of the war generally represented Amer-

·LIFE·

"COME, LET US FORGIVE AND FORGET."

Fig. 7. Charles Dana Gibson, "Come, Let's Forgive and Forget," *Life*, August 11, 1898. Photo: Michael Seneca. The work of a leading New York illustrator, this cartoon speaks directly to the mood of rapprochement with Spain that prevailed in the United States following the 1898 war.

icans either as land-grabbing monsters or gluttonous, money-grubbing pigs. In contrast, Spaniards in America's wartime cartoons were almost invariably depicted as small, swarthy Latins often dressed, as in Gibson's cartoon, in bullfighting apparel, as this was a quick and easy way of referring to the cruelty and bloodthirstiness supposedly inherent in Spain's national character.

As this chapter has attempted to demonstrate, racial stereotyping of this kind was nothing new; it had been integral to the formulation and implementation of U.S. policy toward Spain ever since the earliest days of the republic. In the course of the nineteenth century these same stereotypes acquired yet another negative dimension as the tropes connected to the superiority of the Anglo-Saxon peoples and the deficiencies of the Latins came to the fore. This kind of stereotyping, however, took on new life following the outbreak in February 1895 of a yet another uprising in Cuba that aimed at securing the island's independence from Spain. The earlier one, the Ten Years' War, had ended somewhat indecisively in 1879, when the Spanish government introduced a number of administrative reforms, one of which granted the island's Creoles a voice in the Cortes. Those changes were followed by the abolition of slavery in 1886, but Spain's decision to keep the island under strict military rule served only to rally support in Cuba and among Cuban exiles living in the United States for "Cuba Libre."

The hero and de facto leader of this movement was José Martí (1853–95), a Cuban journalist living in exile in New York. Especially influential was Martí's trenchant essay, "Nuestra América" (Our America), published on New Year's Day, 1891, in New York's *Revista Ilustrada*. In it Martí launched his version of an America-first policy, suggesting that all of the republics of the Americas, together with Cuba, ought to be ruled by Americans as opposed to what he called the "high hats" in Madrid. Martí drummed up further support for the movement with speeches delivered to Cuban clubs in New York, Chicago, Tampa, and New Orleans, and with the assistance of several respected newspapers, especially Charles Dana's *New York Sun*, he elicited widespread support and sympathy for his cause across the United States.[88]

Another boost for the Cuba Libre movement came from the inability of the governments in Washington and Madrid to agree on a workable tariff treaty governing Cuban sugar exports to United States. A breakdown in negotiations contributed directly to the passage in 1894 of the Wilson-Gorman Tariff Act, a measure that sharply increased tariffs on imports of Cuban sugar into the United States and triggered an unexpected collapse in the island's economy, a collapse largely responsible for the revolt that began the following year.

That revolt began on the eastern part of the island but spread quickly, owing principally to the inability of Spanish forces to cope with the hit-run-and-hide guerrilla tactics the rebels employed. Equally successful, and destructive, was the rebels' Sherman-like campaign of laying waste to the island's sugar plantations, many owned by wealthy Americans. That strategy was designed to inflict major economic damage in the hope of generating additional support in the United States for the island's independence and possibly even to provoke the federal government to intervene in the conflict on the pretext of protecting endangered American property.

Despite such threats, Spain's conservative government did not give way. Its initial response to the crisis was to send more troops to the island and to sanction Gen. Valeriano Weyler's so-called *reconcentrado* policy, which entailed the forced, often brutal resettlement of the island's rural population into fortified enclaves. The intended aim of this policy was to deprive rebels of the safe havens they had been previously using to launch guerrilla attacks on Spanish troops, but ultimately it did little to squelch the revolt. On the other hand it generated mounds of negative publicity in the American press, earned Weyler the nickname of "Butcher," and garnered additional support and sympathy for the Cuba Libre movement. It also generated a wave of anti-Spanish sentiment that drew upon the old arsenal of Black Legend themes, together with the kind of racial stereotyping that appeared in Gibson's cartoon.

Theodore Roosevelt, the future Rough Rider, provided a foretaste of this kind of racial thinking in 1893 with the publication of the third part of his best-selling book *The Winning of the West*. Focused on the incursions of Kentucky backwoodsmen into the Spanish-held territories bordering the Mississippi valley at the close of the eighteenth century, Roosevelt's account of this particular episode reflected the New Yorker's well-known Anglo-Saxonist views. He labeled Spaniards as treacherous "weaklings" who necessarily had to give ground to "stouthearted" Kentuckians he alternately defined as members of an "advancing civilization" and as "representatives of a young and vigorous race." Roosevelt also ventured into the realm of social Darwinism when, again with reference to Spain, he offered the opinion that "if a race is weak, if it is lacking in the physical and moral traits which go to the makeup of a conquering people, it cannot succeed."[89]

Racially charged comments similar to Roosevelt's abounded in the 1890s as the prospect of war with Spain over Cuba seemed all but inevitable. Many came from U.S.-based Cubans directly involved in the Cuba Libre movement and who were also the source of articles highlighting (and generally exaggerating) the atrocities committed by Spanish forces as they attempted to quell the revolt. Even more damning was the letter sent to Pres. Grover Cleveland by Máximo Gómez, one of the officers commanding the rebel troops in Cuba, and read aloud in the U.S. Senate in March 1897. "It is logical," Gómez wrote,

> that such should be the conduct of the nation that expelled the Jews and the Moors; that instituted and built up the terrible Inquisition; that established the tribunals of blood in the Netherlands; that annihilated the Indians and exterminated the first settlers of Cuba; that assassinated thousands of her subjects in the wars of South American independence, and that filled the cup of iniquity in the last war in Cuba. It is natural that a people should proceed thus who, by hint of superstitious and fanatical education, and through the vicissitudes of its social and political life, have fallen into a sort of physiological deterioration, which has caused it to fall back whole centuries on the ladder of civilization.[90]

Copy like this sold newspapers, lots of them, especially in New York, where Hearst's *Journal* and Pulitzer's *World* regularly placed reports of Spanish cruelties on the front page. In a pathbreaking book published in 1934, one historian calculated that in the three years from 1896 through 1898 there were only twenty days that these and New York's other newspapers failed to publish articles critical of Spain's Cuba policy. These articles presented Spain as arrogant, insulting, vindictive, and cruel and its people as backward, cowardly, weak, deceitful, divided, and friendless. Editors also drew upon Black Legend themes to emphasize the need for intervention in Cuba. Particularly graphic in this regard was the full-page, illustrated article headlined "Spaniard Unchanged by Time's Flight" and published in the *Chicago Tribune* just prior to the start of the war. Its subtitles reached back into history to find a pretext for war: "Awful Atrocities of the Inquisition," "Contrary to the Generally Accepted Opinion, Isabella Was No Angel: As Bad As Bloody Mary," "Madness and Greed Rule Royalty," "Philip [II]'s Unheard of Savagery Towards the Low Countries Still Alive."[91] As Bonnie Goldenberg has emphasized, Spaniards fared equally poorly in the country's periodical press, with article after article pointing to their multiple failings as both a people and a race.[92]

More of the same appeared in books such as Elizabeth Wormeley Latimer's *Spain in the Nineteenth Century*, a popular history aimed at a general readership, published in 1897 and in a second edition the following year. This Baltimore author had never visited Spain, but in keeping with ideas gathered from other authors, Latimer had few qualms about blaming the Inquisition for the "deterioration of the Spanish character" and turning Spain into an "impoverished, second-rate power."[93]

Other, more highbrow authors expressed similar ideas. One was Brooks Adams, Henry's younger brother. Unlike Henry, who had visited Spain and conducted research in Spanish archives, Brooks's knowledge of Spain and its history derived mainly from his reading of Voltaire, Rev. William Robertson, and other Enlightenment authors. It follows that his *Law of Civilization and Decay*, published in 1895, zeroed in on Spain's multiple failings. The deficiencies of their "race," he suggested, suspended Spaniards in the "imaginative period" of human history and prevented them from developing modern, centralized institutions, let alone a vibrant economy. Adams returned to this theme after the war in *The New Empire* (1902), where, in a comment on the Spanish defeat, he noted that "Spaniards could not assimilate new ideas. They could not think otherwise than they had always thought. They were a primitive type."[94] Bernard Moses, a respected professor of political science at UC Berkeley known for his expertise in the history of Spain's American colonies, harbored similar thoughts. In one influential essay published just after the war, Moses went so far to describe Spain as an "arrested civilization" whose "moral weakness" was attributable to the "orientalized" character of its people.[95]

Gibson's 1898 cartoon is similarly racialized, with its outsized Caucasian Columbia towering over the dark-skinned Spanish matador. Yet as its evocative "Forgive and Forget" label immediately suggests, the cartoon delivers other, more positive messages as well. Columbia, flush with the confidence of victory, offers to make peace with the downtrodden Spaniard, welcoming him as both ally and friend.

How Gibson came to formulate this idea is somewhat mysterious, as his opinions about the war with Spain, together with his thoughts about

Spaniards, are difficult to pin down. Many in the United States, including such literary luminaries as William Dean Howells and Mark Twain, publicly expressed their opposition to the war. Gibson, however, did not. On the other hand, starting months before the outbreak of the conflict, *Life* magazine's publisher, John Ames Mitchell, ran a series of editorials opposing the war, suggesting in one that the country's "strong sympathy for Cuba . . . co-exists with an admiration for Spain and an admiration for her grit and persistence. . . . We don't want to see Spain humiliated, and if we became involved in a war with her we would go in cold-blood, and absolutely without jealousy or animosity."[96] Mitchell also attacked those who believed that the United States possessed a "moral right" to punish Spain by demanding a cash indemnity. Taking away her colonies, he wrote, was punishment enough.[97] Nor was Mitchell, cognizant of Spain's contributions to the history of the Americas, beyond expressing a certain admiration for Spain as it went down in defeat.

As might be expected, the 1898 war sparked new interest in Spain, its history, and the history of its relationship to the United States. The war had already begun, and with Spain's defeat almost a certainty, the editors of the *Atlantic Monthly* asked Henry Charles Lea, a historian famous for his books on the Inquisition, for an essay explaining the historical underpinnings of Spain's impending loss. At first Lea hesitated, as he was opposed to the war and disturbed by the imperialistic drift in America's national politics. But he soon came around, offering an essay that was published in the July issue as "The Decadence of Spain." In it Lea highlighted the country's "stagnation" but attributed this condition less to any defects in Spain's national character than to the lasting and "benumbing" effects of "clericalism" and the Inquisition on its economic and intellectual progress.[98]

Other signs of America's growing fascination with Spain came from the Bay View Association, a nationwide network of more than two thousand reading circles. In June 1898, a moment when reports on the war filled the front pages of newspapers across the United States, the association's directors announced the start of a "Spanish-French Year" that began with Spain. Established in 1875 by a group of high-minded Michigan Methodists and associated for a time with the better-known

Chautauqua movement, the Bay View Association's central mission was education and the promotion of what it called "habits of home study." Toward this end its directors created a series of study courses, many of which aimed at introducing the association's members, the majority of whom were middle-class women, to the culture and customs of foreign lands. Germany had served as the topic of the association's first study course in 1893.[99]

The start of the war against Spain justified the association's decision to create a new study course focused on that country, or as the editorial appearing in the November issue of *Bay View Magazine* explained, "We've been neglecting that people, their institutions, and their civilization, until most people possess the merest smattering of intelligence about the subject."[100] That same issue also initiated a six-month study course that included lists of recommended readings, a detailed fold-out map of both Spain and neighboring Portugal, and questions for study and discussion, as well as a series of well-illustrated articles on Spanish geography, history, politics, literature, and art. John M. Hall, the magazine's editor, also instructed members that studying Spain was important, as its long, often troubled history and recent "decline" offered important "lessons upon the causes of national prosperity and decadence," along with insights into what he uncharitably termed the "the effect of insincerity and untruthfulness, common to all the races of Latin extraction."[101]

Questions of race aside, response to the course was both immediate and enthusiastic, with a member of one reading circle reporting in December 1898, "I got more real information from our November Magazine about Spain than I have found in the newspapers and magazine since hostilities began." Other circles chimed in with reports on the "delights of the Castilian year," how the study course had moved its members from "indifference to enthusiasm" about Spain, and how much they enjoyed "learning about the Spanish." Perhaps the most insightful report, and one certainly in tune with the mood of "forgive and forget," came from the Bloomington, Illinois, reading circle, which explained that its members "had the common American feeling of contempt of Spain, but the course has given a revelation, resulting in an unexpected admiration of so much in that unhappy land."[102]

Seemingly overwhelmed by such comments, in January 1899 Hall candidly acknowledged that "Spain is all the rage this year."[103] Other editors and publishing houses sensed much the same, responding with new travel books dedicated to Spain (see chapter 3) together with reprints of older ones such as John Hay's *Castilian Days*, a volume first published in 1871. Hay had previously served as an aide to President Lincoln, and in 1866 he was appointed secretary of the U.S. legation in Madrid. His arrival in Spain coincided with a particularly volatile moment in Spain's political history, as he witnessed the overthrow of the Bourbon monarchy in 1868 followed by the start of the country's first, and somewhat bumbling, experiment with a republican form of government. These events provided the backdrop for his book, which focused on the shortcomings of Spain's political leaders in addition to providing an introduction to Spanish culture and art. As is well known, Hay (1838–1905) later served as President McKinley's secretary of state, and together with Theodore Roosevelt he emerged as one of the principal advocates of what he famously described as the "splendid little war" that the United States launched against Spain. Hay's prominent role in the conflict also helps to explain why his publisher, Houghton Mifflin, released in 1899 a new edition of *Castilian Days* that was identical to that of 1871. This edition sold so well that Houghton Mifflin soon reissued it in a handsomely illustrated "holiday" edition, albeit with the chapters critical of Spain's leaders stripped out, changes that could only have been done with Hay's permission. In a note to the reader the publisher advised that these changes were to emphasize the more "picturesque" aspects of Spanish society, as reflected in the book's illustrations by the artist Joseph Pennell.[104]

I have not been able to locate Hay's thoughts on the rationale for this new, truncated edition, but the changes he agreed to were consistent with the "forgive and forget" mood prevalent in Washington politics and throughout much of the country in the immediate aftermath of the 1898 war. They also prepared the way for Chadwick's 1909 survey of Spanish-American relations, which, as noted above, underscored the racial differences between the two nations. On the other hand the former naval commander made a point of emphasizing in the course of the

1898 conflict that Spain never lost "the goodwill and kindly regard of the American people."[105]

Chadwick got this right. Resentments lingered, however, especially among veterans who had fought in the war and in families whose sons lost their lives in the conflict. Already in June 1898, with the war still raging, the Larchmont Yacht Club on Long Island's North Shore was honoring the memory of the sailors who had lost their lives in the explosion and fire that had destroyed the *Maine*: the club members erected a display of one of the port-side lights salvaged from the vessel. Commemoration of the war's veterans also figured in the decision of Washington's exclusive Alibi Club to create a special "Spanish Room" with walls "hung with relics of recent battles donated by soldiers and sailors from the war with Spain."[106]

While these and other efforts to preserve memory of the 1898 war continued, they did little to derail the idea of "forgive and forget" announced by Gibson's 1898 cartoon. In fact "forgive and forget" gained traction almost as soon as hostilities ceased. Spain's rehabilitation officially began in February 1899, when the U.S. Senate, after considerable wrangling, ratified the peace treaty that representatives of the two countries had signed in Paris the previous December. This treaty also paved the way toward better, more amicable relations, and by November 1900 the Duke of Arcos, the new Spanish minister in Washington, had reported in one dispatch that his relations with the State Department, if not "cordial," were at least "courteous" and "correct" and showing every sign of improvement.[107]

Among the first signs of improvement was a new commercial treaty the two countries agreed to in 1901. Another came in May 1902, when President Roosevelt, in a gesture of respect for his former foe, had Jabez L. M. Curry, a veteran diplomat with previous experience in Spain, represent the United States as its "extraordinary envoy" at the ceremony celebrating the majority of King Alfonso XIII. The warm reception the monarch accorded to Curry elicited headline news in both Madrid and Washington, where the *Evening Star* headlined its article "Honors for Curry" and noted that he was "treated with greater honor than other extraordinary envoys."[108]

Curry's trip was also an icebreaker, as it opened the path toward a new treaty of friendship and cooperation ratified by both countries in November 1903. Next came a new and expanded commercial agreement, signed in 1906, that lowered tariffs on commodities ranging from American-made machinery to Spanish olive oil and wine. Officially Adams's "natural" enemies were now both allies and friends.[109]

One of the individuals who helped negotiate these new agreements was William Collier, a prominent New York attorney who in 1905 became U.S. ambassador to Spain and served the next four years. Upon his return home Collier published *At the Court of His Catholic Majesty*, a memoir recounting his experiences in Spain and one that is strikingly different in tone from those of most of his ambassadorial predecessors in Madrid. Starting with John Jay, the majority of these emissaries had openly expounded upon the shortcomings of Spain's national character. Others, like Augustus Dodge, Pierre Soulé, and John Hay, lambasted the caliber of the country's political leaders. Collier, in contrast, endeavored to reshape his compatriots' view of Spain, commenting favorably upon his experiences there and the impossibility of finding "a nobler example of the fortitude, perseverance, and constancy of a race than that of the Spaniards."[110]

Rapprochement also moved along other, less formal paths. One was trade, which by 1912 had increased to the point that Spanish authorities set up a permanent display in Philadelphia's commercial museum. In addition to olives, olive oils, wine, and other agricultural products, the display showcased a wide range of Spanish manufactured goods, notably ceramics and high-quality textiles of various sorts. Further rapprochement came from tourism, which, as we have seen with Augustus Saint-Gaudens, resumed almost as soon as the war ended and then reached record highs in the decade following the end of World War I (see chapter 7 and the conclusion). Also new were various educational and organizational exchanges, with Washington's Smithsonian Institution taking the lead. Founded in 1846, the Smithsonian was accustomed to exchanging books and other publications with Spain's Royal Academy of Sciences, but with the outbreak of the war Congress required it to suspend these exchanges, much to the institution's regret. Once the peace treaties were signed, the Smithsonian's secretary initiated conversations with Arcos to renew that exchange, and an agreement to that effect was officially ratified by Spain's Ministerio de Fomento in September 1899, setting in motion a scholarly collaboration that continues to this day.[111]

With the logjam broken, "forgive and forget" quickly gathered momentum as other institutions and organizations across the country moved to embrace the defeated enemy as a friend. One instance of this occurred in August 1900 in Chicago. The city was hosting the thirty-fourth annual encampment of the Grand Army of the Republic, a fraternal organization for veterans of the Civil War, and it was scheduled to honor those who had fought in the more recent war. For reasons he could not easily divine, Arcos, the Spanish ambassador, received an invitation to the event. Initially he hesitated, as Adm. George Dewey, famous for having obliterated the Spanish fleet in Manila in June 1898, was also on the guest list. In the end Dewey did not attend, but the ambassador did in what was clearly meant as a demonstration of friendship and respect. Reporting back to Madrid, Arcos commented favorably on the warmth of his reception in Chicago, noting that nothing was said nor done to dishonor either Spain or its people.[112]

Similar expressions of "forgive and forget" greeted the arrival in Washington of Emilio de Ojeda, Arcos's successor, in November 1902. An experienced diplomat who spoke English fluently, according to the *Los Angeles Times*, Ojeda made a splash with a short article printed in the *New York Herald* in its special New Year's Day edition of January 1, 1903. Headlined "Spain Believes All Enmities Have Ceased and Does Not Regret the Loss of Its Colonies," the article began by inviting Americans to visit Spain, where they would be warmly greeted and received. Ojeda then commented, "It is becoming generally understood, I think, by both countries that the war was due to a misunderstanding. The Americans do not feel enmity to the Spaniards that some would have us believe." In the next paragraph Ojeda, citing the example of Irving and other nineteenth-century American writers known for their interest in Spain, invited would-be authors to follow suit. Politics came next. "As for Spain," Ojeda wrote, "she is better off without colonies," a comment reminiscent of statements made by John Adams and later U.S. politicians and possibly one tailored to appeal to Americans opposed to their own country's imperial turn.[113]

The *New York Herald* article transformed Ojeda into something of a diplomatic rock star. Invitations to address various groups poured in, and Ojeda rarely said no, aiming to do all that he could to improve Spain's image in the United States. In February 1903 Washington's press corps organized its annual banquet at the Gridiron Club. The guest of honor was J. P. Morgan, but Ojeda was also singled out for special attention and invited to offer his reflections on the recent war. No transcript of his remarks survives, but an article reporting on the event and published in the *Washington Evening Star* illustrates the extent to which "forgive and forget" was in the air:

> It was a message of good-will and admiration from the Spanish people to the Americans, a hearty hand-clasp across the sea to a people so lately at war with our own. Tactfully and eloquently Señor Ojeda acknowledged the hospitality of Americans and praised their generosity to a defeated foe, and in connection therewith he paid a fit and admirably expressed tribute to the valor and chivalry of his own countrymen. The storm of applause that followed the speech showed that by it the two countries had been brought to a state of mutuality of sentiment closer than in years past.[114]

In a dispatch sent to Madrid, Ojeda, in addition to remarking on the "standing ovation" his address had elicited, underlined what he described as "repeated expressions of sympathy for Spain." To this he added, "On this and other occasions I have observed that . . . all classes of resentment [to Spain] have passed."[115]

In reality, however, Ojeda's assertion that "all classes of resentment have passed" was an exaggeration. Anti-Spanish sentiment, still fueled by the Black Legend, lingered. Ojeda was otherwise right, especially if his comments are compared to those of one Spanish diplomat who, writing in 1896, worried about the repercussions of the "putrid" atmosphere created by America's newspapers. That atmosphere, he suggested, had convinced most members of Congress, together with the public at large,

that Spain was the "most ignorant, most retrograde, and most impoverished [nation] in the world."[116]

By the time Ojeda spoke at the Gridiron Club, putrid was out, part-
nership in, and such was the theme of the remarks he offered in St. Louis
on May 2, 1903, during the ceremonies marking the second day of the
opening of the centennial exposition celebrating the Louisiana Purchase.
Together with the ambassador of France, Ojeda had received a special
invitation to participate in those ceremonies, and as he soon reported
to his superiors in Madrid, he was delighted that he did. In the invoca-
tion, he noted, the senator from Nebraska, John M. Thurston, not only
offered both ambassadors "our heartiest friendship" but remarked that
"they are our kin. We are their kin. Our forefathers came from every
country that these distinguished guests represent." Ojeda was even
happier when thunderous applause greeted Thurston's remarks about
the passing of the "personal rancor" generated by the recent "deadly
struggle" between his country and Spain and the "wishes of every true
American . . . for the weal of the Spaniard." In his own speech Ojeda
underscored the two countries' shared commitment to both progress and
civilization. He also underscored Spain's formative role in the "early
discovery of this country," possibly gesturing in the direction of the
monumental statue of Hernando de Soto, the explorer credited with the
discovery of the Mississippi River (see chapter 3), erected in the exposition's main plaza as a symbol of Spain's presence in what later became
the American West.[117]

In offering these remarks, Ojeda tapped into one of the key themes
of "forgive and forget," namely, the idea that Spain and America, far
from being natural enemies, were more like brethren-in-arms in a shared
mission to bring both religion and civilization to the Americas, both
North and South. The concept was not new—its origins can be found in
Prescott's histories of Mexico and Peru. It surfaced again in the 1880s as
the process of transforming the early Spanish missions in California into
agents of civilization began (see chapter 2) and subsequently in speeches
delivered in Chicago at the time of World's Columbian Exposition in
1893. After the war, however, the idea of a shared *mission civilisatrice*
evolved into something of a mantra uttered by a host of government

officials, especially on those occasions when representatives of the two countries appeared side by side.

Interestingly enough, one of the first to comment on this idea was Bernard Moses, whose caustic remarks about Spain as an "arrested" and "orientalized civilization" have already been cited. By December 1901, however, after having been appointed to the commission overseeing the U.S. administration of the Philippines, Moses questioned several of his previous assumptions about Spain in a speech delivered in San Francisco. In it he confessed that the United States had been slow recognize Spain's "achievements" in promoting civilization in the archipelago. Americans, he remarked, traditionally "underestimated" what Spaniards had accomplished owing to "political rivalry," "divergences of aims," and the "unlikeness of their national points of view." He then outlined what Spain had achieved, specifically noting:

> The Filipinos under Spanish influence became formally Christians and the church, in the course of the centuries it has dominated them, has impressed upon their minds a large number of practical ideas. Through the influence of these ideas the Filipinos have, to a certain extent, been turned away from the Oriental point of view and made to see things as Spaniards see them. They have been brought with respect to many particulars to occupy the Spaniard's point of view. As the Spaniard, through long contact with the Moors and the infusion of a certain amount of Jewish and Moorish blood, has become something of an Oriental, so the Filipino, through long contact with the Spaniard and the infusion of a certain amount of European blood, has become something of a European.[118]

The straitjacket of national character and attendant notion that "civilization" was contingent upon "blood" runs through these remarks, but Moses's reassessment of Spanish achievements in the Pacific was nonetheless genuine. It also aligned with what other officials were saying, together with the "forgive and forget" theme announced by Gibson's cartoon. Then too it underscores what I am labeling here as the "craze" for Spain that gained momentum following the 1898 war.

One indication of this change in attitude can be found in the comments made by one of the principal proponents of that conflict, Theodore Roosevelt, during the course of his overlooked visit to Spain in June 1914. The rationale for this visit was the marriage of the former president's son, Kermit Roosevelt, to Belle Wyatt Willard, daughter of Joseph E. Willard, then serving as the U.S. ambassador (he was the first to hold that title) in Madrid. When Roosevelt's visit was first announced, the Spanish press was not amused. In an editorial published on June 3, 1914, a few days before Roosevelt's scheduled arrival, the conservative Madrid daily, *El Imparcial*, observed that the former president's upcoming visit was most "undesirable." It also reminded readers that Roosevelt had fought against Spain in the 1898 war and that his actions—the newspaper might have also added his writings, had its editors bothered to read his *Winning of the West*—were generally unfriendly toward Spain. The editorial also commented on the "strong anti-Spanish sentiment" that had prevailed in the United States at the time of war, making note of a circus performance in New York during which a trained monkey was exhibited trampling on the Spanish flag, to the "huge delight of the audiences."[119]

Despite such rants, the newspapers in both Washington and New York reported that King Alfonso XIII and his queen offered Roosevelt a warm welcome at their summer palace at La Granja, in the mountains north of Madrid. Roosevelt was said to have had a "bully time" visiting the palace's sumptuous gardens and engaging in a three-hour discussion with Alfonso that centered on "Spanish history, of which he [Roosevelt] has been a close student." It was also mentioned that Roosevelt "referred to Spain in flattering terms, and declared "that the Spanish language, through the development of South America, might supplant French, and perhaps English, as the universal language."[120]

Back in Madrid, Roosevelt, in addition to attending his son's wedding, played tourist, visiting El Escorial as well as nearby Toledo, where he admired the cathedral and the city's new El Greco museum and where he spoke "volubly . . . on the beauties of the landscape and the architectural curiosities, of the styles, such as Gothic, Arabian, Spanish and Renaissance." But Roosevelt's favorite destination during his trip was the Prado Museum, which he visited together with the Duke of Alba and the Count of Valencia de Don Juan, a former minister of finance and creator of one of the finest private museums in Madrid. According to the *New York Sun*, "Mr. Roosevelt talked endlessly about the pictures he saw, criticising the works of the Spanish, French, Dutch and Italian schools. He was especially impressed by Velasquez, whose work he admired most enthusiastically. The Colonel intends to return to the Prado to-morrow for a farewell to Velasquez." The newspaper also reported that "Col. Roosevelt is enthusiastic over the Spanish people and the picturesqueness of both town and country. He said he wished he might stay in Spain for months and added that he intended to return some day."[121]

Coverage of the colonel's four-day visit to Spain in the *New York Times* was rather more limited, but that newspaper quoted the former president as saying, "This trip is just a spree. And I am not interested in politics now. I want to meet litterateurs and geographers and see the museums."[122] So shall we, moving now from politics to culture, and to the changes in the way Americans circa 1900 viewed their supposed "natural enemy."

ᝐ 2 ᝐ

Sturdy Spain

> To that composite American identity of the future, Spanish
> character will supply some of the most needed parts.
> No stock shows a grander historic retrospect—grander
> in religiousness and loyalty, or for patriotism, courage,
> decorum, gravity and honor. —WALT WHITMAN

Two years before Theodore Roosevelt visited Madrid, on June 8, 1912, to be exact, Washington DC hosted a gathering to dedicate its new Christopher Columbus fountain, which still graces the plaza fronting the capital's imposing Union Station. Designed by Lorado Taft of Chicago, the fountain features a likeness of Columbus: the mariner stands proudly above the prow of a ship, looking something like a visionary, his eyes seemingly fixed on the cupola of the Capitol, symbol of the nation later to dominate the world that he found. Flanking Columbus are two figures: an elderly man, representing the Old World; the other, a Native American with quiver and bow, the New. The rear of the fountain features a medallion with bas-relief likenesses of Ferdinand and Isabella, the Spanish monarchs responsible for Columbus's historic voyage.

Commuters and other travelers who now frequent Union Station tend to rush by this fountain without giving it a second look, but its dedication was reason enough to throw a weeklong celebration that brought work in the capital to a halt. Washington was then the only major American city lacking a public monument honoring the mariner's achievement. New York, Baltimore, Boston, Chicago, New Haven, and other cities had unveiled monuments honoring the mariner's achievement in 1892, when Pres. Benjamin Harrison declared October 12 to be Columbus Day, a national holiday. That same year Congress allocated $10 mil-

Fig. 8. Daniel H. Burnham and Lorado Taft, Columbus Memorial Fountain, Union Station, Washington DC, 1912. The speeches that accompanied the dedication of the fountain celebrated the historic ties between Spain and the United States. Courtesy Library of Congress.

lion for the World's Columbian Exposition, to be held in Chicago in 1893, and the Post Office decided to issue a special commemorative set of sixteen stamps honoring Columbus's achievement. The set included a four-dollar stamp with portraits of both the mariner and his patron Queen Isabella and a five-dollar stamp featuring a portrait of Columbus in profile; it now sells for upwards of $4,000 if in mint condition. On the other hand Congress, in addition to failing to allocate funds for a Columbus monument in the capital, quietly shelved plans to build a triumphal arch honoring the mariner on Sixteenth Street, on a site adjacent to the White House.[1]

Why it did so is still not entirely clear—disagreements over design? Costs? Some combination of the two? But support for a Columbus statue in Washington did not disappear. In May 1906 members of the Fifty-

Ninth Congress warmed to the idea after having listened to James T. McCleary, a longtime representative from Minnesota, read aloud certain passages taken from Washington Irving's famed biography of Columbus. Further lobbying by the Catholic fraternal order known appropriately enough as the Knights of Columbus led Congress on March 4, 1907, to allocate $100,000 for the project. It also established a commission, headed by Secretary of State Elihu Root, Secretary of War William Howard Taft, and a member of the Knights of Columbus, to oversee the monument's design. The commission solicited proposals from sculptors in three countries: the United States, "the land which Columbus gave to the world"; Italy, "the land which gave Columbus to the world"; and, "Spain, the land which made Columbus's achievement possible."[2]

That Spain figured in this list is somewhat surprising in view of the fact that the two nations had recently been at war with each other, but its appearance there reflected the "forgive and forget" theme outlined in the previous chapter. In the end the commission went to Chicago's Daniel H. Burnham, chief architect of the World's Columbian Exposition, and following his death in 1912 the completion of the project was entrusted to his colleague Lorado Taft.

The unveiling of the finished monument drew enormous crowds— tens of thousands by some reports, including many veterans of the 1898 war—who patiently listened to a long line of illustrious speakers led by President Taft. Less well known was the Honorable Joseph Scott of Los Angeles, director of that city's chamber of commerce and one of the founders of its Southwest Museum. It is not clear at which point in the ceremonies Scott mounted the podium, but when he did, he appears to have surprised—perhaps even startled—listeners by criticizing a previous speaker, evidently a New Englander, who had celebrated the role of the Pilgrim Fathers in bringing faith and civilization to North America. Taking issue with that proposition, Scott remarked that "long before the so called Anglo-Saxon had set foot as a colonist upon the American soil, the followers of Columbus had penetrated into the heart of Kansas and gone down as far as Buenos Aires." He continued with the observation that "the Spanish race, with its indomitable faith, pursued almost alone its mission of civilization and evangelization of the aborigines of America," and he concluded his remarks with a reference to the "fortitude of the Spanish race" and the manner in which Spaniards had solved "the Indian problem as it has never been attempted since."[3]

Scott's reference to Spain as the great civilizer would have been greeted with catcalls and boos in 1992 had he been alive to deliver such remarks at the celebrations surrounding the quincentennial of Columbus's voyage. Those celebrations underscored the idea of "encounter" as opposed to "discovery" as a way of elevating the status of America's indigenous cultures and keeping critics of Eurocentrism at bay. The Quincentenary also highlighted the extent to which Columbus and his followers occasioned the destruction of native peoples throughout the New World. But in 1912 Columbus was still a hero and the discovery still a benevolent act. It is likely that some of the veterans in the crowd reacted in dismay as they listened to Scott praise the country they had recently fought, although newspaper reports on the gathering make no mention of criticisms or protests of any sort.

Anglo-Catholic by birth, Scott (1867–1958) had moved to Southern California at the end of the nineteenth century, a moment when the state was busily discovering and celebrating—later critics would say "inventing"—its Spanish roots.[4] As we shall see below, that movement, initiated in the 1870s, centered on the rehabilitation of the memory of the eighteenth-century Franciscan missionary Fray Junípero Serra and the restoration of the missions he labored to create. It would also highlight Spain's role in bringing "civilization" not only to California but to other parts of the South and West. As one of that movement's chief supporters, Scott would have also known that California's efforts to hispanicize its colonial history ran parallel to similar movements in Florida and New Mexico. Dating from the 1880s, these movements were essentially regional in scope, limited primarily to those parts of the country previously under Spanish rule. Scott, in contrast, purposely journeyed to Washington in order to convey the image of Spain the great "civilizer" to a national audience largely ignorant of what he understood as Spain's "civilizing mission" in North America. As his speech readily attests, he linked that image of Spain—call it Sturdy Spain, so different from the Spain of the Black Legend—to the broader trajectory of America's history.

Scott was not alone in establishing this connection. Others included Charles H. McCarthy, professor of history at Washington's Catholic University. His book *Columbus and His Predecessors* (1912), published in conjunction with the dedication of the Columbus memorial, delivered a similar message, and by linking Spain's history with that of the United States, it helped to transform what had begun as a regional phenomenon into one that was truly national in scope. As this chapter explains, this linkage helped give the Spanish craze its start.

That craze also drew inspiration from another, quite different source, namely, the Spain Washington Irving had described as "a land of poetry and romance." That Spain—Sunny Spain—was the source of the "fever" that afflicted Augustus Saint-Gaudens when he visited the country, and it was the Spain that artists and other travelers sought to experience firsthand. Much of the appeal of Sunny Spain lay in the country's perceived difference from the rest of Europe. Part of this difference was attributed to Spain's Muslim heritage, part to its continuing embrace of traditional values that more advanced nations, in their rush to modernize, were said to have lost. James Russell Lowell, a Harvard professor who served as the U.S. minister in Spain for three years starting in 1877, summarized this difference in a letter he wrote in November 1878 in Madrid to the editor of the *Atlantic Monthly*, William Dean Howells: "You can't imagine how far I am away from the world here—I mean the modern world. Spain is as primitive in some ways as the books of Moses and as oriental."[5]

That label "oriental" derived from the notion that Spain's national character had been indelibly influenced by centuries of Muslim rule. "Oriental" also connoted racial difference, as it was linked to a wide spectrum of peoples—from the Spanish in Europe, to Japanese in Asia, along with others in Africa and Latin America—considered resistant to and in some ways unable to change. Lowell was a scholar with a profound appreciation for Spanish literature and culture, but when it came to the "people," he told Howells that "they are still orientals to a degree one has to live among them to believe. . . . They don't care about the same things that we are fools to believe in," such as "ledgers," which suggested a disposition for work and monetary gain. This opinion led

Lowell to conclude that hardworking Americans preferred the economic benefits associated with the "mill-pond," whereas Spaniards preferred the peaceful pleasures associated with the "brook."[6]

That same "brook" had enormous appeal for other American visitors to Spain, many of whom, when they wrote about the country, deliberately ignored signs of progress and change. The Spain they wanted to see was the romantic one, a Spain whose supposed backwardness rendered it relentlessly picturesque, a magic word for most nineteenth-century travelers and one that, starting in the 1880s, helped to transform Spain into a country Americans were keen to learn about and, if they could afford it, to visit as well. Sunny Spain, like the sturdy one, was more imagined than real. It also developed at a time when the country was busily building new railroads and starting new industries of different kinds, but together with Sturdy Spain it figured centrally in the craze for Spain that captured Americans' imagination as the memories of the war of 1898 began to fade.

The Origins of Sturdy Spain

In 1883 a crowd estimated at almost ten thousand people gathered in St. Augustine, Florida, to witness a historic event: an elaborately staged reenactment of the moment in 1513 when the Spanish governor of Puerto Rico, Juan Ponce de León, first stepped ashore in a verdant land he christened La Florida, or Flowered Land. Mainly a local affair, the celebration was important to the extent that it marked a turning point in the way that St. Augustine, and more generally the whole of Florida, constructed its past.

Nowadays the city of St. Augustine unabashedly promotes itself as "America's oldest city," touting its Spanish heritage as a way to attract tourist dollars. Prior to 1883, however, that heritage was generally regarded as a liability and something the local government deliberately endeavored to erase. In the 1820s, when St. Augustine was first envisioned as a winter retreat for "invalids," developers were already doing their best to transform the "ruinous buildings" of the "ancient" Spanish town into what Rufus King Sewall, an enterprising lawyer from Maine, described in 1848 as the "neat, attractive style of American village architecture."[7] As for the old Spanish fort of San Marcos, a structure dating to the mid-eighteenth century and designed to defend the city against English attacks, there was little to be done other than anglicize its name (to Fort Marion) in the hope that visitors would regard it, together with the town's old Spanish gate, as bordering on the picturesque.

What little was left of Spanish culture in St. Augustine was otherwise considered an embarrassment. Originally founded in 1565 as a military outpost, or *presidio*, designed to prevent British and French inroads into a region claimed by Spain, San Agustín, as it was originally known, never amounted to much. Its Spanish population was relatively small: a few hundred soldiers and their families and a handful of clergy, together with a large assemblage of Seminole people and black slaves upon whose labor the Spaniards depended. In 1763 the town, together with the rest of Florida, passed to British control in accordance with the terms of the Treaty of Paris, which ended the Seven Years' War, but it returned to Spanish rule in 1783 in conjunction with the peace treaty in which Britain recognized the independence of its former North American colonies. St. Augustine subsequently remained Spanish until 1821, when, following the signing of the Transcontinental Treaty negotiated by Luis de Onís and John Quincy Adams, the United States annexed the whole of Florida. That transition prompted the majority of the town's Spanish inhabitants to depart, mostly to Cuba. The several hundred who remained were mainly those from Minorca, whom the British had induced to immigrate to Florida during the period (1713–83) when that Mediterranean island was subject to British rule. New American settlers soon outnumbered the Minorcans, but for many years St. Augustine remained an impoverished backwater. One 1823 report described it as "ruinous, dirty, and unprepossessing."[8]

At that point the town's new American managers did their best to eradicate surviving vestiges of the town's Spanish—and Catholic—past. These included the annual Carnival, which marked the beginning of Lent, together with Sherivaree—St. Augustine's equivalent of Philadelphia's Mummers Parade, both viewed as "drunken revels" and "relics of popish superstition and Spanish practice" and associated in the minds of many with the town's old Catholic cathedral. In 1843, two years before Florida became a state, the visiting New York writer William Cullen Bryant happily reported that another old Spanish custom—the Holy Week celebration known as "shooting the Jews"—had disappeared along with the Minorcan families who had kept that tradition alive. Bryant also noted that St. Augustine would probably soon "part with nearly all that is left reminding the visitor of its 'Spanish origin'—its narrow streets, its high garden walls of shell-rock and its overhanging balconies—all but its fine old fort of St Mark—to look like any other American town in the Southern States."[9]

Bryant was right. Starting in the 1840s, when St. Augustine first attempted to build its reputation as a winter retreat, it did so by constructing houses, cottages, and hotels in a purely American or at least English idiom. The first was Magnolia House—built in plantation style and opened circa 1848. Next came the Hotel St. Augustine (1869) and the San Marco, erected in 1885 in the then-popular Queen Anne style. The town was, in short, doing its best to bury its Spanish past, or as the *St. Augustine Examiner* observed in 1863, "the oldest city in the US is, at last, for the first time in the history of the country, fairly, in the possession of the Anglo-Saxon, or rather, dare I say . . . of the Anglo-Yankee."[10]

Another about-face occurred in 1883, when St. Augustine's recently founded historical society elected to sponsor a citywide festival honoring Juan Ponce de León, the Spanish explorer credited with the "discovery" of Florida on Easter Sunday, 1513. As it turned out, that festival was but the first step in a concerted effort to recover St. Augustine's "lost" Spanish heritage and thus to earn its spot on the U.S. tourist map.[11]

This recovery effort began with the work of a brace of historians determined to chronicle Florida's past in ways designed to celebrate its history under Spanish rule. George Bancroft (1800–1891) had addressed this topic in his *History of the Colonization of the United States* (1841) and again in the first volume of his sprawling *History of the United States of America, from the Discovery of the American Continent* (1844). But with his Unitarian background, Bancroft did little to disguise his anti-Catholic prejudices, let alone his antipathy for Spain, a country he regarded as a "dark force" in the history of the Americas and one whose only mission there was "to carve out provinces with the sword . . . to plunder the accumulated treasures of some ancient Indian dynasty, [and] to return

from a roving expedition with a crowd of enslaved captives and a pro-
fusion of spoils."[12]

Such views also colored Bancroft's view of Spanish Florida. In 1835
Theodore Irving—Washington Irving's nephew—had published a "free
English translation" of Inca Garcilaso de la Vega's early seventeenth-
century account of Hernando de Soto's ambitious but ultimately fruitless expedition to Florida and other parts of what is now the American
South in the years between 1539 and 1541. Garcilaso's portrait of De Soto,
dating from 1605, teetered on the edge of hagiography, representing the
conquistador as a Cortés-like chivalric hero, or as Irving put it, "one
of the boldest and the bravest of the many brave leaders who figured in
the discoveries."[13] Bancroft, in contrast, went out of his way to portray
Spaniards as motivated solely by "passions of avarice and religious zeal"
and De Soto as a cruel and heartless captain "blinded by avarice and
love of power" as well as one whose encounters with natives amounted
to little more than "cruelties and carnage."[14]

Bancroft used similar language to describe Pedro Menéndez de Avilés,
St. Augustine's founder. So too did Jared Sparks, a professor of history at
Harvard College. His *Life of Jean Ribault* (1845) was part of the Library
of American Biography, edited by Sparks and probably the most important and widely read biographical series published prior to the Civil War.
Avilés was (and remains) a controversial figure, owing mainly to the
supposed brutality of his 1565 attack on a small Huguenot settlement that
the French naval officer Jean Ribault (sometimes spelled Ribaut) had
established at the mouth of Florida's St. Johns River, just north of St.
Augustine. Protestant accounts of that attack exaggerated its brutality,
traditionally describing it as a bloody and needless massacre. Bancroft
followed suit, castigating Avilés and his soldiers for their "fanaticism,"
"savage ferocity," and "wanton barbarity."[15] He also suggested that
Americans had little reason to place much stock in St. Augustine, owing
to the town's "dark and bloodstained" beginnings. Sparks agreed. The
former Unitarian minister turned historian drew upon the long-standing
Black Legend tropes to highlight Avilés's "inhumanity ... cruelty, and
blood-thirsty bigotry" and to describe him as a representative of "the
engine of oppression and cruelty" that was Spain.[16]

Little of this sat well with Thomas Buckingham Smith (1810–71), the first historian to challenge Bancroft's and Sparks's accounts of Florida's Spanish past. Born in Cumberland, Georgia, but raised in St. Augustine, Smith attended Trinity College in Hartford and then Harvard, where he studied law before returning to Florida in 1839. Once there, local politics together with the settlement of lawsuits arising from old Spanish land titles occupied much of his practice. So too did a report on the feasibility of draining the Everglades, which the Treasury secretary had commissioned with an eye toward turning what was seen as a pestiferous swamp into productive farmland. These projects also piqued Smith's interest in learning about the history of Spanish Florida and locating maps and documents relating to the colonial era. As Smith put it, many of these maps and documents were "buried" in Spanish archives in Havana and Mexico City. So began a personal odyssey to compile an archive of colonial-era materials and to write the history of Spanish Florida and more generally that of Spain in North America.[17]

In truth these subjects first caught his attention in 1824, when at the age of fourteen Smith visited Mexico City, where his father was serving as the U.S. consul to the newly independent Mexican republic. Subsequently, as a student at Trinity, Smith wrote an essay, "Annals of Florida," outlining the state's history under Spanish rule. Additional inspiration came from William Hickling Prescott's stirring *History of the Conquest of Mexico*, one of the best-selling history books of the nineteenth century and almost certainly a book Smith read shortly after its initial publication in 1843. Prescott was the first U.S. historian to write seriously about Spain and its empire, initially attracting a wide readership with his *History of the Reign of Ferdinand and Isabella* (1837), a book that one British reviewer, Richard Ford, condescendingly referred to "as the first historical work which British America has as yet produced."[18]

History of the Conquest of Mexico received even more enthusiastic reviews, especially in the Anglo-American press. As much romance as history, the book by Prescott transformed the battle for Tenochtitlan, the Aztec capital, into an epic struggle between the forces of darkness and light. On the dark side were Moctezuma and the Aztecs, representing barbarism and idolatry, and on the other Christianity and civilization in the guise of Hernán Cortés and the "chivalrous spirit of [Spanish] enterprise." In the end Christianity and civilization emerge triumphant, a victory Prescott credited to the cruel but also bold and foresighted leadership of Cortés, whom he likened to an "instrument selected by Providence to scatter terror among the barbarian monarchs of the western world, and lay their empires in the dust." Particularly memorable in Prescott's telling is the image of Cortés rallying his troops on the eve of one battle with the words, "Great things are achieved only by great exertions and glory has never been the reward of sloth."[19]

Prescott borrowed this phrase from Cortés's first biographer and former personal chaplain, Francisco López de Gómara, but the sentiments they expressed were definitely Washingtonian. Prescott possibly used them to remind readers about the heroic virtues that Mason Locke (aka Parson) Weems attributed to the first U.S. president in his influential *History of the Life and Death of George Washington* (first published in 1800). They also anticipated those that Smith later applied to Álvar Núñez Cabeza de Vaca, Hernando de Soto, and other Spaniards who first ventured into Florida and other parts of the North American South and West.

Cabeza de Vaca came first. One of the few survivors of the doomed Narváez expedition to Florida in 1528, Cabeza de Vaca was among the first Spaniards to come into contact with, and also to write about, the indigenous peoples of North America's South and West. His was a story of courage and adventure: a clash with native warriors near Tampa; a shipwreck that stranded him and a few other companions near what is now Galveston, six years wandering through Texas and other parts of the Southwest in the company of various indigenous groups, and finally a near miraculous encounter with a Spanish expedition in northern Mexico that eventually took him to Mexico City and back to his homeland in Spain.

While Cabeza de Vaca's account (or *relación*) was initially published (in Spanish) in 1542 and again in a more complete edition in 1555, it was slow to appear in English. Samuel Purchas had included some excerpts in the first volume of his compendium of travel accounts, *Purchas: His Pilgrimages*, originally published in 1613. However, the only available

Fig. 9. William H. Prescott (1796–1859), late in life. Engraving by D. H. Pound after a photograph by Whipple and Black. The celebrated but almost blind historian is depicted here with his noctograph, a device that made it easier for him to write. MHS #2722. Courtesy Massachusetts Historical Society.

translation of the complete text dates from 1705. Smith, having purchased
a copy of the 1555 edition in 1848, soon embarked on a new translation
together with the composition of a map reconstructing what he believed
to be the route of Cabeza de Vaca's travels. The completed translation,
privately published in Washington with the assistance of a wealthy banker,
George Washington Riggs, appeared in a limited edition of one hundred
copies for private circulation in 1851.[20]

By this time Smith had already embarked on a more ambitious project to gather additional materials, a kind of mini-archive consisting of
maps, transcriptions of archival documents, and rare books, relating to
Florida's Spanish colonial past. To advance this project he managed to
secure an appointment as a secretary of the U.S. delegation in Mexico
City starting in 1850, using that position to make contact with Joaquín
García Izcabalceta, José Fernando Ramírez, and other Mexican historians with interests similar to his own.

Smith's antiquarian research in Mexico City fed directly into his next
project: a translation of the one surviving contemporary account of Hernando de Soto's explorations. *The True Relation* was a gripping account
of a pioneering Spanish expedition that began in Florida in 1539, peaked
with the discovery of the Mississippi River in 1541, and ended with the
conquistador's death and burial in that same river the following year.
The work of an anonymous Portuguese nobleman known as the Knight
of Elvas and reportedly part of De Soto's expedition, *The True Relation*
was originally published in Portuguese in 1557, translated into English by
Richard Hakluyt in 1609, and subsequently republished in 1846 by Peter
Force in the fourth volume of his collection of documents relating to the
early history of the American colonies. Recognizing the shortcomings of
Hakluyt's translation, together with those he detected in Garcilaso de la
Vega's largely hagiographic account of De Soto and Theodore Irving's
De Soto biography, as well as the biases in Bancroft's history, Smith set
out to locate new documents relating to the De Soto expedition and other
relevant materials for a planned history of Spanish Florida and, more
broadly, of Spain's often forgotten contribution to the discovery and
later settlement of lands ultimately to become part of the United States.

Interest in this last subject had begun with Columbus, the "discoverer of America" Washington Irving had lionized in his best-selling *Life and Voyages of Christopher Columbus* (1828), but it soon extended to De Soto.[21] The latter explorer's reported discovery of the Mississippi received official sanction in 1853 from the congressional committee charged with the selection of the history paintings aimed at illustrating critical moments in the nation's history and intended for display in the rotunda of the new capitol building, still under construction in Washington DC. The first four of the planned eight pictures, all by John Trumbull, depicting key moments of the War for Independence—*Declaration of Independence*, *Surrender of General Burgoyne*, *Surrender of Lord Cornwallis*, and *George Washington Resigning His Commission*—were hanging in the rotunda by 1824. Disagreements over the subjects appropriate for the four remaining pictures stalled the completion of this project for more than a decade, and only in 1836 did Congress manage to instruct the committee to choose subjects that would "illustrate the discovery of America, the settlement of the United States, the history of the revolution, or the adoption of the Constitution."[22] The resulting commissions went to John Vanderlyn for *Landing of Columbus*, a picture that signaled a connection between Spain and the history of the United States; to John Chapman for *Baptism of Pocahontas*; to Robert Weir for *Embarkation of the Pilgrims*; and to Henry Inman for a painting of Daniel Boone's move to Kentucky. The first three were hanging in the rotunda by 1843, but Inman's untimely death in 1846 prevented the completion of the fourth. After several years of indecision, and considerable lobbying as well, in 1853 Congress voted to offer the commission to Inman's favorite disciple, William H. Powell. It also voted to replace the Boone migration with De Soto's discovery of the Mississippi, a subject in tune with the expansionist fervor gripping the country in the wake of the U.S.-Mexico War of 1846–48. Whether Smith ever saw Powell's picture following its installation in the rotunda in December 1853 remains unknown, but he is almost certain to have read some of the press reports it received. These began with a review in the *National Intelligencer* that commented on the "important part played by religion, allied with force, in the conquest of the New World." The hanging of Powell's picture was also accompanied by the publication of several pamphlets explaining its imagery and meaning, among them Henri L. Stuart's *William H. Powell's Historical Picture of the Discovery of the Mississippi by De Soto, A.D. 1541,* which, in keeping with the politics of the moment, announced that De Soto's discovery marked the "opening of a mighty empire and expansion."[23]

Smith's interest in De Soto, however, had less to do with the country's expansionist politics than with the opportunity to advance knowledge of Florida's past and its place in the colonial history of the United States. The opportunity for him to do research on these intertwined projects came in 1855 after he secured a second diplomatic appointment as secretary of the U.S. legation in Madrid. Once in Spain, Smith secured a royal order granting him permission to "examine all documents bearing directly or indirectly on the history of North America, its islands or seas." Armed with this document, he set out to do research in the royal archives in both Simancas and Seville, happily reporting in one letter, "I am having a fine time among the manuscripts." Smith also expressed his enthusiasm about his discoveries in Seville's Archive of the Indies to Ephraim G. Squier, an archaeologist who shared his interest in the history of Spanish America, with the comment, "There are riches for us at Sevilla enough for our utmost indulgence; could I be there permanently."[24]

Over the next two years Smith seemingly devoted himself more to Florida's history than to his duties at the legation, much to the dismay of the American minister, Augustus Dodge, who evinced little interest in either Spain or its history. But Smith persisted and in 1856 published a new and updated translation of the Knight of Elvas's account of the De Soto expedition, including a remarkably frank and objective assessment of De Soto's record. Smith recognized that De Soto was no angel, that he was an explorer whose treatment of the natives was ruthless, even cruel. Smith acknowledged these failings but attributed De Soto's actions to the exigencies of war. As for the explorer's strengths, here too he exhibited a bit of restraint, recognizing that Garcilaso had gone too far in his posthumous praise for the explorer's achievements. Grounding his own assessment in that of the Knight of Elvas and in another contemporary account of the expedition by Luis Hernández de Biedma that he had found in the Spanish archives, the adjectives Smith used to describe De Soto mimicked those Prescott had employed for Cortés: "brave," "prudent," "kindly," and "magnanimous." Smith also went out of his way to praise De Soto and his companions for their "nobility of spirit, compassion towards the natives . . . and manly virtues." He also made a point of describing the Spaniards of De Soto's generation as "refined, enlightened and [as] humane as any [people] of Europe."[25]

Smith's high opinion of Spanish humanity is one with which other historians, Bancroft especially, as well as Francis Parkman Jr., would have certainly disagreed. It was also at odds with the views of Lambert Wilmer, a Philadelphia writer who authored a popular biography of De Soto in 1858, ostensibly to cash in on the publicity surrounding the installation of Powell's De Soto painting in the Capitol rotunda. Wilmer lionized De Soto as the "most humane and heroic" of all the Spanish commanders in the Americas but otherwise drew on the standard repertoire of Black Legend tropes to castigate the character and comportment of the soldiers in the explorer's entourage for their "tyrannous and diabolical cruelty."[26]

These long-standing tropes—and they can also be found in Emanuel Leutze's *The Storming of the Teocalli Temple by Cortez and His Troops* (1848), another "historical picture" that elicited considerable publicity when first displayed in New York's American Art-Union in 1849—were precisely those Smith sought to correct.[27] Smith was no Hispanophile in the strict sense of the term. His interest in creating a more positive image of Spain is instead best related to his determination to endow Florida, or what he would soon refer to as his *patria*, the Spanish term for home- or fatherland, with a "genealogy of virtue" comparable to those of states in the Northeast. The book in question was Smith's *Compendio de varios documentos para la historia de Florida y tierras adyacentes* (1857), a volume whose publication in London was subsidized by his friend, George Washington Riggs, the Washington banker who had previously funded Smith's translation of the Cabeza de Vaca work. Aimed mainly at specialists, it comprised transcriptions of documents relating to Spanish Florida that Smith had located in various Spanish archives and libraries.

Smith also intended the *Compendio* to serve as the starting point for a comprehensive narrative history of Florida under Spanish rule, but his plans for this history were disrupted in 1857 when Dodge, having had enough of Smith's historical interests, summarily dismissed him from his position as secretary and ordered him to leave Spain. The dismissal must have come as a relief, as Smith probably had also had enough of Dodge, whom he later described as "conceited, arrogant, ignorant, and big-fisted . . . he is little else but a mere animal . . . no memory or education . . . he is a monstrous fool."[28]

Upon leaving Madrid, Smith went to Granada, where he visited the Alhambra before returning to his home in Florida. With the outbreak of the Civil War, a conflict he called a "rebellion" on the part of the South, he relocated to New York, where he continued his book purchases and added to his Spanish materials archive until his death in 1871. A year later a wealthy friend purchased this collection from Smith's estate and donated it to the New-York Historical Society, where the Thomas Buckingham Smith Collection can be consulted today.

As for Smith's long-planned history of Spanish Florida, this unfinished project passed to his friend and fellow historian George Rainsford Fairbanks (1820–1901). Born in Waterford, New York, Fairbanks attended school in Montreal and studied law at Union College prior to moving in 1842 to St. Augustine, where he found work as a clerk in the newly created superior court of eastern Florida. Disputes relating to old Spanish land titles led Fairbanks, like Smith before him, to the study of Spanish and then the history of Florida under Spanish rule. In 1856 he joined Smith in helping to establish the Historical Society of Florida (later Florida Historical Society), which was based in St. Augustine and dedicated in part to publicizing its status as North America's oldest town. Asked to deliver the inaugural address at the society's first meetings, Fairbanks gave a talk, "The History and Antiquities of the City of St. Augustine, Florida," using for this purpose copies of documents that Smith had collected in Spain, and in 1858 he published an expanded version of his talk in a slim volume dedicated to Smith.[29]

It was no surprise then that Fairbanks's account of De Soto's adventures closely followed Smith's White Legendish script. He praised De Soto for his "nobility of spirit" and his companions for treating natives with "with greater kindness than any other nation." Fairbanks followed that same script in his account of Pedro Menéndez de Avilés's massacre of the Huguenot colony at Fort Caroline, previously described by both Bancroft and Sparks. Here Fairbanks engaged in a bit of revisionist history with the claim that Domingue de Gourgue, the French soldier who first reported on this particular incident and who also engineered a massacre of Spaniards when he launched a counterattack on Fort Caroline the following year, had deliberately exaggerated the extent of their cruelties "out of vengeance" and in doing so had "unnecessarily and undeservedly besmerched the name and reputation of Pedro Menéndez de Avilés."[30]

Fairbanks was right to challenge the veracity of Gourgue's account of the massacre but left himself open to criticism by failing to consider both Avilés's own report of what had occurred and one that Thomas Buckingham Smith had previously transcribed in Madrid. In this report, dated October 15, 1565, Avilés had specified the number of *luteranos* killed in the attack on Fort Caroline along with twelve others who, having escaped the initial Spanish onslaught, were captured and then stabbed to death. Avilés also indicated, however, that he had spared the lives of women and children living in the fort, as well as the lives of a number of French carpenters and caulkers whose skills were needed at St. Augustine.[31]

Whether Fairbanks ever had the opportunity to consult this letter remains unknown. What's certain is that the account of Avilés and his activities included in Fairbanks's 1871 *History of Florida* was decidedly more balanced than those found in the earlier works of Bancroft and Sparks.[32] It also contradicted the description of Avilés that the Boston-based historian Francis Parkman Jr. (1823–93) offered in *Pioneers of France in the New World* (1865). Parkman acknowledged that Smith had provided him with a transcript of Avilés's letter, but this did nothing to dissuade him from describing the *adelantado* as a "pious butcher" responsible for the massacre of freedom-loving Huguenots or from comparing Spain to a "citadel of darkness, a monastic cell, an inquisitorial dungeon, where no ray could pierce."[33] In contrast Fairbanks openly acknowledged Avilés's "cruelty" and "bigoted" religiosity, but his main concern was writing an unbiased, factual history of Spanish Florida that started with the voyages of Ponce de León and ended with the close of the so-called Florida War in 1821.

Fairbanks's narrative, focused on military and political events, is rather thin. But it is surprisingly evenhanded, addressing both the strengths and weaknesses of Spanish colonial rule. Fairbanks also made explicit reference to the efforts of Spanish friars to Christianize Florida's natives. And whereas Parkman and other historians had questioned the legitimacy of Spain's title to Florida, Fairbanks did just the opposite, defending the legitimacy of Spain's presence in the region and highlighting what he regarded as the repeated and wholly unjustified efforts of the British governors of Georgia to wrest Florida from Spanish control.

Rarely read today, Fairbanks's history represented a pioneering effort to provide a serious examination of Florida's history under Spanish rule. It also served as a counterweight to both Bancroft's and Parkman's Anglocentric approach to the colonial history of the United States, as well as that of such other commentators such as Edward Everett, the U.S. senator whose 1853 essay "The Discovery and Colonization of the Americas" criticized Spain's (and Portugal's) empire for having failed to achieve "anything hopeful for human improvement."[34] Fairbanks had other ideas. Drawing upon transcriptions of the documents Smith had unearthed in Simancas and Seville, he sounded the opening bell in what proved to be a concerted, decades-long effort to document as well as to defend the record of what Scott, in the speech referred to at the start of this chapter, referred to as "Spain's mission of civilization and evangelization" in North America.

Nor was Fairbanks's revisionist brand of history limited to his adopted state. Writing about Florida, he also managed to create what amounted to a new, Spanish-accented template for writing U.S. colonial history that other scholars, especially those interested in the early history of the South and Southwest, would soon employ. But before getting to these scholars, let's return to Florida and recognize the extent to which Smith's template sparked new interest in learning about and also marketing the state's Spanish past as a way of attracting tourists from the North.

This sales pitch began in earnest on March 27, 1883, when the St. Augustine Historical Society organized the first in a decades-long series of historical reenactments of Juan Ponce de León's 1513 landing in Florida. Reports concerning this first Ponce de León festival are somewhat

Fig. 10. Ponce de León celebration program, St. Augustine, Florida. First held in 1883, the festival, designed to increase tourism, marked the start of the town of St. Augustine's embrace of its Spanish past. St. Augustine Historical Society. Photo by the author.

sketchy, but it centered on a celebration of the town's Spanish past, creating what was billed as a "great historical picture" of the moment when Ponce de León and his soldiers first discovered the "land of flowers." The town was draped in the red and yellow colors of Spain; a group of specially recruited Seminole people assembled on the beach to greet Ponce de León, as played by Francis B. Genovar, a local politician and cigar manufacturer of Minorcan extraction, together with forty-six other town residents wearing Spanish period costumes. Next came a high mass sung in the fort, followed by the Parada de los Coches y Caballos, a parade of mounted conquistadors and carriages bearing men and women in Spanish dress. Finally, George Fairbanks, then serving as editor of the *Florida Mirror* in the nearby town of Fernandina, delivered a lengthy oration focused on Florida's discovery by Ponce de León, St. Augustine's founding by Menéndez de Avilés, and ultimately its incorporation into the United States. In a nod to the city's budding tourist industry Fairbanks also touted St. Augustine's "unique foreign character" and how, in the "Ancient City, the spirit of the past endures."[35]

The *Florida Mirror* described the crowd that gathered to witness the event as the largest in Florida's history. The article is unfortunately short on specifics, but other sources indicate that among the listeners gathered to hear Fairbanks sing the praises of Spanish St. Augustine was Henry M. Flagler, the railroad magnate and real estate developer who, as chapter 6 recounts, was soon to give St. Augustine the look of "Old Spain" and, in doing so, spark the beginnings of Florida's discovery of its "lost" Spanish past.[36]

New Mexico: A Tri-Partite Society

The timing was probably coincidental, but 1883 also marked the year Santa Fe, capital of the Territory of New Mexico, chose to showcase its own colonial past. Dubbed the Tertio-Millennial Celebration, it was stuck with a name that created confusion, as not everyone understood what it meant. The celebration's commissioners explained that it referred to the one-third of a millennium, 333 years (the actual number was 338) during which New Mexico was subject to Spanish and then Mexican rule. That era began with Francisco Vázquez de Coronado's pioneering expedition

to the region in 1540 and ended in 1848, when the United States, following its victory in the U.S.-Mexico War of 1846–48, assumed control of
New Mexico, California, and other parts of the Southwest in accordance
with the terms of the Treaty of Guadalupe Hidalgo.[37]

Together with St. Augustine's Ponce de León celebration, the Tertio-
Millennial event had avowedly promotional aims, seeking both to attract
tourists to Santa Fe and to bring investment dollars to the New Mexican territory as a whole. Yet New Mexico's complex racial politics rendered the Tertio-Millennial Celebration quite unique. Subject to military
rule in the immediate aftermath of the U.S.-Mexico War, New Mexico
in 1851 was constituted as a territory with a presidentially appointed
governor and elected legislature that met in Santa Fe, its newly designated capital. That legislature was dominated by delegates drawn from
the elite of the territory's Mexican population, a small but relatively
wealthy group of established merchants, landowners, and ranchers col-
lectively known as the *ricos*. Partly to distance themselves, both culturally
and socially, from the *paisanos*, the poor, largely illiterate agricultural
laborers who constituted the overwhelming majority of the territory's
Spanish-speaking or *nativo* inhabitants, the *ricos* commonly referred
to themselves as *españoles*, claiming in some instances to be the direct
descendants of the conquistadors who had first settled New Mexico in
the seventeenth century.

In contrast, the territory's new American leaders, together with its
rapidly growing population of Anglo immigrants, rarely made such distinctions. In an era when race was believed to condition behavior, temperament, and industriousness, together with adaptability to progress
and change, Anglos tended to classify all Mexicans, rich and poor, rico
and paisano alike, as members of the decidedly and demonstrably inferior Latin "race." Josiah Gregg (1806–50), a transplanted Tennessean,
self-styled "Santa Fe trader," and explorer with considerable experience
in New Mexico and other parts of the Southwest, helped to create such
stereotypes in his widely distributed *Commerce on the Prairies* (1844)
with the comment that "New Mexicans appear to have inherited much
of the cruelty and intolerance of their ancestors, and no small portion of
their bigotry and fanaticism as well."[38] Other observers, notably John

Russell Bartlett, the distinguished linguist and one of the founders of the American Ethnological Society, made some allowance for the ricos, whom he described as "Castilians," but he otherwise categorized the paisanos—whom he labeled mixed-bloods or mongrels—as "human wretchedness in its worst state."[39] Further insights into this kind of highly charged racialized thinking can be found in William Watts Hart Davis's *El Gringo; or, New Mexico and Her People* (1855), a work written while Davis, a Pennsylvania native who had been educated at Harvard, was serving a three-year term (1853–56) as secretary of the new territory.

Notwithstanding the book's curious title—*gringo* was the term Mexicans traditionally applied to foreigners, Americans in particular, who spoke little or no Spanish—Davis intended the volume as an introduction to a region few of his readers would have known much about. Toward this end he coupled a brief survey of New Mexico's history with information about the territory's population and economy along with his thoughts about its prospects for development and growth. Central to his plans was the immigration of gringos, as he believed that the racial limitations of the territory's other ethnic groups constituted a brake on New Mexico's future. These limitations included the "cunning and deceit" of the Pueblo and other indigenous peoples and the "cruelty, bigotry, and superstition" he attached to Spaniards. As for the Mexicans, he pointed to the shortcomings of their "Catholicism" and of their mestizo background, a mixture he likened to an unsavory cocktail of Moorish, Spanish, and Indian blood. Davis here seems to have been thinking primarily of the paisanos, whom he characterized as a "dark, swarthy" people incapable of "improvement."[40]

Not every Anglo shared Davis's prejudices. One such Anglo was Kirby Benedict (1811–74), a lawyer who had moved from Illinois to New Mexico in 1858 to serve as the territory's chief justice, a position he held until 1866. In a speech delivered in Santa Fe on December 31, 1859, Benedict invoked the idea of Christian brotherhood as a unifying factor in New Mexico's past. He also underscored the "heroic qualities" of the Spaniards, whom he credited for having brought "civilization and religion" to a region that, as he described it, was still in the throes of "barbarism."[41]

Benedict's admonitions aside, Anglos were generally reluctant to ascribe any favorable traits to the Mexicans living in the Southwest. Consider the Colorado politician who, in a speech delivered at the time of that territory's admission to statehood in 1876 and intended to honor all of the region's inhabitants, uttered the following remark: "Of the Mexicans, I can believe that I can say nothing in their praise, except that they are very hospitable. As a race, they are low, filthy, and treacherous, and seem to have no wish to improve their condition. . . . I never expected to see such a race in America; they hardly deserve the name of human."[42]

Objection to these and similar comments came from LeBaron Bradford Prince (1840–1922), another transplanted New Yorker. He served as New Mexico's chief justice from 1879 to 1882 and then for a three-year term as its governor starting in 1889. A strong supporter of New Mexican statehood, Prince rallied to the support of what he called the "Spaniards of New Mexico"—his term for the ricos—in a letter published in the New York Times on February 20, 1882, and written in response to a Times article headlined "Greasers as Citizens" and filed by an anonymous writer from Trinidad, Colorado, who was alarmed by the prospect of New Mexico becoming a state. The article claimed that two-thirds of the territory's inhabitants belonged to a "mongrel race known as Mexicans—a mixture of the blood of the Apache, negro, Navajo, white horse thief, Pueblo Indian, old-time frontiersmen with the original Mexican stock . . . distinguished only by its ignorance, lack of literacy, 'paganish Catholicism,' and penchant for crime." It also maintained these same individuals lacked the capacity to wield political power in a responsible and democratic manner.[43]

Prince was indignant in his response. His letter to the Times defended the race purity of the "better classes" of New Mexicans by describing them as "fit representatives of the land of the Cid. And successors of the heroic discoverers and conquerors of the soil." It also quoted a recent report prepared by the territorial governor and indicating that the territory's Mexican citizens were a "well-disposed, patriotic, and liberty-loving people" who rarely committed "heinous crimes." If New Mexico had a reputation for lawlessness, Prince added, responsibility rested chiefly with "desperadoes" from "other localities."[44]

Despite Prince's spirited defense of New Mexico's "Spaniards," the prejudices outlined in the "Greasers as Citizens" article offer a good indication of the way most Anglos residing in the Southwest thought about Mexicans, the paisanos in particular. Put simply, the Anglo view was that they too were greasers, members of a race whose culture and history were distinctly different from, and inferior to, that of the Anglo-American. Such attitudes also help to explain why the first generation of Anglo officials in New Mexico endeavored to americanize the territory as best they could.

This policy of americanization took various forms. It began with the construction of railways in the belief that improved transportation would encourage immigration of Anglo settlers and help speed the "whitening" of the territory. Toward this end local officials created the Bureau of Immigration. Starting in 1879, that bureau orchestrated the publication of a series of promotional pamphlets touting the "resources and advantages" New Mexico offered to (white) "capitalists" and "laborers" willing to join the ten thousand or so "intelligent, patriotic, energetic, economical, honest and frugal" individuals who had settled in the territory between 1846 and 1880.[45] Most of these new arrivals were Anglos hoping to cash in on New Mexico's mineral wealth, while others were former slaves fleeing the South and still others, Jewish merchants and shopkeepers from the Midwest. Compared to the number of Mexicans living in New Mexico, these migrants accounted for only a fraction of the territory's population, but their presence in Santa Fe allowed the well-known naturalist Ernest Ingersoll to describe the city's inhabitants in an 1880 essay as a colorful mixture of "Fra Diavolo–looking Spaniards; negro soldiers; dirt-grimed bull-whackers; grizzled miners; natty clerks with Hebrew noses, and half-breed Mexicans," the latter being a reference to the paisanos he described as "ignorant," "lazy," and "superstitious."[46]

The essay alluded to another aspect of New Mexico's efforts to become more American when Ingersoll noted that the only building in Santa Fe he really liked was the city's "new and splendid cathedral of carved stone."[47] In the mid-nineteenth century Anglos like Ingersoll had little appreciation for or interest in New Mexico's distinctive adobe dwellings, or as W. H. H. Davis scathingly put it in *El Gringo*, buildings made of "mud." The territory's architectural transformation began in 1853, when the U.S. Congress allocated funds to replace Santa Fe's old, Spanish-era, one-story adobe Palace of the Governors with a new territorial capitol. The architect selected was Washington's Ammi Burnham Young, who, working in conjunction with Joab Houghton, New Mexico's first chief justice, designed a Greek revival–style building similar to other state capitols, including one that Young had designed for Montpelier, Vermont. For complicated reasons the building Young designed never became New Mexico's capitol. It was transformed instead into a federal courthouse, but its construction marked the beginning of a concerted attempt to rid Santa Fe of its Spanish past and to give it a more "American" look.

Central to that makeover was the americanization of the old Governors' Palace, a one-story "mud" building whose most distinctive design element was the simple wooden arcade facing Santa Fe's central square (now plaza). A new Greek revival porch was added to the building's façade in the 1850s, and this was followed a few years later with a new classically styled balustrade that stretched along the length of its roof. In the 1870s Santa Fe also acquired something of a Victorian look with a new hotel (the Palace) and other buildings built in the Queen Anne style popular back east, as well as other structures built of stone.

The most dramatic change in the local cityscape got under way in 1869, when construction began on the cathedral mentioned in Ingersoll's essay. The moving force behind the new cathedral was the territorial archbishop, Jean-Baptiste Lamy, a native of Toulouse, France, later immortalized in Willa Cather's famous 1927 novel, *Death Comes for the Archbishop*. Intended to replace the existing adobe church of San Miguel, commonly known as *la parroquía* (parish church), the building was designed in the Romanesque style and modeled after the medieval cathedral of Saint-Étienne that Lamy had known in his youth in Toulouse. After the cathedral was finished in the 1880s, only the interior of the church remained in use, as it became the cathedral's Rosary Chapel. Otherwise, its "mud" was mostly, and discreetly, out of sight.

Yet for all the criticism mud received when New Mexico first became a territory, opinions regarding the adobe that exemplified Santa Fe's

Spanish-cum-Mexican architectural heritage were changing. The initiative here came from the Historical Society of New Mexico, which was founded in Santa Fe in 1859, disbanded during the Civil War, and subsequently reconstituted with help from William G. Ritch, the territorial secretary (and acting territorial governor) who was elected its president in December 1880.

Yet another transplanted New Yorker, Ritch (1830–1904) was instrumental in guiding New Mexico's future. For example, while serving as director of the territory's Bureau of Immigration, he orchestrated the publication of various illustrated pamphlets representing Santa Fe as a mecca for "pleasure-seekers crossing the continent" along with invalids suffering from asthma, tuberculosis, and other pulmonary ailments. Key to these plans was the promotion of what Ritch regarded as one of New Mexico's unique assets: its indigenous and Spanish heritage. Ritch consequently used his inaugural speech as president of the historical society to remind his audience that the society's primary purpose was the discovery and preservation of "the historical facts, manuscripts documents, legends, and memories relevant to this territory" along with historical curiosities, specimen books, and geographical maps. He also indicated that the society needed to correct the "careless misrepresentations" of New Mexico and its history that were regularly appearing in the popular press, citing as a prime example of such misrepresentations an article from a New York magazine that had situated the territory to the south of Arizona. He also urged the society to begin restoration of Santa Fe's old "adobe palace," a building that one visitor had described in 1876 as being as "speckled and spotted as Joseph's coat . . . a disgrace to any civilized and enlightened nationality," with an eye toward creating a "tourist shrine" that would attract visitors to New Mexico.[48]

Efforts to resuscitate—and also to "sell"—New Mexico's Spanish past began on July 4, 1876, during the course of Santa Fe's celebration of the centennial of the United States. On that occasion various speakers made reference to the "heroic annals" of Spain during New Mexico's colonial era, although the only one whose remarks have been preserved is Eugene A. Fiske (1848–1910), an Anglo lawyer and future U.S. attorney in New Mexico. His address, "Spain, the Mother Country of the

Castilian Race in America," referred to Spaniards as a "brave, generous and enlightened people." Fiske also underscored the importance of
the achievement of those men "who carried the name of Spain and the
Christian religion into the heart of a new continent then swarming with
a strange and hostile people."[49]

The reaction of the Anglos who heard Fiske's oration remains
unknown, but it was warmly received by New Mexico's *españoles*, many
of whom claimed to be direct descendants of the Castilians he had
praised. So began the equivalent of a midcourse adjustment in New
Mexico's cultural trajectory, one that gradually steered the territory
(and after 1912, the state) away from the path toward americanization and onto others leading in a number of different, often competing directions. One, the favorite of Anglos such as Ritch, encouraged
New Mexico to embrace, and also to market, its indigenous past. The
other, championed primarily by prominent *españoles* with seats in the
territorial legislature, opted for hispanicization and restoration of the
region's colonial Spanish heritage.

Tensions between these groups meant that agreement over which of
these paths New Mexico should follow remained a source of contention,
and indeed echoes of these disagreements still resonate in New Mexican politics today. But in 1883, when plans first gelled for the Tertio-
Millennial, New Mexico's first major effort to market its history and
culture on a national scale, a compromise was reached. The script for
this celebration was largely the work of LeBaron Bradford Prince and
taken from his *Historical Sketches of New Mexico*, a book whose publication was timed to coincide with the festival's opening day and dedicated to what he defined as New Mexico's tripartite culture. The book's
dedication reads as follows:

> Dedication to the People of New Mexico; threefold in origin and
> language, but now one in nationality, in purpose, and in destiny;
>
>   To the Pueblos, still representing the unchanged form of aborig-
> inal civilization which built the cities and established the systems of
> government and social life which astonished European discovers
> nearly four centuries ago;

To the Mexicans, who in generosity, hospitality and chivalric feeling are worthy sons of the *conquistadores*, who, with undaunted courage and matchless gallantry, carried the cross of Christianity, and the flag of Spain to the ends of the earth;

To the Americans, whose energy and enterprise are bringing all the appliances of modern science and invention to develop the almost limitless resources which nature has bestowed upon us;

To all, as New Mexicans, now united in advancing the prosperity and working for the magnificent future of the territory, of which the author is proud to be a citizen.[50]

Prince's rhetoric is inflated, his characterization of New Mexico's peoples overly essentialized. But in 1883 both were understood as a sharp rebuke to Anglos eager to americanize the territory at the expense of what he regarded as its greatest asset: ethnic diversity and a rich historical past. Elsewhere in the book Prince described the Pueblo people as "industrious, frugal, honest, and hospitable," congratulated Spaniards for their "enterprise and prowess" and their success in bringing Christianity to New Mexico, and described Mexicans as "sons of the conquistadors," his way of dignifying New Mexico's Hispanic population, rico and paisano alike. And while Prince devoted only a few pages to the thirty-odd years New Mexico was subject to Mexican rule, he at least congratulated the Mexican government for sound administration, the creation of public schools—something that Davis claimed they neglected—and the promotion of commerce along the length of the fabled Santa Fe Trail. As for the Americans, Prince studiously steered clear of mentioning New Mexico's querulous politics, choosing instead to thank all of the territory's inhabitants for joining with other citizens of the "Great Republic" in "sustaining the honor of the American nation, enhancing its glory, and fulfilling its great mission."[51]

In keeping with these ideas about the uniqueness and importance of New Mexico's tripartite culture, the Tertio-Millennial celebrated what posters announcing the event referred to as New Mexico's "three great civilizations"—the Aborigine (or Pueblo), the Mexican or Spanish-American (that term was just coming into use), and the American. It

Fig. 11. Tertio-Millennial Celebration, Santa Fe, 1883, promotional poster. Held in Santa Fe, the Tertio-Millennial Celebration celebrated a different era in New Mexico's history and made a special effort to highlight the territory's Spanish past. Box NM 38.s231.1883. Courtesy the Southwest Collection, Special Collections Library, Texas Tech University, Lubbock, Texas.

was no surprise then that each of these civilizations figured centrally in the solemn orations delivered on the fair's opening day, July 2. Yet, in the historical pageant that followed, only the first two were featured; the Americans would have to wait for another day.

Accurate reports of this pageant are few, although one referred to the "unique confusion" that marked a parade headed by groups of Apache, Zuni, and Pueblo people wearing traditional dress. Spaniards came next.

Starting in the 1870s, Santa Fe's Fourth of July Parade reportedly included marchers attired as Don Quixote and Sancho Panza. In the Tertio-Millennial Celebration's pageant, these literary figures were replaced by members of Santa Fe's newly founded Order of Coronado, all costumed as Spanish caballeros in armor and followed by a regiment of Spanish foot soldiers marching in lockstep with a figure dressed as the Goddess of Liberty. Next came some barefooted Franciscan friars carrying the revered image of La Conquistadora, Our Lady of the Conquest. That image, much revered by the territory's Hispanic population, symbolized Spanish efforts to convert the region's aboriginal population to Christianity. The pageant also included floats illustrating "historical scenes" from Santa Fe's past—one representing the arrival of the Spanish in New Mexico, another the Spanish court of justice, and still another depicting Diego de Vargas, the Spanish captain responsible for the "reconquest" of New Mexico that followed in the wake of the Pueblo revolt of 1680.[52]

Over the course of the next month, more historical pageants followed, along with games, horse and burro races, and daily celebrations honoring the territory's different native groups. In the end, however, the Tertio-Millennial Celebration proved a financial flop. Crowds thinned out following the opening day, which reportedly attracted ten thousand. However, apart from the historical pageants and the speeches delivered by the territorial governor, Lionel Allen Sheldon, as well as Prince and the exposition's other commissioner, William Ritch, that day was memorable for another reason—the reading of a letter composed especially for the occasion by the nation's most famous poet, Walt Whitman (1819–92).

Why the organizers of the Tertio-Millennial had solicited Whitman is not entirely clear. The poet had never visited New Mexico, and his experience with the territory was wholly negative: a money-losing investment in bonds issued by the Sierra Grande mining company. But Ritch and Prince were undoubtedly familiar with Whitman's "Prayer of Columbus," a poem that underscored his respect for achievements of the Genoese mariner and the Spanish monarchs who had sent him on his way, as well as his famous "Leaves of Grass," which articulated a conception of racially diverse American society that corresponded to Prince's vision of New Mexico's tripartite society.

The organizers of the Tertio-Millennial originally invited Whitman to compose a special poem in honor of the occasion, but as that invitation only reached Whitman's home in Camden, New Jersey, on June 17, less than two weeks before the celebration's scheduled opening, he politely begged off. But Whitman did manage to write a letter that provided a sketch of what he called "our future national personality." It was also in keeping with Whitman's dream of America as a democratic, classless society and for this reason underscored his respect for the nation's "aboriginal or Indian population." But the letter emphasized what Whitman termed the qualities inherent in the "Spanish character" and more specifically the importance of that character for the "American identity." It reads as follows:

> We Americans have yet to really learn our own antecedents, and sort them, to unify them. They will be found ampler than has been supposed and in widely different sources. Thus far, impressed by New England writers and schoolmasters, we tacitly abandon ourselves to the notion that our United States have been fashioned from the British Islands only, and essentially form a second England only—which is a great mistake. Many leading traits for our future national personality, and some of the best ones, will certainly prove to have originated from other than British stock. . . . To that composite American identity of the future, Spanish character will supply some of the most needed parts. No stock shows a grander historic retrospect—grander in religiousness and loyalty, or for patriotism, courage, decorum, gravity and honor. . . . It is time to realize—for it is certainly true—that there will not be found any more cruelty, tyranny, superstition, etc., in the *résumé* of past Spanish history than in the corresponding *résumé* of Anglo-Norman history. Nay, I think there will not be found so much.
>
> As to the Spanish stock of our Southwest, it is certain to me that we do begin to appreciate the splendor and sterling value of its race element. Who knows but that element, like the course of some subterranean river, dipping invisibly for a hundred or two years, is now to emerge in broadest flow and permanent action?[53]

The language is flowery, but the message crystal clear. Taking direct aim at nativists such as Pierre Soulé, the fiery southerner he is likely to have met during his time as a newspaper reporter in New Orleans during the 1840s, along with the racist ideas of W. W. H. Davis, Whitman clearly regarded Spain's American heritage as integral to the history and culture of the United States.

The reception, let alone the influence, of Whitman's ideas about the importance of what he later called "the Spanish element in our Nationality" is difficult to trace. One Philadelphia newspaper reprinted the text of his letter, and it appeared again in Whitman's *November Boughs* collection of poetry, published in 1888. But Whitman was a controversial figure, and not everyone embraced his idea of the Spaniard, or those we now know as Latinos or Hispanics, as an integral component of the American character. For example, there is Henry Adams's previously quoted 1894 formulation of Spain and America as "natural enemies," as well as current suggestions that Americans of Mexican heritage are not truly American. But the idea of the Spanish as "civilizers," as opposed to destroyers, was definitely out of the bottle, and it soon found supporters in California, yet another part of the country in search of a history with a Spanish-tinged "genealogy of virtue" rivaling the one that Florida was creating and comparable to those of the states in the East.

California Dreaming: Serra, Lummis, and the Romance of Spain

When California entered the union in 1850, the vast majority of the state's new citizens were Mexicans employed in a variety of agricultural pursuits. As in New Mexico, they too were seen as "greasers" in the eyes of the thousands of Anglo-Saxons pouring into the state. Somewhat different was a small group of wealthy ranchers of Mexican extraction, many of whom fancied themselves and were generally known as *californios*, the pure-blooded descendants of the Spaniards who had migrated north from Mexico. One noted californio who thought this way was Gen. Mariano G. Vallejo (1807–90), who in a letter addressed to his friend, the *californio* novelist María Amparo Ruiz de Burton, in 1867 identified the specific attributes of their *raza* that distinguished californios from "Yankees." The latter, he noted, were temperamentally disposed to enterprise and the acquisition of wealth, whereas "we [Hispanics] are better at taste." But he ended the letter with the observation that a mixture of the two races would be "even better, more energetic, stronger, but also sweeter in character, moderate, and thus stronger."[54]

Such "mixtures" were relatively infrequent, but starting in the 1870s californios and Anglo-Saxons joined forces in a search to provide their new state a founding father comparable in stature and importance to the likes of John Winthrop, Roger Williams, or William Penn. The individual they agreed on was Fray Junípero Serra (1713–84), the Mallorcan-born Franciscan friar credited with the founding of sixteen missions in Alta (Upper) California. Leading the charge were two groups of writers, one that Steven Hackel has termed Serra's "secular hagiographers," while the other is best defined simply as hagiographers, as they were mostly Catholics keen on securing Serra's beatification and eventual sainthood.[55]

The hagiographers started first. Their campaign began in 1787, less than three years after the friar's death, with the publication in Mexico City of the *Relación histórica de la vida y apostólicas tareas del Venerable Padre Fray Junípero Serra*. This biography-cum-hagiography came from the pen of Francisco Palóu, Serra's disciple, fellow Franciscan, and longtime companion, and he wrote it in a less than transparent effort to enhance his mentor's credentials for sainthood. Palóu consequently crafted an account of Serra's life that aligned with a particular genre of early modern historical writing centered on the sacrifices, sufferings, and, in some instances, martyrdoms endured by missionaries among non-Christian peoples in various parts of the world.

In the short term little came of Palóu's efforts to promote Serra's candidacy for sainthood, and his *Relación* practically disappeared from view until its rediscovery by William Gleeson, a priest of Irish origin residing in California. Gleeson's 1872 book, *History of the Catholic Church in California*, included several chapters dedicated wholly to Serra. Drawing directly and uncritically from Palóu's *Relación*, Gleeson represented Serra as "noble and godlike," underscoring his activities as a missionary among the "untamed and fierce" inhabitants of Alta California and emphasizing his tireless efforts to deliver the souls of these savages from the Prince of Darkness. He also set out to secure the attention of the papacy's Congregation for the Causes of Saints by emphasizing Serra's role as an apostolic missionary.[56]

Another early hagiographer was Rev. Angelo D. Casanova (?–1893), a priest of Swiss origin serving in Monterey, California. Starting around 1882, Casanova took it upon himself to begin the work of restoring the ruined church of San Carlos Borromeo de Carmelo (Mission Carmel), part of a mission Serra had founded and the place where he and several of his companions were buried. Having located Serra's burial records along with the site of his tomb, Casanova generated support for his project by organizing a public ceremony during which Serra's coffin was opened in order to determine whether the body was actually there and still intact. Precedents for this kind of ceremony dated back to the medieval Church and generally constituted a key step along the road to sainthood.[57]

By the time of this discovery Serra's hagiographers had been joined by the "secular hagiographers," whose interest in the friar had less to do with religious than civic concerns. One of the first of these was Elizabeth Hughes, a progressive writer living in San Francisco and the author of a short history of California's missions published in 1875.[58] Relatively little is known about Hughes or the reasons for her interest in the history of the missions, but she was determined to present Serra and the work of the friars in a wholly favorable light. In doing so, Hughes took issue with the Scottish writer Alexander Forbes, whose *California: A History of Upper and Lower California* had appeared in 1839. No friend of the Catholic Church, Forbes had expressed grudging respect for Serra as an individual but criticized the missions for having achieved little more than the transformation of California's "free savages into pusillanimous and superstitious slaves." Hughes had a different view. Writing for a primarily Protestant, eastern audience, Hughes reminded her readers that even though she was not a Catholic ("I am no advocate of Romanism"), they would do well drop their prejudices against missionaries such as "Jumpero Lerra [*sic*]," whom she presented, along with other Franciscan fathers, as humane teachers who managed the spiritual conquest of California through the "feminine power of love and inspiration."[59]

Similar messages could be found in the work of Helen Hunt Jackson (1830–85), the author who can be credited with bringing Serra's achievements to a national audience with her two-part essay "Father Juniper and His Work," first published in a popular periodical, the *Century Magazine*, in May and June 1883. Jackson's interest in Serra and the missions sprang from her work as an activist for Native American rights. Her reading of Palóu's life of Serra, together with several visits to California, had evidently persuaded her of the flawed character of U.S. Indian policy and how much the nation's leaders could learn from the "admirable simplicity and system" of the missions that had guaranteed the well-being and the welfare of "savages" by instructing them in "all the laborious occupations known to civilized society."[60]

Jackson's description of both Serra and his followers was also couched in language designed to appeal to Protestants skeptical of anything remotely connected with Roman Catholicism. She did so by representing Serra primarily as a Franciscan, a member of a religious order famous for being "helpers of men" and one to which America was "pre-eminently" in debt owing to the support it had provided Columbus. In addition, by describing Serra's work as one of "struggle, hardship, and heroic achievement," Jackson employed rhetoric traditionally applied to New England's Puritan pioneers, and she reiterated this point by favorably comparing the work of the Franciscans in the West to the better-known history of the Puritans in the East. Whereas the latter were "driving the Indians further and further into the wilderness every year, fighting and killing them," she maintained that Serra and his followers were "gathering the Indians by thousands into communities, and feeding and teaching them." Jackson made her point, determined as she was to present Serra and the friars as moral exemplars deserving both admiration and respect, together with a place in American history textbooks.[61]

A similarly secularized Serra appeared in the opening volume of Theodore Hittell's *History of California*, first published in 1885. A San Francisco lawyer and politician—he served as a state senator from 1880 to 1882—Hittell was no friend of the missions and had little respect for what the missionaries had achieved. He characterized them as an "obstacle to civilization" and criticized them for having taught California's native peoples "little or nothing of value." His opinion of Serra, however, was decidedly more favorable, as he characterized him as a "remarkable

Fig. 12. *The Home of Ramona*, 1888. Cover page from an album of photographs compiled by Charles F. Lummis. This album comprised photographs of places featured in Helen Hunt Jackson's novel *Ramona* (1884). This best-selling book presented California's Spanish missions in a wholly sympathetic light. Huntington Library, San Marino, California.

and in some respects great man" to be respected for his faith, devotion, and evangelical zeal. And though Hittell himself was not Catholic, he considered Serra worthy of canonization, noting, however, that the friar's "memory will live longer and be preserved greener as the Founder and First of Pioneers of Alta California than either as a missionary or a priest or even a saint."[62]

The agendas of Serra's secular hagiographers differed, but ultimately they shared a common goal: to downplay the friar's Catholicism and present him simply as a Christian, a refocusing that would allow the friar to become a transcendental religious figure who could be credited with bringing both "Christianity" and "civilization" as opposed to Catholicism to California. The overarching idea was to make Serra into the state's spiritual father, its first citizen, and a patriot to boot.

This secularized Serra first came into public view on October 8, 1876, during San Francisco's centennial celebration of the founding of the Mission San Francisco de Asís but popularly known simply as the Dolores Mission, owing to its location at the intersection of Mission and Dolores

Streets. Organized under the auspices of the Society of California Pioneers, the celebration was a decidedly ecumenical event, as the speakers included not only Joseph Sadoc Alemany (1814–88), San Francisco's first archbishop, but also Oakland's mayor, John W. Dwinelle (1816–81), who at the start of his oration pointedly reminded his listeners that he was a Protestant. Another speaker was the aging californio Mariano G. Vallejo, whose speech, delivered in Spanish and without an interpreter, likely went over the heads of a crowd said to have numbered "upwards of 5,000." Alemany spoke first. Mindful that the majority of his listeners were Protestant, he downplayed the Catholicism of Serra's achievements, emphasizing instead his "heroic sacrifices" and success in delivering California from "the darkness of Paganism." As for the other friars, they were remembered as "heroic, disinterested Christian pioneers," and Alemany, carefully avoiding any reference to their efforts to win converts to Catholicism, credited them for "establishing Christianity in this country."[63]

The day's chief speaker and evidently the one the crowd most wanted to hear was Mayor Dwinelle. He reminded the crowd that Spain's "colonization of California" was primarily "religious . . . the work of the Roman Catholic Church . . . [and] to convert the native savages into Christians, afterwards into citizens, with organized civil institutions and then leave them in the possession of the conquered, civil and Christianized territory." Such was the importance and magnitude of that achievement, he continued, that it transcended the Church's quest for souls to become one worthy of the "American Republic." As for Serra, by describing him as a "man of fervent piety, indomitable will, irrepressible energy and unconquerable fortitude," Dwinelle, surely mindful that 1876 also marked the centennial of the United States, invoked qualities commonly associated with the country's Founding Fathers. Once again, the idea was to broaden the friar's appeal and to represent him as the founding father of the state.[64]

The apotheosis of this reformulated Serra came in 1884, the centennial of this death. In April of that year the California state legislature voted to declare August 29—as opposed to August 28, the actual date of the friar's death—a legal holiday. That action was symbolic, but it heralded a fundamental change in Serra's status—from that of a Catholic missionary

into a more Columbus-like figure credited with bringing all of the benefits of civilization to California. That same year also brought the start of
a carefully orchestrated campaign to increase public awareness of Serra.
It included publication of an English translation of portions of Palóu's
biography and a fundraising campaign endorsed by the governor, the
mayor of San Francisco, and Archbishop Alemany and intended to raise
the monies needed to complete the work of restoring Mission Carmel.
The pamphlet announcing this appeal referred to Serra as a "pioneer"
and a "venerable man" but purposely downplayed his Catholicism in an
apparent effort to attract the support of Californians of every creed.[65]

A similar theme marked the unveiling in 1891 of the first Serra statue,
which was funded by Jane Stanford, wife of Leland Stanford, founder of
Leland Stanford Junior University (now Stanford University). Designed
and executed by John W. Combs, a sculptor living in San Jose, and erected
on a site near what was thought to be Serra's first landing place in Monterey, the statue depicted the moment when Serra, perched on a small
landing craft, first set foot on California soil. It depicts him wearing Franciscan robes but not a crucifix, which, in an apparent nod to California's
Protestants, was conveniently left in the boat in a place where it was difficult for onlookers to see. The accompanying plaque also reflected the
secular hagiographers' agenda. It described Serra as a "philanthropist,"
a "hero," a "faithful servant of His Master Lord." Significantly, the word
"Catholic" did not appear, nor was it mentioned in the accompanying
ceremonies, which, though organized in part by the Reverend Casanova,
trumpeted Serra's contributions to California and, more broadly, the
United States, as opposed to the Roman Catholic Church.[66]

The next step was to insert Serra, and all of the Spanish missionaries
in California, into the broader narrative of the history of the United
States. This movement had its critics, among whom the California publisher turned historian Hubert Howe Bancroft (1832–1918)—no relation to the above-mentioned historian George Bancroft—is probably
the best known, owing partly to the university library in Berkeley that
still bears his name. Bancroft assiduously collected documents relating
to the era in which California was subject to Spanish rule, but his opinion of Spaniards and their legacy was rather low. His *California Pastoral*

Fig. 13. John W. Combs, Father Serra monument, Monterey, California, ca. 1897. Erected in 1891 with funds provided by Jane Stanford, this Serra statue was part of a well-orchestrated campaign designed to transform this Spanish Franciscan missionary into California's "founding father." Courtesy the University of Southern California and California Historical Society.

(1888) criticized Spain for its "ultra-religiosity" and blamed the Church for having reduced Spaniards to "ignorance and fanaticism." As for the country's contribution to America, Bancroft likened the Spanish Empire to a backward-looking "system of destruction" that did its best to prevent innovation and to quash liberty.[67]

Such criticisms, though powerful, did little to derail the campaign promoting the image of Serra and more generally that of Spain. If anything, that campaign, backed by commercial interests seeking to promote investment and tourism in Southern California, gained traction as the century drew to a close. Support for this campaign also derived from the runaway success of Helen Hunt Jackson's novel *Ramona*, first published in 1884. Set in Mexican as opposed to Spanish California, *Ramona* had little to do with Serra per se, but its romanticized portrait of the missions as places where kindly "Spanish" friars taught Native Americans the benefits of work, religion, and the arts presented Spaniards in roles diametrically opposed to those associated with the Black Legend. Jackson's Spaniards also anticipated those described in the address Joseph Scott later delivered in Washington DC. Inspiration for Scott's speech, however, derived less from Jackson than from the work of his close friend Charles F. Lummis (1859–1928), another author known for his efforts to defend Native American rights but also one equally determined to celebrate the Spanish heritage in California and other parts of the Southwest.

Born in Lynn, Massachusetts, Lummis was brilliant but unpredictable. Son of a Methodist preacher, he attended Harvard, but after having secretly married during the course of his junior year, he dropped out without taking a degree. He moved shortly thereafter to Ohio, where he worked for a time as a reporter for the *Chillicothe Leader*, the state's oldest newspaper. The indigenous cultures of the Southwest soon captured his fancy, and sometime in 1884 he succeeded in persuading the newspaper's editors to finance a trip to California, promising to provide them with colorful weekly stories as he wound his way out west.

This "tramp," as Lummis called it, began in Cincinnati in November 1884 and ended 143 days later in Los Angeles. Once there Lummis worked as a reporter for the city's *Daily Times*, but he again grew restless and soon convinced that newspaper's editors of the need for stories

Fig. 14. Charles F. Lummis, 1897. Photographer unknown. This ardent admirer of Spanish colonization in the Southwest often wore rugged corduroy suits. He had a special preference for wide-wale corduroy loomed in Barcelona, Spain. Courtesy Library of Congress.

relating to the U.S. Army's efforts to capture the fabled Apache war-rior known as Geronimo. In 1888 Lummis relocated to New Mexico, where he spent almost four years, paling around with the Swiss-born anthropologist Adolph Bandelier, then engaged in a study of the region's native peoples, as well as Amado Chávez, an elderly rico then serving as speaker of New Mexico's House of Representatives. Subsequent trips took Lummis to Mexico, Guatemala, Ecuador, and Peru, but by 1894 he was back in Los Angeles—raising a family and working as the first editor of the *Land of Sunshine*, a journal financed by members of Los Angeles's business community and designed to promote investment and tourism in Southern California.[68]

Throughout his long and often tumultuous career as an editor, writer, and, starting in 1907, founding director of Los Angeles's Southwest Museum, Lummis devoted himself, and tirelessly so, to the protection of native peoples in California and other parts of Southwest. The region's Spanish-cum-Mexican heritage became another of his passions. As an undergraduate at Harvard, Lummis had studied German, along with Latin and Greek. Spanish came later, a language he learned piecemeal, initially during the course of his tramp out west and later during his four-year stay in New Mexico and subsequent trips to Mexico and South America. As for the Mexicans he met during his tramp, his initial reaction aligned with the Anglo-Saxon prejudices of the day. He too called them "greasers," although he modified this epithet, adding that, as a people, they were not "half bad." Impressed, however, by the generosity and hospitality of the "greasers" he met, within a matter of weeks he began referring to them in the weekly letters he published in the *Chillicothe Leader* as members of "one of the kindest races in the world."[69]

Lummis's opinion of Spaniards and their contribution to New Mexi-can society also changed. When he first arrived in New Mexico in 1884, the Black Legend seemingly colored his observation that "those old Spaniards appear to have been Southern Democrats . . . every mother's son of them, for they stuffed the ballot boxes, bull-dozed the majority, and kept the poor Pueblos down in regular slave fashion." Nor was he much impressed by Santa Fe. In his view the town's Hispanic heritage rendered it a "dead old trunk" that only "Americanization" could bring back to life.[70] By 1892, however, after having resided four years in New Mexico, learning Spanish, and undoubtedly having been influenced by Amado Chávez's stories about his illustrious "Spanish ancestors" and their glorious deeds, Lummis offered a wholly different and far more positive view of New Mexico's, and California's, Spanish past. The first hint of this turnabout can be found in his *Tramp across the Continent* (1892), a published account of his trek across the country eight years earlier, in which Spaniards, especially Franciscans like Serra who had established missions in California, New Mexico, and other parts of the Southwest, are represented as heroes deserving the country's acclaim. In keeping with the White Legend view of Spain, Lummis also used this book to comment on the "dense popular ignorance as to Spanish doings in the beginning of the New World, and particularly of the beginning of the United States[;] our partisan histories, even our encyclopedias, are either strangely silent or as strangely biased. They do not seem to realize the precedence of Spain, nor the fact that she made in America a record of heroism, of unparalleled exploration and colonization never approached by any nation anywhere." He also took direct aim at the Black Legend and especially George Bancroft, Francis Parkman Jr., and other historians critical of Spanish settlement practices in the Americas. "We talk about the cruelty of the Spanish conquests," Lummis wrote, "but they were far less cruel than the Saxon ones. He conquered the aborigine, and then converted and educated him and preserved him—with a scholarship, a humanity, and zeal of which, to our shame be said, our own history does not furnish the hint of a parallel." The Spanish, he finally observed, were "the most humane neighbors the American Indian ever had."[71]

Lummis's newfound Hispanophilia was equally evident in *The Spanish Pioneers*, his first best seller and a work reprinted in no fewer than eight revised and expanded editions between its initial publication in 1893 and 1928.[72] That same volume also marked the beginning of Lummis's lifelong effort to connect the history of Spain with that of the United States and to offer what he called a new, more truthful history of the conquest of the American West. In doing so, he relied on the scholarly research of Frank W. Blackmar (1854–1931), a historian at the University of Kansas who was determined to revise the ideas of one of his mentors, the Johns

Hopkins historian Herbert Baxter Adams, about the so-called Teutonic origins of the institutions that governed colonial America. Adams had argued that these institutions, together with the country's notions of liberty, were outgrowths of European "germs" found among Teutonic tribes inhabiting the forests of medieval Germany and later spread via Anglo-Saxon England to New England's colonial towns.[73]

Blackmar had other ideas. Having lived for a time in California's San Joaquin Valley, he learned that many of California's laws and practices, notably those governing water usage, were Mexican, and thus ultimately Spanish in origin. He subsequently used his doctoral dissertation, *Spanish Colonization in the Southwest* (defended in 1889, published by Johns Hopkins in 1890) to argue that the governing institutions of the southwestern part of the United States had less to do with the medieval German forest than with Spanish adaptations of even older Roman practices. He elaborated on this thesis in his *Spanish Institutions of the South-west* (1891), which asserted that the Spanish origins of the institutions governing the Southwest ought not to prevent that region from being considered an "integral component part of the American commonwealth." The region's history was both Spanish and American, and though he failed to elaborate, Blackmar reminded his readers that "there is much in modern life relating to old Spanish life and institutions" that his book, focused on institutional and legal issues, did not describe.[74]

Blackmar's call for additional research into Spanish life and institutions did not go unanswered. One of the first to respond was Woodbury Lowery (1853–1906), a wealthy Washington lawyer who, after having ended his practice in patent law in 1897, invested both money and time in gathering maps, documents, and other materials for what he envisioned as a comprehensive political and religious history of Spain's record in North America. A member of an old New England family of Protestant Scotch-Irish descent and a graduate of Harvard (class of 1875), Lowery developed his interest in this particular subject at some unknown point, but he seemingly received encouragement from José Ambrosio Brunetti (later Duke of Arcos), a Spanish diplomat who married Woodbury's sister, Virginia Lowery, in 1895. Brunetti also facilitated Lowery's visits to archives in Mexico, as well as others in Madrid and Seville, where he ordered transcriptions of documents relevant to the history of what he later referred to as the "outlying, neglected and half-forgotten province of the [Spanish] Viceroyalty of Mexico." These documents served as the starting point for Lowery's *Spanish Settlements within the Present Boundaries of the United States* (1901), a volume he hoped would "arouse the interest . . . of treatment of [the] Spanish history of our own country."[75]

Blackmar also found a follower in Edward G. Bourne (1860–1908), a professor of history at Yale. Bourne's interest in Spanish America began in 1892 with the publication of a series of scholarly articles devoted to such subjects as the Line of Demarcation, which divided the New World between Portugal and Spain by order of Pope Alexander VI in 1493, and the naming of America. Further impetus for Bourne's interest in the history of Spanish America came from his reading of Martin Hume's *Spain: Its Greatness and Decay (1479–1788)*, published in 1899. Bourne rightly complained that Hume, a British historian, had failed not only to accord much attention to Spain's involvement in the Americas but also to recognize the importance of that involvement for the overall trajectory of Spain's national history. "She [Spain] undertook," Bourne writes, "the magnificent if impossible task of lifting up a whole race numbering millions into the sphere of European thought, life, and religion. . . . She failed but left an ineffable impress on succeeding ages."[76] So began the start of a productive decade during which Bourne, in addition to writing his invaluable *Spain in America, 1450–1580* (1904), published as part of Albert Bushnell Hart's series The American Nation: A History, endeavored to "integrate Spain into American history" with a study on the workings of Spain's overseas empire and a new translation of De Soto's chronicles, together with a history of the Spanish Philippines.[77]

The third historian to follow in Blackmar's footsteps was Herbert E. Bolton (1870–1953), who began his career at the University of Texas and subsequently moved to the University of California, Berkeley, where he taught the history of the American Southwest. Bolton is also generally credited as a pioneer in the field known today as borderlands studies. Starting with his early publications on Spanish frontier institutions in Texas, Bolton attempted to disprove the notion that Spaniards were little more than "mere" explorers whose experiments with colonization had "failed." Following the Spanish-accented template originally laid out by Smith and Fairbanks for Florida and keyed by the writings of his friend Charles Lummis, Bolton published an important article in 1917 defending the missions as important frontier institutions and praising the "vigor and vitality" of Spain's frontier forces, as well as the success of that small Iberian nation in spreading "her culture, her religion, her law, and her language over more than half of the two American continents, where they still are dominant and still are secure—in South America, Central America, and a large fraction of North America."[78] Bolton extended these arguments in his foundational study, *The Spanish Borderlands: A Chronicle of Old Florida and the Southwest*, first published in 1921, and subsequently in other books and articles. In 1943, despite his Methodist background, Bolton provided evidence supporting Serra's candidacy for sainthood and, more broadly, defending the work of the Franciscan missions in California and other parts of the Southwest.[79]

Compared to these academic historians, Lummis wrote about Spaniards, and the missions, in a different way. An avowed popularizer with little patience for starchy historical discourse, he went so far in his book on Spanish pioneering to assert that Spanish accomplishments in North America were nothing less than the "most marvelous feat in manhood in all history." He also turned a blind eye to writers who criticized the conquistadors for cruelty and the missionaries for running the equivalent of slave camps. Instead he boldly claimed that Spanish pioneering was marked by a "humane and progressive spirit . . . from first to last."[80]

Lummis expanded this idea in the revised editions of *The Spanish Pioneers* printed in the aftermath of Spain's defeat in the war of 1898. Together with Mark Twain, Charles Dudley Warner, and other prominent writers, Lummis had opposed U.S. intervention into what he regarded as Cuba's civil war, going so far as to label Manifest Destiny—the concept the war's supporters used to justify it—as "manifest thievery." As a way of criticizing the United States' new fondness for imperialism and territorial expansion, Lummis pointedly reminded his readers that "had there been no Spain four hundred years ago, there would be no United States today" and thus "there would be no Los Angeles, no San Francisco, no San Diego, and almost certainly no American state west of Kansas."[81]

Lummis's take on Serra and the legacy of the California missions was equally hyperbolic. Borrowing Thomas Carlyle's notion that "the history of the world is the story of its great men," he observed that "the story of the Franciscan missions of California, which gave the United States continental scope, is the story of Junípero (Hoo-*nee*-pe-ro) Serra and a hero of a kind that Puritans never produced."[82] As early as 1894, moreover, having recognized the potential of the missions as a magnet for tourism, Lummis emerged as the driving force behind the creation of Los Angeles's Landmarks Club, an organization dedicated to raising funds for the restoration and preservation of the missions, many of which were in an advanced state of decay. He consequently forged close ties with members of the Los Angeles business community, many of whom, having grasped the importance of the missions and the region's Spanish heritage as a draw for tourists, adopted Lummis's ideas about the importance of Spain's *mission civilisatrice* together with his understanding of the many links between Spain's long history and that of the United States.

That linkage was definitely overwrought, although it was already pictorially evident in William H. Powell's *De Soto* hanging in the Capitol rotunda, as well as the grisaille *Frieze of American History*, designed by the Italian American artist Constantino Brumidi (1805–80) for that same space just prior to the Civil War and whose installation began in 1878. Tracing the advance of civilization in America, which Brumidi presented allegorically in the opening scene, the frieze continued with highlights drawn from Spain's colonial past: *Landing of Columbus*, *Cortes and Montezuma at the Mexican Temple*, *Pizarro Going to Peru*, and *De Soto's Burial in the Mississippi*, each of which reflected what Prescott had earlier described as the "chivalrous spirit of [Spanish] enterprise." Next came scenes from British North America—they included *Captain John Smith and Pocahontas*, *Landing of the Pilgrims*, *William Penn and the Indians*, *Colonization of New England*, and *Oglethorpe and the Indians*—before moving on to others from the annals of U.S. history. These next scenes began with the *Battle of Lexington* and continued on to the U.S-Mexico War and the *Discovery of Gold in California* in 1849. (Scenes added in 1951 carried the story forward from end of the Civil War to the beginning of the aviation era.)[83]

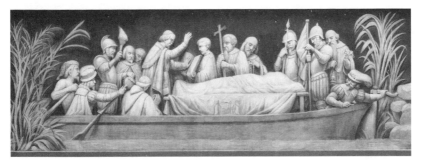

Fig. 15. Constantino Brumidi, *The Burial of Hernando de Soto*, frieze in the Capitol rotunda, ca. 1870–80. This bas-relief frieze featured key moments in the history of the United States. The scene featuring De Soto underscores one of Spain's contributions in that narrative. Courtesy Architect of the Capitol.

The overall scheme for Brumidi's frieze is said to have begun with suggestions from the architect of the Capitol, Gen. Montgomery C. Meigs, but ultimately it needs to be traced to Prescott's notion that Spain deserved credit for having taken the lead in the struggle against the forces of barbarism in the New World.[84] As such, the frieze provided a corrective to the standard Black Legend image of the conquistadors, along with Henry Adams's formulation of Spain and the United States as natural enemies. It suggested instead that the two nations shared a mutual endeavor—to foster the spread of both Christianity and civilization in the Americas. As Scott suggested in his Washington address, Spain's sturdy soldiers and courageous missionaries had initiated that campaign in the sixteenth century. He then added that in the wake of Spain's defeat in the war of 1898, responsibility for seeing that mission through to completion shifted to the new standard-bearer of the Americas: his country, the United States.

This same linkage also led to the idea that, whatever the political differences separating Spain from the United States, these were but superficial and temporary inasmuch as the culture, the language, and indeed the history of two countries were deeply and profoundly intertwined. Much of this was pure invention, but at the dawn of the twentieth century it offered Americans an opportunity to exchange the Black Legend view of Spain for one more closely aligned with the white one Lummis endeavored to propagate. At the same time, it enabled them to embrace Spanish culture to an extent never before possible. Much of this, as already noted, began in California and other parts of the Southwest, where it was coupled with a growing nostalgia for an older, simpler, overly romanticized way of life associated with the region's Spanish past.[85] But such ideas quickly spread to other parts of the country and contributed directly to the start of the Spanish craze. They also allowed Spanish-style houses—and I should add Spanish tiles, furniture, music, and dance—to be understood in terms of "dignity," "honesty," and "sincerity," which are attributes that writers such as Alexis de Tocqueville and Mark Twain had already used to describe the essence of the American character. From this perspective the Spanish craze was not so much the United States' discovery of Spain but America's discovery of itself.

Despite this discovery, old antipathies lingered, as several of the country's most prominent Hispanophiles readily understood. Lummis for one recognized the extent to which "foolish race-prejudice" continued to color American views of both Mexico and Spain.[86] As we shall see in a later chapter, sharp increases in the number of students studying Spanish in and around the time of World War I sparked considerable criticism on the part of other language instructors, on the grounds that Spain's culture had little to offer compared to that of Italy or France. Spanish officials seeking to attract U.S. tourists to their country also recognized that prejudices originating in the Black Legend erected obstacles they found difficult to surmount. In one memorandum drafted circa 1925, one of these officials noted that "in the United States of North America the state of opinion with respect to both [Spain] and Spanish is not especially favorable to our Nation and in fact is openly unfavorable."[87] The memorandum did not specify the source of such feelings, but the responsible official was clearly referring to the extent to which the Black Legend continued to influence Americans' images of Spain.

Yet for all the pull of that legend, other factors intervened to enhance the appeal of Spain and, more generally, that of Hispanic culture broadly conceived. Of key importance here was what Lummis called the "romance of Spain," with romance, as he defined it, representing "a thing of the spirit—of ideal, of imagination" as opposed to anything more concrete.[88]

3

Sunny Spain

Everything is bewitching. For once, my dreams
have been realized, and I have seen Spain as I have
imagined it. —HARRIET TROWBRIDGE ALLEN

The "romance of Spain"—when Charles F. Lummis wrote these words, he pinpointed a key component of the Spanish craze: the image of a country brimming with poetical associations of a kind that visitors to the country, Americans among them, would never find at home. Those associations were more imagined than real, but they emerged as key components of the "fever" that Augustus Saint-Gaudens contracted during his hurried visit to Spain in 1901. They also figured in the way the celebrated writer Edith Wharton reacted to the country in 1914. Wharton was an avowed Francophile, yet her motor trip through various parts of northern Spain during the summer of 1913 elicited the comment, "Spain in July is the most delicious place imaginable."[1]

Unlike Wharton, Lummis never managed to visit Spain. The romantic country he envisioned was purely a mental construct, one that he likened to a "beautiful dream." Writing to a Spanish friend in 1919, he remarked,

It would be a crowning experience in my life to be in Spain even for a month or so. . . . How wonderful it would be to visit the scenes so sacredly linked with that marvelous chapter of noble romance which has fascinated me all my mature life. To know of Spain today, and those who are leading its thought and progress; to trace in the home life of its people the secret springs from which welled that matchless tide of conquest and colonization; and to stand reverently in the Holy places associated with history—it would be a good deal nearer heaven than I ever expect to get![2]

Lummis's failure to travel to Spain was nothing out of the ordinary. Prior to World War I tens of thousands of Americans traveled to Europe each year, but relatively few—several thousand at most—visited Spain. Their failure to do so constituted a problem that the Marqués de la Vega-Inclán, founding director of Spain's Royal Commission on Tourism, endeavored to redress. He did so by arranging for the printing and distribution of thousands of tourist brochures, improving the Spanish infrastructure for tourists, and making the country's monuments and museums more accessible. It did not take long before these investments in overseas tourism promotion paid a handsome return. The number of American tourists arriving in Spain rose exponentially during the 1920s, reaching a figure of forty thousand per year by 1925. That number declined during the 1930s owing to the Great Depression and what proved for Spain an era of political turbulence and, starting in 1936, civil war, but it increased again starting in the 1950s. Today Spain, a country of more than forty million inhabitants, attracts upwards of eighty million foreign tourists each year, among them well over a million or so from the United States.[3]

These are astonishing figures, but at the start of the twentieth century Spain for most Americans was far away and the expense of getting there a luxury few could afford. For these stay-at-homes, as for Lummis, Spain was a country imagined, rather than seen, and partly for this reason it was easy to portray as one of romance.

That romance—what I am calling here Sunny Spain—has a history. Its origins date to the end of the eighteenth century and the start of the Romantic era in literature, music, and art. It was then that foreign visitors to Spain "discovered" landscapes, people, and buildings that inspired poetic imaginings and were deemed "picturesque," a term that conjured up encounters with the unexpected and the unusual, along with sights and scenes worthy of a painter's brush. Previously, "picturesque" was not a word visitors to the country were apt to employ. Most—count John Adams among them—carried with them preconceptions colored by the Black Legend. They saw Spain through a dark lens—it was backward, impoverished, a country where travelers had to contend with poor lodgings, execrable food, and brigands ready to relieve them of their purse. Typical was the comment made by Voltaire, the illustrious French *philosophe* who never actually visited the country but could still venture the remark that "Spain is a country with which we are no better acquainted than with the most savage parts of Africa, and which does not deserve the trouble of being known."[4] Similar sentiments came from the anonymous English writer who offered would-be visitors to the country the following advice in a 1778 essay published in the *London Magazine*:

> Nothing but necessity can induce a man to travel to Spain; he must be an idiot if he makes the tour of this country from mere curiosity, unless he has a design to publish memoirs of the extravagancies of human nature. In that case, he cannot do better, for he will find everywhere—pride, baseness, poverty, ignorance, bigotry, superstition, and ridiculous ceremony. This is a faithful abstract of the character of the Spaniard. . . . The common people, the citizens, and the middling gentry, are just the same ostentatious, solemn, vain, poor wretches they were in the time of Philip II.[5]

Harsh as it seems, the comment neatly summarizes what Pere Gifra-Adroher defines as the Enlightenment view of Spain.[6] In the United States that view was surprisingly long-lived, kept alive, as in Britain, by deep-seated Protestant suspicions of Roman Catholicism, along with a series of territorial squabbles—over the Mississippi River, West Florida, and finally Cuba—which only ended with the Spanish-American War in 1898. Afterward it practically disappeared, only to surface in phoenix-like fashion following the victory of the fascist forces led by Francisco Franco during Spain's bloody civil war of 1936–39.

Yet for all its tenacity Voltaire's dark view of Spain began to compete with another view that imagined the country, much as Lummis did, as one of "noble romance." This new take, starting around 1800, was first voiced among foreign visitors by the young English poet (and future poet laureate) Robert Southey (1774–1843). After having visited his uncle in Lisbon in 1794, the young Southey spent much of the following year traveling about Spain, looking for what impressed him as different or unusual and then transcribing his reactions into verse. His 1797 poem "Recollections of a Day's Journey in Spain" is famous for this line: "How did the lovely landscape fill my heart!" Southey's *Letters Written during a Short Residence in Spain* (1797) also made note of the poetic qualities he observed in the Spanish landscape, along with a national character that rendered Spaniards quite unique, so much so that "we almost fancy them a different race from the rest of mankind."[7]

As he aged, Southey tempered his youthful, overly sentimentalized portrait of the country, but other writers, especially those with a romantic bent, soon portrayed it in similar ways. One was his contemporary, the Scottish novelist Walter Scott (1771–1832), whose admiration for Don Quixote, Sancho Panza, and the other characters he encountered in Cervantes's *Don Quixote* helps to explain why he connected Spain with the "idea of Romance." Yet Scott introduced another element into the emergent romantic view of Spain in his 1814 "Essay on Chivalry" with the observation that the country's "oriental character" disposed Spaniards to "heroic deeds."[8]

"Oriental" in this context derived from the notion that Spain's Moorish past connected it to the Muslim cultures of the Middle East and North Africa. That same history allegedly endowed Spain with a national character so markedly different from those of other European countries that it allowed the great French novelist Victor Hugo to allude to its "Oriental" qualities in the preface to his 1829 book, *Les orientales*. Expounding, perhaps, on memories he had collected during his boyhood years in Spain (1806–13), Hugo remarked, "L'Espagne, c'est encore l'Orient, l'Espagne est à demi africaine" (Spain is still the Orient, Spain is half-African).[9] This comment was later shortened into the phrase "fait commencer l'Afrique aux Pyrénées" (Africa begins at the Pyrenees), an expression commonly but erroneously attributed to his fellow French novelist Alexandre Dumas.[10]

Africa in this instance meant Moorish, and Moorish meant Oriental. The term cut two ways. On the one hand "Moorish" was freighted with notions of racial inferiority and cultural backwardness. On the other, and in keeping with the lasting popularity of such books as *The Thou-*

sand and One Nights, it conjured up images of moonlit gardens, luxurious palaces, and harems filled with exotic beauties. By definition, everything Moorish was romantic.

Such was Lord Byron's reaction during his visit to Seville, Cádiz, and other Andalucian cities in 1809. In one letter Byron writes, "I am enamoured with the country," and he announces his particular fondness for Cádiz (and its women) with the comment, "Cádiz, sweet, Cádiz—it is the first spot in creation."[11] Byron's affection for Cádiz was even more pronounced in his poetry, especially *Childe Harold's Pilgrimage* (published initially in 1812):

> Fair is proud Seville; let her country boast
> Her strength, her wealth, her site of ancient days;
> But Cadiz, rising on the distant coast,
> Calls forth a sweeter, though ignoble praise.
> Ah, Vice! how soft are thy voluptuous ways!
> While boyish blood is mantling, who can 'scape
> The fascination of thy magic gaze?
> A Cherub-hydra round us dost thou gape,
> And mould to every taste thy dear delusive shape.[12]

As for Spain, Byron summarized his feelings in one memorable phrase: "Oh, lovely Spain! renowned, romantic land."[13]

It turns out that Byron and Scott were the two British writers most admired by Washington Irving, the first American author to break from the Enlightenment view of Spain and present it in a new, romantic light. Irving's fascination with Spain's history began during his childhood in New York. He was equally enamored with Spanish literature: Cervantes and the seventeenth-century playwright Pedro Calderón de la Barca were two of his favorite writers. And as he later observed, Moorish Granada was another of his passions: "From earliest boyhood, when, on the banks of the Hudson, I first pored over the pages of old Gines Perez de Hyta's [*sic*] apocryphal but chivalresque history of the civil wars of Granada, and the feuds of its gallant cavaliers, that city has ever been a subject of my waking dreams, and often I have trod in fancy the romantic halls of the Alhambra."[14]

Irving here referred to Ginés Pérez de Hita's *Historia de los bandos de los Zegries y Abencerrajes*, more commonly known as *Guerras civiles de Granada*, or *Civil Wars of Granada*. The first part of that book, a romanticized account of life in Muslim Granada and the region's eventual loss to the Christians in 1492, was published in 1595, although Irving probably read the 1803 English translation by Thomas Hold. He was also familiar with Henry Swinburne's *Travels through Spain in the Years 1775 and 1776*, published in London in 1777, one of the first travelogues to offer a detailed description of the Alhambra, the fortress-cum-palace complex that served as the court of Granada's Muslim rulers. Swinburne was no romantic, but when it came to the Alhambra, he made reference to the "agreeable sensations" he experienced during his stroll through that "magic ground."[15]

Irving's view of the Alhambra's romantic halls and patios can also be traced to the one described in François René de Chateaubriand's *Les aventures du dernier Abencérage* (issued in translation as *The Last of the Abencerrajes*), first published in 1826. This work tells the story of Aban Hamet, a member of the clan that ruled Granada prior to 1492. Inspired by his visit to Granada in 1807, Chateaubriand described the Alhambra as something straight out of the Arabian nights: "The walls, decorated with arabesques, imitated to the eye those Oriental fabrics that the caprice of some slave girl weaves amidst the boredom of the harem. Something sensual, religious, and yet warlike, seemed to breathe through this magical edifice; a kind of cloister of love, a mysterious retreat in which the Moorish kings tasted all the delights, and forgot all the duties, of life."[16] It is not clear when Irving first read Chateaubriand's book, but it helped nurture his view of the Alhambra as a "stately pleasure dome" comparable to the one in Xanadu that Kubla Khan "decreed" in Samuel Taylor Coleridge's famous poem of 1816.

Irving is also likely to have learned more about the Alhambra in 1819, when, living in London, he met George Ticknor, fresh from his own visit to Spain and soon to take up his position as Harvard's first Smith Professor of Romance Languages. The journal Ticknor kept during the course of these travels suggests that his general opinion of Spain aligned with that of other Enlightenment writers: he criticized the despotic Bourbon monarchy, the ignorance and indolence of the nobility, the fanaticism

Fig. 16. Washington Irving (1783–1859), ca. 1855–60. The romanticized image of "Sunny Spain" Irving created in *Tales of the Alhambra* (1832) achieved lasting popularity. Irving served as the U.S. minister to Spain from 1842 to 1846. Photograph by Mathew B. Brady. Courtesy Library of Congress.

of its clergy. On the other hand Ticknor writes that, upon visiting the Alhambra, his reaction was one of "riotous, tumultuous pleasure."[17]

Whether Irving experienced anything similar when he first toured the Alhambra on March 10, 1828, is not at all clear. He had arrived in Spain about two years earlier, initially residing in Madrid and devoting much of his time to writing what soon became his best-selling *Life and Voyages of Christopher Columbus* (1828). Irving's journals and letters indicate that he regarded Spain as a "romantic" country right from the very start. He also viewed it as picturesque, noting in one letter that "Spaniards even surpass Italians in picturesqueness" and in another that Spaniards are "wonderfully picturesque in all their attitudes, groups, and costumes." As for Granada, he described it as a "most picturesque and beautiful city," its outskirts a place where "the imagination is excited to pleasant dreams and reveries."[18]

These comments provide the backdrop for Irving's *The Alhambra: Tales and Sketches of the Moors and the Spaniards*, published in 1832 and dedicated to his friend, the Scottish artist David Wilkie. As the preface explains, Irving credited Wilkie for having encouraged him to write a book about the Alhambra, so long as he infused it with "a dash of that Arabian spice which pervades everything in Spain."[19] Irving did just this, and in doing so fashioned an image of Spain that other authors did not hesitate to copy. That same image later figured in Lummis's view of the country as one of "noble romance" and, more broadly, in the craze for Spain that followed the war of 1898.

Integral to that image was the sketch of Spain that Irving offered in the opening chapter of *The Alhambra*, which recounted his adventures in Andalucia along a route leading eastward, from Seville to Granada. He described that Spain as a "land of adventure," that travel there was a "romance," and that it was a place where visitors would discover that "the habits, the very looks of the people, have something of the Arabian character." He then larded his account of that journey with a series of picturesque encounters with peasants, *contrabandistas*, gypsies, and muleteers. Especially noteworthy was when he and his traveling companion—a Russian prince—witnessed in the courtyard of a village inn an impromptu performance of flamenco dance and guitar music. According to Irving, "The scene was a study set for painter."[20]

Later chapters offered a spiced-up description of the Alhambra, followed by a series of stories ("arabesques") based on what Irving termed the Spanish "oriental passion for story-telling." Central to these stories, the star, if you will, is the Alhambra, a complex he describes as "the most remarkable, romantic, and delicious place in the world." Following Chateaubriand, Irving invests the Alhambra with the "power of calling up vague reveries and picturings of the past, and thus clothing naked realities with the illusions of memory and the imagination," a description that does much to explain why so many movie palaces constructed in the United States at the start of the twentieth century carried the Alhambra name. (Granada was another favorite; see chapter 6). Most of that power emanated from the Alhambra's Court of the Lions, which seemingly possessed magical powers and functioned in ways similar to the "power points" central to today's New Age philosophy. These powers were primarily psychic and enabled Irving to experience a vision of a "turbaned Moor quietly seated near the fountain," along with other reveries featuring lovelorn princesses, moonlit walks along fragrant garden paths, the music of nightingales, and, perhaps most important, to "escape from the bustle and business of the every day world."[21]

Published concurrently in London and Philadelphia in 1832, Irving's *Alhambra* was an instant editorial success, reedited in numerous editions and quickly translated into French, Spanish, and other European languages. But Irving's airbrushed image of Spain was not to everyone's taste, and it was certainly far different from the one outlined in Alexander Slidell Mackenzie's *A Year in Spain by a Young American*, first published in 1829 and subsequently in several revised editions. Slidell, as he was originally known, was a young naval officer whose initial visit to Spain overlapped that of Irving. The two met in Madrid and became friends, and Irving subsequently helped with the publication of Slidell's book, even though its portrait of Spain was markedly different from his own. Slidell, for example, highlighted Spain's troubled politics, a subject that Irving's *Alhambra* studiously avoided. Nor did Slidell's Spain offer much in the way of romance. To put it bluntly: Irving's brigands told stories, while Slidell's murdered and robbed.[22]

More direct criticism of Irving's Spain could be found in Richard Ford's *Handbook for Travellers in Spain* (1845). Ford was an English writer who went to Spain in 1829, initially residing in Seville. Following Irving's example, he moved to Granada in 1830, taking up residence in the Alhambra, which he used as base for excursions to different parts of the country undertaken over the course of the next five years. These travels led to a book equivalent to Michelin Green and Red guides rolled into one, as it offered detailed descriptions of places Ford deemed of touristic value together with practical information regarding conveyances, currency, lodging, eating, tour guides, and so on.

Ford's Spain differed from Irving's in several notable respects. Like Irving, his was "romantic, racy, and peculiar" but deficient in what Irving had labeled picturesque. Consider their respective descriptions of the Alhambra. Irving's was magical. In contrast Ford advised readers planning to visit the monument to discard their "over-exaggerated notions" of a place *granadinos* likened to "a *casa de ratones*, or rat hole." So began a rather sober account of a monument Ford described as "decayed and fallen," as a result of centuries of despoilment and neglect, as well as one "disfigured by invalids, beggars, and convicts, emblems of [he adds "Spanish" in the third edition] weakness and poverty." Ford also contended that the keepers in charge of the monument were hardly the picturesque personages Irving had described. "The power of romance," he writes, "can gild the basest metals." Ford thus represents Mateo Ximenez, Irving's storied guide to the Alhambra, as little more than a "chattering blockhead," and his wife, Tia Antonia, as "cross and crabbed," a far cry from the charming woman who emerged from Irving's fanciful pen.[23]

Even harsher criticism of Irving's romanticized vision of Spain came from the Baltimore lawyer-cum-Hispanophile Severn Teackle Wallis. Wallis (1816–94) initially crossed swords with Irving in 1841 in a series of essays published in the *Southern Literary Messenger*. These pieces berated the "Old Knickerbocker" for his uncharitableness and failure to acknowledge the research of certain Spanish scholars in his *Life and Voyages of Columbus*. Wallis offered more criticisms in his *Glimpses of Spain* (1849), a travelogue studded with philosophical reflections of various sorts, and in his *Spain: Her Institutions, Politics and Public*

Men (1853), an insightful analysis of life, culture, and politics in mid-nineteenth-century Madrid. Both offered a spirited defense of Spanish culture, primarily by attempting, much as Alexis de Tocqueville had done for the United States, to explain it on its own terms rather than in light of ideas and attitudes imported from abroad.

It follows that Wallis criticized virtually every foreigner who had written about Spain, especially those who, like Irving, presented Spain as a land of romance. In addition to Irving, Wallis's list of targets included the French romantic writer Théophile Gautier, whose *Voyage en Espagne* (1846) conjured up the image of a country wallowing in the "picturesqueness" of its peasants and muleteers, a country whose "simple" culture had little in common with the "civilizations of northern Europe." According to Wallis, Gautier (and Alexandre Dumas, who also received a mention)—was wrong. These French writers, Wallis claimed, having arrived in Spain armed with biased national *prescriptions*, created a Spain that did not exist: a *tableau vivant* composed of Figaro, Almaviva, and other characters drawn from *Le Barbier de Séville* (1775), the Beaumarchais comedy that Rossini transformed into a light opera, *Il Barbarie di Siviglia*, in 1816.[24]

For reasons left unexplained, Wallis's list of authors responsible for having created this tableau was far from complete. It did not include Benjamin Disraeli (1804–81), the English writer whose popular 1832 novel *Contarini Fleming* highlighted the "calm voluptuousness of Spanish life" and instructed readers to visit Seville because "Figaro is in every street, and Rosina [another of Beaumarchais's characters] in every balcony."[25] Nor did Wallis refer to Henry Wadsworth Longfellow (1807–82), the American poet whose impressions of Spain had appeared in his travelogue *Outre-Mer: Pilgrimage beyond the Sea* (first edition 1833, with nine more before 1900).

Longfellow's Spain aligned neatly with the one Wallis abhorred, as it was largely modeled on Irving's, representing the country as a romantic retreat peopled by a colorful mixture of beautiful *señoritas*, dashing gallants, fancifully dressed muleteers, and white-robed Carmelite friars. Interestingly, the portrait of Spain depicted in *Outre-Mer* was far more romantic, and decidedly far more Irvingesque, than the one Longfellow had originally recounted in letters he wrote during his one visit to the country in 1827. Gone, for example, were his previous comments to his brother and his sister about the "barrenness" and "melancholy" of the countryside outside Segovia. As for the hardscrabble mountain village of Villanueva del Pardillo, in his letters Longfellow described it as "the most picturesque village I have seen in Spain." In *Outre-Mer* the village became a veritable pastoral paradise, a "quiet, happy place" whose "orderly and industrious" inhabitants, come every evening, spontaneously organized dances to the accompaniment of guitars, tambourine, and castanets.[26] Music, dance—these too served as hallmarks of Sunny Spain. Gypsies came next, and here the contribution of the English writer George Borrow (1803–81) was key. Borrow first arrived in Spain in 1835 as a Protestant missionary intent on spreading the Gospels as an agent of Britain's Bible Society. He subsequently recounted his somewhat unsuccessful efforts at evangelization in *The Bible in Spain* (1843), a runaway best seller in both Great Britain and the United States and one in which Borrow explained that Spaniards were not the "fanatic" people Protestants commonly imagined.[27]

Borrow was also the author of *Zincali: Gypsies of Spain* (1841), a pioneering study of the lives and traditions of Spain's Roma people, known in Spanish as *gitanos*, a term derived from the Spanish name (*egipcios*) for the inhabitants of Egypt, their supposed original homeland. Records of their existence in Iberia date to the fifteenth century, by which time gitanos were already a marginalized people and, together with Jews, candidates for expulsion, partly because their lives as itinerant pastoralists and traders put them at odds with the more settled agriculturalist peasantry. Gypsies were also synonymous with all manner of criminality and reputed for leading generally disreputable lives.

Borrow's *Zincali* was no work of scholarship, but it was among the first studies to examine the culture of the Roma in serious fashion. Yet as some of the book's first reviewers recognized, Borrow was not a dispassionate ethnographer. His approach to the Roma was uneven, shifting quickly from the objective to the romantic, as the following description (worth quoting at length) of the "wandering gitana" he encountered in Seville readily attests:

She is of the middle stature, neither strongly nor slightly built, and yet her every movement denotes agility and vigour. As she stands erect before you, she appears like a falcon about to soar, and you are almost tempted to believe that the power of volation is hers; . . . her face is oval, and her features are regular but somewhat hard and coarse, for she was born amongst rocks in a thicket, and she has been wind-beaten and sun-scorched for many a year . . . ; there is many a speck upon her cheek, and perhaps a scar, but no dimples of love; and her brow is wrinkled over, though she is yet young. Her complexion is more than dark, for it is almost that of a Mulatto; and her hair, which hangs in long locks on either side of her face, is black as coal, and coarse as the tail of a horse . . . she is a prophetess . . . ; she is a physician . . . ; she is a procuress, though she is not to be procured; she is a singer of obscene songs, though she will suffer no obscene hands to touch her; . . . she is a cutpurse and a shoplifter whenever opportunity shall offer . . . she comes to flatter, and to deceive, and to rob, for she is a lying prophetess, and a she-Thug; she will greet you with blessings which will make your heart rejoice, but your heart's blood would freeze, could you hear the curses which to herself she murmurs against you. . . . There is no female eye in Seville can support the glance of hers, so fierce and penetrating, and yet so artful and sly . . . ; her mouth is fine and almost delicate, and there is not a queen on the proudest throne between Madrid and Moscow who might not, and would not, envy the white and even rows of teeth which adorn it, which seem not of pearl but of the purest elephant's bone of Multan. . . . Huge rings of false gold dangle from wide slits in the lobes of her ears; her nether garments are rags, and her feet are cased in hempen sandals. Such is the wandering Gitana, such is the witch-wife of Multan, who has come to spae the fortune of the Sevillian countess and her daughters.[28]

Borrow's wandering gitana was a tantalizing, dangerous femme fatale but thoroughly picturesque, a combination that enabled her to become one of the stock figures of Sunny Spain. That same gitana made her literary debut in Prosper Mérimée's novella *Carmen*, published initially as a series of installments in the *Revue des Deux Mondes* in 1845 and the following year as a book. Mérimée's Carmen was every bit as dangerous as Borrow's wandering gypsy, but she was younger, more alluring, and definitely more eroticized:

> She wore a very short red skirt, which revealed white silk stockings with more than one hole, and tiny shoes of red morocco, tied with flame-coloured ribbons. She put her mantilla aside, to show her shoulders and a huge bunch of cassia, which protruded from her chemise. She had a cassia flower in the corner of her mouth, too, and as she walked she swung her hips like a filly in the stud at Cordova. In my province a woman in that costume would have compelled everybody to cross themselves. At Seville every one paid her some equivocal compliment on her appearance, and she had a reply for every one, casting sly glances here and there, with her hand on her hip, as impudent as the genuine gypsy she was.[29]

Mérimée claimed that his Carmen came from a story told to him by a Spanish noblewoman, the Countess of Montijo, during his visit to Spain in 1830, but he also acknowledged his debt to Borrow. Whatever the source, Carmen proved irresistible, and she quickly became a model for other writers interested in seeking to capture something of the romance of Spain. In 1868, for example, the English writer George Eliot transformed Carmen into Fedelma, the gypsy dancer featured in her epic poem *The Spanish Gypsy*. A few years later Carmen became the seductive protagonist in Georges Bizet's now famous opera by that name, first performed in Paris on March 3, 1875. *Carmen* arrived in the United States in 1884, with almost simultaneous performances in Boston, Philadelphia, and New York. Critics had little positive to say about the quality of the singing in any of these performances, but Carmen was now a star, along with her male counterpart, the dashing toreador, both being integral to the idea of Spain, land of romance.[30]

To be sure, contrary images of the country are not difficult to find. As noted earlier, neither Alexander Slidell Mackenzie nor Severn Teackle Wallis made much allowance for romance; both were more interested Spanish politics and the country's difficulties in establishing the stable governing institutions it needed to develop and grow. Kate Field had similar concerns. Field was a New York journalist who visited Spain in 1873 shortly after the start of the country's first, but short-lived, experiment with a republican form of government. Her avowed aim was to interview the prime minister, Emilio Castelar, which she did, and to determine whether his particular brand of republicanism had any chance of lasting success. What she discovered proved discouraging. Most of the people she encountered in the course of her hurried visit were monarchists, few of whom had much faith in Castelar, let alone democracy. Nor did Field take much liking to the deputies of the Cortes whom she met, commenting mainly on what she perceived as their lack of "self-control," as expressed in their apparent readiness to expectorate on carpets and not into spittoons. As for sightseeing, she liked Madrid's "picture-gallery," but otherwise the country described in her *Ten Days in Spain* (1875) had little in common with the Sunny Spain Irving and Longfellow had described. She regarded it instead as "dreary," where all was "monotony," Philip II's Escorial "a hideous burlesque," Toledo a city where every stone told "tales of bloodshed and violence," and Spaniards little more than a "grim parody of humanity." She also observed, quite originally, that "Spain is the mother of all dust."[31]

Field's Spain was darker and far dustier than most but, when it came to politics, not all that different from that of John Hay's *Castilian Days* of 1871. This volume, a compilation of essays that Hay had published in the *Atlantic Monthly* when he was attached to the U.S. legation in Madrid, offered one of the more insightful inquiries into Spanish governance by any nineteenth-century American observer. An accomplished man of letters, Hay recognized the importance of what he called the "panorama" of Spain's history and culture. He was also taken with the charm of some of the more "picturesque" aspects of Spanish society, notably in Toledo, where in one letter he commented that "I felt the coil of cares slipping away from me and leaving me young and appreciative again" upon seeing the city's "adorable doorways" together with "picturesque beggars dressed in rags of the period." On the other hand, with the exception of the qualities of the pictures he encountered in the Prado Museum, the Spain outlined in Hay's *Castilian Days* offered little in the way of romance. It appeared instead as a backward society, where "modern civilization" was lacking, politicians corrupt, the administration plagued by "financial phthisis," and democracy hampered by "political indifferentism." It was a country whose outlook for the future was muddled at best.[32]

The Alhambra

Hay's pessimistic view of Spain and its politics is important to the extent that it undoubtedly factored into his support for the war against Spain while he was serving as President McKinley's secretary of state in 1898. On the other hand neither Hay's book nor Field's managed to derail Americas' growing fascination with Sunny Spain. For most Americans living in the decades after the Civil War, that Spain was primarily the one they wanted to read about, and especially to see for themselves. My evidence here derives partly from the continuing popularity of Irving's *Alhambra*, which he revised and expanded in 1851 with the addition of new picturesque encounters, or "arabesques," and the concluding comment that his time in Granada and the Alhambra had represented "one of the pleasantest dreams of my life."[33] Adding to the "dream-like" atmosphere of the new edition was a series of specially commissioned and decidedly orientalized illustrations provided by the New York illustrator Felix O. C. Darley. That book alone provided the incentive for a growing number of Americans who traveled to Granada looking for Carmen and also expecting to experience something of the magic of the monument Irving described.

Extant visitor registers in the Alhambra tell the story. These registers began in 1829, and the first visitor to enter his name in the register was Washington Irving. He did so on May 9, 1829.[34] The next name to appear was that of Irving's nephew, Edgar—he signed on May 12, 1829—followed by those of Caleb Cushing, a leading Massachusetts politician, and his wife, Caroline. They were both there in February 1830. Caleb's clearly written signature belies his description of the Alhambra as the equivalent of an orientalist "phantasmagoria" that appeared in his 1833 book, *Reminiscences of Spain*.

On the whole American visitors to the Alhambra were few as compared with those hailing from Britain and France. During the 1830s only

Fig. 17. Title page illustration by Felix O. C. Darley for *The Alhambra* (revised ed., 1851), by Washington Irving. Darley never visited the Alhambra. The elaborate archway depicted in this illustration reflected the romanticized image of the monument that Irving had created. Photo by the author.

two dozen Americans signed the visitor book, but thereafter the figure moves up: 33 or so during the 1840s, more than 70 in the 1850s, and 160 in the 1860s. In the 1870s, the decade when a rail line finally reached Granada, the number jumped to more than 500, and by all appearances the next decade brought even more, although by then the overall volume of tourists visiting the Alhambra reached the point at which signing the register was no longer expected or even required.

Who were these Americans? It is difficult to know, as most signed only their name and place of residence, and no more than a handful saw fit to enter a comment. One who did was Charles F. Willis, a resident of New York City (and possibly a relative of the well-known journalist Nathaniel Parker Willis). "My astonishment," he wrote on August 1, 1846, "is so great on visiting this place that I have not language to express it." Another was Emilio Pritchard from Brooklyn. In a September 21, 1875, comment reminiscent of Irving's moonlit strolls through the Alhambra, he noted the time of this visit: "One hour after midnight by the light of the moon." Another visitor was Severn Teackle Wallis. He was there on June 7, 1847, and although he neglected to leave a comment in the visitor book, he did offer an extensive and generally favorable description of the monument in his 1849 travelogue, *Glimpses of Spain*. Other notable visitors included James Russell Lowell, who together with his wife and several other Bostonians first toured the monument on April 23, 1855, making a return visit on February 11, 1878, while he was serving as head of the U.S. legation in Madrid.

Other easily identified visitors include the antiquarian Thomas Buckingham Smith, who was there, accompanied by his wife, Julia, on February 3, 1858, just prior to returning to the United States; Cornelius Roosevelt, grandfather of Pres. Theodore Roosevelt—he signed the register on March 31, 1868; and the prominent Philadelphia merchant and art collector William O. Wilstach, together with his wife, daughter, and two other travelers, on April 11, 1870. On December 31, 1878, close to the end of his visit to Spain, the former president of the United States, Ulysses S. Grant, also signed the visitor book.

The reaction of one other visitor to the Alhambra deserves comment, as it reveals the extent to which travelers from the United States used

Fig. 18. J. Laurent and Company, interior of the gallery and west pavilion of the Court of the Lions, Alhambra, Granada, 1871. Inspired in large part by Irving's *Alhambra*, American tourists who visited Spain rarely missed an opportunity to visit this important Muslim monument. Courtesy Library of Congress.

Irving as their guide, not only to Granada but also to Spain as a whole. That visitor was the Ohio native and intrepid travel writer Harriet Trowbridge Allen (1845–1926), who recorded her impressions of Spain—she too referred to the country as the "land of romance"—in a diary published in 1879 as *Travels in Europe and the East during the Years 1858–1859 and 1863–1864*. The diary indicates that she toured the Alhambra on May 9, 1864, describing it as "fairy-like, exquisite beyond description." She then added, "I have taken great pleasure in tracing the steps of Mr. Irving, using his exquisite tales of the Alhambra as my guide . . . everything is bewitching. For once, my dreams have been realized, and I have seen Spain as I have imagined it."[35]

"Spain as I have imagined it." The Alhambra apart, the phrase evoked the idea of Carmen along with Figaros, Almavivas, and toreadors as opposed to the inept politicians who figured in books by Kate Field and John Hay. Journalists and politicians generally sought to report on the problems confronting the Spanish government, such as squabbles over tariffs and Cuba that had poisoned relations between Spain and the United States. But as the Gilded Age dawned, the Spain that captured Americans' fancy, the way most "imagined it to be," was Sunny Spain and all that image evoked.

Images of Spain

Part of this interest can be related to what Kristin Hoganson has called the "cosmopolitanism" inherent to the start of the Gilded Age.[36] For the wealthy, that cosmopolitanism translated into travels abroad and the collection of bric-a-brac from distant lands. For others, particularly the stay-at-homes, cosmopolitanism expressed itself in the perusal of travel books, along with attendance at travel-oriented lectures of the kind for which John L. Stoddard (1850–1931), starting in the 1870s, was especially famous. Featuring lantern slide (aka stereopticon) projections of photographs taken during his travels, Stoddard's lectures, whether delivered singly on in a series, played to sell-out audiences in cities, large and small, scattered throughout the United States. In total Stoddard is said to have delivered more than twenty-five hundred lectures, eventually reaching an audience estimated at more than four million. Having visited Spain in 1877, he first started lecturing about the country on January 19, 1881, with a series he presented at Chicago's Central Music Hall. The first lecture, titled "The Land of the Moors, or Saunterings in Sunny Spain," introduced the audience to Toledo, Córdoba, Seville, and Granada, as well to the bullfight. In later years Stoddard trimmed this series of lectures to one, calling it "Travels in Sunny Spain." In New York, for example, Stoddard's regular venue was Daly's Theatre, and it was there, on April 8, 1883, he arranged for an orchestra to play the so-called Toreador Song from Bizet's *Carmen* in order to prepare the crowd for what they were about to see and hear in his lecture. When he delivered that same lecture, apparently sans orchestra, in Washington DC in 1888, a review on the front page of the *Washington Post* noted that "Mr. Stoddard weaves through his lectures a charming thread of Spanish romance and tradition." By this date, moreover, one version of Stoddard's "Travels in Sunny Spain" lecture, accompanied by engravings based on photographs he had taken, had appeared as the opening section in his first travel book, *Red-Letter Days Abroad* (1884).[37]

For those unable to attend one of Stoddard's lectures, there were other ways to catch a glimpse of Carmen and other aspects of Sunny Spain. Art offered one possibility. By the 1830s Spanish themes were already figuring centrally in the work of two painters from Britain: David Roberts and John Frederick Lewis. Few of their canvases came to the United States, but folio-sized volumes of their engravings of the Alhambra and picturesque scenes in Granada and Seville were best sellers, in both Britain and the United States. Harder to find were the pictures of Spanish gypsies by the Scottish artist John Phillip. These were popular in Britain, where most quickly found their way into private collections, but a few also found their way into American homes. Much better known in this respect were the images of gypsies by the French artist and illustrator Gustave Doré, as these circulated as illustrations in Abbé Léon Godard's handsome travel folio, *L'Espagne, mœurs et paysages, histoire et monuments*, published in 1862.[38]

As the art historian M. Elizabeth Boone has ably demonstrated, one of the first American artists to produce similar images of the country was Samuel Colman (1831–90), a landscape painter associated with New

Fig. 19. Title page, John L. Stoddard, *Red-Letter Days Abroad*, 1883. "Sunny Spain" ranked among Stoddard's most popular travel lectures. It was also the lead chapter in this illustrated travelogue. Photo by Thomas Hensle.

York's Hudson River school. How Colman became interested in Spain is not altogether clear, but his attraction can probably be traced to his fellow New Yorker Washington Irving and several other friends who had previously visited Granada. What's certain is that Colman had a romanticized view of the country well before 1860, when he embarked on an extended European journey that included Spain. Once there he made a beeline for Andalucia, visiting Córdoba, Granada, and Seville and making sketches of monuments and scenes he deemed picturesque. He later transformed one of these sketches into his majestic *Hill of the Alhambra* and another into a hazy view titled *Harbor of Seville*, both of which, together with other Spanish-themed pictures, private collectors snapped up soon after they were first put on display in a New York gallery in 1865.

It did not take long for other American artists, encouraged in part by Colman's success, to visit Spain in search of picturesque themes. In November 1869, for example, three Philadelphia artists—Thomas Eakins, Harry Humphrey Moore, and William Sartain—were studying in Paris when they decided to travel to Spain, apparently at the suggestion of their mentors, Jean-Léon Gérôme and Léon Bonnat, both of whom had a particular interest in the art of Velázquez and other Spanish Old Masters. Eakins was the first to go, and letters written to his father during his time in Spain provide a hint as to how the young artist spent his time. His first destination was Madrid, where he visited the Prado, mainly to study the artistry of Velázquez. "I have seen big painting here," Eakins writes. He then went to Seville, where he was joined by Moore and eventually Sartain. Eakins's letters home record daily walks in the country together with Moore, as well as the kinds of people ("I know ever so many gypsies, men and women, circus people, street dancers, theatre dancers, and bull fighters") he was particularly eager to meet ("The Spanish I like better than any people I ever saw and so does Harry Moore") and also to paint.[39] Still new to what he called "picture-making," Eakins during the course of his six months in Seville—he returned to Paris early in June 1870—executed only a handful of Spanish-themed paintings, but they included his celebrated *Street Scene in Seville*, which featured Carmel-

Fig. 20. Thomas Eakins, "San Bernardo" Spanish sketchbook, 1870. Eakins was among the first U.S. artists to discover Spanish art and paint "typically" Spanish scenes. His sketchbook includes this little-known drawing of what appears to be a liquor advertisement featuring a *torero* preparing to kill a bull. From Charles Bregler's Thomas Eakins Collection. Courtesy of the Pennsylvania Academy of the Fine Arts, Philadelphia.

ita, the seven-year-old daughter of gypsy dancers. Moore and Sartain were more productive, especially Moore, who extended his stay in the country, visited the Alhambra (he signed the register on June 10, 1870), and eventually executed dozens of canvases depicting gypsies, matadors, dancers with castanets, and señoritas holding fans—in other words, the same picturesque types that had fascinated Eakins and the same ones Americans had come to associate with Sunny Spain.

On the heels of this trio of artists came various others in the 1870s and 1880s. As with Eakins, these artists journeyed to Spain partly to study the work of Velázquez and partly to paint images reflecting the country's fabled romance. One was Mary Cassatt (1844–1926), who, following her initial training together with Eakins in Philadelphia's Pennsylvania Academy of the Fine Arts, went to Paris to study with Gérôme and other artists. In a letter written during the course of her first visit to Seville during the fall and winter of 1872–73, Cassatt trumpeted the opportunities Spain offered artists such as herself: "I see the immense capital that can be drawn from Spain, it has not been exploited yet as it might be and it is suggestive of pictures on all sides."[40] That capital meant pictures of gypsies, matadors, and other picturesque types. It was much the same for other artists, such as John Singer Sargent, J. Carroll Beckwith, J. Alden Weir, Charles S. Reinhart, William Merritt Chase, Francis Hopkinson Smith, Frank Duveneck, and Robert Henri, all of whom had a common interest in painting the Spanish picturesque and whose canvases featuring these subjects found a ready market among collectors across the United States.[41]

How many Americans saw these pictures? It is difficult to say, as the majority went directly into private collections and were rarely exhibited to the general public. Such was the history of Samuel Colman's Spanish pictures, and Cassatt's as well. It also applies to John Singer Sargent's *El Jaleo*, arguably the one picture that best illustrates America's growing fascination with the romance of Spain. The son of a wealthy Philadelphia couple who spent much of their time in Europe, Sargent (1856–1925), born in Florence, lived much of his early life in Paris, and it was there, after having demonstrated an aptitude for painting and drawing at an early age, he entered the atelier of Carolus-Durand when he was still in his teens. Carolus-Durand, together with Gérôme and Bonnat, was another devotee of Velázquez, and he encouraged the young Sargent to visit the Prado in order to study and learn from the Spanish master's technique. Sargent undertook this journey in 1879, and in addition to visiting the Prado, he journeyed to Seville, where, in a café, he made sketches of an alluring flamenco dancer and the guitarists who accompanied her.

Back in Paris these sketches served as the source for *El Jaleo*, meaning hubbub or ruckus, a term that refers to the clapping, foot-stomping, *olé*s, and other shouts of encouragement offered by dancers and also by the audience during a flamenco performance. Sargent's monumental picture—almost twelve feet wide and seven high—fails to convey these sonorous elements of the dance but otherwise captures the atmosphere and the excitement of the performance he witnessed. The completed picture first went on public display at a Paris salon in May

1882, and it was purchased shortly thereafter by the wealthy Bostonian Thomas Jefferson Coolidge, who brought the canvas to the United States shortly thereafter.

At that point *El Jaleo* disappeared from public view until January 28, 1888, when, together with Sargent's provocative portrait *Madame X*, it was exhibited for two weeks at Boston's St. Botolph Club. According to the *Boston Sunday Globe* edition of February 19, 1888, that exhibit attracted more than five thousand visitors, among them the prominent Boston socialite and collector Isabella Stewart Gardner, who fell in love in with *El Jaleo* and attempted to buy it from Coolidge, who also happened to be her nephew. It took Gardner more than twenty years to persuade Coolidge to part with the picture. As for the public, they were unable to see *El Jaleo* until 1914, when Gardner opened to visitors her newly refurbished and remodeled house museum near Boston's Fenway Park (see chapter 5).[42]

But if *El Jaleo* and similar pictures by other artists remained largely out of sight, books and magazine articles allowed other Americans to catch a glimpse of Sunny Spain. That glimpse generally began with the arabesques and fanciful illustrations included in Irving's *Alhambra*, but Sunny Spain also figured in a seemingly endless string of articles published in such popular periodicals as *Frank Leslie's New Family Magazine*, *Century Magazine*, *Harper's New Monthly Magazine*, and *Scribner's Magazine*. Some of these articles—their numbers exploded in the 1870s—attracted readers with such tempting titles as "Spain, Her Ways, Her Women, and Her Wines" and "Madrid from Noon to Midnight." In others illustrations were the hook, as in those accompanying "From Gibraltar to the Bidasoa," a two-part travel essay published in *Frank Leslie's New Family Magazine* starting in September 1856. The work of an anonymous artist, these images depicted beggars, gypsies, and other picturesque types. A roughly similar cast of characters could be seen in the illustrations included in Susan Carter's "Street Life in Spain," published in *Century Magazine* in 1889. In this instance they were the work of William Merritt Chase, the noted New York artist instrumental in helping to whet the appetite of wealthy American collectors for choice examples of Spanish Old Master Art (see chapter 5).[43]

Travel books provided yet another way for Americans to experience, albeit vicariously, something of Spain's romance. Ford's *Handbook for Travellers*, originally published in 1845, remained an important vade-mecum for readers in both Britain and the United States. Even more popular was Ford's *Gatherings from Spain*, an abbreviated version of the *Handbook* dating from 1851, and the lighthearted *Gazpacho: Or, Summer Months in Spain*, by another British author, William George Clark, also published in 1851. As its title suggests, this book provided readers with an introduction to the cold soup that is practically synonymous with today's Spanish cuisine, but, as Clark described it, gazpacho then had no trace of tomato but consisted solely of olive oil, some vinegar, garlic, and mashed bread.

The popularity of these books soon prompted American travel writers, together with their publishers, to provide their own travel books to readers. One such writer was the poet and inveterate traveler William Cullen Bryant (1794–1868). The year 1850 marked the appearance of his *Letters of a Traveler*, a volume that included Bryant's impressions of cities ranging from Florence and Edinburgh in Europe to St. Augustine in the United States. Bryant followed this volume with his *Letters from Spain and Other Countries in 1857 and 1858*, a compilation of dispatches originally published in the *New York Post*. Bryant's impressions of Spain—"a curious old place, with many picturesque and interesting peculiarities"—varied; some were sunny, others not, but given his fame as a travel writer, the book whetted Americans' appetite for reading about and, for those who could afford it, traveling to Spain.[44]

America's Civil War occasioned a temporary halt in the publication of travelogues of this sort, but they began reappearing in 1869 with the publication of Bayard Taylor's *By-Ways of Europe*, which included chapters touching on the author's impressions of Catalonia and the Balearic Islands; John Hay's *Castilian Days* (1871); the relentlessly sunny account of Spain that Harriet Trowbridge Allen included in her *Travels in Europe and the East* (1879); and James Albert Harrison's erudite travel book, *Spain in Profile: A Summer among the Aloes and Olives* (1879). A professor of modern languages at Virginia's Washington and Lee University, Harrison (1848–1911) was a scholarly jack-of-all-trades; his books included a life of George Washington, an Anglo-Saxon grammar, a study of *Beowulf*, another on French syntax, and, most famously, several books dedicated to the life and works of Edgar Allan Poe. The Mediterranean was yet another of his interests, and, piqued by what he called the "adventure of Spain," Harrison spent several months there in 1876, taking time out from his travels to pay a call on James Russell Lowell, the U.S. minister in Madrid. Lowell provided Harrison with the equivalent of a crash course in Spanish politics, sharing with him his admiration for the new king, Alfonso XII, his thoughts on the shortcomings of the country's new "papier-mâché" constitution, together with praise for its *ayuntamientos*, the institutions of local governance he regarded as the "chief strength of Spain." Harrison's book—a collection of what he called a "series of profiles projected more or less vaguely by a Spanish sun"— included his overwhelmingly favorable impressions of the country, the one exception being the bullfight, which, like most Americans who had witnessed the spectacle, he considered a "ghastly drama."[45]

The decade of 1880s, a period of relative tranquility in Spanish politics, brought with it new interest in and opportunities for travel to Spain. Publishers responded with a host of new travel books outlining the delights awaiting tourists able to visit the country. The banner year was 1883, with the publication of no fewer than seven almost lookalike books focused on the sunnier side of Spain. The most original and entertaining of them was "Lizzie" Williams Champney's *Three Vassar Girls Abroad: Rambles of Three College Girls on a Vacation Trip through France and Spain for Amusement and Instruction*, the inaugural volume in what became that writer's popular Three Vassar Girls series. Champney's Spain was relentlessly sunny, a "land of romance and mystery." As for Spaniards, they were invariably "gay and picturesque."[46]

Next came Henry Day's *From the Pyrenees to the Pillar of Hercules* (1883), a volume that had its origins in the author's travels through Spain in 1876. Day's Spain was a "picturesque country" and the Spaniards a people who embraced an "everlasting tomorrow."[47] More of the same could be found in William Howe Downes's *Spanish Ways and By-Ways* (1883), which emphasized Spain's "shiftless picturesqueness, her squalid grandeur, and her lazy dignity." The fastidious Downes, however, only

Fig. 21. Charles S. Reinhart, *A Mandurra Solo*. Frontispiece in George Parsons Lathrop, *Spanish Vistas*, 1883. *Spanish Vistas* was Lathrop's only travel book. Reinhart's illustrations, based on sketches made from life, featured picturesque, typically "Spanish" scenes. Photo by Thomas Hensle.

recommended Spain for travelers with a "mania for the picturesque and a not overfastidious stomach."[48]

Yet another 1883 publication was George Parsons Lathrop's *Spanish Vistas*, a volume one reviewer judged a "delightful book," as it managed to capture both the "romance and reality" of Spain.[49] Adding to the volume's appeal were illustrations by Charles Stanley Reinhart (1844–91), an artist who had accompanied Lathrop on his trip across Spain. Those illustrations featured a stock array of picturesque types: dancing boys, peasants in a marketplace, the night watch, and, more menacingly, two assassins in long cloaks.[50] Illustrations also enhanced Marvin Richardson Vincent's *Shadow of the Pyrenees*, which focused on the Basque Country, a part of northern Spain that had little in common with Andalucia in the south but where the author was still able to locate dancing gypsies and declare that the city of San Sebastián approached "perfection."[51] More high-quality drawings illustrating different aspects of Sunny Spain could also be found in W. Parker Bodfish's *Through Spain on Donkey-Back*. An artist and book illustrator, Bodfish described Spain as a "nation of singers and dancers and" Spaniards as a "sun-basking, siesta-loving" people, virtually all of whom, men and women alike, played the guitar.[52]

Yet another of the Spanish travelogues appearing in 1883 was aimed at readers contemplating a visit to Spain accompanied by their children—and apparently many did, judging by the number of American families who signed the Alhambra's visitor register. This was Susan Hale's *Family Flight through Spain*, a thoroughly lighthearted account issued by the same publisher—Boston's D. Lathrop & Co.—as the travelogue by Bodfish but aimed at a different audience and filled with comments ("Andalusia, the land of romance and sunshine") that echoed those of both Irving and Gautier.[53] In contrast, Susan's brother, Rev. Edward Everett Hale, offered a somewhat more sober account of the country in *Seven Spanish Cities*, a book that began with his trip to Spain, together with Susan and her children, in 1882. Hale informed readers that "I have wanted to go to Spain ever since I can remember," and he attributed this desire to a combination of factors: the Spanish "bon-bons" his uncle, Edward Hill Everett, Irving's patron and a former U.S. minister in Madrid, had brought him when he was a child; his study of Spanish, starting at the age of sixteen; his reading of Prescott's histories of Spain, Mexico, and Peru; his stint working as Latin American editor for Boston's *Advertiser*; and a lifelong fascination with Columbus that would later yield Hale's biography of Columbus, a book he completed in 1891, just in time for the celebrations honoring the four-hundredth anniversary of the mariner's famous achievement. It follows that when Hale finally got to Spain, he went straight to Palos, the small Andalucian port from which the mariner had set sail, and then Seville, where he visited the General Archive of the Indies as well as the Columbiana, the library begun by Columbus's son Ferdinand. His book mixed sightseeing with reflections on Spain's complex politics, together with its checkered relationship with the United States. "We hate the Spaniard," Hale wrote, "in a certain sense, as Drake and Hawkins and Arnyas Leigh hated Spain. But this only means Charles V and Philip II . . . the Inquisition and its iniquities. . . . We love Columbus. Then Isabella the Good. And Mexico." He then added, in a comment referring to the emergent notion of Sturdy Spain, "We cannot but see how much we owe to Spain."[54]

The simultaneous appearance of so many travel books dealing with Spain defies easy explanation, but it allowed one reviewer to announce the start of a "rediscovery of Spain by Americans."[55] That rediscovery moved along several parallel but interlocking paths. One, just noted, was art. History was another, much of it centered on documenting Spain's history in America but also extending to such books as Edward Hale and Susan Hale's *The Story of Spain*. This 1886 volume (and subsequent editions) offered a wholly sympathetic overview of the country's history, beginning in antiquity and ending with the challenges confronting its young monarch, Alfonso XIII, and in doing so it adroitly avoided any mention of such hot-button issues as the tensions over Cuba that plagued relations between Spain and the United States.

The same rediscovery also occasioned the publication of still more travel books and essays, the majority focused on the more romantic and supposedly traditional aspects of Spanish society as opposed to the changes that were gradually aligning the country with other European countries, such as England, Germany, and France. Put another way, America's "rediscovery of Spain" emphasized what Henry M. Field (see below) termed "old" Spain—the carefree Spain of romance—as opposed to "new" Spain, replete with banks, coal mines, Basque iron foundries, Catalan textile factories, railways, and other hallmarks of modernization, progress, and change. Traditional Spain was also a "safe" Spain to the extent that it allowed authors, together with their publishers, to avoid thorny political topics such as Cuba, as well as the restrictions that the Spanish constitution of 1876 imposed on Protestant churches seeking to gain a foothold in Spain. Better to avoid controversy and emphasize the more palatable and popular folkloric aspects of Spanish culture, and this in fact is what most travel writers of this era, following Irving's tried and true formula, did. They included Samuel Parsons Scott (1846–1929), an Ohio lawyer for whom Irving's *Alhambra* kindled a lifelong fascination with the influence of Islamic culture on Spain. Scott's visit to Spain in 1879 led initially to a series of articles featuring Granada, Córdoba, Seville, and other Spanish cities he regarded as "Moorish" and subsequently to his 1886 book *Through Spain: A Narrative of Travel and Adventure in the Peninsula*, similarly fastened onto Moorish themes.[56] That same year brought the publication of Francis Hopkinson Smith's *Well-Worn Roads of Spain, Holland, and Italy travelled by a painter in search of the picturesque* (1886). Born and educated in Baltimore, Smith was a structural engineer who assisted with the design of the stone foundation for the Statue of Liberty. He subsequently became an artist and travel writer specializing in books featuring his own watercolor illustrations and reproduced in the newly invented phototype process. Scribner's, his publisher, used this technology in *Well-Worn Roads*, which opened with several chapters devoted to Andalucia and featuring picturesque accounts of scenes and characters copied from or at least inspired by those of Irving, as his description of one street in Seville readily attests: "It is a narrow, winding, crooked thoroughfare, shaded by great awnings stretched between the overhanging roofs, and filled with balconies holding great tropical plants, strings of black hats, festoons of gay colored stuffs. Sly peeping señoritas, fruit sellers, aguadores [water sellers], donkeys, beggars, and the thousand and one things that make up Spanish life."[57]

"Things that make up Spanish life": the phrase is telling, as Smith made no mention of those things most on the of mind Seville's inhabitants in 1886, among them delays in the construction of the city's urban tramway (it only began service in 1887) or the challenges confronting the newly widowed Queen María Christina as regent of Spain's one-year-old monarch, King Alfonso XIII.

These challenges made a cameo appearance in Henry M. Field's *Old Spain and New Spain*, a volume first printed in 1886. A veteran travel writer, Field (1822–1907) made a point of emphasizing the ways in which Spain was changing, dedicating several chapters to its constitutional monarchy, vibrant periodical press, and what politicians such as Antonio Cánovas de Castillo and Emilio Castelar had told him was the country's steady progress toward democracy. Yet, so as not put off too many readers, Field reminded them that much of "Old Spain," that is, Sunny Spain, was still to be seen, especially in small villages and among the peasantry. "The common people of Spain, who till the soil," he wrote, "are of the right stuff: simple and honest, brave in war and industrious in peace in the country's basic way of life."[58] He also envisioned these villagers as symbols of a bygone era that cherished values—hard work and a simpler, agrarian style of life—that he, together with the likes of Henry Adams, believed had already vanished in the fast-paced, rapidly industrializing and urbanizing United States.

This same "Old Spain," sunny and bright, figured centrally in most of the travel books published during the decade leading up to the 1898 war. Disputes over tariffs and, starting in 1895, Cuba's civil war placed new strains on relations between Spain and the United States, but these tensions and the growing clamor for war did little to deter a new crop of travel writers from representing Spain in wholly positive—read romantic—ways. Subject-wise, these books are practically interchangeable. They include Charles A. Stoddard, *Spanish Cities* (1892; second edition 1893); Hobart Chatfield-Taylor, *Spain: Land of the Castanet* (1896); Louise Chandler Moulton, *Lazy Tours in Spain and Elsewhere* (1897); Fanny Bullock Workman's *Sketches Awheel in Modern Iberia* (1897), a charming account of her experiences during a bicycle tour across various parts of Spain in 1895; and Mary F. Nixon-Roulet's somewhat oddball *With a Pessimist in Spain* (1897).

This last title is of particular importance. It appeared at a moment when anti-Spanish rhetoric was blazoned across the front pages of news-

Fig. 22. (*top*) E. C. Potter, equestrian statue of De Soto. Louisiana Purchase Exposition, St. Louis, 1904. Courtesy Library of Congress.

Fig. 23. (*bottom*) William H. Rau, *Spanish Students on the Streets of Seville*. Louisiana Purchase Exposition, St. Louis, 1904. Sturdy Spain—in the guise of the De Soto statue—and Sunny Spain—as represented by these "Spanish" singers and an arcade called the "Streets of Seville"—were both on display at the fair. Courtesy Library of Congress.

papers in the United States, but Nixon-Roulet deliberately ignored it, opting instead to offer a wholly romanticized view of Spain and its people. Nor did the war with Spain, nor the anti-Spanish, Black Legend–like propaganda appearing in the newspapers owned by Pulitzer and Hearst do anything to diminish this author's enthusiasm for the country. In fact that propaganda may have done just opposite. In keeping with the theme of "forgive and forget," Nixon-Roulet returned to Spain on several occasions soon after the 1898 war had ended. These visits led to her charming *Fernando, Our Little Spanish Cousin* (1906), part of a series aimed at a teenage audience. Next came *The Spaniard at Home*, directed at a more mature readership and published in several editions starting in 1910. In the preface Nixon-Roulet announced that this book aimed at "portraying Spain of to-day as she really is" and from a wholly "Spanish point of view." This perhaps explains why, in a section devoted to Spanish industries, she announced that "decadent Spain was a thing of the past" because the loss of Cuba and its other overseas colonies had enabled its government to concentrate on improving the welfare of its citizens.[59] On the other hand most of the book served up the familiar stereotypes typical of "Old Spain" and those that readers had come to expect: descriptions of the Alhambra; gypsy girls dancing the fandango; streets cluttered with guitar players, water carriers, and other picturesque types. That Spain was fast disappearing, especially in cities such as Barcelona and Madrid, but it remained the stuff of fantasy and romance.

That same image of the country also helps account for the popularity of the arcade exhibit known as "Streets of Seville" and located on the "pike," or main thoroughfare of the Louisiana Purchase Exposition held in St. Louis in 1904. A privately organized commercial venture, "Streets of Seville" had no formal connection to the Spanish government nor did it make reference to the image of Sturdy Spain evoked by the Spanish ambassador, Emilio de Ojeda, during the exposition's opening ceremonies (see chapter 1) and epitomized by Edward C. Potter's colossal equestrian statue of De Soto that was erected in the exposition's central Plaza of St. Louis. Rather it served up a familiar hodgepodge of offerings lifted from the idea of Sunny Spain: a replica of the Alhambra's Court of the Lions; actors dressed as gypsies and performing flamenco dances; a troop of singers in Mexican dress but identified as "Spanish students"; a bullfight staged with puppets; a model bullring; and most famously *The Girl from Madrid*, a somewhat racy vaudeville show that was billed as a fashion show.[60] This Spain, Sunny Spain, was more imagined than real, but together with Sturdy Spain it too served as the spark that ignited Americans' emergent craze for Spanish culture, language, and art.

$\widehat{}$ 4 $\widehat{}$

Hispanism, *Hispanismo*, and the Hispanic Society of America

The sons of Hispania are closest to nature's man
and woman and most moved of primordial forces.
—ARCHER MILTON HUNTINGTON

In a little-known article dating from 1909 Martin Hume, lecturer in Spanish history and literature at the University of Cambridge, analyzed what he considered the "instinctive mutual attraction" of Spain and the United States. Employing the hallowed principle that opposites attract, Hume argued that this attraction derived from the "extreme dissimilarity of character" of the two nations, or as he condescendingly expressed it, "A strenuous people [i.e., the Americans] find in the repose of the Spaniards an antidote for their restlessness; a nation of businessmen are brought into contact with a people, the keynote of whose character is an almost disdainful disregard for laborious and calculated gain; on the one hand, keen acquisitiveness, on the other a languid magnanimity incite in their opposites the wondering admiration that engenders a kind of humorous and tolerant affection on both sides." Such affection, Hume continued, expressed itself in myriad ways: "social intercourse" (he did not provide any example); Spain's interest in what he called the "advanced institutions of the anglo-saxon world" (no example here either); and, on the other side of the coin, the interest of the United States in the language and literature of Spain.[1]

Elaborating on this last point, Hume commented that the United States and its universities "now stand absolutely pre-eminent in this branch of learning" and continued by listing the names of such well-known students of Spanish culture as Archer M. Huntington, founder of the Hispanic Society of America; Dr. Hugo Rennert (1858–1927), a professor of Spanish literature at the University of Pennsylvania and author of several important books on the history of the seventeenth-century Spanish theater; and two historians: Henry Charles Lea (1825–1909), a scholar whose many books included a monumental study of the Spanish Inquisition, and Samuel Parsons Scott, whose *History of the Moorish Empire in Europe* appeared in 1904.[2]

Few of today's scholars pay much attention to Hume's racially based assessment of Spanish-American relations; in fact it is mostly forgotten and rarely read. But it is worth noting that Hume's remarks about the excellence of Spanish studies in the United States echoed those of Spain's most prominent man of letters, the philosopher and critic Miguel de Unamuno (1846–1936). In an interview with the Spanish newspaper *La Nación* in August 1906, Unamuno is likely to have shocked some of his compatriots with the announcement that "one can honestly say that the United States of North America is today the nation in which the things of Spain are studied most and best. All of its great universities offer courses in Spanish language and literature, and these courses are becoming more and more popular. The number of young people dedicated to the study of our culture (*cosas de España*) grows year by year. This has gained momentum, as a consequence of our last war, of the decision of the United States to keep Puerto Rico and to intervene in Cuba."[3] Unamuno's comments, together with those of Hume, speak directly to one important, indeed crucial aspect of the Spanish craze: America's enthusiastic embrace of Spanish language and literature, or what I will refer to here as Hispanism, in the immediate aftermath of the war of 1898.

Hispanism

At the heart of this phenomenon is what James D. Fernández aptly calls Longfellow's Law. By this "law" Fernández asserts that U.S. interest in Spain is primarily mediated by U.S. interest in Latin America. The law itself derives from the advice that the young poet Henry Wadsworth Longfellow, residing in Paris, received from his father in 1826: "Such are the relations now existing between this country [the United States] and

Fig. 24. Henry Wadsworth Longfellow, self-portrait en route from Málaga to Granada, 1828. Together with Washington Irving and George Ticknor, who was his predecessor in Harvard's Smith Professorship of Romance Languages, Longfellow was among the first Hispanophiles in the United States. MS Am 1340172, Henry Wadsworth Longfellow Papers, Houghton Library, Harvard University.

Spanish America that a knowledge of the Spanish is quite as important as French. If you neglect either of these languages, you may be sure of not obtaining the station which you have in view." Heeding his father's counsel, Longfellow dutifully packed his bags, hurried to Madrid, and promptly undertook study of the language and literature of Spain.[4]

Longfellow's father was by no means the first to suggest that the relationship between the United States and Latin America should be the reason why Americans ought to study Spanish. Thomas Jefferson had similar ideas. Jefferson himself could read Spanish, and *Don Quixote*—which he apparently read in English translation—ranked among his favorite books, and he urged his daughter Martha to read it and study Spanish as well. Prior to becoming president Jefferson was also in correspondence with a number of Spanish scientists, and his library—the core of today's Library of Congress—contained hundreds of Spanish books.[5] In 1779, moreover, Jefferson introduced modern languages, Spanish among them, into the curriculum of the College of William and Mary, and in 1818 he made certain that instruction in the language would be offered when the University of Virginia opened its doors in 1825.[6]

Jefferson's interest in Spanish derived in part from the quality of Spain's literature. It was also connected to what its explorers, geographers, and other men of letters had contributed to the understanding of the New World. But as a letter Jefferson directed in 1787 to Thomas Mann Randolph, the son of a wealthy Virginia planter and student at William and Mary, suggests, commercial and geopolitical concerns were also involved. Jefferson writes, "With respect to modern languages, French, as I have observed, is indispensable. Next to this the Spanish is the most important to an American. Our connection with Spain is already important and will become daily more so. Besides this, the ancient part of American history is written in Spanish."[7]

A year later Jefferson offered similar advice to his nephew, John Rutledge, then traveling in Europe. Jefferson, thinking about the future of the United States, urged him to visit both Lisbon and Madrid, specifically noting, "I should think the knowledge of their language, manners, and situation, might eventually and even probably become more useful to yourself and country than that of any other place you will have seen. The womb of time is big with events to take place between us and them, and a little knowledge of them will give you great advantage over those who have none at all."[8] In this instance Jefferson did not define what he meant either by "useful" or "advantage," but commerce with Spain's American colonies was clearly on his mind. So too was the day when Spain's American colonies, independent and democratic, would enter into close association with the United States. More specifically, "useful" and "advantage" referred to the acquisition of Florida and Louisiana by the United States, a process of expansion that President Jefferson initiated when he negotiated (albeit with Napoleon) the Louisiana Purchase in 1803 and opened preliminary discussions with the Spanish monarchy over the possible sale of Florida to the United States.

Despite Jefferson's interest in promoting Spanish, few Americans, Rutledge among them, ever bothered to learn the language. Throughout most of the nineteenth century and part of the twentieth as well, the arts curriculum in most secondary schools, whether public or private, was rooted in the classics—the study of Latin and occasionally Greek. Modern languages were an add-on, and French, aided by its associations with Enlightenment culture and diplomacy, was the one language customarily taught. German came next, owing in large part to its close connection with scholarship, medicine, and science.

In comparison, few secondary schools outside California and other parts of the Southwest invested very much in the teaching of Spanish. One exception was Round Hill School, a private academy founded in 1823 in Northampton, Massachusetts. Round Hill was the brainchild of George Bancroft and Joseph Green Cogswell, two Harvard professors who left their positions at the college to start a school with a curriculum modeled on those they had previously encountered during their studies in Germany and travels in other parts of Europe. Round Hill emphasized the importance of modern languages, Spanish included, justifying its addition by pointing out that "the great changes which are taking place in the southern parts of our continent give it at this time peculiar importance." But if Round Hill was a trailblazer, few followed in its path. Financial difficulties led to the school's closure after only ten years, and possibly for this reason few other private academies saw fit to offer their students the opportunity to study Spanish.[9]

As for public secondary schools, Philadelphia's innovative Central High School was the pioneer. It introduced Spanish into its curriculum as an elective in 1838, only to drop it (along with its classes in Anglo-Saxon and Greek) in 1854.[10] The situation in New York City's secondary schools was somewhat similar even though that city was home to the largest Spanish-speaking population in the East. In fact, as documented in an important survey published by the U.S. Bureau of Education in 1913, Spanish was taught only "sporadically" in most of the country's high schools until after the start of the twentieth century.[11]

As for the nation's colleges and universities, here too instruction in Spanish was slow to take root. The 1749 constitution of Philadelphia's Public College—later to become the University of Pennsylvania— called for instruction in Spanish, but it was only in 1766 that the college's trustees hired Paul Fooks to teach Spanish along with French. Little is known about Fooks except that he was a Huguenot, a "Notary and Tabellion Publick" residing in Philadelphia, and, starting in September 1766, the Province of Pennsylvania's newly appointed "Interpreter of French and Spanish Languages."[12] Later he served in a similar capacity for the Continental Congress. Records documenting his teaching at the college are few, evidently because Fooks's appointment as a language instructor was irregular; he never received a salary nor did his classes figure in the college's curriculum. He taught them instead on an hourly, fee-paying basis, and in order to drum up business he regularly placed advertisements announcing these classes in the *Pennsylvania Gazette*, the newspaper founded by Benjamin Franklin. These indicate Fooks taught out of his home, offering private lessons to young ladies in the morning and young gentlemen in the afternoon. On July 3, 1776, just one day before the Founding Fathers signed the Declaration of Independence in Philadelphia, Fooks published in the *Gazette* a substantive essay, "On the Advantages of being acquainted with both the French and the Spanish languages." The essay reminded readers that knowledge of these languages would allow an individual to become a "Citizen of the World." It also emphasized their practical benefits in matters of commerce and trade with "France and Spain in their settlements in the West-Indies, and Gulph of Mexico" and also included Fooks's thoughts on the comparative worth of the two languages he taught. French, he suggested, was "the most universal," especially among men of learning, with Spanish being less so, owing partly to Spain's "severe laws and customs," the "slavish submission" caused by the Inquisition, and a press subject to "tyrannical inspection." Despite such obstacles, he noted, the Spanish language was "majestic and expressive," and even though it did not have as many authors "worth perusing" as French, it still offered "a Quevedo, a Cervantes, a Calderon, a Marquis of Santa Cruz, a Feijoo, a Sarmiento, etc." Fooks could easily have listed other authors as well, among them Spain's famous seventeenth-century playwright, Lope de Vega, but at the moment when Fooks offered these observations, no better defense of the learning of Spanish existed in the English-speaking world.[13]

It remains to be determined whether Fooks's advertisements—these appeared on a weekly basis—brought him any pupils. All that is known is that Fooks, in addition to serving as an interpreter for the Continental Congress and becoming a member of the American Philosophical Society, maintained his attachment to the Public College until shortly before his death in 1781. Was he replaced? Apparently not. By the 1780s, as François Furstenberg has eloquently argued, Philadelphia was a city that "spoke French." Under the circumstances the college had little incentive to hire a full-time Spanish instructor as opposed to others versed in French, the "universal" language and evidently the one Philadelphians were most eager to learn.[14]

Even so, Spanish did not altogether disappear from Philadelphia. The American Philosophical Society, the city's premier institution of learning, regularly played host to visitors from both Spain and its American colonies, among them the Canary Islander Antonio Josef Ruiz de Padrón, an associate of Franklin who in 1784 presented a lecture—in French?—on the evils of the Inquisition. Philadelphia also hosted a number of printing houses that produced Spanish-language books destined for the South American market. In 1794, for example, one run by Francis Bailey printed *El desengaño del hombre*, a fiercely antimonarchical treatise authored by

Santiago (aka James) Felipe Puglia, an Italian-cum-Spanish political exile who had immigrated in 1790 to Philadelphia, where he filled the vacancy left by the death of Fooks by offering lessons in Spanish as well as Italian. The list of subscribers who helped Puglia with the publication of his book included Alexander Hamilton, Thomas Jefferson, and Richard Worsam Meade, a Philadelphia merchant soon to become the U.S. vice-consul in Cádiz. Other Philadelphia-based printers producing books in Spanish included the Irish exile Mathew Carey (1760–1839) and his brother James. Puglia worked with both. In 1799 James Carey printed *Reflexiones sobre el comercio de España con sus colonias en América, en tiempo de guerra,* signed by "A Spaniard in Philadelphia." Authorship of this treatise—a screed inspired by Adam Smith's arguments on free trade and one that argued in favor of allowing U.S. merchants unfettered access to Spain's American colonies—is customarily assigned to Puglia, although it has also been attributed to the Marqués de Casa Yrujo, then serving as the Spanish minister in Philadelphia. But whoever was responsible for the treatise, it sold well enough for Carey to invest in printing an English translation, which was released in 1800, just before James decided to move shop to New York City.

At this point his brother Mathew, founder of Carey and Son, became the Philadelphia printer of record not only for Puglia but also for other Spanish-language publications, many of which, like *Reflexiones*, were meant to provide encouragement and support for the nascent independence movements in Spanish America. Imprints included translations of Rousseau's *Social Contract* and Thomas Paine's *Rights of Man*, copies of which were exported directly to Havana (often in exchange for what Carey called "segars") and other Caribbean ports. In 1822 he also published a two-volume Spanish dictionary intended mainly for export. In the 1820s Philadelphia printers also produced several Spanish-language newspapers, among them *El Habanero*, which carried subversive messages to readers in Cuba and Spain's other American colonies. Philadelphia in these years may have spoken French, but its printers knew Spanish as well. For this reason "la famosa Filadelfia," as one of Ecuador's first presidents, Vicente Rocafuerte, called the City of Brotherly Love, was also known as a "bastion of [South American] liberty."[15]

If Philadelphia's printing houses maintained their interest in Spanish, the trustees at what became the University of Pennsylvania did not. Instruction in the language apparently ended with the death of Fooks— there is no evidence that Puglia had any connection with the university— and Spanish did not return until 1825 (and then only on a temporary basis), when the university hired Felix Marino on a four-year contract. His successor was Augustus Willis, but he too left after four years. After that the position of Spanish instructor (as opposed to those in German and French) was left vacant until 1867, the year in which Penn's trustees authorized the "Department of Arts . . . to make temporary arrangements for instruction in the Spanish language and literature." That position went to León de la Cova, who was contracted to teach four lessons per week and paid $1.50 for each. This ad hoc arrangement lasted only three years, and only in 1892, with the appointment of Hugo A. Rennert as professor of Romantic languages, did Penn finally begin to offer instruction in Spanish language and literature on a regular basis.[16]

Nor were the difficulties that Spanish encountered at Penn unique. William and Mary's first professor of modern languages, hired in 1779, was a Florentine exile, Carlos Bellini. As might be expected, Bellini offered more classes in his native Italian, as well as in French, than in Spanish, and after his death in 1803 teaching of the language all but disappeared at the college until after the Civil War. The situation of Spanish at the University of Virginia was equally precarious, despite the attention it received in Jefferson's original program of instruction. George Blaetterman, the university's first professor of modern languages, specialized in German, but he was a polyglot who offered classes in French, Spanish, and Italian until he left the university in 1840. His successor, Macmillan Schere de Vere, a Swiss national, commanded several languages but farmed out Spanish classes to a series of instructors, few of whom taught on a regular basis.[17]

As for other universities, Yale hired its first Spanish instructor in 1826, and Columbia followed suit in 1830 with the appointment of Mariano Velázquez de la Cadena, compiler of what became a standard Spanish-English dictionary that was issued and updated in many revised editions (I used this dictionary in my high school Spanish classes).[18] At other institutions Spanish generally played second fiddle to French, as at the University of Michigan, which appointed a French scholar, Louis Fasquelle, to its newly established professorship of Romance languages in 1847. Once in Ann Arbor, Fasquelle taught French on a regular basis, although he did manage to offer a Spanish course on a one-time basis in 1848, possibly in response to the interest generated by the country's acquisition of California and other Spanish-speaking territories in the wake of the U.S.-Mexico War. Spanish subsequently disappeared from Michigan's offerings until 1868, when it was offered on an alternate basis with Italian. Continuous instruction in the language only began in 1886.[19]

The one university where Spanish did best was Harvard, but even then its history was fraught. In 1816 the college's president, John T. Kirkland, named the young Boston scholar George Ticknor to Harvard's newly endowed Ariel Smith Professorship of French and Spanish Languages. At the time Ticknor was in Germany, studying literature and improving his German at the University of Göttingen, but he readily accepted the new post. Before doing so, he visited Spain, partly to improve his Spanish and also to purchase books he might need. Back in Boston, Ticknor wrote Kirkland in August 1819 about his teaching plans: one course in French literary history, another on Spanish literary history. He also indicated that he required the assistance of two language instructors, one in French, the other in Spanish. By the time Ticknor submitted this request, however, Kirkland had already hired Francis Sales as an instructor to teach both languages. A French refugee from the South of France, Sales had lived for a time in Spain before moving to Boston in 1793, earning a living by offering private lessons similar to those Fooks had taught in Philadelphia. One of his pupils happened to have been George Ticknor, who is likely to have recommended Sales to Kirkland; another pupil was the historian William Hickling Prescott. Sales also published a Spanish grammar tailored especially for merchants. It was first printed in London in 1807, and a Boston publisher issued a revised version in 1817, the year Sales began teaching at Harvard.[20]

Ticknor's relationship with Sales is not especially well documented. As holder of the Ariel Smith Professorship, Ticknor mainly taught literature, while Sales taught language, principally French, as the number of students enrolled in those classes generally outnumbered those in Spanish by three and sometimes four to one. As for Spanish literature, in 1823 Ticknor prepared a *Syllabus of a course of lectures on the history and criticism of Spanish Literature*, although it is not clear whether he offered these lectures on a regular basis. What we do know is that Ticknor resigned his professorship in 1835 following a series of squabbles with the university over matters of curriculum reform. At that point Ticknor set about transforming his syllabus and lecture notes on Spanish literature into what became his *History of Spanish Literature*, which appeared in three hefty volumes in 1849. It was the first survey of its kind ever to be written in English and remained standard reading for those interested in the subject for well over fifty years.[21]

Ticknor's immediate successor as Smith Professor was the young poet and Harvard graduate Henry Wadsworth Longfellow. Following his trip to Europe in 1827–28 and the advice of his father to study Spanish, Longfellow landed a professorship at Maine's Bowdoin College, where he apparently taught courses in both French and Spanish literature and language. He also made use of his time at Bowdoin to publish several articles on Spanish poetry, another on the history of the Spanish language, and an English translation of Spain's most important fifteenth-century poet, Jorge Manrique. He also completed his *Outre-Mer*, his "European sketch book" that recounted, as noted earlier, somewhat romanticized accounts of experiences in Spain and other parts of Europe. Once at Harvard—he started there in 1836—Longfellow's interest in Spanish literature continued; he even completed a play, *The Spanish Student*, which can be dated to around 1840. Longfellow later noted that inspiration for this play derived partly from the "exquisite" Spanish dances of a woman—almost certainly Fanny Elssler, a Viennese ballerina who toured the United States in 1840–42 and whose repertoire included English hornpipes and Spanish folk dances in addition to classical ballet—whose movements not only reminded him "of days gone by" but also stirred his romantic imagination (and, possibly, something else).[22]

Longfellow's tenure at Harvard was not an altogether a happy experience. Curricular reforms introduced in 1840 required students to study French; all other modern languages—German, Italian, and Spanish—

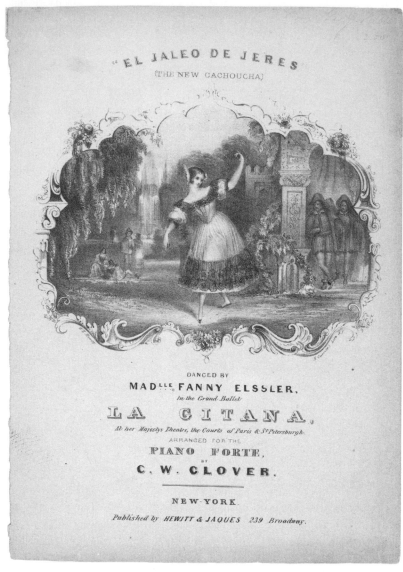

Fig. 25. *El Jaleo de Jeres (The New Cachucha), with Fanny Elssler,* playbill, 1840. Elssler was famous for her "pagan" rendition of the Spanish dance known as the *cachucha* when, starting in 1840, she embarked on an extended tour in the United States. Her diaphanous dresses assured sell-out performances. Courtesy the New York Public Library.

would become electives. The result: sharp increases in the number of students taking French. A crisis ensued when Sales, apparently overwhelmed by his French classes, refused to teach anything except Spanish. At that point the Harvard Corporation stepped in and forced Longfellow to teach language classes in addition to his required lectures in literature. Longfellow grumbled, "I have now under my charge 115 students in French, and 30 in German. Of course, with so many pupils my time is fully occupied. I can exercise but little superintendence over the Department, and have no leisure for the prosecution of those studies, which are absolutely requisite for the proper discharge of the duties originally prescribed to me."[23]

This standoff ended when Harvard agreed to appoint a new French instructor and allowed Sales to focus exclusively on Spanish, an arrangement that enabled Longfellow to teach only literature. By this time, however, Longfellow had abandoned the general survey in Spanish literature that Ticknor had pioneered and replaced it with lectures on Dante, Molière, and Goethe. As for *Don Quixote*, Longfellow devoted only one course to Cervantes's famous novel, and only in 1838, apparently as a favor to Sales, whose new edition of the novel had appeared in 1836.[24]

Yet the troubles for Longfellow, and for Spanish, at Harvard were far from over. The aging Sales had difficulties meeting his teaching obligations and, according to some reports, also failed to maintain discipline in his classes. Citing his "feeble state of health," Sales, having reached the age of eighty-two, resigned his instructorship in 1852, at which point Spanish temporarily disappeared from the college's offerings inasmuch as the Harvard Corporation took more than six years to hire a replacement. In the interim Longfellow, faced yet again with the prospect of teaching language as opposed to literature, abruptly resigned from the Smith Professorship in 1854. Longfellow's successor was a Harvard graduate and distinguished man of letters—James Russell Lowell—but his appointment did little to improve the college's offerings in Spanish. In fact it was just the reverse. Upon accepting the Smith Professorship, Lowell asked for and received a two-year leave of absence from his teaching duties, claiming that he needed to travel to Europe in order to improve his language skills, especially in German and French.

It follows that when Lowell actually took up the post, his lectures focused on German and French authors, with some Dante as well. In the meantime he relegated the teaching of Cervantes, Calderón, and other Spanish authors to a string of part-time language instructors. Among them, Santiago Cancio-Bello, a native Cuban hired to replace Sales in 1861, was probably the most successful.[25] Lowell's command of Spanish improved following his three-year stint as the U.S. minister to Madrid from 1876 and 1879, but other than developing an interest in the work of Calderón and publishing one insightful essay on Cervantes, there is no indication that he ever taught Spanish literature prior to resignation from the Smith Chair in 1886.[26]

By then the place of Spanish in Harvard's curriculum was parlous at best. Charles William Eliot (1834–1926), a German-trained chemist who was appointed Harvard's president in 1869, was a reformer determined to modernize what he considered Harvard's hidebound curriculum, mainly by placing greater emphasis on instruction in the sciences along with graduate instruction and research. The first inkling of what Eliot was up to, and where modern languages fit into his program, came in the form of a two-part essay that appeared in the *Atlantic Monthly* magazine, one of the country's most respected journals, toward the very start of his presidency. Eliot believed that students entering the sciences did not need Latin nearly as much as French or German, languages he considered essential for keeping abreast of the latest advances in Europe. As for students preparing for a bachelor's degree in philosophy, Eliot was more a traditionalist, recommending that they needed a solid grounding in Latin before studying French, a language he considered a "necessity." So while Harvard continued to offer instruction in Spanish, it remained an elective, limited to those students who had already mastered French.[27]

Making matters worse for Spanish was the absence of a departmental head following Lowell's resignation in 1886. Given Eliot's emphasis on science, the Harvard Corporation was slow to hire his successor let alone accord much attention to courses related to either Spain or Spanish America. But pressure to do so was building, especially around the time of the 1898 war and the country's growing interest in the history, politics, and culture of the broader Hispanic world. Other universities were investing in both Spain and Spanish America in ways that Harvard was not. In 1879, for example, Yale broke precedent by appointing William I. Knapp (1835–1908), a specialist in Spanish literature, as its second Street Professor of Romance Languages. Over the course of the next decade or so Knapp published a series of important books and monographs on Spanish language and literature, arguably becoming the country's foremost expert in that particular field.[28] Knapp resigned his professorship in 1892 to take up another at Chicago, leaving the teaching of Spanish to his colleague, Frederick Bliss Luquiens. In 1895 Yale also appointed Edward Gaylord Bourne (1860–1908), a specialist in the history of Spain's overseas empire, as professor of history, making Yale the first U.S. university to teach the history of Spain and Spanish America on a regular basis. Following Bourne's retirement in 1907, Yale maintained that tradition with the appointment of his former student, Hiram Bingham III, a historian also interested in archaeological studies and who, as a leader of the Yale Archeological Expedition, is now credited with the "discovery" of Machu Picchu in the Peruvian Andes in July 1911.[29]

Other institutions of higher learning, including the Universities of California, Chicago, Columbia, Pennsylvania, and Texas, soon followed Yale's lead with similar appointments in the Hispanic field.[30] Another breakthrough occurred in 1902, when Smith College offered a professorship in Romance languages to Caroline Bourland (1871–1956), a Bryn Mawr PhD and specialist in Spanish literature. As Bourland later recalled, "When I went to Smith there were *at the most six* Spanish books in the Library." To this she added, "I believe that I was the first woman in the United States to have the title of full professor of Spanish in an institution of learning."[31]

The trend for colleges and universities to do more with both Spain and Spanish America was clear. In 1885 there were only about ten Spanish professorships in the entire country. By 1900 there was scarcely a major U.S. institution of higher learning that failed to offer students opportunities to take classes in both Spanish language and Spanish literature, and occasionally Spanish and Spanish-American history as well.[32] Even Harvard got the message. In 1903 its history department hired Roger B. Merriman (1876–1945), a medievalist with interests in Spain's overseas empire, and in 1907 the Harvard Corporation finally filled the Smith Chair, vacant since 1886, with the appointment of Jeremiah D. M. Ford (1873–1958), a well-regarded specialist in Spanish literature. As for Johns Hopkins, my own university and one whose reputation was largely based on its embrace of German academic culture, it hired its first *hispanista*, Charles Carroll Marden (1867–1932), in 1904.[33]

Pan-Americanism

The momentum behind this wave of appointments came from various sources. One was the attention accorded Spain—here the idea of Sturdy Spain was paramount—as a country whose history was integrally tied to that of the United States. Another was the publicity, mostly favorable, that Spain had received at the wildly popular World's Columbian Exposition of 1893. Although Spain's national pavilion and its other exhibitions were not especially impressive—Spanish observers were especially critical, suggesting that they conveyed the image of a "poor, backward country" that had yet to embrace the modern world—the exposition itself highlighted aspects of the country Americans customarily connected with Spain. These included the Columbus statue; replicas of his caravels, the *Niña*, *Pinta*, and *Santa María*; a replica of the Franciscan monastery of La Rábida where Columbus supposedly conjured up his plan to reach Asia by sailing westwards across the Atlantic; and various exhibits featuring maps, documents, and other artifacts associated with the discovery of the New World.[34]

To be sure, not everything Spanish at the exposition redounded to the country's credit, such as the controversy over the independent, freewheeling ways of the cigarette-smoking Infanta Eulalia de Borbón during the course of her visit to the exposition in June 1893. She was the first member of the Spanish royal family to visit the United States, and the exposition's organizers went out of their way to greet her, declaring June 8 as Infanta Eulalia Day. During the course of her stay in Chicago, however, the infanta's seeming arrogance reportedly aggravated many of her hosts, especially Mrs. Bertha Palmer, president of the exposition's Board of Lady Managers. Upon Eulalia's departure from Chicago on

Fig. 26. Infanta Eulalia de Borbón (1864–1958), ca. 1893. As the first member of the Spanish royal family to travel to the United States, Eulalia attracted wide attention in 1893 when she visited the World's Columbian Exposition in Chicago, but her cigarette smoking and independent ways upset her hosts. Print Collection, Miriam and Ira D. Wallach Division of Art, Prints and Photographs, the New York Public Library, Astor, Lenox and Tilden Foundations.

June 14, the city's *Tribune* newspaper printed a stinging editorial commenting on her impoliteness:

> Royalty at best is a troublesome customer for republicans to deal with and royalty of the Spanish sort is the most troublesome of all. . . . There is an insuperable chasm between the effete monarchism of Spain and the fresher civilization of the New World. The former is old and haughty, and indeed has little left except its pride. . . . As the result of these differences the effort of Chicago to consort with Castile and Aragon has not been particularly happy or successful. Some things that we did evidently were not appreciated by the Spanish guests. It is certain that several things done by the latter were distasteful and offensive to their American hosts.[35]

Yet the bitterness surrounding the infanta's visit faded quickly. It was also limited to Chicago. Elsewhere the lighthearted image of Sunny Spain prevailed, assisted by the metaphorical Carmen, who, though only a fiction, added immeasurably to the allure of both Spain and its culture. More help—and this was decisive—came from the emergent interest in the Spanish heritage of Florida, as well as California, Texas, and other parts of the Southwest. Mixed together, these developments focused new attention on both Spanish and Spanish-American culture and in doing so provided new incentives for the study of Spanish in schools and colleges across the United States.

The foundation for a major turnabout was therefore already in place when, on April 25, 1898, the United States unilaterally declared war on Spain. As is well known, this conflict led to the country's acquisition of Puerto Rico and the establishment, albeit temporary, of U.S. protectorates in both Cuba and the Philippines. It also provided support for a movement to develop closer commercial and political ties—what was already called pan-Americanism—between the United States and Spanish-speaking parts of America.[36]

Pan-Americanism's official start in the United States dates to 1889 and the creation in Washington of the government's Bureau of International Affairs (later renamed the Pan-American Union), but the first major public expression of the movement was the Pan-American Exposition that opened in Buffalo, New York, in September 1901 with hemispheric cooperation as its principal theme. Designed in what its organizers called a "Spanish-American" style (see chapter 6), the exposition proved popular, attracting more than eight million visitors in the course of only eight months. It also brought new attention to the importance and lasting influence of the language and culture of Spain throughout the Americas—North, Central, and South.[37]

Pan-Americanism received an additional boost from the construction of the Panama Canal, begun under the administration of Pres. Theodore Roosevelt in 1904 and completed in August 1914. Although one of the canal's principal purposes was to facilitate the movement of U.S. warships between the Atlantic and Pacific Oceans, its promoters downplayed its strategic uses, presenting it instead as an integral component of hemispheric unity—"All American" in the words of John Barrett, the director of the Pan-American Union. Promoters also touted the benefits, both commercial and cultural, its completion would bring. In other articles and essays Barrett also urged Americans to "get ready for the Panama Canal."[38]

Responses to Barrett's call to action differed. One way Americans, especially young Americans, got "ready" was to study Spanish as opposed to French and especially German, a language whose instruction suffered a catastrophic collapse immediately after the outbreak of World War I on August 4, 1914—two weeks shy of the opening of the canal. Numbers tell the story. In 1910 fewer than five thousand high school students were studying Spanish, well under 1 percent of all who were studying a foreign language. By 1915 that number had jumped to more than thirty-three thousand (or 2.7 percent of the total). Over the course of the war that number continued to move higher, especially on the East Coast, where Spanish had never previously made much of an inroad into secondary schools.

New York offers a prime example. Between 1914 and 1918 the number of students studying Spanish in the city's high schools jumped, on the order of 1,000 percent.[39] As for the reasons driving this increase, in 1914 William T. Morley, president of the New York High School Teachers Association, in his annual report had pointed to both pan-Americanism and the war against Germany: "The opening of the Panama Canal and the great European war have tended to bring these two great peoples [those of the United States and South America] much closer together."[40]

Numbers of students studying Spanish at colleges and universities also skyrocketed. Exact figures are few, but according to one study the number of students enrolled in German classes declined by a whopping 40 percent over the course of the war. In contrast the number of students studying French increased on the order of 13 percent, and for Spanish the increase was an incredible 452 percent. In 1917–18 Spanish-language students totaled 9,579, just about half the number (19,352) studying French.[41] Total enrollments in Spanish thus still trailed well behind those in French, and according to Archer Milton Huntington, one of the strongest supporters of Spanish studies in the United States, most students studying the language did so for practical purposes, or to gain what he called "commercial Spanish."[42] Huntington's observation was probably correct, but whatever the rationale for studying the language, enrollments in Spanish courses shot up so rapidly that many observers thought it would soon become students' number-one choice. These increases also constituted one of the more tangible and measurable aspects of the Spanish craze.

For some observers, the meteoric rise of Spanish-language study was an unwelcome development and for some critics yet another sign that "culture" in America was taking a turn for the worse.[43] Arguments levied against language were several. One was "nimiety"—an old English word for excess, or too-muchness; another was that Spanish was "easy" and lacking the intellectual challenges needed to help develop and strengthen young minds; another was its supposed lack of "cultural" as opposed to "practical" value. Some critics even questioned whether "commercial" Spanish had any practical worth. One skeptic was William R. Price, New York's state supervisor for instruction in modern languages. A longtime advocate of instruction in both German and French, Price complained vociferously in a series of speeches about the rapidly rising demand for classes in Spanish: "Why Spanish? Why not Hottentot? Why not Choctaw? Why not Italian?—for which through the Renaissance we derive our culture?"[44]

Equally vitriolic was the attack launched by Ernest Hatch Wilkins (1880–1966), a professor of Italian and a respected scholar of Petrarch at the University of Chicago. In an address delivered to a meeting of foreign language teachers in Boston in 1918, Wilkins offered his own estimates of what was happening in the nation's schools and colleges. In schools, he suggested, 200,000 students were taking French and 150,000 Spanish, as compared to only 23 taking Italian. The spread at the collegiate level was much the same: 75,000 in French as compared to 50,000 for Spanish, and a paltry 200 in Italian. "Is this state of things satisfactory? My answer is No." He then followed this "no" with a series of homilies ("I have both knowledge and love of the Spanish language and literature"; "I have taught Spanish for years"; "I have the happiest memories of Spain") before questioning the rationale for studying the language. Spain's literature, he argued, had little intrinsic value as compared with that of France or Italy. He also indicated that students were mistaken if they—and their parents—believed that knowledge of the language would lead to commercial gain as the United States developed its trading links with Spanish America:

> I deplore the increasing tumefaction of the study of Spanish in this country. That Spanish should be widely studied I agree; but that it should be studied in such overwhelming numbers is but added evidence to the old indictment that we Americans see only that which is at hand. That Spanish should be studied for its literary value I agree, but I believe that no sane critic who knows the several European literatures would rank Spanish literature with Italian or with French in universal value. That Spanish should be studied for its commercial returns I agree, provided that it be studied in commercial courses; that Spanish should be studied by tens of thousands in our high schools and colleges for the sake of its money-making value I deplore, both because the motive is one that should not dominate study in such schools, and because the promised gain is so largely illusory. Not one boy in fifty of those who crowd the Spanish courses will ever be a *perro chico* [a nickname for a small Spanish coin] the richer for his work.

Wilkins ended the talk with the comment: "I think the time has come when Spanish should be deliberately checked." What he wanted was more instruction in French and, if possible, Italian, his own specialty.[45]

Wilkins's remarks about the "tumefaction" of Spanish—tumefaction refers to swelling, like a blister or sore, exactly the image Wilkins sought to convey—triggered a torrent of outraged responses, most coming, understandably, from teachers of Spanish. With the demand for their skills and services increasing astronomically, in 1917 New York's Spanish teachers founded the first regional chapter of the American Association of the Teachers of Spanish, an organization that soon spread nationwide as the AATS. With financial assistance provided by Juan Carlos Cebrián, a Spanish mining entrepreneur who had made a fortune in California and served as the Spanish consul in San Francisco, along with Archer Milton Huntington, in 1917 the AATS launched a new professional journal, *Hispania*, which provided members with a place to publish scholarly articles on topics relating to both Spain and Spanish America and served as a forum for the discussion of pedagogical methods and ideas.[46]

The AATS was far from a united group. Many of its members were unreformed Hispanists, instructors whose support for the teaching of Spanish language and literature derived primarily from their interest in the traditional culture of Spain. Others, enthusiasts for pan-Americanism, invoked this doctrine as the principal reason why Spanish merited instruction. Particularly outspoken on this issue was Frederick Bliss Luquiens (1875–1940), professor of Spanish in Yale's Sheffield Scientific School, forerunner of what is today the university's School of Engineering and Applied Science. Luquiens began his scholarly career writing about the Middle Ages and is best known for his 1901 edition and translation of the *Song of Roland*, one of the classics of French medieval literature. Some years later, however, Luquiens, possibly influenced by the interest of the Sheffield School's students in careers relating to Latin America, jumped on the pan-American bandwagon and by 1915 had emerged as one of the nation's foremost champions of the neglected field of Spanish-American literature. Luquiens outlined his thoughts on the subject in his essay "The National Need for Spanish," published in the *Yale Review*. There Luquiens argued that schools and colleges "must teach the Spanish of South

America, not, as now, the Spanish of Spain. . . . Only South American Spanish can give us what we need," with "need" here defined as better relations with the United States' neighbors to the south. To help satisfy this need, in 1917 Luquiens published his *Elementary Spanish-American Reader*, a textbook designed to provide students with an introduction to the geography, history, and literature of Spanish America.[47]

Luquiens was far from the only member of the AATS who expressed support for the intrinsic importance of Spanish for purposes of "hemispheric" unity. He had an important ally in Henry Grattan Doyle (1889–1864), professor of Romance languages at George Washington University. Doyle was also the author of "Tumefaction in the Study of Spanish," an essay that refuted Wilkins's criticisms of the spread of Spanish-language instruction in the United States. Yet Doyle also used this essay to present a powerful case for the different ways Spanish could promote closer ties—"politically, intellectually, commercially, socially"—between North and South America.[48] Another Luquiens ally was Charles Alfred Turrell (1875–?), professor of Romance languages at the University of Arizona and a specialist in the drama of both Spain and Spanish America. Turrell was also one of the first university instructors to teach the history of Spanish-American literature, as opposed to that of Spain, and to help his students he published a reader that first appeared in 1920.[49]

Outside the AATS, support for Luquiens's remarks about the importance of studying Spanish America—as opposed to Spain—came from various quarters, none perhaps more influential than the remarks made by Theodore Roosevelt during the course of his visit to Spain in June 1914. As noted earlier, Roosevelt embarked on this journey in order to attend his son Kermit's wedding in Madrid. Roosevelt's visit was short—only four days—but thoroughly Rooseveltian, as his schedule was full: a meeting with the Spanish monarch, Alfonso XIII; tours of several palaces, including El Escorial; a day in Toledo, where visited the city's old Jewish synagogues, the House of El Greco, and the cathedral and other churches. Even on the day of the wedding he went early to the Prado to see works by Velázquez, Goya, and other Spanish artists. Energetic as ever, Roosevelt found time for several interviews with Spanish reporters eager for his opinions about both Spain and its people. Just prior to his arrival in Madrid one newspaper published an editorial attacking the former president for his participation in the 1898 war and for a building a canal it branded an instrument of Yankee imperialism. In his interviews Roosevelt took the high road, telling the reporters about his admiration for Spain's diverse landscape, its historic monuments, and the paintings he saw in the Prado Museum. In addition, in a statement that represented an about-face from those he expressed in his *Winning of the West*, he also commented on the "vigor" of the Spanish "race" and his desire to explore some of its small, remote villages in order to get a better sense of Spain's national character.[50] Roosevelt also addressed the importance of Spanish as a language, but his precise words were not recorded. They were paraphrased, however, in an editorial published on June 11, 1914, in the *Washington Times*. In a nod toward pan-Americanism the editors observed that Roosevelt had commented that the "Spanish language, through the development of South America," had the potential to become a "universal language."[51]

These remarks were clearly intended to please Roosevelt's Spanish hosts, but they also reflected his long-standing support for the pan-American movement. As Roosevelt undoubtedly understood, most of the demand for the study of Spanish in the United States derived from the country's new and, many might say today, belated recognition of Spanish America as a place—and a culture or cultures—vastly different from that of Spain. Advocates of the unique quality or Americanness of Spanish American culture were not hard to find, but their ideas clashed with the concept of *hispanismo* (also known as *hispanoamericanismo* in Spain), or the idea that Spaniards and Spanish Americans—Mexicans, Peruvians, Argentinians, and so on—were essentially one people, a *raza*, endowed with a unique set of characteristics and traits that were fundamentally different from those of, say, the Anglo-Saxons residing in Great Britain and the United States.

Hispanismo drew much of its support from intellectuals and politicians in Spain—members of the so-called Generation of '98, who, following their country's defeat by the United States, sought to make common cause or build a bridge with their former colonies in the Americas, partly as a way of adding prestige and importance to what they touted as common culture determined by a shared racial inheritance. The movement also found supporters throughout the Americas, notably in Puerto Rico, where, as the late Christopher Schmidt-Nowara has trenchantly argued, post-'98 politicians used it as a means to defend what they perceived as the island's cultural integrity against that of their new masters in the United States.[52]

Today the idea of a common pan-Hispanic *raza* finds little support, as it is a formulation that privileges "Spanishness" or *hispanidad* at the expense of the all-important indigenous component that differentiated Spanish America so markedly from Spain. The concept of hispanismo also fails to reflect the extent to which *la raza* was inflected with the blood of African slaves whose arrival in the Americas dated to the time of Columbus. But in 1914 these racial differences tended to be swept under the rug and were generally ignored. Hispanismo was all about raza, and that raza was supposedly "pure." It was for this reason Spain's government, starting in 1918, declared October 12, the traditional holiday celebrated in recognition of Columbus's discovery of the Americas, to be the Día de la Raza. By that time several Latin American countries had done so as well.[53]

It follows that hispanismo's proponents, whether in Spain, Argentina, or the United States, found common cause in arguments favoring the universality of Spanish, or Hispanic, culture. One such individual was John D. Fitz-Gerald (1873–1946), professor of Romance languages at the University of Illinois. His essay, *Importance of Spanish to the American Citizen*, distributed in the form of a pamphlet starting in 1918, constituted another reply to critics claiming that Spanish was worth studying only for commercial purposes. To make his case Fitz-Gerald, apart from highlighting the importance of Cervantes and other famous Spanish golden age writers, listed the manifold contributions of Spaniards in such fields as history, philosophy, religion, science, theology, and so on. Nor did he omit Spanish America, noting in purplish prose that "from the loins of this glorious Spain there have emerged eighteen sovereign independent and sovereign nations" that, together with Spain, shared a "general culture." He listed the contributions of a raft of "Hispano-Americans" in different areas as further justification for the study of Spanish.[54]

Similar ideas can be found in the speeches and writings of other prominent members of the first generation of AATS members. They included Lawrence A. Wilkins, a New York teacher who served as the organization's first president and who was equally upset by arguments suggesting that Spanish had little of cultural value to offer students. And while Wilkins acknowledged the growing importance of Spanish America, his pan-Americanism was somewhat guarded, as he was more interested in having students read the literature of Spain, as opposed to that of Mexico, Argentina, Chile, or Peru.[55]

Another argument in favor of Spanish as a "universal language" came from Federico de Onís (1885–1966), a Spanish philologist who had been appointed Columbia University's first professor of Spanish language and philology in 1919. Columbia's president, Nicholas M. Butler, had established that professorship in 1918 in an effort to provide Spanish studies with a stronger, more secure base in New York City. Butler's first choice was Archer Milton Huntington, founder of the Hispanic Society of America and an accomplished scholar in the field of medieval Spanish literature, but Huntington rejected the offer, recommending Onís instead. A direct descendant of Luis de Onís, the diplomat who had negotiated the Transcontinental Treaty with John Quincy Adams in 1819, Onís was a former student of Miguel de Unamuno at Salamanca and a professor of philology at the University of Oviedo in northern Spain.[56] Onís accepted, assuming his duties in 1919, a moment when nationwide enrollments in Spanish were soaring and American interest in Hispanic culture was greater than ever before.

A year later, during a summer's visit to Spain, Onís presented a talk to his former colleagues at Salamanca on the topic "Spanish in the United States." Central to his lecture—later published in *Hispania*—was the extent to which *panamericanismo* was responsible for what he likened to a "collective fever, the desire to know Spanish and everything relevant to the peoples who speak the language." From his perspective, this fever began with the 1898 war, and to support this point he trotted out figures documenting recent increases in the number of students enrolled in Spanish courses. He admitted that in the course of the nineteenth century the United States had produced Hispanophiles such as Washington Irving,

Fig. 27. Miguel de Unamuno (*left*) with two disciples: Federico de Onís (*right*) and Licinio Perdigón. Salamanca, May 26, 1905. Attracted by the country's growing interest in Spanish language and literature, Onís moved to New York in 1916 to teach at Columbia University. Courtesy Creative Commons.

together with such distinguished Hispanists as Prescott and Ticknor, but only after the war did the country develop a new, generalized interest in Spanish language and civilization. Onís attributed this development mainly to pan-Americanism and growing interest in the character, customs, history, and literature of Spanish America, but so as not to step on the nationalist sensibilities of his Spanish audience, he invoked the notion of raza with the assertion that the "Hispanic-American peoples were the children of Spain."[57]

Onís, however, also reminded that same audience that America's Spanish fever should not to be attributed to impersonal forces alone. Help, he suggested, came from individuals, mainly the growing number of Hispanists teaching in colleges and universities across the United States. He also underscored the influence of writers such as Irving and

Lummis, together with that of a number of Spanish scholars who had recently appeared on the international stage, most notably Santiago Ramón y Cajal, winner of the 1906 Nobel Prize in Physiology. Onís also went out of his way to highlight the work of Archer M. Huntington and to thank him for his tireless efforts to enlighten Americans about the art, literature, and culture of Spain. Huntington, he suggested, was a "better Spaniard than we are" (*mejor español que nosotros*) and an individual to whom Spain owed an enormous debt, although he might have added Spanish America, inasmuch as Huntington also embraced hispanismo and the idea of the Spanish as a raza whose multifaceted contributions to civilization needed to be better known, especially in the United States.[58]

Huntington and the Hispanic Society of America

My love of Spain? Where it came from I cannot guess. As a boy you filled me with English and French reading, so it seems strange that this country should have so overwhelmed me. There is a fine reckless bravery about these hearts, which are homes of charm and grace, and to know them is to love them. These natural soldiers who have laid aside guns for banderillas, are still strong, even if impulse and ideals have taken on bright plumaged words. But they have a strange passionate sincerity, a faithfulness and sense of humour which needs no questioning. These, with all the faults and miseries that go with them, still reign and have always reigned in this land of light hearted lover; of woman and wailing song.[59]

The quote is from an undated letter Archer Milton Huntington (1870–1955) sent from Seville to his mother, the noted New York socialite and art collector Arabella Huntington, during the spring of 1898. Huntington was in Seville to purchase books for a planned museum-cum-library devoted to the arts and literature of Spain and to the promotion of a culture few Americans knew much about. That project soon became a reality. Following the death of his stepfather, the wealthy railroad magnate Collis P. Huntington, in 1900, Huntington inherited a fortune, all that he needed and more to establish what he founded in 1904 as the Hispanic Society of America.

Situated on a plot of land in New York City's Washington Heights that once belonged to the famous naturalist John James Audubon, the Hispanic Society of America (HSA) had as its stated purpose "the advancement of the study of the Spanish and Portuguese languages, literature, and history, and advancement of the studies of the countries wherein Spanish and Portuguese are or have been spoken."[60] Yet the HSA did far more than this. Officially opened to the public in January 1909, its art gallery offered visitors a comprehensive survey of pictures, sculpture, tapestries, ceramics, and other objects that Huntington had purchased over the course of a decade. In keeping, moreover, with the importance that Huntington accorded to scholarship and research, the HSA sponsored the publication of a monograph series on Spanish literature, history, and art. It also developed and maintained an extensive photographic archive meant to preserve images of Spain's historic monuments together with others documenting the country's traditional customs and way of life. By 1920 that collection amounted to some twenty-eight thousand items, but Huntington wanted even more, as he regarded photographs an ideal means to educate Americans about Spain and its culture. He made just this point to a Spanish friend with the comment, "We must have photographs and photographs and more photographs. It is the very thing which reaches the general public and instructs it regarding Spain. . . . We have 28,000, and should have 100,000 at least."[61]

This archive, together with books, manuscripts, pictures, and other objects, was central to Huntington's effort to advance HSA's didactic mission. In addition the HSA served as an outlet for Huntington's philanthropy, providing financial support to other institutions, both domestic and foreign, whose aims and purposes matched his own. These included France's *Revue Hispanique*, a scholarly journal specializing in Spanish culture the HSA began to support in 1905; Toledo's Casa del Greco, which was founded by the Marqués de la Vega-Inclán in 1909 in an effort to promote awareness of paintings by El Greco and, more generally, the evolution of Spanish art; and, starting in 1912, another of Vega-Inclán's creations—the House (or Casa) de Cervantes in the Castilian city of Valladolid. Huntington also authorized the HSA to serve as the U.S. distributor of a series of promotional pamphlets published by Spain's

Royal Commission on Tourism, an agency that Vega-Inclán created in 1911 for the purpose of attracting foreign tourists, Americans especially, to visit Spain.[62]

As Spain's champion in the United States, Huntington supported hispanismo in all its aspects, together with the pan-American ideal. An early indication of his interest in both these movements can be found in a 1902 letter he sent to Arthur Hadley, president of Yale. Hadley had asked Huntington for his advice on the advisability of allowing the university's Spanish instructor to take a year's leave of absence in Spain. In response, Huntington suggested that the instructor's leave could be better spent in Spanish America, given that "South American letters in their relation to Spain form an all but unknown field." To this he added, "Your students will be most anxious to learn about South America. Our relations with those Governments will be after all the chief object of Spanish study and the literature would naturally lead to the mother country for any student who wished to continue."[63]

Huntington followed these suggestions by helping to finance a series of Yale-sponsored archaeological expeditions to Spanish America, including Hiram Bingham's to Peru. In 1911 the HSA also underwrote the costs of sending Benjamin Chew (1878–1938), a well-known photographer and one of Huntington's close friends, on an eight-month expedition to the Andes meant to assemble a photographic record of the region's colonial Spanish architecture. Huntington also anticipated Roosevelt's Good Neighbor policy by several years when, starting in 1927, he established an endowment for what soon became the Hispanic Division of the Library of Congress. If the HSA tilted more in the direction of Spain than Spanish America, the Hispanic Division did just the reverse, although in both places the overarching idea was to showcase the intellectual achievements of Hispanic peoples the world over.

Huntington's astonishing philanthropy extended well beyond the Hispanic world. The Mariners' Museum in Newport News, opened in 1930, was another of his creations, and he also provided the endowment that led to the creation of what is now the Blanton Museum of Art at the University of Texas at Austin. But Huntington's crowning achievement, and the one for which he is best remembered today, is the HSA, an institution that, for its time at least, was utterly unique. Apart from Spain's royal academies of language and history, both dating from the eighteenth century, it was the first institution wholly dedicated to the study and promotion of Spanish (and, to a lesser degree, Portuguese) culture. As a museum, moreover, it was arguably the first whose collections were wholly dedicated to a particular "people" or what Huntington, in keeping with prevailing nineteenth-century ideas about the distinctive genetic makeup of individual nations, often referred to as a race. At the time most large public museums—the list includes Britain's National Gallery along with Louvre in Paris, the Prado in Madrid, Berlin's Gemäldegalerie, and New York's Metropolitan Museum of Art—took pride in the "universal" character of their holdings. Purely "national" museums existed. These included London's National Portrait Gallery (1856), the Musée de l'Histoire de France (1867) in Paris, and London's National Gallery of British Art (1897; renamed the Tate Gallery in 1932), the last being a collection originally intended to showcase modern—in the sense of Victorian—British art. Even so, Huntington's idea of devoting an institution to offering a comprehensive view of a single people was unusual, if not unique.

So too was the multifaceted character of the collections of the HSA. A possible model here was London's British Museum, whose collections were meant to display different aspects of human artistic and intellectual achievement—books, art, handicrafts, and so forth—across the ages. Another was Washington's Smithsonian Institute (now Institution), founded in 1846 for the "increase and diffusion of knowledge."[64] The HSA would do just this, but primarily with respect to the language, literature, and culture of the broader Hispanic world, encompassing regions most Americans, especially those of Anglo background, traditionally regarded as decadent and whose chief language, *castellano* or Spanish, few bothered to learn.

Huntington's *hispanofilia*, coupled with his manifold efforts to promote Spanish culture, defies easy explanation, as there was little in his family background that explains his love for Spain. His mother, born Arabella Yarrington Duval (1851–1924), was an ardent Francophile and a collector whose taste in art ran more toward the Old Masters from the north of

Europe as opposed to those from Spain. Over the years, however, a bit of Archer's *hispanofilia* rubbed off on his mother. Shortly after the end of the war with Spain, for example, Arabella is likely to have raised some of her guests' eyebrows by organizing a dinner party around a Spanish theme for some her New York friends in San Francisco.[65] In 1909, moreover, Arabella paid what amounted to a record sum for a canvas by Velázquez that she subsequently gifted to the HSA (see chapter 5).

Nor did Spain much figure in the interests of Archer's stepfather, Collis P. Huntington (1821–1900), one of founders of the Southern and Union Pacific Railroads and director of an important shipyard in Newport News. Collis's railroad investments also extended into Mexico, and he visited there—once with young Archer in tow—on several occasions. As a collector, his purchases initially centered on choice examples of western art—the panoramic landscapes of Albert Bierstadt were among his favorites—and later, following his marriage to Arabella in 1884, French paintings and others from the north of Europe, as opposed to the work of Spanish artists.[66]

The best guide to Huntington's thinking about Spain is the typewritten (and still unpublished) "autobiography" he prepared for Arabella, circa 1920, on the occasion of her seventieth birthday. This autobiography is something of a potpourri: excerpts of diaries that Huntington kept, starting at the age of twelve; extracts of letters written to his mother, other relatives, friends, and associates; and retrospective comments aligned with what is more generally understood as the autobiographical genre.[67]

The autobiography (cited as the AMH Diaries) begins in 1882, when Archer was twelve years of age. What we know of his life before then is relatively sparse and also confused, partly because there are some doubts about his paternity inasmuch as Arabella, though married, was rumored to have been having an affair with Collis Huntington prior to Archer's birth in New York in March 1870. Before long, Arabella sent her baby to live with her mother in San Marcos, a small Texas town located midway between Austin and San Antonio. Details about young Archer's life in San Marcos are sparse; it is not even certain when he returned to New York to live with his mother. Texas, however, did make at least one lasting impression on him, as he later remembered: it was there he heard Mexicans referred to as "greasers," a slur that may well account for his lifelong determination to change the way Americans thought about Spanish speakers as a whole.[68]

The next clue to the origins of Archer's "love for Spain" dates from 1882, when Arabella took her twelve-year-old to Europe on the equivalent of a grand tour. Their first stop, in June, was in Liverpool, the city in which Archer, already a bookish type, began keeping a diary, portions of which are incorporated in the narrative he later compiled for his mother. The first entries recall his visit to the Walker Art Gallery ("an agreeable experience") and his initial encounter with collecting rare coins. It was also in Liverpool that Huntington purchased a copy of George Borrow's *Zincali*. Borrow's evocative account of the gypsies—remember the allure and the power of his Sorceress of Seville—captured the boy's fancy; he referred to it in his diary as "the most interesting book I have found here. Spain must be much more interesting than Liverpool." That diary entry sparked Huntington's retrospective comment: "Soon I became quite enthusiastic about Borrow. Here was something new. Adventure, and all alive, and when years later I went to Spain it was though I were not entirely in a new world. I read him over and over. Perhaps this was the first step, and I owe to this strange person credit as an influence in the days ahead. The *Bible in Spain* followed, and I was launched on a sea of wonder and questions. Johnny Appleseed had passed my way."[69]

Apples are tempting, as Eve learned in Eden. Archer's Eve is likely to have been the eleven-year-old Spanish girl he met two months later in Paris. Identified only as the daughter of a marquis, she prompted him to write the following comment in his diary: "Spain must be a nice country. Asked mother why we didn't go there, but she said it is too hot and she is too busy. The Spanish girl is going to a place called Deauville. I showed her my coins. She gave me a Spanish one." So began what eventually mushroomed into Huntington's collection of more than three thousand rare Spanish coins.[70]

In retrospect, this was the moment when the die setting out Huntington's future was seemingly cast. Etched into that die were two abiding passions: one for museums, the other for Spain (let's forget for a moment whatever thoughts lingered about that young Spanish girl). In 1884, his diary notes that he "built a small museum out of boxes, with pictures [cut] out from magazines and newspapers. Seven boxes with seven galleries 12 inches deep 20 wide and 35 long." As for Spain, he later recalled that "I was 14 and the memory of Borrow's *Zincali* and his other books had left a roseate glow. . . . I was soon over my head, and a professor was called in. A terrible lady, who made me learn irregular verbs through long bitter hours." But as she was a native of the Castilian city of Vall-adolid, he remembered that he "managed to tempt her into talks about that city and Spain. She brought me a map and went over it with me day by day, and she gave me a Spanish history to read when she was not there, but my Spanish was not quite up to it yet."[71]

The year 1884 also marked out Archer's future in another and equally important way. On July 12—referred to in his diary as "a new day"—his mother married Collis P. Huntington.[72] It is not clear whether Huntington formally adopted Archer as his son, but whatever the boy's legal status, Collis treated him as if had, earning Archer's lasting love and respect. Both regularly, and lovingly, referred to one another as father and son.

As for Archer's passion in Spain, books were key. Homeschooled with the help of private tutors, the teenaged Huntington was an avid reader. In 1886 he writes, "I am reading Prescott and Ticknor and began to read a long history," possibly a reference to Edward Everett Hale and Susan Hale's recently published *The Story of Spain*, which traced the country's history from antiquity to the present. These books also prompted him to embark on one of his own: a chivalric novel featuring "Roderick the Goth as hero [along with] battles and deeds of mighty men." To this he added, again retrospectively, "Adventure now filled me with yearning for high deeds, the rescue of bereaved maidens, and I read *Amadis of Gaul*. The trees became giants, and the great house a castle of dreams."[73]

"A castle of dreams"—the phrase is telling, one that recalled Longfel-low's *Castles in Spain*, a poem the young Huntington undoubtedly read. Aged sixteen, Huntington already displayed several of the symptoms of the fever that would later help fuel the craze for Spain. He had much to learn, however. There were more Spanish lessons—one of his teachers was Alberto Bernis, also a Spanish instructor at the Harlem Evening School; others in French, Greek, and, more unusually, Arabic; and what he called a "serious plunge into history: French, English, Spanish, Italian." The bookish Archer had little time for sports. "'Books' they [his friends] call me. I was fat," and worse, it seems, he "had to get glasses."[74]

There were travels as well: to California in 1886 with his parents; in 1887 to Europe, where he met a professor in London who had lived in Salamanca and with whom he discussed Borrow's life; to Texas, Southern California, and other parts of the American Southwest; and in 1889 with his father to Mexico, where, in addition to having an opportunity to practice his Spanish, he met the president, Porfirio Díaz. The trip to Mexico, he later wrote, was a "revelation": "From books I had gathered impressions of it and California had already given me broken bits of meaning but when reality suddenly came! This, of course, was my first encounter with something which was to fill my whole life, and all at once I felt a curious, feverish eagerness. . . . And my museum dreaming became clear and took new forms. I had become bound up in a vague plan."[75]

By 1890 that vague plan had started to crystallize. "Full of plans for Spain," he writes. "They keep me awake. And always it is the museum. I have it on the brain." By then Archer had even formulated his museum's design, writing his mother that "I am working on more plans for a museum which will amuse you, I would like to know how much wall space is wasted in U.S.A. museums by windows. The windows of an art museum should be pictures."[76] No surprise then that when his architect cousin, Charles Pratt Huntington (1871–1919), finalized plans for the building that would house the HSA, skylights would constitute the only source of natural light.

The path toward what the young Huntington already started to refer as his "Spanish museum" was not always smooth. As he later wrote Arabella, "Friends had already, as you know, begun to try to divert me to other fields." One of these "friends" was his older cousin, Henry E. Huntington, who, following Collis Huntington's death, married the widowed Arabella in 1913 and, with her assistance, established what was to become the Huntington Library, Art Collections, and Botanical Gardens in San Marino, California. When the two cousins met on December 9, 1890, Henry was openly critical of Archer's plans, as Huntington's diary makes clear: "Saw H E Huntington today, and he asked me many questions about books, of which he knows very little. In fact he is rather frankly contemptuous of book collecting and especially my own. He repeated several times, 'but why Spain?' And rather laughed at me." Another of his friends, Charles Wickliffe Throckmorton, was equally critical: "He also said that I was making a great mistake wasting my time on Arabic and Spanish. Why did I not go into my father's office and make money."[77]

A still more forceful challenge to the young Huntington's plans came from Morris Ketchum Jesup (1830–1908), a wealthy financier and leading philanthropist who, starting in 1883, served as president of New York's American Museum of Natural History. Jesup was also a connoisseur, later bequeathing his rather substantial collection of pictures and sculptures to New York's Metropolitan Museum of Art, but like most other Gilded Age collectors he had little use for either for Spain or its art. It follows that when Huntington visited him in his office in January 1891, Jesup counseled him on the importance of science and scientific research. "He [then] made clear," Huntington wrote, "that my place was there [in the Museum of Natural History] and not in what he indicated was a 'dead and gone' civilization the study of which would bring me small reward or satisfaction. I told him I was not seeking a reward, that rather [I] had hopes of presenting a picture by book or otherwise of what was, had been, and might be. I did not venture to use the word Museum which had filled me with a dream for as long."[78]

Despite his interest in a "dead and gone civilization," Archer had his father's support. At one point the elder Huntington attempted to persuade his adopted son to follow in his footsteps and enter the business world, but he soon relented, or as one entry in Archer's diary reads, "'Archer I can see that you know what you want, and I believe you can do it. Go on as you like and do the thing well.' (I shall not forget these words)."[79]

Additional encouragement for the study of that civilization appears to have come from another, more unusual source: the Spanish gypsy dancer Carolina Otero, during her inaugural visit to New York in the fall and winter of 1890. Spanish flamenco dancing was then something of a novelty in the United States, but it had already gained its first star, Carmencita, about whom more will be said later. Carmencita's rival

Fig. 28. Archer Milton Huntington in Spain, 1892. The year 1892 marked Huntington's first trip to Spain. Later visits centered on the acquisition of books, manuscripts, and other objects destined for his "Hispanic museum" in New York. Courtesy Hispanic Society of America, New York.

was "La Belle" Otero, described by one reporter as "a woman of great beauty, a magnificent bust, and [who] carries herself with the bearing of a queen."[80] Otero's singing and dancing were not nearly as proficient as Carmencita's, but her performances at the Eden Musée, a popular, all-purpose amusement center located on Manhattan's Twenty-Third Street, were regular sell-outs, partly for reasons connected to Otero's revealing costumes, reportedly displaying ample portions of her "magnificent bust." Otero also pretended to be a countess, and this does much to explain part of her attraction for the Vanderbilts, the Belmonts, and other members of the city's wealthy elite, the social set to which Huntington and his parents belonged. The musical tastes of these families generally ran in the direction of opera, the symphony, or classical ballet, as opposed to the lowbrow vaudevillesque atmosphere characteristic of the Eden Musée.[81]

The circumstances of Huntington's meeting with Otero remain somewhat murky, but the possibilities were many: one of the teas the Vanderbilts organized in her honor at their sumptuous Fifth Avenue mansion; an after-theater party at Delmonico's or the Plaza Hotel; or, given Huntington's historical interests, the day at the Eden Musée when Otero unveiled a wax sculpture of "Columbus being received by Ferdinand and Isabel." But whatever the occasion, Huntington's diary indicates that Otero encouraged him to visit Spain, southern Spain in particular.[82] Whether Huntington and Otero ever met again his diary does not say, but he did manage to visit Andalucia during his second visit to Spain in 1893, again in 1898, and on numerous occasions thereafter.

For the moment, however, those trips were on hold, although in 1891 Huntington visited St. Augustine, the Florida city then in the midst of transforming itself into a "Spanish" city, and Havana as well. That was also the year when Huntington established an agenda for writing and research: "I had already chosen a period [the Middle Ages] and soon I was to be at work on a translation of the poem of the Cid and as the other flowers grew in my garden, it became in each case easier to get the general view which was to make possible the working out of my one object—a Museum which more or less should present the culture of a race and its chronological backgrounds."[83]

Enter now William Ireland Knapp, the Spanish literature specialist then teaching at Yale. In 1890 Huntington had declined an offer to take a degree at Yale, preferring to continue his studies independently. He was determined to visit Spain and to retrace the steps of the Cid, the legendary warrior featured in the *Poem of the Cid*, the medieval ballad that Huntington was later to edit, translate into English, and publish in three handsome volumes starting in 1897. So with Collis paying the bills, Knapp was invited to accompany Archer to Spain as a kind of cicerone, tutor, and travel companion rolled into one.[84]

The meticulous Huntington readied himself for this long-awaited journey in various ways. He reread *Don Quixote* and prepared "a note book which I call *Questions* [that] lies on my table and grows fatter day by day. These are the things I want to find out about Spain, books, pictures, architecture, etc. But chiefly I must know the people and see them as they are, and as they were. The two lock and define each other. What are the inherited ideas and acts and what the outside inheritances." A month later, following a meeting with Knapp, he writes, "The thing now is to get to Spain. I am so stuffed with questions that if I do not get there soon I shall forget—or bust! The first trip must be cities, the country and the people. Then book collecting and library work and last History and Archeology. They will overlap of course but it is best to [go] with a plan to cover several trips."[85]

The long-awaited trip began toward the end of June 1892, when Huntington and Knapp left New York for Europe. On July 4 they boarded a train in Paris en route to Spain: "At last! We are on the train leaving Paris. Every click of the rails plays an accompaniment of a dream come true. All these years! Well I must prepare to repaint my picture. Surely the thing I am about to find will be quite unlike what I have built up. I can see Spain ahead dotted with palaces and fortresses, with cathedrals and walled cities, with bearded warriors and great ladies. Of course it is all wrong. Isabella the Catholic will not be in Madrid and I am sure to miss Visigoths and Almazor. But there will be footprints."[86]

Footprints indeed. He found the first ones near the city of Burgos, in the village of Vivar del Cid, the reported birthplace of the famed Spanish hero. Huntington's reactions were mixed: "Alas there is no Cid's palace and nothing of a town to speak of. A plain and the small river Ubierna, bare hills, one of which may have been fortified. But I was so filled with Rodrigo Diaz [del Cid] that the river grew to a torrent and the hills put on their lost forest. I talked with a dozen inhabitants. There was rather a vague interest in *The Cid*." But by the time he got back in Burgos, Huntington was thrilled: "I had seen Vivar! The footprints of Babieca [Cid's horse] I imagined all over the place."[87]

These imaginings, this search for footprints of the legendary hero, marked out much of the itinerary Huntington followed. Knapp, he remembered, was often "tired and bored," as the two traveled around the north of Spain before heading to Madrid. Once in the capital, Huntington visited the Prado Museum, where, as he later recalled, "I had my first real vision of Velazquez. Stunning, amazing, a discovery, and cannot be talked about." He subsequently set out to retrace the Cid's route across La Mancha ("imagine on the plain windmills of the days of its hero [Don Quixote]") to Valencia, before exiting Spain via Barcelona.[88]

Fig. 29. Carolina "La Belle" Otero, ca. 1890. Famous for her revealing outfits and striking physique, this Spanish flamenco dancer regularly performed to packed houses on her U.S. tour in 1890–91. She received an especially warm welcome among members of New York's high society. TCS 2, Box 372, Harvard Theater Collection. MS Am 1340172, Houghton Library, Harvard University.

In the course of these travels Huntington met a number of individuals who shared his scholarly concerns. One was the German art historian Carl Justi, whose important *Diego Velázquez and His Times* had appeared in English translation in 1889. Huntington met up with Justi in the northern town of Logroño and described him as "a scholar of some distinction," but he otherwise found the German somewhat snobbish and a bit cold. Worse: "he has very little use for American scholarship[,] saying that only the Germans know the meaning of the word. As this is typical I said little. But it gives one to think!" As for Spaniards, in Madrid Huntington made friends with the medals specialist Pablo Bosch y Barrau (1841–1915), who introduced him to "no end of books and people."[89] He also met Juan Riaño y Gayangos (1865–1939), a diplomat who later helped negotiate the peace settlement between Spain and the United States in 1899. In 1903 Riaño also became the first postwar secretary of the Spanish legation in Washington DC and a year later married a "celebrated Washington belle," Alice Ward. Elevated to the rank of ambassador in 1914, Riaño by then was a close friend of Huntington, a strong supporter of both the HSA and AATS, and outspoken in his support for the study of Spanish culture in the United States.

As for the "people" he was apparently so eager to meet on that initial visit to Spain, Huntington fondly recalled his encounter in the Castilian town of Aranda de Duero with a tailor who repaired his torn trousers. He also remembered the "freethinker" he met on a train. "The man," he wrote, "asked why he, an American, is visiting Spain." His response: "I came to see your people and your country. We Americans have a feeling that we owe a great deal to Spain."[90]

The 1892 trip proved the first of many, but it left such an impression that Huntington later cobbled together the letters he had written to his mother during the course of the journey into a travelogue that was published, only weeks shy of the start of 1898 war, as *A Note-Book in Northern Spain*. At first glance, the travelogue was little different from those published by other American travelers, and many of his observations about the country simply repeated what others had written before him. Taking note, for example, of Spain's failure to develop as rapidly as other parts of Europe, Huntington echoed Adam Smith and other

Enlightenment figures with the comment that "Spain lacks the trading spirit," that is, "the great primitive developing agency." Somewhat more original was Huntington's reluctance to assign Spain a single national character. Rather he presented it as a "composite" nation comprising a collection of different peoples, each with its own unique, albeit stereotypical, character. These included "the brawny Aragonese, the hard-tongued, industrious Catalán, the Celtic-souled Gallegan, the dignified gentleman of Castile and Leon, the fiery, knife-loving Andaluz."[91]

Unlike most other visitors, however, Huntington had less interest in Sunny Spain—Carmen was not his first priority—than in Sturdy Spain and the qualities that had once made the country capable of producing such men as El Cid and Cortés. He found his answer in what he described on the very first page of the *Note-Book* as the country's "wondrous, melancholy landscape, unvaried, sullen, monotonous to-day, to-morrow ablaze with a fiery life; impetuous, restrained, indifferent, responsive. Look deep enough into its heart and you may read the heart of the Spaniard."[92]

The idea that the "heart of the Spaniard" lay in rural Spain, in its *pueblos* and peasants, spoke directly to the age-old tradition about the influence of environment on temperament. Since at least the time of the Renaissance, European humanists had contrasted the "honesty" and "virtue" of rural life with the "cosmopolitanism" and "corruption" of the city. With respect to Spain, Ticknor had also believed that its common folk, especially the peasantry, best represented Spain's traditional character. The Bostonian also maintained that those common people were the ultimate source of Spain's greatest literature, especially Huntington's favorite, the *Poem of the Cid*. Many Spanish writers had similar ideas. Among those writers were the celebrated romantic poet Gustavo Adolfo Bécquer (1836–70) and the philosopher Miguel de Unamuno, whose famous essay *En torno al casticismo*, published in 1895, located the roots of Spain's "eternal tradition" (*lo castizo*) in the heartland of Castile and in Sancho Panza, the quintessential peasant. Following Unamuno, various members of the famed Generation of '98 had similar ideals, as virtually all of them looked to the *pueblo* as opposed to the city in their quest for the traditional values—*lo castizo*—

that would aid their country's recovery from the loss it suffered at the hands of the United States.[93]

The authentic, *lo castizo*—it was this aspect of the country that also caught Huntington's eye; it was one of those "footprints" he set out to find. "It is in the back country," he wrote, "that Spain can be known, in the bare lands that once were covered with great forests and are now inhabited by a scattered and tradition filled population, one which has preserved the true type better than elsewhere." That true type, he believed, was still to be found among Spain's villagers, the people he described as the "amazing peasants . . . men and women of another age . . . preserving an independence and character of truth and honesty which fills one's heart with a sense of freshness and integrity. . . . I talk with everyone. . . . From these talks I learn so much more than I can get from many a more instructed friend. Here are the sources of national values. The blood that runs in these veins is the national blood undiluted by recent contacts with the world outside."[94]

To emphasize this point the *Note-Book* included photographs of some of these "undiluted" types. They included images labeled as follows: "Peasants of Lerida" (the photo features a man and a woman, presumably his wife, in festive dress); "A Spanish Gypsy"; "Women of the Province of Calatayud"; "Washerwomen" (the photo shows a group of women clustered on the banks of a river near the Aragonese mountain town of Jaca); and "Maragatos"—the name traditionally given villagers from the northern Spanish province of León and whose dress was erroneously thought to be "Moorish" in origin. Others featured bullfighters and a *mozo de cordel*, a street porter likely to have figured among the working-class men (*gente de bronce*) he observed on Madrid's Toledo Street, or calle de Toledo, during his second visit to Spain, in 1893. That street impressed him so much that he referred to it in one letter as a place "where the people, the real people, growing fewer and fewer from day to day, still come, and still talk like real Spaniards, of which I used to dream."[95]

For Huntington these folkloric types constituted emblems of the Spain he had initially encountered in books. It was also the Spain he believed was destined to disappear due to the forces of modernization,

212 HISPANISM, *HISPANISMO*, AND THE HSA

combined with the onslaught of tourism. As he wrote one friend who was visiting southern Spain in 1902, "I want you to get as much of the spirit and taste of Spain as you can, before it is invaded. The time is up: Spain is sure to become a tourists' country in the next ten years, and all the old customs will be swept out as they have been in Italy, or preserved in the future, when they are kept up, for the benefit of the globe trotters. What a dreadful day it will be when [the palace of] San Telmo, in Seville, is turned into a hotel, and fig gypsies dance in the Patio!"[96] That "spirit and taste," Spain's very essence, is what Huntington determined to capture in a museum that was "to touch widely on arts, crafts, letters . . . [and] condense the soul of Spain into meanings, through works of the hand and spirit." Huntington's search of these items began circa 1894, the year he likened to "a hopeful time when I began to buy seriously" and also one during which, as he later recalled, "my notes and lists were full."[97]

The buying began with books, largely because Huntington subscribed to the well-established notion that a nation's true character could be found in its literature. As noted above, the first record of his book buying was his 1882 purchase of Borrow's *Zincali* in Liverpool. Thereafter, the buying never seemed to stop. In 1894 he notes "books flowing in from Europe," and in March 1896, in the midst of his third trip to Spain, his diary reads, "Books and more books. The days when I had to search are over. They tumble in. Dealers, friends, and strangers bring them. And now come first editions and other flowers of type." More such flowers were soon to arrive. In 1897, for example, on the eve of yet another trip to Spain, he informs Arabella, "This is a book trip. My claws are sharpened and I carry a large bag. In Sevilla there is material to be had. There are some splendid collections nesting by the Guadalquivir. Frankly, I am tired of angling in the shallow streams of the north [of Spain]. Perhaps I may this time catch something larger than a *merluza* [hake]." To this he added, "My lists are made. The idea of the museum of which I told you grows so great that I cannot see around it. . . . Already I see the librarian at his desk, the objects in cases, pictures and tapestries on walls, each a flower from fields wherein I have loved to walk, the whole something of a cross section in miniature of the culture of a race. It is no longer a mere dream. It has become so[m]nambulistic and I begin to feel that it can be done." Once again he explained, "On this trip it is books, books, and yet again books! . . . Of pictures on this trip I shall have nothing to say, not even time to look at them. . . . They are for another day. Moreover, as you know, I buy no pictures in Spain, having the foolish sentimental feeling against disturbing such birds of paradise upon their perches. Let us leave these beloved inspiration builders where they were born or dwelt, but for Spain I do not go as a plunderer. I will get my pictures outside. There are plenty to be had. Books and people only this time." He also informed her that "I am collecting for a purpose you know quite well. That small compact museum of Spanish culture will take all the time left me in this world. Others can then come and write beautiful books hot off the shelves—and still others may write books hot off these. I wish to know Spain as Spain and so express her—in a museum. It is about all I can do. If I can make a poem of a museum it will be easy to read" [in pencil again: "easy to read"].⁹⁸

Once in Seville—he arrived there in January 1898—Huntington had little difficulty acquiring the books he sought. As news of the wealthy American's interests spread, he informed Arabella that "eager ears are listening, and books creep out of their hiding places to be sold to the fool American at fantastic prices for the worthless specimens, and far below the value of others." Yet books were not the only reason Huntington had gone to Seville. Archaeology was another, or as he wrote in his diary in 1896, "Archeology. Oh yes, I am deep in it now."

Archaeology too would help him illustrate the "culture of a race." Yet Huntington recognized that archaeology had its limits. "Archeology," he wrote, "is to be sure an interesting way of learning of the past but to most it is a dead past." For this reason he endeavored to combine ethnographic fragments from the past with others garnered from "the bodies of the living. Surely the past is there as well as in fragments from graves." In his museum, what he called "specimens" illustrative of living Spanish folkways—these included embroideries, weavings, ceramics, glass, even kitchen utensils—were to be displayed alongside objects from earlier eras and together they would provide visitors to the museum insights into the soul of Spain itself.⁹⁹

But Huntington still needed artifacts to illustrate earlier epochs in Spain's long history, and for this reason, once in Seville he made it a point to make contact with a pair of archaeologists then in the city. One was George Edward Bonsor (1855–1930), the French-born British archaeologist known for his excavations at the nearby city of Carmona and one from whom Huntington later purchased several crates of Roman ceramics, figurines, and glass that had been uncovered on that particular site. The other was Arthur Engel (1855–1935), a Frenchman who had excavated Italica, a former Roman city whose ruins were located on the outskirts of Seville. This site exercised a special hold on Huntington. "Italica," he wrote, "enveloped me. It was a place of whispers. . . . On what were streets one might almost hear cries that [an] Arab uttered a thousand years ago, mingled with Latin footsteps of earlier Roman soldiers and the clink of armor. . . . For a moment all that I read about it came back to me. Kings, nobles, ladies, retainers, Romans, Arabs, Greeks, and Goths tread the unreal streets and ruins."[100] Eager to get closer to that past, and also to try his hand at archaeology, Huntington hired a team of workers and with help from Engel directed a series of excavations that yielded, in addition to a horde of Roman coins, other objects he eventually had shipped to New York.

Unfortunately for Huntington, politics brought this project to an abrupt and somewhat unexpected halt. He liked Seville, describing it to his mother in Irvingesque language as a city where "romance and song and laughter dance together." But all that levity seemingly came to an end in the weeks immediately following the explosion of the uss *Maine* in Havana's harbor on February 15, 1898. News of that disaster prompted Arabella to write a letter to Huntington in which she expressed worry about her son's continuing residence in Spain at a moment when members of Congress were already beating the drums of war. Huntington responded without delay: "Your letter about the *Maine* disaster was not a surprise as the news has turned people wildly here. Everyone is on edge and trouble seems probable. The talk in the clubs is lurid." At the same time, he reminded his mother that he had little interest in Spain's politics: "There is one field in Spain on which I have never trespassed in Spain—Politics. . . . On this *mare nostrum* [I] will not sail."[101]

By late March and early April the waves in that sea had grown even more turbulent. By April 3, which was Palm Sunday and the start of Seville's famous Holy Week processions, Huntington had admitted that he was sensing "a spirit of anticipation, of hesitation, of nervousness, of anxiety" in the city and that Spain stood on the verge of a "great struggle . . . a possible war with a great power." Huntington halted the excavations at Italica, packed up his bags and books, and hurriedly left Seville on April 13 for Gibraltar, then Marseille, where on April 23— the day the U.S. Senate declared war on Spain—he embarked on a P&O steamer bound for New York.[102]

No record exists of what Huntington thought about during the course of that voyage. In an 1896 interview with a reporter from the *New York Herald* he had openly aligned himself with the Spanish government in regard to the civil war that had erupted in Cuba the previous year. On this occasion he remarked, "I am positive in my belief that Spain is right and that her course [is] perfectly justifiable in the Cuban affair. In case of war my sympathies would be with my native land, yet I earnestly believe the United States is entirely wrong."[103]

But wrong or right, the war Huntington feared had begun. Records of his opinions about it are scarce, but he clearly sided with Mark Twain, Charles Lummis, and others opposed to his country's decision to declare war on Spain. As the battles raged, in the Philippines with Commodore George Dewey's devastating attack on the Spanish fleet in Manila and then in Cuba, Huntington seemingly found solace in what he described to his mother as the "quieter landscape of the common [Spanish] man and in it [I] find the sources of truth and worth and self."[104]

The war, however, did little to dampen Huntington's enthusiasm for Spain. "My job is marked out. I have no choice but to continue," he noted. And continue he did. In 1895 Huntington started publishing facsimile editions of several of the rare Spanish imprints he had acquired. He also made certain to distribute copies of these facsimiles to scholars in Spain, partly as a way of demonstrating his commitment to furthering the cause of Spanish letters.[105] These gestures served him well, especially in 1902, when he negotiated what was arguably the greatest book purchase of his life: the library of the Marqués de

Jérez de los Caballeros in Seville. Huntington had had his eye on this collection for a number of years, but the marqués had been reluctant to sell. The war changed his mind, however, and at the start of 1902 Huntington made a special trip to Seville and successfully negotiated the sale of what he tersely described to his mother as a "large library," with twenty thousand books, papers, and manuscripts that were soon to be shipped to New York.[106]

As news of this acquisition leaked out, a scandal ensued, as a number of prominent Spanish scholars, including Marcelino Menéndez y Pelayo, director of the country's National Library, considered it an enormous loss. In a letter to a friend in Seville the director wrote, "I do not have any relation, direct or indirect, with Huntington, and I must confess that I have a profound antipathy toward him, as he is despoiling Spain and making a show of his wealth." Citing the popular refrain *de un lobo un pelo*, which translates as "better something than nothing," he then added a reference to Huntington's facsimiles: "But, in the end, from a wolf, at least something; and if he continues making reproductions of some of the books he has taken, we will all be better off."[107]

Huntington was well aware of the scandal his purchase had sparked but justified his acquisition, at least to himself, with the idea that once his Hispanic library was opened to the public it would further the interests of Spain by strengthening its image abroad. He outlined his thoughts on this sensitive issue in a letter written to his mother in 1902: "As you may imagine the jerez library sale was not long in becoming news in Seville. . . . Letters came from friends all over Spain. Many regretted it as a loss to the country, and said so frankly, but one or two others grasped its influence to spread in America knowledge of Spanish letters. Of course on the whole Spain loses nothing." He then commented on the overarching significance of the library, indicating his intention of maintaining the collection intact: "It has been a great and glorious blessing to me to be able in this way to hasten my collecting, saving me many a month of search for books otherwise unobtainable. Certainly the making of this library has become one of the most laborious and delightful undertaking[s] imaginable, and here I have obtained material which could never be duplicated."[108]

With the acquisition of the Jérez de los Caballeros library, Huntington's book-buying effort began to slow. Prices of the items he wanted were starting to rise, partly because Spanish booksellers had locked onto his interests. Huntington complained about these increases in a letter dating from 1904: "I have already found that it is quite impossible for me to buy books in Spain owing to the extraordinary prices which have suddenly been placed upon them, and it is unfortunate because there are many things which I should be very glad to acquire, but which now are placed at such astonishing figures that it would be foolish to consider buying them."[109]

Price rises aside, the completion of the HSA's building in Washington Heights in 1905 also helps account for the gradual tapering off of his book-buying effort. Previously he had stored his books in Plaisance, the house in the New York suburb of Baychester that his father had given him some years before. The transfer of these books to the HSA began in November 1905, a move that Huntington reported to his mother with some regret: "Thus begins the departure of some of my best friends. . . . But it hurt none the less to see them go taking with them so many memories of the kind a collector loves to cherish but I am no 'collector' as you know. Everything I buy is bought with the idea of its place in my little [museum]." Two days later he wrote her again, announcing, "I have turned over my library to the HSA in New York and am no longer purchasing rare books myself."[110]

That was not quite true. In 1906 Huntington purchased a copy of Juan José Eguiara y Eguren's *Biblioteca mexicana* from Karl W. Hiersemann, a bookseller from Leipzig he derogatorily described "as a funny little Hebrew."[111] Other acquisitions followed, and by 1908, when the HSA first opened its doors, its library consisted of approximately fifty thousand volumes, many of them rare incunabula and other early imprints relating mainly to Spain and Spanish America. There was no other comparable library in North America, and that remains true today.

Art was Huntington's next priority. His first recorded purchases of pictures date from 1894, when he acquired two unspecified items from Avery's, an art dealer in New York. His subsequent acquisitions are difficult to track, but they remained somewhat sporadic until 1900, when, following the death of his father, he inherited sufficient funds to acquire pictures and other objects for his museum. At this point he went on a veritable spending spree, visiting dealers in London, Paris, and Frankfurt on a regular, almost annual basis. The best source of what he was up to on these trips comes from his diary. One entry dating from 1904 is particularly revealing:

> The stay in Paris was active. I was collecting furiously but carefully in view of the necessary completion of those lines, chiefly book collecting and minor arts. I collected always with the view to definite limitations of the material to be had, always bearing in mind the necessity of presenting a broad outline without duplication. These limitations greatly aided me by reduction of the number of pieces adequate to present a comprehensive whole, and I often astonished my dealer friends by refusing an object which most collectors would have seized upon with enthusiasm. Moreover, I was most eager to complete those lines of which I had serious knowledge, for I had already learned by experience that the dealer is not so much the collector's friend as his own. As I was best equipped for the collecting of books, it was pleasant to find that my rivals were few, and opportunities many.[112]

The quote offers several important insights into the rationale underlying Huntington's purchases for his museum. According to HSA director Mitchell Codding, Huntington never fancied himself as a "collector" in the classic sense of the term. As early as 1898 he reminded his mother that "I have often said I venture to flatter myself that I am not a 'collector,' rather an assembler for a given expression," that expression being a survey of Spain's and, to a lesser degree, Spanish-America's artistic and literary creations across time.[113] For this reason, he proved reluctant to spend huge quantities of money for the kind of acknowledged masterpieces that were attracting the attention of other wealthy American collectors.

Evidence for this policy can be found in his correspondence with Francis Lathrop (1849–1909), a prominent New York decorative artist who served as Huntington's principal art advisor until shortly before his death in 1909. Lathrop had helped to decorate the interior of Collis Huntington's New York mansion in 1891 and subsequently became a close friend of the Huntington family, Archer in particular. A collector in his own right, Lathrop fancied himself a connoisseur of Old Master art and starting in 1901 began recommending various pictures that he believed Huntington should purchase. It was then, for example, that he suggested Huntington should bid on one of El Greco's masterworks, *Assumption of the Virgin*, formerly in the collection of the late Infanta María Cristina de Borbón and soon to go on sale in Madrid. Lathrop writes, "It is really a grand picture and as good a specimen of Greco at his best as you could possibly have," but Huntington, apparently eager to avoid the negative publicity triggered by his purchase of the Jérez de los Caballeros library, did not bite. Nor did Huntington pull out his checkbook when Lathrop suggested in 1902 that he acquire a Velázquez from the Morritt collection at Rokeby House shortly before the picture went up for auction in London. The picture in question was the Spanish master's *Venus with a Mirror*, otherwise known as the Rokeby Venus. Using the kind of high-pressure language similar to that of professional art dealers, Lathrop told Huntington, "If you owned this picture you would have the most important Velázquez outside of Spain." The cost? Somewhere north of $100,000, and in order to get Huntington to bid, Lathrop offered to halve his "usual 10% commission," so that the total cost would be somewhere $125,000 and $150,000. "If you are not prepared to lay out such a sum after your library purchase," he added, "would your mother be willing to do it for you?"[114]

Once again Huntington failed to act, in this case for reasons that had less to do with the cost of the picture or its Spanish provenance than with a museum he envisioned less as a collection of individual masterpieces than as an assemblage of pictures illustrative of different periods of Spanish art and the "genius" of the Spanish people as a whole. In the end Lathrop did manage to persuade Huntington to purchase a dozen or so other Spanish pictures, among which Velázquez's portrait of an Italian cardinal, Camillo Astalli Pamphili, dating from 1651, was by far the best. In 1908, however, Huntington, having decided that he no longer needed Lathrop's artistic advice, informed his friend, "I find it much better to consult no one so that responsibility may rest with me alone. Moreover, as I am collecting with a fixed plan no one would agree with me."[115]

Integral to that "fixed plan" was a studied effort to avoid what he called "duplication." With reference to such artists as Velázquez, El Greco, or Goya, avoidance of duplication meant acquiring selected, as opposed to serial, examples of their most representative work. Avoidance of duplication also explains why Huntington, starting around 1912, was able to write that "the buying of books and pictures draws to an end." Around that time he also made an effort to avoid contact with dealers, although his correspondence indicates that they continually pestered him with offers of various kinds. The start of World War I also served to put a brake on Huntington's buying trips to Europe, and by January 1916 he had more or less decided to put an end to his purchases, informing a friend, "I am no longer adding to my collection nor is the Hispanic Society."[116]

Another key aspect of Huntington's buying was his determination to avoid being seen as a "plunderer" out to despoil Spain's artistic patrimony. He first articulated that policy to his mother in 1898 and reiterated it on several occasions thereafter. In 1910, for example, the Spanish artist Joaquín Sorolla wrote Huntington, asking whether he might consider the purchase of several pictures in Spain. Huntington paraphrased his response in a letter to his mother that is included in his diary: "I have explained to him that I do not care to buy much of importance in Spain, owing to the fixed rule that I have been following outside the Peninsula only. The things come to Paris eventually and one is saved the long bargaining which is enough to drive one mad. It is an inheritance from an Oriental background. But I do not go to Spain to buy (with the exception of books)."[117]

"Oriental" here means Arab, and the racial slur was similar to others Huntington used with reference to booksellers and art dealers who were Jewish or whose prices he judged excessive. His "fixed rule" also requires qualification. As Huntington himself often remarked, it did not apply either to books or to manuscripts. Nor did it necessarily embrace the so-called minor arts inasmuch as Huntington regularly acquired, either by purchase or by gift, pottery, glass, embroideries, and even some archaeological objects in Spain, nor did he hesitate to acquire choir stalls and other antiques that he (or his agents) purchased in Lima and other cities in Latin America.[118] But unlike most other major

American collectors, such as William Randolph Hearst or Henry Clay Frick (see chapter 5), Huntington refrained from making any major purchases in Spain itself.

But this policy was somewhat hollow. Huntington had his favorite dealers, among them Samuel Avery and Ehrich Brothers in New York, Conalghi Gallery and Lionel Harris in London, and Joseph Duveen, Charles Sedelmeyer, and Jacques Seligmann in Paris. Well apprised of his interests, they managed to circumvent the "fixed rule" by importing to their galleries various Spanish objects that they later sold to Huntington. A case in point: Huntington's 1906 acquisition of several magnificent Renaissance tomb sculptures that rank among the prize objects in the collections of the HSA. Those sculptures, originally housed in a Franciscan convent in the Castilian town of Cuéllar, were purchased in 1905 by the Duke of Sesto, who subsequently lent (or sold) them to Lionel Harris, a London dealer whose business, the Spanish Art Gallery, specialized in acquiring objects from Spain and selling them to a select international clientele, Huntington among them. It is doubtful whether Huntington bears any responsibility for the export of these sculptures from Cuéllar, but Harris is more than likely to have acquired them with the New Yorker in mind and in doing so enabled Huntington to uphold his "fixed rule" regarding the acquisition of important works of art.[119]

Long in the planning, Huntington's Spanish museum finally opened to the public on January 20, 1908. The immediate response was mixed, as Huntington readily acknowledged. But the opening did not go unnoticed in the New York press. A *New York Times* article, headlined "Another Fine Museum Added to the City's List," thanked for Huntington for his philanthropy and highlighted many of the treasures he had assembled, including the fifty thousand volumes in the HSA's library; pictures by Velázquez, Goya, Murillo, and El Greco; the tomb sculptures from Cuéllar; archaeological objects from various Spanish sites; and Hispano-Moresque pottery, tilework, coins, and so on. It also mentioned "Indian" wall paintings with scenes depicting the Spanish conquest of Mexico and, somewhat discordantly, several medieval bronzes that Huntington had purchased in Egypt and were evidently intended to demonstrate Spain's "Oriental" (i.e., Arabic) roots. The article also made reference to the museum's double-sided glassed frames that allowed for several maps, charts, and prints to be viewed at once.[120]

Yet for the all praise the article lavished on Huntington's creation, its anonymous author hinted that the HSA was not "everyman's museum," describing it instead as a "special museum for students" and again as "a special museum for students of Spanish literature and art."[121] That assessment was essentially correct. Although the HSA did not charge admission and even opened its galleries on Sundays, it was not geared to the interests of the general public. Huntington instead conceived of the HSA's principal mission as one of scholarship and research and that of the museum as "the protection of distinguished achievements or objects of historical interest."[122] For these reasons, and referring again to Lawrence Levine's understanding of the hierarchical divisions in early twentieth-century American culture, it was a "small collection of objects" that catered principally to students, specialists, and honorary members of the society as opposed to being a collection organized and presented to serve the needs of the ordinary visitor.[123]

An inkling of what Huntington was up to can be found in a 1920 letter to his mother in which he outlined the workings of the HSA. There he explained that he wanted his staff to concentrate on the production of "leaflets and monographs listing all of the relevant facts and which would be available for purchase at a price below actual cost." Such publications, he argued, would allow the staff to dedicate themselves to scholarship and not have to bother with "the myriad enquires of the ignorant, trivial and uninformed, who are the bane of scholars and the devourers of priceless time."[124]

Elitism aside, what Huntington was articulating here was the idea that the chief obligation of museum curators (known as keepers in the United Kingdom) was to be a subject specialist and engage in scholarship directly pertinent to the objects in the collection as opposed to attending to the needs of visitors. That concept, originating in nineteenth-century Germany, was relatively novel in the United States and situated the HSA at the forefront of an important museological trend that continued throughout most of the twentieth century. (Nowadays museums are eager to be friendlier to the public.) Huntington was also a pacesetter in another way. He firmly believed that women were the individuals best suited for the kind of detailed curatorial scholarship he wanted; as he wrote to Arabella in 1920, "I am convinced more than ever that this is women's work."[125]

The statement is telling, as it suggests that Huntington had a gendered view of art history as a field of research, one that separated broader, more synthetic scholarship—a male domain in his view—from the more focused, monographic research museum work required. What is certain is that over the years the HSA regularly employed women, as both librarians and curators. One of the first was Georgiana Goddard King (1871–1939), founder of the art history department at Bryn Mawr College and a scholar with a special interest in the architecture of medieval Spain. King's collaboration with Huntington began around 1911, when he commissioned her to produce a new edition of George E. Street's *Some Account of Gothic Architecture in Spain*, a work originally published in 1865. He subsequently provided her with the financing she needed to travel to Spain and begin the research that led to *The Way to Saint James*, her important three-volume work focused on the architecture of pilgrimage churches in northern Spain, which the Hispanic Society of America published in 1920. By this time, however, King and Huntington no longer saw eye to eye. She wanted the freedom to direct her own research, while he wanted her to focus on topics related directly to the aims and ambitions of the HSA. One bone of contention: an art journal King sought to establish at Bryn Mawr but that Huntington refused to support. The dispute was relatively minor, but it led Huntington to question whether he could work in the future with King, as one entry in his 1918 diary readily suggests: "Miss King is very sure of herself and rather too impressed with her own ability. She has a sharp way of talking and does not take advice at all. But she also works hard and with rather bad methods[.] She will break down one day when she least expects it."[126] King's opinion of Huntington is difficult to determine, but it is telling that his name does not appear among those listed in the acknowledgments in the first volume of *The Way to Saint James*. Whatever the exact reason for their falling out, by 1923 King regretted, as she put it, having "mortgaged her ink-pot" to the HSA.[127]

Fig. 30. Charles W. Hawthorne, *Georgina Goddard King*, 1905. A pioneer in the field of Spanish art history and a longtime professor at Bryn Mawr College, Georgiana Goddard King conducted research for a time for the Hispanic Society of America. She later regretted having "sold her ink-pot" to Archer M. Huntington, that institution's director. Philadelphia Museum of Art.

Huntington's determination to keep his employees on a narrow path also helps to explain his break with Mildred Stapley Byne (1875–1941) and her architect husband, Arthur Byne (1884–1935), in 1921. The two, married in 1910, had a particular interest in the art, architecture, and history of Spain, a country in which they had traveled extensively. How Huntington learned about the couple is not altogether clear, but he was undoubtedly familiar with Mildred's essay "The Great Queen Isabel," published in the popular *Harper's Monthly Magazine* in June 1912 and was much taken with Byne's expertise in the architecture of medieval Spain.[128] Collaboration began in 1914, with Huntington and the HSA supporting the publication of the couple's *Rejería of the Spanish Renaissance* (1914)—a book on window grilles—and *Spanish Ironwork* (1915). In 1916 Huntington also arranged for the Bynes' joint appointment as the HSA's curators of architecture and allied arts, each with an annual salary of $2,500. In the years that followed the HSA commissioned the Bynes to go on several trips to Spain, partly in an effort to secure photographs of medieval churches and other buildings Huntington wanted for the HSA's photographic archives. These trips also led to Arthur Byne's *Spanish Architecture of the Sixteenth Century* (1917), as well as the couple's jointly authored *Decorated Wooden Ceilings in Spain* (1920), both published under the auspices of the HSA.

This cozy relationship was not to last. The Bynes and Huntington were increasingly at loggerheads, mainly because the couple, much like King, felt constrained by the kinds of projects Huntington wanted. The first signs of tension surfaced in January 1919, when Huntington scribbled the following note: "they [Bynes] have their limitations which may be hard to conquer. Vanity is their danger."[129] Partly at issue here was a planned book on Spanish Romanesque architecture. The Bynes wanted to extend the volume to include early Gothic architecture, but Huntington thought otherwise, insisting in one letter that "it [the Gothic] is not part of the present plan" and in another, after Mildred broached the idea of a book on Spanish furniture, the need to "stick with the original plan."[130] Huntington also frowned on the Bynes' relationship with the architect Julia Morgan, an old friend of Mildred, and her connection with the newspaper magnate William Randolph Hearst, along with

Fig. 31. Joaquín Sorolla exhibition, Hispanic Society of America, New York, 1909. Sorolla's 1909 exhibition at New York's Hispanic Society was a veritable block-buster, attracting more than 160,000 visitors in less than three months' time. Courtesy Library of Congress.

the couple's interest in becoming dealers in art and antiques. The end came in January 1921, when the Bynes wrote Huntington announcing their "desire to sever our connection with the Hispanic Society" (and receive severance pay of $3,000) and agreeing to deposit six hundred photos that they had taken under the auspices of the HSA in the society's archives, albeit on the condition they be granted "the right to use them in future, [with] each photo to be stamped 'Byne Stapley Expeditions 1919–1920.'"[131] Huntington accepted these conditions, at which point Mildred and Arthur settled in Madrid, establishing themselves as dealers specializing in the sale of Spanish art and antiques to various American collectors and museums (see chapter 6).

Both King's and the Bynes' experiences with Huntington indicate that he was a demanding taskmaster, one who expected his staff to adapt to own way of doing research and to support his personal commitment to the enhancement of Spain's image in the United States. Concern for that image, together with the somewhat lukewarm reception the HSA received

when it first opened to public in 1908, also convinced Huntington that the HSA needed to do more, or at least try something different, to attract the general public to Washington Heights. Huntington was never keen on temporary exhibitions, especially those focused on, as he put it, the work of "dead painters. They should be honorably hanged (painlessly) in museums." He thought differently, however, about "modern pictures, by living artists," which should be exhibited (mainly by dealers), discussed, and "above all else bought."[132] It is not clear when exactly Huntington formulated this idea, but in a determined and indeed studied effort to give Spain and its culture a secure place on New York's cultural map he arranged for the HSA to host two back-to-back temporary exhibitions in 1909. Both featured the work of two "modern artists," both from Spain: Joaquín Sorolla y Bastida (1868–1923) and Ignacio Zuloaga (1870–1945).

Sorolla's exhibition came first, and it was a wise choice. Sorolla had previously exhibited some of his paintings at the Chicago World's Columbian Exposition in 1893, and his reputation as Spain's outstanding "painter of light" preceded his arrival in New York for the exhibition's opening in February 1909. It proved a spectacular success—160,000 visitors in less than two months; more than 20,000 catalogs sold; repeated interviews with the New York press; commissions for portraits from J. P. Morgan and other prominent New Yorkers; and on top of all this an invitation in April to dine at the White House, where he met with President Taft, spoke Spanish with Mrs. Taft, and in the days that followed painted the president's official portrait. Huntington also arranged for the Sorolla exhibit to travel to other venues, in Boston, Buffalo, and St. Louis, where its reception was comparable to its initial showing in New York.

Writing some years later, Huntington happily recalled the exhibition's success:

> It was called a triumph. The [New York] artists looked upon it as an invasion. . . . The collectors welcomed it. . . . The dealers secretly snarled and wrote me enthusiastic messages. One said: "Spain sank low in our defeat of her, she has replied with the lightnings of art." Everywhere the air was full of the miracle. People quoted figures of attendance. There was eternal talk of "sunlight." Nothing like it had ever happened in New York. Ohs and ahs stained the tiled floors. Automobiles blocked the street. Orders for portraits poured in. Photographs were sold in unheard of numbers. And through it all the little creator sat surprised, overwhelmed yet simple and without vanity . . . and then it was all over.[133]

Yes, but not quite. The Sorolla exhibition set the stage for Zuloaga, whose exhibition of thirty paintings opened at the HSA two weeks after Sorolla's had closed. Critics applauded it, although they regretted the fact that Zuloaga, unlike Sorolla, had decided to remain in Europe rather than accompany his pictures to New York. As for the general public, the Basque artist's cool palate and often dark subject matter had less in the way of popular appeal than Sorolla's sunnier and brighter canvases. Even so, Zuloaga's pictures still managed to attract as many as 70,000 visitors to the HSA.

In this respect Huntington's "love for Spain" resonated with the public but in ways he probably did not predict. In subsequent years the HSA, in keeping with Huntington's interest in photography, organized exhibitions of photographs of Spain that also commanded considerable attention in and around New York. So too did the permanent installation in 1926 of Sorolla's large-scale series of paintings illustrating different scenes of Spain's traditional pastimes and ways of life. Yet it was the 1909

Sorolla exhibition that really captured New York's and, more broadly, the country's attention. As one journalist, Henry Tyrell, observed, the success of that exhibition was part of a broader "Spanish Revival in the United States that has blossomed out exuberantly." Tyrell attributed this "revival" to "Spanish-American good fellowship," which, as he saw it, the "late Spanish-American unpleasantness" had failed to erase. That fellowship, he added, also embraced U.S. interest in Spanish omelettes, Spanish dancing, Spanish music. "Spanish dancers are here," he writes, and "more are coming and Spanish-American is at its height." Without saying so directly, Tyrell was alluding to the start of the emergent craze for Spain, although he failed to mention growing U.S. interest in Spanish-themed architecture or, save for the pictures assembled by Huntington at the HSA, the race among wealthy collectors to purchase choice examples of Spanish art. These key elements in the craze for Spain are those the following chapters address.[134]

5

Collectors and Collecting

Art that one cannot see cannot be understood.
—ARCHER MILTON HUNTINGTON

A special predilection for Spain and Spanish Art has become
a peculiarity of the Americans through the war with Spain.
—WILHELM BODE, *New York Times*, January 6, 1912

When the doors of the HSA opened in January 1908, Spanish art, though still a novelty, was already in demand.[1] Across the country wealthy collectors were vying with museums to acquire choice works by Spanish Old Masters, especially El Greco, Murillo, Velázquez, and Zurbarán. A spirited market also existed for Goya's pictures, together with those by Sorolla, Spain's most famous contemporary artist. In 1908 only a handful of Americans had ever heard of the young avant-garde artist known as Picasso, but he too would leap to prominence following the presentation of his cubist canvases and other works at the New York Armory Show of 1913. Put briefly, Spanish art was in vogue.

The prices commanded by Spanish Old Master pictures, especially those attributed to Velázquez, provide one marker of the strength and velocity of the growing appetite for Spanish art. In 1896 Bernard Berenson (1865–1959), soon to become one of the United States'—and Europe's—most famous art critics and connoisseurs, was young and relatively unknown, his knowledge of Spanish art minimal at best. Yet Berenson had a nose for trends and where the art market was heading. For this reason he urged his friend and fellow Bostonian Isabella Stewart Gardner, one of the first American collectors of Old Master art, to purchase a portrait of King Philip IV of Spain by Velázquez then on sale

Fig. 32. Diego Velázquez and Workshop, *King Philip IV of Spain*, ca. 1626–28. The noted art dealer Bernard Berenson helped Isabella Stewart Gardner acquire this picture in 1896. The purchase sparked the interest of other American collectors in paintings attributed to this famed seventeenth-century Spanish artist. Isabella Stewart Gardner Museum, Boston.

at London's Colnaghi Gallery. The price was 14,000 pounds sterling, or roughly $36,400. Gardner, though interested in acquiring a picture by Velázquez, hesitated, informing Berenson that the price was well beyond her means. Berenson, no doubt eager for the commission the sale would bring, responded by racheting up the pressure. "You are of course aware," he replied, "that Velázquez both with artists and buyers stands now at the very top, and is of all painters the most sought after for these artists." Still Gardner dithered. She even asked for a discount, but when Berenson informed her that Colnaghi would not budge, she finally bit the bullet and bought the portrait at the asking price.[2]

Was Gardner overcharged? Perhaps. But her timing was perfect. Eight years later another somewhat similar Velázquez portrait of Philip IV came up for sale in a Paris gallery. Critics disagreed about its authenticity, but the Museum of Fine Arts, Boston, eager to add to its expanding collection of Spanish art, bought it for 60,000 francs, or just over $41,000, roughly 20 percent more than Gardner had paid just a few years earlier.[3]

The trend was clear. As more museums and private collectors clamored for pictures by Velázquez, prices for canvases attributed to the great Spanish master spiraled sharply upward. In 1905 Gardner acquired a second Velázquez—for $96,000, or more than double the cost of her first one. But this figure was a steal as compared with the $400,000 Arabella Huntington paid for Velázquez's portrait of the Count-Duke of Olivares in 1908, let alone the astonishing $500,000 that Henry Clay Frick, the Pittsburgh industrialist turned New York collector, paid in 1911 for another Velázquez portrait of Philip IV.

With prices at this stratospheric level, only a handful of collectors and museums could afford to purchase a Velázquez. One such collector was Benjamin Altman, a New York department store magnate. Eager to enhance the quality of his growing collection of Old Master art, in 1912 Altman paid a whopping $1 million for two of Velázquez's portraits—one of Olivares, another of Philip IV. To be sure, ownership of a Velázquez was a privilege, reserved for a privileged few, but the price Altman paid for the two pictures illustrates yet another, admittedly pricey, facet of the craze for Spain.[4]

Art for the Nation

The demand for these pictures also speaks to changes in Americans' artistic tastes. One shift, already referred to, was increased cosmopolitanism and new interest in the cultures and customs of faraway lands. Cosmopolitanism took many forms, most tangibly in the acquisition of objects imported from abroad. These ranged from cheap bric-a-brac and other household paraphernalia to such pricey objects as Chinese porcelains and lacquerware, Turkish rugs, and, at the very top of the scale, European Old Master paintings.[5]

An early expression of this cosmopolitanism—and a clarion call for more of it—can be found in a letter Henry James wrote to a friend in 1867. James remarked, "I think to be an American is an excellent preparation for culture . . . we can deal freely with forms of civilisation not our own; we can pick and choose and assimilate and in short (aesthetically etc) claim our property wherever we find it."[6] James's words neatly summarize one of the many reasons why the art and artifacts of foreign cultures had such enormous appeal for Gilded Age collectors in the United States. Without a long and distinguished heritage of their own, Americans, especially wealthy Americans, looked abroad to create the artistic and cultural patrimony their nation supposedly lacked. In 1867, however, the year in which James wrote this letter, such collecting had scarcely begun. Yet James proved prophetic, and when in 1875 his novel *Roderick Hudson* first appeared, it helped to establish an agenda that many collectors would adopt, namely, the idea that collecting, whatever its aesthetic pleasures, was not only socially useful but patriotic, in other words, something every red-blooded American with the means could and should pursue.

Roderick Hudson centers on the character of Rowland Mallet, who, as James describes him, "was extremely fond of all the arts and had an almost passionate enjoyment of pictures." As a good citizen, Mallet believed he should go abroad and secretly purchase valuable specimens of the Dutch and Italian schools and then present them to an American city.[7] To be sure, not all collectors were so altruistic; many bought art simply as markers of their wealth and cultivated taste. But in creating

Mallet as the central character of his novel, James helped popularize the idea—call it "art for the nation"—of collecting, or what Neil Harris has defined as a "valued activity" invested with "social worth."[8] In addition, James—one of the most widely read and influential authors of the Gilded Age in the United States—helped move collecting into the zone of what Thorstein Veblen defined in 1899 as "conspicuous consumption."[9] It is difficult to determine which of these two forces—art as a marker of individual status and prestige, or the idea of art collecting as a civic or patriotic activity—carried more weight, but they combined to help spawn Americans' growing and seemingly insatiable appetite for European art.

The real markers of status and wealth were choice examples of the art of Europe's Old Masters. Demand for these pictures gathered momentum during the 1880s and 1890s and received an additional boost in 1909 with Congress's passage of the Payne-Aldrich Tariff Act. Previously collectors had had to pay a 20 percent duty on imported antiques, paintings included. The new act ended those duties, opening the floodgates to artworks entering the country from abroad. The tax break proved a boon to the likes of J. P. Morgan, one of many collectors who had lobbied for the change, but it terrified Europe, as Henry "Hy" Mayer's cartoon, *How we strip Europe of her Treasures of Art*, published in the February 19, 1911, edition of the *New York Times*, attests. Part of a series entitled Impressions of the Passing Show, the cartoon features a portly gentleman who can be identified as the wealthy banker and industrialist J. P. Morgan entering a long gallery lined with portraits. The sitters in these portraits, animated by the sight of Morgan and seemingly terrified at the prospect of being shipped to the United States, make a collective dash to safety as fast they can.[10]

"Priest-Ridden Work"

At the outset of this art-buying spree Spain had relatively little to fear from the likes of Morgan and other American collectors, few of whom expressed much interest in Spanish as opposed to Dutch, Flemish, or Italian art, let alone that of China and the rest of East Asia. There was one exception, however: pictures by Bartolomé Esteban Murillo (1617–

82), the seventeenth-century Sevillian artist known for his airy renderings of the Virgin Mary and street urchins. Starting in the eighteenth century, Murillo's works had captured the attention of British and other European collectors, and such was his fame that in the course of Spain's Peninsular War, Maréchal Jean-de-Dieu Soult, one of the Napoleon's generals, spirited several of Murillo's most important works to Paris, including the monumental *Immaculate Conception*, now in the Louvre.[11]

The first Murillo to arrive in the United States is likely to have been his now-lost picture *Jacob and Rebecca at the Well*. According to a letter later written by Harvard's Spanish instructor, Francis Sales, in 1793, the young Boston merchant Thomas Foster (1772–1863) and Sales sailed from Cádiz to Boston aboard the *Bald Eagle*. Foster had previously journeyed to Spain in order to obtain some merino sheep, a species prized for its long-staple wool but one whose export was strictly prohibited. With help from Sales, whom he had apparently met in Cádiz, Foster successfully managed to smuggle three merinos—one ram and two ewes—onto the vessel along with "a valuable painting of 'Rebecca at the well,' by Murillo, [the export of which was] prohibited under severe penalties." Sales then adds, "The painting I found a few years ago, (being reminded by you [S. W. Jewitt, the Vermont landowner to whom the letter was addressed] of its existence) in Col. Sargent's [probably Paul Dudley Sargent] garret. I gave it to the Boston Athenaeum, where it is much valued."[12]

The next pictures attributed to Murillo that arrived in the United States came via Richard Worsam Meade (1778–1828), the Philadelphia merchant we encountered in the last chapter as one of the subscribers supporting the publication of works by the exiled writer Santiago Puglia. Meade, son of George Meade, an Irish Catholic merchant who had helped finance George Washington's army, had commercial ties in the West Indies before he relocated from Philadelphia to Cádiz in 1804. Once there he presided over a flourishing "commercial establishment" that imported flour from Philadelphia and Baltimore and exported olive oil, wine, and wool in return. Starting in 1806, Meade also served as the U.S. vice-consul and used that position to forge a close relationship with the provisional government, or junta, which took refuge in Cádiz following Napoleon's invasion of Spain in 1808. In effect Meade served as one of the junta's financiers, a connection that proved his undoing following the defeat of Napoleon and the return of the exiled King Ferdinand VII to Spain in 1814. Arrested on trumped-up charges of fiscal malfeasance, Meade spent almost three years in prison, until John Quincy Adams, as part of the Transcontinental Treaty negotiations with Luis de Onís, secured his release. Returning to Philadelphia in 1820, Meade initiated a claim against the Spanish government for money owed him. That claim was only settled by his heirs—among them Gen. Gordon Meade, commander of the victorious Union forces at the Battle of Gettysburg—in 1859.

Details about Meade's collecting are few, but during his time in Cádiz he acquired no fewer than 165 works by Italian and Spanish masters, among them four pictures (and a miniature painted on copper) attributed to Murillo and which included a *Roman Charity* previously belonging to Manuel de Godoy, the Spanish minister whom Henry Adams later described as "the most contemptible of mortals." The circumstances surrounding Meade's acquisition of this canvas are somewhat murky, but at the time of Godoy's fall from power in 1808, it was in the possession of a Spanish artist, Tomás López Enguídanos, who soon sold it to Obadiah Rich (1777–1850), an American merchant then serving as the U.S. consul in Valencia. Rich then sold it to Meade, probably in Cádiz. Meade entrusted the picture to his wife, Margaret Coates Butler, who brought it with her on a trip to Philadelphia in 1811. It was first exhibited at Philadelphia's Pennsylvania Academy of the Fine Arts in 1815, and Meade subsequently donated the picture, along with some of his other Spanish pictures, to the academy, but the story has a tragic ending. The *Roman Charity* was destroyed in a fire that swept through the academy's building in 1845.[13]

Meade's other Murillos escaped that fate, but as his widow discovered after a failed attempt to sell them at a New York exhibition sale in 1831, few other American collectors of that era shared her deceased husband's interest in Spanish Old Master art.[14] Two decades later, however, the tastes of these collectors began to change, owing in large measure to the excitement generated in Paris in May 1852 by the sale of the famed *Immaculate Conception* belonging to Maréchal Soult. That auction received wide press coverage on both sides of the Atlantic, especially in New York, where one anonymous writer, after commenting upon the frenetic bidding the picture elicited, emphasized the "immortality" of Murillo's artistic genius with the statement, "Gold, titles, scepters, what are these compared with the pencil of Murillo[?]"[15]

That "pencil" did not figure in Meade's Murillos, all of which were acknowledged to be copies of the master's work. On the other hand, the publicity surrounding Soult's picture helps account for the sale of these pictures during yet another auction of the Meade collection, held in Philadelphia on March 15, 1853.[16]

In this respect, the Soult auction, especially when combined with the publicity accompanying the wildly successful May 1853 auction of the Spanish pictures formerly in the possession of the French monarch Louis-Philippe (see below), was a tastemaker to the extent that it increased the awareness of American collectors to the value and importance of Murillo's art. One such collector was Baltimore's William T. Walters (1820–94), who had developed an interest in Old Master European art. Walters purchased a *Virgin Mary* attributed to Murillo at an auction sale in 1855, although this was the only Spanish picture he ever bought.[17]

Works by Murillo and other Spanish artists also figured in the collection assembled by Thomas J. Bryan (1800–1870), a native Philadelphian who lived for almost twenty years in Paris. As a collector, Bryan sought pictures illustrative of each of the so-called "national" schools of European art. In 1852, after returning to the United States and taking up residence in New York, Bryan opened his Gallery of Christian Art, aimed at educating the public about "progress" in the arts. Located in Bryan's residence on Lower Broadway, the gallery held 230 pictures, more than half of which were Dutch, Flemish, and Italian. Representing the Spanish school were five pictures: two attributed (wrongly) to Velázquez (a landscape and a portrait of King Philip IV as David) and three alleged Murillos, among them an *Adoration of the Shepherds* (possibly the one now in Florida's St. Petersburg Museum of Art) that he had purchased at the Soult auction in Paris.[18] The Spanish school also made a cameo appearance in the collection of Louis Durr (1821–80), a New Yorker of German origin who made a fortune refining silver and gold. Durr owned several hundred pictures, among them two attributed to Murillo and another to Velázquez. Following his death in 1880, Durr's executors in 1882 donated his collection to the New-York Historical Society.[19]

The only nineteenth-century U.S. collector to make a habit of buying Spanish pictures was William H. Aspinwall (1807–75), a New York merchant with important investments in Panama as well as the East and West Indies. In 1857 Aspinwall acquired what he thought was a genuine Murillo—an *Immaculate Conception* now in the Detroit Institute of Art; critics described it as a "wonderful picture" after he placed it on public display. Aspinwall later acquired two other canvases attributed to Murillo, together with a pair of male portraits attributed (wrongly) to Velázquez, among them *A Knight of Malta*. This picture later became the property of James Renwick Jr. (1818–95), who subsequently bequeathed it to New York's Metropolitan Museum of Art in 1895. At the time the Met's only other Spanish picture was a *Holy Family* (now in the Ringling Museum of Art, Sarasota, Florida) attributed to Murillo and acquired from the estate of the noted philanthropist John Jacob Astor III (1822–90).[20]

Aspinwall's well-known appetite for Murillo, as well as the interest of other American collectors in the work of this artist, may also have figured in one of the more bizarre nineteenth-century incidents relating to pictures by this important Sevillian master. One of Murillo's masterpieces and certainly his largest work, measuring eighteen by twelve feet, was his *Vision of St. Anthony of Padua*, executed for the baptistry chapel in the Cathedral of Seville in 1656. After the canvas had been hanging undisturbed for several centuries, a cathedral guard discovered on November 5, 1875, that the painting had been "mutilated," with the figure of St. Anthony "cut out" from the canvas. Spanish authorities quickly sent cables announcing the theft to diplomats in various countries, including the United States, and offering an astonishing $10,000 reward for the fragment's recovery. Two months later, in early January 1875, two Spaniards, one calling himself Fernando García, walked into the New York gallery of the respected art dealer William Schaus, who recognized the picture they brought with them for what it was—the stolen Murillo—and purchased it for $250. Schaus immediately contacted

Fig. 33. Bartolomé de Murillo, *Vision of St. Anthony of Padua*, 1656. In 1876 thieves cut out the figure of the saint from this picture and smuggled the piece to New York, hoping to cash in on the demand for paintings by Murillo. The scheme backfired, and the canvas was returned to Seville, where the mutilated picture was repaired and restored. Seville Cathedral. Photo: Pepe Morón, Seville.

the police as well as Hipólito de Uriarte, the Spanish consul in Madrid. García was soon arrested and sent to Spain via Cuba along with the Murillo fragment, which was returned to Seville. The theft, together with Schaus's discovery of the stolen Murillo, received press coverage in several cities, especially in New York, where it was front-page news.[21]

Except for Murillo, however, the U.S. market for works by Spain's Old Masters was, as the *New York Times* correctly reported in 1877, "indifferent" at best.[22] That indifference fed partly on ignorance. Murillo, described as the "first painter of Spain" by one connoisseur, was a known quantity and works attributed to him occasionally went on public display, but most other Spanish artists, even Velázquez, were not well known.[23] A handful of pictures attributed to this artist were briefly on view in an exhibition held in Boston's Athenaeum in 1830, while others could be seen in Bryan's Gallery of Christian Art. In 1853 an enterprising English antique dealer, John Snare, also exhibited what he believed was a genuine but long-lost Velázquez portrait in New York's Stuyvesant Institute. The picture generated considerable publicity, even a long review in the *American Phrenological Journal*.[24]

But the Snare Velázquez was the exception. Connoisseurs truly interested in seeing genuine works by this artist and Spain's other Old Masters had few options except traveling to Europe. Britain's private collections boasted numerous Murillos, along with various pictures by Velázquez, although access to these collections was difficult. As for public galleries, the Dulwich Picture Gallery, opened in 1817, included several Murillos, and London's National Gallery, opened in 1824, had in addition to pictures by Murillo and Velázquez others by Jusepe de Ribera and Alonso Cano.

A once-in-a-lifetime opportunity to see a far broader sampling of Spanish pictures occurred in 1857 with the opening of the Manchester Art Treasures Exhibition, which gathered more than twelve thousand pieces from among private collections in Britain. The Spanish paintings— fewer than fifty in all—would have been easy to miss among hundreds of others categorized as "antique masters," although one vestibule was devoted exclusively to Murillo (with twenty paintings) and Velázquez (six works). Elsewhere in this exhibit hung works by El Greco (a portrait said to be of his daughter), Zurbarán, and other, lesser known Spanish artists. Attracting more than a million visitors in less than five months, the Manchester exhibition was a true blockbuster, probably the world's first. Among the Americans who saw it were George Ticknor and the writer Nathaniel Hawthorne, who admired the Murillos on exhibit but failed to comment on the pictures by Velázquez and Zurbarán.[25]

As for the rest of Europe, Americans visiting Paris prior to 1849 would have had the opportunity to view the Galerie Espagnole, which the French monarch, Louis-Philippe, had assembled at the Louvre. Opened in 1838, this gallery contained almost five hundred pictures, including important works attributed to Murillo, Velázquez, El Greco, and Zurbarán. An instant success, the gallery elicited favorable critical attention in addition to kindling new interest in Spanish art among the leading French artists of the day, including Jean-Léon Gérôme, Carolus-Duran, and Jean-François Millet, along with the young Édouard Manet. Yet for all its importance in introducing France—and presumably many foreign visitors to Paris as well—to Spanish art, the Galerie Espagnole closed after Louis-Philippe's abdication in 1848 and his death in 1850. In 1852 its contents were shipped to London and sold at Christie's auction house the following year. A few items, including Zurbarán's haunting *St. Francis in Meditation*, which was purchased by London's National Gallery, entered into public collections, but most quickly found their way into private ones. A small sampling of these pictures occasionally appeared in temporary expositions such as the one held in Manchester, along with another held in Boston in 1874 (see below), but for the most part they remained hidden from public view.[26]

To be sure, other European museums, notably those in Berlin, Dresden, and Vienna, owned Spanish pictures, but as William Cullen Bryant recognized after his tour through Spain in 1859, "the full merit of the Spanish painters could not be known to those who have never visited Spain."[27] To be more precise, Bryant was recommending a visit to Madrid's Prado Museum, which had opened to the public in 1819. Among the first Americans to visit the Prado was Washington Irving, who visited the "gallery of paintings" on March 4, 1826, and again on four different occasions over the course of the next two years.[28] Curiously, Irving's journal records nothing about these visits, a silence that becomes significant—and perhaps even telling—when compared to his entries recording his visits to Madrid's Royal Academy of Fine Arts, the Escorial monastery, and various churches in Seville, all of which reveal that he had definite ideas about pictures. Irving's visit to, for example, the Royal Academy of Fine Arts on March 26, 1826, elicited the following comment: "A superb painting by Murillo on a nauseous subject: Queen Isabella washing the sores of the mendicants; two fine paintings by him, the *Dream of a Nobleman and his wife about the founding of St Peters at Rome*." Similarly, Irving used the terms "beautiful," "fine," "noble," and "superb" to describe the Murillos he saw during his visit to Seville's Hospital de la Caridad, when he was accompanied by the Scottish painter David Wilkie.[29]

From one of his letters we also know that Irving, ever the good romantic, practically swooned when in January 1828 he watched the beautiful young wife of one diplomat stage a "*tableau vivant* of Murillo's *Virgin of the Inmaculate [sic] Conception*," although in this instance I would venture that it was the lady in question—the young wife of the Russian ambassador—rather than Murillo, who captured Irving's fancy: "It was more like a vision of Something Celestial than a representation of anything mortal."[30]

In view of these enthusiastic comments about Murillo, how are we to account for Irving's silence about Velázquez and the other Spanish artists whose work he would have seen in the Prado, probably for the first time? Indifference? Hostility? Whatever the answers to these questions, I draw attention to Irving's silence because similar silences can be found in the reactions of other visitors to the Prado, and these voids complicate our understanding of the ways in which nineteenth-century Americans (not to mention other visitors) who saw that collection interpreted Spanish art.

Irving's may be the first recorded visit to the Prado by an American, but his journal indicates that he did not go there alone. His fellow visitors are likely to have been members of the U.S. diplomatic delegation in Madrid, among them the delegation's secretary, Obadiah Rich, the merchant responsible for the sale of Murillo's *Roman Charity* to Richard Meade and later to become a bookseller in London and a dealer in engravings after pictures by Murillo, Titian, and Velázquez.[31] Another of Irving's companions was the head of the delegation, Alexander Hill Everett, an accomplished man of letters who, upon returning to the United States in 1829, became the editor of Boston's prestigious *North American Review*. There, in a review of an exhibition of pictures held at the Athenaeum in 1830, an exhibition that included Murillo's *Jacob and Rebecca at the Well*, Everett wrote what is arguably the first critical assessment of Spanish art ever published in the United States. Couched in eighteenth-century notions of the sublime popularized by the philosopher Edmund Burke (1729–97) together with the idea that painting should be judged by its power to stir the emotions, the review was judgmental and subjective, focusing on coloring, drawing, composition, and subject matter, all measured against an ideal standard of beauty epitomized by antique sculpture and the work of such Italian Old Masters as Titian and Raphael.[32] But Everett demonstrated that he was somewhat ahead of his time when he lauded the merits of Velázquez at a moment when Murillo ranked as the acknowledged champion of Spanish art. Velázquez, writes Everett, is less well known than Murillo, but he is the "superior artist," because his "truth to nature" allowed him to approach "the point of actual perfection" in art. Despite such praise, Everett confessed that Velázquez's realism left him "rather cold," whereas Murillo succeeded in moving his imagination because of his "felicity of composition" and "brilliancy and charm of his coloring." Even so, he observed somewhat critically that Murillo's "charming simplicity and sweetness of expression" led to "childish weakness" as opposed to "poetical expression."[33]

Following Everett, other Americans who visited the Prado prior to the Civil War and wrote about their experiences there also drew upon Burke's aesthetics to record their encounters with Spanish art. For example, subjectivity similar to Everett's permeated Caroline Cushing's impressions of the Prado's pictures and was included in the narrative of her Spanish travels published after her untimely death in 1831. Cushing (1802–32), née Caroline Elizabeth Wilde and wife of Caleb Cushing, was the first American woman to write about Spanish art. Many of her observations, though interesting, echo Irving's to the extent that she regarded Murillo's *St. Elizabeth of Hungary Tending the Sick* as a "splendid painting" even though she deemed the subject unpleasant.[34] The language Alexander Slidell Mackenzie used to describe the pictures by Murillo and Velázquez he had encountered in the Prado and that he published in his *Spain Revisited* (1836) is much the same. Impressed by the work of both artists, Slidell considered Velázquez the "greater genius" but recognized that he had derived "more pleasure" from Murillo.[35]

As subjective as these reactions may strike us today, these travelers were not alone in writing about art in such a personalized way. However, somewhat more objective accounts could be found in Juan Agustín Ceán Bermúdez's *Diccionario histórico de los más ilustres profesores de las bellas artes en España* (1800), as well as Louis Viardot's *Notices sur les principaux peintres de l'Espagne* (1839), but the readers of these works were mostly specialists. Something of a breakthrough occurred in 1848 when William Stirling-Maxwell's *Annals of the Artists of Spain* first appeared. A Scottish writer and connoisseur, Stirling-Maxwell reportedly developed his interest in Spanish artists during his first visit to the Prado in 1842, although it is likely that he had also seen works by Murillo and other Spanish artists in the Louvre's Spanish gallery. Three years later he was back in Madrid and then Seville, and he purchased engravings of some of the pictures he saw with an eye toward writing a book about Spanish art. The *Annals*, published in three substantial volumes, was the result. Though riddled with errors, the *Annals* represented the first comprehensive, English-language survey of the subject —it was also the first to employ an early photographic technique known as talbotypes to illustrate the pictures described in the text—and it remained standard reading, for collectors and critics alike, for decades to come. Stirling-Maxwell (1815–78) was also a collector—his collection still can be seen in Glasgow's Pollok House, his family's ancestral home— and the author of *Velázquez and His Works* (1855), the first monograph exclusively devoted to this artist.[36]

As for the Americans able to visit the Prado and appreciate its holdings in Spanish art, the *libros de apuntes* (visitors' registers) housed in the museum's archives offer an invaluable guide. These registers— they begin in 1846 and end in the early 1870s—record the names, places of origin, and profession of foreigners and certain other visitors who toured the collection, and together they provide a fascinating (although still understudied) glimpse of those individuals who visited the Prado during that era. These visitors ranged from Spanish workers taking a day off to admire their country's artistic treasures to important foreign dignitaries, as well as such literary luminaries as Théophile Gautier—he signed the book on October 5, 1846, and again on July 18, 1864—and Hans Christian Andersen (he signed on December 8, 1862). Another noteworthy visitor was the French artist Édouard Manet. His visit to the Prado on September 1, 1865, apparently contributed to his decision to employ a style reminiscent of that of Velázquez and to execute a series of important canvases featuring bullfights and other Spanish themes.[37]

Mingling with these Europeans was a small but steady stream of Americans. By the time Manet visited the Prado, an average of one hundred or so Americans were visiting the Prado on an annual basis. Among those who can be easily identified are John Jacob Astor III—he signed the register together with four traveling companions on February 11, 1845—and the writer William Cullen Bryant—he was there in January 1857 and recorded his impressions of what he saw in an essay published New York's *Evening Post*. That essay failed to mention Velázquez, praised Murillo, and complained about the lack of landscapes in the Spanish school, curiously attributing their absence to Spain's lack of "country life."[38] Another noteworthy visitor was Millard Fillmore. The former president and his wife signed the register on February 23, 1866, together with Horatio Perry, the secretary of the U.S. legation in Madrid, and John L. O'Sullivan, the Democratic politician whose belief in "manifest destiny" had previously led to his support of Narciso López's filibustering expeditions to Cuba. Another distinguished visitor was Henry Adams, who toured the museum on February 18, 1869, but whose impressions of the Spanish pictures he saw there remain unknown.[39]

In general the Americans visiting the Prado in the mid-nineteenth century were much like the ones who toured the Alhambra: wealthy businessmen hailing from East Coast cities, especially Boston, Philadelphia, and New York; diplomats attached to the American legation in

Madrid; a handful of artists, lawyers, students, and professors; and others who simply identified themselves as gentlemen and *rentiers* who tended more often than not to visit the museum in small clusters comprising both family and friends. A few came from California, the South, and the Midwest. One gentleman from New York, insulted by the thought of having to state his profession, simply wrote, "None." Others opted for anonymity, referring to themselves simply as "traveler," although starting in the 1850s, a few opted for the word "tourist."[40]

The reactions of these visitors to what they saw in the Prado are, like Irving's, difficult to assess. William Cullen Bryant was favorably impressed, as was Severn Teackle Wallis, whose Hispanophilia rendered him incapable of writing anything too critical of Spain, let alone its art. These positive assessments of the Spanish school clashed with those of an author identified only by the initials E.L. (possibly Elias Lyman Magoon, a writer known for essays on a variety of religious themes), who was the author of the article "Spain, Her Ways, Her Women, and Her Wines," published in 1850. E.L. attributed the predominance of religious themes in Spanish art to national character, or what the writer called Spain's "national spirit," which E.L. claimed was fixed during the course of the Middle Ages and especially by the Reconquest, the centuries-long struggle to expel Muslims from Iberian soil. Together with Ticknor, Prescott, and other writers of the era, E.L. romanticized the Reconquest and exaggerated its importance to the point that it became the key determinant of a national spirit that supposedly incorporated certain war-like elements—defiance, independence—along with religious intolerance and hate. Blended together, this peculiar admixture accounted for the "indelible tone of intense fervor and severe simplicity" E.L. equated with Spanish art. The writer then added that this tone, canonized by the Church and the Inquisition, ultimately denied Spanish artists access to "the heaven-born inspiration of beauty" associated with Italian art. Such observations led to the conclusion that "Spanish art . . . became confined to its narrowest channel, and preying upon itself, fell, as it were into a monomania" that focused on "solemn friars, grim warriors, and stiff, haughty courtiers, legends of impossible miracles . . . [and] the most impressive episodes in the history of Christianity."[41]

"Monomania" seems a bit harsh but only marginally different from other contemporary assessments of Spanish art, especially those by American critics. Influenced by the Black Legend, these writers tended to judge the value of any work of art as the direct by-product of the society in which it was produced, and for this reason few had anything positive to say about any Spanish artist, with the notable exception made for Murillo. This certainly applies to John Hay, the diplomat we have encountered in previous chapters and whose views on Spanish art appeared in his book *Castilian Days* (1871). As noted earlier, Hay had little positive to say about Spain's politicians, let alone its national character, which in his view comprised an odd mixture of "Northern individualism and Latin association" and consequently rendered the country unsuitable for republican forms of government. That same combination of racial traits permeated Hay's description of the character of the pictures in the Prado's Spanish gallery and alluded to the "forbidding" array of "prim portraits of queens and princes, monks in contemplation, and holy people," together with an "indefinable air of severity and gloom." In keeping with this generalization, Hay offered more detailed descriptions of some of the pictures he found there, among them Jusepe de Ribera's *Prometheus* (a "picture of horrible power") and another featuring a "*chiarascuro* [*sic*] monk," possibly Zurbarán's *Apparition of Saint Peter to Saint Peter Nolasco*, and one he dismissed as a "gloomy and terrible work." Hay had more positive things to say about Velázquez, "with his steady devotion to truth," and Murillo, on account of "his virile devotion to beauty" and ability to paint "the perfect feminine," yet his overall impression of Spanish art was preconditioned by Black Legend themes. Thus this remark: "there is the dim suggestion of the fag[g]ot and [the] rack about many of the Spanish masters."[42]

The reaction of H. (Henry) Willis Baxley (1803–76), a medical doctor with a penchant for travel writing, was much the same. Having visited the Prado in 1872, Baxley compiled his thoughts about Spanish art and published them three years later in his book *Spain: Art-Remains and Art-Realities* (1875). He admired Murillo's pictures but criticized most of those by Velázquez, describing him as "a copyist, not a creator." Baxley especially disliked what he referred to as the "besotted sensualism" of this artist's *Borrachos*, a composition he called "a vulgar carousel, a triumph of drunkenness," and that he dismissed as "a piece of realism well suited to his [Velázquez's] talents."[43]

Additional fuel for these prejudices derived from the British art critic John Ruskin (1819–1900). Ruskin's ideas about the "organic" unity linking individual artists with the society they inhabited influenced generations of art criticism in the United States. Equally influential was Ruskin's idea that great art could flourish only in democratic or republican societies as opposed to aristocratic and autocratic regimes.

For these reasons Ruskin was particularly drawn to artists who worked in the city-states and republics of medieval Italy, and the same was true of most of his followers in North America, among them Harvard's Charles Eliot Norton and Yale's James M. Hoppin, two of the founders of art historical studies in the United States.[44]

Another influential art critic (and collector) who adopted Ruskin's ideas was James Jackson Jarves (1818–88). Jarves expressed his ideas about art in *Art-Idea* (1864), which articulated the notion that the art of a particular society reflected the "underlying spirit" of the times. He subsequently refined and elaborated on this idea in *Art Thoughts* (1874), in which Jarves emphasized that "art itself is less dependent on blood or climate than on intellectual influences." In keeping with this premise, as well as his deep-seated hatred of the Catholic Church and a somewhat exaggerated view of Spain as a country where "the temporal and ecclesiastical powers acting in conjunction have sufficient force to stifle every manifestation of the popular will not acceptable them," Jarves used *Art Thoughts* to reduce the entire Spanish school of art to what he called "the lowest ascetic standard, scarcely one grade above fetishism."[45] He then dismissed its importance as anything worthy of serious study:

> We need not look for the poetical or imaginative in Spanish art; seldom for very refined treatment, and never for any intellectual elevation above the actual life out of which it drew its restricted stock-motives. What could be expected of painting in a country where masked inquisitors visited every studio and either destroyed

and daubed over any details that did not accord with their fanatical scruples of sculpture which was dressed or painted to imitate actual life, and where an artist could not destroy the labor of his own hands, if [*sic*] a sacred image, without risk of being put to torture for sacrilege? There are admirable points in Spanish painting, but it is not a school of popular value or interest. Besides its two chief names [Velázquez and Murillo] it has no reputation beyond its own locality. The fixed purpose of its priest-ridden work was to stultify the human intellect and make life a burden instead of a blessing.[46]

Jarves's dismissal of Spanish art went further than most, partly because his preferences ran toward Italian art, but he was by no means alone. The popularity of Ruskin's ideas about the "organic" unity of art and society, as well as the prevailing view of Spain as a country and a culture crippled by the absence of political liberty, the powerful Catholic Church, and an excess of popular religious zeal, combined to influence the views of American visitors to the Prado and to enable that handful who wrote about their experiences there to find similar qualities in the country's art. One writer, arguing deductively from Jarves's "underlying spirit" of the times, asserted that Spanish painters shared a special "capacity for conviction" that accounted for the singular "fervor of devotion "and "intensity of supplication" of their art.[47]

This same cocktail of ideas seemingly influenced Henry James's attitudes toward Spanish art when in 1874 he wrote a critical review of Spanish pictures then being exhibited at the Boston Athenaeum. The pictures in question belonged to Antoine Marie d'Orléans, Duke of Montpensier (1824–90), the youngest son of Louis-Philippe of France and the husband of a Spanish princess. Partly as a way of safeguarding his collection during a moment of political turmoil in Spain, the duke had been hoping to exhibit his collection, customarily housed in Seville, in London, but when that fell through, an American merchant arranged for them to be shipped—free of cost—to Boston. The exhibit included twenty-one Spanish pictures, including three canvases attributed to Velázquez and one Murillo. The best pictures—five featuring scenes from the childhood of Christ that the duke had acquired at the London

auction of his father's pictures in 1852—were those by Zurbarán, an
artist then virtually unknown in the United States.

The Montpensier pictures represented the first major exhibition of
Spanish art in the United States, and partly for this reason newspapers in
Boston, New York, Chicago, and even faraway San Francisco reported
on it. Yet critics, quite rightly as it turned out, disagreed over the quality and condition of the pictures on view. James's review, published in
the *Atlantic Monthly* in November 1874, was by far the most critical.
James had never visited the Prado, and his one visit to Spain, in 1876,
was limited to the time he crossed the border from Biarritz to attend a
bullfight in the nearby Basque town of Irun.

On the other hand, after having embarked on a grand tour of Europe
in 1869 with Charles Eliot Norton, James had become familiar with
the continent's major museums and had seen pictures by Murillo and
Velázquez in London's Wallace Collection, as well as Velázquez's portrait of Pope Innocent X in the Doria-Pamphili palace in Rome. James
was also an admirer of Ruskin and for this reason not especially inclined
toward Spanish art, noting at the outset of his review that visitors to the
Montpensier exhibit ought not to expect very much since, compared to
other European schools, "the Spanish school is of all the schools the
least valuable," although he expressed some admiration for the "noble
gravity and solidity" of Velázquez and described him as "one of the
most powerful of painters." For James, however, the only "gem" in the
exhibit was Murillo's *Virgin Dressed in Swaddling Clothes* (now in a private collection), which is far from that master's best. As for the three
Velázquez pictures on display, James observed that two were of "ques-
tionable authenticity" and judged a third, described as a "small head,"
much inferior to the painter's *Innocent X*. He consequently labeled it
"an admirable sketch" that would "offer a liberal education to a young
American portrait painter."[48]

James's view of the exhibit's other Spanish pictures was hardly better.
A "shadow of mediocrity" burdened those by Zurbarán, Ribera's portrait of the Cato the Younger was little more than a "disagreeable curi-
osity," and all the others were "indifferent" at best. The review ended
by thanking the duke for his "liberality" in sharing his Old Masters with

the American public but suggested that visitors should not be deceived or have any particular reverence for the pictures on view.[49]

Much of this is typically James, whose elitism and snobbishness are well known. On the other hand, his skepticism about the merits (or lack of same) of the Spanish school was nothing out of the ordinary. A similar skepticism was also attached to colonial-era pictures from Mexico and other parts of Spanish America. U.S. collectors, especially those of Protestant background, found it difficult to stomach the religious character of many of these pictures, the majority of which were originally commissioned by churches and convents. Nor did they much like the staid portraits of Spanish prelates and viceroys, let alone those featuring nuns, another well-established colonial-era artistic subject. For this reason, Spanish-American colonial art was virtually unknown in the United States, which helps to explain why Henry Adams, on a visit to Mexico in 1894, expressed surprise about the sheer number of pictures he encountered in Puebla, Mexico City, Guadalajara, and other cities. "In Guadalajara alone," he wrote, "[there is] more good art than in all our cities altogether, putting museums and collections out of the question." Adams quickly added, however, that is "it is baroque and Spanish, and altogether sweet and decadent," and evidently not to his taste, undoubtedly on account of the overwhelmingly religious (read Catholic) character of the pictures he saw.[50]

One American with a more positive assessment of these pictures was Robert H. Lamborn (1835–95), a civil engineer who lived in Mexico from 1881 to 1883 and supervised the construction of several railways. A collector with wide-ranging artistic and ethnographic interests, Lamborn owned examples of pre-Columbian pottery, Egyptian and Etruscan antiquities, and coins, especially those made of copper, a metal he especially liked. As Clara Bargellini has explained, Lamborn's fascination with copper may also explain his interest in colonial-era pictures, many of which were painted on thin copper sheets as opposed to canvas.[51] But whether it was a question of copper, style, or subject matter, Lamborn assembled a collection of approximately eighty colonial Mexican paintings and prints, including a portrait of the famous seventeenth-century nun Sor Juana Inés de la Cruz; another, painted on copper, of Santa

Rosa de Lima, the first New World saint; and a religious painting by the eighteenth-century Mexican artist Miguel de Cabrera.

Upon leaving Mexico in 1883, Lamborn had his collection shipped to New York and temporarily deposited at the Metropolitan Museum of Art, evidently hoping to persuade its director to put them on permanent display. That director, Luigi (or Louis) Palma di Cesnola (1832–1904), had other ideas. Son of an Italian nobleman who immigrated to New York in 1858, Cesnola had served as a colonel in the Union army during the Civil War. He was later appointed U.S. consul in Cyprus, where he supervised archaeological excavations at various ancient Greek sites and in doing so amassed a substantial collection of antique pottery that he sold to the Met in 1872. Seven years later the Met's trustees, impressed by Cesnola's archaeological credentials, appointed him to be the museum's first full-time director.

According to the Met's 1870 charter, the museum had been established for the purpose of "encouraging and developing the study of the fine arts, and the application of arts to manufacture and practical life, of advancing the general knowledge of kindred subjects, and, to that end, of furnishing popular instruction."[52] The charter did not define "fine arts," but at the start of the Gilded Age and in keeping with Ruskin's artistic ideas, the term was virtually synonymous with antiquities and European art. According to Charles C. Perkins (1823–86), a wealthy art critic who figured among the founders of the Museum of Fine Arts, Boston, in 1870, that institution was "to aim at collecting material for the education of a nation in art." The art in question was to help "refine and elevate" the nation's taste, and for Perkins this translated into a collection organized around the art and sculpture of Europe, starting in the ancient Mediterranean and then proceeding through the Middle Ages, Renaissance, and so on. In such a scheme, the art of colonial Mexico seemingly had little or nothing to offer.[53]

As the Met's first director, Cesnola rarely made any public pronouncements about either art or museums. Yet his readiness to give his Cypriot collections pride of place when the Met moved to its new Fifth Avenue building in 1880 suggests that Cesnola's understanding of "fine art" seemingly approximated that of Perkins. So when Lamborn offered to donate his collection of Mexican art to the Met in 1888, Cesnola said no. Lamborn, a native Philadelphian, immediately turned to the Pennsylvania Museum of Art, whose curator, Dalton Dorr, readily accepted the donation with the promise that the Mexican pictures and pottery were to be placed on public display. With that expectation, Lamborn wrote and paid for the publication of *Mexican Paintings and Painters* (1891), the first book on the subject by an American author and one that included a catalog of his collection. In the book's introduction Lamborn contended that Mexican painting constituted "a memorable chapter in the record of human culture," and later in the book, cognizant no doubt of the cold shoulder he had received in New York, he groused openly about the "conspiracy of silence" surrounding the "the Mexican branch of the great Spanish school."[54] Such a conspiracy probably never existed, although the New York publisher and bookseller J. W. Bouton, in his review of the book, questioned whether Mexican painting was as "memorable" as Lamborn maintained.[55]

Whether Dalton Dorr's assessment of the artistic and educational value of Mexican painting accorded with Bouton's is difficult to judge. For several years Lamborn and Dorr discussed how his Mexican pictures and pottery might be best displayed. A photograph from around 1892 suggests that the paintings, together with other objects from Lamborn's collection, were housed together in what resembled a small study room—notice that in the photograph one of the vitrine's glass doors is open and various objects are on the floor—as opposed to one of the museum's public galleries. Lamborn's correspondence with Dorr indicates his desire to have all Mexican objects gathered in a single "Mexican" room for the purpose of illustrating the "civilization . . . from which they were drawn." Dorr had other ideas, and despite negotiations that continued until Lamborn's death in 1895, the Mexican pictures appear to have remained where they were—in the room shown in the photograph.[56]

What happened next is difficult to track. Following Dorr's death in 1900, the museum appointed a new curator, Edwin Atlee Barber (1851–1916), an archaeologist with a particular interest in ceramics and pottery. He also embraced the German notion of *Kulturgeschichte* and the idea that art objects should be displayed in coherent historical rooms designed

Fig. 34. Robert Lamborn Collection, ca. 1890. Photographer unknown. Lamborn pioneered the collecting of Spanish colonial art in the United States. Having donated his collection to Philadelphia's art museum, he is depicted here along with Dalton Dorr, the museum's director. Philadelphia Museum of Art.

to highlight the particular character of the countries and cultures where they originated. In keeping with this idea and drawing upon his museum's own collections and various loans, in 1910 Barber created several "period" rooms, among them a seventeenth-century English room, two American colonial rooms, and even a seventeenth-century "Spanish room" fitted out with a carved wooden ceiling along with several pieces of Spanish furniture, wall-hangings, and so forth.

How did Lamborn's Mexican objects fit into this scheme? Barber's new period rooms were consistent with the "Mexican room" Lamborn had envisioned when he first donated his collection to the Pennsylvania museum. As with Dorr before him, however, Barber resisted such a grouping, evidently because he regarded these objects, especially the colonial-era pictures, as being short on both "culture" and "refinement." As a result he treated these pictures more like problematic foster children who could be easily moved about—from the museum's music room where in 1903 several were displayed somewhat incongruously alongside a sixteenth-century harpsichord, armor, and display cases with coins and subsequently in the museum's north corridor, which served as a kind of catch-all space crammed with cases filled with metalwork, wax seals, and other small objects, as well as several antique cannons. Extant museum records do not account for these moves, but it appears that Barber did not subscribe to Lamborn's notion that "the Mexican branch of the great Spanish school" deserved a space of its own.[57]

The Spanish Turn

If the "Mexican branch of the great Spanish school" was slow to take root in Philadelphia and museums in other American cities, other expressions of that school, as Barber's "Spanish room" suggests, met with increasing success. An early indicator of progress occurred in 1900, when the trustees of the Pennsylvania Museum of Art, acting on the recommendation of the prominent Philadelphia collector John G. Johnson, agreed to purchase a *Crucifixion* by El Greco. The picture in question was not to everyone's taste (see below), but the acquisition suggests that some of the prejudices previously surrounding the appreciation of Spanish art were beginning to soften. Was the Black Legend dead? Hardly. But attitudes about the inherent inferiority of the Spanish school changed as more and more Americans, whether through travel or through reading, learned about its art.

Much of the impetus for these changes came from artists who, following their French counterparts, had "discovered" Spanish Old Master art. The date of this discovery is difficult to pinpoint, but it predates the Civil War. It was then that Charles C. Perkins—the same Perkins who later helped to establish the Boston museum—left his studio in Paris in 1854 in order to visit Spain and learn about its art. Once there he paid

Fig. 35. El Greco (and Workshop?), *Crucifixion*, ca. 1610. When Philadelphia's art museum purchased this picture by El Greco in 1900, it marked the beginning of an important trend. Other museums and wealthy collectors quickly followed the Philadelphia museum's lead. Philadelphia Museum of Art.

homage to Velázquez and copied his work.[58] Other artists, as noted in the previous chapter, soon followed suit, among them Thomas Eakins and Mary Cassatt.[59]

Velázquez loomed even larger in the career of John Singer Sargent (1856–1925). Sargent's parents had taken him as a five-year-old child to Spain in 1861, but it was only later, when he was an art student in Paris, that he became interested in Spanish art. Sargent returned to Spain on an extended visit in 1879, mainly to study the paintings by Velázquez in the Prado. Once there, and as the museum's records indicate, Sargent made of copy of Velázquez's most famous composition, *Las Meninas*; that copy is now in a private British collection. Sargent returned to the Prado on numerous other occasions to copy other works by Velázquez, and in 1895 he made a special trip to copy works by El Greco.

Another influential artist especially enamored with Velázquez was William Merritt Chase (1849–1916). Chase first traveled to Spain in 1881, and, like many other U.S. artists (see chapter 3), he went there in search of picturesque themes. Following his initial encounter with the Velázquez pictures he saw in the Prado, Chase announced that Velázquez was "the greatest painter that ever lived."[60]

In the years that followed, Chase, by now one of New York's leading artists, returned to the Prado again and again, and starting in the 1890s he led groups of art students to the museum so that they too could have the opportunity to study and learn about Velázquez and his technique. Photographs of Chase's Tenth Street Studio reveal that he decorated it with copies of Velázquez's work. Chase moved about the city, presenting lectures on the merits of Spanish art, at least one of which addressed the "sublime example of Velázquez."[61] Chase's admiration for Velázquez also extended to his wife and family, who dressed up in costumes modeled after those featured in *Las Meninas* and then appeared in *tableaux vivants* inspired by that famous painting.[62] I shall return to Chase's ideas about Velázquez and Spanish artists below, as they were essential in helping to initiate the "Spanish turn" among art collectors and connoisseurs in the United States.

One early but tangible sign of this shift in taste occurred in August 1882, when the wealthy New York banker and collector Henry G. Marquand (1819–1902) learned that an art dealer in London was selling a portrait, *Prince Baltasar Carlos*, by Velázquez. Marquand immediately wrote a letter, informing the dealer, "I am crazy for that Velázquez," and he soon purchased it for 2,000 British pounds, roughly $9,740. Over the next five years Marquand acquired another three canvases attributed (erroneously) to Velázquez, in addition to a picture of the archangel Michael that a dealer in Cádiz identified as a genuine Zurbarán. (The alleged Zurbarán work *Saint Michael the Archangel* is now in the Met and attributed to another Sevillian artist, Ignacio de Ries.) Marquand also purchased another four pictures believed to be by the hand of Velázquez, a sure sign that this collector, otherwise known for his interest in important work by Dutch masters (Marquand was the first American to acquire a genuine Vermeer) and Flemish artists such as Van Dyck, had acquired at least some affinity for Spanish art. Other collectors were soon to follow in his path.[63]

In April 1889 Pedro Alcántara de Borbón y Braganza, Duke of Dúrcal and a close relative of Alfonso XIII, the infant king of Spain, arrived in New York. Hoping to take advantage of what one newspaper had referred to as "the race for Old Master" pictures among American collectors, the duke brought with him his family's collection of drawings and paintings with the idea of placing the entire lot up for auction at the headquarters of the American Art Association, then located in Chickering Hall on the busy corner of Eighteenth Street and Fifth Avenue in Manhattan. The sale included works attributed to such well-known Spanish artists as Murillo, Velázquez, and Zurbarán, along with others still relatively new to American collectors, such as El Greco, Juan Carreño de Miranda, Juan de Juanes, Juan Labrador, Antonio de Pereda, and so on. Lucy Wharton Drexel, wife of the financier Joseph W. Drexel, came away with two pictures: an infant Christ attributed to Murillo, and an *Agnus Dei* supposedly by Zurbarán, whereas Dr. W. Duncan McKim, a prominent physician whose writings about eugenics and the dynamics of race remain controversial today, purchased at the bargain price of $1,000 an equestrian portrait of the Count-Duke of Olivares attributed (wrongly it seems) to Velázquez. On the other hand, many of the pictures that one reporter attributed to "obscure Spanish artists," El Greco among them, did not sell.[64]

Much the same can be said of the auction of another collection sponsored by the American Art Association at the beginning of April the following year. Brought to New York by Francesc Guiu i Gabalda, a paint manufacturer from Barcelona, the collection contained Spanish and Italian works, along with some Flemish pictures, in addition to ceramics, embroideries, furniture, and more—more than twelve hundred objects in all. From the outset critics doubted the authenticity of many of the items Guiu had brought to New York. A *Times* article headlined "Queer Old Pictures" questioned the attributions given to the Old Master pictures, called the one Spanish colonial picture in the collection "bad beyond conception" and suggested that "the collection resembles, indeed, the contents of several bric à brac shops in some moldy old town of Spain."[65] The anonymous critic was right, as most of the objects up for sale, starting with the jeweled Renaissance cask marketed as having belonged to Columbus, either turned out to be modern fakes or spurious attributions. A few items found buyers—William Schaus, the art dealer who had discovered the stolen Murillo some years before, purchased the alleged Columbus casket for a little more than $1,000—as did the pictures attributed to Murillo and Velázquez. Otherwise the Guiu sale did little to further the demand for or enhance the reputation of Spanish art.[66]

Enter now Isabella Stewart Gardner (1840–1924), whose acquisitions of Spanish pictures and, equally important, the manner in which she displayed them, created a pattern other collectors would emulate. Gardner's interests in both Spain and Spanish artists derived in large part from her friendship with John Singer Sargent. Acting, it seems, on Sargent's advice, in 1888 Mrs. Gardner and her husband embarked on an extended visit to Spain, mainly to learn more about its art. Traveling by rail from Paris, they began their journey by visiting Burgos and then Madrid, where Gardner documented her visit (or visits) to the Prado with photos of pictures by Velázquez, Murillo, Ribera, and Zurbarán that she later incorporated into a travel scrapbook meant to serve as an aide-mémoire. The couple's next stop was Seville, where they lingered for almost six weeks—visiting churches and convents along with that city's museum, witnessing its haunting Holy Week processions, attending bullfights, and even participating in the annual springtime festival, or *feria*, photographs of which (in Gardner's scrapbook) show her lunching with members of the local elite. Gardner also used Seville as a base to visit other Andalucian cities, including Granada, where, in addition to visiting the Alhambra, she attended a performance of a gypsy dance, and Córdoba, to visit that city's famous mosque. She subsequently returned to Madrid, using the capital as base to make side trips to Lisbon, Salamanca, Segovia (with its great Roman aqueduct), and León, along with the Escorial and Toledo, where she visited the parish church of Santo Tomé in order to pay homage to El Greco's masterpiece, *The Burial of the Count of Orgaz*. Gardner exited the country at Barcelona before returning to Boston via Paris and New York.

The scrapbook documenting this visit underscores the extent to which Gardner succumbed to the same fever that plagued other foreigners who visited Spain. In addition to featuring photographs illustrating the places she visited, the pictures she saw, and the people she met, it records how quickly Gardner warmed to the culture and customs of Spain. "Quien dice España," she writes, "dice todo" (Spain says it all). Seville in particular caught her fancy. "Here one *feels* existence," she noted. An existential experience? Signs of the same fever that Sargent diagnosed? Perhaps both.[67]

Prior to visiting Spain, Gardner was already a collector, but she had limited her purchases to paintings by Sargent, James Whistler, and other contemporary artists. In Seville she bought her first Old Master: a *Virgin of Mercy* attributed to Zurbarán that she subsequently hung in the private parlor of her Boston home.

That acquisition is important, as it marked the beginning of Gardner's Spanish turn and, to a certain extent, that of other American collectors as well. Together with Marquand, however, Gardner was ahead of the curve. Her tastes were eclectic, and throughout her collecting career she aimed at acquiring examples of the work of Europe's most famous artists, including Raphael, Rembrandt, Titian, and Vermeer. But following her visit to Spain and the acquisition of the Zurbarán, she determined to buy more Spanish pictures, making her preferences known to Bernard Berenson, even though this connoisseur generally considered Spanish art far inferior to that of Italy. Yet Gardner persisted, writing Berenson

Fig. 36. Patio de la Fonda de Madrid, Seville. Isabella Stewart Gardner Travel Album: 4:15, Spain, 1888. Already a seasoned traveler, Gardner visited Spain in 1888. She especially liked Seville, noting, "Here one *feels* existence." The trip also led to her first purchase of a Spanish picture—*Madonna and Child*, by the seventeenth-century artist Francisco de Zurbarán. Isabella Stewart Gardner Museum, Boston.

in 1895 that she was interested in a *"very* good" Velázquez in addition to pictures by Filippino Lippi and Tintoretto. The following year Berenson found her a portrait by Velázquez—now known as studio piece—which she bought at the asking price of just over $36,000.

At this point Berenson got the message and began a search for other Spanish pictures that might interest her. In 1901 Gardner was ready to acquire another Velázquez—another portrait of Philip IV—that Berenson had located in London, but Boston's Museum of Fine Arts managed to buy it first. Three years later Berenson recommended she acquire an *Adoration of the Magi* by El Greco that he had found in a Paris gallery. The picture, he wrote, was the "best Greco that is ever to be sold," but he warned Gardner that she needed to act quickly as there were other American buyers, Huntington among them, looking at it as well. Gardner was tempted but considered the asking price of $40,000 to be "preposterous" and "impossible" for her to afford.[68]

Gardner never got that picture—El Greco's *Adoration of the Magi*, one of the artist's last works. It went the following year to New York's Metropolitan Museum of Art at the discount price of $35,000. In 1905, however, still determined to add another Velázquez to her collection, she paid more than $96,000 for a portrait of Pope Innocent VIII that Berenson attributed to Velázquez and described to her as a "whacker." Berenson was wrong: the picture was actually a seventeenth-century copy, not an authentic work.[69]

As for her other Spanish pictures, Gardner generally fared better when she acted on her own instincts as opposed to relying on Berenson. In 1900, for example, she purchased an exquisite panel painting, *Santa Engracia*, by the fifteenth-century artist Bartolomé Bermejo, that she is likely to have seen in Rome. Next came her acquisition in 1906 of Zurbarán's stately portrait *Doctor of Laws at Salamanca*, a picture she saw at New York's Ehrich Galleries, which had come to specialize in Spanish art. She wrote Berenson straight away, describing the picture as "splendid" and one she had acquired "just of pure love! . . . I do like the young Salamanca student!" She also took pride in having bought the picture from under the nose of other collectors, crowing that she "snapped it up just in time to prevent Mr H[untington] getting it for his Spanish Museum, or Mr Philip Lydig [another New York collector] for his red room! Mr H is cursing himself for his delay, for he saw it months ago."[70]

Even before this Zurbarán entered the collection, Gardner, perhaps recalling her time in Seville, was planning to "hispanicize" Fenway Park, her ornate Venetian-styled residence-cum-museum. She did so with a series of renovations that incorporated a new, Spanish-themed cloister and an adjacent Spanish-style chapel into the building's ground floor. As Ellen Prokop has explained, Gardner envisioned the new cloister as the ideal setting for John Singer Sargent's *El Jaleo*, his haunting picture of a Spanish gypsy dancing in a Sevillian café and one that Henry James judged comparable in quality to a Velázquez. Gardner had seen the picture in Paris shortly after its completion in 1882, but, as noted earlier, it was purchased by Thomas Jefferson Coolidge, one of her relatives by marriage. By constructing the cloister, outfitted with a Hispano-Moresque-style window, more than two thousand colorful Mexican tiles, and other objects that were not necessarily Spanish but meant to evoke a Spanish mood, she hoped to persuade Coolidge either to sell her the picture or donate it to her. The plan worked. When Coolidge first saw the completed cloister in 1915, he reportedly "gave Isabella the picture, there and then." As for the Spanish chapel, it too was a hybrid, mixing stained glass from the north of Europe with a fifteenth-century recumbent marble figure of a Spanish knight she had bought in Paris in 1906, but Gardner designed it as the appropriate setting for her first Spanish picture: the Zurbarán she had acquired in 1888.[71]

Opening the Market

My account of Gardner's Spanish collecting is far too brief, but what Gardner seemingly began, other collectors, ignoring the earlier criticisms of Jarves and James, would continue. Help here came from the English art critic R. A. M. Stevenson, whose *Art of Velázquez* (1895) touted the influence of the Spanish master upon such modern artists as Courbet, Manet, Monet, Whistler, Degas, and Sargent.[72] Stevenson's book quickly attracted the attention of a number of prominent New York art critics, especially Royal Cortissoz (1869–1948)—one of his

Fig. 37. The Spanish Chapel, Fenway Court, Boston, ca. 1926. Adjacent to Fenway Court's Spanish Cloister, this chapel, dedicated to Isabella Stewart Gardner's deceased son, speaks to her continuing fascination with Spain. It contained a sixteenth-century Spanish altar front, Zurbarán's *Madonna and Child*, and (not shown) the tomb sculpture of a Spanish knight. Isabella Stewart Gardner Museum, Boston.

ancestors was Spanish—and Russell Sturgis (1836–1906), who together helped popularize what William Merritt Chase pointedly referred to in an 1896 lecture as the "extreme modernism" of Velázquez's work.[73] Further excitement for Spanish pictures came from the exhibition of several hundred Spanish Old Master pictures in London's New Gallery in 1895–96. That exhibition, the first of its kind in England, received wide press coverage in the United States, including a lengthy and favorable review in *American Architect and Building News*, a professional journal published in Boston and distributed nationwide.[74]

But whether it was a question of criticism, one of taste, or some combination of the two, collectors did not hesitate to follow Gardner into the Spanish turn. Among the first to do so was a wealthy Philadelphian named Peter A. B. Widener (1834–1915), who began life as a butcher, later founded the Philadelphia Tractor Company, and made a fortune investing in cable and trolley cars in cities nationwide. As a collector, Widener's taste initially ran toward contemporary French pictures, but he reportedly became interested in Spanish art following his acquisition of Édouard Manet's *Dead Toreador* in 1894. Widener's first recorded purchase of a Spanish picture was Murillo's *Gallegas*, an enchanting, mildly provocative genre piece of two women in a window (now *Two Women in a Window*, National Gallery of Art) he purchased at an estate sale in England in 1894. Next came a trio of works identified as genuine pictures by Velázquez—a portrait, *Infanta María Teresa*; a small version of the artist's *Los Borrachos* (The drinkers) in the Prado; and *Satyr and Travelers*, but as Widener soon discovered, all were either copies or by other artists. Widener had a similarly negative experience with two supposed Goya pictures and another two attributed to El Greco, all of which he "de-accessed" in relatively short order.

After these initial mistakes, Widener finally got it right in October 1906 with the acquisition of El Greco's *St. Martin and the Beggar* and *Madonna and Child with Saint Martina and Saint Agnes*, both previously part of an altarpiece ensemble in Toledo's Capilla de San José, the family chapel for which they were originally commissioned in 1597. In 1906 that chapel was still in private hands, but the family who owned it, eager for cash, arranged to sell the two pictures noted above to a French dealer,

Boussod, Valadon & Cie., which quietly arranged for their transport to Paris, which is where Widener purchased them.

When news of this acquisition leaked out, it sparked a furious debate in Spain's parliament, the Cortes, with some deputies calling for tough export controls on the nation's artistic treasures and others defending the right of private individuals and churches to dispose of these treasures as they saw fit. But as the Cortes debated this issue, Widener had his prize El Grecos shipped from Paris to his sprawling hundred-room home in the Philadelphia suburb of Elkins Park, promptly giving them pride of place in the mansion's central gallery.[75]

Next in the lengthening line for Spanish pictures was the wealthy banker and financier J. Pierpont Morgan. An avid collector of books and manuscripts, Morgan was not especially interested in pictures, but in 1896 he acquired what he thought was a genuine Velázquez portrait of the Infanta María Teresa from Agnew's in London. (It is now at the Met, where it is attributed to Juan Bautista del Mazo, a follower of Velázquez.)[76] After Morgan came the sugar magnate Henry O. Havemeyer (1847–1907) and his wife Louisine (1855–1929), two New York collectors whose interest in Spanish art was much influenced by Mary Cassatt, a friend of Louisine since childhood. The Havemeyers started collecting in the 1880s, mainly buying works by impressionists, especially Degas and Manet, both close friends of Cassatt. Cassatt, however, also had an interest in Goya, and the Havemeyers, acting on her advice, purchased a pair of Goya portraits in 1897, eventually adding to their collection another ten pictures attributed to this artist.

Cassatt's next move was to introduce the Havemeyers to El Greco, indicating in one letter to Louisine that "El Greco's merit is that he was two centuries ahead of his time, and that is why painters, Manet amongst them, thought so much of his art."[77] To help them learn more about El Greco, Cassatt took the couple to Spain in the spring of 1901, first to Madrid, then Toledo, so that the Havemeyers could have a look at El Greco's masterpiece, *The Burial of the Count of Orgaz*. When Henry first saw the picture, he is said to have remarked that it was "one of the greatest pictures I have ever seen, yes, perhaps the greatest." The picture was not for sale, but others were. In Madrid, Cassatt spotted a small

El Greco (*Christ Carrying the Cross*) in the window of an antique shop and persuaded Louisine to buy it. Thanks to Cassatt's sleuthing, the Havemeyers also had the opportunity to view other works by this artist, works that would later find their way into the Havemeyers' New York residence. They included his impressive *Portrait of a Cardinal* (acquired in 1904) and haunting *View of Toledo* (acquired in 1909). These acquisitions allowed Louisine to boast that she alone had created a market in the United States for works by these artists, or to quote her directly, "We were, so to speak, to open the market for Grecos and Goyas, at least in the United States."[78]

Louisine was not exaggerating, although additional support for the opening of that market came from New York's Ehrich Galleries, which organized the country's first-ever sale of Spanish Old Master pictures, in November 1905, and continued thereafter to cater to collectors interested in Spanish art.[79] In New York alone the list of these collectors approximated a Who's Who of the city's moneyed elite. It began with Henry Clay Frick (1849–1919), who was still living in Pittsburgh when, in the course of a visit to Spain in 1904, he acquired a small self-portrait by Murillo similar to one that he might have previously seen in London's National Gallery. The following year Frick bought El Greco's portrait of a cardinal, identified as *Saint Jerome*, from Émile Parés, a dealer in Paris. The picture had previously belonged to the Valladolid Cathedral, and its sale in 1904 to Parés sparked debate in Spanish newspapers about the right of the Church to sell pictures judged vital to the preservation of Spain's artistic patrimony (see below).

Whether Frick caught wind of that debate is unknown, but when the picture got to New York, he placed it, like a hunting trophy, above the mantel in the upstairs parlor in his sumptuous new residence on New York's Fifth Avenue. But Frick was far from through with Spanish art. Later acquisitions included two other pictures by El Greco: *Christ Driving the Money Changers from the Temple* and a portrait of Vincenzo Anastagi, both purchased in 1914; a bust-length portrait of María Teresa, Infanta of Spain, attributed to Velázquez and purchased in 1908 but traded in 1913 as the down payment for a Van Dyck after acquiring in 1911 a second, far more impressive Velázquez, which was the artist's full-length rendering *Philip IV in Red and Silver*. This buying spree ended with the acquisition of a trio of Goyas, the last of which, *The Forge*, a subject reminiscent of Frick's career in the iron and steel industry, entered his collection in 1914.[80]

Apart from Archer M. Huntington, whose search for pictures to include in his Spanish museum began in earnest around 1902 and continued until around 1915, other New Yorkers looking for top-quality Spanish art included Benjamin Altman. His collecting began in 1882 with Chinese porcelain vases, and only in 1905, after having settled into his lavish Fifth Avenue home, did Altman turn his attention to Old Master art. Rembrandt was Altman's favorite—he eventually had a dozen of this artist's pictures— but Velázquez was also high on his shopping list. Velázquez's *Supper at Emmaus* entered his collection in 1907, and as previously noted, he bought two very expensive portraits by this same artist in 1913.[81]

By then a number of other wealthy New Yorkers had also entered the race for Spanish pictures. One was Philip Lehman (1861–1947), son of the founder of the investment bank Lehman Brothers, and the other George Blumenthal (1858–1941), head of Lazard Frères, another investment firm. Blumenthal also served for a time as president of the Metropolitan Museum of Art. In 1913 Lehman acquired *Saint Jerome* by El Greco and, the following year, the Velázquez portrait of María Teresa previously owned by Frick. As for Blumenthal, he first demonstrated an interest in Spanish pictures in 1912 with the acquisition of no fewer than four canvases within a matter of months, and each was attributed to El Greco. These back-to-back purchases made news, seemingly prompting a *New York Times* article headlined "Increasing Popularity of El Greco, the Spanish Painter, among Collectors in This Country."[82]

But El Greco represented only the beginning of Blumenthal's quest for Spanish art. His most spectacular and—for Spaniards at least—most controversial acquisition was the Renaissance patio previously part of the castle of Vélez Blanco, a small town in southeastern Spain. A Parisian dealer had purchased the patio in 1904, dismantled it, and shipped it via wagon and train to Paris. One prospective buyer was Huntington, who described it in 1913 as "a piece of plunder of some interest," but he refrained from buying it, suggesting instead that the dealer offer it to William Randolph Hearst, the newspaper baron who had recently started collecting Spanish art (see below).[83] In the end the patio went to Blumenthal, who had shipped it to New York and reassembled in the interior of his new residence to give it a more "Spanish" look. His heirs later bequeathed it to the Met, where it can be seen and admired as a truly spectacular example of Spanish Renaissance architecture.

New Yorkers, however, were not the only competitors in the race for Spanish pictures. As already noted, Philadelphia's Widener was an early entrant, but another Philadelphia collector with an eye for Spanish pictures was Widener's close friend John G. Johnson (1841–1917), one of the most prominent—and wealthy—lawyers of his day. Something of an autodidact when it came to art, Johnson had eclectic tastes, and as early as 1901, while serving as trustee of the Wilstach Fund of the Pennsylvania Museum of Fine Arts (forerunner of today's Philadelphia Museum of Art), he did not hesitate to recommend the purchase of the *Crucifixion* attributed to El Greco. At the time no other North American museum owned an El Greco, partly because El Greco's unique—some critics called it "extravagant"—style of painting was just starting to catch on.

Other museums soon rushed to follow the lead of Philadelphia's museum. After months of negotiation, the Museum of Fine Arts, Boston, acquired an important El Greco portrait in 1904, and in 1905 the Met purchased his *Adoration of the Magi* for $35,000, a figure that one of the museum's supporters, in an article published in the *New York Times*, considered outrageous for what he dismissed as a hopeless jumble of carelessly drawn figures that was essentially "worthless." Such criticism figured in the Met's decision in 1906 to turn down an offer to purchase another work by El Greco—the majestic *Assumption of the Virgin* that Francis Lathrop had recommended that Huntington acquire a few years earlier. The Met's loss proved to be Chicago's gain, however. The Art Institute there acquired the picture in July 1906 and placed it on display, apparently without controversy, in January of the following year.[84]

As for Johnson's personal collection, his preferences generally ran in the direction of Dutch, Flemish, and Italian art, and he gradually assembled an astonishing array of more than twelve hundred pictures.

Fig. 38. Vélez Blanco patio. Home of George Blumenthal, New York, ca. 1920[?].
At the start of the twentieth century American collectors craved Spanish art and
antiques. Blumenthal purchased this Renaissance patio in 1913 to give his New York
mansion a more "Spanish" look. The Metropolitan Museum of Art, New York.

Of these only twenty-one were of the Spanish school. These included two attributed to Velázquez; three by El Greco—one turned out to be an out-an-out fake even though it had been recommended to him by Roger Fry, the influential English connoisseur who served for a time as the Metropolitan Museum's curator of European paintings; three Goyas, of which of only was authentic; and a smattering of works by lesser known artists such as Juan de Juanes, Luis de Vargas, and Pedro de Orrente.[85]

The difficulties Johnson encountered in acquiring genuine works by the great Spanish masters was another, albeit problematic feature of the Spanish turn. The sudden growth in demand for Spanish pictures, coupled with the skyrocketing prices collectors were willing to pay for them, flooded the market with pictures that owners and dealers believed to be genuine but, as many later discovered, turned out to be studio pieces, contemporary copies, and downright fakes reminiscent of those Guiu had put up for auction in 1890. Among the more reliable dealers was London's Lionel Harris. His Spanish Gallery, opened in 1898, served as a conduit for important works that had been recently (and generally illegally) removed from churches and convents across Spain; one previously noted example, the Cuéllar sculptures, Huntington purchased in 1906. The inventories of the Spanish Gallery are no longer extant and its sales require detailed study, but Harris used various contacts in Spain to build up his inventory in the knowledge that a Frick, or a Gardner, or a Huntington, or a Widener might soon be knocking at his door. Nor it did take long before other dealers, sensing the growing demand for Spanish art, followed his lead. They included Pau Bosch, Paul Durand-Ruel, and Jacques Seligmann and Charles Sedelmeyer, all based in Paris; Berenson in Florence; Joseph Duveen in London; and, in New York, Ehrich Galleries and Knoedler's.

One challenge that both dealers and collectors had to confront was the shortage of detailed *catalogues raisonnés* of the work of individual Spanish artists. That shortage led to a lack of consensus on which works were "genuine" and which were not. In 1883 Charles B. Curtis published his *Velázquez and Murillo: A Descriptive and Historical Catalogue*, but this work, meant to correct errors in William Stirling-Maxwell's *Annals of Spanish Art* and this same author's monograph on Velázquez, committed others of its own. The English-language translation of Carl Justi's exhaustive biography of Velázquez (1889) provided new information about this artist's life, and it was soon complemented by Aureliano de Beruete's *Velázquez* (1898), which appeared in English translation in 1906.[86] Yet many of Beruete's attributions, including one in his private collection that he expected to sell to a wealthy foreign collector, turned out to be wrong. The same was true of many of the pictures that the Spanish scholar Manuel B. Cossío attributed to El Greco in his 1908 catalog of this artist's oeuvre. Nor did any of Germany's leading art historians—the list includes Carl Justi, Wilhelm von Bode, Valerian von Loga, and Julius Meier-Graefe—who were supposedly knowledgeable about Spanish art, do much better. Equally prone to errors of judgment were those American artists claiming expertise in Spanish art, among them Sargent, Chase, and Mary Cassatt, along with Huntington's art advisor, Francis Lathrop.

Faulty judgments made for faulty deals, and these help to explain why, when it came to buying expensive Old Masters pictures, collectors such as Gardner, Huntington, and Johnson often preferred to rely on their own assessments as opposed to those of dealers anxious to make a sale. Even then mistakes were plentiful, as Huntington learned in 1906 after purchasing three works by El Greco from Charles Sedelmeyer in Paris. Of the three, only one turned out to be genuine.

Johnson and Widener made similar errors, as did William C. Van Horne (1843–1915), a wealthy American railroad executive based in Montreal. Van Horne started collecting toward the end of the nineteenth century but only entered into the Spanish turn around 1905 with a bit of a push from his artist friend William Merritt Chase. He started with El Greco's *Gentleman of the House of Leiva*, a portrait he purchased from the same Parisian dealer who had sold El Greco's *Saint Jerome* to Frick. The portrait turned out to be genuine. Over the course of the next decade Van Horne acquired a raft of other Spanish pictures, so many in fact that at the time of his death in 1915 his *New York Times* obituary noted that "Spanish art in particular interested him and holds the most prominent place in his gallery."[87] Whoever made that observation was correct. In addition to the El Greco, Van Horne had acquired a first-class Zurbarán (*Saint Casilda*, now in Museo Thyssen-Bornemisza, Madrid) that, together with a few other Spanish pictures, he proudly displayed in the central corridor of his Montreal mansion. But most of Van Horne's other Spanish acquisitions, including several works attributed to Velázquez, turned out to be either copies or fakes, at which point he withdrew from what had become a no-holds-barred competition to purchase Spanish Old Master art. In doing so, Van Horne is apt to have remembered the advice offered him in 1911 by his friend August F. Jaccaci, a writer in the process of editing a series of books on important art collections in the United States. Traveling in Europe with a friend, Jaccaci was visiting dealers in Paris when he wrote Van Horne, "There is an incredible number of poor or spurious stuff. Spanish and Flemish. Legions of Grecos and Goyas. Heaps and Heaps of triptychs and polydiptychs! But if we stayed there a while and knew real people[,] who knows, *Quien sabe?* Especially if luck was a bit in one's favor."[88] Luck, however, was not always a trustworthy companion, as many collectors like Van Horne often learned when they entered the Spanish turn.

Deering's Chateau en Espagne

Such challenges did little to deter Chicago's Charles Deering (1852–1927), a collector whose unbridled enthusiasm for Spain and its art persuaded him to acquire, quite literally, his very own castle in Spain. Born in 1852 in South Paris, Maine, Deering entered the Naval Academy at Annapolis in 1869, the same year his father founded a small manufacturing company. He soon moved the company to Evanston, Illinois, where it became the Deering Harvester Company, a giant in the field of agricultural machinery. Following twelve years in the navy, Charles began working for this company in 1881. In 1902 he began chairing the company, but he resigned in 1910 in order to devote more attention to his growing collection of art.[89]

Exactly when Deering began his collecting career is poorly documented. One letter indicates that he had a "collection of stamps" by the age of nine, but the year of his transition from postage to pictures and other objets d'art remains unknown.[90] It might have been 1876, when he first met John Singer Sargent, the artist who became his lifelong friend and whose pictures figured prominently in the collection Deering later amassed. Another possibility is 1893, when he met Anders Zorn at the World's Columbian Exposition and began acquiring drawings and then pictures by this important Swedish artist. What we know is that Deering, shortly after his initial meeting with Zorn, journeyed to Paris, ostensibly to perfect his own painting technique by studying in Zorn's studio but also to acquire works by other contemporary artists. He began with Giovanni Boldini, a Paris-based Italian painter best known for his portraits; the postimpressionist American artist James Whistler; and Ramon Casas, a bohemian Catalan artist whose work Deering first encountered in Munich in 1901 and who subsequently took him, together with Sargent, to Barcelona in 1903. Casas soon became Deering's favorite artist. He also introduced the Chicagoan to Miquel Utrillo, another Catalan artist who helped Deering acquire works by other contemporary Spanish artists, including Santiago Rusiñol, Joaquín Sorolla, Josep Maria Sert, and Ignacio Zuloaga. And while it has been suggested that Utrillo and his artist friends were largely responsible for awakening Deering's interest in Spanish Old Master painting, it is equally plausible that credit should go to Sargent, given this artist's well known fascination with Velázquez and El Greco.

The origins of Deering's Hispanophilia are difficult to trace. Writing to his friend, the Marqués de la Vega-Inclán, in 1912, Deering explained that at the time of his first visit to Spain as a midshipman in September 1873, he thought that "one day I'd like to live there."[91] Nothing about this initial visit is known, but given Deering's background and education—graduating second in his class from the Naval Academy—he was undoubtedly familiar with Irving's *Tales of the Alhambra* and, like so many other Americans of his generation, had probably read Prescott's histories as well. His friend Sargent would have told him more about Spain, almost certainly urging him to visit it as well.

As for Deering's introduction to Spanish art, that likely occurred in 1893, when the judges for the art competition in the World's Columbian Exposition honored Joaquín Sorolla with first prize for his picture *¡Otra Margarita!*, a strikingly somber composition depicting a young woman—a thief? a runaway adulteress? a prostitute?—in the clutches of Spain's feared Guardia Civil, or rural police force.[92] Sorolla was not in

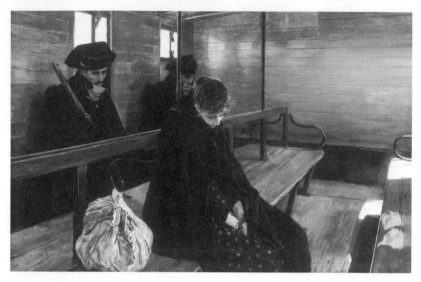

Fig. 39. Joaquín Sorolla y Bastida, *¡Otra Margarita!* (Another Marguerite!), 1892. Oil on canvas, 51 ¼ × 78 ¾ in. Charles Deering's introduction to Spanish art is likely to have begun in 1893 at the World's Columbian Exposition in Chicago, where this picture by Sorolla won first prize. Gift of Charles Nagel Sr., 1894. Mildred Lane Kemper Art Museum, Washington University in St. Louis.

Chicago to receive the prize, as he only arrived there in 1909 to accompany an exhibit of his paintings at the Art Institute. Sorolla reported that three thousand guests attended the opening reception, and Deering was almost surely in attendance.

Deering's purchases of Spanish Old Master art began in 1911. The competition for such works was sharp, but Deering's pockets were deeper than those of many other collectors and his taste almost as broad as Huntington's. But what truly distinguishes Deering from the other collectors who followed the Spanish turn was his desire to live in Spain. The place selected was Sitges, the small seaside town just south of Barcelona that he first visited, together with Casas, in 1909. Sitges was also the site of Santiago Rusiñol's Cau Ferrat, a house museum often described as a temple of Catalonia's avant-garde *moderniste* movement and a frequent gathering place for Casas, Picasso, Utrillo, Sert, Zuloaga, and other artists. The house itself was (and still is) filled to the rafters with all manner of Spanish ironwork, furniture, and other bric-a-brac, together with pictures by El Greco—one of Rusiñol's favorites—and other Spanish artists, along with examples of Rusiñol's own work. Sitges even boasted a monument to El Greco paid for by public subscription and erected in 1898.

It was love at first sight. Sitges captured Deering's fancy, and with Casas's assistance he purchased the shell of an old hospital and adjacent properties just down the street from Cau Ferrat. It was then that the fast-talking Utrillo—he knew both English and French—entered Deering's life, serving simultaneously as an architect, interior designer, and artistic advisor rolled into one.[93]

Utrillo's first project for Deering was the restoration of the hospital, renamed Maricel de Mar. It served as Deering's residence, housing his study, a sumptuous Gothic-style dining room, and other rooms decorated with pictures by Zorn, Casas, Rusiñol, Sargent, Sorolla, and Zuloaga. Also in Maricel was a series of mural paintings celebrating the allied victory in World War I; Deering had commissioned them from Josep Maria Sert in 1918. Across the narrow street—and connected by a bridge—was the refurbished building known as Maricel de Terra. It had a fanciful roof garden of Islamic design and several grand salons that together served as a museum. These showcased Deering's growing collection of Old Master pictures, along with carpets, tapestries, furniture, sculpture, and other decorative objects, the majority obtained with Utrillo's help between 1909 and 1918.

Photographic records of these galleries—the Golden Room, the Blue Room, and so on—are incomplete, and their contents shifted with time, but showpieces included a grand Gothic chimneypiece from the Aragonese town of Jaca; a pair of Goyas (*Truth, Time and History* and *Allegory of Poetry*); Zurbarán's *Saint Romanus*; and Bernat Martorell's *Saint George and the Dragon*, one of the finest examples of fifteenth-century Catalan art. The Martorell had belonged to an old Catalan family, but in July 1917 Utrillo, acting on Deering's behalf, purchased the painting for a figure estimated at somewhere between 100,000 and 350,000 pesetas (roughly $26,000 to $100,000).[94] There was also a special place in Maricel de Terra for the great fourteenth-century Ayala altarpiece from a chapel in the Basque town of Quejana—one report put it in the

Fig. 40. Maricel de Mar, Sitges, Spain. In 1911 the Chicago industrialist Charles Deering purchased a medieval hospital in the Catalan seaside town of Sitges. Subsequently refurbished and christened Maricel—Catalan for sea and sky—it housed his important collection of Spanish art. Photo by the author.

Fig. 41. Golden Room, Maricel, ca. 1915. This salon featured some of the most important objects in Charles Deering's collection. The fourteenth-century Ayala altarpiece (now in the Art Institute of Chicago) hangs on the rear wall. Courtesy Arxiu Fotogràfic de Barcelona.

"Grand Gallery," presumably the Golden Room. Also in this building were four El Grecos (though Deering claimed to have purchased no fewer than seven works by this artist); a *Saint John the Baptist in the Wilderness* bought as a Velázquez; several Murillos; an important fifteenth-century panel attributed to Fernando Gallego, one that Deering later bequeathed to Toledo's El Greco Museum; Palomino's *The Virgin Presenting the Rosary to Saint Dominic* (now in the Seattle Art Museum); and what one newspaper article referred to as an uncounted number of "Catalan, Castillian, Aragonese, Valencian and Navarrese retables."[95]

Owing to the lack of detailed inventories, it is difficult to determine the total size of Deering's collection in Sitges, although it was estimated to have been in the vicinity of four thousand objects.[96] Nor is it possible to determine exactly when and where Deering made his purchases. He and Utrillo motored around Spain on several occasions, plucking retables, frontals, and other items from churches, monasteries, and other ecclesiastical institutions in need of cash. Deering orchestrated this kind of deal in 1916 with the impoverished archbishop of Tarragona, who sold him a ruined castle in Tamarit, a town just south of Sitges. The castle was Deering's most spectacular purchase in Spain, but he used it mainly as a depository for works that did not fit into Maricel.

Other items came from dealers in Barcelona and in Madrid—Deering reportedly bought Zurbarán's *Saint Romanus* (now in the Art Institute of Chicago) from the *madrileño* antiquarian Apolinar Sánchez. He acquired others in Paris—at least two of his Goyas came from the gallery of Durand-Ruel—and in New York—Knoedler's was the source of his small version of El Greco's *Saint Martin and the Beggar*. The others, Deering once wrote, were purchased directly from their "owners," which probably means churches and monasteries he visited in Spain. Deering also had recourse to Lionel Harris, the London dealer from whom he acquired in 1913 the spectacular medieval retable known as the Ayala altarpiece. Dating from 1396 and commissioned by Don Pedro López de Ayala for a family chapel in the Dominican convent of San Juan Bautista in the small Basque town of Quejana, the circumstances of the altarpiece's removal from the chapel and how Harris then managed to acquire it remain a mystery. According to one report, Harris initially offered the altarpiece to Huntington, but when he refused, Harris sold it to Deering, who promptly installed it in Maricel.[97] In most instances, however, Deering preferred to buy his art—"to fish" (*pescar*), as he once put it—in Spain as opposed to buying through dealers such as Harris.[98]

Whatever the source of Deering's pictures, his purchases generally went through Utrillo and Casas, both of whom seemingly profited from dealers' kickbacks and by acting as intermediaries between Deering and their artist friends. This was definitely the opinion of Ignacio Zuloaga's uncle, Daniel, who in a letter to his artist nephew in February 1916 wrote, "Let's see if the American living in Sitges buys anything from you. It appears that he is sequestered there by Utrillo and Casas. He is a multimillionaire and does not do anything except what Utrillo and Casas tell him to do."[99]

Sequestered may not be the right term to describe this artistic ménage à trois, but Utrillo took full advantage of Deering's absences, when he was back in the United States. Surviving letters suggest that Deering had entrusted the Catalan with the equivalent of a power of attorney that entitled him to supervise Maricel's restoration as well as to purchase works of art, property, and more. But Utrillo proved both unscrupulous and corrupt; whenever Deering was away, Utrillo reportedly behaved as if Maricel were actually his. He appropriated for himself entire rooms, even the wine cellar, in addition to lining his own pockets with money Deering had presumably set aside for other purposes.

Matters came to head after the end of World War I in 1918, when Deering and his wife, Marion Whipple, returned to Sitges with the idea of retiring there and making Maricel their permanent home. Signs of an impending bust-up began after Utrillo—a "reptile-like" creature, according to one Spanish observer—refused to sign certain papers connected to Deering's plan to create a foundation and cede Maricel and all of its art to the Spanish state for the purpose of creating "a great art center in which artists and students of art would come from all [over] the world to study and produce works of art."[100] Mrs. Deering and Utrillo were soon at loggerheads—one letter writer called it a tug-of-war—and in the end she succeeded in getting Utrillo out of her husband's life.

What happened next is somewhat fuzzy, owing to a documentary lacuna partially explained by Deering's fondness for drink—one observer sadly referred to him as a "chronic and senile alcoholic."[101] The final break occurred in April 1921, when Deering informed his New York lawyer, Elbert Gary, that he had engaged an English accounting firm in Barcelona to investigate Utrillo's accounts. He also reported that he was having difficulty recovering ownership of fourteen properties that Utrillo had purchased in his name. "I may have to sue him," he writes, and then commented that Utrillo "has seemingly been dishonest in his use of my funds for his own benefit, but I have the whip in hand, and he is very foolish to do what he is doing. Not to say insane. But the man became thoroughly imbued with the conviction that he was master here, and when I came for a month it didn't matter, but when I began living here I encroached upon his high mightiness, and no vainer man lives."[102]

Events now moved swiftly. By June 1921 Deering, aged almost seventy, had decided to abandon Sitges and ship most of his collection back to Florida and his residence at Cutler, just south of Miami. Rumors to this effect caused something of an uproar in Sitges—on July 18 the town's mayor and its citizens presented Deering with a petition urging him to stay. Deering had previously been one of the town's principal benefactors, endowing a hospital and several schools. In addition, Maricel, although never formally opened to the public, had attracted a steady stream of distinguished visitors—artists, prominent Spaniards, and members of Deering's own family, including his brother James, owner of the grand Miami estate known as Vizcaya—who helped initiate Sitges's transformation into the tourist town it has now become.[103]

But Deering, old navy man that he was, had already charted his course. Obstacles emerged in the guise of protests from various groups involved in the preservation of Catalonia's artistic patrimony. Catalan politicians intervened, hoping to use laws banning the export of valued works of art to forestall Deering's removing his collection from Sitges or at the very least to require him to pay an export tax equivalent to 10 percent of the collection's value, something that Deering—no friend of taxation of any sort—steadfastly refused to do. Letters currently housed in Spain's Archivo de la Nación document this particular tug-of-war together with the frenzied efforts by Vega-Inclán, acting as intermediary, to work out a compromise that would enable Deering to export his collection free of tax on the condition he donate the Ayala altarpiece either to the El Greco museum in Toledo or Barcelona's museum of Catalan art. These negotiations came to naught. On September 25, 1925, the Ayala altarpiece left Barcelona, together with Deering and hundreds of crates holding most of his collection, on a ship bound for New York and then Miami. Left behind was the chimney from Jaca—it is now in Barcelona's Pedralbes Museum—as well as several medieval retables, which Deering's heirs later moved to Tamarit in 1954, although these were put up for auction after that castle was sold in 1986 and today can be found in several Spanish museums.[104]

As for the items that went to Deering's home in Florida, Deering's lawyer had one idea: "If you are determined to donate your splendid collection for the benefit of the public," he wrote, "you could build up for yourself and descendants a fine monument by establishing a museum in New York, or better still Chicago, or still better Miami, and call it the Charles Deering Collection; and then place it in the hands of self-perpetuating trustees to be named in your will and in that way give your descendants, as well as the public, the benefit and opportunity to see and enjoy these fine works of art."[105]

The suggested brick-and-mortar museum never materialized, but the Charles Deering Collection was reconstituted as a family trust with Deering's heirs, starting with his daughters, serving as trustees. Dispersion of the collection began in 1924, when Deering helped arrange for the loan of the Ayala altarpiece to the Art Institute of Chicago. Deering, however, retained ownership of the rest of his collection until his death in 1927, at which point his two daughters determined its fate: many of the prime Spanish items went to the Art Institute; others were sold, although a few pictures by Ramon Casas, one of Deering's favorite artists, can today be seen at the Deering Estate in Cutler, Florida; still others belong to members of the Deering-McCormick family.

So ended Deering's Spanish turn, together with his dream of a castle—and in his case an old hospital as well—in Spain. As for his collection, it is now dispersed, unlike the one that Huntington assembled for the HSA. Both Deering and Huntington shared a commitment to Spain and its art, but the two were rivals, often competing for the same works of art.[106] Huntington's opinion of Deering as a person and as a collector is not all that clear, but he kept close tabs on Deering's purchases, thanks in part to reports provided by Arthur Byne, his curator at the HSA. In 1917, for example, Byne provided Huntington with a report on the "museum" Deering was creating in Sitges: "It is one of the sights of Spain and the people are very proud of it, especially as it is to be left to them as a museum. We don't know Deering well. We are told he speaks little Spanish and comes seldom to Sitges. But [he] has invested [a] half million in his 'Spanish hobby.'"[107] What's certain is that Huntington never offered Deering membership in the HSA.

As for Deering, he was definitely leery of Huntington, suspecting that dealers like Harris offered "everything" first to Huntington. As noted earlier, he also questioned whether Huntington kept to his promise of refusing to buy pictures in Spain.[108] For this reason he resented the many accolades Huntington received in Spain, including an honorary degree from Madrid University, membership in the Spanish Royal Academy, and the Grand Cross of Alfonso X. Such resentments also help to explain why, prior to leaving Sitges, Deering announced that while Huntington was buying Spanish treasures in order to bring them to the United States, he was doing the opposite and purchasing them so as to return them to their native land. The irony here is, thanks in large measure to Utrillo's treachery and his subsequent run-in with the Spanish treasury, Deering would soon close Maricel and have his collection shipped to the United States. It practically goes without saying that he never received any honors from the king of Spain.

"Ravaging the Country"

If Deering's Spanish turn ended by depleting Spain's artistic patrimony, then in the eyes of many Spaniards, that of William Randolph Hearst was far, far worse. As the title of a 2012 book published in Spain suggests, Hearst was the "great hoarder," a collector whose seemingly unquenchable appetite for Spanish art and antiques resulted in wholesale "destruction" of Spain's artistic and architectural patrimony. The primary author of this book, a respected architect, catalogs these losses in meticulous detail. They include roughly eighty wooden *artesanado* ceilings dating from the sixteenth and seventeenth centuries, nearly all stripped out of different palaces and churches across Spain; a wide array of choir stalls and screens, the most famous of which, originally in the cathedral of Valladolid, stands now in the central hall of New York's Metropolitan Museum; and the cloisters of two medieval monasteries, both disassembled, their pieces numbered and shipped secretly to New York. One is currently in Florida, the other in northern California. Add to this list hundreds of Hispano-Moresque lusterware plates, dozens of pictures, reliquaries, furniture, tapestries, and more. The scale and scope of Hearst's acquisitive habits explains why the Italian writer Umberto Eco referred to it as "incontinent collectionism." In contrast, José Merino de Cáceres, the architect and author who calls Hearst "el gran acaparador" (the great hoarder), referring to the simulacrum of Hearst that appears in Orson Welles's 1941 film *Citizen Kane*, attributes it simply to megalomania.[109] Other explanations are equally plausible.

COLLECTORS AND COLLECTING 285

Mary Levkoff, an art historian and the author of an important book on Hearst's collecting, adopts a different and decidedly less polemical and psychological interpretation of Hearst's collecting. She attributes Hearst's acquisitiveness to his outlandishly extravagant lifestyle and determination to furnish all of his residences—they included the famous Hearst Castle and two other large residences in California, a monstrous five-story apartment in the Clarendon building on New York's Riverside Drive, an estate on Long Island's North Shore, and a castle in Wales—in the cluttered, cosmopolitan style typical of the Gilded Age. She also attributes some of Hearst's buying to his long-standing desire to establish in California a museum dedicated to the arts of the Middle Ages and Renaissance and to the memory of his mother, Phoebe Apperson Hearst, a collector in her own right and undoubtedly partly responsible for nurturing her son's artistic interests.[110]

As for Hearst's interest in Spanish antiques, Levkoff dismisses the notion that it had anything to do with personal animosity toward Spain per se. It is true, she admits, that in the run-up to the 1898 war Hearst newspapers repeatedly printed sensationalist stories representing Spanish soldiers in Cuba as "cruel and merciless," lobbied both President McKinley and Congress to intervene in the conflict, and, after the explosion of the *Maine* in February 1898, urged them to declare war on Spain and then congratulated them when they did. Hearst in fact believed that his newspapers helped to make the war happen. In 1899 he confessed to his mother that "I really believe I brought on the war," only to castigate himself afterward for having failed, unlike Roosevelt, to volunteer to fight. Other observers also attributed the war to Hearst, calling it Hearst's war, and Hearst himself did little if anything to suggest otherwise.[111]

But is there a connection between Hearst's collecting and the war? As I see it, that connection is best found in Hearst's outspoken Americanism on the one hand and his disdain for Europe's monarchies, Spain among them, on the other. Monarchy for Hearst represented the past; democracy, especially American-style democracy, the future. Monarchy was a relic, a medieval holdover, or as he put it in one editorial commenting on the birth of a Spanish prince in 1907, there was little to celebrate, as the child represented the "tail-end of a worn-out line."[112]

He also blamed the institution of monarchy for the poverty he encountered during a visit to Portugal (and Spain) in 1911: "I can't see how a
country can run down so. I guess the trouble is with the kings. Kings
are a sort of a permanency. If a country draws a good one the result is
immensely beneficial but if it draws a bad one it has to suffer under a
selfish and stupid government until the miserable old failure dies. Two
or three bad kings in succession put a country on the bum. Kings are
all right if a country has the recall and can [dethrone?] a King who isn't
making good."[113]

Hearst's aversion to monarchy became even more pronounced in several editorials he published just after the outbreak of World War I. The
war, he averred, was a disaster, to be blamed entirely upon "monarchi-
cal systems, the imperial policies, the mediaeval traditions, the aggression of states and the arrogance of kings which are responsible for this
inexcusable destruction of our fellow human beings." Apart from the
human costs of the conflict, he also envisioned serious material ones,
writing that "the accumulated treasures of centuries are being destroyed,
treasures not merely of money but of art and architecture which can
be never be replaced, and whose refining and elevating and civilizing
influence will forever be ended in the world." The war, in short, marked
what he called "the destruction of civilization in which we Americans
are part possessors."[114]

"The destruction of civilization"—here in my view lies the key to
Hearst's "incontinent collectionism." That collectionism had less to do
with psychology than ideology, especially Hearst's idea that Europe's
aging institutions could no longer guarantee, let alone be trusted with,
the protection and preservation of its accumulated "treasures of centuries." Better that these treasures, together with the civilization they represented, be safeguarded in the United States, a country he envisioned
as a new Venice, standing "at the center of the world's commerce" and
serving as "the custodian of its wealth."[115]

It is difficult to pinpoint when Hearst first formulated such ideas, but
1898 is plausible, as he is likely to have interpreted the relative ease of
America's victory and the speed of Spain's defeat in two different ways.
To begin with, that combination played to his Americanism, as it pro-

vided tangible proof of his country's industrial and military might and the superiority of its democratic form government. Hearst may also have interpreted Spain's defeat as yet another sign of the inherent weakness of monarchy, which in Spain's case had so weakened the country that it was no longer capable of defending its remaining overseas colonies. Hearst was also apt to have been aware of the crisis—economic, political, even psychological—that the war triggered in Spain itself. Spanish intellectuals and political pundits reacted negatively to their country's defeat, searching for new and better institutions and modes of governance they hoped would strengthen the country's political institutions, its economy, and its way of life. But while the intellectuals—members of the Generation of '98—pondered the country's future, workers and peasants took to the streets with a wave of strikes. Anarchism, socialism, and anticlericalism and other forms of radical republicanism were also on the rise, reaching an apparent climax during the "tragic week" in Barcelona in 1909, which resulted in considerable loss of life. From Hearst's perspective such agitation offered proof positive that Spain's "worn-out line" was no longer in a position to protect the country's valued artistic "treasures" from popular agitation and unrest. His response: assume the role of Hercules and shoulder that responsibility himself, although he put it rather more crudely in a letter to his mother in 1905, a letter written just prior to crossing the border from France and visiting Spain for the first time: "We [he was traveling with his wife] will burst through the Pyrenees into Spain and ravage the country. How does that strike you?"[116]

Upon close inspection, Hearst's "ravaging" began well before the 1898 war, let alone the crisis that rocked Spain in the ensuing years. He had studied Spanish during his two years as a student at Harvard (he never earned a degree), and as early as 1889, upon learning that the Duke of Dúrcal was selling his pictures in New York, he wrote his mother, an avid but eclectic collector, urging her to attend the auction and "get a Murillo or a Velázquez. Don't get four or five old masters that nobody ever heard anything about. Get a Murillo or a Velázquez. Or get a Murillo *and* a Velázquez if you can but at least get one good picture."[117] Phoebe does not appear to have attended the auction, and even if she did, the two Murillos and the equestrian portrait attributed to Velázquez that were part of the sale went to other buyers. In fact the only "good" Spanish picture Phoebe ever acquired was one by the late seventeenth-century artist Claudio Coello (*Virgin Appearing to Saint James*, now at Hearst San Simeon State Historical Monument, owned by the California State Parks).

But if his mother dithered, Hearst did not. His began buying pictures in the course of a trip to Europe in 1889, but it was apparently the trip to Spain and Portugal in 1905—he visited again in 1911—that piqued his lifelong interest in Spanish architecture along with the art, furniture, and antiques of that country. One of his stops on the first trip was Ronda, an Andalucian town famous for a stone bridge spanning an adjacent gorge. Hearst loved Ronda, later celebrating the town and its pleasures in a short poem (see below). The mixture of styles—Mudéjar, Gothic, Renaissance, and plateresque—incorporated into the town's Collegiate Church of Santa María la Mayor also captured his attention, so much so that in 1919 he instructed his architect, Julia Morgan, to use its bell tower as the model for the towers of the main house, the fabled Casa Grande, at San Simeon. The architecture of Casa Grande was equally varied, although when still in the planning stage Hearst explained to Morgan that he wanted something approximating what he called "Spanish baroc [*sic*]."[118]

That same trip took Hearst to the northern Spanish city of Burgos, where he made his first documented attempt to purchase one of the country's "treasures" and ship it back to the United States. The item in question was the elaborately carved Renaissance patio of the Casa (or House) of Miranda. In 1910 its Spanish owner offered to sell the house to the city of Burgos, but when the city fathers refused, it was sold instead to two out-of-town buyers, one Spanish, the other French. How they got in touch with Hearst remains unknown, but in April 1910 he purchased the patio for $51,000, paying the owners a deposit of $16,000 with the balance due when the patio was en route to New York. Hearst evidently wanted to incorporate the patio into his quintuplex at the Clarendon, but a series of legal obstacles prevented him from doing so.

These obstacles cropped up almost as soon as news of his purchase leaked out. An outcry in Burgos led authorities there to issue a tempo-

Fig. 42. Panoramic view of Enchanted Hill, San Simeon, California, ca. 1930. In 1919 Hearst commissioned his architect, Julia Morgan, to build a "castle" for him in "Spanish baroc [*sic*] style." The towers of the main house (Casa Grande) were modeled after those of a church Hearst had seen in southern Spain some years earlier. Courtesy California History Room, California State Library, Sacramento, California.

rary injunction ordering the dismantling of the patio to stop. When news of this outcry reached New York, the incident prompted the *New York Times*, possibly for the only time in its history, to offer its sympathy for Hearst with an article that read, "It is good for the people of Burgos to be alive to the worth of its treasures . . . foreign folk ought to be grateful to the American collectors . . . for stirring up their pride."[119]

Hearst's agents in Spain—they included Joseph Willard, the U.S. ambassador—subsequently appealed this injunction to Spain's supreme court, which, after a five-year delay, in June 1915 announced a verdict supporting the right of the "seller to sell [the patio] and the purchaser [Hearst] to take [it]."[120] At this point King Alfonso XIII, acting on the advice of the Royal Academy of Fine Arts, intervened. On October 17, 1915, Alfonso issued a royal decree declaring the Miranda patio a national monument. That decree effectively blocked the patio's export—it still can be seen in Burgos—much to Hearst's chagrin, who considered himself the patio's rightful and legitimate owner. In a letter sent in 1919 to his architect, Julia Morgan, and in which he referred to "the patio in Bergos [*sic*]," Hearst commented, "By the way I own [that patio] but cannot get it out of Spain."[121]

The Burgos incident seems not to have diminished Hearst's determination to acquire more Spanish treasures and export them to the United States. His drive instead seemed even greater. The chronology of his early acquisitions, both Spanish and non-Spanish, remains somewhat uncertain, as catalogs recording his purchases only begin in the 1920s, when Hearst created the International Studio Corporation for the purpose of crating, shipping, storing, and inventorying his dizzying number of purchases.

When it came to collecting, Hearst's first love was ancient Greek vases; he first purchased several during the 1890s. Tapestries were another; he wanted these to decorate the walls of his New York apartment and other residences. As for his Spanish treasures, he began with the acquisition of Hispano-Moresque lusterware plates—he eventually owned almost three hundred—which were initially meant for the "Spanish Gallery" located on the mezzanine of his New York quintuplex. Armor, furniture, and other objects soon followed, but the pace quickened in 1919, when he finally decided to build his estate at San Simeon, California, in a combination of Moorish, Gothic, and Renaissance styles he labeled as "Spanish."[122]

That decision rested partly on Hearst's desire to find an architectural style that harmonized with California's Spanish past. He did not have much use for the plain style of California's missions—"too bare and clumsy." He also rejected the elaborate plateresque style more typical of Spanish colonial architecture: "too elaborate," too "baroc [*sic*]." He instead wanted something more akin to the architecture he had encountered in Ronda and in line with that depicted in some of the photographs included in Arthur Byne's *Spanish Architecture of the Sixteenth Century* (1917), a book he sent to Julia Morgan to help her reach a final design.[123]

As it turned out, Morgan already knew about these photographs; Byne (née Bein) and his wife, Mildred, a friend of Morgan since her student days in Paris, had been in regular communication since at least 1914. As noted in the previous chapter, Arthur was a trained architect, albeit one who preferred photographing old buildings than designing new ones, whereas Mildred was an intrepid traveler who became enamored of Spanish art after hearing William Merritt Chase lecture on the subject—"it set my imagination on fire," as she later recalled. The two married in New York in 1910 and soon went off to Spain, to write, take photographs, and explore. By 1914 the couple was in contact with Archer Milton Huntington, who two years later appointed them curators of architecture and allied arts at the HSA. By 1919 the couple's relationship with Huntington was fraying, with the final break coming in 1921, by which time the Bynes, having become thoroughly "españolized," as Mildred put it, established themselves as independent antique dealers in Madrid, just in time, in other words, to help Hearst, as well as Morgan, find the treasures he needed to furnish the complex at San Simeon.[124]

Morgan wasted little time in recommending the Bynes to Hearst, partly as a way of helping the couple get their new business off the ground. In January 1920 she wrote Hearst, telling him about "the wonderful collection of Spanish photographs made by Mr and Mrs Byne whose book 'Spanish Architecture of the sixteenth century' you sent me. They work up at the Hispanic Museum, and if you want any particular material such as ceilings, grilles, etc., I am sure they would gladly send you down a fine collection to look over." A few months later—on May 13, 1920, to be exact—Morgan sent Hearst a copy of the Bynes' latest book on ceilings, drawing his attention to the "interesting ones on pages 13, 16, 41 and especially 4, 5, 6, 7. In fact the ceilings on pages 4 and 7 are so quaint and interesting that I think we should steal them for some part of the building. They would go well in [the] big refectory room. . . . I think they would be wonderful there. They are near enough to the Spanish, because they have a bit of Moorish influence too." In the meantime Hearst's purchases of furnishings for the yet unbuilt house and surrounding cottages had already begun, as he informed Morgan that his recent purchases included "three large important window grilles from Spain; also a tremendous door grill[e] . . . 2 fine hispano moresque columns 13th c for loggias house." As for the refectory Morgan had already mentioned, he wrote her that he was thinking of "a large mantelpiece" and above it "a big contemporary copy of a Murillo, with a nice spanish frame."[125]

With Morgan serving as intermediary, and after having learned of Hearst's interest in *artesanado* ceilings of the kind featured in their *Decorated Wooden Ceilings* book, the Bynes sent Morgan photographs and a detailed description of one sixteenth-century ceiling from a house in Granada that they believed they could purchase, dismantle, and ship abroad. The offer was tempting. Hearst was interested, but as news of the impending sale leaked out, the Spanish government intervened, declared the house and its contents a national monument, and effectively blocked its sale, much to the Bynes' regret. But the couple soon located another, somewhat similar ceiling, cabling Morgan that it was a now-or-never deal and that Hearst had to act quickly, which he did. Even before this sale was concluded, however, they informed Morgan that, should Hearst be interested, they were in a position to offer sixteen more ceilings.

In the meantime Morgan, acting as the equivalent of a mole, sent the Bynes a string of letters and telegrams intended to provide them with a sense of the size and scale of the project under way at San Simeon and information about the character of Hearst's acquisitions: "We are building for him a sort of village on a mountain-top overlooking the sea and ranges of mountains, miles from any railway, and housing incidentally, his collections as well as his family. Having different buildings allows the use of very varied treatments . . . also hillside location requires endless steps and terracing." Mildred replied, "Knowing, as we do now, the charm of the traditional Spanish house we envy you architects in California [and] your opportunity to create something fine in this line. . . . If we can't build Spanish residences, we can furnish them."[126] Her husband then assured Morgan that "no one in all Spain is in touch with saleable treasure to the extent that we are" and that they were in a position to provide Hearst with "whatever objects he might need." He also noted that her prices would be well below those of "rapacious professional antiquarians."[127]

As for Hearst's purchases, Morgan told Mildred that "he probably is the largest buyer of Spanish antiques at present in the country." She also sent her the following list of his recent acquisitions:

I had probably best tell you a little more of what he is doing. So far we have received from him, to incorporate into the new buildings, some 12 or 13 cartloads of antiques, brought from the ends of the earth and from the prehistoric down to the last Empire in period, the majority, however, being of Spanish origin. They comprise vast quantities of tables, beds, armoires, secretaries, all kinds of cabinets, polychrome church statuary, columns, door frames, carved doors in all stages of repair and disrepair, window grilles, votive candlesticks, torcheres, all kinds of chairs in quantity, six or seven well heads (only one of these Spanish), marble and wood columns and door trims[,] a few good wooden carved ceilings, one very nice gilt and polychrome ceiling hexagonal in shape, one very nice rejería about 18' wide and 17' high, a marble sanctuary arch from the entrance of some choir, and pictures—most of these of early type painted on wood, with a few good canvases; a number of Donatellos, lots of Della Robbia. I don't see myself where we are ever going to use half suitably, but I find that the idea is to try things out and if they are not satisfactory, discard them for the next thing that comes that promises better. There is interest and charm coming gradually into play.[128]

But there was more interest—I will not vouch for the charm—to come. On November 16, 1921, Hearst wrote Morgan that "we will want a tremendous [amount] of stuff for the big house, bath house, etc. and probably we could do much better from her [Mildred Byne] than from the average antiquary."[129] What this meant is that Hearst, having determined that the Bynes had severed their previous connections with Huntington, decided to have the couple serve as his agents in Spain. So began a relationship that lasted until Arthur Byne's tragic death in an automobile accident on the outskirts of Madrid in July 1935.

Before then, Hearst was by far the Bynes' best but no means only American client, as the couple had managed to develop close ties with a number of other collectors, as well as museums in New York, Boston, Philadelphia, Cleveland, and Kansas City, all of which expressed interest

Fig. 43. William R. Hearst, Arthur Byne, and others in Toledo, Spain, ca. 1924[?]. Arthur Byne and his wife, Mildred, were Hearst's principal buying agents in Spain. Byne is the second from the left; Hearst is wearing a white hat. ©Hearst Castle®/ CA State Parks.

in precisely the classes of Spanish objects that interested Hearst, namely, ceilings, choir stalls, grilles, paintings, architectural fragments, and so on.

Over the years the Bynes played this fiercely competitive aspect of the craze for Spain to their own advantage, partly as way to put pressure on Hearst, their best client by far. Yet Hearst proved a constant source of frustration, regularly agreeing to buy something but failing to pay, at least in a timely fashion. Hearst was also a two-timer, as he often bought Spanish "treasures" from sources other than the Bynes, including the annual New York auctions organized by Raimundo and Luis Ruiz, two enterprising *madrileño* antique dealers who were almost as adept as the Bynes in evading Spanish export laws, bribing officials, and shipping different objets d'art out of the country.[130]

The Bynes, however, had one sales advantage Hearst's other supplier lacked—insider information provided by Morgan as she regularly apprised them of precisely the kinds of objects the press baron was seeking. Starting in 1923, for example, Morgan cabled the Bynes with such tips as, "What we would like are ceilings, especially door trims, interesting architectural motifs—not so much furniture as objets d'art"; "locate large size material like moorish columns gothic stone doorways cloisters, write facts and figures"; "is collection of sixteen ceilings still available[?] client wants fine collection twelve or more important ceilings and fine cloisters church *rejas* [iron grilles] whole large architectural units such as fine large choir stall sets stairways. Cable him NY what available and price serious proposition this time"; "he is very anxious to get a large cloister, a big well—mantels like illustrated in the magazine you sent once—an important doorway; an alabaster railing—the bigger, more architectural things we need just now. You must wonder what we do with it all!"[131]

These last tips led to one of Hearst's most spectacular Spanish acquisitions: the cloister of an abandoned Romanesque monastery near the village of Sacramenia (Segovia), which the Bynes claimed they were able to purchase, dismantle, and then ship to New York. That possibility energized Hearst, who acted without delay, cabling the Bynes the money they needed to get the project under way. Morgan subsequently informed the Bynes that Hearst was planning to incorporate the cloister into a museum to be erected on the campus of the University of California, Berkeley:

> The cloister you have bought will in all probability be built into that building. Idea to link objects on display with rooms, courts that are contemporary. I imagine you are laughing, you and Mildred, when you get this request, but Mr Hearst said last night "You know we sent Mr Byne a perfectly good set of pictures of possible looking patios and cloisters, and surely some of those Signors, Dukes, etc., are hard enough up to part with *one* of them." I have in my charge something like four cartloads of objects. . . . We need big things to use to make settings for them.[132]

Big things indeed! With the work at San Simeon nearing completion— the main house, the Casa Grande, was dedicated in 1926—Hearst began

Fig. 44. Cloister, Sacramenia monastery, Segovia, Spain, and reconstructed in Miami, Florida. Expecting to incorporate the cloister into his house at San Simeon, Hearst purchased it from the Sacramenia monastery in 1925. It was then dismantled and shipped to New York, but Hearst never made use of it. The cloister was later sold and reconstructed in Miami, Florida. Segovia image courtesy of the B. Davis Schwartz Memorial Library, LIU Post Library, Greenvale, New York. Miami image from Creative Commons.

to make plans for a beach house (for his girlfriend, Marion Davies) in Los Angeles and a huge country residence at Wyntoon in northern California, neither to be built in plateresque style. Morgan provided the Bynes a hint of what was to come: "If I read him correctly, no long[er] interested in material of Cistercian period as he does not consider it residential—for his house in LA. His eye is on something more richly ornamental, rather than something of value from the purity of its architecture."[133] The term "richly ornamental" described perfectly the great iron grille the Bynes located three years later in the old Castilian city of Valladolid. Arthur informed Morgan about this discovery on April 25, 1929: "just found great grille fifty feet wide forty high. 17000 dollars. urge purchase. can ship instantly. . . . It is from cathedral in Valladolid. Formerly enclosed the choir but it was taken down 12 years ago after a reform, early 17th C. The price I consider cheap and I doubt if another example will ever present itself. Furthermore, it has the advantage that it is definitely in my possession—no beating around the bush for a year with a bishop and his chapter." Four days later, Morgan replied, "You have me lying awake nights imagining what on earth to do to house a 40 × 50 iron reja!—particularly without the least idea of its type! For once you are ahead of Mr H in scale! And I am glad." Two weeks later Hearst enters into the exchange: "I am not interested in great grille. it is too severe and not the one I want = Hearst."[134] But Hearst soon changed his mind, claiming that he had been misled by inadequate photographs of the grille. Another cable from Byne also helped sway him:

> The cathedral is a cold, classic church but the grille is richly orna-mented and gilded and neither cold nor classic. It is the work of one of the greatest spanish ironsmiths, Juan Baptista Celma. Bal-asters are beaten out of solid iron four inches in diameter at the turnings, capitals are beautifully wrought, the cresting quite florid. I am sending it at my own expense to NY. I am sure that once you see it you will reconsider. It is a magnificent piece of work which compares favorably with the finest grilles in the country. In the event of your not being interested I will try to place it in an Amer-ican museum. The 13,000 you advanced will be credited to your account, but judge the grille "without prejudice." It is a question of striking while the iron is hot. Another such opportunity will never present itself for double the money.[135]

The sales pitch, typically Byne, worked. Hearst bought his "richly ornamental" grille, apparently thinking of it as something for the new wing he was planning for the Casa Grande or his new house in Wyn-toon. Soon after the grille arrived in New York, however, he changed his mind and warehoused it in the Bronx, where it moldered until 1956, when it was acquired by the Metropolitan Museum of Art. It went on display in 1957 following a series of complex negotiations between that museum and the Spanish government.[136]

Once the Great Depression pinched Hearst's finances, the mogul's buying habits changed, although he did not abandon the Bynes—far from it. In 1930 the couple sold Hearst a series of *artesanado* ceilings, doors, furniture, and more. Hearst's purchases of "big things," however, were gradually coming to an end, partly for reasons connected with his financial difficulties—Hearst declared bankruptcy in 1937—but, equally important, with difficulties in getting such objects out of Spain.

Fig. 45. Choir screen, Valladolid Cathedral, Spain, 1763. One of Hearst's more spectacular purchases, this gilded and painted choir screen was gifted to New York's Metropolitan Museum of Art in 1956. The Metropolitan Museum of Art, New York.

Spain's first laws restricting the export of important art objects date to the end of the eighteenth century, but enforcement of these laws remained lax and they were easily avoided with the help of bribes. Furthermore, the laws in question did not apply to property belonging to the Church. Other complications arose from the government's policy

of sponsoring exhibitions featuring Spanish artistic treasures in various
foreign countries. One especially popular exhibition was that organized
in 1902 at London's Guildhall. In addition to works by such living artists as Sorolla and Zuloaga, it included others by Murillo, Ribera, Zurbarán, and Velázquez, all lent by private Spanish owners and available
for purchase.[137]

By the start of the twentieth century pressure to change this laissez-
faire policy was on the rise. Huntington's well-publicized acquisition of
the library of the Marqués de Jérez de los Caballeros in 1901 led several
of the country's most prominent scholars to question the wisdom of
allowing such exports, but the incident that really triggered the demand
for new laws to protect the country's artistic patrimony was the Valladolid Cathedral's sale of two pictures by El Greco to a French dealer in
1904. The pictures in question were the *Portrait of the Gentleman of the
Leiva*, soon to become the property of William Van Horne, and the *Saint
Jerome* that Frick was to buy. That sale, widely discussed in the Spanish
press, prompted demands to place new restrictions on the sale of Church
property, as did the pair of El Grecos that Peter Widener purchased in
1907, leading to a heated debate in the Spanish Cortes. Some deputies,
citing recent Italian laws restricting the export of fine art, called for laws
prohibiting the export of objects determined to be "of special artistic
or historic value and worthy of a place in public museums," while others defended the rights of private individuals, as well as the Church, to
dispose of their property as they saw fit.[138]

Combined with the Payne-Aldrich Tariff Act of 1909, the resulting
standoff added to the momentum of the Spanish turn to the extent that
it did nothing to prevent, and may even have accelerated, the export of
Spanish art and antiques to the United States. Yet the debate over the
merits of such exports did not go away. It surfaced again after Hearst's
attempt to export the patio of the Casa de Miranda in 1910. On that occasion he had been prevented from doing so when Alfonso XIII declared
the patio a national monument, and in 1921 the monarchy had accorded
a similar status to the sixteenth-century *artesanado* ceiling that the Bynes
had located in Granada's Casa de los Tiros. Yet in other instances the
monarchy failed to intervene, as in 1913, when an important altarpiece

Plate 1. William H. Powell, *Hernando de Soto Discovers the Mississippi River*, 1847. Powell's imagined interpretation of De Soto's "discovery" belonged to an ongoing effort to connect the history of Spain's *conquistadores* to that of the United States. Capitol rotunda, Washington DC. The Architect of the Capitol.

Plate 2. Samuel Colman, *Hill of the Alhambra*, 1865. American artists "discovered" Spain starting around 1850. They were especially attracted to picturesque scenes. One favorite was the Alhambra, the medieval Muslim fortress in Granada. The Metropolitan Museum of Art, New York.

Plate 3. John Singer Sargent, *El Jaleo*, 1881. Depicting a scene from a café in Seville, *El Jaleo* (The ruckus) captures some of the picturesque elements in Spanish society—guitar players, flamenco dancers—that travelogues of the period regularly described. Isabella Stewart Gardner Museum, Boston.

Plate 4. (*opposite*) Francisco de Zurbarán, *A Doctor of Law at Salamanca*, ca. 1635. When Isabella Stewart Gardner first saw this canvas in New York's Ehrich Galleries in 1906, she "made an offer, just out of pure love!" She was lucky to get it, as other collectors were interested as well. Isabella Stewart Gardner Museum, Boston.

Plate 5. Sir Gerald Kelly, *Henry C. Frick in the West Gallery*, 1925. Painted after Frick's death, this canvas shows him standing in the picture gallery of his New York home. The two pictures behind him—Velázquez's *King Philip IV* and El Greco's *Vincenzo Anastagi*—attest to his interest in Old Master Spanish art. Frick Art and Historical Center, Pittsburgh, Pennsylvania.

Plate 6. George Washington Smith, Casa del Herrero, Montecito, California, 1925. With its whitewashed adobe walls, red-tile roof, iron window grilles, and ornamented entrance, Smith's "farm-house" interpretation of Spanish revival architecture served as a model for architects and builders across the United States. Carol M. Highsmith, photographer. Courtesy Library of Congress.

Plate 7. (*opposite*) Daniel Sayre Groesbeck, Spanish colonial history mural at the Santa Barbara County Courthouse, Santa Barbara, California, 1929. Groesbeck's mural formed part of Santa Barbara's effort to hispanicize the city's—and California's—history. This detail depicts the landing of the Spanish explorer Juan Rodríguez Cabrillo at what is now San Diego in 1542. Courtesy the Jon B. Lovelace Collection of California Photographs in Carol M. Highsmith's America Project, Library of Congress, Prints and Photographs Division.

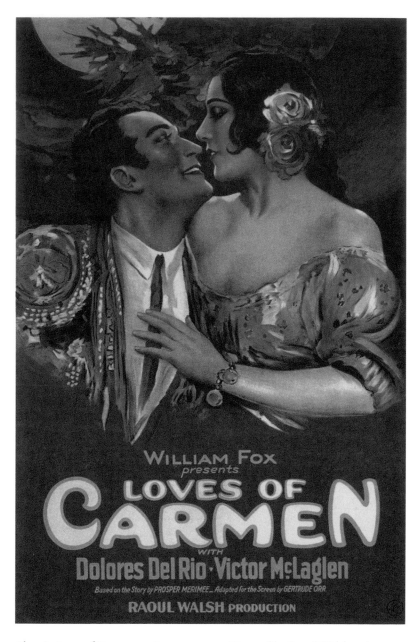

Plate 8. *Loves of Carmen* movie poster, 1927. Directed by Raoul Walsh and starring the Mexican singer Dolores del Río, *Loves of Carmen* was among the many Hollywood films to capitalize on the "romance and love" formula evoked by the craze for Spain. Reproduction after the original; collection of the author.

by the fifteenth-century Flemish artist Hugo van der Goes was removed from a private chapel in Monforte de Lemos, a small town in northwestern Spain, and sold to a dealer from Berlin.

The uncertainties in Spanish export laws afforded the Bynes extraordinary latitude, essentially enabling them to get their fledgling antiques business off the ground. But those days were numbered. In 1922 Spain's minister of finance, alerted by Deering's determination to export the contents of Maricel to the United States, proposed the imposition of a 10 percent duty on the value of art objects going abroad. That duty was never enacted, but in 1926 the government empowered the Royal Academy of Fine Arts and the Royal Academy of History to prevent the export of objects determined to be in Spain's national interest. The Bynes, together with the Ruiz brothers and other dealers found ways to avoid such restrictions, mainly by keeping their purchases secret and, whenever necessary, bribing local officials to keep quiet. Such loopholes allowed the owners of an eleventh-century tomb sculpture to sell it, albeit surreptitiously, to Harvard's Fogg Museum in 1926.[139]

But the noose was beginning to tighten, as conditions in Spain were changing fast. Following elections in the spring of 1931 that ushered in the start of Spain's Second Republic, the government enacted new laws restricting the right of private citizens and the Church to dispose of objects determined to be of artistic or historical interest. Although unevenly enforced, these laws caused the Bynes no end of headaches, as their correspondence with Morgan and Hearst readily attests. Other changes stemmed from the breakdown in public order that accompanied the start of the new government. Across the country anarchists and other anticlerical groups took to the streets, many churches and convents were attacked, and strikes were rampant. Amid the turmoil the Bynes soldiered on, occasionally voicing their complaints to Morgan: "Conditions in this country are very uncertain and contradictory laws are being turned out by the bushel every day."[140]

Hearst's view of this situation is difficult to assess, but as a staunch anticommunist opposed to "bolshevik" politics of any sort, he is certain to have looked upon the left-wing tilt in Spanish politics with alarm. From his perspective the combination of Spain's unsettled politics, the rise of left-wing parties, and anarchist riots represented yet another dangerous threat to the country's artistic treasures, possibly far worse than the one previously posed by its old, tired monarchy. That calculus seemingly figured in his decision in 1931 to proceed with the acquisition of yet another monastery—Santa María de Oliva (usually referred to as Monte Oliva or La Oliva)—the Bynes had located the previous winter. Hearst agreed to purchase Monte Oliva in February, paying a deposit of $25,000 and promising an equal amount to come. The second installment, however, was slow to arrive, a situation that left the Bynes in the lurch, as they had gone ahead and hired no fewer than ninety-two workers to begin dismantling the monastery, numbering the stones, and putting them into crates. Come summer a frustrated Byne cabled Morgan, complaining that the only reason that he was able to proceed with the project was that he had managed to convince Spain's minister of labor that, in a time of high unemployment, his ability to hire workers outweighed whatever artistic importance Monte Oliva possessed. Still the money did not arrive, prompting yet another, even more indignant cable, informing Morgan that "at the moment am sweating blood in Spain, transporting a whole monastery in the midst of a revolution and anarchy all for mr H's sake I am in no mood to listen to such tom-foolery as this."[141] In the end the money arrived, Monte Oliva was dismantled and shipped to San Francisco, only to suffer the same fate as Sacramenia: storage for years in a warehouse inasmuch as Hearst had not decided what to do with it.

The Monte Oliva monastery represented the last "big thing" Hearst bought from the Bynes. He made a few relatively minor purchases over the course of the following years, but these ended following Byne's unexpected death in July 1935. After Arthur's death Mildred made an effort to sell more antiques to Hearst, but these sales ended with the start of Spain's bloody civil war in July 1936 and the press magnate's declaration of bankruptcy the following year. Hearst's "ravaging" of the country had come to an end.

Ronda—A Spanish Song

Hearst is not known for his poetry, but at some point, possibly sometime after Spain's Second Republic government came to power in 1931, he composed an ode. Actually he called it a song that was dedicated to Ronda, Hearst's favorite Spanish town and one whose architecture had inspired the design for San Simeon and, along with it, his acquisition of countless treasures from Spain. "Ronda—A Spanish Song" recalled the "rapturous hours" Hearst had spent in Ronda's Fonda de Cádiz, evidently the inn where he stayed in 1905. According to Baedeker's *Handbook for Travellers to Spain and Portugal*, the only *fonda* then listed for Ronda was the Fonda Rodeña, a *pensión* described as "unpretending" but that offered wine at a modest price. Over the years Hearst might have easily forgotten the inn's exact name, but the Fonda de Cádiz described in the poem appears to have been the product of Hearst's imagination, the way he wanted to remember Ronda, and Spain, as it is nothing less than a paean to the fonda's wonderful cuisine:

> Did you ever have breakfast
>   at Ronda, In the fonda De Cadiz?
> Did you ever have coffee, more creamy, Hot and steamy?
>   You're a practiced and persistent eater
> Did you ever taste ham that was sweeter,
>   Or bread that is whiter, Or rolls that are lighter
> Than those that they serve you at Ronda, ·
>   At the fonda De Cadiz.[142]

Judging from one of the letters Hearst wrote to his mother when traveling through the "wilds of Spain," Hearst's hotel experiences in Ronda and other towns were not nearly so pleasant, nor the cuisine so delectable:

> We have gotten so we can eat everything boiled in oil and saturated with garlic, but we can't somehow learn to sleep on barbed wire mattress with a boiled hay bolster and sack of potatoes for a pillow—especially when we are not the only occupants of the bed. Moreover, the hotels always have cafes under them and the Spaniards never go to bed. They drink and play billiards and sit up and sing and then go out on the sidewalk and talk it over then go back in the cafe and begin all over again. At daylight we get a few winks and then get up and bump along for the day over the dusty roads.[143]

If this letter correctly captures Hearst's experiences in Ronda, he was evidently resistant to the fever that plagued Saint-Gaudens and other U.S. visitors to Spain. On the other hand, Hearst succumbed to the ailment sometime after he left, most probably in the luxurious Spanish-like surroundings of his plateresque castle in San Simeon. If so, Hearst was not alone. As the next chapter suggests, other Americans of his generation were equally keen on living in their own version of a castle in Spain, albeit on a scale decidedly less grandiose than the one Hearst constructed in California on a sun-drenched hilltop overlooking the sea.

⫷ 6 ⫸

"Castles in Spain Made Real"

Mea culpa, mea culpa, mea maxima culpa. (My fault, my fault,
my most grievous fault.) —RALPH CRAM, quoting the
Latin *Confiteor* from the Roman Catholic mass

Sunny Spain will always live in the Plaza. —J. C. NICHOLS,
developer of Country Club Plaza, Kansas City, Missouri

Ralph A. Cram, one of the most prominent architects in the United States, made a confession, a *mea culpa*, at the start of his 1924 essay "Renaissance in Spain." His "fault," Cram admitted, related to the "unkind things" he had previously written about the architecture of the Renaissance. "I said this in my haste," Cram added, "for then I had never been to Spain." All that changed following the architect's six-month trip, together with his family, to Spain in 1920.[1]

When Cram (1863–1942) made this confession, he did so as a convert to the beauty of a style of architecture particular to late fifteenth- and early sixteenth-century Spain and Portugal. The style is the one commonly known as plateresque (from the Spanish *plateresco*, meaning "in the manner of a silversmith") and that referred to a composite style of architecture combining elements of Gothic, Renaissance, and Moorish (or *mudéjar*) architecture and one distinguished by ornate, often elaborately carved and decorated entryways and window surrounds. Today some critics call it late Gothic, others early Renaissance, still others a transitional form of architecture combining elements of both, but Cram and other architects of his generation regarded it as uniquely Spanish and something utterly different from the styles of architecture encountered elsewhere.

Cram regarded his trip to Spain—he rented a house in Seville over-looking the gardens of the former Moorish palace or *alcázar*—as utterly transformative, as it seemingly altered his understanding of the history of Western architecture. Ever since the 1880s, when he started as an archi-tect in Boston, Cram had favored buildings of Gothic design, a style he considered especially suitable for churches, colleges, and universities owing to what he perceived as the links of these institutions to the Mid-dle Ages. Much influenced by John Ruskin's ideas about the "organic" quality of architecture and the essential unity between buildings, the character of the surrounding society, and the era in which they were built, Cram outlined the advantages of the Gothic in a 1907 book, *The Gothic Quest*, which centered on his notion of the style of architecture best suited to "Christian civilization." The volume offered a dim view of Renaissance architecture on the grounds that the classical elements inherent in that style were essentially pagan and thus incompatible with Christianity. It instead applauded the Gothic as a style whose intricate design and "absolute beauty" not only harmonized with the "Christi-anity of the Middle Ages" but spoke to the present because its "men-tal attitude" was one of "supreme calm, self-restraint and immitigable law." To this Cram added that the Gothic epitomized "heroism, sacri-fice, chivalry, and worship," qualities he considered in short supply in the modern, industrializing world.[2] It was undoubtedly for this reason that the trustees of Princeton University endorsed the Gothic design Cram proposed for the new Graduate College (built in 1908) in con-junction with his new master plan for the university's campus. Similarly, the values Cram attached to the Gothic help to explain why the officials in charge of the construction of New York's Cathedral of St. John the Divine voted in 1912 to change that building's original Romanesque design to a Gothic one proposed by Cram.[3]

Cram's love for the Gothic acquired a wholly new meaning during his trip to Spain. By his own admission Cram felt overwhelmed upon entering Seville's massive late Gothic cathedral, a building he later described as "the crowning demonstration of the breadth, the compre-hensive individuality, and the universality of Gothic architecture." That visit also marked what Cram referred to in his 1936 autobiography as the start of a "new revelation" seemingly renewed and reinforced by his subsequent visits to other Spanish cathedrals, in Toledo, Burgos, León, Barcelona, Gerona, Segovia, Salamanca, and especially Palma de Mallorca, the location of "one of the great cathedrals of the world," which he described in meticulous detail in a monograph published in 1932. These churches, he wrote, not only modified his puritan ideas about pure style but also enabled him to understand that "progress" in architecture did not end with the Gothic. Such progress, in Spain at least, instead continued on to the plateresque and after that to the elaborate form of baroque architecture associated with the late seventeenth-century architect José de Churriguera and known as "Churrigueresque."[4]

Nor was Cram's "new revelation" limited to Spanish architecture. It embraced "all the other arts of the Iberian peninsula." Those other arts included the "beautiful Primitives with their Flemish quality . . . best seen in the churches and museums of Catalonia; the mystical splendour of El Greco; the occasional charm of the early Murillos in Seville; the magnificent mastery of Velasquez in Madrid; . . . the sculpture of [Alonso de] Berruguete, metal work; cabinet work of the Mudejar period," as well as Toledo's Mozarbic liturgy, which he described as the "sole survivor in the West of the primitive ceremonial of the undivided Church."[5]

When Cram prepared this list, Ruskin's ideas linking art organically with society were still fresh in his mind. So too were others gleaned from Ángel Ganivet's *Idearium español* (1897) about the fundamentally "spiritual" as opposed to "materialist" quality of Spain's national character and from his own reading of the Spanish philosophers Miguel de Unamuno and José Ortega y Gasset, both of whom emphasized nonmaterialist interpretations of the Spanish character. This cocktail of ideas allowed Cram to connect Spanish art and architecture with "the quality of the Spanish race and its essential culture; that strange synthesis of austerity and magnificence, of profound philosophy and the devouring passion for adventure."[6] He added that these were

the inherent qualities persisting for a thousand years. . . . The continuity of creative force is unbroken. Goldlust and colonial cruelty, monstrous as they were; the unleashed passion of the Inquisition; the blind unreason of Republican interludes; the insanity of imported and alien communism and syndicalism—all these are extraneous to the deep and noble Spanish spirit, the *Idearium Español* so clearly revealed by Angel Ganivet. Above all this is the controlling and lasting energy, from San Juan de la Cruz and Santa Teresa, through Cervantes even to the present day, with Unamuno and Ortega y Gasset revealing the persistence of a great idea that lasts with all its integrity while democracies and communes and materialistic, atheistic episodes live their little hour only to die in dishonour.[7]

The "new revelation" Cram experienced on his first visit to Spain strikes me as a variant of the "fever" to which other visitors to the country had reportedly succumbed. Shortly after the end of that visit Cram published a series of essays on Spanish architecture, including four that appeared in the *American Architect and Architectural Review*, a professional journal read mainly by his fellow architects, presumably an audience whose ideas about Spain approximated the ones he had had prior to his eye-opening journey. The series began with "Spanish Notes: An Introduction," in which Cram criticized himself for his "indifference" to Spain, an indifference that ended following "six months of revelation" in the country. Afterward, he claimed, no other architecture interested him, not even little English villages, the cathedrals of France, or the hill towns of Italy, let alone Venice, Palermo, or Carcassonne. "My only call," he wrote, "is back to Spain," a country he likened to a "sacred preserve" that had successfully managed to retain the "real values in life long lost in other highly-civilized and progressive nations."[8]

Cram's romanticized view of Spain was nothing new. As already discussed here, similar sentiments could be found in the writings of Washington Irving, in the observations of James Russell Lowell, and those of many of the writers whose views of the country I have grouped under the label of "Sturdy Spain." For Cram these values translated into an "impeccable sense of style" and a blending of architectural "magnificence curbed by austerity." He continued by writing a series of essays for *American Architect and Architectural Review* that amounted to a capsule course in Spanish architectural history. The series began with an essay outlining Spain's success in "moulding and transforming" the Romanesque into a distinctive national style; here Cram signaled the importance of the work of a friend, the Harvard professor Arthur Kingsley Porter, whose two-volume *Romanesque Sculpture of the Pilgrimage Roads* (1923) had just appeared.[9]

Among the other essays, one focused on the originality of Spain's Gothic cathedrals and included a detailed account of the edifice in Seville ("There never was anything quite like it on earth, and I suppose never can be again"), another on the inventiveness and originality of plateresque architecture, and yet another devoted to domestic architecture and the "pictorial quality" of the country's paneled (*artesanado*) ceilings, shutters, and doors, its "right balance of simplicity and directness," "noble richness," and success blending "tradition" with "modernism." Cram further suggested that the simplicity of Spanish domestic design offered an ideal living environment, or "frame," for both people and furniture. "Until the architect has seen Spain," Cram observed, "he knows only half of architecture."[10] And to help his colleagues acquire that knowledge, he appended a short bibliography devoted to the history of Spanish architecture as well as Spanish decoration and design. Books in the last group included Arthur Byne and Mildred Byne's *Decorated Wooden Ceilings in Spain* (1920) and their *Spanish Interiors and Furniture* (1921), the same books Julia Morgan was using to help design Hearst's houses at San Simeon; Austin Whittlesey's *The Minor Ecclesiastical, Domestic, and Garden Architecture of Southern Spain* (1917), and Winsor Soule's *Spanish Farm Houses and Minor Public Buildings* (1924). Also on the list, and to help his fellow architects acquire a better sense of the Spanish temperament, were Ganivet's *Idearium* together with books by Unamuno and Ortega y Gasset. He also included *Rosinante to the Road Again* (1922) by John Dos Passos, one of a generation of American novelists (see chapter 7) who, together with Cram, considered Spain no less than a "revelation."[11]

Cram practiced what he preached. His "Spanish" buildings were never very many, but they did prove influential. One of the first was the Blanche Harding Sewall house (1924) in Houston's exclusive River Oaks neighborhood, and it triggered a Texas-sized rush for houses of similar design. Even more impressive was Houston's Julia Ideson Library (1923), a building whose façade was modeled after that of the University of Alcalá de Henares, a sixteenth-century building designed by Rodrigo Gil de Hontañón, one of Cram's favorite Spanish architects.[12] That building, and Cram's copy of it, also served as the model for the administration building of Texas Technological College (now Texas Tech University) in Lubbock, designed by a Cram disciple, William Ward Watkin. At his mentor's urging, Watkin traveled to Spain to study its architecture firsthand and later explained that he had selected the Spanish style because the "simple splendor" of the architecture he had seen in León, Alcalá, Salamanca, and Toledo was reflected in "the early history of Texas as enshrined in old Spanish missions such as San Antonio." That same style, Watkin added, was in keeping with "the bonds of tradition, the old history and new, the past, the present, and the hope for the future."[13]

But to return to Cram, he designed Spanish-style buildings for places other than Texas. They included Pittsburgh, where he designed the majestic Holy Rosary Church (1928), modeled after the cathedral of Palma de Mallorca, one of Cram's favorite Spanish churches, as well as the Knowles Chapel (1931) at Rollins College in Winter Park, Florida, a building whose restraint and simplicity reflect one of Cram's observations concerning the defining features of Spanish architecture.

These buildings—think of them as Cram's homage to Spain—were not the first Spanish-style buildings built in the United States, but they were important given Cram's prestige as an architect. As such they constituted a major contribution to the Spanish turn in the aesthetics of American architecture. The start of that turn can be traced to the closing years of the nineteenth century, but it gathered momentum, together with other facets of the Spanish craze, in the decades following the end of the 1898 war.

Beginnings: The Ponce de León

March 27, 1883, marked the day of the St. Augustine Historical Society's celebration of Juan Ponce de León's landing in Florida, and Henry M. Flagler, railroad magnate and Florida developer, was on hand to enjoy

Fig. 46. William Ward Watkin, architect, Administration Building, Texas Tech University, 1924. Watkin modeled the façade of this building after the 1537 façade that the Spanish architect Rodrigo Gil de Hontañón designed for the Colegio de San Ildefonso in Alcalá de Henares, Spain. Photograph by W. L. Daniels. Heritage Club Collections, c666-1, 1924. Southwest Collection, Special Collections Library, Texas Tech University, Lubbock, Texas.

it. Flagler had already decided to transform St. Augustine into a luxurious winter resort, a veritable Newport of the South. The town had one elegant hotel, the San Marco, a wooden Victorian-style building, but Flagler wanted something grander, something, as he later recalled, in "keeping with the character of that place."[14]

Keep in mind that the character of St. Augustine in 1883 was arguably more American than Spanish. Following the acquisition of Florida by the United States, most of the town's former Spanish inhabitants, including those from the Mediterranean island of Minorca who had come to Florida under the auspices of the British, had left. As more and more Americans of Protestant origin arrived, St. Augustine came to resemble what one visitor called an "American village." Remnants of the town's Spanish heritage included its eighteenth-century Spanish fort (renamed Fort Marion), a ceremonial town gate erected by the Spaniards in 1812, and a pair of streets lined with houses that had overhanging balconies or *piazzas*. Most visitors, however, tended to describe St. Augustine as "quaint" rather than "Spanish." Flagler went further. He called it "dull." The circumstances surrounding his decision to build a new hotel in harmony with the town's character are not altogether clear, but the events marking March 27 almost certainly played their part in convincing him to give St. Augustine the look of Old Spain.[15]

The look in question began with the construction of the Ponce de León Hotel, which opened its doors in January 1888 and was celebrated with a gala dinner that included "chicken a la espagnole."[16] Designed by the young New York architect Thomas Hastings (1860–1919), the massive hotel, now Flagler College, amounted to a pastiche of Old Spain that included entryways with plateresque-like decorated surrounds; door lintels etched with the word *bienvenida*, meaning welcome; entrance ways flanked with rondels incorporating Spanish proverbs and shell designs meant to evoke the traditional Spanish pilgrimage route to Santiago de Compostela; a rotunda with murals by the artist George W. Maynard (1843–1923) that included feminine allegories representing the glories (adventure, discovery, conquest, and civilization) of Spanish exploration; and in the hotel's lavish dining room—with stained-glass windows by Louis C. Tiffany—a vaulted ceiling with painted escutcheons rep-

Fig. 47. Thomas W. Hastings, architect, Ponce de León Hotel, St. Augustine, Florida, 1887. Henry Flagler wanted the design of Florida's first grand hotel to evoke the leisure, luxury, and picturesque qualities of Old Spain. Other developers in Florida would soon do the same. Courtesy Library of Congress.

resenting the cities and provinces of Spain and held aloft by maidens Hastings condescendingly referred to as "Spanish dancers." That same ceiling boasted inscriptions of old Spanish proverbs ("El buen vino no ha menester pregonero" [It is not necessary to advertise good wine]; "De la mano a la boca pierde la sopa" [From the hand to the mouth the soup is lost], etc.) designed to both educate and amuse the diners seated below. Yet the hotel's decorative pièce de résistance is likely to have been Thomas Moran's monumental *Ponce de León in Florida* (1877–78), a painting that had hung for a time in the Capitol in Washington and that Flagler later purchased in 1886 for his new hotel, then still under construction. It remained there, adding to what critics and visitors alike perceived as the resort's historic Spanish atmosphere, until 1906, when Flagler moved it to his new home in Palm Beach.[17]

As for the Ponce de León's overall design, little, with the possible exception of the red-tile roof and white plaster walls, was distinctly Spanish. It was rather a somewhat mongrel mixture of diverse design elements that has triggered endless scholarly discussion. One historian refers to the building as a prime example of "academic eclecticism," another as one that captures the "Spanish picturesque."[18] What's certain is that when the Ponce de León first opened, critics referred to it as a mixture of both Spanish and Moorish design, one that successfully created a "Spanish atmosphere" in a building emulating the "palaces of old Spain."[19]

Inspiration for this atmospheric design derived in part from Villa Zorayda, a neo-Moorish fantasy house that the Boston millionaire merchant Franklin W. Smith (1826–1911) had built as his winter residence in St. Augustine in 1883.[20] An intrepid traveler, Smith had a penchant for both ancient and exotic cultures, and it had taken him to southern Spain and the Alhambra in 1882. Smith later wrote that his visit to Granada inspired him to build his new villa—named after one of the Moorish princesses featured in Irving's *Tales of the Alhambra*—in the Moorish style. Constructed out of Portland cement mixed with coquina stone, the villa's central courtyard, modeled after one in the Alhambra, boasted a series of horseshoe arches inscribed with phrases from

Fig. 48. Thomas Moran (American, 1837–1926), *Ponce de León in Florida*, 1877–78, oil on canvas, 64 ¾ × 115 ⅞ in. Thomas Moran depicted the first meeting of the famed Spanish explorer Ponce de León and Florida's Seminole people as a peaceful encounter. Henry Flagler acquired the picture for display in St. Augustine's Ponce de León Hotel. Cummer Museum, Jacksonville, Florida. Acquired for the people of Florida by the Frederick H. Schultz Family and Bank of America. Additional funding from the Cummer Council, AP.1996.2.1.

the Quran and furnishings that Smith had acquired in both Granada and Morocco.[21]

Currently fitted out as a small house museum, Villa Zorayda is an oddity, but Flagler is likely to have seen it, *pace* Irving, as a building that evoked the romance of Spain—precisely the mood he wanted the Ponce de León to convey. Flagler subsequently conveyed these ideas to Hastings, an architect trained in the Beaux-Arts style in Paris and one who, starting in 1884, had joined the fashionable New York architectural firm of McKim, Mead and White. Why Flagler selected the young Hastings for the project is not altogether clear, but the choice may best be explained by Hastings's familiarity with the architecture of southern Spain. Following the completion of his studies in Paris, Hastings journeyed to Andalucia in 1882 and toured the Alhambra, signing the visitors' book on November 24 of that year. His arrival in New York also coincided with the publication of a series of articles on Spanish architecture published in the *American Architect and Building News* starting in 1885.[22] The extent to which these articles—the equivalent of a crash course in the subject—influenced Hastings's design decisions remains to be determined. What's certain is that the style selected was consistent with what he called "the spirit of old [meaning Spanish] Saint Augustine." He also invoked something of the spirit of Irving's Alhambra by calling the hotel an "American Xanadu."[23]

Ultimately the design of the Ponce de León was Flagler's. Having familiarized himself with Spain's history and literature, subjects that reportedly had first captured his attention in his youth, Flagler indicated in one interview that the hotel managed to capture the "bright side of the Spanish race" and dispel hackneyed ideas about the "dark and forbidding" nature of Spain's national character. As for why he chose the name Ponce de León, that of the first European to explore what is now Florida in 1513, Flagler explained it was partially inspired by "the romantic quest" of this "redoubtable knight and discoverer."[24] In keeping with that quest he conceived of the hotel as a pleasure dome, thus connecting it to Irving's view of Spain as a land of Oriental luxury and delight but, as the hotel's interior decorations were meant to suggest, also a country whose accomplishments were integral to both Florida's and America's colonial pasts.

Flagler's determination to capture something of Spain's early history in the Ponce de León was much more than a passing whim. In the 1880s, just as plans for the hotel were taking shape, what scholars call "medievalism" was all the rage inasmuch as the Middle Ages was thought to embody many of the values—authenticity, honesty, integrity—that America's fast-changing society had supposedly lost. Medievalism led in one direction to places—Spain among them—whose backwardness supposedly assured the preservation of those traditional values, and in another direction—to paraphrase the historian T. J. Jackson Lears—to homegrown "places of grace" meant to be accessible to vacationers and offer a modicum of respite from the pressures of the workaday world.[25]

These linkages—Spain, romance, adventure, pleasure dome, luxury, escape—were central to the Ponce de León. Similar ideas also account for the vaguely Spanish-cum-Moorish design of two other hotels, the Alcázar (also designed by Hastings) and the Cordova (originally Casa Monica)—associated with Flagler's efforts to transform St. Augustine into the country's finest and most luxurious winter resort.

But these Spanish-style hotels were only part of Flagler's master plan to infuse St. Augustine with the look, feel, and atmosphere of Old Spain. Integral to that plan was an effort to persuade the town council to hispanicize the names of St. Augustine's streets, a plan that met with only partial success. The town council agreed to change the name Washington Street to Granada Street, Gregg Lane to Cadiz Street, Hospital Street to Aviles Street, and so on, but it refused to transform the community's main thoroughfare, King Street, into the Alameda, a Spanish name reminiscent of the elm-lined walkways and parks found in Seville and Granada, along with others in Lima and Mexico City.[26] On the other hand they did agree that the Ponce de León festival should be an annual event so as to enhance St. Augustine's "Spanish" atmosphere, attract visitors, and fill the town's coffers. Over time this festival, complete with replicas of Spanish vessels, landings of the Spanish explorers, groups of "friendly" Seminole natives welcoming the foreigners ashore, and cavalcades featuring locals fitted out in armor and Spanish period dress became ever more elaborate. Minus the "friendly natives," that festival continues today.[27]

Giraldas

In the summer of 1890 the City of New York inaugurated a new Madison Square Garden, the second arena known by that name. The first, built in 1879 at the corner of Madison Avenue and Twenty-Ninth Street, had proved too small, and the Garden's owners, following a design competition, opted to replace it with a new, more sumptuous arena designed by Stanford White, one of the city's most prominent architects. The new Garden's main building, built in Italian Renaissance style, housed a ten-thousand-seat amphitheater, then one of the largest in the world. But what was particularly striking about the new Garden was its brightly illuminated 304-foot tower, an altitude topped only by the New York World skyscraper on Park Row.

Even more remarkable was the tower's unusual design. The first skyscrapers in New York, Chicago, and other American cities were typically constructed in a neoclassical idiom, either Roman or Greek. White wanted something different, unusual, a real crowd pleaser. He consequently modeled the Garden's tower on Seville's Giralda, a minaret that dated from the twelfth century and the era in which that city was part of al-Andalus. Miraculously the Giralda survived Seville's conquest by Christian forces in 1248 and later served as the bell tower of the Gothic cathedral constructed on the site previously occupied by a mosque. In the sixteenth century the Giralda was "Christianized" to the extent that it acquired a spire of Renaissance design topped by a weathervane in the form of an angel, known as the Giraldillo, and intended to symbolize the triumph of Christianity over Islam. Otherwise the Giralda, with its intricate, interlaced brickwork, impressed most visitors to Seville as a striking reminder of Spain's Muslim past. It also epitomized, together with the Alhambra, much of the romance that Irving and other visitors associated with southern Spain.

Presumably the Garden's Giralda-like tower was meant to do the same, although White, having incorporated what he called his "snuggery"—his name for a small bachelor's apartment—into one of the tower's upper

Fig. 49. Stanford White, architect, Tower of Madison Square Garden, New York, 1890. The design of this tower was modeled after Seville's Giralda, a twelfth-century minaret that was later transformed into the bell tower of the city's cathedral. Courtesy Library of Congress.

floors, evidently defined romance in more corporeal ways. In keeping with that mood White brazenly replaced the statue of the angel with an eighteen-foot-tall gilded copper figure of a naked Diana, Roman goddess of the hunt, a sculpture confected by his artist friend Augustus Saint-Gaudens.

Fig. 50. Augustus Saint-Gaudens, *Diana*, Madison Square Garden, New York, 1890. This twenty-one-foot-tall statue of Diana was soon replaced by a somewhat smaller version. The statue's naked torso challenged contemporary moral standards. Courtesy Library of Congress.

When this Diana was first unveiled in October 1891, her glistening naked body, together with her massive height, elicited considerable comment, mostly negative, in the New York press. Even White admitted that the Diana was too tall and out of scale with the rest of the tower. So she was soon removed and sent to Chicago, where she found a new perch on top of the Agriculture Building at the World's Columbian Exposition that opened in 1893. In the meantime Saint-Gaudens fabricated another, smaller—only thirteen feet tall—but still unclothed Diana, who was installed atop the Garden's tower in November 1893.

The unusual design of the Garden's tower was also a source of comment. Some critics thought it too tall, while others considered it less elegant than the Giralda in Seville. Still others pondered the need for copies or replicas of older structures as opposed to buildings of original, American design. Nor were critics able to decide what to call the tower's architectural style. One labeled it "baroque"; others more accurately termed it Spanish. And while one critic described the Garden as the "Ponce de León [Hotel] converted into a Roman palace," most seemed to agree with Mariana Griswold Van Rensselaer, who in an essay published in the *Century Magazine* asserted that White's Madison Square Garden was a building of "unforced" genius and "so big and so beautiful that it will never be removed."[28] (She was wrong; see below.)

Why White modeled his tower after the Giralda remains a mystery. He had previously traveled extensively in Europe but never to Spain, so he likely learned about the country from his artist friends, John Singer Sargent and William Merritt Chase. These artists also introduced White to the famed Spanish dancer Carmencita, even arranging for him to meet her at a private performance organized in Chase's Tenth Street Studio shortly before the Garden was opened to the public in June 1890. Those same friendships also explain why one critic could write that White "was and is profoundly interested by Spanish architecture and Spanish decorative art."[29]

Yet little of that interest was evident in 1887, when White originally conceived of modeling the Garden's tower after the one in Seville. As he had never visited Spain, let alone Seville, possible sources for his design included David Roberts's well-known lithographs of the monument; the paintings of Seville by the New York artist Samuel Colman, a close friend of White's father; the illustrations by Francis Lathrop, a friend of White, published in *Harper's New Monthly Magazine* in 1882 as accompaniments to the essay "Spanish Vistas" written by Lathrop's brother, George Parsons Lathrop; and the detailed fold-out view of the monument featured in the December 1885 issue of the *American Architect.*[30] White's Giralda replica was also in keeping with the so-called

Moorish revival (or mudéjar) style of architecture that initially made its appearance in New York in 1868 in the guise of Leopold Eidlitz's Temple Emanu-El on Fifth Avenue and subsequently in the Casino Theatre designed by Francis Hatch Kimball and opened on the corner of Broadway and Thirty-Ninth Street in 1882. This eye-catching music hall, said to echo the "Saracenic" architecture of Spain, featured an elaborately carved interior vaguely modeled after the designs of the Alhambra.[31]

Neither the Garden nor its magnificent tower lasted for very long. In 1925 new owners demolished the building, although the Diana was saved; she now hangs in the central hall of the Philadelphia Museum of Art. But well before that occurred, White's Giralda inspired other architects to build their own versions of the Giralda—twenty in all—in what amounted to a nationwide effort to bring something of the romance of Spain to such cities as Chicago, Cleveland, San Francisco, and Miami, which eventually boasted three such towers. Among these American Giraldas, the most unusual was the Electric Tower, constructed at Buffalo's Pan-American Exposition grounds in 1901 (see below). Another notable example was the one designed by William Reynolds and festooned with red hearts. It was built in 1903 in the center of Dreamland, an amusement park on New York's Coney Island.[32]

The first of these copycat Giraldas was the short-lived version at the World's Columbian Exposition in Chicago in 1893. Constructed somewhat incongruously atop the fair's Cold Storage Building, this Giralda, evoking both Spain and Seville, was in keeping with the exposition's Columbian theme. It also complemented the fair's other two other Spanish buildings: a replica of the La Rábida monastery, outfitted with various memorabilia of Columbus, and that of Valencia's Lonja, or Merchants' Exchange, a building that served as Spain's national pavilion and was meant to symbolize Spain's business acumen. But few of the fair's two million or so visitors had an opportunity to visit the tower, as it was destroyed by fire on July 15, 1893, only a few short weeks after the fair had opened. Much more durable was the Giralda replica that served as the clock tower for San Francisco's new Ferry Building, completed in 1895. With the exception of its original brick facing, whose color resem-

Fig. 51. A. Page Brown, architect, Ferry Building, San Francisco, California, 1906. The Ferry Building's tower was one among many replicas of Seville's Giralda built in the United States. It withstood the 1906 earthquake, but its original ocher facing was soon painted white. Courtesy Library of Congress.

bled the original in Seville, the tower withstood the tremors of the 1906 earthquake owing to its interior steel frame. This Giralda was the work of a Stanford White disciple, A. Page Brown (1859–96), a New York architect who had moved to San Francisco in 1890 and who subsequently served as principal designer of the California State Building erected at the World's Columbian Exposition. The commission responsible for the competition for that building had specifically solicited a design combining what was called the "Mission and Moorish types" and did so in the belief such a mixture "would be distinctive and typical of the earliest architecture of California."[33] The commission would not have known it then, but in making that decision they initiated an architectural style that spread across not only California but the whole country.

Fig. 52. A. Page Brown, architect, California State Building, Chicago, 1893. *Campbell's Illustrated History of the World Columbian Exposition*, 1894. Designed in what was originally defined as a mixture of Moorish and mission-style architecture, this building was meant to evoke California's Spanish past. Courtesy Special Collections, University of Wisconsin–Milwaukee.

Mission and Moorish

Inherent in the mixture of mission and Moorish architecture was the notion that Spanish culture, following centuries of Muslim rule during the Middle Ages, was profoundly "Oriental." Spanish soldiers and friars supposedly brought this same Oriental or "Moorish" culture to the Americas in the sixteenth century and ultimately to "el Norte," the old Spanish term for the Southwest. From there came the idea that the simple design of the region's eighteenth-century Franciscan missions—solid adobe construction, plain whitewashed walls, red-tile roofs, and minimal decoration—reflected Spain's Muslim heritage as well.[34]

Such reasoning had also underscored another California landmark: Palo Alto's Leland Stanford Junior University, today's Stanford University. When Stanford first decided in 1884 to establish a university, he wanted it to be built in "Moorish" style. A few years later, however, advice received from the Boston architect Charles Allerton Coolidge persuaded Stanford to discard "Moorish" and build the new campus in the more established Romanesque style of architecture popularized by Coolidge's noted mentor, H. H. Richardson. In the end Stanford and Coolidge arrived at a compromise. The campus was to be Romanesque, but in keeping with California's Spanish heritage, its buildings were to have red-tile roofs along with distinctive Spanish names.

That same Spanish heritage also figured in the frieze of the memorial arch erected on the Stanford campus in 1899. That frieze, drawing upon the idea of Sturdy Spain as outlined by Prescott and subsequently popularized in California by Lummis, followed the course of Spanish colonization in the Americas, starting with figures of Cortés, Pizarro, and the other conquistadors who blazed the path that Jesuit and Franciscan missionaries would later follow. On the other hand nothing in the frieze evoked the "noble romance" that Lummis and other late nineteenth-century writers associated with California's Spanish past.

However, hints of that romance figured in Page Brown's decision to top the Ferry Building in San Francisco with a Giralda, as well as in his earlier design for the California State Building at the Chicago fair, built in what he called "semi-Spanish Renaissance." In keeping with the design commission's mandate, the building's plain white stucco walls and red-tile roofs harked back to California's old missions. The "Moorish" component was harder to find, although some observers located it in the building's roof garden, while others saw it in the dome designed by Brown's assistant, Bernard Maybeck, an architect who had collaborated with Thomas Hastings on the Ponce de León Hotel.

But whether the building was mission, Moorish, Spanish, or something in between, one promotional article declared that the California State Building "will take the beholder back to the days when the Fathers, with their Missions, started the march of civilization in the Golden West."[35] In addition to being one of the most visited sites at the fair, the California State Building helped popularize the vogue for what came to be known as Spanish mission or mission revival architecture, a style generally associated with plain, whitewashed stucco walls, red-tile roofs, and, according to one of its chief proponents, Irving Gill, "long, low lines, graceful arcades, tile roofs, bell towers, arched doorways and walled gardens." For Gill the mission style was also "tradition, history, and romance."[36]

Other observers had similar ideas. One such observer was George Wharton James (1858–1923), a transplanted Briton turned California booster whose *In and Out of the Missions of California* (1905) was one of the first guidebooks to these old Spanish monuments. Echoing Lummis, James applauded the missionaries for having transformed "rude savages" into "tens of thousands of happy, contented, progressive people," a statement unlikely to have found favor among Native Americans at any time.[37] In another book, *Through Ramona's Country* (1909), James indicated that the Spanish missions offered Californians "lessons of simplicity, dignity and power," and in an unpublished essay he suggested that the mission-style houses popping up across southern California constituted a "silent tribute to the genius" of Franciscan missionaries who first brought "civilization" to California. He also praised the style's "native simplicity and elegance, . . . frank honesty of adaptability to purpose, [and] . . . freedom from extraneous unnecessary adornment."[38]

Early California examples of the new mission style included Los Angeles's Casa de Rosas (1893), whose architect, Sumner P. Hunt, was a friend and associate of Charles Lummis; the Tevis house in Bakersfield, designed by Henry A. Schultze and part of a complex known as Los Portales; the Hacienda del Pozo de Verona, designed by A. C. Schweinfurth for William R. Hearst and his mother in 1896 in Pleasanton; Pasadena's Hotel Green (Frederick Roehrig, architect), an 1898 building whose style was described as a mixture of Spanish and Moorish; and the special favorite of George Wharton James, Riverside's Glenwood-Mission Inn, designed by Arthur B. Benton, built in 1902 with financing from Henry E. Huntington, and boasting a large collection of religious art, wax figures of Pope Pius X and his pontifical court, a row of mission-style arches, a courtyard, a campanile, and more.

From its California base the mission style spread quickly to other parts of the South and West, to mining towns such as Ajo, Arizona (designed in 1906 by the architects William Kenyon and Maurice Maine and incorporating a "Spanish Mediterranean" plaza), and Tyrone, New Mexico (designed in unornamented Spanish style by Bertram Grosvenor

Fig. 53. Arthur Benton and Myron Hunt, architects, Old Adobe, Glenwood–Mission Inn, Riverside, California, ca. 1920. Built in various stages between 1902 and 1914, the Mission Inn is a classic example of mission- or Spanish colonial–style architecture. Courtesy Library of Congress.

Goodhue in 1914).[39] Variants of this same style appeared in many of the depots constructed by the Atchison, Topeka, and Santa Fe Railway in California, Arizona, New Mexico, and Texas, and others in Bismarck, North Dakota, and Battle Creek, Michigan. With its distinctive red-tile roof, the Burlington Station in Hastings, Nebraska, dating from 1900, represented yet another iteration of the same style, as would other public buildings and private houses in other states.

Aiding the style's spread—and this is key—was the readiness of numerous observers to declare the "Spanish style" the equivalent of an autochthonous "American" style of architecture comparable to that of Puritan meetinghouses of colonial New England. Interest in locating such a national style had been growing since the 1880s following the example of Great Britain, which had determined that Gothic revival architecture, as reflected in its new Houses of Parliament designed in 1840 by Charles Barry with help from Augustus Pugin, best embodied the country's temperament, whereas France opted for neo-Renaissance style in the design of Paris's new Hôtel de Ville, which replaced an older structure destroyed in 1871. Starting in the 1880s, Spain did something similar, building bullrings and train stations in a neo-mudéjar style in the belief that it aligned with the country's Muslim past.

In the United States a similar consensus proved difficult to reach. Charles Eliot Norton and other writers lamented lack of a national, quintessentially "American" style of architecture, while others declared that America's ethnic and ecological diversity required a series of regional styles. The debate over this issue lasted for decades. In the meantime the mission or Spanish style continued to spread, aided in part by the emergent pan-American movement and the idea of hemispheric cooperation and exchange. These two movements coalesced starting around 1895, when initial planning for yet another world's fair, to be known as the Pan-American Exposition and to be celebrated in Buffalo, New York, began. The 1898 war delayed the exposition for several years, but when it finally opened, in May 1901, its organizers had already determined that since the aim of the exposition was "to celebrate the achievements of civilization during 100 years of development in the Western Hemisphere," the one style of architecture that best expressed that idea, together with the notion of hemispheric unity, was fundamentally Spanish.[40]

The Pan-American Exposition's official handbook offers a guide as to how that decision was reached. The organizers' mission was clear: "This is to be an American Exposition—North, South and Middle Americas and our Islands of the Seas. Neither Greece nor Rome, nor yet Turkey come into this thing. It shouldn't be particularly classic, Gothic or Byzantine. Perhaps we cannot get away altogether from the old principles of construction, but we can at least make an effort to exemplify American architectural ideas, if we can find them."[41]

The organizers initially agreed that those ideas were best expressed in the "Spanish-American mission style," but at some point the exposition's chief architect, John M. Carrère, Thomas Hastings's partner in the firm of Carrère and Hastings, intervened and reportedly opted for

Fig. 54. John Galen Howard, architect, Electric Tower, Pan-American Exposition, Buffalo, New York, 1901. Designed as another replica of Seville's Giralda, the tower had a "Spanish" style in keeping with the exposition's pan-American ideal, meant to evoke the unity of the peoples North and South America. Courtesy Library of Congress.

"formality picturesquely developed." The simplicity of the mission style subsequently developed into something more elaborate, as it incorporated the use of color for different buildings, hence the nickname Rainbow City for the exposition as a whole. The exposition's centerpiece moreover was the four-hundred-foot-high Electric Tower modeled after the Giralda, decorated with hundreds of electric lights and topped not by a naked Diana but a respectfully clothed "Goddess of Light."[42]

The Pan-American Exposition in Buffalo—known popularly as the "Pan"—is remembered today as the site where, on September 6, 1901, President McKinley was shot by an assassin. The exposition, like so many other expositions of that era, was not an overwhelming commercial success, but it did manage to attract a steady stream of visitors during the six months it was open to the public. Many, however, found it difficult to find the right words to describe its architectural style. As one visitor put it, "Of all the buildings created, some speak of old mission architecture and some do not. But, still, happily, although their work ran the whole gamut of architectural orders, combinations and modifications, yet it came together in harmony. Much of it is Renaissance of the freest sort; but the Spanish-American idea is dominant there, and makes itself felt throughout." Other terms used to describe the architecture included "quasi-Spanish style," "free-form Spanish-oriented structures," "fantasy buildings of a freely interpreted Spanish style," or, as the official guide defined it, "free treatment of the Spanish Renaissance."[43]

As for the merits of this "Spanish" architecture, opinions differed once again, although one critic, Robert Grant, summed up prevailing opinion with the observation that it was "dignified but not tawdry," also "picturesque and interesting."[44] The journalist Julian Hawthorne (the son of the famous writer Nathaniel Hawthorne) offered another, decidedly more racialized comment on the exposition's architecture in a report published in *The Cosmopolitan* magazine in 1901. "Technically," Hawthorne observed, "it is a liberal rendering of the Spanish Renaissance, but it symbolizes our welcome to the genius of the Latins to mingle their strain with the genius of the Anglo-Saxon."[45]

Such language is out of place in today's world, but in this description Hawthorne, in addition to expressing his support for the pan-American movement, was suggesting that "Spanish" architecture was an "American" architecture ideally suited for and possibly capable of helping to unite the country's increasingly cosmopolitan culture. Additional support for the "American-ness" of Spanish architecture came from the organizers of the South Carolina Interstate and West-Indian Exposition, which opened in Charleston in December 1901. The architectural heritage of the Carolina Low Country was primarily English, but, in keeping with the ideals of pan-Americanism, the fair's organizers determined to adopt the "rich and beautiful Spanish Renaissance architecture."[46] That decision, coming on the heels of the "Pan," allowed Enos Brown, a California writer, and Frank Chouteau Brown, a Boston architect, to imagine the "Spanish type of architecture" as the possible "foundation upon which our national type of architecture may be erected." They also suggested that the "picturesque remains" of California's Spanish missions had the potential to become "proto-types for a new type dwelling that bids fair to become so immensely popular as to overrun the country."[47]

As it turned out, that prognostication was half wrong, half right. It was wrong because enthusiasm for the original "plain" style of mission architecture was, according to one article that appeared in the California journal *Architect and Engineer* in 1909, a "waning fad."[48] But it was right to the extent that the mission style served as the starting point for a newer, more elaborate, and more luxurious interpretation of Spanish architecture, known as Spanish revival or Spanish colonial, that spread like wildfire across the United States as the decade often known as the Roaring Twenties got under way.

"A City in Old Spain"

The transition from mission to Spanish colonial style began with yet another exposition—the Panama-California Exposition held in San Diego in 1915. That same year San Francisco organized the much larger Panama-Pacific International Exposition, choosing as its principal architectural scheme a Beaux-Arts, neoclassical style reminiscent of the Chicago exposition of 1893 as well as of the St. Louis World's Fair, held in 1904. The organizers of the San Diego exposition opted instead for a style more in keeping with the city's Spanish-cum-Mexican past. The city fathers had already starting celebrating the region's Spanish heritage in 1892 with a series of historical pageants featuring the landing of the Spanish captain Juan Rodríguez Cabrillo near San Diego in 1542, partly as a way of attracting visitors to the city, much in the same way St. Augustine used Ponce de León to enhance its reputation as a prime tourist destination.[49]

The 1915 exposition had even more ambitious aims. As Matthew Bokovoy has explained, local leaders envisioned it as a way to promote San Diego's newly constructed city center, located about a mile south of the original Spanish settlement. The new development, to be called Old Town and situated adjacent to the old Franciscan mission, was meant to demonstrate further the commercial advantages that San Diego's proximity to the newly opened Panama Canal offered to both shippers and investors. In addition, having determined to organize the event around a pan-American theme, the exposition organizers offered Old Town as a way of demonstrating the strength of San Diego's Spanish heritage and uniting a city whose population included large numbers of Spanish-speaking Mexican field hands and laborers.[50]

To showcase that heritage and provide a more suitable setting for the exposition, the name of the site selected for the exposition was changed from City Park to Balboa Park. The still popular mission revival style was also selected as the exposition's architectural theme, and to help with matters of planning and overall design the organizers selected Frederick Law Olmsted Jr., son of the famous designer of New York's Central Park and head of the firm of Olmsted and Bros., as their chief landscape architect. Olmsted, never a fan of the simplicity and sobriety of mission style, recommended something more elaborate than mission style for the exposition's overall design and in 1910 suggested the appointment of the New York architect Bertram Grosvenor Goodhue (1869–1924) as the exposition's principal consulting architect. The organizers agreed.[51]

A partner in the firm of Cram, Goodhue, and Ferguson, Architects, Goodhue, together with Ralph Cram, was keen on Gothic revival–style architecture, as demonstrated in his design for St. Thomas Church in New York. Yet Goodhue also had experience working in California, having assisted with the neo-Moorish-cum-neo-Spanish design of El Fueridis,

the Montecito estate built for his friend James Waldron Gillespie. Goodhue was also enamored with the baroque architecture of colonial Mexico.
Inspired in part by Robert Lamborn's book on Mexican colonial painting,
in 1890 Goodhue, then age twenty-one, journeyed to Mexico. That trip
inspired his rather impressionistic and romanticized travel book *Mexican
Memories*, published in 1892. The volume recounts Goodhue's fascination with different aspects of Mexican culture, especially his admiration
for the architectural grandeur of its colonial-era churches, especially the
elaborate Churrigueresque decoration of Mexico City's imposing cathedral. A few years later Goodhue returned to Mexico, accompanied by the
Boston-based writer Sylvester Baxter and a photographer, Henry Greenwood Peabody. It was a trip that resulted in a massive twelve-volume
collaborative study, *Spanish-Colonial Architecture in Mexico* (1901), for
which Goodhue provided the drawings of the elevations and plans of
individual buildings. It was the first major book on the subject ever published in English, and together the authors expressed their admiration for
the manner in which Mexico's colonial architects had managed to transcribe and adapt Spanish architecture into another style they described
as "inexhaustibly picturesque and enchantingly spectacular."[52]

Picturesque and spectacular are both terms that can be applied to the
architectural scheme that Goodhue, together with his assistant, Carleton M. Winslow, developed for Balboa Park. Drawing directly upon
his experiences in Mexico, together with another trip to Spain in 1901,
Goodhue envisioned the San Diego exposition as the equivalent of a
"city in Old Spain," albeit one that combined the simple stucco walls
of mission-style architecture with ornamented doorways and window
surrounds, iron grilles and balconies, all based on the baroque churches
in Mexico. This mixture of styles had different names, although it was
most commonly referred to as Spanish revival, Spanish colonial, or simply as Spanish, as it supposedly exuded the spirit of "Old Spain." That
spirit infused Goodhue's designs for the exposition's principal buildings,
especially its centerpiece, the California State Building, whose tiled,
polychromed dome was loosely modeled on that of the cathedral in the
Mexican city of Puebla. The building, still extant, currently houses the
San Diego Museum of Man.

Fig. 55. Bertram G. Goodhue, architect, California State Building, Panama-California Exposition, San Diego, California, 1915. Goodhue's mixture of Mexican and Spanish elements in this building epitomized what came to be known as the Spanish revival style. Courtesy Library of Congress.

Goodhue's design decisions proved an instant success. Even before the fair opened, local newspapers welcomed its innovative style. One reported that "the Exposition might have gone ahead and erected buildings of Greek or Roman type, or other conventional types which have appeared at all world's fairs of the past. Beyond a doubt the result would have been beautiful . . . [but] . . . the Exposition adopted a different plan, and now offers to the world something which is not only wondrously beautiful, but also is creative in that it has brought about a genuine renaissance of the glories of Spanish art and architecture."[53] And closer to the fair's actual opening in January 1915, another observed, "The Spanish atmosphere has been carried out to the finest detail. The guards and attendants of the Exposition will be garbed as caballeros and conquistadors, and the dancing girls, who will move to the hum of the guitar and the click of the castanets, will be Spanish dancing girls in the bright costumes of Old Spain, in the dances which have been performed for hundreds of years in the plazas of Castile. It is all very quaint and very romantic and very beautiful."[54]

Together with most other world's fairs of that era, the Panama-California Exposition failed to bring San Diego the economic windfall its organizers had imagined. But it served to generate nationwide publicity for the city, adding to its reputation as a tourist destination where visitors could admire not only Balboa Park but also the city's newly reconstructed mission and Old Town, which included what was billed as "Ramona's House" (see fig. 12). The exposition also attracted a number of top-drawer celebrities, including President Taft and Theodore Roosevelt, the former president.

The exposition's free interpretation of Spanish architecture also proved a powerful aesthetic, inspiring other architects, developers, and in some instances entire communities to emulate Goodhue's "Spanish" designs. The architects included Los Angeles's Myron Hunt, whose first Spanish-style building—Riverside's First Congregationalist Church, completed in 1912—incorporated some of the ornamentation that Goodhue employed; George Washington Smith, designer of El Hogar, one of the first Spanish revival–style houses to be built in Montecito, an exclusive community located just east of Santa Barbara; and Richard Requa, the architect hired by the glass manufacturer Edward Libbey to supervise the reconstruction of Ojai after that community's destruction by fire in 1917. Following Requa's advice, Ojai was the first California town to be built exclusively in the Spanish revival architectural style. It also established a model for several other developments. Among them were Rancho Santa Fe, where the supervising architect was Requa's disciple Lilian Rice, and Palos Verdes Estates, outside Los Angeles, a development whose covenant, in addition to limiting construction to a "Latin"—read Spanish or Mediterranean—style, allowed only Caucasians as residents. Another such community was San Clemente, founded by a Swedish émigré, Ole Hanson. Advertised as a "Spanish village by the Sea," it was also a development whose covenant stipulated that it be a "whites only" community. That same covenant, following the example of Palos Verdes, also required houses to have white stucco walls and red-tile roofs in order into preserve California's "Spanish tradition."[55]

As previously noted, that same tradition and accompanying aesthetic figured in Julia Morgan's design for William Randolph Hearst's sprawling hilltop "castle" at San Simeon, California, as well as in the city of Santa Barbara's efforts to embark on a systematic program of architectural hispanicization starting in 1919. Santa Barbara owed its origins to a mission established by the Franciscans in 1782 and the soldiers stationed in a nearby garrison, or *presidio*. In the mid-nineteenth century many of the old, whitewashed adobe homes and buildings were still intact, but after California entered the union in 1849, that situation changed, as it did in other parts of the state. Newcomers, most of them Protestants from New England and the Midwest, brought with them a taste for other, more familiar architectural styles. Already by 1874 an article in a local newspaper had complained that "the old landmarks and most charming characteristics of Santa Barbara are disappearing among the march of 'improvements.'" Typical of these improvements were the thin wooden posts that replaced the existing stocky and stuccoed pillars on the front porch of the De la Guerra house (1817–26), one of the city's oldest adobe homes. During the "boom" years of the 1870s the newly constructed Arlington Hotel featured Victorian design, and the new courthouse was in the Greek revival style. So many were these "improvements" that in 1882 Helen Hunt Jackson, author of *Ramona*, compared Santa Barbara to "one of a dozen New England towns—stodgy, smug, correct, and uninteresting."[56] The neo-anglicization continued after the coming of the railroad to Santa Barbara in 1887, and by the mid-1890s one guidebook was describing the city's few remaining old adobe houses as "the crumbling ruins of Spanish glory" and "picturesque."[57] These losses notwithstanding, Santa Barbara's Spanish heritage survived in many of its street names, and in 1886, as a way of marking the centennial of its Franciscan mission, the local government organized parades and other festivities celebrating the city's colonial past.

Despite such developments, Santa Barbara's Anglo inhabitants expressed little interest in the growing mission revival movement until well after the end of the 1898 war. Construction on its first mission-style building, the new Arlington Hotel, designed by Arthur Benton, architect of Riverside's Glenwood-Mission Inn, followed the loss of the older Victorian-style hotel building to a fire in 1906. Other mission-style buildings soon followed. By 1920 local planners, inspired by the example of Ojai and San Clemente, set out to use architecture as a means of restoring Santa Barbara's Spanish tradition and augmenting its attractiveness as a place to visit as well as to live. Key players in this movement included Pearl Chase and especially the transplanted New Yorker Bernhard Hoffmann, both members of the city's civic league and planning commission. For advice Hoffmann turned to Goodhue, who was then spending part of every year in Santa Barbara; his disciple Carleton Winslow, designer of Casa Dorinda, another of Montecito's Spanish villas; and the architect George Washington Smith, designer of the Casa del Herrero, one of the country's finest examples of "Spanish farmhouse"–style architecture and one whose owner, George Steedman, was particularly keen on decorating the house with Spanish art and antiques. What followed was a project to transform Santa Barbara into a city that was Spanish, in the sense of southern Spanish or Andalucian.[58]

This ambitious project began with the construction of El Paseo (also known as the Street of Spain), which was to be lined with buildings having white stucco walls and red-tile roofs meant to create the equivalent of "a quaint little street in the South of Spain." When Charles Lummis first saw it in 1924, he was effusive, describing El Paseo "as the best thing of its kind in the United States—a dream of architectural beauty and of faithfulness to the spirit and the detail [of Old California]."[59]

Local builders soon broke ground on similar projects: a new Spanish-style city hall, the Lobero Theatre (designed and reconstructed by George

Fig. 56. William Mooser III (with J. Wilmer Hershey), architect, Santa Barbara County Courthouse, Santa Barbara, California, 1929. Following a destructive earthquake in 1925, Santa Barbara remodeled itself as a "Spanish" town with a new courthouse and other Spanish-style buildings. Other communities did the same. Picture from *Santa Barbara: Tierra Adorada (A Community History)*, 1930. Photographer unknown. Courtesy Creative Commons.

Washington Smith), and various Spanish-themed office buildings. The earthquake that struck Santa Barbara on June 29, 1925, devastated much of the old city center, but it also afforded local planners and developers a unique opportunity to accelerate the city's hispanicization. Central to the rebuilding project was a new Spanish-style courthouse (completed in 1929 and decorated on the interior with a wall mural by artist Daniel Sayre Groesbeck depicting key moments in the history of Spanish California). Santa Barbara's makeover also included the construction of a series of affordable, bungalow-style houses built in loose Spanish-cum-Mediterranean design.[60]

Through these and other projects Santa Barbara endeavored to recover the "romance" that Californians, like other Americans, had come to associate with Spain. For this same reason, as well as to attract visitors, in August 1924 Santa Barbara organized its first Old Spanish Days festival, which was modeled after Pasadena's Carnival of Roses Festival but with a decidedly more historical bent. Publicity for the festival came from the Dons and Donnas Society, an organization whose participants, mainly of Anglo-Saxon ancestry, wore Spanish period dress. The fiesta itself began with a parade that included a Spanish galleon, a group of Santa Barbara Kiwanians dressed as "historically accurate Indians" meeting the Spanish captain Juan Cabrillo after he stepped ashore, and a parade that included marchers dressed as Spanish and Mexican soldiers and a magnificent palomino horse meant to serve as the "living symbol" of the entire fiesta, as it demonstrated the interconnectedness of Spain—its country of origin—Mexico, and California. Other activities included musical performances featuring Spanish dancers playing castanets, Spanish and Mexican songs, and nighttime serenades.[61]

The emphasis Santa Barbara accorded its Spanish as opposed to its more immediate Mexican past does much to explain why the journalist Carey McWilliams, writing in the 1940s, was so outspoken in his criticism of what he called "improvised traditions and manufactured legends," such as the ones that emerged around Helen Hunt Jackson's fictional Ramona. He also labeled California's Spanish heritage a "fantasy," one invented primarily for commercial purposes and that barked racial prejudice, as the state's heritage was far more Mexican than Spanish.[62] McWilliams was right. California's "Spanishness," centered on the near mythic figure of Junípero Serra, had been wildly overblown. Nor was McWilliams the first to express the idea that California's supposed Spanish heritage had been invented primarily for commercial ends. Charles Lummis, the writer responsible for creating much of that fantasy heritage, had similar concerns. In 1925, on the eve of the first Old Spanish Days festival, Lummis worried that "pirates and materialists and money-changers will try to vulgarize and commercialize that beautiful occasion" and tarnish what he understood as "the old romantic beauty that was California."[63]

Lummis's worries, however, did little to deter the proponents of Santa Barbara's hispanicization. They were predominantly Anglos whose interpretation of pan-Americanism leaned more in the direction of Old Spain than toward America's Spanish-speaking neighbors to the south, let alone the culture, language, and customs of the Mexicans they employed as gardeners, servants, and cooks, or the itinerant farmworkers still known derogatorily as "greasers," or the fierce-looking Pancho Villa–like *bandidos* (Donald Trump's "bad hombres") regularly featured in Hollywood westerns (see chapter 7). Old Spain, in contrast, evoked images of dashing caballeros, seductive gypsies like Carmen, and the trio of luxury, leisure, and romance. Those same connections were also responsible for movie theaters named Granada, Alhambra, and Seville; they inspired new luxury resorts and hotels built in the Spanish style; and they helped fuel a nationwide demand for houses built in the Spanish style.

Spanish Castles, American Style

In 1921 the South Florida real estate boom was just heating up, with new housing developments popping up across the state. One of the largest and most ambitious was the one George E. Merrick (1886–1942) planned for Coral Gables plantation, a citrus grove located on the southern outskirts of Miami. Merrick envisioned Coral Gables as a utopian "garden community" suburb modeled on New York's Forest Hills. But Forest Hills was a Tudor-style development, and Merrick wanted Coral Gables to be "Spanish," a style he believed consistent with Florida's colonial heritage as well as its semitropical climate.

Fig. 57. Edward Eichenbaum, architect, Granada Theatre, Chicago, 1926. Demolished in 1990, this theater was one among hundreds of "atmospheric" movie palaces of the 1920s bearing Spanish names. Courtesy Library of Congress.

Inspiration for Coral Gables's Spanish design came from several sources. Merrick partly attributed it to the architecture he had seen on a previous trip to Mexico and Central America. That journey supposedly convinced him of the need to satisfy the everyman dream of owning a "castle in Spain" in the guise of an affordable Spanish-style house.[64] Other sources included the colonial-era buildings Merrick encountered on a trip to Havana, along with the Ponce de León and other Spanish-style resort hotels in St. Augustine, as well as the mansions Addison Mizner was building in Florida's Palm Beach (see below). Then there was the Villa Serena, the Spanish-cum-Mediterranean revival house in South Miami built for William Jennings Bryan in 1916, and the similarly designed El Jardin, a house completed in 1919 for John Bindley, president of Pittsburgh Steel, and in Coconut Grove, then an independent community immediately adjacent to Coral Gables.

Merrick's uncle, Denman Fink, served as his chief planning assistant and artistic advisor. Fink had never visited Spain, but he had read Prescott, Irving as well, and knew enough about Spain and its culture to encourage Merrick's efforts to give Coral Gables a thoroughly Spanish feel. The community was still on the drawing boards when Fink explained to one reporter that "we are endeavoring to transplant from the old world, the wealth of color, the beauty, the romance of the Spain of Ferdinand and Isabel."[65]

Fink expanded on this theme in an article published in the *Miami Herald* as part of the promotional campaign that Merrick orchestrated in conjunction with the formal opening of Coral Gables to the public on November 24, 1921. Headlined "Castles in Spain Made Real," the article explained that "we have taken for our motif such old Spanish cities as Cordova, Salamanca, and Toledo, and lovely old Seville" and that Coral Gables would be a "really faithful rendering of the fine old Spanish atmosphere" updated to serve modern needs. Fink also conjured up the image of "broad plazas, cloistered walls and vine-glad pergolas" together with the "charm," "dignity," "quaintness," and "restfulness" of a community visualized "along purely Spanish lines of the real old type."[66]

As the new community took shape, the "lines" of Coral Gables were not as purely Spanish as Fink had suggested. The architects involved in the project—Richard Kiehnel, H. George Fink, and the landscape designer Phineas Paist—persuaded Merrick to broaden his vision of what Coral Gables should be. The result was a Mediterranean mishmash, with Spanish and what Merrick in one interview called "Italian, Venetian, North African and Mayan" thrown into the mix.[67]

Whatever Coral Gables was (and remains), Merrick marketed it as distinctly Spanish, because Spanish, in keeping with the success of Spanish-themed buildings elsewhere, was America's style du jour, simple yet refined, luxurious as well. Spanish also could be marketed—and sold—as "American" in ways that Venetian and Moorish could not, and this was the pitch that Merrick, a marketing genius, employed in November 1921 when lots in Coral Gables first went on sale. That pitch, a multimedia event, included promotional articles such as the one Fink had authored; posters announcing "Follow the Golden Galleon: Where Your Castle in

Fig. 58. "Follow the Golden Galleon" promotional poster for Coral Gables, Florida, 1925. The developer George Merrick promoted Coral Gables as a "Spanish" community where home buyers could purchase their own version of a "castle in Spain." Courtesy State Archives of Florida.

Spain Is Made Real" and tacked up on trees and signposts across South Florida; sales agents dressed as Spanish caballeros; and, on the opening day of the sale, a Spanish musical fiesta that reportedly attracted more than five thousand potential buyers. Merrick organized similar promotions in various northern cities, including one in New York City's Grand Central Palace that featured rooms decorated with Spanish paintings and antiques and was described in the *New York Times* as "a piece of Old Spain in Gotham."[68]

Adding to what Merrick billed as Coral Gables's "fine old Spanish atmosphere" were Spanish street names (Granada Boulevard, Ponce de León Boulevard, Alhambra Plaza, Balboa Plaza, Segovia Street, and the grand Puerta de Sol (now Douglas) entrance way; fountains with Spanish names (including one named after Hernando de Soto); a city hall with a façade festooned with escutcheons of the ancient kingdoms of Castile and León; and the development's centerpiece, the Ritz-Carlton Hotel, with a tower that was yet another replica of Seville's Giralda. (The hotel opened in 1925.) One departure from the Spanish motif was the Venetian Casino, with a freshwater pool crisscrossed by a small flotilla of gondolas Merrick imported from Venice. But Coral Gables's other amenities were distinctly Spanish. They included the Alhambra Arcade, which was a shopping mall, along with the Granada Shops, an emporium where the owners of newly constructed Spanish-style bungalows and houses—the everyman Spanish castles that Merrick had previously envisioned—could purchase reproductions of Spanish paintings, furniture, and antiques.[69]

There were more such shops in Palm Beach, which, together with Boca Raton, constituted another epicenter of South Florida's Spanish craze. Much has already been written on the architectural and design history of these resorts, but what was arguably Spanish—or at least Mediterranean—in both was mostly the handiwork of the famed architect Addison Mizner (1872–1933). Born in California, educated in Guatemala (where his father was the U.S. ambassador), Mizner, unlike Merrick, had visited Spain, studying (perhaps Spanish history or literature) for about a year at the University of Salamanca. That trip to Spain, he later wrote, was a pilgrimage: "I turned to Salamanca as inevitably as a Mohammedan seeks Mecca. There I learned to give expression to my boyhood longings."[70] Those longings entailed additional travels to Europe, a stint as an antiques dealer in New York, and the desire to design and decorate houses in a Spanish or Mediterranean mode. What's interesting about Mizner is that he kept a detailed graphic record of his travels in the form of sketches and photographs that he later incorporated into a series of twenty-five albums that are currently housed in the King Library of the Society of the Four Arts in Palm Beach. These include three albums labeled "Spain," "Spain and Its Provinces," and "Spain and Its Colonies," along with others designated "Gothic," "Furniture," "Textiles," and the like. There is even one entitled "Architecture of the United States," which, as one recent study suggests, is basically a tribute to the work of one of Mizner's mentors, Stanford White.[71] These hefty volumes contain page after page of drawings of houses, gardens, and various architectural details together with a multitude of articles and clippings from newspapers and magazines, and photographs of houses, gardens, grilles, and ceilings cut out of the books published by Arthur Byne and Mildred Stapley Byne and other volumes on different aspects of Spanish architecture, gardens, furniture, and design. Mizner used these albums as a kind of aide-mémoire, and according to one of his many biographers, he would "mull over his pictures and assemble a set of them" at the start of every new project and continued to do so throughout the course of his long and productive career as an architect.[72]

More direct evidence as to the manner in which Mizner planned his houses can be found in a 1930 newspaper interview focused on Playa Riente, the largest house he ever designed in Palm Beach and one whose owner expressly wanted a "Spanish palace." Using a 1920 edition of the Spanish design magazine *Arte y Decoración en España* as his principal source, Mizner acknowledged that Playa Riente incorporated design elements from the La Cartuja monastery in Burgos, the cloister of the church of San Juan de los Reyes monastery in Toledo, Valencia's Lonja, and still others from houses he had visited in Madrid. He also he admitted, "I based my design largely on the old architecture of Spain—with important modifications to meet Florida conditions and modern ways of living."[73]

Mizner began his career as an architect during the 1890s in Southern California, where he served as an apprentice for Willis Polk, an early

Fig. 59. View of the Everglades Club from Lake Worth–Palm Beach, Florida, ca. 1928. Completed in 1918, the Everglades Club introduced the exclusive community of Palm Beach to what became Addison Mizner's signature Spanish-cum-Mediterranean style of architecture. Black-and-white photonegative, 4 × 5 in. State Archives of Florida, Florida Memory.

proponent of mission-style architecture.[74] Mizner then moved to New York, where, as an apprentice in the firm of McKim, Mead and White, he worked with and befriended Stanford White. His first Spanish-style houses date from 1911–12, both built for wealthy clients on Long Island's North Shore. But whether it was these houses, Mizner's personal charm, or some combination of the two, Mizner caught the eye of the heir to the Singer sewing machine fortune, Paris Singer, who regularly spent his winters in Palm Beach. Singer subsequently invited Mizner to that budding resort community and in 1917 commissioned him to design a convalescent home for army officers wounded in World War I. That building, still extant, later became the community's exclusive Everglades Club. In his autobiography Mizner writes that he originally imagined the home as "a Moorish tower, like one on the south coast of Spain, with an open loggia at one side facing the sea, and on this side a cool court with a dripping fountain," but when he actually saw the building site, which fronted Lake Worth, he also envisioned a "Spanish building . . . something religious . . . a nunnery, with a chapel built into the lake . . . a mixture built by a nun from Venice, added onto by one from Gerona, with a bit of new Spain in the tropics." He then added an orange court to render the complex even more Spanish and more picturesque.[75]

The resulting conflation of styles was typically Mizner—his trademark—and it proved infectious. Starting with El Mirasol, the house he designed in 1919 for the wealthy New York banker Edward T. Stotesbury, Mizner was responsible for dozens of large, sumptuous houses—almost seventy in all—built in what one of his biographers termed a "Bastard-Spanish-Moorish-Romanesque-Gothic-Renaissance-Bull-Market-Damn-the-Expense Style."[76] Mizner, in contrast, considered his designs "Spanish," mainly because he regarded Spain as an architectural melting pot that combined a mixture of styles—Roman, Moorish, Gothic, and plateresque. He then reassembled these different styles into a hodgepodge of design elements gleaned from his scrapbooks but that, in his mind at least, adhered to "Spanish tradition."[77] In keeping moreover with the prevailing notion that Spanish style suggested luxury, leisure, and romance, these mansions generally sported Spanish names, as in Casa Juanita, Las Campanas, Casa de los Arcos, Hogarcito, Nuestro Paradiso, El Sarmiento, Playa Riente, and in the case of Mizner's own house, Sin Cuidado. Mizner's efforts to hispanicize Palm Beach also extended to the lanes and patios he designed for Worth Avenue, Palm Beach's main thoroughfare. These included the Via Mizner, which, as one article reported, managed to capture the "romance and colorful grandeur of the Alhambra."[78]

Mizner did more than simply design buildings. He also endeavored to create an entirely "Spanish"—read leisured, luxurious, romantic, and picturesque—way of life by providing clients with Spanish furniture, paintings, and other antiques he purchased during annual buying trips to Spain, once returning with "half a boat load" of different objects. His secretary, Alex Waugh, remembering his trip with Mizner in 1922, explained that, having arrived first in Madrid, "my instructions were

Fig. 60. Addison Mizner, architect, El Mirasol, Palm Beach, Florida, 1919. El Mirasol was the first "Spanish"-style mansion Mizner designed for wealthy clients in Palm Beach. It was also a trendsetter, inspiring other architects active in Palm Beach and other Florida resort towns to build in a similar mode. Courtesy Florida Memory, Creative Commons.

to set about buying antique furnishings for three houses, soup to nuts and don't spare the horses." Soon Mizner arrived, and what amounted to a multicity shopping spree began. "When Addison bought," Waugh observed, "he bought. . . . He had a precise knowledge of exactly what he wanted for each room in each house—we, or rather I, had made lists[,] but Addison spurned them—and he set about his purchases with an intent venom, induced by suffering [his leg injury and ulcers] and need to complete the job, which confounded me." After Madrid, Mizner traveled to Granada, Seville, and Burgos, "each of which yielded up its treasures and in each of which Addison poured out riches of their history as from a fountain."[79]

When imports did not work or items were difficult to find, Mizner adopted the creed, "If you can't get it, make it."[80] And so he did, rep-

licating something of the "romance and colorful grandeur" of genuine
old Spanish furnishings through "antiqued" reproductions produced
by Mizner Industries and the adjacent Las Manos Tile Company, two
workshops he established in West Palm Beach to produce handmade
pottery, tiles, grilles, and furniture of Spanish and Mediterranean design.
According to one exuberant report published in the *Palm Beach Post* in
1923, "This factory where the beautiful Spanish type of tiles in their
soft colorings and uneven contours are produced probably has the distinction of being the only tile manufactory in the United States without
machinery of any sort, every [roof] tile being fashioned by hand and
shaped over the thigh, according to the ancient custom, and the pottery
when . . . also made here in delicious colorings and wonderful Spanish
and Italian glazes, is also shaped on the potter's wheel entirely by hand."[81]

The reporter who wrote the article was mistaken, however, as Mizner
Industries was far from the only manufactory producing reproductions
of this kind. Others had been established in California, Michigan, and
New York, but Mizner Industries was integral to Mizner's grand though
never fully realized plan. This plan aimed at transforming Boca Raton
("rat's mouth" in Spanish), then a sleepy seaside village located seven-
teen miles to the south of Palm Beach, into a full-fledged Spanish city
similar to the one Merrick was constructing in Coral Gables. In a nod
toward Henry W. Grady's famed 1886 remarks about the future of the
southern United States, Mizner marketed Boca Raton as an embodi-
ment of the "spirit of the New South." One advertisement went even
further, noting that Boca Raton "represents the spirit of Americanism
at its highest, for its motive in building was to create a finer and happier
place for human abode."[82]

Americanism perhaps, but Mizner colored his Americanism with a
Spanish hue. Boca Raton's principal landmarks included a spiraling water
tower modeled after the Giralda; a broad central thoroughfare called the
Camino Real; a grand Ritz-Carlton hotel, the Castillo del Rey, with a
dining room similar to the refectory of a fifteenth-century hospital Mizner
had seen in the Catalan city of Vich; an administrative building meant
to replicate El Greco's house in Toledo; and a mission-style depot and
town hall. Also in the development was a Spanish village with Spanish-

style houses and bungalows, and for his own house, Mizner envisioned a mock Spanish castle, complete with drawbridge and moat.[83]

The back-to-back hurricanes that devastated much of South Florida in 1925 and again in 1926, combined with the collapse of Florida's land boom, put most of these plans on hold. By then, however, the Spanish-themed architecture that Mizner and Merrick helped popularize went viral, cropping up in different parts of the Sunshine State. Starting in 1925, for example, Perry Snell, Tampa's largest developer since 1909, set out to build "Spanish castles" in various shapes and sizes along that city's Coffee Pot Boulevard. Snell also created a new Spanish-themed subdivision called Granada Terrace, and another Tampa business operator, Harry E. Prettyman, transformed an office building in the city's downtown into what one reporter described as a "replica of a Spanish home in the time of Ferdinand and Isabel."[84]

More in line with the prevailing trend for Spanish-styled resorts was St. Petersburg's Hotel Rolyat, built by I. M. "Jack" Taylor at the tail end of the Florida land boom of the 1920s. Taylor designed the Rolyat (Taylor spelled backward) to be a Spanish walled town complete with a *plaza mayor*, a bridge modeled after one in Toledo, and an octagonal tower that was a replica of Seville's Torre del Oro.[85]

As the Rolyat was taking shape, the architect Howard Major, in an important article published in the journal *Architectural Forum*, as well as with his book, *The Domestic Architecture of the Early American Republic: The Greek Revival* (1926), launched what amounted to a frontal attack on the then popular "Spanish" style. A strong proponent of a national architectural style, Major argued that the Spanish style "was totally at variance with our Anglo-Saxon temperament" and failed to express America's "national character."[86] That character, Major suggested, could be better served by the use of Greek revival architecture of the kind first popularized during the early part of the nineteenth century or, failing that, colonnaded colonial (or what he called British colonial), as seen on plantation houses throughout the South.

What Major failed to recognize in this critique is that the Spanish style was less of a foreign import than he imagined. Starting with the writings of the Florida historian T. Buckingham Smith and his nineteenth-century counterparts in California and the Southwest and to a certain degree Walt Whitman as well, Americans had discovered that the elements of Spanish culture and living examples of what was then often termed the Spanish *raza* were essentially homegrown and visible throughout much of the country as well. That realization was especially important in California, New Mexico, and Florida, where it connected with an earlier but often forgotten colonial history. By the start of the twentieth century a recognition of that same history was in the process of making inroads into the other parts of the country, fueling the growing craze for Spain, providing the country with countless examples of the "Spanish house."

American Homes, Spanish Style

Randolph Williams Sexton (1884–?) was another architectural critic in search of national style, yet he refused to believe that America's national character or temperament could be expressed in any one style or design. Adaptability was Sexton's creed, and in books devoted to the design of theaters and apartment houses he credited the country for its success in absorbing, adapting, and ultimately transforming imported European—he might also have added Asian—styles into something that was recognizably and uniquely American. The Spanish style figured among those America had successfully absorbed, and his thoughts on this topic appeared in his book *Spanish Influence on American Architecture and Decoration* (1927).

Sexton was far from the only writer interested in the character and quality of Spanish architecture, decoration, and design. Others, as previously noted, included the Bynes, whose books were essentially pictorials meant to provide a visual introduction to the basic elements of Spanish architecture and design as opposed to an exhaustive analysis and history of the subject. Similar books included two by Austin Whittlesey, a California architect who had traveled to Spain in 1917 to study its architecture and who later worked as an associate with Bertram Goodhue. The first of these two books was *Minor Ecclesiastical, Domestic, and Garden Architecture of Southern Spain* (1917), with a preface by Goodhue that criticized the "very crude and very unarchitectural" quality of mission revival buildings as opposed to the more "honest" and "substantial" design of

Spanish colonial architecture.[87] Next came *Renaissance Architecture of Central and Northern Spain* (1920), a pictorial or pattern book meant to be used by architects interested in learning more about the increasingly popular Spanish style. Winsor Soule's *Spanish Farm Houses and Minor Public Buildings* (1924) was another pictorial meant to be used in similar fashion, as was William Lawrence Bottomley's *Spanish Details*, also published in 1924.[88] That Bottomley, an architect best known for his houses of classic colonial design, wrote this book is surprising, but he apparently conceived of it in conjunction with a commission from a Virginia client interested in a house of Spanish design, and in 1916 he even visited Spain in order to learn more about its architecture. Like Cram, he returned a convert, extolling "the dignity, austerity, and distinction" of Spanish architecture and attributing its "blending of classic tradition and Moorish influence . . . [to] the strong individuality of the Spanish race."[89]

Together these portfolio books—and there were others—were invaluable resources, as Ralph Cram recognized in his bibliography on Spanish architecture.[90] These volumes provided architects and decorators, especially those who had never been to Spain, with guides to the kind of Spanish-style houses their clients were demanding. But Sexton's book was different. He was a critic, not a practicing architect, and less interested in Spain per se than in analyzing changes in America's architectural scene, among them the rapidly evolving type of American architecture based on the "Spanish style." He therefore aimed at providing readers with an overview of that style, illustrated with photographs, together with an explanation for why the Spanish style was so popular. The style, he observed, was particularly appropriate for semitropical locales, among them Florida and Southern California, where it first made its presence felt, but he also maintained that it was equally "suitable for non semitropical places." Sexton's argument centered on the design elements found in most Spanish-style houses: solid stucco walls, shutter-style windows, and interior garden patios. These, he argued, rendered "Spanish" houses suitable for a variety of climates, as they are "warm in winter, cool in summer . . . [provide] light, air and sunshine . . . [and also afford] privacy." He also listed the style's other advantages: "individuality," "absence of sham and meaningless applied ornament," "dignity," and a

1 Story
Front Gable
Offset Attached
Porch

Barcelona (1929-1931 Ready-Cut)
1929 ($1575), 1930 ($1645), 1931 ($1597)

"The Barcelona has every latest Wardway feature. It is ultra modern from the brick step in front, through every room to the service entrance off the kitchen. The fashionable and architecturally excellent design comes from old Madrid in Sunny Spain. The Barcelona stands out, imposing, beautiful on any street. It marks the man of taste - discrimination - individuality! It brings you beauty that lasts.

Everyone says "It's the smartest home in town". Those who favor the bungalow say there is no home so beautiful, so fashionable and so comfortable as the new Barcelona. It's the home of homes to hundreds of people - to city man, suburbanite and country dweller alike.

The Spanish effect stucco is applied over metal lath on ship-lap - the best construction known. 5-2 Perfect Red Cedar - the best grade wood shingles made - are supplied for the roof. Stain them red and you will obtain a most striking and colorful effect, much admired by all."

- 1929 Wardway Homes

Fig. 61. By the end of the 1920s the Spanish style was accepted as an American style. Both Montgomery Ward and Sears Roebuck & Co. offered customers inexpensive home-building kits for Spanish-style houses and bungalows. "The Barcelona," advertisement for a Montgomery Ward "Wardway" home, 1930. Photo by the author.

Fig. 62. Palace of the Governors, Santa Fe, New Mexico, 1890. Courtesy Library of Congress.

Fig. 63. Palace of the Governors, Santa Fe, New Mexico, after 1911. As part of a campaign to hispanicize Santa Fe, municipal officials in 1912 ordered the removal the wooden, New England–style balustrade from the building's façade. Courtesy Palace of the Governors Photo Archives (NMHM/DCA), HP.2007.04.

sense of spontaneousness, as well as "sincerity and honesty in design," all of which harked back to the qualities that critics previously attached to the housing designs associated with the earlier arts and crafts movement. That same movement, and possibly Mizner Industries as well, also figured in Sexton's suggestion that the Spanish-style house was helping to "awaken craftsmanship in this country." He also believed that it could serve as a "hedge" against mass-produced, characterless houses of the type listed in such publications as the *Sears Homes Catalogue*, although Sexton might have changed his mind on this topic had he ever seen the Sears catalog advertisement for a "San José" Spanish-style home kit or Montgomery Ward's for a Barcelona-style "Sunny Spain" bungalow.[91]

Factors other than style, however, figured directly in Sexton's argument favoring the Spanish-style house. That style, he noted, was an "import" but one that had been successfully modified and updated by "American common sense, good taste, and insistence on comfort and convenience." The Spanish style, he added, was "old," yet one that had been adapted to American tastes and in the process became one certified as "American design."[92]

The "Americanness" that Sexton and other observers attached to the Spanish style does much to account for its spread to parts of the country lacking a Spanish, let alone a Mexican past. In California, Texas, and Florida proponents of the style defended its presence on the basis of history and local tradition. Take New Mexico, especially Santa Fe, where, starting around 1910, local boosters moved to rebrand their city as an old Spanish (or at least Mexican) "adobe city," partly by implementing new municipal ordinances requiring buildings in the city center, especially those surrounding the central plaza, to be built in what was referred to as the "new" but "old Santa Fe" style.[93] The first building to be remodeled in this fashion was the old Palace of the Governors, which had its Victorian-era balustrade and other adornments on its façade removed. Others soon followed. These changes impressed visitors, albeit in differing ways. Writing in the 1920s, the essayist and writer Katharine Fullerton Gerould observed that Santa Fe, "visually speaking[,] . . . is more Spanish than American, and more Mexican than Spanish." Her favorite building: the Palace of the Governors, the epitome of what she

Fig. 64. Isaac H. Rapp, architect, Scottish Rite temple, Santa Fe, New Mexico, 1914. Completed in 1914, the temple's planners believed that the "Moorish-style" architecture reflected Santa Fe's Spanish roots. Photographer: Jesse Nusbaum, Courtesy Palace of the Governors Photo Archives (NMHM/DCA), #061379.

called the "Spanish type." Otherwise Gerould dismissed the new-old Santa Fe architecture as a "graceless blend of Spanish and Hopi." Still, Gerould concluded her assessment of Santa Fe with the comment that "the Spaniard . . . still owns the New Mexican soul."[94]

Archetypes for these new-old Spanish-style buildings varied. Edgar Lee Hewett (1865–1946), an archaeologist then serving as director of the newly created Museum of New Mexico, together with his archaeologist friend and close collaborator Sylvanus Griswold Morley (1883–1948), opted for a design that harmonized with the region's ethnic diversity. The resulting cocktail was heavy on adobe, mixing Moorish, Spanish, and indigenous elements into the new, yet old, Santa Fe style, later to become known as Pueblo style. There were some outliers, as in the unusual design of the city's new Scottish Rite or Masonic temple, to which Hewlett belonged. Planning for that building began in 1909. The original temple, a classic Beaux-Arts design reminiscent of the World's

Columbian Exposition of 1893, came from the Colorado-based architect Isaac Rapp. But it was judged incongruous with New Mexican traditions, and Rapp was dismissed. His replacement was the Los Angeles architectural firm of Hart and Burns, known for their work in the mission style. The new architects designed a neo-Moorish, Alhambra-like building complete with horseshoe arches, which, however incongruous with Masonic traditions, impressed both Hewlett and Morley as one that reflected New Mexico's Spanish past.

As with the mission style, the connection was forced but consistent with Hewlett's attempts to establish a link between New Mexico's Santa Fe and the original Santa Fe, the military encampment laid out by King Ferdinand and Queen Isabella in the form of a cross in 1491 and subsequently used as a base to launch the crusade to conquer and then Christianize Granada, the last remaining Muslim outpost in peninsular Spain. Hewlett is best remembered as a champion of indigenous culture, yet in 1910, as part of a movement to link Santa Fe with its Spanish past, he presented a lecture, "Spain the Motherland," which honored the memory of Ferdinand and Isabella and their role in bringing religion (as opposed to Catholicism) and civilization to the New World. Other New Mexicans had similar ideas, among them one member of the state legislature who, in a speech delivered to his colleagues in 1910, evoked Santa Fe's Spanish past by referring to its Hispanic population as "descendants of the Conquistadors, who wrested the South West from the savage tribes of Indians."[95] Spain, conquistadors, civilization—the connections seemed clear and were evidently the reason why Hewlett, Morley, and the city's other planners approved the neo-Moorish design for the Scottish Rite temple.

Dedicated in November 1912, that temple today is one of Santa Fe's most striking landmarks. Located a few blocks north of the plaza and standing atop a small knoll, it is almost impossible to miss; its pinkish adobe exterior and horseshoe arches surrounding the entrance way have little in common with the stockier, more geometric shapes and earthen tones of the other adobe buildings in the city center. Contemporary reaction to the temple's striking design is difficult to come by, but it seemingly reflected the efforts of both Hewlett and Morley to inject a bit of Spain into Santa Fe. In addition, and as Chris Wilson has observed, the temple's neo-Moorish features harmonized with New Mexico's multi-layered ethnic past. But the symbolism goes further. Medieval Spain was a tripartite culture, a sometimes uncomfortable mixture of Christian, Jewish, and Muslim peoples and customs. As noted in chapter 2, New Mexico was another tripartite culture, a mixture of indigenous, Spanish, and American. Medieval Spain in this respect foreshadowed and indeed gave birth, historically speaking, to New Mexico.

These connections became even more apparent in the murals for the interior of the temple commissioned in 1915 from the Chicago artist E. A. Vysekal. These murals remain in place today. One, painted above the proscenium arch, depicts Ferdinand and Isabella being handed the keys to the city of Granada by Boabdil, the last Muslim ruler to live in the Alhambra, in January 1492. The other, painted on the stage curtain itself, offers a prospect of the original Santa Fe as seen from the Alhambra. The symbolism in these images is clear: the citizens of the new Santa Fe, the direct heirs to those in the old one, had also conquered, civilized, and Christianized what had been a pagan land.[96]

Other efforts to give Santa Fe a more distinctly Spanish atmosphere ran parallel to the construction of the new temple and in most instances followed the model pioneered by St. Augustine and its efforts to hispanicize (or re-hispanicize) itself through architecture and the renaming of its streets. In Santa Fe, the former New York Street, to cite but one example, became the Calle Santa Fe, whereas various wards were designated barrios and given their old Spanish names: Ward 1 became Barrio San Miguel; Ward 2, Guadalupe; Ward 3, Rosario; Ward 4, San Francisco; and so on. The overarching idea, as in St. Augustine, was to render Santa Fe more attractive to tourists and to transform it into what one planner called "a residence and resort city."[97]

Elsewhere other ideas, none more important than the equation of Spanish with leisure, comfort, refinement, and romance, played their part. That equation aligned with, and in some ways embodied, the general tenor of the country during an epoch of growth and prosperity remembered as the Roaring Twenties. Make no mistake: the "roaring" was not for everyone. White Americans benefited far more than black, income inequalities increased, and only a tiny percentage of Americans

Fig. 65. Warren & Wetmore, architects, Eagle's Nest, Centerport, Long Island, New York, ca. 1926. William K. Vanderbilt II's summer residence—originally built as an English-style cottage—was one of countless Spanish-style homes built in the United States during the 1920s. Courtesy of the Suffolk County Vanderbilt Museum, Centerport, New York.

could afford one of the luxurious "Spanish" mansions George Washington Smith and other architects were designing in Montecito, let alone Mizner's Palm Beach or, to cite a more northerly example, Eagle's Nest, the house the New York architect Ronald Pearce designed in 1928 for William K. Vanderbilt in Centerport, a wealthy retreat on Long Island's North Shore. Eagle's Nest was originally built as a small English cottage, suitable for a small number of guests. By the mid-1920s, however, Vanderbilt was eager to expand it and, in keeping with the vogue for Spanish-style houses, sent Pearce on a trip to Spain to study its architecture. Pearce returned with the designs for a large, "rambling Spanish house" that included a "Moorish court."[98]

These large Spanish mansions were relatively few in number, but the publicity they generated helped to create the aura of a particular way of life that adhered to the Spanish style and was one to which other Americans, though lacking Vanderbilt's money, could still aspire. The appeal of that same lifestyle is precisely what George Merrick promoted in his advertisements highlighting the "romance" attached to the relatively modest Spanish bungalows he was building in Coral Gables. Mizner did the same with advertisements announcing his Spanish bungalows, available for the sum of $7,350 in the "Spanish village" section of Boca Raton.

Nor did it take long for developers in other parts of the country, hoping to capitalize on what critics were calling the vogue for Spain, to begin marketing Spanish-style houses to urban residents seeking a more leisured, and possibly more romantic, suburban style of life. In 1926, for example, Brooklyn's *Daily Eagle* ran a real estate ad announcing the sale of "Beautiful Spanish Style Homes" in the Shores of Seville, a development in the town Massapequa, on Long Island's South Shore. These dwellings, the ad noted, offered a "Touch of Old Spain." Advertisements promoting "Waterfront Spanish Villas" on Long Island's Manhasset Bay appeared shortly thereafter, and in 1928 another developer ran an advertisement announcing "Your Spanish Castle at Bay Ridge," with Bay Ridge referring to a new suburban subdivision of Brooklyn and "castle," to a modest house with a Spanish tile roof and patio.[99]

Spanish-style apartment houses were also the rage. The forerunner here, in New York City at least, was the sprawling luxury complex located on Manhattan's Central Park South and popularly known as the Spanish Flats. Constructed during the 1880s by José Francisco de Navarro, a wealthy Basque businessman who had settled in New York, the Spanish Flats comprised a series of eight buildings with separate entrances, each with a Spanish name, such as Madrid, Barcelona, Cordova, Granada, and even Tolosa, the Basque town where Navarro was born.[100] Others were later built in Brooklyn, in several towns, including Haverford, along Philadelphia's elegant Main Line, and in Baltimore, where such a building was constructed at 230 Stony Run Lane in the mid-1920s and where I had the privilege to live during the 1970s.

Nor were Spanish-style houses, subdivisions, and suburbs limited to the East Coast. One example is Cleveland's Alcazar Hotel, a residential hotel that opened in 1923. The hotel's name was part of its allure. *Alcázar*, derived from Arabic, was the generic Spanish term for a fortress, or fortified place, but it referred more specifically to the

Fig. 66. Spanish-style homes were not just for the rich. Home builders' advertisements in newspapers across the United States reflected the "Americanization" and democratization of the Spanish style. "Shores of Seville," *Brooklyn Daily Eagle*, May 11, 1926. Photo by the author.

one in Seville that was appropriated by the Christian kings of Castile in the mid-thirteenth century and subsequently transformed into an elegant royal palace. Known for its richly ornamented interior arabesques and attendant gardens, the Alcázar figured in the itinerary of most visitors to Seville, the city usually favored by foreigners visiting Spain. Together with the Alhambra, it was a synonym for Oriental luxury and delight.

No surprise then that Edna Florence and George Hale, owners of Cleveland's Alcazar, used similar language to promote the new hotel, whose architect was Harry T. Jeffery. Located in Cleveland Heights, an affluent suburb immediately adjacent to Cleveland itself, the Alcazar was marketed as a residence as opposed to a travelers' hotel. Its design was not demonstrably Spanish, although it was definitely promoted as Spanish, its lobby adorned with fourteen different designs of Spanish tiles, its front entrance announced "Esta es la Casa de Usted," which was poorly worded Spanish for "This house is your house." Advertisements in the *Cleveland House Despatch* claimed that the Alcazar was "built for those who know how to live graciously and well," whereas a promotional story published in *Cleveland Town Topics*, a local newsletter, explicitly established the connection between such a lifestyle and the hotel's Spanish design: "Picture yourself living in a castle of sun-blessed Spain . . . dreams of architectural perfection have come true; the tiles used in the floors and walls imported directly from Spain. The beautiful fireplace and the wonderful stairs are exact duplicates of those in the famous Casa del Greco in Old Spain."[101]

Similar marketing strategies accompanied the roll-out of Country Club Plaza, a Spanish-style suburban development and shopping center in Kansas City, Missouri, inaugurated in 1922. Its developer, Jesse Clyde Nichols (1880–1950), had decided upon a "general Spanish type of architecture" as he considered it both "classic" and "adaptable."[102] Toward this end Nichols sent his architect, Edward Buehler Delk, on trips to both Mexico and Spain. The results were striking. The Spanish revival–style theater, shops, and other buildings lining the plaza's perimeter were meant to replicate what Delk envisioned as "harmony of design, color, and height," what Nichols regarded as Spanish architec-

Fig. 67. Edward Buehler Delk, architect, Country Club Plaza, Kansas City, Missouri, 1930. The plaza's developer, J. C. Nichols, wanted the Country Club Plaza and surrounding district to mimic the picturesque qualities of an old marketplace in Spain. A replica of Seville's Giralda was added later. Courtesy Missouri Valley Special Collections, Kansas City Public Library, Kansas City, Missouri.

ture's "beauty of design," and also to create "the feeling of an old market place of picturesque Spain [in] Kansas City."[103] The plaza's original design also included a replica of a Spanish fountain from Seville along with a squat seventy-foot-high but still recognizable replica of Seville's Giralda, although that tower was not completed until after Nichols's death. Why Nichols and Delk selected the Spanish style for the plaza is still not altogether clear. Kansas City's historical heritage was far less Spanish than French, but the decision to organize Country Club Plaza with a Spanish theme harmonized with Nichols's ideal that Kansas City marked the beginning of the old Santa Fe Trail linking America's heartland with the Southwest. It also aligned with the prevailing idea that Spanish equaled luxury and, judging from the kind of luxury shops located in the new shopping center, free spending as well. For this reason

Fig. 68. Edwin H. Clark, Plaza del Lago, Wilmette, Illinois, 1927. This shopping center was part of a larger development meant to capture the beauty of "ancient Spain." Digital File#199501_120423_004. Edwin H. Clark Papers, Ryerson and Burnham Libraries, the Art Institute of Chicago.

Country Club Plaza offered free parking, another innovation, although ownership of the private houses adjacent to the plaza was enjoined by a restrictive whites-only covenant similar to those governing Ojai and other Spanish-style developments on the West Coast.

Still another Spanish-style shopping center built in a region with no apparent connection with Spain was the Spanish Court in the northern Chicago suburb of Wilmette, Illinois. Designed by Edwin H. Clark (1878–1967), the Spanish Court (its name was changed in 1967 to Plaza del Lago) included a cinema, the Teatro del Lago, which opened in 1927, together with shops and small apartments. One local newspaper (*Wilmette Life*) compared the style of the new complex with the "quaint old missions of the Pacific Coast." Next to be constructed was Vista del Lago, a posh Spanish-style club advertised as a "jewel of Spanish splendor" and one whose beauty would rival that of "ancient Spain." Much of that beauty rested with a ten-story tower modeled after Seville's Giralda, but even though that tower was never built, club members could still enjoy a five-hundred-foot "esplanada del Sevilla," a "Hispano" roof garden, the "fiesta" ballroom, and other amenities. The developer also constructed another adjacent Spanish complex known as the Miralago ballroom, but it was heavily damaged by fire in 1932 and never rebuilt.[104] All that remains of this Spanish-style development on the shore of Lake Michigan is the Plaza del Lago, which includes a high-end Spanish restaurant together with tiled walkways and fountains fashioned after those in Seville.

As for the rest of the Chicago area, it too experienced the same vogue for Spanish middle-class suburban houses as New York. Starting in 1925, advertisements—"Here's the Spanish Bungalow You're Seeking"— announcing the sale of Spanish-style homes began to appear in Chicago's *Tribune*. The March 21, 1926, issue of the *Tribune* included a sketch of such a dwelling with a label calling it a "picturesque Spanish type." The headline read, "This home costs $9,500; it looks like a million." Following the article's suggestion that Spanish houses were becoming "increasingly popular," builders in and around Chicago jumped on the fashion for houses of Spanish design, as anyone who today drives around Wilmette, Illinois, can still appreciate. At the peak of the craze in 1928 one developer announced the construction in Park Ridge of an entire "Spanish town," although the reporter asked to write about this development astutely observed that the town in question is "reminiscent of a town in Spain, or at any rate of the Cuban or Californian conception of one."[105]

Whether the new town was Spanish, Cuban, or a copy of Ojai, the developer, Durchslag by name, was selling not just houses but the dream of a Spanish castle whose size did not matter. The marketing worked. The Spanish house had evolved into the equivalent of a powerful narcotic capable of conjuring up the image of a lifestyle predicated on luxury, leisure, and romance. The demand for that lifestyle also accounts for what amounted to an unprecedented vogue for Spanish-style furniture, especially portable wooden writing desks known as *bargueños*, colorful Spanish tiles, and grille-work. Some of these were true antiques of the kind the Ruiz brothers had offered in their annual New York auction sale. To be sure, these sales catered primarily to wealthy buyers such as Hearst and others able to afford Mizner's fanciful creations in Palm Beach, but they also helped foster a growing demand for a "Spanish

Fig. 69. D. Paul Witmer, architect, Castilian Court, Hershey Hotel, Hershey Park, Pennsylvania, 1934. Opened just as the Depression took hold, this hotel symbolically marks the end of the Spanish craze in the United States. Postcard courtesy author's collection.

home." As early as 1923 John Wanamaker's New York department store organized a special promotion, "The Spanish House," featuring Spanish-style furniture and "antiques." But as the number of Spanish-style homes increased, the demand for Spanish furnishings grew exponentially, and by 1926 the *New York Times* critic Walter Rendell Storey had written a long feature article, "Old Spain Enters the American Home," that signaled the "growing interest of America in things Spanish." Citing examples from Boston as well as Joliet, Illinois, Storey attributed this interest to the "intrinsic" beauty of the "simplicity" of Spanish design, and with respect to the design and organization of the Spanish house, he noted the importance of the interior patio as an "allurement" that, even in northern climates, introduced a measure of light and the outdoors into the domestic interior. As for Spanish-style furnishings, he observed that they were so popular that many of the country's Spanish-style houses were "more Spanish than many a house in Spain."[106]

Storey, together with other critics, recognized that Spanish-style houses were best suited for the southern parts of the country as opposed to the colder regions, where their stucco exteriors might require special treatment and their patios allow in too much air, especially in winter. Such drawbacks help to explain why the vogue for Spanish houses never reached much farther north than West Hartford, Connecticut, where Grace Spear Lincoln constructed what is still known as the city's "Spanish house."[107] Lincoln built it, so it is said, because she had once lived in Spain and wanted something that reminded her of her stay. For others, such houses, whether large or small, offered, quixotically perhaps, the promise of the leisured, relaxed lifestyle associated with Spain. Part of that demand was met by Spanish-themed hotels and resorts in California and Florida but also by the Hotel Arlington in Hot Springs, Arkansas, which was rebuilt in the Spanish style following a fire in 1925. Similar "Spanish" hotels could be found on St. Simons Island, Georgia, where Addison Mizner designed the Cloister Inn (1928), and also in Hershey, Pennsylvania, where the "Chocolate King," Milton Hershey, the town's owner and developer, built the Hershey Hotel in a style reminiscent of ones he had seen in Cuba, where he owned several sugar plantations. Designed in large part by Hershey's architect, D. Paul Witmer (1894–1981), the hotel featured a Spanish-style courtyard or patio; the Castilian Ballroom; and the atmospheric Iberian Lounge, with a mural by Robert von Ezdorf, the architect responsible for the hotel's mock-Spanish interior furnishings and design. Completed in 1934, the mural depicted a Spanish waterfront scene, several buildings of vague Moorish design, and a galleon evidently meant to evoke the Spanish voyages of discovery to the New World.

Yet by the time the Hershey Hotel opened to guests, the Spanish craze was just about over; a combination of the Great Depression and changing tastes had seen to that. Still, architectural remnants of the craze remained. One was La Ronda, the sprawling Spanish-cum-Mediterranean castle-like mansion that Addison Mizner designed for Percival E. Foerderer and his wife, Ethel, in Bryn Mawr, Pennsylvania, and completed in 1929. La Ronda's name was Spanish, but its design was a characteristically Miznerian mixture of Gothic, Spanish, and Italian. Mrs. Foerderer's taste in art and furniture was less Spanish than Italian, but among La Ronda's more unusual features was a series of glazed Spanish wall tiles

Fig. 70. Addison Mizner, architect, La Ronda, Bryn Mawr, Pennsylvania. Undated photograph. La Ronda marks the end of an era, as it was completed in 1928, a moment when Spanish-style houses were ebbing in popularity. The house was demolished in 2009. Courtesy William Morrison Collection, Lower Merion Historical Society, Bala Cynwyd, Pennsylvania.

with scenes from the adventures of Don Quixote, the knight famous for his dream in which windmills turned into giants.

La Ronda, with fifty-one rooms and eighteen thousand square feet, was a giant in its own right, Percival and Ethel's version of a fanciful castle in Spain. But with its pastel stucco walls, red-tile roofs, and rounded turrets, La Ronda had little in common with the other mansions and estates of Bryn Mawr, a wealthy suburb on Philadelphia's Main Line. One or two of these mansions were also castles, even larger than La Ronda, but, constructed mainly of brick and stone, their designs were generally Tudor or colonial design and, in keeping with the community's heritage, often boasted English (or Welsh) names. La Ronda, moreover, had little in common with Bryn Mawr's famous women's college (now university), whose architecture was primarily neo-Gothic and whose only link to Spanish art and architecture was through its noted instructor, Georgiana Goddard King. In other words La Ronda definitely looked out of place, a kind of eyesore, and once the Foerderer family sold it in 1969, it was soon abandoned, a relic of a bygone era in which Spain and its architecture were in vogue. In 2009, despite the efforts of diehard preservationists to save it, La Ronda, together with one family's dream of a castle in Spain, fell to the wrecker's ball.

Epilogue

The extent of the spread of Spanish style during the decade of the 1920s is difficult to chart. Mission/Spanish revival is one of the categories listed on the National Register of Historic Places, which provides a state-by-state, city-by-city guide to buildings judged of historic importance, but it is far from complete or entirely accurate. From personal experience I know that it fails to list the magnificent Spanish-style (ca. 1925) pink stucco and red-tile roof house dating from ca. 1925 on Stratford Road that I often admired on my morning jogs in the Guilford section of Baltimore, nor does it include the nearby Spanish-style apartment complex located at 230 Stony Run Lane where I once lived. It also fails to include innumerable Spanish-style houses, hotels, apartment blocks, theaters, gas stations, and other public buildings that were constructed during the 1920s but are no longer extant.

☙ 7 ❧

The Spanish Blaze

The winter of 1915–16 beheld the Spanish blaze.

—CARL VAN VECHTEN

On October 31, 1917, *The Land of Joy* (*La tierra de la Alegría*), a Spanish musical revue, opened at New York's Park Theatre. The timing was far from ideal. War was raging in Europe, and the *New York Times* and other newspapers were filled with reports about American casualties. Even so, hopes for the success of *The Land of Joy* ran high, and, according to a review in the *Times*, the opening night's audience responded with "spontaneous enthusiasm" throughout the performance. Ten days later a second article in the *Times* likened the revue to a "breath of Spain" and to an escape, though fleeting, from the war and the worries of everyday life.[1]

The music in *The Land of Joy* was the work of Joaquín "Quinito" Valverde (1875–1918), the Spanish Victor Herbert and thus a composer well known for lighthearted *zarzuelas*, or light operas. Although popular in both Spain and Spanish America and performed regularly in London's Alhambra Theatre, a music hall on Leicester Square, the *zarzuela* was not a musical genre American audiences knew much about. On the other hand the lead dancer in the revue, the Argentine-born but Spanish-trained Antonia Mercé y Luque, aka La Argentina, was a known quantity. Famous for her seductive *seguidillas*, *sevillanas*, and other classical flamenco dances, she had made her American debut the previous year in Maxine Elliott's Theatre in New York, albeit to mixed reviews. Carl Van Vechten, a writer and music critic whose *Music of Spain*, the first book on the subject by an American author, would appear in 1918, was unimpressed, using the phrase "mild enthusiasm" to describe the reception of La Argentina's "café-concert dances." Other critics reacted more positively. One reviewer in the *Times* raved about the "native fire" of this "great Spanish beauty," another compared her with such legendary flamenco dancers as La Carmencita, aka "The Pearl of Seville," and Carolina "La Belle" Otero, both of whom who had captivated audiences in New York and other cities during the 1890s. In the end La Argentina had a successful run of six months of performances in New York, subsequently embarking on an extended tour that took her to Chicago, St. Louis, and Washington.[2]

Expectations therefore mounted after the theater-going public learned that La Argentina—billed as "Spain's Greatest Dancer"—would be appearing again in *The Land of Joy*. The opening occurred on October 31, and Van Vechten was there. He described the performance as "extraordinary," a far cry from his previous throwaway line of "mild enthusiasm." Yet in this instance "extraordinary" seemingly had less to do with La Argentina than with another, considerably younger dancer, Doloretes. Van Vechten described her as capable of heating the blood of Faust with "the clicking of her heels, the clacking of her castanets, now held high over her head, now held low behind her back, the flashing of her ivory teeth, the shrill screaming, the passion of her performance." Dazzled by the "abandoned perverse bewitchery" of Doloretes and La Mazantinita, another young "gypsy" dancer, Van Vechten observed that by the end of the performance the normally reserved New York audience, having discarded the straitjacket characteristic of traditional genteel behavior in American culture, "became hysterical, and broke into wild cries of *Ole! Ole!* Hats were thrown on the stage."[3]

The wild cries of "Olé!" belonged to what Van Vechten called a "Spanish blaze"—other critics referred to it as "Spanish vogue," others a "Spanish fad"—that raced across New York's theaters, music halls, and other venues starting in 1915. That blaze—part of my Spanish craze—encompassed much more than music. A keen observer of New York's passing scene, Van Vechten detected signs of the conflagration in the city's galleries and museums—here he specifically made reference to the popularity of both Sorolla and Zuloaga—or, as another critic put it, "Just at the moment, Spain is all over the place."[4] Van Vechten also took note of the

Fig. 71. *The Land of Joy* playbill, 1916. Friedheim Music Library, Johns Hopkins University, Baltimore, Maryland. This musical helped ignite what one influential critic described as the "Spanish blaze" that engulfed New York and other cities in 1916. Photo by the author.

blaze's impact on the world of fashion. "Our womenfolk," he observed, are wearing "Spanish garments," including the "the hip-hoops of the Velasquez period, the lace flounces of Goya's Duchess of Alba, and the mantillas, the combs, and the accroche-coeurs of Spain, Spain, Spain."[5]

Other commentators, together with magazine and newspaper advertisements announcing the arrival of new shipments of Spanish shawls, Spanish sherry, pimiento-stuffed olives, and other Spanish foodstuffs, bear witness to these more quotidian aspects of this particular blaze. What Van Vechten neglected to mention was the impact of "Spain, Spain, Spain" on the motion picture industry and, as we shall see later in this chapter, on writers belonging to what Gertrude Stein labeled the Lost Generation, whose notables included as John Dos Passos and Ernest Hemingway.

"Spain, Spain, Spain" also set the stage for the flamenco sensation who would thrill audiences in New York and other cities: Raquel Meller (1888–1962), a songstress—she called herself a Spanish *diseuse*—who took the United States by storm in 1926. Already a hit in London, Paris, and Buenos Aires, Meller received nationwide publicity upon her arrival—with forty-two trunks and six Pekingese dogs—aboard the ss *Leviathan* in New York on April 4 and for her opening performance at the Empire Theatre on April 14. As the *Chicago Daily Tribune* and other newspapers reported, tickets to her opening commanded a record-breaking $26.50 each, and among those in attendance at that opening performance was New York's mayor, John Walker; the singer Al Jolson; the former U.S. ambassador to Spain, Alexander Moore; and various other celebrities. By all reports they were not disappointed. Having played the role of Carmen in a 1926 French film version of Bizet's famous opera, Meller was known for gypsy dances, and the audience, warming to what one reporter termed "her swaying hip and the saucy toss of her head," greeted Meller's opening dances with shouts of "Brava! Brava!" These *bravas* grew even louder when Meller performed "La Violetera," leaving the stage dressed as a street vendor, dancing up and down the aisles, and offering bunches of violets as the audience rose to its feet. The critics raved. One called her "a bit of a sorceress," another announced that

TIME

The Weekly News-Magazine

National Affairs

Foreign News

Books

The Theatre

Music

Cinema

Education

Religion

Medicine

Science

The Press

Business & Finance

Sport

Aeronautics

Miscellany

Milestones

SENORITA RAQUEL MELLER
—*nine golden bangles*
(See Page 18)

APRIL 26, 1926

Fig. 72. Señorita Raquel Meller, *Time* magazine, April 26, 1926. The popularity of this Spanish singer landed her on the cover of this national magazine. It also helped trigger a vogue for Spanish-style dress. Courtesy author's collection.

"her art is an exotic radiance, less than music, less than great acting, but more than these put together."[6]

Whatever the sources of Meller's appeal, and her vibrant Spanishness was apparently one, her three-week stay at the Empire occasioned even more publicity, another fad for Spanish dress, and, most spectacularly, a photograph of Meller wearing a Spanish hair comb and mantilla on the cover of the April 26, 1926, issue of *Time* magazine.[7] That photograph, together with the *Time* article about her performance, ensured that Meller's subsequent appearances—in Boston, Chicago, Washington, St. Louis, and Los Angeles—would be sell-outs as well. Van Vechten's Spanish blaze, raging for almost a decade, had seemingly reached its peak.[8]

"Flowers of Our Lost Romance"

The start of Van Vechten's blaze can be traced to the concert halls of both Paris and London, where the music of Isaac Albéniz (d. 1908), Enrique Granados (d. 1916), and other modern Spanish composers delighted audiences long before it reached the United States. The success of these composers rested on what critics perceived as their "Spanishness," which translated into their ability, as native-born Spaniards, to draw on the traditional rhythms of Spanish folk music and to create works understood as organically "Spanish" as opposed to the Spanish-themed music popularized by Bizet, Chopin, Lalo, Chabrier, Debussy, and other foreign composers. Put briefly, their music was "authentic" and intrinsically "truthful" in ways that Spanish-sounding music—or what been called Spanish-idiom music—written by other composers was not.[9]

With the exception of Bizet's *Carmen*, premiering in North America in 1884 at New York's Metropolitan Opera, which incorporated it into the company's repertoire shortly thereafter, the nation's leading symphonic orchestras traditionally had little interest in Spanish music, whether "authentic" or not, possibly for reasons connected with the Black Legend and also because Spanish music did not form part of the classical repertoire. High culture it was not, at least in the United States. The Boston Symphony Orchestra broke the ice in 1887 with a performance of the French composer Édouard Lalo's *Symphonie espagnole*, dating from 1874. In 1897 that same orchestra also premiered Emmanuel Chabrier's

España, which had been written in 1883, and in 1908 it was the first U.S. orchestra to play Rimsky-Korsakov's *Capriccio espagnol*. In comparison, orchestras in Chicago, Philadelphia, and New York dragged their feet until after the start of World War I, the moment when, as Van Vechten observed, all things Spanish were in vogue.

As for the "authentic" Spanish music, the Chicago Symphony Orchestra got the ball rolling in November 1915 with the U.S. premier of *Dante*, a lilting symphonic poem by Enrique Granados, one of Spain's most famous composers. A month later Granados crossed the Atlantic to attend the world premier of his new opera, *Goyescas*, at New York's Metropolitan Opera on January 28, 1916. Inspired by Goya's scenes of life in eighteenth-century Madrid, the opera had originally been scheduled to debut in Paris, but the ongoing war in Europe prevented it. *Goyescas* was the first Spanish opera the Met ever produced, but it proved so popular that it figured among the sparks that ignited the Spanish blaze to which Van Vechten referred. A review in the *Times* noted that its score was "intensively Spanish . . . coming from the brain and heart of a real Spaniard" as opposed to those of other composers who borrow "Spanish rhythms, Spanish melodic traits, Spanish musical colors." It also raved about entire performance—music, singing, staging, costumes, and so on.[10]

The Met's decision to stage Granados's *Goyescas* helped establish a trend, as it did not take very long before New York and other cities played host to a new roster of talented Spanish musicians. They included the young Catalan cellist Pablo Casals (1876–1973), billed as "world's greatest cellist"; Miguel Llobet (1878–1938), a virtuoso classical Spanish guitarist; María Barrientos (1883–1946), a soprano from Barcelona who made her debut at the Met on January 31 singing Lucia, the title role in Donizetti's *Lucia di Lammermoor*, and who was such a hit that she was invited to join the company on a permanent basis; Andrés de Segurola (1874–1953), a basso singer who also joined the Met's company in 1916; and Isabel Rodríguez, another flamenco dancer who, according to Van Vechten, managed to transform New York's recently opened Winter Garden Theatre into the equivalent of a *maison de la danse* in Seville. Van Vechten also reported that for "ballroom dancers," the tango, a dance that was Argentine in origin but understood as generically Spanish, was also "in." Audiences also flocked to the Met's new production of *Carmen*, which featured the American soprano and film star Geraldine Farrar singing the role of the cigarette girl; the fabled Italian tenor Enrico Caruso playing the ill-fated José; and the young Italian maestro Arturo Toscanini conducting the orchestra.

Such was the rage for this new *Carmen* that film producers quickly produced two different dramatic versions of the opera. One, the work of Raoul Walsh, was filmed at Fox Studios in Fort Lee, New Jersey, and starred Theda Bara, the sexpot of the silent film era, while the other, produced by Cecil DeMille in Hollywood, starred Geraldine Farrar. Both met with critical success, although censors in Philadelphia removed several supposedly scandalous scenes from the version DeMille had produced. The noted comic Charlie Chaplin also got into the act with his "burlesque" version of *Carmen*, released in December 1915. There was more to come. In 1918 the German director Ernst Lubitsch filmed yet another silent version of *Carmen*, this time starring the Polish actress Pola Negri. It reached the United States in 1921 with the provocative title *Gypsy Blood*.

Carmen aside, no blaze lasts forever, although the Spanish one Van Vechten described in 1916 was slow to burn out, as the enthusiastic reception Raquel Meller received ten years later in cities across the United States readily attests. Like all fires, moreover, this blaze left a lasting mark on the country's musical and cultural landscape. In 1918 Van Vechten published his *Music of Spain*, a volume that introduced Americans to the history of a subject few knew anything about. Van Vechten was no musicologist, but he had done his homework and offered what amounted to an enthusiastic endorsement of both Albéniz and Granados, as well as another contemporary Spanish composer, Manuel de Falla (1876–1946), who wrote the music for a ballet, *The Three-Cornered Hat*, which premiered in New York in 1923. Van Vechten's book was far from a best seller, but it apparently served to persuade orchestras in New York and other cities to expand their repertoire with more in the way of "authentic" Spanish music.

Growing interest in Spanish music found other expressions as well, leading folklorists, for example, as well as musicologists to search for songs that were part of the country's Spanish-cum-Mexican heritage.

Fig. 73. Pola Negri in *Gypsy Blood*, poster containing movie still, 1921. Hollywood silent filmmakers were quick to capitalize on the "love and romance" formula as embodied in the alluring Spanish gypsy featured in Bizet's most famous opera, *Carmen*. Courtesy author's collection.

American popular music had long been influenced by the music of both Spain and Spanish America, and as the musicologist Louise Stein reminded us, the first European music ever to be heard in North America was Spanish. One of the soldiers who accompanied Cortés to what is now Mexico City in 1519 played the *vihuela*, a guitar-like instrument, in addition to instructing natives in Spanish music and dance. In the centuries that followed, Spanish missionaries introduced natives to that same musical tradition in California and other parts of the Southwest. By the nineteenth century songs sung in Spanish, accompanied by the guitar and the banjo, an instrument whose origins can be traced to West Africa, could be heard across the region and elsewhere.[11]

Historians have long recognized that the "winning of the West" also occasioned losses, both human and material, among them the disappearance of much of the region's Spanish musical heritage. Starting early in the twentieth century, however, writers with folkloric interests, such as Charles F. Lummis and Eleanor Hague, endeavored to collect, transcribe, and even record as much of that musical heritage as possible. Lummis led the way. In the 1880s, in the course of his trek across the Southwest, the New England transplant was already keeping notes on Spanish-language songs sung by the New Mexican *paisanos* he met. Lummis later published annotated and translated transcripts of a dozen of these songs in his 1893 book *The Land of Poco Tiempo*, a paean to New Mexico's traditional cultures, both native and Spanish.[12]

Once settled in Los Angeles, Lummis continued the preservation effort by transcribing the songs associated with southern California's Spanish-speaking population and those of native peoples. Starting in 1898, he published transcripts and translations of several of these songs, including "El viejo" (The old man) and "Angel del amor" (Angel of love), arranged under the title "Real Spanish Folk Songs" in his published journal *Land of Sunshine* and subsequently in its sequel, *Far West*. To help with the work of collecting these songs, Lummis turned to the Southwest Society of the Archaeological Institute of America, and with their assistance acquired a portable Edison Home Phonograph, which utilized wax cylinders for both the recording and reproduction of sound. The device was clumsy, but starting around 1903 Lummis was able to use it to record no fewer than five hundred songs, at least four hundred of which were in Spanish. His 1907 report on this project offers a sense of what Lummis was able to accomplish:

> The Southwest Society has been so fortunate as to ferret out and enlist a number of those who still remember [these songs]. Some are old, some are only old-fashioned enough to care. A poor old washerwoman, proud of her race, was a perfect bonanza of the early California songs; while a rich young matron, a famous toast, equally cherishes her inheritance. A blind Mexican lad has been one of the staunch props of the work; and several brave young women

who could ill afford the sacrifice of time, have contributed to science far more in proportion than does many a rich "patron." The most extraordinary achievement has been that of Miss Manuela C. Garcia, who has sung the records of no less than 150 songs, with full words! Few can do that in any language, from sheer memory. Sofia Adelaida Kamp, of Ventura, comes next with sixty-four records. . . . And with the assistance of the music critic and composer Arthur Farwell, he began the arduous work of transcription and annotation.[13]

Arthur Farwell (1872–1952) was a critic, composer, and musicologist from Boston with a special interest in Native American music. The Southwest Society engaged him to help with the arduous work of transcribing, annotating, and harmonizing the songs that Lummis had previously been recorded. Additional assistance came from another folklorist, Henry Edmond Earle, who later admitted that many of the songs Lummis had recorded were Spanish-language versions of songs borrowed from Mozart, Donizetti, Schubert, and other European composers, while others were demonstrably Mexican.[14] But Lummis was stubborn, as well as determined to classify most of these songs he recorded as Spanish, as that was what fit neatly with his romantic view of Old California as fundamentally Spanish rather than Mexican. Lummis also traveled around the state, lecturing audiences about life in Old California and entertaining them with his own vocal renditions of songs he referred to as "flowers of our lost romance," a phrase he later made the title of his last book on Spanish pioneering in North America.[15] According to a letter he wrote to a Spanish friend, Lummis told his listeners that the "Spanish californians who taught me these songs a third of a century ago have nearly forgotten them themselves, and when we sing together it is I who have to prompt the words. *Que barbaridad!* [What a disaster!]."[16]

In 1907 Lummis and the Southwest Society made plans to publish a collection of these songs, but the project stalled after Farwell left California to take up a new position in New York. (He returned around 1919 and served as a kind of musical promoter.) Nor did Lummis's increasingly sour relations with the directors of the Southwest Society do anything to move this project along. He also had to contend with a rival: Elea-nor Hague (1875–1954), a relatively unknown but apparently wealthy folklorist from Stockbridge, Massachusetts, who had recently moved to California to assemble, if not necessarily to record, her own collection of old Spanish songs. Little has been written about how Hague went about her work, let alone about her informants, but she managed to publish a sampling in her book *Spanish American Folk Songs*, published under the auspices of the American Folklore Society in 1917. What Lummis thought of Hague's collection is unknown, but it apparently served as the spark he needed to raise the money to fund publication of the first volume—he planned on three—of his *Spanish Songs of California, Collected and Translated by Charles F. Lummis*, in 1923.

With only fourteen songs, the volume was thin, but Lummis was justifiably ecstatic. Soon after its appearance he wrote to his friend, Juan Riaño, the Spanish ambassador in Washington DC: "There is nothing I know of which can do so much for the development of friendly feeling as to bring about the popular singing by our modern American generation of the Songs that were characteristic of California 'before the Gringo came.'" In another letter to Riaño he noted, "You would understand my meaning if you could go with me to one of Mr. Farwell's 'Community Sings' in millionaire Pasadena—and there see a thousand Gringos, from all parts of the United States, but mostly the Middle West, fairly 'eating up' these Spanish songs. They sing them with even more joy and swing and gusto than the old favorites that have been the joy of the American people for more than half a century."[17]

A few months later Lummis wrote to Julián Ribera, a Spanish musicologist, thanking him for his review of *Spanish Songs of California*. Lummis reported that the book, though privately printed, had sold more than five thousand copies. He also expressed hope that the songs, part of what he called America's "heritage of beauty," would provide his compatriots with an alternative to jazz as well as "a better feeling . . . toward the Mother Country of the Three Americas [i.e., Spain]." To this he added, rather confidently, "I find that this is coming true. These songs are being sung today by thousands of people who never knew a Spanish song before—and by a surprisingly large number of them,

Fig. 74. Charles F. Lummis, *Spanish Songs of Old California* songbook cover, G. Schirmer, 1923. Friedheim Music Library, Johns Hopkins University, Baltimore, Maryland. As part of his ongoing efforts to preserve the culture of "Spanish" California, Lummis recorded and transcribed the scores of hundreds of folk songs. Only a handful made it into this book. Courtesy author's collection.

in the Spanish! And it gives them a new and a gentler feeling towards a race as to whom they have inherited so many prejudices from the English birthright."[18]

As usual, Lummis exaggerates. The prejudices he referred to, especially those directed toward Mexicans and Hispanics in general, continued and still continue today. But the songbook, as Lummis rightly reported, proved a commercial success. It also brought new attention to this dimension of California's musical past, as many of the songs he transcribed were broadcast on radio stations in Los Angeles and San Diego (and possibly elsewhere). Others are known to have been sung at the "community sings" that his old friend and collaborator Farwell was organizing and in various festivals such as Santa Barbara's Old Spanish Days. On the other hand, none ever came close to becoming a hit or anything resembling the success enjoyed by the Spanish-themed songs coming from another contributor to the musicological component of the Spanish blaze: Tin Pan Alley.

Enthusiasts know that the "alley" in question was actually a street: Manhattan's Twenty-Eighth Street between Fifth and Sixth Avenues, a block where New York's composers and publishers had clustered since the end of the nineteenth century. The most famous songs written there at the start of next century included such all-time hits as George M. Cohan's "Give My Regards to Broadway" (1914) and Irving Berlin's "God Bless America" (1918). The Alley's most famous composers tended also to be Jewish or African American. Few were Hispanic, but this did little to protect them from the fallout coming from Van Vechten's Spanish blaze.

One Alleyite was the Ohio-born lyricist Ballard MacDonald (1882–1935), a composer best remembered today for such soupy hit songs as "The Trail of the Lonesome Pine" (1913), "Back Home in Indiana" (1917), and "Second-Hand Rose" (1921). In 1920, however, MacDonald jumped on the Spanish bandwagon with his quirky "That Wonderful Kid from Madrid," a song recorded by Al Jolson (1886–1950), one of the leading popular singers of the day and one whose rendition of "The Spaniard That Blighted My Life," a comic song about a flirtatious toreador, sold more than a million records in 1913. "That Wonderful Kid

from Madrid" did not do quite so well, but it achieved a certain noto-
riety by evoking gypsy dancers similar to the ones who had brought
New York audiences to their feet. That song occasioned others, none
too memorable, all released in 1920: "The Spanish Beauty" (José Partipilo), "Spanish Cavalier" (Edith Hatch), and finally "Spanish Infanta"
and "My Spanish Rose" (both by José Padilla). Far more successful was
the romantic ballad "Way Down Barcelona Way" (first line: "There
came a gay serenader, Who played a wicked guitar"), by Fred Fisher,
a songwriter whose best-known hits include "Peg O' My Heart" and
"Chicago (That Toddlin' Town)," recorded by Fred Hillebrand. Next
came George Gershwin's "Spanish Love" (1920), written specifically to
promote Avery Hopwood's similarly named romantic comedy *Spanish
Love*, starring a young William Powell, later famous for his role in *The
Thin Man* and its sequels. *Spanish Love* opened during the summer of
1920, and the show proved a real hit, possibly because it was sufficiently
risqué to be labeled "hot stuff."[19]

Whether hot or not, more Spanish-themed songs also made it to
the charts. Titles include "In Old Madrid," a languid love ballad sung
by Emilio de Gogorza (1872–1949), a much recorded American born
baritone of Spanish heritage, released in 1920; "Spain," a jazzy serenade
recorded in 1924 by the Chicago-based songwriter and bandleader Isham
Jones; and "Valencia: A Song of Spain" (opening lines: "Valencia / In
my dreams I hear you softly call for me / Valencia / where the orange
trees forever scent the breeze beside the sea"), recorded in 1926 by the
Isham Jones and Paul Whiteman orchestras in New York and by a popular group known as the Revelers. The year 1926 also marked the release
of "My Castle in Spain" (first line: "Behold my dream / I dream of my
castle in Spain") and one of the big hits of that year, "In a Little Spanish Town," with music by the Brooklyn-born songwriter Mabel Wayne
(1890–1978) and lyrics by Sam M. Lewis and Joe Young. Originally
recorded by Paul Whiteman's orchestra with vocals by Jack Fulton (and
later by many other singers, including Bing Crosby and Dean Martin),
this love ditty topped the best-seller charts for eight weeks.

But the biggest "Spanish" hit of the decade was unquestionably
"Ramona," a romantic ballad with lyrics by L. Wolfe Gilbert (1886–

WEEK BEGINNING MONDAY EVENING, AUGUST 23, 1920
Matinees Wednesday and Saturday

WAGENHALS & KEMPER CO.
Presents

SPANISH LOVE

A Drama in Three Acts with Music
By AVERY HOPWOOD and MARY ROBERTS RINEHART
Adapted from the Work of Josè Feliu y Codina, Carlos de Battle and Antonin Lavergne
Music by H. MAURICE JACQUET
From the Popular Airs of the Province of Murcia

In a far-off distant corner of southeastern Spain lies the Kingdom of Murcia. It is a land of simple faiths and simple people. There they worship God—and water.

Nowhere else do the sun's rays beat down quite so hot. Nowhere else is the soil so productive. And the people of no other land are quite so lazy.

As God made Murcia, it was an arid wilderness. By irrigation, man has made it a land of plenty. "Drive a cane in the rich soil of the huerta and the day after it will bear blossoms," runs an oft-quoted adage of Murcia.

To the rest of Spain, the Province of Murcia is the Garden of Passions. The envies, the jealousies, the hates and—the loves, particularly the loves, of these people of Murcia, have furnished legends which date to antiquity.

This, then, is Murcia, the land from whence has come the play, "Spanish Love."

And now, as the play begins, you'll meet in turn:
ROQUE ....WALLACE HICKMAN
ALVAREZ. ....MANOLO THESTINO

PROGRAM CONTINUED ON SECOND PAGE FOLLOWING

Fig. 75. Playbill for *Spanish Love* at Maxine Elliott's Theatre, New York, 1920. The "Spanish" musical blaze first described in 1916 received added fuel from this musical review. One critic called it "hot stuff." Billy Rose Theatre Division, the New York Public Library for the Performing Arts, Astor, Lenox, and Tilden Foundations.

Fig. 76. Sheet music for "In a Little Spanish Town," lyrics by Sam Lewis and Joe Young, music by Mabel Wayne, 1926. In the 1920s composers in New York's Tin Pan Alley churned out dozens of songs focused on the "romance" of Spain." "In a Little Spanish Town" was among the most popular. Courtesy author's collection.

1970) and music by Mabel Wayne. Reportedly the first theme song ever composed for a movie, it was meant to promote the 1928 silent film based on Helen Hunt Jackson's novel of 1884. Dolores del Río (1904–83), the Mexican actress who starred in the film, first recorded the song, but the version that went to the top of the charts, reportedly selling as many as two million records, was the one by Gene Austin, a singer best remembered today for his recording of "My Blue Heaven."[20] Yet a third version, sung by Ruth Etting (1896–1978), a famous Broadway songstress, sold almost equally well.

After "Ramona" Tin Pan Alley did not produce many more Spanish-themed hits, although enough had already been written to fill the songbooks of such popular ensembles as De la Plaza and Juanita with Their Spanish Serenaders. By the end of the 1920s, however, the Spanish musical blaze, together with most other aspects of the Spanish craze, had run its course, only to be replaced by a new version of "Spanish" music that adopted more of a hemispheric or "Latin" beat. Aiding this transition was the start of the Good Neighbor policy in 1933 coupled with the growing popularity of Xavier Cugat, Carmen Miranda, and other Latin performers. It is only fitting therefore that the haunting, waltz-like tone of the song "Ramona," inspired by the book that helped launch the Spanish craze, marked its symbolic end.

The Spanish Screen: "A Country of Romance and of Love"

Another medium in which the story of Ramona marked both the symbolic beginning and end of the Spanish craze was motion pictures. Between 1910 and 1936, four different versions of the story appeared. The first version, released in 1910, came from the Biograph studio of D. W. Griffith (1875–1948), the director famous for his controversial 1914 classic, *The Birth of a Nation*. Starring the celebrated actress Mary Pickford (1892–1979), the *Ramona* film was shot on location at Mission San Gabriel, where Ramona was supposedly born, as well as Rancho Camulos, allegedly the home of the Moreno family and where Jackson's young heroine was living when she met her Indian lover, Alessandro. Echoing Helen Hunt Jackson's passionate defense of Native American rights, Griffith's adaptation of *Ramona*, subtitled *A Story of the White Man's Injustice to the Indian*, cast the Anglo American settlers of California as murderous villains who dispossessed Alessandro of his traditional lands. The only white person who comes off well in the film is Padre Salvierderra, the kindly Franciscan friar who, in keeping with Jackson's romanticized view of the Spanish missions, helped both to civilize and Christianize the Temecula and, in the case Alessandro, teach him to play the mandolin. Griffith purchased the film rights to *Ramona* from Hunt's publisher, Little, Brown, for $100, and the film, though only seventeen minutes long, was reportedly the most expensive film ever made up to that time.[21]

If Griffith's *Ramona* established records, the next *Ramona*—produced by the Los Angeles promoter and theater owner W. H. Clune, directed by Donald Crisp, starring Adda Gleason as Ramona, and released early in 1916—set others. The film was a "five-reeler," running for more than three hours, or an hour more than the previous record holder, Griffith's *Birth of a Nation*. To make it as authentically "historical" as possible, Clune invested lavishly in elaborate sets, which included a seventy-six-foot-high replica of Mission Santa Barbara and another of Rancho Camulos. He also hired artists, designers, and a small army of seamstresses to fashion period costumes reminiscent of Spanish California, and his team prepared an illustrated twenty-one-page promotional pamphlet that, in addition to retelling Ramona's tragic story, promised theatergoers "Padres–Spanish Ladies–Spanish Dons–Lady Dancers–Indians" and more. When the film opened in Los Angeles on February 5, 1916, ticket holders saw a veritable multimedia extravaganza that, in addition to the film, featured a live orchestra, a chorus, and actors as well.

Despite reviews describing the film as "tedious," which it most assuredly is, the success of Clune's elaborate rendition of *Ramona* was practically assured as millions of Americans knew the story of the half-blood Ramona and her Indian lover, Alessandro, and of Father Salvierderra and other characters in Jackson's novel practically by heart. In Los Angeles the film played to packed houses for more than ten weeks. Clune then shipped his elaborate sets to New York, where, starting at the end of March 1916, the show played to packed houses at the Forty-Fourth Street Theatre and, according to one report, added to the "rage" for "Spanish things," including "gowns, dishes, and 'atmosphere.'" Clune's *Ramona* seemingly had the same effect in other cities, including Boston, Cleveland, Detroit, Chicago, and San Francisco.[22]

The success of Clune's *Ramona* set the stage for the performance of a play, also based on Jackson's novel. It was first staged in 1923 in Hemet, California, where it is still performed today. The story's enduring popularity also contributed to the success of the song "Ramona" recorded by Dolores del Río in 1928, along with director Edwin Carewe's silent screen version starring Del Río. This film differed from Griffith's and Clune's versions of *Ramona* in significant ways. Technically innovative, it was one of the first silent pictures to have a synchronized score, and with the onscreen presence of Del Río, an actress whom George Bernard Shaw described, together with the Taj Mahal, as two of the most beautiful things in the world, tickets sold well. But Carewe had little interest in romanticizing life in Spanish California, and at Del Río's insistence he emphasized her Mexicanness and that of southern California as well. As Carewe himself was part Native American, he introduced a measure of violence that was noticeably absent in Jackson's novel and did so with scenes in which gringos, in their greediness to appropriate land, did not hesitate to massacre Indians, indiscriminately shooting men, women, and children alike.[23]

Carewe thus managed to introduce into the Ramona story a measure of reality that the earlier version lacked, and together with Del Río's vocal performance the film represents the symbolic end of an era in Hollywood filmmaking in which Spanish-themed pictures, excluding those with borderlands themes, were in vogue. The borderlands cinematic vogue began in New York around 1908 with the release of a series of early westerns filmed in vaguely southwestern settings. These films regularly featured actors dressed as Mexicans (wearing outsized sombreros) and cast in the role of bandoleros and bad guys of various sorts. Several of these borderlands films came from D. W. Griffith's original Biograph studio in Manhattan, although his films often focused on more romantic themes, among them two eminently forgettable shorts, *The Vaquero's Vow: The Undying Love of a Mexican Cowboy* (1908) and *Mexican Sweethearts* (1909).[24] After moving to Hollywood in the winter of 1910, Griffith stuck with this particular genre, releasing several more films expressly

Fig. 77. *Ramona* movie poster, 1928. Reproduction after the original. The seemingly endless popularity of Helen Hunt Jackson's novel *Ramona* led to no fewer than three film interpretations. The 1928 version, directed by Donald Crisp, was the most successful. Courtesy author's collection.

inspired by the "romance" of the Spanish Southwest and the missions, as recounted in Jackson's novel, along with such other books as Hubert H. Bancroft's *California Pastoral* (1888) and Lummis's *Spanish Pioneers* (1893). Among these releases was a string of "mission" pictures, including *In Old California*, a short released in March 1910 and reportedly the first film ever made in Hollywood; *Thread of Destiny* (1910), starring Mary Pickford and partially filmed on location at Mission San Gabriel; *Two Brothers*, which, as described by the film historian Dominique Brégant-Heald, refreshingly juxtaposed the "dreamy languor" of the *californios* against "Progressive [read Anglo] society, which valued efficiency and diligence"; and his *Ramona*, by far the most memorable—"pictorially perfect," according one critic, and a "pure spirit of poesy," according to another—and popular of the lot.[25]

Inspired by the success of Griffith's *Ramona*, other California directors followed with mission pictures of their own. They included William Selig, whose Selig Polyscope Company produced *Ramona's Father* (1911); Hobart Bosworth, whose films *The Padre*, *A Cup of Cold Water*, and *The Convert of San Clemente*, all released in 1911, attracted viewers by repeating the theme of the benevolent Spanish friar; and Cecil DeMille's *Rose of the Rancho*, a 1914 release. Gaston Méliès, a French-born filmmaker based in San Antonio, Texas, used one of that city's missions as the backdrop in a series of now-lost "one-reelers," among them the aptly named *The Mission Waif* (1911) and *The Mission Father* (1912). Together these films, as well as others like them, helped establish a vogue for films that romanticized the lives of the *californios* and other southwesterners "before the gringos came." These films were unabashedly racist, indiscriminately representing both Spaniards and Mexicans as "Spanish," or as one astute filmgoer, in response to the 1910 short *A Mexican Lothario*, observed, "A picture that is supposed to happen in Spain will show men wearing tall hats like those worn in Mexico, and a picture supposed to be in Mexico will show girls dressed in attempted imitations of Spanish girls." The same could have been said of Frank Montgomery's 1911 film, *A Spanish Wooing*, promoted as "An Exceedingly Picturesque Romance of Old Mexico" but a Mexico populated exclusively by white actors wearing unmistakably aristocratic Spanish dress.[26]

The conflation of Spain and Mexico also appeared in the two Zorro classics, *The Mark of Zorro* (dir. Fred Niblo, 1920) and its 1925 sequel, *Don Q, Son of Zorro* (dir. Donald Crisp), both starring one of the great male stars of the silent era, Douglas Fairbanks Sr. (1883–1939). The first, based on Johnston McCulley's 1919 novel, *The Curse of Capistrano*, was set in a California that was arguably more Spanish than Mexican; neither "Mexico" nor "Mexican" appears in McCulley's text. As for Don Diego Vega, aka Zorro, the "Spanish" equivalent of Robin Hood, he allies with the Spanish friars, whose "empire of missions" was suffering from the depredations of corrupt, presumably Mexican officials. Zorro's Spanish heritage is even clearer in the sequel, which features Don Cesar Vega, Zorro's son, a "Californian" born of old and noble Spanish blood. Based loosely on H. Hesketh-Prichard's *Don Q's Love Story* of 1909, the film, centered on the adventures and misadventures of Don Q, is set in what its titles indicate is "Old Spain . . . a country of romance and of love." That setting may also explain why the *New York Times*, in keeping with the prevailing vogue for Spain, judged it one of the "top ten films" of 1925.[27]

"Old Spain . . . a country of romance and of love"—the trope sold tickets. It also explains why it figured in nearly all of the films related to the craze for Spain. The first was the short featuring Carmencita, the Spanish dancer who was all the rage during the 1890s. Filmed at Thomas Edison's Black Maria Studio in West Orange, New Jersey, in 1894 and based on her performances at Koster and Bial's Music Hall in New York between 1890 and 1894, Carmencita can be seen going through part of her standard dance routine with a series of kicks and swirls (see fig. 2). Originally meant to be viewed on Edison's Kinetoscope, the film was short—only twenty-one seconds—but pioneering, as it was the first time a woman—and a young Spanish woman at that—had ever been filmed in the United States. For this reason the film earned Carmencita the title of the "first female star."[28]

Yet stardom can be fleeting, and with the start of the 1898 war, producers temporarily shelved any thoughts of films featuring Spain, "land of romance and of love." Those interested in Spanish-themed subjects turned instead to "borderland pictures" of the kind described above, but

Fig. 78. *Don Q, Son of Zorro* movie poster, 1925. Starring Douglas Fairbanks, one of Hollywood's greatest stars, the film reportedly captured the ambience of "Old Spain . . . a country of romance and of love." Reproduction after the original; photo by the author.

in 1911 D. W. Griffith returned to the romance and love formula with the release of *Spanish Gypsy*, a film loosely based on Mérimée's *Carmen* and depicting a tortuous love affair between Pepita, as played by Vivian Prescott, with Wilfred Lucas in the role of José. That same love and romance formula figured in later Edison productions such as *The Spanish Cavalier* (1912) and *A Proposal from a Spanish Don* (1913), now both lost, and subsequently in a series of films from the early 1920s, a moment when the Spanish craze in the motion picture industry reached its stride.[29]

The year 1921 marked the release of *Serenade*, a lighthearted film directed by Raoul Walsh and based on *María del Carmen*, a love story by the Catalan author José Feliu i Codina. In 1922 the director Rex Ingram brings the Spanish writer Vicente Blasco Ibáñez's best-selling novel *Blood and Sand* to the silver screen with the great Hollywood heartthrob Rudolph Valentino (1895–1926) in the role of Juan Gallardo, the matador whose infatuation with the wealthy Doña Sol leads him into a life of dissipation and ultimately to his senseless death in the bullring as the film draws to a close. Moviegoers had been introduced to Valentino the previous year in Ingram's *The Four Horsemen of the Apocalypse*, another adaptation of a Blasco Ibáñez novel that recounted the story of a wealthy Argentine landowner of Spanish descent who immigrated to Paris only to witness the horrors of World War I, the loss of his fortune, and a tragic death. That film, together with his role in *The Sheik* and *Blood and Sand*, rocketed Valentino to stardom and helped make *Blood and Sand* one of the first films ever to gross more than $1 million.

Soon other producers, sensing the popularity of Spanish-style houses, Spanish furniture, and the fashion world's "Spanish fever" and the demand for "long and flowing skirts," along with the vogue for cinema palaces with Spanish names, opted for lighthearted, Spanish-themed movies as well. Never very numerous, they included two lookalike films, both loosely based on Jules Massenet's *opéra comique* of 1872, *Don César de Bazan*, and Victor Hugo's *Ruy Blas* (1838), a novel set in the seventeenth-century Spanish royal court. One was Herbert Brenon's *Spanish Dancer* (1923), described by a *Washington Post* reviewer as "a flaming love story of Old Castile," evidently because it starred the Pol-

Fig. 79. *Blood and Sand*, a Paramount picture, movie poster, 1922. Vicente Blasco Ibáñez's *Blood and Sand*, the tragic story of a Spanish bullfighter, was an immediate best seller following its publication in English in 1919. The 1922 movie version, starring Rodolph Valentino, was the first Hollywood film to earn more than $1 million. Reproduction after the original; courtesy author's collection.

ish femme fatale Pola Negri in the role of a gypsy fortune-teller. Critics lauded her in this role as the "primitive woman type" and "almost as untamed as Carmen."[30] The other was *Rosita*, the first Hollywood production of the German director Ernst Lubitsch. Billed as "A Spanish Romance," it starred Mary Pickford in the role of a guitar-strumming "Alluring, Beguiling, Capricious, Coquetish little Street Singer of Sunny Spain." One New York reviewer called it "delightfully charming," another in Chicago labeled it "real art."[31]

Artistry aside, the technologically most important film of 1923 was Lee De Forest's *From Far Seville*, which employed his "phonofilm" technique to produce one of the first "talkies" ever made. Premiered in New York (on April 12) and subsequently screened in thirty-four theaters that had been wired for sound, this eleven-minute short featured a singing, dancing, and castanet-playing Conchita Piquer (1906–90), a Spanish dancer who had made a name for herself in New York, Chicago, and other cities for her thrilling performances in *The Wild Cat*, a "Spanish music drama" featuring bandits, bullfights, gypsies, love affairs, and Seville—in other words, the ingredients characteristic of Spanish romance.[32]

One critic, a teacher of Spanish in New York, criticized these films for their "sensual, sentimental, and sleazy" portrayal of Spaniards and also for ignoring the more "spiritual" as opposed to the "romantic" elements in Spain's traditional culture.[33] The teacher had a point, but the formula proved successful at the box office and consequently reappeared in Raoul Walsh's *The Spaniard*, a film based on Juanita Savage's 1924 novel by the same name. Set in Seville, the quintessential city of Spanish romance, it centered on the loves of a Spanish grandee and featured the hackneyed array of bullfights, cafés, and gypsy dances. The same could be found in *A Spanish Romeo* (1925), directed by George Marshall; *La Fiesta* (1926), a Vitaphone sound short featuring the soprano Anna Case, the Metropolitan Opera chorus, and the Cansino dancers all outfitted in traditional Spanish dress; *The Loves of Carmen* (1927) starring Dolores del Río; *Visions of Spain* (1927), another Vitaphone short starring the well-known singer Lina Basquette; and *Spanish Fiesta* (1929/1930), a musical featuring the tenor Roberto Guzman singing "La Paloma," "Te quiero," and other well-known Spanish songs.[34] By 1930, however, the Spanish love and romance formula was tired and the Spanish craze in movies, as in other media, almost at an end, as Paul Terry, founder of Terrytoons, understood. He poked fun at the entire subgenre in his whimsical spoof *Spanish Onions* (1930), an animated cartoon featuring matadors dancing hand-in-hoof with the bulls they were otherwise supposed to kill.

In 1936 Twentieth Century Fox, still hoping to cash in on Helen Hunt Jackson's novel, released yet another version—in Technicolor—of *Ramona*, albeit one stripped of the political messages Carewe had infused in his 1928 rendition of the story. Directed by Henry King and starring Loretta Young (described by a *Washington Post* reviewer as looking "more Egyptian than Indian") as Ramona and a young Don Ameche as Alessandro, this *Ramona* took its cue from Shakespeare's *Romeo and Juliet*. It was a romantic take centered on two star-crossed lovers, one Indian (described by the *Post*'s reviewer as Ramona's "primitive mate,") and the other *mestizo*, whose marriage ended in tragedy. The Spanish missions came off fairly well in this version, and so too does the "Castilian" Morena household, but the details did little to prevent the critic who reviewed it in the *New York Times* from dismissing it as a "piece of unadulterated hokum."[35] With Spain's brutal civil war making headlines, by 1936 sympathy for Spain's role in bringing civilization to North America had all but disappeared. The cinematic craze for Spain had reached its end.

Life and Literature

Bulls, matadors, flamenco dancers: together with the supposed authenticity, or what Gertrude Stein called the "primitive" quality, of Spanish culture, this combination of factors underscored why Spain also positioned itself close to the center of America's literary imagination as World War I drew to a close. Spain's popularity had dual sources. One derived from the readiness of avant-garde authors to question the rampant materialism of American life and the emphasis accorded industrial progress, urbanization, and incessant change. Another was antimodernism of the kind associated with Henry Adams, the historian and intellectual who, beginning with his *Mont-Saint-Michel and Chartres* (1905) and *The Education of Henry Adams* (1907), questioned the artificiality of modern industrial society and championed what he considered the more natural, organic quality of the Middle Ages.

If Adams found an antidote for the ills of modern society through medievalism and an escape to a romanticized past, other writers located it in societies viewed as having managed to preserve traditional values that the world's supposedly advanced nations had lost. Potential candidates here were many, but by the time of World War I Spain had emerged as an odds-on favorite owing partly to the romantic qualities associated with its history and a national character most observers, both Spanish and foreign, considered unique. Ángel Ganivet's widely read *Idearium español* suggested that Spain's national character was sui generis and divorced from those of the rest of Europe. In Spain the book helped trigger a national debate that became even more heated following the country's defeat by the United States in the war of 1898.

Contributors to this particular debate are grouped under the rubric of the Generation of '98 and include such well-known figures as the journalist Ricardo Macías Picavea; the novelist Emilia Pardo Bazán; two philosophers, Miguel de Unamuno and his disciple José Ortega y Gasset; the historian Rafael Altamira; and a host of other prominent intellectuals and writers. Their views differed, but together they set out to determine the particular elements in Spain's character that, apart from having contributed to its rapid and humiliating loss to the United States, constituted a "national problem" that required resolution if the country was ever to progress. Was it, as some argued, excessive individualism? A quixotic tendency toward idealism and thus the lack of a practical, make-do spirit? Or inbred religious enthusiasm?

In the United States discussion of Spain's national character went off on a different tack. During and immediately after the 1898 war, it focused on the defects in the Spanish temperament in an effort to explain the rapidity of the Spain's defeat. Yet it did not take long before this discussion, in keeping with the idea of "forgive and forget" (see chapter 1), took a more positive turn, a development reinforced by the influence of Havelock Ellis's *The Soul of Spain*, first published in 1908 and reprinted on repeated occasions thereafter. A British polymath famous for his pioneering (and then controversial) work on homosexuality, Ellis (1859–1939) had a particular interest in Spain, a country he had visited on numerous occasions and one whose "spirit" he struggled to understand. Ellis's understanding of this spirit derived partly from his own observations, partly from his interpretation of Spanish literature and art, and partly from his reading of Ganivet, Unamuno, and other members of the Generation of '98 whose ideas, otherwise only available in Spanish, he summarized and translated into English. From these sources Ellis determined that Spain's national spirit rested upon a bedrock of "passion, virility, and moral rigor." He also concluded that spirit, or what he designated "essential Spain," represented the "supreme manifestation of a certain primitive and eternal attitude of the human spirit, an attitude of heroic energy of spirit and exaltation, directed not chiefly towards comfort nor towards gain, but towards the more fundamental facts of human existence."[36]

Enthusiastically reviewed in the *New York Times* as nothing less than "enlightening," Ellis's book, combined with his sympathetic approach to Spain, proved enormously popular, establishing itself as another of the elements feeding into the craze for Spain.[37] It resonated especially among the generation of writers caught up in what the Berkeley historian Henry F. May, writing in the mid-1950s, labeled the "cultural revolution" that America experienced during and after World War I.[38] That revolution, triggered by the horrors of World War I and the Bolshevik Revolution of 1917, was relatively peaceful, but, anticipating that of the 1960s, it entailed a generational division that pitted young against old. "Old" here represented writers, intellectuals, and other individuals aligned with what the Spanish-born Harvard philosopher George Santayana had defined in 1911 as the "Genteel Tradition."[39] As described by Santayana, that tradition, an offshoot of Calvinism, championed Victorian morality, privileged education, high culture, and social refinement; supported communitarian values over individualism; and, with respect to racial matters, avowed the superiority of the Anglo-Saxon over and above other peoples, whether of Latin, Asian, Slavic, or African origin.

May's "young" are roughly synonymous with members of a generation that another historian, T. J. Jackson Lears, identified as those who subscribed to the "therapeutic ethos" owing to their interest in the Freudian ideas and concomitant concern with issues related to identity and self-realization.[40] Gertrude Stein coined the most famous term for this same group of writers when she told Ernest Hemingway in conversation that he, together with Ezra Pound and John Dos Passos, belonged to the *génération perdue*, or lost generation of American writers.[41]

Whether "therapeutic" or "lost," many members of this generation, John Dos Passos in particular, flirted with Marxism and other radical movements. Others—and here Hemingway serves as a prime example—opted for individualism and, having rejected the straitjacket of Victorian morality, invested heavily in self-fulfillment and the pursuit of fulfilling personal needs, both emotional and physical. They tended also to embrace emotion as opposed to self-control, openness over restraint, spontaneity over mannered politeness. At the same time, this same generation of writers manifested a nostalgia for older, simpler, supposedly more natural modes of existence together with societies in which individual needs were seemingly met apart from the emergent ethos of consumerism and materialism. For this reason members of this new generation—some have called them "transnational"—often felt at home with and identified with cultures whose values differed sharply from those they knew at home.

Scholarly literature relating to this generation is copious, far too copious to summarize here. But what historians often forget—and this includes May, Lears, and most other commentators—is the extent to which Spain figured in the works of the generation of writers who rose to prominence just after World War I. As earlier chapters have noted, such interest was not unprecedented. Starting with Mordecai Noah, Irving, Slidell Mackenzie, Prescott, and Longfellow, an increasing number of writers in the course of the nineteenth century seemed to have Spain looming large in their imagination, and that interest increased during the Gilded Age. Novelists such as James Fenimore Cooper and Edgar Allan Poe had also written about Spanish topics.[42] What was new in the twentieth century, as noted in chapter 4, was the dramatic and unprecedented increase in the number of Americans who, for whatever reason, studied Spanish as opposed to German or French.

Accompanying this Spanish turn was new scholarly interest in Spanish history and literature, the creation of new university chairs devoted to the study of these subjects, and the emergence of specialized scholarly journals such as the *Hispanic American Historical Review* and *Hispania*. In 1917 in *El hispanismo en Norte-América* Miguel Romera-Navarro, a transplanted Spaniard teaching at the University of Pennsylvania, drew attention to this sea change in Spanish studies—his term was "renaissance"—and the extent to which this phenomenon redounded to the benefit of his native land. The book offered readers a checklist of U.S. scholars whose contributions to Spanish letters—in language and literature, along with history or art—Romera-Navarro considered worthy of note. That list began predictably with Irving, Ticknor, and Prescott but also included Henry Charles Lea (1825–1909), author of what Romera-Navarro considered the "most impartial and complete" history of the Spanish Inquisition ever published. He also made reference to scores of other *hispanistas* whose recent entrance into the field had in his judgment rendered the study of Spanish letters in the United States second to none (see chapter 4).[43] Today Romera-Navarro's *Hispanismo* is little more than a period piece, but the book serves as an excellent guide to the "renaissance"—my Spanish craze—that rendered Spanish studies a respected academic discipline, comparable in many respects to the older, more established ones in French, German, and Italian. It says very little, however, about the field of literature and Spain's magnetic appeal for a host of writers caught up in May's "cultural revolution."

WILLIAM DEAN HOWELLS

The pioneer in this cultural revolution was no revolutionary, let alone one who belonged to the generation Stein described as lost, as he died shortly after the end of World War I. I refer to the so-called dean of American letters, William Dean Howells (1838–1920), longtime editor of the *Atlantic Monthly*, respected novelist, critic, and travel writer. Howells also epitomized what the Genteel Tradition was all about. On the other hand he was politically progressive, outspoken in his support for the women's suffrage movement, and doggedly opposed, both in public and in private, to the war with Spain in 1898, once describing it as "a wicked, wanton thing."[44] Howells was also something of a rebel when it came to language, coming regularly to the defense of literature written in languages other than English, Spanish in particular. As a writer, Howells is often described as a charter member of the social realist school of nineteenth-century literature associated with Leo Tolstoy in Russia and Émile Zola in France—two authors Howells greatly admired. That characterization is perhaps best expressed in his novel *The Rise of Silas Lapham* (1884), a rags-to-riches story set in the Midwest.

Howell's penchant for literary realism helps also to explain his lifelong infatuation with Spanish literature. In his autobiography, *Years of My Youth* (1916), Howells remembered that, growing up in northern Ohio, he developed a "passion for things Spanish which was the ruling passion of my boyhood."[45] That passion began with Cervantes's *Don Quixote* and was subsequently strengthened by his reading of Irving's *Conquest of Granada*, a book that inspired the young Howells and his friends to team up and play war games pitting Spaniards against the "Moors of Granada."[46] Other favorite readings included Longfellow's *Spanish Student*, which magically enabled him to "spirit" to Spain. Howells also reported that with the help of the Spanish grammar textbook his father bought from a veteran who had served in the U.S.-Mexico War, "I had taught myself to read Spanish, in my passion for Don Quixote, and I was now intending, as the age of fifteen, to write a life of Cervantes."[47]

In the end Howells never wrote that biography, but his knowledge of Spanish led him to the "famous picaresque novel, *Lazarillo de Tormes*," which conjured up "the atmosphere of Don Quixote, and all the landscape of that dear wonder-world of Spain, where I had lived so much." The *Lazarillo* also whetted Howells's appetite for the kind of literary realism associated with the picaresque genre. He admired that genre's "honest simplicity in the narration ... pervading humor and ... rich feeling for character," so much so that he recommended every "intending author of American fiction ... to study the Spanish picaresque novels; for in their simplicity of design he will find one of the best forms for an American story."[48]

If Howells's enthusiasm for Spanish literature began with *Don Quixote* and the picaresque, by the end of the nineteenth century it had expanded to include various contemporary Spanish authors whose untranslated works were virtually unknown in the United States. Already in 1895 he was recommending the "realistic" novels of Armando Palacio Valdés, Benito Pérez Galdós (Howells wrote the preface for the 1891 English translation of this author's famous novel *Doña Perfecta*), and Emilia Pardo Bazán (1851–1921), an author Howells described as one of "the great realists of her country and age." He also observed, somewhat enigmatically, that Pardo Bazán possessed "that humor [realism?] of her race, which brings us [i.e., Americans] nearer the Spanish than any other non-Anglo-Saxon people."[49] His admiration for these writers also allowed him, at the time of the Spanish-American War, to offer a stinging criticism of America's policy toward Spain. Howells first expressed his opposition to that conflict when, on 3 April 1898, just as Congress was debating whether to declare war on Spain, he wrote his sister that "we have no right to take on Cuba, and we have no cause of quarrel with Spain." He subsequently expressed his opposition in a letter of 31 July 1898 to Henry James, and again in a draft version of his *Literature and Life* (1902): "We Americans are apt to think, because we have banged the Spanish war-ships to pieces, that we are superior to the Spaniards; but here, in the field where there is always peace, they shine our masters. Have we any novelists to compare with theirs at their best? . . . Our money would have been far better spent if we had acquired three Spanish novelists—Pérez Galdós, Palacio Valdés, and Emilia Pardo-Bazán, instead of Cuba, Porto Rico, and the Philippines."[50]

Howells's next literary find was Vicente Blasco Ibáñez (1867–1928). This Valencian novelist achieved worldwide fame with his international best seller *Four Horsemen of the Apocalypse* (1914), but his earlier novels, *La catedral* (1903; English translation, *The Shadow of the Cathedral,* 1919) and *Sangre y arena* (1908; English translation, *Blood and Sand,* 1919) captured Howells's attention well before that. These novels so impressed Howells that in the course of an interview published in *Harper's New Monthly Magazine* in 1915 he lauded *La catedral* as a "synthesis of the soul of Spain," *Sangre y arena* as a "study, mighty, dramatic, of the Spanish nature as expressed in bull-fighting," and Blasco Ibáñez for his ability to write "truth to life." He also observed that "no living

Fig. 80. William Dean Howells, unknown photographer, 1903. A lifelong Hispanophile, Howells—known as the "Dean of American Letters"—was outspoken in
his praise for the excellence of Spanish literature, especially that of Vicente Blasco
Ibáñez and other contemporary novelists. Courtesy Library of Congress.

novelist, now that the incomparable Tolstoy is dead, can be compared to this author" and suggested that with the "Spanish . . . you have first-class modern fiction, easily surpassing the fiction of any other people of our time, now the Russians have ceased to lead."[51]

Howells's enthusiasm for Spanish literature also extended to the country itself. In 1911 Howells, at the age of seventy-four, finally realized his lifelong dream: a trip to Spain and a visit to the places first encountered in the pages of *Don Quixote*, *Lazarillo de Tormes*, and the other Spanish books he loved so much. The journey was a literary quest, and according to one of his biographers, he took with him a copy of *Don Quixote* as "a sort of guide."[52] Howells's itinerary included the cities where Cervantes had resided, the windmills of La Mancha that Don Quixote took to be giants, Toledo and the cathedral that figured in Blasco Ibáñez's *La catedral*, a bullfight reminiscent of those described in *Sangre y arena*, Irving's Granada, and every tourist's favorite, Seville. The trip led to a series of essays that appeared in the *North American Review* and *Harper's Monthly* before Howells brought them together in his *Familiar Spanish Travels* (1913), a curious, entertaining, and typically Howellsian mixture of autobiography, literary commentary, reflection, and travelogue.

As he looked back on those travels, Howells admitted having experienced a few unexpected surprises and several awkward encounters with the Spaniards he met; though he read Spanish, he did not speak it. But his impressions of the country were wholly favorable, save for one unfortunate encounter with a disagreeable bank clerk in Valladolid. Even so, in one letter to his son, Joseph, Howells confessed that "the Spain I have been seeing is not the romantic Spain of my boyish dreams, it is far better."[53] No wonder then that Howells at the very end the book proclaimed that "they [Spaniards] are the honestest people in Europe."[54] Yet he recognized that Spaniards, like all peoples, including Americans—and remember here that he thought the "humor" of the two peoples was very much alike—offered certain contradictions that he found difficult to understand. Thus the conclusion:

> In Italy I never began to see the cruelty to animals which English tourists report, and in Spain I saw none at all. If the reader asks

how with this gentleness, this civility and integrity, the Spaniards have contrived to build up their repute for cruelty, treachery, mendacity, and every atrocity; how with their love of bull-feasts and the suffering to man and brute which these involve, they should yet seem so kind to both, I answer frankly, I do not know. I do not know how the Americans are reputed good and just and law-abiding, although they often shoot one another, and upon mere suspicion rather often burn negroes alive.[55]

Compared to other writers associated with the Genteel Tradition, Howells's passion for Spain and its literature was unusual. His friend Henry James had none of it. James's one visit to Spain, in September 1876, amounted to little more than a day trip from the French town of Saint-Jean-de-Luz to the nearby Spanish town of San Sebastián. His French friends took him there so that he could attend a *corrida*. Predictably James described it as "beastly" but found more to enjoy in the spectacle—"extreme picturesqueness" and "gallantry and grace on the part of the *espada*"—than he expected. But James never returned to Spain and in 1911 pointedly ignored Howells's invitation to meet him in Madrid.[56] As for Howells's other friends and associates—a prominent assortment of men of letters that included James Russell Lowell, John Hay, Mark Twain, and Charles Eliot Norton—most recognized the genius of Cervantes, together with that of Velázquez and other giants associated with Spain's golden age of literature and art. In sharp contrast with Howells, however, they distanced themselves from the culture and literature of modern Spain.

GERTRUDE STEIN

That distance—call it a separation between Spain and the United States—all but collapsed with May's "cultural revolution" and the emergence of the new generation of modernist writers who came of age during World War I. The first of them bent on ending that separation, identifying with, and finding inspiration in Spain was the avant-garde author and art collector Gertrude Stein (1874–1946). Residing in Paris after 1903, Stein today is closely connected with French culture and art. Often forgotten is Stein's lifelong interest in—or passion for, according to some critics—Spain and its culture. That fascination seemingly began with Stein's first visit to Spain during the summer of 1901, in the company of her brother Leo. With the Spanish-American War still in the news, why she decided to visit Spain just then remains unclear. Neither Spain nor Spanish had been part of her education, either at Bryn Mawr or later at Radcliffe, although she is likely to have learned something about Spanish culture from Santayana, one of her professors in Cambridge. Even then, since Paris was her and Leo's ultimate destination, why they elected to go there via Spain remains a mystery.

What's certain is that when Stein visited Spain, she carried with her the stigma, perhaps even the disappointment, of having failed to complete her program of studies in psychology at Johns Hopkins. By all reports she was busily attempting to "find herself" on various levels—emotionally, intellectually, sexually. Information about her time in Spain is scarce, but she was there for just over two months, initially in Andalucia and then Madrid, where she visited the Prado Museum and other places. A letter to her friend Mabel Weeks, written from Granada and dated July 10, 1901, suggests that Stein warmed immediately to Andalucia. The region's sunburnt hills reminded her of her childhood in California, and the Alhambra sparked an Irvingesque romantic escape back to the era of al-Andalus. "I love the Moors so much it is almost a pain," she writes, quickly adding that "the Alhambra, and the sunshine and the brown legs and the smells are all mine all mine."[57]

The depth of Stein's identification with Andalucia, together with other parts of Spain, is difficult to ascertain, but subsequent writings, starting with her first novel, *QED* (an initialism for *quod erat demostrandum* [1903]) provide clues. In *QED* Stein's avatar, Adele, sits in the (Lion?) court of the Alhambra "watching the swallows fly in and out of the crevices in the walls, bathing in the soft air filled with the fragrance of myrtle and oleander and letting the hot sun burn her face and the palms of her hands, losing herself thus in sensuous delight she would murmur again and again 'No it isn't this, it's something more, something different. I haven't really felt it but I have caught a glimpse.'" Whatever that "something"—peace, ecstasy, a sense of wholeness?—was, Adele's chance encounter with a "young Spanish girl" provided her with a "near perfect experience." Sitting beside her on a hillside overlooking Granada, Adele experienced "a feeling of complete companionship, their intercourse saved from the inter-change of common-places by their ignorance of each other's language." They then parted, "as quiet friends part," with "a gentle wave."[58]

That "gentle wave" was less of a goodbye than the start of Stein's lifelong connection with Spain. Support for that connection came from Stein's intimate friendship with Pablo Picasso, an artist she identified as quintessentially Spanish soon after their first meeting in Paris in 1905. David Murad has recently argued that Picasso's artistic genius altered Stein's view of Spain in important ways, notably by moving her away from the romantic view of the country embedded in *QED* and toward an understanding of Spain as a country whose racial difference from the rest of Europe infused it with a creative energy other places lacked.[59] What's certain is that the young Picasso became Stein's muse. Changes in his style of painting, especially the shift toward "primitivism" that occurred around 1906, followed by his "cubist" turn circa 1910, reportedly prompted her to alter her own style of writing and move it closer to the continuous, often repetitive "stream of consciousness" style associated with such avant-garde authors as Marcel Proust and James Joyce. According to Stein, she inaugurated that "modern" style in her short story "Three Lives" and subsequently in *The Making of America*, a history of her family written (or at least rewritten) between 1906 and 1909. Picasso's presence in that history is palpable. In 1906 Picasso, together with his lover (and future wife) Fernande Olivier, spent the summer in Gósol, the mountain village in Catalonia where he abandoned his earlier "blue" and "rose" style of painting, altered his palette, and embarked on a new series of ocher-toned works that foreshadowed the primitivism that was so dramatically expressed in his pathbreaking *Les Demoiselles d'Avignon* of 1907. Gósol in this sense represented a place of beginning, of transformation and change. In *The Making of America* Gósol became Gassols, Stein's name for East Oakland, California, where her family moved and began anew after leaving Breakpoint (her name for Baltimore).[60] Picasso also enabled Stein to establish certain affinities between Spain and the United States, especially in matters of aesthetics, where she ventured the opinion that "Spaniards and Americans have a kind of understanding of things which is the same."[61]

Stein's view of Spain did not come from Picasso alone. From 1913 until 1918 and the end of hostilities in Europe, Stein and Alice B. Toklas visited Spain annually, often for extended periods of time. Spanish neutrality, in addition to giving the country's economy an enormous boost during the course of the war, also meant that it served as a place of refuge and offered Stein and Toklas an opportunity to escape the Zeppelin raids threatening Paris. Their favorite destination was Palma, capital of the Mediterranean island of Mallorca, but they visited other parts of the country, or as Stein remembered in her third-person work, *The Autobiography of Alice B. Toklas* (1933), "We went several times to Spain and I always liked it more and more." The "more and more" eventually mushroomed into Stein's claim in the *Autobiography of Alice B. Toklas* that she was "impartial on every subject except that of Spain and Spaniards" (see the introduction). Stein returned to this same subject in *Everybody's Autobiography*: "I used to say that the only thing about which Alice Toklas was not impartial was Spain. Anything can bias me but the only thing that could bias her was the charm of Spain."[62]

Over the course of six years successive trips took the two of them to Barcelona, a city where Stein claimed to have discovered an imaginative shop display that was the source of Picasso's cubist turn. Other discoveries followed, as in the Madrid music hall where she attended the performances of La Argentina, the flamenco dancer soon to debut in New York. So taken was Stein with La Argentina that she recommended her enthusiastically to her friend Carl Van Vechten.[63] It was also Madrid where Stein met up with her old college friend Georgiana Goddard King, then on assignment for the Hispanic Society of America, and where she and Toklas attended their first bullfights. As Stein later reported, Picasso had told her that the bullfighting was not a sport but a ritual. Even so she admitted that "at first they [the bullfights] upset me and Gertrude Stein used to tell me, now look, now don't look, until finally I was able to look all the time."[64] That advice was not only to look but also to encourage Ernest Hemingway (see below) to go to Spain, attend a bullfight, and learn as much about it as he could.

Fig. 81. Gertrude Stein, photographer unknown, ca. 1930. Stein's interest in Spain began with her first visit there in 1899. It was subsequently piqued by her friendship with Picasso and further trips starting in 1913. Courtesy Library of Congress.

Other Spanish cities on Stein's itinerary included Valencia (more dancing, but not as good as what she saw in Madrid, Cuenca ("We delighted in Cuenca and the population of Cuenca delighted in us"), and Ávila, where she reportedly lost her "heart." Ávila, she writes, was the city of Saint Teresa, "a heroine of Gertrude Stein's youth" and the saint who, together with Ignatius of Loyola and Saint Francis, her two favorite saints, figured in the libretto of her 1925 opera, *Four Saints in Three Acts*. As her friend the composer Virgil Thompson later recalled, when they first began their collaboration on that opera, its subject was "undecided," but as "Gertrude had been a great deal to Spain, and she loved Spanish saints and she said, 'What about that?' I said, 'It's OK by me. I've never been to Spain, but you find any saints you like.' So she worked with that idea, and turned out a Spanish landscape, peopled with Spanish saints with whom she had, so to speak, geographical contact."[65] Ávila did more than inspire Stein's opera. It was also there that she began writing *Tender Buttons* (published 1914), another of her modernist works and one that critics called cubist to the extent that it focused on quotidian objects, dissecting each with enigmatic plays on words.[66]

Stein's return visit to Granada proved equally important to the style and content of her work. In *Alice B. Toklas* she recalls that "we stayed there for some time and there Gertrude Stein worked terrifically. . . . We enjoyed Granada, we met many amusing people english and spanish . . . and it was there and at that time that Gertrude Stein's style gradually changed. She says hitherto she had been interested only in the insides of people, their character and what went on inside them, it was during that summer that she first felt a desire to express the rhythm of the visible world."[67] That desire led to what she described as a "long tormenting process," which led to a series of Spanish-themed stories that included "Susie Asado" (first lines: "Sweet sweet sweet sweet tea. Susie Asado"), "Preciosilla," "In the Grass (on Spain)," and "A Sweet Tail (Gypsies)," all of which appeared in her *Geography and Plays*, a collection of her writings published in 1922.

For Stein, Spain was many things—a source of inspiration but also transformational to the extent that her experiences there, coupled with her friendship with Picasso, enabled her to discover her unique, albeit controversial literary voice—George Santayana, for example, called Stein "an infantile writer." Stein never returned to Spain after 1918, but her ties to the country and its culture remained extraordinarily close, as repeated references to the "charm of Spain" and the impossibility of her being "impartial" to Spain in her two autobiographies attest. Nor did Stein's passion for Spain wane over time. As late as 1945, just one year before her death, in the middle of a conversation with the African American writer Richard Wright, Stein remarked, "'Dick, you should go to Spain.' 'Why?'" he asked her. Stein's response: "You'll see the past there. You'll see what the Western world is made of. Spain is primitive, but lovely. And the people! There are no people such as the Spanish anywhere. See those bullfights, see that wonderful landscape.'"[68]

If Wright's recollection of that conversation is at all accurate, Stein's view of Spain as backward but appealing was by no means unusual. Rather it aligned closely with those of other Americans, so many of whom, starting with the likes of James Russell Lowell, likened the country to a kind of refuge from the humdrum of the modern, workaday world. Stein had experienced that Spain during her first visit there in 1899 and again on subsequent visits around the time of World War I, trips that evidently fostered a sense of belonging that rivaled the one she felt for the United States. An alter ego? Perhaps. But it clearly provided her with an identity distinct from, yet complementary to that of being an American. In *The Autobiography of Alice B. Toklas* Stein suggested that "America and Spain have something in common," insisting that both were "abstract and cruel," and she made the same point in *Everybody's Autobiography* by comparing America's love for football with the Spanish affinity for the bullfight. In this latter work she also explained that, as opposed to the busy-body French and English, "Americans, like Spaniards," excelled at "doing nothing."[69]

JOHN DOS PASSOS

"Doing nothing" was far from John Dos Passos's view of America, let alone Spain. Nor did he believe that the two countries had very much in common. He highlighted their differences in a 1920 essay, "America and the Pursuit of Happiness," which records a heated exchange he reportedly overheard while riding in a cart along Spain's southern coast. One passenger, an older peasant, upon learning that Dos Passos was an American, ventured the opinion that "in America there is liberty." At this the young *arriero*, or mule driver, responds, "En América no se divierte" (In America people don't enjoy life). The peasant shouts back, "In America there is freedom . . . there are no rural guards; road menders work eight hours and wear silk shirts and earn fabulous sums; there is free education for children and at forty everyone owns an automobile," to which the *arriero* responds, "I don't care if the whole country is made of gold. . . . People don't enjoy life there. . . . It's not gold people need, but bread and wine and to enjoy themselves. We are poor here and have to work all day long, but we have dances and fine weather and pretty girls and this coast is so beautiful this gentleman [pointing to Dos Passos] has come all the way from Madrid just to see it."[70]

In many ways this exchange summarized Dos Passos's conception of Spain. The country for Stein was a source of inspiration; for Dos Passos it was one from which America had much to learn. Those lessons began in October 1916 when, having recently graduated from Harvard, Dos Passos (1896–1970) went to Spain, evidently at the suggestion of his father. He had already traveled extensively in Europe and the Middle East, but Spain had eluded him. His first destination was Madrid, where he enrolled in the Centro de Estudios Históricos, took courses in both language and literature, and endeavored to learn as much about the country and its culture as he could. He had been in Madrid only a few weeks when wrote home that "I am quite settled here in Madrid now, feel as if I'd lived here all my life."[71] In another letter he added that the city offered a fascinating mixture of old and new, with "little yellow French trains and American automobiles and German locomotives all in a tangle together."[72] On this trip Dos Passos also arranged to get out of Madrid and visit Andalucia—an excursion that evidently included a ride in a mule cart along the coast—along with Valencia. The result: ecstasy, or so he suggests in another letter: "I am so fascinated by Spain. I am just beginning to fathom a little, to understand a little." He also saw Spain as a "temple of anachronisms" where the marks of past civilizations— Celtic, Roman, Visigothic, and Muslim—were everywhere visible.[73]

Inherent in these visits to different parts of the country was a literary quest, similar in some respects to those of Howells and Stein, yet also different. Howells went to Spain in search of Cervantes, Stein to find a muse. Dos Passos wanted something different. He was en route to Madrid when his first major piece, an essay entitled "Against American Literature," appeared in the October 14, 1916, issue of the *New Republic*. In keeping with the dissatisfaction roiled up by Henry F. May's "cultural revolution," the essay had all the markings of a young man searching for a better future, as the work offered a brash, yet brilliant critique of American literature, specifically its lack of what Dos Passos called an *âme nationale*, a national spirit or soul. "Our books," he observed, "are like our cities; they are all the same. Any other nation's literature would take a lifetime to exhaust. What then is lacking in ours?" His answer: "For one thing, American literature is a rootless product."[74] The literature of other countries—Russia was his prime example—was by contrast

> the result of long evolution, based on primitive folklore, on the first joy and terror of man in the presence of the trees and scented meadowlands and dimpled whirling rivers, interwoven with the moulding fabric of old dead civilizations, and with threads of fiery new gold from incoming races. The result is glamour, depth, real pertinence to the highest and lowest in man. It is to be found, in one form or another, beneath the temporary scum of every established literature. This artistic stimulus, fervid with primitive savageries, redolent with old cults of earth and harvest, smoked and mellowed by time, is the main inheritance of the civilizations, the woof upon which individual artists may work the warp of their own thoughts. America lacks it almost completely.[75]

The "it" here was what Dos Passos called America's lack of "earth-feeling . . . our lack of root, out of our lack of spiritual kinship to the corn and wheat our fields grow, out of our inane matter-of-factness."[76]

Dos Passos discovered in Spain the "earth-feeling" America lacked. Soon after his return to the United States in April 1917, he wrote to his friend Roland Jackson, "I am still drunk with Spain—even if I am not there."[77] That same feeling led to his next essay, "Young Spain," published in the December 1917 issue of the avant-garde New York journal *Seven Arts*. That essay introduced readers to Dos Passos's "baker of Almorox," a villager he had apparently met on an excursion outside Madrid. Dos Passos presents him as a whole and complete individual whose life centered on devotion to both family and work and who is well versed in the history and traditions of his village. The baker, moreover, epitomizes the "earth-feeling" that America lacked: "In him I seemed to see the generations wax and wane, like the years, strung on the thread of labor, of unending sweat and strain of muscles against the earth. It was all so mellow, so strangely aloof from the modern world of feverish change, this life of the peasants of Almorox. Everywhere roots striking into the infinite past."[78]

Dos Passos explains that these roots, that infinite past, are both the "the strength and the weakness of Spain," as they gave rise to an "intense individualism." That individualism, he adds, was "born of a history whose fundamentals lie in isolated village communities—*pueblos*, as the Spaniards call them—over the changeless face of which, like grass over a field, events spring and mature and die[. This] is the basic fact of Spanish life."[79] He also explains that these same pueblos, rooted in the land, account for the individualism of Don Quixote, an idealist out to change the world, and that of his partner, Sancho Panza, the pragmatist who cares for nothing but a full belly, as well as the creativity, originality, and genius found in Spain's literature and art.

What follows is a rapid-fire survey of all that Dos Passos had seen and read in the course of his short stay in Spain: the diversity of Spanish geography, the genius of El Greco, Velázquez, and Goya, as well as that of Cervantes and the playwright Lope de Vega. But Dos Passos's pantheon of Spanish genius was not limited to the artists and writers of Spain's fabled golden age. He also referred to Zuloaga and this artist's skill in capturing the "peculiarities—the picturesqueness—of Spanish faces and landscapes"; the contemporary composers such as Isaac Albéniz, Enrique Granados, and Manuel de Falla, whose music had managed to escape "Viennese tinsel and syrup" and draw instead on the wellspring of the country's folk and historical traditions; and finally a raft of contemporary writers that included Blasco Ibáñez, Pío Baroja, and the poet Antonio Machado.[80]

It is hard to fathom how Dos Passos, after a visit that lasted only four months, was able to absorb so much of Spain's history and culture. On top of this he learned something about its politics and even had the opportunity to witness a general strike on December 18, 1916, to protest increases in the costs of fuel and food. He interpreted that event in two sharply different ways, one as part of "the restless industrial world of joyless enforced labor and incessant goading war" and the other as a manifestation of Spanish tradition and the idealism of Don Quixote. He ended by concluding that whatever changes modernization was bringing to the country, "Old Spain"—the "earth-feeling" he found in its pueblos—and what he called "the gospel of Sancho Panza" would not disappear.[81]

When "Young Spain" first appeared in print, Dos Passos had already returned to Europe and was driving an ambulance, along with Hemingway, for American troops. The experience was disillusioning, so much so that wanted to leave the front and go back to Spain, admitting to a friend that he longed for "Spain—Spain—garlic and roses and mountains tawny as panthers."[82]

Those tawny mountains soon came his way. After his discharge from the army, Dos Passos made a beeline for Spain, arriving there in late August 1919. This second visit lasted eight months, and he was busy: hiking with his friend Dudley Moore through the Basque Country and the Picos de Europa in northern Spain; attending a bullfight ("It's stupid, it's ugly, it's splendid"); walking along the Mediterranean coast near Málaga, a region he described as a "wonderful part of the world. The people in the towns hire a fig tree for the summer and go out under it with their pigs and goats and cats and chickens and eat the figs and enjoy the shade. Life has no problems under those conditions."[83] At one point Dos Passos wrestled with a nasty bout of rheumatic fever but still managed to write most of his bitter antiwar novel, *Three Soldiers*, which appeared in 1921.

Over the next three or four years, excited by the discovery of the "earth-feeling" he believed was enabling Spain to hold on to its past in ways other countries had not, Dos Passos returned to the country again and again. In 1921 he went together with another promising young

American writer, the poet E. E. Cummings, and just over a year later he returned with another writer friend, Ernest Hemingway. The two had recently met in Paris, and in July 1923 they traveled together to Pamplona to attend the annual San Fermín festival and to watch bullfights, which Hemingway especially wanted to see (see below). They were together in Pamplona—more bullfights—in July 1924. By this time Dos Passos had published no fewer than twenty essays and reviews focused on Spain—think of it as his personal version of the Spanish craze. They included "America and the Pursuit of Happiness," which suggested that the United States, unlike Spain, had forgotten what "liberty and the pursuit of happiness" were all about (*The Nation*, December 1920); "Andalusian Ethics" (*The Freeman*, February 1922), which elaborated on the themes previously explored in "Young Spain"; and reviews of his favorite Spanish authors, among them Pío Baroja ("Novelist of Revolution"), Blasco Ibáñez ("Inverted Midas"), and Antonio Machado ("Poet of Castile"); *A Pushcart at the Curb* (1922), a book of poetry that captured street scenes Dos Passos had witnessed in Madrid, the seaside town of Dénia, and other towns; and *Rosinante to the Road Again* (1922), a collection of previously published essays interspersed with others that were new.[84]

Rosinante to the Road—its title was inspired by the name of Don Quixote's horse—stands out among Dos Passos's other Spanish writings as the only one that met with a modicum of commercial success. It also summarized virtually everything Dos Passos admired about Spain and what he hoped to discover there. His alter ego in the volume is a Spanish-speaking version of Telemachus, the son of Homer's Odysseus and Penelope, who had set out on a journey to gather news about his long-absent father and in the process learn about himself and the world. In this Spanish version of *The Odyssey* Telemachus, together with his companion Lyaeus, sets out on a different sort of quest; he seeks to locate the "gesture" that epitomizes what Dos Passos calls *lo castizo* and *lo flamenco*, words he used to refer to the essence or spirit of Spain and all that is traditional in Spanish life. That quest, Telemachus admits, is burned into his blood: "I can't help it. . . . I must catch that gesture, formulate it, do it."[85] As for the mysterious gesture, there were several. Lyaeus remembered the bullring: "When Belmonte turned his back suddenly on the bull and walked away dragging the red cloak on the ground behind him I felt it. . . . That gesture, a yellow flame against maroon and purple cadences . . . an instant swagger of defiance in the midst of a litany to death the all-powerful. That is Spain . . . Castile at any rate." Another was the one "a mule-driver makes when he tosses off a glass of aguardiente."[86] Telemachus found another gesture, more predictably, in Pandora Imperio, a gypsy flamenco dancer reminiscent of Mérimée's Carmen; the Carmencita who captivated John Singer Sargent, William Merritt Chase, and Stanford White; and the Doloretes who had brought Carl Van Vechten and other New Yorkers to their feet. Telemachus watches Pandora dance:

> Her face is brown, with a pointed chin; her eyebrows that nearly meet over her nose rise in a flattened "A" toward the fervid black gleam of her hair; her lips are pursed in a half-smile as if she were stifling a secret. She walks round the stage slowly, one hand at her waist, the shawl tight over her elbow, her thighs lithe and restless, a panther in a cage. At the back of the stage she turns suddenly, advances; the snapping of her fingers gets loud, insistent; a thrill whirrs [sic] through the guitar like a covey of partridges scared in a field. Red heels tap threateningly.[87]

Later reflecting on her performance, he recalls the image of her dancing, "standing tense as a caryatid before the footlights, her face in shadow, her shawl flaming yellow; the strong modulations of her torso seemed burned in his flesh. He drew a deep breath. His body tightened like a catapult. 'Oh to remember that gesture,' he muttered. The vague inquisitorial woman-figures had sunk fathoms deep in his mind."[88] Thanks to Pandora, through Telemachus, Dos Passos had discovered what he believed was the essence of Spain and, with it, the antidote that enabled Spain to remain indifferent to "the Mammon of business, the great God of our time."[89]

Rosinante to the Road Again marks the beginning of the end of Dos Passos's Spanish craze. In 1931, as a way of flattering Dos Passos and persuading him to meet him again in Spain, Hemingway reportedly told his friend, "Dos—You are the great writer of Spain."[90] But it was almost too late. Dos's passion had moved elsewhere, to Russia and to Mexico, both of which were in the midst of revolutionary movements in tune with his own increasingly radical politics. Yet Hemingway persisted, and in 1933 he again invited Dos to meet him in Spain. On this occasion Dos Passos said yes, eager to show his wife, Katy Smith, some of his old haunts and also to learn something about the policies of the country's new Republican government, then in its second year and headed by an old friend, Manuel Azaña. As he wrote to Hemingway, "Damn Tootin we'll be in Spain, dead or alive," and he explained that in order to obtain the money he needed to finance the trip, "I just signed a contract to write a book (short book) about the Second Republic which will be burned by Hitler, pissed on in the Kremlin, used for toilet paper by the anarcho syndicalists, deplored by the *Nation*, branded by the *New York Times*, derided by the *Daily Worker*, and left unread by the Great American Public."[91]

That excitement disappeared soon after he arrived in Madrid in July. The government was not nearly as revolutionary as Dos Passos wished, and Azaña himself told the writer that he was not about to institute the radical land reform policies the PSOE, Spain's socialist workers' party, was demanding. After attending a PSOE party rally, Dos Passos also reached the conclusion that its leaders were more interested in cronyism and in providing jobs and favors for friends than in attending to the needs of the country's workers or helping its peasants to secure access to land.

Disappointment morphed into disillusionment. It is no surprise then that the book on Spanish politics Dos Passos was commissioned to write never materialized, although he did manage several short essays gathered under the title "The Republic of Honest Men" and included in his 1934 book *In All Countries*. They are not fun to read; the tone is dark, the optimism of *Rosinante to the Road Again* absent. Several were satires and poked fun at the comfortable lives of the "lawyers, doctors, socialist professors and lecturers" running the PSOE and "steeped in academic ignorance of life that besets the intellectual and professional classes the world over."[92] For Dos Passos these "honest men" were far more interested in feathering their own nests than instituting the land reforms meant to improve the lives of Spain's landless peasantry.

Dos Passos's next—and last—visit to Spain was in 1937. The civil war was raging; the forces of the Republican government were divided and barely able to hold against the rebel armies headed by Francisco Franco and supported by Hitler and Mussolini, and conditions throughout the country were extremely harsh. Dos Passos ostensibly embarked on this visit to patch up what was by then his rocky friendship with Hemingway, and he did so by agreeing to collaborate on the production of *The Spanish Earth*, a documentary film—critics called it propaganda—designed to drum up international support for the beleaguered Republican government. He was equally keen to investigate the murky circumstances surrounding the disappearance and death of another old Spanish friend, the writer José Robles. Hemingway maintained that Robles was shot by supporters of the Republican government for being a Francoist spy. Dos Passos disagreed.

Once in Spain, Dos Passos discovered that Hemingway was mistaken; Francoists had engineered Robles's disappearance and murdered him along with other writers for his leftist views. This discovery led to a permanent rift between Dos Passos and Hemingway, and in a 1939 essay he sadly described the death of Robles as "one story among thousands in the vast butchery that was the Spanish civil war."[93]

This same visit to Spain also led to several short essays documenting different aspects of Dos Passos's experiences there, and they were included in his 1938 book *Journey between Wars*. One essay was "Madrid under Siege," a vivid account of the bombing of Madrid, and another, "The Villages Are the Heart of Spain," recounted the challenges faced by the fishermen of Sant Pol de Mar, a Catalonian coastal village just north of Barcelona. Dos Passos records their complaints: "'If only the fascists would let us alone.' 'And the anarchists,' somebody added . . . 'We could be very happy in San Pol.'"[94] These comments led Dos Passos to ponder Spain's future: "How can they win, I was thinking? How can the new world full of confusion and cross-purposes and illusions and dazzled by the mirage of idealistic phrases win against the iron combination of men accustomed to run things who have only one idea binding them together, to hold on to what they've got."[95] It was his last paean to the virtues inherent in Old Spain, to the baker of Almorox.

Fig. 82. Playbill for the film *The Spanish Earth*, 1937. John Dos Passos had already lost faith in Spain when he collaborated with Hemingway on this film documenting the horrors of the country's civil war of 1936–39. Courtesy Speiser and Easterling-Hallman Foundation Collection of Ernest Hemingway, Irvin Department of Rare Books and Special Collections, University of South Carolina Libraries, Columbia, South Carolina.

And with Franco's victory in the war almost a certainty, Dos Passos's Spanish craze came to an abrupt and tragic end.

WALDO FRANK

The same happened to Waldo Frank (1889–1967), yet another American writer who "discovered" Spain in the wake of World War I. A Yale graduate of Jewish origin living in New York, Frank made headlines with *Our America* (1919), a critical inquiry into the "nature" of the United States. Together with Dos Passos, Frank had little patience with consumerism. He also maintained that industrial progress had severed most Americans from history as well as from the land they inhabited. The book also outlined Frank's ideas for what a less materialistic, more spiritual America might become.

History in *Our America* revolved around what his friend Van Wyck Brooks called Frank's "search for a usable past." That past centered mainly on New England's Puritan pioneers and (no doubt owing to the influence of Lummis) touched briefly on the Spanish pioneers in the Southwest. Frank's interest in Spanish pioneering had taken him to Colorado and New Mexico in 1918, where, in addition to being introduced to Pueblo culture, he also managed to learn something about their Mexican neighbors. Brooks summarized Frank's experiences in the region with the comment, "In that poor and exiled fragment of the world of the Spaniards, in our own Southwest, he [Frank] had sensed at once that it had something for him and our people. It was something the absence of which made our proud industrial world, with all its triumphant success, a danger and delusion." Brooks also recalled that Frank's search for that "something" sent him first to Spain and later to Mexico and Argentina "to find the source of the strength this [Spanish] world possessed."[96]

In his memoirs Frank tells a slightly different story. He recalls that after having finished *Our America*, he began a search for other topics to engage him, possibly one related to Europe. He asked himself, *Why not Spain?* His answer: "The Hispanic in the American Southwest had moved me; I had acknowledged that in *Our America*; I had not looked to understand why I was moved. *Why not Spain?* . . . I'd like to see Spain. I'd write a few picturesque pieces for magazines to defray the expenses.

I made satisfactory arrangements with the editors of several well-paying periodicals—*castanets, get ready*."[97]

If Frank's initial motive for visiting Spain was to write a travelogue, it was a travelogue of a special sort. Again his memoirs provide clues. They indicate that after Frank, en route from Lisbon, arrived in the Spanish border town of Badajoz, he got other ideas about what to write. Recalling an encounter with a small contingent of Spanish soldiers at the train depot, he notes, "With dramatic sharpness, I saw their abrupt difference from the human stock of Western Europe. They had a tone of their own, a resonant *soundness* like a good violin. . . . Something was in these men, something I had not felt before, and *something I must find out*, because in an unregistered way I knew it was important."[98]

Little of this makes much sense, but Frank continues by reporting that he was still in Badajoz when he purchased a copy of Luis Araquistáin's *El peligro yanqui* (The Yankee danger) at a local kiosk. The book's title intrigued him even though his command of Spanish was minimal. Fortunately Frank knew both Latin and French and managed to muddle through a text that offered an extended criticism of the existential threat that the military power, cultural ascendance, and racial prejudices of the United States posed to the cultures of both Spain and Spanish America. Nor could Frank help but notice that Araquistáin cited *Our America* throughout the book, heaping praise upon its author. The memoirs also indicate that Frank, after arriving in Seville, managed to locate Araquistáin's address, wrote him a letter of thanks, and received a quick reply together with an invitation to visit the Spanish writer at his home in San Sebastián in the Basque Country, in the north of Spain. To prepare for this visit, Frank remembered, he bought a Spanish dictionary, a grammar, a copy of Ángel Ganivet's *Idearium español*, along with one of Juan Valera's novels, probably his best-selling love story, *Pepita Jiménez*. Once the American had arrived in San Sebastián, Araquistáin, communicating mainly in French, introduced Frank to a brace of novelists, including Azorín and Ramon Pérez de Ayala, along with the noted philosopher José Ortega y Gasset. It was then, Frank writes, that he abandoned the idea of writing "picturesque magazine articles": "I knew I was going back to Spain, not exploit it."[99]

Much of this story is pure invention, and Frank's biographers tell it differently, noting that Frank actually went to Spain at the invitation of Araquistáin. Whatever the truth, after this initial visit Frank, hooked on Spain, decided to find there what his memoirs describe as "some quality of living that the Western World did not give me." Further support for this search reportedly came from the Mexican poet Alfonso Reyes, who met Frank in Paris and encouraged him, in the spirit of *hispanidad*, to learn more about the culture of both Spain and Spanish America. So began the road that led to Frank's *Virgin Spain* (1926) and subsequently to his later books on Spanish America.[100]

Frank returned to Spain, via North Africa, in 1923. He did not go unprepared. Following his initial visit, he read *Don Quixote* (in Spanish) together with other Spanish literary classics. History was also on his reading list—Prescott of course, also with Roger B. Merriman's *Rise of the Spanish Empire* (1918), several books on Muslim Spain, possibly Samuel Parsons Scott's *History of the Moorish Empire in Europe* (1910) among them, along with several books by members of Spain's Generation of '98, a list that would almost certainly have included José Ortega y Gasset's recent book, *Invertebrate Spain* (1923), as he was an author Frank had previously met. Such was Frank's growing passion for the country—think of it as his version of Saint-Gaudens's fever—that in his memoirs he recalled, "I knew that I was in love with Spain."[101]

Frank's return visit began in Algeciras, a port city in the south where he reportedly experienced a revelation similar to the previous one he had had upon seeing the soldiers in Badajoz: "I felt it at once. These townspeople of Spain had a vigor, a vibrant erect vigor, like a tumescence. These men were *man*. These ample-bodied women *woman*; almost motionless although they were walking, as in a balance of forces. Did I love this because it was the true human condition? And was it lost to the men and women in the West?"[102]

Frank had found something special, and unique, in Spain, or so he believed. Subsequent conversations with members of the Generation of '98—Ortega again, along with the poet Juan Ramón Jiménez, the novelist Pío Baroja, and others—seemingly reinforced his belief that the *Homo hispanus* was a living reality, a separate being whose peculiar admixture of races and civilizations—Roman and Visigothic, Celtic and Christian, Arab and Jewish—gave the Spaniards a particular spirit, a special essence uniquely their own. Influenced in large part by Ortega, together with Spain as it appeared in Ganivet's *Idearium español*, as well as Ellis's *Soul of Spain*, Frank soon determined that "the average Spaniard was an integrated person" in contrast to the inhabitants of those countries where "industry and science and machine have alienated man from his intellectual counterpoint with his earth, his group, and his self."[103] The Spaniard's salvation, Frank explains, was a "temperament" that imparted to Spain a "completeness," a "spirit" that enabled it to cope with the stultifying effects of economic progress and change. In this respect Frank, like the young Dos Passos, was an optimist, one determined to break from the long tradition of foreign writers who classified Spain as a backward, retrograde country. He rather envisioned it as a beacon illuminating a path that other countries could follow toward a brighter, happier future.

Frank was still in Spain, often working in the cavernous and frequently chilly central reading room of Madrid's National Library, when he began writing *Virgin Spain*. The book's title is likely to have come from the first page of Ganivet's *Idearium español* and the suggestion that "in our old age we [Spain] have come to find ourselves still virginal in spirit," that is, unspoiled, naïve, yet ripe with promise.[104] Such was Frank's Spain, and he spelled it out in a series of essays appearing in *The Nation*, the *New Republic*, and the *North American Review* prior to uniting them together in his book *Virgin Spain*, which appeared in 1926.

The subtitle, *Scenes from the Spiritual Drama of a Great People*, is misleading, as it suggests what readers were about to encounter was a kind of theatrical piece divided into acts. In the preface, however, Frank labeled the book a "Symphonic History" with different "movements," each exploring the interplay between "climate, geography, historical events, literature, manners, custom, laws and arts."[105] Starting with the Muslim invasion in the eighth century, the book's chapters each centered on psychological portraits of various personalities—some fictional, others real—to explain the complexities of the Spanish essence. His pantheon included the empire builder Queen Isabella the Catholic, Torquemada the nefarious inquisitor, Saint Teresa of Ávila the mystic, Saint Ignatius of Loyola, founder of the Jesuit order, Lazarillo de Tormes the rogue, and Cervantes the novelist, along with El Greco and Velázquez. The final movement, dealing with the present, featured portraits of individuals Frank judged crucial to Spain's "awakening." They included the educator Francisco de los Ríos, Miguel de Unamuno the philosopher, the poet Juan Ramón Jiménez, and the artist Pablo Picasso. The book also offered detailed accounts of the Basque Country, life in Madrid, and an erotically charged, Freudian description of the bullfight as an epic contest between a penetrating male (the matador) and a passive female (the bull). The volume ended with an imagined conversation between Columbus and Cervantes over where America was going. The dialogue is difficult to follow, but it suggested that Spain, "mother of beginnings," bore America, but over time America, having fallen prey to the twin forces of commercialism and industrialization, had lost its way and stood desperately in need of spiritual redemption that only the "seed" of Spain could provide.[106] Frank never gets around to defining what was inside the seed or what it might bear, but once again Van Wyck Brooks provides a few insights. The seed, he explains, was at once spiritual and linked to Frank's understanding of Spain's "mystical tradition," but it also contained a traditional element guaranteeing the preservation of long-standing customs that more practically minded, business-oriented countries had lost. Left to germinate, the seed would blossom into an "organic body, whole and free," comprising both Spain and Spanish America. Spain thus offered a path toward the realization of *hispanidad*, or what Frank called a "true New World, a true America."[107]

Frank's notion that Spain offered hope for America's future accounts for the warm reception *Virgin Spain* received throughout the Hispanic world. In comparison the book's reception in the United States was considerably cooler, save for that of M. J. Bernadete, a Spanish instructor at New York's Hunter College whose review in the professional journal *Hispania* compared the book to Voltaire's *Lettres philosophiques* for its spiritual and didactic qualities. Bernadete also praised Frank, "an American artist of genius," and his successful attempt to "get at the marrow of the psychological mechanics of Spain, at her unbribable core." Yet the character of that core puzzled other critics, including Muna Lee, a reviewer for the *New York Times*. The book, Lee noted, offered a "vivid pageant of her [Spain's] civilization" but was otherwise "uneven" and overwhelmed by the author's "verbal[ly] pyrotechnic, too self-conscious" style.[108]

That verbally pyrotechnic style also bothered John Dos Passos, who criticized Frank's "ornamental verbiage" in a review published in the Marxist journal *New Masses*. He liked the book's description of the bull-fight but dismissed the rest as a "mere library piece," "academic, rather than real," and, more predictably, given his political inclinations, criticized the failure to comment on the plight of Spain's working classes.[109] The most damning review came from the British writer and art critic Sacheverell Sitwell in the Chicago-based journal *Dial*. Decency prevented Sitwell from writing what he really thought of *Virgin Spain*, but that did not keep him from including in his review several quotations indicative of what he considered the book's "terrible passages of vulgarity and affectation." He also indicated that it would have been "kinder if Frank *had* left Spain a virgin," which was his way of saying that Frank—no "writer of genius," in his view—ought not to have written, let alone published, the book.[110]

As for Hemingway, he never got around to publishing a review but initially expressed his thoughts on *Virgin Spain* in a letter to his writer friend Isidor Schneider. There he candidly expressed indignation at the book's title: "Imagine it being Virgin Spain. The country that lost its virginity the first of any . . . Waldo probably imagines it was Virgin until he planted his gigantic phallic tool in the innermost uterus of the Picos of Europa. I'll tell you, I'll review it for you and you can say on the jacket—Waldo Frank is young full of [laughter] horseshit and he can't write."[111]

At the heart of Hemingway's vulgarities was his belief that Frank's understanding of Spain was overly bookish and overly dependent on effete literary types, whereas his drew on personal experience and engagement with ordinary Spaniards he met in bars and cafés. Hemingway exaggerates. In 1926 Frank's knowledge of Spanish history and literature was arguably more extensive than Hemingway's, though Hemingway did have a certain familiarity with several of Spain's modern writers, as a letter sent to Ezra Pound in 1925 indicates. Hemingway asks his friend, "Do you like to read Spanish. [There] Are some nice Y[ou]ng. Spanish writers not near so full of shit as 'Y[ou]ng' French 'writers.'"[112] As for art, it was more of a tie. Both expressed admiration for El Greco, with Frank citing the biography of this artist by the Spanish art historian Manuel Cossío and Hemingway citing that of the German art critic Julius Meier-Graefe. Velázquez received praise from both, though only Hemingway made reference to Goya.

The one arena where Hemingway held a distinct advantage over Frank was the bullring. The *corrida*—the Spanish word for bullfighting—was the source of Hemingway's personal fascination with Spain. He first wrote about bullfights when he was a reporter for the *Toronto Star* and later he featured them in *The Sun Also Rises* (1926) and *Death in the Afternoon* (1932) and finally in his posthumously published novella, *The Dangerous Summer* (1985). Starting in 1923, the year he first went to Pamplona, Hemingway made a habit of traveling with and hanging out with *cuadrillas*, the group of bullfighters—*picadores*, *bandilleros*, and the like—in the entourage of every *matador*. It follows that Hemingway's view of the bull's role in the corrida differed sharply from Frank's, who poetically likened the bull to an artist whereas Hemingway saw it as animal trained to kill. No surprise then that he objected to Frank's Freudian interpretation of the corrida, which he dismissed as naïve, though he is likely to have used saltier language to describe it. For Hemingway the corrida was a tragedy, an epic struggle between life and death, whereas Frank defined it as a "gross comedy of blood; sex, dionysian and sadistic."[113] Their difference on this issue undoubtedly figured as the principal reason—others might have been Frank's Jewishness, his membership in the Communist Party after 1931, and interest in mysticism and other spiritual matters—for Hemingway's devastating attack on *Virgin Spain* in *Death in the Afternoon*, in which he mocked it as a "one-visit" book marred by Frank's "erectile"—does he mean florid? expansive? overblown?—style of writing together with his "pseudo-scientific" approach to Spain.[114]

Frank's response to Hemingway's commentary remains unknown—he did not mention it in his memoirs—but by 1932 and the publication of *Death in the Afternoon*, he had moved on. His "love" of Spain was essentially over, replaced by a new passion for Spanish America, along with pan-Americanism and the concept of *hispanidad*. This new love affair dates from 1929, when Frank received invitations to lecture in both Mexico and Argentina. He foreshadowed his change of heart in *Virgin Spain*, which he dedicated to "those brother Americans whose tongues are Spanish and Portuguese whose homes are between the Rio Grande and Tierra del Fuego but whose America like mine stretches from the Arctic to the Horn."[115] These concerns came to the fore in Frank's *America Hispana: A Portrait and a Prospect* (1931) and then in a torrent of other books and publications dealing with Spanish American themes. As with Dos Passos, Spain's civil war briefly rekindled Frank's old love affair. In 1936, at the very start of the war, he published a short essay in *New Masses*, expressing his support for the Republic and its rallying cry that it was better to be dead than alive under the rule of the fascists. "Spain," he added, "is fighting the good fight."[116] Two years later, with a fascist victory in Spain's civil war all but a certainty, he briefly visited the country, evidently to check on what was happening to the awakened Spanish spirit whose future he had touted in *Virgin Spain*. Evidently distraught to see that part of that spirit had aligned with Franco, in a trio of short essays published in the *New Republic* Frank bravely managed the thought that the war had transformed Spain's old spirit into the struggle "to stand up against the machinery of the Fascists." He then concluded, albeit without much confidence, that "Spain's men and women are awake. They read Marx but they have not forgotten San John of the Cross. They read about Einstein but they have not forgotten Don Quixote de la Mancha. . . . Spain, in agony but not in terror, resolutely moves toward the freedom in which she may create a society with the measure of her genius, the sense of the whole man, whose feet are rooted in Spanish soil and whose head breathes the airs of the world."[117]

Frank's last expression of interest in Spain occurred in 1942, when a second edition of *Virgin Spain* appeared. The text was identical to the 1926 original save for a new concluding chapter, "The Awakening Passion." That chapter analyzed the reasons for the Republic's defeat. Frank argued that the Republic was out of touch with the "people"; suggested that the clash between Spain's old spirit and the modernizing West had produced the divisions that led to the war; explained that many of the people who sided with Franco believed they were fighting for "God and Spain"; and finally offered an updated version of his old prophecy with the observation that Spain, its recent disaster notwithstanding, had still succeeded by gifting its old spirit to the world. But gift or no gift, few cared. In 1942 Americans had other, more pressing worries, and outside a handful of academic readers, interest in the new edition of *Virgin Spain* was practically nil. The Spanish craze was long over, as was Frank's.

ERNEST HEMINGWAY

The last writer—or at least the last I will deal with here—to succumb to the craze for Spain was Ernest Hemingway (1899–1961). But what, if anything, is there new to say about his love for the country? Literary critics specializing in Hemingway have been writing about this topic for decades, and the volume of literature dissecting his novels and short stories relating to Spain is enormous and, as of this writing (in July 2017) still growing. But what I see and what critics, along with Hemingway's many biographers, often forget is that the start of Hemingway's lifelong engagement with Spain roughly matches that of the other writers the current chapter examines.[118] It also corresponds to the other aspects of the craze for Spain explored in this book and to the moment when travel to Spain became the "in" thing for American tourists to do. According to a 1925 *New York Times* article that used information supplied by the Marqués de Vega-Inclán, the head of Spain's tourist agency, approximately three thousand Americans visited Spain in 1923. By 1925 that number had leaped to almost forty thousand, a twelvefold increase in less than two years.[119]

Hemingway represented little more than a tiny drop in this torrent, but unlike most tourists who visit a foreign country only once, Hemingway returned to Spain again and again: annually every summer between 1923 and 1927, again in 1929 and 1931, and for six months in 1937–38, when he worked as a war correspondent for the North American Newspaper Alliance and helped with the production of two documentary films: *Spain in Flames* and *The Spanish Earth*. Franco's victory in Spain's civil war suspended these visits, as Hemingway vowed to avoid Spain so long as any of his friends remained in Franco's jails. In 1953, however, just after the United States, as part of its Cold War policy, recognized Franco's government and President Eisenhower flew to Madrid to meet Franco and welcome Spain into the family of nations allied against Russia, as well as to secure his permission to establish a string of air and naval bases in Spain, Hemingway, with the excuse that his friends had already died, went there as well, staying for about a month. Other short-term visits followed in 1954 and 1956. Partly to complete work on *Dangerous Summer*, the last in his trio of books dealing with bullfighting (the earlier ones were *The Sun Also Rises* [1926] and *Death in the Afternoon* [1932]), he went for six months in 1959. That visit was his last.

These visits aside, Spain engaged Hemingway throughout most of his writing career. His first publication dealing with the country was a short article on the Galician town of Vigo (see below) that appeared in the *Toronto Star Weekly* in 1922. Spain subsequently figured in five of his major books, starting with *The Sun Also Rises* (1926) and *Death in the Afternoon* (1932), later in his famed novel about the civil war, *For Whom the Bell Tolls* (1940), and finally in two posthumous novellas, *The Dangerous Summer* (1985) and *The Garden of Eden* (1986). It was also central to many of his short stories, including the text of *In Our Time* (1924) and "The Undefeated" (1927), both focused on bullfighting; "Hills Like White Elephants" (1927), featuring two lovers drinking Anís del Mono in a café near Zaragoza; "A Clean Well-Lighted Place" (1933), centered on matadors in Madrid; incidentally in "The Mother of a Queen" (1933), with more matadors; and "The Capital of the World" (1936), also with matadors in the Spanish capital. Spain's civil war figured in *The Fifth Column* (1938), Hemingway's only full-length play, and in five short stories ("Under the Ridge," "The Butterfly and the Tank," "Night before Battle," "The Denunciation"—which included an homage to Chicote, the *coctelería* and one of Hemingway's favored drinking haunts in Madrid— and "Nobody Ever Dies," written in 1938 and published the following year). Spain also made a cameo appearance in *The Strange Country*, an unfinished novel Hemingway worked on between 1946 and 1951. With so much attention, there is every reason to believe that Hemingway was sincere when on the very first page of *The Dangerous Summer* he referred to Spain as "the country I loved more than any other except my own."[120]

The affair began in Vigo, a seafaring town in Galicia, on Spain's northwestern coast, that Hemingway briefly visited during the summer of 1921. That was also likely to have been the first time Hemingway ever set foot on Spanish soil. On his return from Italy after the war, in 1919, the ship on which Hemingway was traveling stopped briefly at Gibraltar, which is just across the bay from Algeciras, but if Hemingway went there he wrote nothing about it.

Vigo made much more of an impression. Hemingway and his wife Hadley were en route to Le Havre when their ship, the ss *Leopoldina*, put in at Vigo for a stopover lasting no more than four hours. Hemingway disembarked, walked along the quay, watched the local fishermen at work, and visited the local fish market, where he was impressed by the array of tuna and other fishes on display. A few months later he wrote to his old fishing buddy from Michigan, Bud Smith: "Vigo, Spain. That's the place for a male. . . . Gaw, what a place." He continued by telling Smith about Vigo's enormous tuna, that three-year-old wine cost only two *pesetas* a quart and cognac four pesetas a liter, and he ended by saying, "We're going back there," which he did.[121] He also wrote a short article about Vigo that appeared in the *Toronto Star Weekly*, the newspaper for which he worked. Hemingway's description of Vigo as "a pasteboard looking village, cobblestone streets, white and orange plastered, set up on one side of a big, almost land-locked harbour that is large enough to hold the entire British Navy" offers a sense of why he liked the place so much. But Vigo's real attraction for Hemingway, already an avid fisherman, was fish. The article lists "long, slender Spanish mackerel, big heavy-shouldered sea-bass with odd, soft-sounding names," along with sardines and trout, and especially "the king of all fish, the ruler of the Valhalla of fishermen," the large "silver and blue tuna that local fishermen were trolling" with lines cast from "small, lateen-sailed boats."[122] Hemingway relishes the thought of catching one of these monsters, and he writes about doing so in language that foreshadows the way another fisherman, Santiago, struggles to catch an enormous swordfish off the coast of Cuba in *The Old Man and the Sea*: "If you land a big tuna after a six-hour fight, fight him man against fish when your muscles are nauseated with the unceasing strain, and finally bring him up alongside the boat, green-blue and silver in the lazy ocean, you will be purified and be able to enter unabashed into the presence of the very elder gods and they will make you welcome."[123]

So began Hemingway's lifelong love affair with Spain. But if that relationship began with fishing, bullfighting added an additional spark. Hemingway knew very little about the subject until 1923, when he was living in Paris and became friends with Gertrude Stein and Alice B. Toklas. Both were true *aficionados*, and if what he later wrote on the opening page of *Death in the Afternoon* is credible, the two women sparked his interest in bullfighting: "Once I remember Gertrude Stein talking of bullfights spoke of her admiration for Joselito and showed me some pictures of him in the ring and of herself and Alice Toklas sitting in the first row of the wooden barreras at the bull ring at Valencia with Joselito."[124]

What happens next is well documented. In 1923 Hemingway, accompanied by Robert McAlmon, a writer and wealthy publisher friend of his who paid for the trip, spent May and June in Spain and attended bullfights in several cities. A letter written after Hemingway's return to Paris outlines his itinerary: "I went all over Spain traveling with a cuadrilla of bull fighters, Madrid, Seville, Ronda, Malaga, Garanada [*sic*] and ending up in the north."[125] The "north" here refers to Pamplona. Shortly after this trip ended, Hemingway returned to Spain in early July to attend Pamplona's San Fermín festival. These trips led to a series of articles on bullfighting that appeared in the *Toronto Star Weekly* the following October. The first, "Bullfighting Is Not a Sport—It Is a Tragedy," offered a detailed description of the corrida and various actors involved; the second, "World's Series of Bull Fighting a Mad, Whirling Carnival," reported on San Fermín and the early-morning ritual of the running of the bulls through the city's streets.[126]

Further indications of Hemingway's passion for the bullfight and for Spain can be found in his correspondence. On October 11, 1923, the day after his son was born, he writes Stein and Toklas from Toronto, telling them that his "young Gallito"—the diminutive of El Gallo, a matador he had seen the previous summer—bore an uncanny resemblance to the "king of Spain." What he failed to mention is that the baby was named John Hadley Nicanor Hemingway, with Nicanor referring to Nicanor Villalta, another matador he admired.[127]

As for Spain, on November 7, 1923, Hemingway writes his father, Clarence, from Paris: "Galicia in Spain has the best trout fishing in Europe. All free. You just need a licence and the rivers are full of trout. It is a great country. Spain, I think, is the best country in Europe." He repeats that thought in the letter to James Gamble that describes his bull-fighting experiences of the previous summer. Using language likely to have echoed Gertrude Stein's ideas about Spain's "primitive" qualities, Hemingway writes, "Spain is the very best country of all. It is unspoiled and unbelievably tough and wonderful."[128]

Hemingway was hooked—on Spain, its bullfights, trout streams, cheap booze, and more. The country also struck him, as he put it in another letter, as an ideal place for a "male," an idea that harked back to the concepts of Sturdy Spain and of Spain as a country that had man-aged to preserve its traditions in ways others had not. But whatever the precise mixture of ingredients in Spain's attraction for Hemingway, bullfighting was key. Together with Hadley, Howell Griffiths Jenkins, and John Dos Passos, whom he had recently met in Paris, he returned to Spain for two months during the summer of 1924, to fish for trout in Navarre's Irati River near the mountain village of Burguete, to attend the San Fermín festival, and to have fun. "Big trout," he writes. "Had-ley caught six in less than [an] hour out of one whole [sic] where they were jumping a falls. Water ice cold and virgin forests, never seen an ax. Enormous beech forests and high up, Pines." Once in Pamplona he participated in the amateur bullfights that were part of the festival, with the "noted Espadas Howell Griffiths Jenkins and Ernest de la Mancha Hemingway representing the Stock Yards of Chicago." He was in love, less with Hadley than with Spain: "The godamdest wild time and fun you ever saw. Everybody in the town lit for a week. bulls racing through the streets every morning, dancing and fire works all night. . . . Honest to Gawd Carper there never is anything like it anywhere in the world. Bullfighting is the best damm stuff in the world."[129]

Figs. 83 and 84. Postcard from Ernest Hemingway in Pamplona, Spain, to Gertrude Stein and Alice B. Toklas, July 13, 1924. Stein had introduced Hemingway to Spanish bullfights. Here Hemingway participates in a *novillada*, an amateur bullfight with young (and not especially dangerous) bulls. ©1924, printed with the permission of the Ernest Hemingway Foundation. This correspondence appears in *The Letters of Ernest Hemingway: Volume 2, 1923–1925*, published by Cambridge University Press. Postcard courtesy Beinecke Rare Book and Manuscript Library, Yale University.

More praise for the country followed in Hemingway's attempt to persuade his old fishing buddy, Bud Smith, to join him in Spain the following summer. His language is relentlessly masculine: "Bull fighting is the best damn stuff in the world. . . . The people have any people in the world skinned. They're all as good guys. . . . Spain is the only country left that hasn't been shot to pieces. They treat you like shit in Italy now. All lost war fascisti, bad food and hysterics. Spain is the real old stuff. And you can have a hell of a good time and spend hardly any money."[130] More such hype can found in another letter, dating from February 1925—yet another effort to get Smith to join him in Spain. "Spain," writes Hemingway, "is the most Christ wonderful country in the world."[131] Smith failed to make it to Pamplona that summer, but Hemingway did, and he went again in 1926, the year marking the publication of *The Sun Also Rises*, his first full-length novel and one dedicated in large part to the pleasures of bullfighting, as well as eating roast suckling pig and drinking Rioja in one of his favorite eateries, Madrid's Casa Botín. In 1927 Hemingway was back in Spain, accompanied by his new wife, Pauline Pfeiffer, and visiting Santiago de Compostela and then fishing for trout in Galicia. His enthusiasm for the country was growing, but he also wished that his Spanish was better, noting that Spain is "bloody, fine country . . . wish the hell I'd been born there and could write Spanish—by Gad wouldn't a man be a writer then."[132] Hemingway skipped Spain in 1928, but he returned for three months in 1929 and for four in 1931, ostensibly to put the finishing touches on *Death in the Afternoon*, although it was a text that he revised even when it was already in galleys. It was at that stage, for example, that he excised from the final chapter that Spain was a "strange" country, difficult for foreigners to fathom, together with another autobiographical comment, yet one that can also be read as a slap at the efforts of Dos Passos and Frank to capture Spain's special essence or spirit: "As an American I know it is very presumptuous of me to write about Spain and I have avoided diagnosing her soul."[133]

Presumptuous perhaps, but Hemingway was not about to give up on Spain, as his later publications attest. By 1932 Hemingway's infatuation with the country, together with that of other Americans, had begun to cool. The annual visits stopped as he spent more and more time in Cuba

Fig. 85. Original book jacket, Ernest Hemingway, *Death in the Afternoon*, 1932. Hemingway's paean to the *corrida* can also be read as his critique of the more romanticized interpretation previously offered by another American writer, Waldo Frank. Photo by the author.

and Key West, although he returned in 1937, mainly to report on the civil war. Franco's victory in that conflict led to a rupture that only ended in 1953, when Hemingway's love for bullfighting brought him back for several last visits and *The Dangerous Summer*, which highlighted the rivalry between two Spanish matadors and reprised many of the topics found in *The Sun Also Rises* and *Death in the Afternoon*. By the 1950s, however, the magic was over; the dangers and the thrill of the corrida Hemingway had previously managed to capture were mostly gone. Thus when Hemingway referred to Spain on the first page of *The Dangerous Summer*, one senses a bit of regret. The Spain of his youth, and his own youth, were but memories, things of the past. Hemingway's Spanish craze lasted far longer than America's, but the end had finally come.

Conclusion

The "Back-and-Forth" Style

"Americans have no interest in Modern Spain other than the comfort and the sanitary conveniences that their travels demand. They want to see traditional Spain in all of its different manifestations, and they are surprised when they meet an educated Spaniard who is not a good catholic and who gives more importance to his country's modern industry than to its artistic treasures and traditions."[1]

This advice appeared in *De interés nacional* (Of national interest), a special report prepared by Spain's Comisaría Regia del Turismo in 1924. Founded in 1911, this commission was the brainchild of Benigno Vega Inclán y Flaquer, Marqués de Vega-Inclán (1858–1942), an erudite nobleman and a close friend of the Spanish monarch, Alfonso XIII. Vega-Inclán served as its director from 1911 until its dissolution in 1928.

High on the commission's agenda was the creation of the touristic infrastructure Vega-Inclán believed necessary to attract well-heeled foreign travelers, Americans especially, to Spain. In 1905 Spain's government had established a national tourist commission tasked with attracting visitors from abroad. The new commission achieved relatively little, but the idea of attracting foreign tourists Spain did not disappear, and in 1906 the government authorized municipalities to create tourist agencies of their own. A handful, Barcelona and Palma de Mallorca among them, did just this, setting their sights mainly on visitors from nearby countries, France in particular.[2]

Vega-Inclán had a much wider, almost global vision of what tourism in Spain might become. Just prior to the outbreak of World War I hundreds of thousands of Americans were traveling to Europe on an annual basis, but as Vega-Inclán recognized, only a fraction—several thousand at most—visited Spain.[3] Having resided for several years in Paris and traveled to other parts of Europe, Vega-Inclán also believed he understood what these tourists wanted: modern, comfortable accommodations, especially in towns and cities other than Madrid; first-class communications; streets devoid of beggars and hucksters; and easily accessible historical monuments and museums. Spain becoming a tourist mecca—this was Vega-Inclán's dream, his way of helping Spain to recover from the "disaster" of 1898. It was also in tune with the reformist, "regenerationist" ideas formulated by the intellectuals belonging to the Generation of '98, many of whom were his close friends and associates. One of the aims of the regenerationists' agenda was the protection of Spain's artistic and cultural patrimony. Another was tourism, and together they helped persuade the government to create a special commission in 1905 for the purpose of attracting foreign visitors to Spain. As for Vega-Inclán, his plans to promote tourism in Spain focused on the Comisaría Regia del Turismo (CRT), an institution that he urged Alfonso XIII to create. Integral to that program was the determination to strengthen "the spiritual, social and economic ties linking Spain to America," with America here referring to Spain's former colonies as well as the United States.[4]

Vega-Inclán's interest in the Americas stemmed in part from his father, a lieutenant general in the Spanish army who was stationed for many years in Puerto Rico. Vega-Inclán visited him there in 1884 and traveled to various countries in South America as well.[5] It also reflected his interest in *hispanidad*, the movement advocating closer ties between Spain and Spanish America and one best interpreted as the Hispanic world's counterpart to the Anglo-Saxonism prevalent in nineteenth-century Britain and the United States. The movement rested on the principle that native-born Spaniards together with individuals of Spanish descent belonged to a single *raza* whose shared characteristics and interests transcended national boundaries. It was no surprise then that the movement took off on both sides of the Atlantic. As the late Christopher Schmidt-Nowara demonstrated, *hispanidad* also took on political meanings in Puerto Rico following the island's annexation by the United States in

1898, whereas supporters in Spain urged the government to promote closer ties with its former colonies in the Americas as way of compensating for the country's humiliating loss to the United States. Toward this end Alfonso XIII announced that the traditional October 12 national holiday—still celebrated in North America, albeit with increasing dissent, as Columbus Day, would be the Día de la Raza. That holiday was first celebrated in 1918.[6]

As for Vega-Inclán's interest in the United States, the artist Domenikos Theotokopoulos, aka El Greco, provided the crucial link. Why El Greco? The answer, though complex, can be explained by El Greco's growing appeal to collectors and museums on both sides of the Atlantic but especially those in the United States. For centuries El Greco had been forgotten, but toward the end of the nineteenth century artists in both France and Spain came to the conclusion that the origins of "modern" art could be found in this artist's highly individualized, somewhat idiosyncratic style, often referred to as an "extravagant" mode of painting. They also interpreted El Greco's willingness to break with convention as being the forerunner of efforts by Cézanne, Picasso, and other moderns to break from the rigid confines of nineteenth-century academic art.

Collectors agreed. Starting in the 1890s, El Greco, notwithstanding his Greek origins and artistic training in Venice and Rome, came to be seen as a quintessentially Spanish artist, one whose artistry exemplified the mystical soul or spirit of Spain as expressed in Ganivet's *Idearium español* of 1897. Partly for this reason the Prado Museum in 1902 organized the first-ever exhibition of El Greco's paintings, many lent by collectors close to Vega-Inclán. As for Vega-Inclán's own interest in El Greco, much of it can be attributed to his learned friend Manuel B. Cossío (1857–1935), author of the first catalog of El Greco's oeuvre. Often acting on Cossío's advice, Vega-Inclán made his first acquisition of works attributed to the artist in 1902, and by 1905, after Cossío had informed him that a house adjacent to the palace where El Greco once lived and painted during his time in Toledo was for sale, Vega-Inclán began to contemplate the creation of a museum dedicated to this artist's work.[7]

It was also when Vega-Inclán's interest in tourism and, coincidentally, in North America first crossed. With an eye toward creating a new museum centered on the art of El Greco and designed to lure tourists to Toledo, Vega-Inclán purchased the dwelling Cossío had told him about, personally underwriting the costs of transforming the derelict building into the Casa-Museo de El Greco, a house museum fitted out with sixteenth-century furniture and meant to demonstrate how the artist might have lived. As for pictures by El Greco to put on display, in addition to donating several from his own collection to the new museum, Vega-Inclán made use of his ties with the Spanish monarch to arrange for the transfer of approximately forty works attributed to El Greco and poorly housed in the Museo Provincial in Toledo to the Casa-Museo, and he did so by agreeing to pay for the restoration of these pictures out of his own pocket.

But Vega-Inclán's pocket was not all that deep. Desperate for funds yet motivated by what a friend diagnosed as his *manía* for El Greco, Vega-Inclán made use of his connections in Paris to enter the international art market, partly by selling paintings from his own family collection and partly by acting as an intermediary and helping his Spanish friends find buyers for whatever objects they wanted to sell. His previous stay in Paris had given him a good sense of the character of that market, especially the growing demand among wealthy American collectors for Spanish Old Master art.[8]

Vega-Inclán's career as an art dealer began roughly around the same time that the bills relating to work on the Casa-Museo de El Greco first came due. Information about his buying and selling is scarce, as he endeavored to keep much of it a secret, but in 1905 Peter A. B. Widener, the wealthy Philadelphia collector, acquired (via Paris) *Family of El Greco*, a picture then attributed to El Greco and one that had come from Vega-Inclán's personal collection. In 1908 Vega-Inclán sold a second reported work by El Greco, a portrait identified as the artist's wife, to John G. Johnson, another Philadelphian in the market for works by this Spanish artist. Nor did Vega-Inclán's dealing—de-accessing might be another word to describe it—end there. Expenses related to the Casa-Museo de El Greco continued to mount, and in a letter of May 6, 1909, addressed to his artist friend Joaquín Sorolla, Vega-Inclán reported on how he helped to arrange, again via Paris, the sale of a picture attributed

Fig. 86. Rafael Doménech, *La Casa del Greco*, 1911, from the series El Arte en España. Toledo's El Greco Museum formed part of the Marqués de Vega-Inclán's efforts to attract American and other foreign tourists to Spain. Courtesy author's collection.

to Goya to the Havemeyers in New York. On this occasion he also expressed regret for having failed to charge more for the picture, attributing his eagerness to sell to "my endless dirty business" (*mi eterna cabronada*) in Toledo.[9]

That "dirty business" ended with the opening of the Casa-Museo de El Greco in 1909, by which time Vega-Inclán had persuaded Alfonso XIII to assume responsibility for the building's maintenance and the care of its collection. Yet there were other bills to pay, especially those attached to his work as director of the CRT. "Spain," he observed in one document, "is a monument, an enormous museum," but each and every one of the programs the CRT instituted to make that museum accessible and attractive to foreign tourists required money. Making matters worse was that CRT had no official line in the Spanish budget. From 1911 to 1913, no matter what the commission's expenses, Vega-Inclán agreed to pay them himself. Nor did the CRT receive much governmental support thereafter. According to one calculation, its annual budget was set at 75,000 pesetas, a paltry figure that did not begin to cover expenses, putting even more pressure on Vega-Inclán to find the money to finance his many projects. The CRT in this sense was Vega-Inclán's hobby, and a costly one at that.[10]

The CRT also explains why Vega-Inclán remained involved, albeit surreptitiously, in the international art market for several years to come. Old Master paintings were valuable assets and easily turned into cash if sold to wealthy foreigners. How Vega-Inclán justified these sales of the artistic patrimony that he had pledged to protect is not entirely clear, but he apparently did so by likening each picture exported abroad to an advertisement—*propaganda* in his language—announcing the different kinds of artistic and cultural treasures awaiting Americans (and other foreigners) who elected to visit Spain. He also believed that tourism was essential for dismantling "the myriad of legends and falsehoods that weigh upon Spain," his way of describing what was just becoming known as the Black Legend.[11] Vega-Inclán's ideas on this issue also aligned with those of his close friend, the New York Hispanophile Archer Milton Huntington. In a letter sent to Joaquín Sorolla in 1912 Huntington informed the artist that 1912 was a bad year for the sale of

Spanish pictures in New York, adding, "I am naturally sorry because it [the sale of these pictures] is a chief means of keeping an interest in Spanish things in the minds of people."[12]

Keeping all things Spanish in the minds of people, foreigners in particular, perfectly describes Vega-Inclán's raison d'être as director of the CRT. One of his first and, for its time, more innovative projects called for the restoration of the late fourteenth-century synagogue in Toledo known as El Tránsito, a building described as "the most important symbol representative of the influence of the semitic race in Spain," together with the creation there of a "Center for Hebraic Studies," both with the thought of attracting tourists, many of them Jewish, as well as Hebraic scholars to Spain.[13] A second was the creation of another house-museum in the Castilian city of Valladolid, this one to be dedicated to Spain's greatest writer, Miguel de Cervantes. As with the Casa-Museo de El Greco in Toledo, this project entailed the purchase and restoration of an old house near where Cervantes might have lived in the city, together with the creation of a library and reading room open to the general public. Huntington did not have much interest in the Tránsito, but he wrote a check equivalent to 50,000 francs to pay for the books to be placed in the library of the Cervantes house-museum.[14] Also on the CRT's agenda, again requiring Vega-Inclán's personal participation, was the restoration of parts of the palace of the Alcázar in Seville together with several courtyards in the Alhambra.[15]

In the meantime Vega-Inclán, determined as ever to bring more tourists to Spain, coordinated the preparation of a series of guides, El Arte en España (Art in Spain), with each guide printed in three languages (Spanish, English, and French). The first item in the series, *La Casa del Greco*, published in 1913 and dedicated to the figure of El Greco, was the work of his friend Rafael Doménech, director of Madrid's Museo de Artes Decorativos. Velázquez, Murillo, and Goya figured in the series' other pamphlets, and still others, each written by a respected scholar, focused on the art and architecture in particular regions or towns and were intended to highlight the creativity and diversity of Spanish culture. The personal contribution of the seemingly tireless Vega-Inclán was a guide to the churches and other sights tourists traveling along the famed Camino de Santiago would encounter.[16]

The logical source for these tourists was northern Europe, especially France and Great Britain. To attract more British visitors, Vega-Inclán in conjunction with the CRT sponsored a dazzling but money-losing tourist exhibition that opened in London's Earl's Court Pavilion in February 1914. Predictably titled *Sunny Spain*, the exhibition featured a "grand panorama of thirty of Spain's most beautiful cities," Spaniards dressed in national costume, flamenco dancing (the famed Carmencita, though aging, helped organize these performances), an orchestra from Córdoba, a café serving "real" Spanish food, a replica of the Prado Museum, and a magnificent set of sixteenth-century tapestries illustrating the Emperor Charles V's conquest of Tunis in 1536 (on loan from Madrid's royal palace). Unfortunately for both Vega-Inclán and Spain, the start of World War in August 1914 meant that few of the Britons who visited the exhibition ever visited Spain. The exhibition, in other words, proved a flop, and with war raging in the north of Europe, the tourists that Vega-Inclán wanted would have to be found elsewhere.[17]

One alternative was South America. The Unión Iberoaméricana, an association dedicated to the principle of *hispanidad* and the common concerns of the peoples who belonged to the Spanish "race," had been founded in 1885. As noted earlier, the Spanish government was keen on promoting hispanidad, and, in keeping with the policy, in 1912—four years before the first Día de la Raza celebration—Vega-Inclán announced in Buenos Aires that the CRT would "facilitate voyages . . . to Spain and for Spain . . . and to ensure that the thousands of South American tourists who go to Europe each year do so via Spain, even if they are only passing through, and to do so by organizing excursions, trips, and civic peregrinations to the Mother Country."[18] A few months later he expressed similar sentiments in an interview with a Spanish newspaper: "In world tourism there is a very important current that can result in great benefits for Spain. I refer to American tourism. The tourist who comes from America needs to be flattered when he visits Spain. Here he will find his history, his ancestry, his language."[19]

Such ideas are likely to have resonated favorably with Americans such as Amado Chávez and Guadalupe Vallejo, who claimed for themselves and their families a pure Spanish heritage, although those of indigenous or mestizo background were apt to have other ideas. Nor were Vega-Inclán's hopes of capitalizing on hispanidad much helped by the start in 1910 of Mexico's turbulent revolution against the government of its longtime dictator, Porfirio Díaz, let alone the high costs of travel between Spain and Argentina, then one of the richest nations in Spanish America. Whatever the exact cause, hispanidad failed to yield many tourists in search of the delights the "Mother Country" had to offer.

Vega-Inclán fared much better with Americans from the United States. His art dealings in Paris had taught him that the wealthiest among these Americans were willing, and able, to spend money—big money—buying Spanish art, a lesson reinforced by the runaway success in New York and other cities of the 1909 exhibition featuring the work of Sorolla, one of his closest friends. The next step was getting these and other Americans to visit Spain. In a letter addressed to Sorolla in July 1911 Vega-Inclán expressed the "*transcendental*" importance of "*the spiritual and economic ties linking Spain with the United States*" (emphasis in original).[20]

The transcendental character of this relationship received an additional boost in the course of Vega-Inclán's one and only visit to the United States, which started in December 1912. The official rationale for this visit, underwritten in large part by King Alfonso XIII, was to explore the possibilities for Spain's participation in the Panama-Pacific International Exposition, scheduled to be held in San Francisco in 1915, and also to determine how the CRT might be able to attract more American tourists to Spain. On a more personal level and with an eye toward earning money, Vega-Inclán was also keen to meet American collectors with an interest in Spanish art. It was no surprise then that his shipboard baggage included several paintings, among them one by Goya. Upon his arrival in New York, he quickly consigned these pictures to the Ehrich Galleries, a dealer specializing in the sale of Spanish art.

Vega-Inclán's host in New York was Archer Milton Huntington, who he had previously met in Paris and with whom he had already collaborated on several projects, including the Cervantes house in Valladolid. After visiting New York Vega-Inclán went to Washington for a meeting with the Spanish ambassador, Juan Riaño y Gayangos; then Chicago, where he met Charles Deering, who had recently begun making the purchases necessary to transform his "house" in Sitges into the equivalent of a museum of Spanish art; Texas—probably San Antonio; then westward, by way of Santa Fe, to Southern California, stopping first in Los Angeles, where in addition to meeting Lummis he visited Riverside's Spanish revival–style Mission Inn, a stopover that led to an interview in which he announced, "I find myself as if I were in my Patria, Spain."[21]

Vega-Inclán's next stop was San Diego, where he visited the recently restored Franciscan mission and discussed the city's plans for its Panama-California Exposition. A motor journey northward along the newly refurbished Mission Trail came next. Once in San Francisco Vega-Inclán met with the organizers of the upcoming Panama-Pacific International Exposition, in addition to giving several speeches in which he expressed the idea that he felt at home in California, as California was essentially Spain. He then returned to the East Coast, stopping first in New York, where Huntington introduced him to Benjamin Altman and other collectors, then Boston and Washington, where he dined with President Taft at the White House and presented a lecture on U.S.-Spanish relations at the recently established Spanish-American Athenaeum. Next came a quick stopover in Princeton to meet with President-elect Wilson and finally the return voyage to Spain, with Vega-Inclán carrying picture postcards of the Spanish missions in California to show Alfonso XIII.

Exhausting as it appears, the trip proved a real eye-opener, California in particular, as it deepened Vega-Inclán's understanding of what he perceived as the Spanish imprint on the Southwest. Just before he returned to Spain, a *New York Times* article devoted to Vega-Inclán's visit rightly used the phrase "California is Spain" to summarize his view of the state.[22] The same visit also confirmed his conviction that Spain could reap untold economic benefits if it were able to attract more American tourists.

So began a concerted campaign to raise Spain's profile, both commercial and cultural, in the United States. Trade came first. Only a few months after his visit to the United States, Vega-Inclán wrote to Alfonso XIII, emphasizing the importance of organizing displays of Spanish commercial goods at the upcoming international fairs in San Francisco and San Diego. Education came next, mainly in the guise of *cursos de verano*, which were specially organized summer courses in language and literature in Madrid that were designed for foreigners and taught by some of Spain's top scholars.[23] Spain's embassy in Washington distributed letters and brochures announcing these courses to colleges and universities across the United States. As for the pamphlets and tourist brochures prepared by the CRT, Huntington and the Hispanic Society helped to distribute these, as did the Southern Pacific Railroad, whose director, Ernest O. McCormick, Vega-Inclán had met in California. The success of this "propaganda" campaign is difficult to assess, as many of Vega-Inclán's initiatives, among them the creation of a Spanish tourist office in New York, never materialized. Even so, as Huntington commented in a letter to Vega-Inclán in 1922, "I am doing all that I can at the Hispanic Society here to urge those who visit it to go to Spain, and I think we have had some results."[24]

New hotels catering primarily to foreigners constituted the last and most costly component in Vega-Inclán's campaign to promote tourism. Help here came from the private sector and various investors, both Spanish and foreign, who financed the construction of several new luxury hotels, among them the Ritz (opened 1910) and the Palace (opened in 1912) in Madrid, the Alhambra Palace (opened in 1910) in Granada, and several more. Vega-Inclán recognized the importance of these and similar luxury establishments, but over time he also recognized the need for tourist accommodations targeting visitors different from those he labeled "transatlantic multimillionaires"—read Americans—with "prodigious suitcases and unimaginable trunks piled up to the ceiling and which make entering any of their rooms the equivalent of a true alpine ascent."[25] The others included students coming to Spain to study its language and culture and those interested in alpinism, nature, and the countryside, as well as those who gravitated toward museums and historic monuments. These visitors, he believed, would be happy with new "modest" hotels of modern design that also harmonized with the country's varied regional architecture.

Vega-Inclán began with Seville, Spain's principal tourist destination. His attention there focused on the city's centrally located old Jewish quarter, or *judería*, known popularly as the Barrio de Santa Cruz. Visitors to

Seville in the nineteenth century regarded the barrio's narrow, twisting, unpaved streets and derelict old houses as quintessentially picturesque. Others, local officials in particular, saw them differently. At the start of the twentieth century city managers viewed them as lacking in harmony with their efforts to modernize Seville by widening and straightening the city's streets.[26]

Enter Vega-Inclán, who was determined to preserve the traditional character of the Santa Cruz barrio yet also improve it with modern sanitation and other amenities. He consequently engineered a series of reforms that included the installation of sewers, pebble-paved streets, and flower-lined walkways, as well as the creation of several intimate plazas designed to give Santa Cruz the look and feel of a garden city, albeit in miniature. Above all he wanted it to look "Spanish." Starting in 1911, and with his own funds, he purchased houses on several of the barrio's more picturesque streets, initially on the callejón del Agua, which ran along the wall facing the gardens of the Alcázar palace, followed by calle de Justino de Neve, and the calle Pimienta. Following his trip to the United States he began the work of converting these houses into small residences, or *hospederías*, catering especially to tourists and students from the Americas. Superficially these residences, with whitewashed exterior walls, iron door and window grilles, red-tile roofs, and garden-like interior courtyards, resembled the traditional Andalucian style of domestic architecture, but Vega-Inclán admitted that inspiration for the new hospederías came principally from California, where he had encountered "cute but spacious residences [I think he meant bungalows] . . . filled with air, vegetation and flowers, each with their small rooms [*departamentos*] installed in the middle of grassy parks, yet also adjacent to a central hotel." Such lodgings, he claimed, were "hard to find in the great cities of Europe, let alone in the eastern part of the United States" but "common along the Pacific Coast, both in the guise of the grand hotels built by California's railroad companies, as well as in all kinds of private residences in San Diego, Los Angeles, Monterrey [*sic*], etc., up to the north of California."[27]

He had also plans to build a series rural hospederías—the forerunners of today's *paradores*—to cater principally to the "tourist looking for the countryside, small villages, and close proximity to [out of the way] mon-

Fig. 87. Patio of a house in the Barrio de Santa Cruz, Seville, ca. 1920. Vega-Inclán refurbished several old houses in Seville to make them look more like the Spanish-style houses he had seen during a visit to California in 1914. Courtesy Museo del Romanticismo, Madrid.

uments."[28] The first, and the only one he was directly responsible for, was the hospedería built in the mountain village of Gredos just north of Madrid. Opened in 1916, it still caters to visitors today.

The idea of making Spain, or at least southern Spain, look more like California may seem odd, but in 1930 Antonio Mendez Casal, a Spanish architectural critic and journalist, understood that this was exactly what Vega-Inclán was attempting to do. Mendez Casal called it the *estilo de ida y vuelta* (back-and-forth or round-trip style), his term for a style of architecture that originated in Spain, moved to California, and then returned, cleaned up and modernized, to the place it began.[29] The *estilo de ida y vuelta* for small, tourist-oriented hotels and residences also represented another way Vega-Inclán hoped that his country could capitalize on and profit from America's Spanish craze.

He was not mistaken, because for a decade or so his efforts to promote American tourism to Spain proved successful. Accurate figures are scarce, but with so much of Europe devastated by World War I, Spain's attractiveness as a tourist destination, as Hemingway admitted in 1924, steadily increased. As noted previously, by 1925 a record number of Americans (roughly forty thousand) were visiting Spain on an annual basis.

As one article famously put it, "the American is a migratory animal," keen on travel abroad.[30] That may be true, but in the 1920s Americans were quite fickle as to where they wanted to go, and Spain was only one destination among many. According to one set of statistics published in 1929, only 27,672 Americans had entered Spain during the previous year, or one-third fewer than the number of those who had done so in 1925, and by all indications that number dropped even further as the Depression took hold and Spanish politics, starting in 1931, became increasingly turbulent and unstable.[31] Nor were Vega-Inclán's efforts to attract American visitors much helped by a southward tilt in U.S. foreign policy. This tilt had begun in 1921 when Pres. Warren Harding compared Simón Bolívar, the "great liberator" of Venezuela, to George Washington, and it continued through a succession of presidents—Calvin Coolidge, Herbert Hoover (who embarked on a ten-nation goodwill tour to Latin America as president-elect in November 1928), and then Franklin D. Roosevelt, who embraced the Good Neighbor policy in an effort to end the "big-stick" diplomacy and heavy-handed interpretation of the Monroe Doctrine that had characterized so much of U.S. policy toward Latin America for almost a century.

This shift in policy was far from complete, as the country's subsequent meddling in Cuba, Santo Domingo, Chile, and Nicaragua readily attests, but political change occasioned certain cultural changes as well. As Helen Delpar has ably demonstrated, the Latin turn in U.S. diplomacy helped alter U.S. attitudes toward Mexico, a country previously associated with the "greasers" living in California and the rest of the Southwest and depicted on the silver screen as if it were a country populated exclusively by mustachioed bandits and heavily armed desperadoes. In the course of the 1920s that image began to evolve, with help from popular, left-leaning writers such as Katherine Anne Porter, who first visited Mexico in 1920 and started publishing articles about the country in 1923; John Dos Passos, who, following his first trip to Mexico in 1926, realized that it possessed the same "earth-feeling" he had previously discovered in Spain; and Waldo Frank, whose travels to Mexico led to his 1931 pronouncement that "for intelligent North Americans to visit Mexico is getting to be a custom."[32]

"Intelligent North Americans," and presumably some others as well, also discovered in Mexico the work of a new generation of Mexican artists who, as an exhibition at the Philadelphia Museum of Art has demonstrated, managed to "paint" what Mexico's revolution was all about in the guise of vast public murals and other works. Foremost among these artists were Diego Rivera, José Clemente Orozco, and David Alfaro Siqueiros, all of whom, starting around 1930, received invitations to bring their realistic style of mural paintings to the United States. Of the three, Rivera, the husband of Frida Kahlo, an important artist in her own right, was the best known, especially after an exhibition of his work at New York's Museum of Modern Art in 1931. Shortly thereafter Americans also acquired a taste for certain Mexican foods; chile con carne—heavy on beans, short on meat—was standard Depression-era fare. Such developments allowed one *New York Times* reporter to comment in 1933 on "the present enormous vogue of things Mexican."[33]

That a Mexican craze succeeded the Spanish one was no accident. To begin with, geography worked in Mexico's favor. Katherine Dos Passos reminded readers of *Woman's Home Companion* in 1932 that Mexico was, as the article title indicated, "Just Over the Border," and she suggested that a "trip to Mexico is more exciting than a trip to Europe, because the country is not standardized or touristed, and even the most inexperienced traveler makes his own discoveries."[34] How many Americans visited Mexico as tourists is impossible to calculate, but in the course of the 1920s U.S. tourist expenditures in Mexico went from approximately $12 million to $38 million by 1930. Comparable figures are not available for Spain, but a bonanza on that scope was one that exceeded Vega-Inclán's wildest dreams.

Demography also favored Mexico as opposed to Spain. The number of Spanish émigrés living in the United States fell well short of 100,000 in 1930. In comparison the number of Mexicans in the United States more than doubled during the 1920s, growing from approximately 730,000 to more than 1.4 million by 1930. At the same time, the American colony residing in Mexico—San Miguel de Allende and Cuernavaca were favored "gringo" retreats—registered increases that Madrid or Seville could hardly begin to match. As for language, the study of Spanish in the United States skyrocketed starting with the opening of the Panama Canal in 1914, but in most schools the Spanish being taught came with a Mexican accent. *Castellano*, with its distinctive soft *c* sound—like a *th* before vowels such as *e* or *i*—was rarely taught. In this respect words alone worked in Mexico's favor, much to the detriment and in some cases dismay of Spain. One final blow—a singular snub to Huntington's efforts to promote Spanish culture in the United States—came in 1929 when the John Simon Guggenheim Foundation, in keeping with President Hoover's efforts to promote closer relations with the United States' southern neighbors, launched special fellowship program for residents of Latin America and the Caribbean, one that continued up to 2017.[35] That foundation, however, did nothing to earmark special fellowships for Spain, nor did Huntington and the HSA.

It is difficult to assign an exact date when the changeover from the Spanish craze to the "enormous vogue for things Mexican" actually occurred. The *New York Times* article mentioned above suggests the early 1930s, but the vogue for Mexican art, and archaeology, was gaining traction well before then. As for the end of the Spanish craze, it is easy, perhaps too easy, to link its demise with the final, violent months of the Second Spanish Republic and the failed army putsch on July 18, 1936, that spiraled into a bloody three-year civil war. Make no mistake: that conflict did little to help the Spanish cause in the United States. Franklin Roosevelt's government, fearful of Moscow's increasing influence over Spain's elected officials, declared neutrality, distancing itself from the Republican cause while turning a blind eye to the readiness of Texaco to provide the upstart Nationalist forces with the petroleum needed to fuel their trucks, tanks, and airplanes. As for the Hispanophiles in the United States, they split into two camps. Some sided with Huntington, whose fear of communism and whose willingness to protect and support what he considered Spain's traditional way of life translated into a grudging sympathy for the Nationalist cause. In contrast, Dos Passos, together with Frank, Hemingway, and Stein, went the opposite way, lending their support to the country's elected Republican government and then distancing themselves from Spain following Franco's victory in 1939.

Franco's victory, followed by his willingness to ally with Hitler at the start of World War II, did more than put a damper on relations between Spain and the United States. It also helped revive old Black Legend ideas about Spanish backwardness and the country's seeming inability to adopt democratic values and embrace both progress and change, ideas reinforced by Hemingway's famous 1940 novel, *For Whom the Bell Tolls*, which highlighted the civil war's brutality and the failure of Spain's Republican forces to put up a united front against fascism. Starting then, both Spain and Spanish culture, having made important inroads into America's colleges and universities at the start of the twentieth century, beat a hasty retreat that lasted until the death of Franco in 1975.

But if Franco helped drive the proverbial nail into the coffin of the Spanish craze, the death of that craze occurred well before the self-styled "Generalissimo" ever took power. I date its demise to 1928, and for several reasons. As noted earlier, 1928 marked the construction of Addison Mizner's last great Spanish fantasy home—La Ronda, in Bryn Mawr, Pennsylvania—as well as the resignation of George Merrick from his position on the Coral Gables Development Commission, effectively ending his efforts to transform southern Florida into a tropical Spanish paradise. The year 1928 also marked the death of Charles Lummis, arguably Spain's greatest champion in the United States and one whose ideas about the romance of Spain, second only to those of Washington Irving, had served as a catalyst for the Spanish craze, especially in California and the Southwest.

That year also marked the completion of the U.S. national pavilion designed and constructed for Seville's Ibero-American International Exposition, a fair that opened the following year. Huntington and the HSA supported the exposition—and America's long-standing links to Seville—by gifting to the city a bronze equestrian statue of El Cid Campeador, the Spanish medieval hero synonymous with bravery and courage, that was the work of his wife, Anna Hyatt Huntington. That statue, similar to the one standing in the courtyard of the HSA and others Huntington presented to San Diego, San Francisco, and Buenos Aires, still can be seen in Seville today.

As for America's national pavilion in Seville, the members of the commission in charge of the design competition opted for one in the "Spanish-American style of architecture," a decision consistent with the then-current vogue for Spanish-themed architecture. It was also meant to provide tangible evidence of the historical connections between Spain and the United States, a linkage that several generations of historians and other writers had worked to establish.[36] Such a design, however, represented a significant break from precedent. U.S. national pavilions at previous international world's fairs were built either in colonial style, as at the 1900 Universal Exposition in Paris, which a featured a design modeled on the White House and submitted by the prominent the Boston architect Charles A. Coolidge—or the classical Beaux-Arts style, as at the World's Columbian Exposition at Chicago in 1893 and subsequently the Turin world's fair of 1911. Yet early in 1927 the commissioners opted for the "Spanish-American" style in the belief that it best represented Spain's manifold contributions to the culture and civilization of the United States.

The winning bid came from William Templeton Johnson (1877–1976), a San Diego architect who had previously collaborated with Bertram Grosvenor Goodhue on the design of several of the Spanish-style buildings erected at San Diego's Panama-California Exposition in 1915. Johnson was especially proud of that exposition's majestic California State Building, once describing it as nothing short of a Spanish masterpiece. He also contended that "there is no finer façade in Spain, and the tower holds its own with the gorgeous towers of Cordova and Seville."[37]

Following the end of that exposition, Johnson struck out on his own, designing several Spanish-style houses in and around San Diego and the La Jolla Library (now Athenaeum) in 1926, followed by the San Diego Museum of Art, which incorporated an intricately carved Spanish plateresque façade. His last Spanish-style building in San Diego was the Junípero Serra Museum, but reflecting the work of the building's namesake, its design, though Spanish, was closer to the earlier, and simpler, mission style.

In keeping with the guidelines of the competition, Johnson's winning design for the main building of the U.S. pavilion in Seville was a combination of mission and Spanish revival. He then made a special journey to Seville to survey the construction of the building together with that of an adjacent cinema and exhibition hall—buildings intended only for temporary use whereas the pavilion was built to last.[38]

Once completed, the pavilion's simple whitewashed exterior and red-tile roof was remarkably similar to the "California-style" hostelries that Vega-Inclán had constructed in the nearby Barrio de Santa Cruz. During the run of the fair, which opened in May 1929, the building served as a residence for art students from the United States who wanted to learn more about Spanish art. It also housed a reading room and library that included old Spanish maps of California and the American Southwest together with books and manuscripts intended to highlight the historic connections between Spain and the United States. Following the fair's closure in June 1930, the pavilion became the U.S. consulate in Seville and served in this capacity until 2006, when, in keeping with the original terms for the land on which it was built, ownership passed to Seville's municipal government. It currently serves as the home of a nonprofit foundation supporting education and exhibitions in the fine and applied arts as well as research in environmental studies.

Johnson's building looks authentically Spanish as opposed to American. In fact to the casual passerby the building's design is virtually indistinguishable from that of many of Seville's other palaces and homes. Yet, if one looks closely at the façade, two small telltale details emerge. Flanking both sides of the central entranceway is a small armorial escutcheon, similar in design to those found on the façades of many old Spanish palaces, which often display the rampant lion and castle symbolizing the ancient kingdom of Castile and León. In contrast, Johnson's escutcheons proudly display the U.S. stars and stripes. It is easy to miss them, but their presence in Seville serves as an enduring reminder of Vega-Inclán's effort to bring the image of Spain that he encountered in California back to his native land. The two escutcheons also attest, albeit in miniature, to that moment when the United States wholeheartedly embraced the arts, architecture, and culture of Spain.

Fig. 88. William Templeton Johnson, architect, former U.S. consulate, Seville, Spain, 1928. Photo by Amparo Graciano.

Fig. 89. Medallions, former U.S. consulate, Seville, Spain. Originally meant to serve as the U.S. pavilion at the Seville world's fair of 1929, the building's Spanish design symbolized the historic connections between Spain and the United States. Photo by Amparo Graciano.

Epilogue

In 1998 the *New York Times* ran an editorial headlined "Forget the *Maine*: Spain Is Back."[1] The article focused on Spain's growing influence in Europe and Latin America, but what it had to say about the country's seemingly ever larger footprint applied also to the United States. Spain's footprint continues to grow.

In many respects Spain is everywhere. It is also part of our daily life in ways that Archer Milton Huntington and other early twentieth-century advocates of Spanish culture could never have imagined and, given their elitist attitudes, are likely to have abhorred. Just listen for it—Spanish now is spoken in virtually every state in the Union, although with an accent more likely to be from Mexico or other parts of Central America, or from Cuba or Puerto Rico. Just taste it: *sangría* is a pool-side favorite; *tapas*, otherwise known as small plates, are restaurant standards; Spanish-style *chorizo* is available in most supermarkets; and Spanish wine, Rioja in particular, is sold nationwide. Go shopping for clothing: Zara, still owned by the Galician entrepreneur who founded it and is now one of the world's richest men, can be found in main streets and malls; Desigual, a clothing brand headquartered in Barcelona, and the Mallorcan firm of Camper, a footwear company, both have a nationwide presence. Save money: branches of the Cantabrian bank Banco Santander, each with its bright red logo, are ubiquitous throughout New England and parts of the Middle Atlantic as well. In Center City Philadelphia, where I currently live, two such branches are only steps away. Less visible but no less important are several Spanish companies with a secure foothold in the U.S. economy. They include the energy firm Iberdrola, owner of Avangrid, which is part of the New England electric grid; Abengoa is a major supplier of biofuel (ethanol) and solar energy; Agroman, a construction company; Cintra, which manages toll highways in Indiana and Texas; and Repsol, a Spanish energy company that in March 2017 announced a massive petroleum discovery on Alaska's forbidding North Slope.

Spain's current presence in the United States has little to do with the Spanish craze this book has addressed. The end of that craze roughly coincided with the start of the Depression, the turbulent politics of Spain's Second Republic (1931–39), the start of its civil war (1936–39), and the victory of Franco's Nationalist armies in 1939. Hemingway's *For Whom the Bell Tolls* appeared the following year. Symbolically the bell in question signaled not only the demise of the second Spanish Republic but, for a time at least, Hemingway's and, more broadly, America's embrace of Spain and its culture. At the same time, the start of Franco's fascist dictatorship, compounded by his close relationship with Germany's Hitler and Italy's Mussolini, breathed new life into the Black Legend, raising anew doubts about Spain's ability to maintain a viable democracy and Spaniards' ability to adapt to the exigencies of the modern, industrializing world.

It was thus no surprise that the start of the Franco regime—lasting until the death of the *generalísimo* in 1975—initiated a marked turnabout in Spain's relative presence in the United States, essentially erasing or at least reversing what had been a steady advance. Save for California and other parts of the Southwest, interest in learning Spanish dwindled, as I can personally attest. In 1957, when I was about to start high school, my father, owner of a small factory—it manufactured nonferrous wire, principally aluminum and brass—in northern New Jersey, embarked on month-long sales trips to Latin America in an effort to drum up sales. Thinking that I would one day enter and possibly inherit the business, he encouraged me—in what amounted to his interpretation of Longfellow's Law—to study Spanish, which I dutifully did, for four years in high school and another two in college. I soon discovered that in my high school—a private day school in Elizabeth, New Jersey—Spanish was for "dummies," useful mainly for commercial purposes owing to the supposed general weakness of Spanish literature and culture.

That situation was little different than the one I encountered in college—at Columbia University—starting in 1961. My history courses rarely touched on Spanish topics other than the Spanish Armada's defeat and the Spanish civil war—both serving as symbols of Spanish backwardness. Nor did my courses in art or architectural history have much to say about Spain. Picasso, though born in Málaga and trained in Barcelona, was classified as French. In fact if I wanted to learn something about Spanish art and history, the only place to do so on campus was in the confines of the Spanish department. Specialists in those subjects were otherwise far and few between, a lesson I learned firsthand when in the course of my senior year I decided to eschew my father's wire business and pursue a doctorate in early modern Spanish history. In the end I earned my doctorate abroad, at Cambridge University, where I had the good fortune to study with John H. Elliott, then and now the world's preeminent historian of Spain and its empire.

I completed my degree in 1968, a year in which available teaching jobs for young historians were plentiful, but only a few universities had much interest in my chosen area, that of imperial Spain. In contrast, however, the study of Latin American history was flourishing, owing partly to area studies funded by the Ford Foundation and various governmental agencies. Once again, Longfellow's Law worked in my favor. The history department at Indiana University, Bloomington, one of the beneficiaries of the Ford program, saw fit to offer me a job, justifying the appointment on the grounds that, as someone knowledgeable about Spain's history, I was in a position to offer a bit of "background" to students in the Latin American field.

As for my next job, at Johns Hopkins University beginning in 1972, again I was lucky. In an effort to break out of the mold of area studies and encourage more in the way of comparative history across different geographical specialties, the Rockefeller Foundation had recently funded the university's new program in comparative Atlantic history and culture. Under these circumstances, the Johns Hopkins history department, then under the leadership of Jack P. Greene, was prepared to hire me in view of the centrality of Spain's centuries-long position in the history of the Atlantic world.

In those years the study of Atlantic history was still in its infancy and Johns Hopkins's interest in the subject quite unusual. In other colleges and universities Spain's place in the curriculum rarely extended beyond the departments of Spanish or other Romance languages. Its language and literature could be studied, but its art history was generally ignored; only three institutions—Brown, Chicago, and New York University's Institute for Fine Arts—had a bona-fide specialist. The situation in history was not much better, as very few departments were prepared to allocate a position to a country best known for the Inquisition, repeated failures at democracy, and a dictatorship seemingly at odds with the democratic traditions of western Europe let alone the United States. They seemingly understood, in keeping with advertising issued under the direction of Franco's Ministry of Tourism, that "Spain is different."

In many ways those departments were right. In the 1950s and 1960s Spain *was* different, something I personally experienced in 1965 upon crossing the bridge spanning the Bidasoa River and leading from France into Spain. It was then I first encountered the country's feared Guardia Civil. I encountered difference again in the newspaper kiosks in Madrid, where the handiwork of Franco's censors—and what was later known as "self-censorship" on the part of the country's newspapers— was visible almost daily. The cinema was yet another site of Spain's difference, again in the sense of ham-handed censorship meant to placate the most conservative elements of the country's Roman Catholic hierarchy. Where else would censors remove from the 1965 film version of Rodgers and Hammerstein's *The Sound of Music*—as true a family film as any—those frames in which the Mother Abbess and the abbey's other nuns sing secular songs. Spanish difference under Franco could be sensed at swimming pools replete with signs that, in addition to prohibiting ball-playing, reminded their clientele that anything judged offensive to "Spain's traditional way of life" (read bikinis, overt signs of affection, talk critical of the regime) would be prosecuted. Difference could also be found in James Michener's *Iberia* (1965), in which the opening line—"I have long believed that any man interested in either the mystic or the romantic aspects of life must sooner or later define his attitude concerning Spain"—echoed the supposed eternal qualities that nineteenth-century writers such as Irving assigned to Spain. For many Americans, Michener's best-selling book was the closest they got to Spain. For others it served as a guidebook, steering them away from the hard politics of Franco's Spain, a topic that the author did his best to avoid. For many Americans the Spain they knew, and remembered, was the one symbolized by the Inquisition as it appeared in Mel Brooks's 1981 film *History of the World: Part I.*

Spain fared better, much better, in the decade that followed. Franco's death in 1975 cleared the way for a return to democracy, as guaranteed in the country's new constitution in 1978. Spain's position in the world soon improved. Following Franco's victory in the Spanish civil war of 1936–39, the country had become a pariah, shunned by most every Western democracy and denied membership in the United Nations, let alone access to the largesse the United States offered to other western European countries via the Marshall Plan. Nor did Franco's antipathy to democratic forms of government do anything to improve his, let alone Spain's, image in the American press. As some studies have indicated, Franco was the subject of ridicule and Spain was depicted as a down-trodden country suffering under the weight of "Franco's heel."[2] The start of the Cold War, coupled with Franco's efforts to package himself as a staunch anticommunist and thus a potential ally of the United States, initiated a period of gradual rehabilitation for Spain. In 1953, with a treaty called the Pact of Madrid, the United States agreed to provide Franco's regime with economic and military aid in exchange for military bases that figured in Eisenhower's strategy to contain the Soviet Union and fight the spread of communism. Two years later, after having been strong-armed by the United States, the United Nations finally agreed to admit Spain to membership. Franco's death, coupled with Spain's return to democracy, opened the doors to more international cooperation: entrance into NATO in 1982, admission into the European Union in 1986, and in 1992 the celebration of a world's fair in Seville quickly followed by the Olympics in Barcelona during the summer of 1992. By then Spain had earned both Europe's and America's admiration and respect. Its political system was also judged worthy of study, largely because its peaceful transition from dictatorship to democracy was widely considered a model for eastern European countries transitioning away from communist rule.

Spain, in short, was "in," especially among "foodies" attracted by the emergence of avant-garde, high-quality (and high-priced) restaurants such as San Sebastián's Arzak, which earned its third Michelin star in 1989; El Bulli (two stars in 1990, three in 1992); and Girona's El Celler de Can Roca (three stars in 2009), judged the world's best restaurant in 2011, although dropping to third place in 2017, a year in which two other Spanish restaurants ranked in the top ten. The first Spanish restaurants in the United States, located on New York's Fourteenth Street and in the area known as Little Spain (as it was there that Spanish and Cuban immigrants tended to cluster), dated from the era of the craze discussed in this book, but few of these establishments survived the Depression. In the 1960s, when I lived in New York, "Spanish" restaurants were mostly Cuban, and I distinctly remember one in Greenwich Village where paella arrived in a covered, cast-iron pot and, rice excepted, had little in common with the traditional, open-pan Valencian version of that dish. I can say the same for Baltimore's Tio Pepe, an eatery founded by one of the cooks attached to a restaurant in the Spanish Pavilion of the 1964 New York World's Fair but whose cuisine, at least when I first dined there in 1969, bore little resemblance to anything Spanish.

All this changed starting early in 1987 with the opening of Alcalá, arguably the first New York restaurant to serve authentic Spanish tapas, quickly followed by Solera (opened 1991) and Marichu (opened 1994), the latter being the first in Manhattan to offer Basque cuisine. Soon other Spanish restaurants, many specializing in tapas—Washington's El Jaleo (opened 1993) being a prime example—appeared in cities across the United States.[3]

To be sure, not everything ran in Spain's favor. One dark note was the Columbian Quincentenary of 1992. Although organized around the theme of "encounter" as opposed to "discovery," the event triggered numerous protests focused on the issue of genocide and the destruction of the indigenous cultures occasioned by Columbus's voyages and by the Spanish *conquistadores* who followed in his wake. Part of that movement was Kirkpatrick Sale's *The Conquest of Paradise* (1991), an imaginative though largely utopian reconstruction of the pre-Columbian world that included a Black-Legendish account of the destruction, both human and ecological, that the "discovery" wrought. From those beginnings came today's efforts to change the name of the Columbus Day holiday (October 12) to Indigenous Peoples Day.

Otherwise the 1990s were good years for Spain's image in the United States. Economic growth in both countries fostered closer relations, both political and diplomatic; more American tourists were visiting Spain; there was more in the way of scholarly publication and exchange, a series of major art exhibitions featuring Spain's most famous artists, and growing acclaim for two leading Spanish novelists, Javier Marías and Arturo Pérez Reverte, as well as for the Spanish film director Pedro Almodóvar, whose *All About My Mother*, starring Penelope Cruz, won the Academy Award for Best Foreign Film in 1999.

As the 1998 *New York Times* article rightly observed, Spain was indeed "back." To be sure, the country's recovery never blossomed into a full-blown craze comparable to the one this book has attempted to describe, but the current century began on a positive note for Spain's image in the United States. The year 2001, for example, brought the inauguration of an imposing, stand-alone building for Dallas's Meadows Museum, the so-called Prado of the Prairie and the one North American collection other than the HSA to specialize in Spanish art. That same year marked the opening of the Milwaukee Art Museum in a new building designed by Santiago Calatrava, the Spanish architect whose futuristic designs in the United States now include New York City's soaring—and far too costly, critics say—World Trade Center Transportation Hub, opened in March 2016. Spain received an additional boost from two of its most famous movie stars, Penelope Cruz and Javier Bardem, both featured in Woody Allen's widely acclaimed (except in Catalonia) *Vicky Cristina Barcelona* (2008), which earned Cruz an Academy Award for Best Supporting Actress. Additional polish for Spain's image came from the tennis champion Rafael Nadal and from the soccer world, with the victory of Spain's national team in the FIFA World Cup championship of 2010 and the perennial excellence of the country's premier football clubs, "Barça" (FC Barcelona) and Real Madrid, winner of the Champions League in 2018.

Soccer apart, some of the luster Spain accrued as the century began evaporated as the Great Recession of 2008–14—what the Spanish refer to as *la crisis*—took hold. For Spain that recession was actually a depression, with an unemployment rate that regularly reached 25 percent, sharp reductions in government spending, and a good measure of political instability as well. *La crisis* also helped fuel Catalonia's demands for independence, leading to the arrests of several prominent Catalan separatists and what has become a full-blown constitutional crisis centered on the relationship between Spain's central government and the Generalitat, the government of Spain's autonomous community of Catalonia, together with a larger debate over the definition of Spanish nationhood.

This crisis, especially the arrests of prominent Catalan separatists, received widespread press coverage throughout the United States, but it did little to diminish Americans' continuing interest in what they perceive as "Spanish" language and culture. The result is that the study of Spanish in the United States, driven in large measure by Longfellow's Law, continues to increase. According to one study, the number of Spanish-language teachers in the nation's public schools is five times greater than those providing instruction in the second most popular foreign language, which is French, and the number of students enrolled in postsecondary Spanish-language courses surpasses the number of those studying all other foreign languages combined.[4] More often than not, American students studying Spanish learn a language inflected with Mexican accents, and their vocabulary is generally more Spanish American than Spanish.

Even so, Spain, *la madre patria*, lurks in the background in much the same way Britain does for English-language students throughout the world. And Cervantes, like Shakespeare, continues to be read as the epitome of Spanish culture, in much the same way as the adventures of De Soto, Cabeza de Vaca, and Serra are now—and are likely to remain—deeply etched into America's colonial history. What the future will bring, especially as the number of Americans of Hispanic origin continues to increase, few can predict, but Spain's presence in America, whether through language, memory, architecture, or art, is likely to remain both vibrant and alive. I wish I could be around to see what will happen, but to quote Doris Day, "Que será, será."[5]

Notes

Abbreviations

AGA	Archivo General de la Administración
AGPR	Archivo General de Palacio Real
AMAE	Archivo del Ministerio de Asuntos Extranjeros
BRL	Braun Research Library
CRT	Comisaría Regia de Turismo
HSA	Hispanic Society of America
HSPBC	Historical Society of Palm Beach County
KL	Kennedy Library
leg.	legajo (file)
RAH	Real Academia de la Historia
TBSP	Thomas Buckingham Smith Papers
WRHP	William Randolph Hearst Papers

Introduction

1. As cited in Linderman, *Mirror of War*, 121.
2. For Sargent's advice as to the itinerary Saint-Gaudens should follow, see Sargent to M. Gaudens, 18 November 1899, boxes 17–20, Augustus Saint-Gaudens Papers, Rauner Library, Dartmouth College.
3. Saint-Gaudens, ML 4 (69.7), Memoirs, Saint-Gaudens Papers.
4. R. Bushman, *Refinement of America*; Levine, *Highbrow/Lowbrow*.
5. Archer M. Huntington Diaries, January 1891, HSA.
6. Hoganson, *Consumers' Imperium*.
7. For Rich's research in Simancas, see Kagan, "Secrets of Simancas," 439.
8. W. Irving, *Journals and Notebooks*, 4:140. Irving had been invited to Madrid by Alexander Hill Everett, the American consul, to translate the first volume of Manuel Fernández de Navarrete's *Colección de los viajes y descubrimientos que hicieron por mar los españoles desde el fin del siglo XV*.
9. I refer to Juderías, *La leyenda negra*. For Juderías, see Español Bouché, *Leyendas negras*. The literature on the origins and history of the Black

Legend is immense but can be approached through Maltby, *Black Legend*; M. Sanchez, "Anti-Spanish Sentiment"; Schmidt, *Innocence Abroad*; García Carcel, *La leyenda negra*; and Friedrich Edelmayer, "The 'Leyenda Negra' and the Circulation of Anti-Catholic and Anti-Spanish Prejudices," *European History Online* (*EGO*), 29 June 2011, available at http://www.ieg-ego.eu. For the history of the Black Legend in the United States, see Powell, *Tree of Hate*; J. Sanchez, *Spanish Black Legend*; the essays gathered in Kagan, *Spain in America*; and DeGuzmán, *Spain's Long Shadow*.

10. Edgar Allan Poe, "The Pit and the Pendulum," 18, accessed at Ibiblio, https://www.ibiblio.org/ebooks/Poe/Pit_Pendulum.pdf.

11. On this legend, see Hauben, "White Legend against Black."

12. DuVal quoted in Weber, *Spanish Frontier in North America*, 358.

13. Wharton, *Letters of Edith Wharton*, 325–26.

14. G. Stein, *Autobiography of Alice B. Toklas*, 145.

15. Jarves, *Art Thoughts*, 42. See chapter 5.

16. G. Stein, *Letters of Gertrude Stein and Carl Van Vechten*, 51 (letter dated Palma, 10 April 1916); "ABC en Nueva York," *ABC*, 12 February 1917, 6.

17. W. Howells, "Editor's Note."

18. For these crazes, see Tafton, *Egypt Land*; Brier, *Egyptomania*; Hutchinson, *Indian Craze*; Lancaster, *Japanese Influence*; Cohen, *East Asian Art*; Yoshihara, *Embracing the East*; A. Scott, *Holland Mania*; and Delpar, *Enormous Vogue of Things*.

19. Motley, *Rise of the Dutch Republic*, preface. Reprints of this book numbered more than twenty before 1900. More would follow. For another example of cultural transfer, see Tatlock and Erlin, *German Culture*.

20. G. Vallejo, "Ranch and Mission Days."

21. Statistics relating to Spanish immigrants vary considerably, but see "Spaniards in the United States"; and Gomez, "Spanish Immigration in the U.S." For Tampa's Spanish population in 1808, see letter of 10 February 1908, box 54/8248, AGA; and "Estado mas aprosimado de los españoles residente en este distrito Consular," caja 1987, AMAE (which, in addition to New York and environs, includes estimates for other states). Other studies include González, *Pinnick Kinnick Hill*, a fictional account of one Spanish family residing in West Virginia (the preface by Suronda Gonzalez is especially revealing); Varela-Lago, "Conquerors, Immigrants, Exiles"; and Fernández and Argeo, *Invisible Immigrants*, which provides an invaluable photographic record of Spanish immigrants in the United States.

22. For more on elasticity of the term "Spanish" and the notion that Spaniards and Spanish Americans belonged to the same race (or *raza*), see Nieto-Phillips, *Language of Blood*, 177.

23. J. Hawthorne, "Some Novelties," 485.

1. Rival Empires

1. Wills, *Henry Adams and the Making of America*, introduction.

2. "Treaty of Friendship, Limits, and Navigation between Spain and the United States," signed 27 October 1795, accessed at Avalon Project, Yale Law School, http://avalon.law.yale.edu/18th_century/sp1795.asp.

3. Henry Adams, *History of the United States*, 1:334–51.

4. Henry Adams, *History of the United States*, 1:176. For Adams's evolving ideas about national character, see Sutherland, "Viscous Thought."

5. Henry Adams, *History of the United States*, 1:340–41

6. Henry Adams, *Letters of Henry Adams*, 2:373, 379, 381 (letters of 13 September 1879, 24 October 1879, and 21 November 1879).

7. Henry Adams, *Letters of Henry Adams*, 2:343 (letter of 21 August 1878).

8. Henry Adams, *Letters of Henry Adams*, 2:379, 381 (letter of 21 November 1879).

9. Jefferson quoted in Henry Adams, *History of the United States*, 1:404.

10. John Adams, *Diary and Autobiography of John Adams*, entry for 13 November 1779. The diary is available online at Adams Family Papers: An Electronic Archive, http://www.masshist.org/digitaladams/archive/diary/. His notes on this trip to Spain may be found in part 3: entries from 13 November 1779 through 23 January 1780. For a detailed account of his impressions of Spain, see Kagan, "Accidental Traveler."

11. John Adams diary, 8 January 1780, Adams Family Papers electronic archive.

12. J. Q. Adams, *Diary of John Quincy Adams*, 1:25 (entry for 27 December 1779).

13. Mrs. Henry Adams, *Letters of Mrs. Henry Adams*, 195.

14. Kagan, "Prescott's Paradigm."

15. Chadwick, *Relations of the United States and Spain*, 3–4, 587.

16. McCadden, "Juan de Miralles and the American Revolution." For documentation of Miralles's slave trading, see Ribes, "Nuevos datos biográficos sobre Juan de Miralles."

17. Jay, *Correspondence and Public Papers of John Jay*, 2:113 (16 September 1781); Jay and Jay, *Selected Letters of John Jay and Sarah Livingston Jay*, 74–119; Jay, *Diplomatic Correspondence of the United States*, 6:105, 281.

18. Henry Adams, *History of the United States*, 1:340.

19. Jay, *Correspondence and Public Papers of John Jay*, 2:113. The best English-language biography of Jovellanos remains Polt, *Gaspar Melchor de Jovellanos.*

20. For Jay's and Sarah's reactions to Madrid, see Jay and Jay, *Selected Letters of John Jay and Sarah Livingston Jay.* For his mission in Madrid, see Sánchez Mantero, "La misión de John Jay en España." Other relevant literature includes Yela Utrilla, *España ante la Independencia de los Estados Unidos*; T. Chávez, *Spain and the Independence of the United States*; and Botero, *Ambivalent Embrace.*

21. *Diplomatic Correspondence of the American Revolution*, 7:281 (Madrid, 11 May 1780).

22. Jay, *Correspondence and Public Papers of John Jay*, 2:195 (25 April 1782). Jay left Madrid on 21 May 1782.

23. Morse, *American Universal Geography*, 2:394. See also the entries for Spain in Morse, *Geography Made Easy*, together with those cited in Fell, *Foundations of Nativism in American Textbooks*, 37; and Fitzgerald, *America Revisited*, 49.

24. Spanish resistance to Napoleon's army, especially that of the Aragonese city of Zaragoza, site of a brutal and protracted siege by French forces, attracted sympathy and support in a number of American cities, especially Boston, where merchants staged a special dinner in January 1809 to honor the "patriots of Spain." For more on this dinner, see Kagan, "From Noah to Moses," 26–27.

25. For this letter, see Josef Yznardy to Thomas Jefferson, Cádiz, 3 August 1809, an attachment to Luis de Onís to Thomas Jefferson, Georgetown, 17 October 1809, available at Founders Online, https://founders .archives.gov/documents/Jefferson/03-01-02-0475.

26. The best study of Onís's mission remains Río, *La misión de Don Luis de Onís.*

27. Jefferson, *Catalogue of the Library of Thomas Jefferson*, 3:46.

28. Monroe, *Writings of James Monroe*, 3:273–74, 299.

29. Verus [Luis de Onís], *Passage of the President's Message which deals with the forcible occupation of Western Florida.*

30. Madison to Congress, 2 February 1810, in Madison, *Papers of James Madison Digital Edition*, Presidential Series, vol. 3. For an overview of Madison's foreign policy, see Stagg, *Mr. Madison's War.*

31. As cited in Río, *La misión de Don Luis de Onís*, 225 (letter of 16 April 1812 ["Nuestra cosas aquí van mal"]).

32. Monroe, *Writings of James Monroe*, 5:301 (letter of 7 December 1814).

33. Luis de Onís, letter to the Secretary of State [. . .], 30 December 1815, as reproduced in *Message from the President of the United States*, 26 January 1816, 5, 6, 8.

34. Luis de Onís, letter to the Secretary of State [. . .], 30 December 1815, as reproduced in *Message from the President of the United States*, 26 January 1816.

35. Monroe, *Writings of James Monroe*, 5:316 (27 June 1816); see also Founders Online, http://founders.archives.gov/documents/Madison/99-01 -02-5219. Onís wrote this note in response to the capture of a U.S. brig in Cartagena, but it applies equally well to Florida.

36. Monroe, *Writings of James Monroe*, 6:33 (letter to Madison, 24 November 1817). Monroe made this comment with reference to some minor disputes with Spain over incidents involving U.S. vessels off the coasts of Algiers and Peru, but Florida was clearly on his mind.

37. Monroe, *Writings of James Monroe*, 6:60—61 (letter to Jackson, 19 July 1818).

38. "Trait of the Spanish Character," 30. This article appears to have been a sequel to "Character of Spain, and the Spaniards: Taken chiefly from the speech of Dr Antonio Ruiz de Padrón, Deputy to the Cortes, spoken Jan 18, 1813, and from 'Bread and Bulls' by Don Gaspar Jovellanos, 1813," *North American Review* 3 (May 1816): 54—58, an article whose theme was the Inquisition's pernicious influence on Spain's national character.

39. Verus [Luis de Onís], *Observations on the existing differences*, 6—7.

40. Verus [Luis de Onís], *Observations on the existing differences*, 17.

41. J. Q. Adams, *Writings of John Quincy Adams*, 6:306 (letter to George Erving, 20 April 1818).

42. J. Q. Adams, *Memoirs of John Quincy Adams*, 4:329.

43. For Erving, see Kagan, *Spain in America*, 7; and Curry, *Diplomatic Services of George William Erving*.

44. Clay, *Speeches of Henry Clay*, 1:143, 244; Remini, *Henry Clay, Statesman for the Union*, 174. Clay also argued that Spain, having failed to protect "the industry of its subjects," had become "one of the poorest countries in Europe." Clay, *Papers of Henry Clay*, 2:518 (speech of 24 March 1818 on the emancipation of South America).

45. Onís to Adams, 27 February 1818, in J. Q. Adams, *Memoirs of John Quincy Adams*, 4:56.

46. Onís to Adams, 1 November 1818, in Río, *La misión de Don Luis de Onís*, 245.

47. Clay, *Speeches of Henry Clay*, 1:212 ("Speech on the Spanish Treaty," 3 April 1820).

48. J. Q. Adams, *Diary of John Quincy Adams*, 2:255.

49. Río, *La misión de Don Luis de Onís*, 247.

50. Río, *La misión de Don Luis de Onís*, 253–54 (letter to his son, 29 June 1819, noting, "con estos solos [Cuba and Philippines] puntos puede la España recuperarse en restableciendo el orden de su hacienda; sin ellos, no le queda esperanza alguna de restablecimiento").

51. L. de Onís, *Memoria sobre las negociaciones entre España y los Estados Unidos* [. . .], published in translation as *Memoir upon the negotiations between Spain and the United States* [. . .] (1821).

52. Botero, *Ambivalent Embrace*.

53. Pettigrew, *Notes on Spain and the Spaniards*, 415.

54. For López, see Chaffin, *Fatal Glory*. For Fillmore's order, see Fillmore, *Millard Fillmore Papers*, 1:341 (Fillmore to Secretary of State Daniel Webster, 16 April 1851), where the president admitted there was little to be done to prevent López from embarking for Cuba. President Polk, although keen to purchase Cuba from Spain, had also expressed his opposition to the filibusteros and their raids. See French, "Foundations of Empire Building," chap. 2.

55. Strong, *Diary of George Templeton Strong*, 2:62 (entry for 24 August 1851).

56. Pettigrew, *Notes on Spain and the Spaniards*, 422–23, 428.

57. W. Irving, *Letters*, 3:179 (letter of August 1842).

58. For Saunders and Spain, see Bowen, *Spain and the American Civil War*, 23.

59. Calderón de la Barca, *Attaché in Madrid*, 72.

60. The classic study on this movement is Curti, "Young America." For a more recent work, see Eyal, *Young America Movement*.

61. J. Q. Adams quoted in Bemis, *John Quincy Adams and the Foundation of American Foreign Policy*, 341.

62. O'Sullivan quoted in Ettinger, *Mission to Spain of Pierre Soulé*, 99.

63. Calderón de la Barca quoted in Ettinger, *Mission to Spain of Pierre Soulé*, 156, 213.

64. Lester quoted in Ettinger, *Mission to Spain of Pierre Soulé*, 163, 186.

65. Soulé quoted in M. Field, *Memories of Many Men and Some Women*, 81.

66. Soulé quoted in Manning, *Diplomatic Correspondence of the United States*, 11:729.

67. Soulé quote from dispatch in Manning, *Diplomatic Correspondence of the United States*, 11:729.

68. Ettinger, *Mission to Spain of Pierre Soulé*, 237.

69. *La España* (Madrid), 27 June 1855; *La Época* (Madrid), 30 August 1854, 18 October 1854, 8 November 1854, 27 June 1855, 29 June 1855, 20 November 1855.

70. Ettinger, *Mission to Spain of Pierre Soulé*, 361.

71. As quoted in Lorenzo, "Black Warrior Affair," 295.

72. *La España*, 5 November 1854, 2, and 8 November 1854, 4. With reference to Soulé's penchant for troublemaking, the Spanish press widely reported the decision of the French government, citing his previous fight with Ambassador Turgot, to deny Soulé access to France on his return to Madrid from Belgium. See also Moors, "Pierre Soulé," 206.

73. *La España*, 27 June 1855.

74. Ettinger, *Mission to Spain of Pierre Soulé*, 461 (Soulé to Lord Howden 13 January 1855).

75. Pettigrew, *Notes on Spain and the Spaniards*, 430.

76. Pelzer, *Augustus C. Dodge*, 211–12, 230; Manning, *Correspondence*, 11:874 (Dodge to Marcy, 12 July 1855). For Schurz in Madrid, see Schafer, *Intimate Letters of Carl Schurz*, 263; Donne, "Carl Schurz, the Diplomat"; Brauer, "Appointment of Carl Schurz as Minister to Spain"; and F. Bancroft, *Speeches and Political Papers of Carl Schurz*, 1:198–99. For Koerner, see his *Memoirs of Gustave Koerner*, 2:287. See also Cortada, "Spain and the American Civil War."

77. Seward delivered a speech on the subject of Cuba to the Senate on 26 January 1853. See Baker, *Works of William Henry Seward*, 3:605–18.

78. Ulysses S. Grant, "Seventh Annual Message," 7 December 1875, *The American Presidency Project*, edited by Gerhard Peters and John T. Woolley, http://www.presidency.ucsb.edu/ws/?pid=29516.

79. Keneally, *American Scoundrel*, 337.

80. Fish's diary as cited in Corning, *Hamilton Fish*, 88.

81. Ulloa quoted in Fish's diary as cited in Corning, *Hamilton Fish*, 88.

82. Philadelphia Centennial Announcements, Manuel de Orovio, 13 August 1875, and Carlos Navarro y Rodrigo, 28 November 1875, leg. H 310, AMAE.

83. Strahan's comments can be found in Strahan, *Masterpieces of the Centennial International Exhibition Illustrated*, 1:239. For U.S. collectors of Fortuny's work, see W. Johnston, "W. H. Stewart, the American Patron of Mariano Fortuny."

84. U. Grant, *Papers of Ulysses S. Grant*, 26:29, 32.

85. The literature on 1898 is enormous. Valuable surveys include Gould, *Spanish-American War and President McKinley*; Trask, *War with Spain in 1898*; J. Smith, *Spanish-American War*; Perez, *War of 1898*; and Schoonover, *Uncle Sam's War of 1898 and the Origins of Globalization*. For U.S. perceptions of Spain and Spanish politics prior to 1898, see Sánchez Padilla, "Entre la modernidad y el absolutismo."

86. *Life*, 11 August 1898, 110–11.

87. See DeGuzmán, "Consolidating Anglo-American Imperial Identity."

88. An English version of Martí's article is available at http://writing.upenn.edu/library/Marti_Jose_Our-America.html.

89. Roosevelt, *Winning of the West*, 3:107, 4:2. One can only wonder whether Roosevelt's views on Spanish weakness later figured in his decision to resign from his position as secretary of the navy and volunteer for military service at the start of the Spanish-American War, although in light of the stiff resistance that he and other members of his famous Rough Riders troop encountered during the charge of San Juan Hill, it is likely that he revised some of his previous ideas about the ability of the Spanish soldiers to put up a courageous fight.

90. Máximo Gómez, "Letter to U.S. President Grover Cleveland," 9 February 1897, as recorded in *Journal of the Senate of the United States of America* (Washington DC: Government Printing Office, 1897), 35, www.historyofcuba.com/history/gomez4.htm.

91. *Chicago Tribune*, 29 March 1898.

92. See Goldenberg, "Imperial Culture and National Conscience" and especially her *From Liberation to Conquest*. See also Wisan, *Cuban Crisis as Reflected in the New York Press (1895–1898)*.

93. Latimer, *Spain in the Nineteenth Century*, 10.

94. Brooks Adams, *New Empire*, 104. See also Brooks Adams, *Law of Civilization and Decay*, esp. chap. 10, "Spain and India."

95. Bernard Moses, "The Old Regime and the New in the Philippines," as reported in *San Francisco Call*, 10 December 1903. For Moses and U.S. policy in the Philippines, see Kramer, *Blood of Government*.

96. "Spain and Us," editorial, *Life*, 4 November 1897.

97. Editorial, *Life*, 21 July 1898.

98. Lea, "Decadence of Spain," 40.

99. For more on the Bay View Association and its "Spanish-French Year," see French, "Foundations of Empire Building," chap. 3.

100. Hall, "Around the Study Lamp," *Bay View Magazine* 6, no. 1 (1898): 36.

101. Hall, "Around the Study Lamp," *Bay View Magazine* 6, no. 2 (1898): 76.

102. Hall, "Around the Study Lamp," *Bay View Magazine* 6, no. 2 (1898): 78; 6, no. 5 (1899): 206, 208.

103. Hall, "Around the Study Lamp," *Bay View Magazine* 6, no. 3 (1899): 125.

104. Hay, *Castilian Days* (1903), publisher's note.

105. Chadwick, *Relations of the United States and Spain*, 587.

106. Larchmont Yacht Club from *New York Times*, 6 June 1898, 2; Alibi Club from "The Most Exclusive Club in Washington," *Washington Times*, "The Most Exclusive Club in Washington," 30 March 1902, 2.

107. Duke of Arcos, dispatch, 4 December 1900, leg. H 1481, carpeta E 33, AMAE.

108. "Honors for Curry," *Washington Evening Star*, 14 May 1902, 13. Curry's political career is the subject of Chodes, *Destroying the Republic*.

109. For an exhaustive examination of U.S.-Spain relations following the end of the 1898 war, see Montero, *El despertar de la gran potencia*, together with the various essays in Sánchez Mantero, Álvarez Rey, and Macarro Vera, *La imagen de España en América, 1898–1931*.

110. Collier, *At the Court of His Catholic Majesty*, ix.

111. For the renewal of these exchanges and the start of other ones, see report of 2 July 1899, carpeta E 33, leg. H 1481, AMAE.

112. Duke of Arcos, report of 4 September 1900, leg. H 1481, carpeta E 33, AMAE.

113. Emilio de Ojeda, "Spain Believes All Enmities Have Ceased and Does Not Regret the Loss of Its Colonies," *New York Herald*, 1 January 1903, 1.

114. "Noble Speeches—Rumor Says," *Washington Evening Star*, 2 February 1903, 2. On the same day the *Washington Post* published a similarly laudatory résumé of Ojeda's speech.

115. Dispatch of 2 February 1903 (which includes a clipping from the *Washington Post*), leg. H 1481, carpeta E 166, AMAE. Reports on Ojeda's remarks also appeared in the *Washington Times* and *Washington Evening Star*.

116. Tomás Faril al Duque de Tetuan, 21 September 1896, leg. H 1481, carpeta E 444, AMAE.

117. Dispatch from *St. Louis Republic*, 2 May 1903, 2, leg. H 1481, carpeta E 166, AMAE. Although Spain did not build an official pavilion at the St. Louis fair, the exhibit called *Streets of Seville*, located on the exposition's main thoroughfare or "Pike," offered visitors glimpses of "Spanish" life. See chapter 3.

118. Bernard Moses, "The Old and New Regime in the Philippines," as reported in "Gives Spain Some Credit," *San Francisco Call*, 10 December 1903, 7.

119. *El Imparcial* (Madrid), 3 June 1914, 1.

120. "Spain Kind to T.R.," *Washington Post*, 10 June 1914; "A Boom for Spanish," *Washington Times*, editorial, 11 June 1914.

121. "Kermit Roosevelt Weds Miss Willard in Madrid," *New York Sun*, 11 June 1914, 3.

122. "Roosevelt in Madrid," *New York Times*, 9 June 1914. See also the full press record, both Spanish and American, of the former president's visit to Madrid in leg. 54/1825, AMAE.

2. Sturdy Spain

1. On 28 May 1890 the Rep. Charles O'Neill (R-Pennsylvania) proposed the construction of a bronze statue honoring Columbus at the western entrance to the Capitol (51st Cong., 1st sess.). It was reported in late 1892 that Congress had allocated $75,000 for the statue and also contemplated the construction on Sixteenth Street of a triumphal arch honoring Columbus. W. Curtis, "Columbus Monuments," 138. William Curtis, first director of the Bureau of the American Republics (later known as the Pan-American Union), organized as part of the U.S. exhibit at the Exposición Histórico-Americano in Madrid in 1892 an exhibition featuring copies of portraits of Columbus together with photographs of Columbus monuments in the United States. For a checklist of objects in the U.S. exhibit, see *Catálogo general de la Exposición Histórico-Americana*, 1.

2. For this commission, see H.R. 13304, 59th Cong., 2nd sess. (1907), chap. 2932, p. 1413, available online at http://legisworks.org/congress/59/session-2/publaw-267.pdf.

3. For Scott's speech, I relied on the version available in Correspondencia, leg. H 1481, carpeta E 1101, AMAE. The program of the celebration and the text of the speeches by President Taft and other luminaries are available at "The 1912 Dedication of the Columbus Memorial," National Christopher Columbus Association, http://christophercolumbus.org/the-1912-dedication.html. See also McCarthy, *Columbus and His Predecessors*.

4. One such critic was the journalist Carey McWilliams, who first articulated his ideas about California's "invented" Spanish past in his *South California Country* (1946), especially chap. 1, and in his *North from Mexico* (1949), especially chap. 2.

5. Lowell, *Letters of James Russell Lowell*, 2:221 (letter to W. D. Howells, 2 May 1879).

6. Lowell, *Letters of James Russell Lowell*, 2:235 (letter to Thomas Hughes, 17 November 1878). For more on Lowell in Spain, see his *Impressions of Spain*; and Kibble, "James Russell Lowell's Residence in Spain."

7. Sewall, *Sketches of St. Augustine*, 11–12.

8. Vignoles, *Observations upon the Floridas*, 19.

9. Bryant, "Letters of William Cullen Bryant from Florida," 262. See also Bloomfield, *Bloomfield's Illustrated Historical Guide*, 78.

10. Clipping from *St. Augustine Examiner*, 23 December 1863, in box 3, TBSP, New-York Historical Society.

11. For these changes, see Graham, "Henry Flagler's St. Augustine," 9.

12. G. Bancroft, *History of the United States*, 1:35, as cited in Saulnier, "'You could there write the fates of nations,'" 93. See also Billias, "George Bancroft"; and Handlin, *George Bancroft*.

13. T. Irving, *Conquest of Florida by Hernando de Soto*, 165.

14. G. Bancroft, *History of the Colonization of the United States*, 1:15; G. Bancroft, *History of the United States of America* (1888), 1:38.

15. G. Bancroft, *History of the United States* (1844), 70–71.

16. Sparks, *Life of Jean Ribault*, 91, 113.

17. Smith still awaits a biographer. For his life, see box 1, TBSP, which contains a short biography by Charles V. Tettle, Esq.; and John Gilmary Shea, "Memoir of Thomas Buckingham Smith," included as an appendix in Cabeza de Vaca, *Relation of Alvar Núñez Cabeza de Vaca*, 261–73. See also Van Tyne, "Translated Conquests," chap. 3. Smith's report on the Everglades is discussed in Hollander, *Raising Cane in the 'Glades*, 31–34.

18. Ford quoted in Robertson, *Richard Ford, 1796–1858*, 169. For other early reviews of Prescott, see Jaksic, *Hispanic World and American Intellectual Life, 1820–1880*; and Van Tyne, "Translated Conquests," chap. 2.

19. Prescott, *History of the Conquest of Mexico*, 1:217, 258, 261.

20. De Soto, *Narrative of the Career of Hernando de Soto*, trans. Smith. Subsequent editions appeared in 1856 and 1871. The best modern edition and translation is Cabeza de Vaca, *The Narrative of Cabeza de Vaca*, edited and translated by Rolena Adorno and Patrick Charles Pautz (2003).

21. For the "discovery" of Columbus, see C. Bushman, *America Discovers Columbus*; Materassi and Ramalho Sousa Santos, *American Columbiad*; and Bartosik-Vélez, *Legacy of Christopher Columbus in the Americas*.

22. Report of the Select Committee, 28 February 1836, as cited in Tilton, *Pocahontas*, 104.

23. Stuart, *William H. Powell's Historical Picture*. For more on the politics surrounding Powell's picture, see Fryd, *Art and Empire*.

24. Thomas Buckingham Smith to George H. Moore, 31 October 1855, Madrid; Smith to Ephraim G. Squier, undated, both in box 1, TBSP.

25. De Soto, *Narrative of the Career of Hernando de Soto*, trans. Smith, xxv–xxvi.

26. Wilmer, *Life, Travels, and Adventures*, 520, 524.

27. For more on Leutze and this picture, see Truettner, "Art of History"; and Groseclose, *Emanuel Leutze, 1816–1868*.

28. Thomas Buckingham Smith, undated letter quoted in a typed biography of Smith, box 1, TBSP.

29. Fairbanks, *Early History of Florida*; Fairbanks, *History and Antiquities of the City of St Augustine, Florida*. On Fairbanks, see Lynch, *George Rainsford Fairbanks*.

30. Fairbanks, *Early History of Florida*, 8, 17.

31. Pedro Menéndez de Avilés to King Philip II, 15 October 1565. Buckingham Smith sent a copy of his transcription of this letter to Francis Parkman, who translated it into English in 1870. It is currently in the collection of the Massachusetts Historical Society and available at The New World, http://thenewworld.us/the-letters-of-pedro-menendez-aviles/4/.

32. Fairbanks, *History of Florida*. The book was reprinted in 1884 and again in 1904.

33. Parkman, *Pioneers of France in the New World*, 86, 114.

34. E. Everett, *Orations and Speeches on Various Occasions*, 3:203.

35. *Florida Mirror*, 21 March 1885, 1, 28 March 1885, 1 (which reproduces Fairbanks's oration), 14 April 1885.

36. For a reprint of the account of this festival originally published in the *St. Augustine Evening Record* on 3 April 1885, see *El Escribano* 5, no. 2 (1988): 4–5. For the festival's influence on Flagler, see Martin, *Henry Flagler*, 106.

37. See Mauzy, "Tertio-Millennial Exposition"; and B. Ellis, "Santa Fe's Tertio-Millennial Exhibition."

38. Gregg quoted in Paredes, "Mexican Image in American Travel Literature," 7.

39. Bartlett quoted in Paredes, "Mexican Image in American Travel Literature," 7; Bartlett, *Personal Narrative of Explorations and Incidents in Texas, New Mexico, California, Sonora and Chihuahua*, 2:74.

40. W. Davis, *El Gringo*, 214–16.

41. Hunt, *Kirby Benedict*, 175. See also Stensvaag, "Clio on the Frontier," 203.

42. Quoted in Montgomery, *Spanish Redemption*, 60.

43. "Greasers as Citizens," *New York Times*, 6 February 1882; LeBaron Bradford Prince, "The People of New Mexico and Their Territory," letter to the editor, *New York Times*, 28 February 1882.

44. LeBaron Bradford Prince, "The People of New Mexico and their Territory," letter to the editor, *New York Times*, 28 February 1882. Prince's advocacy of the "better class" of Mexicans was partly conditioned by his efforts to shorten New Mexico's path to statehood by creating the image of a state populated by peoples worthy of American citizenship. For more on Prince, see Chancy, *In Memoriam of L. Bradford Prince*; and Montoya, "L. Bradford Prince."

45. *Official Reports of the Territory of New Mexico for the Years 1882 and 1883: Illustrated New Mexico* was printed in four editions totaling sixteen thousand copies in 1882–83. See also Ritch, *Aztlan*.

46. Ingersoll, "La Villa Real de Santa Fe," 678, 680.

47. Ingersoll, "La Villa Real de Santa Fe," 673.

48. Ritch, *Inaugural Address*, 5, 9; Montgomery, *Spanish Redemption*, 115. For more on Prince, see Nieto-Phillips, *Language of Blood*, 160–69; and his "When Tourists Came, the Mestizos Went Away."

49. Eugene A. Fiske quoted in *Centennial Celebration*, 51.

50. Prince, *Historical Sketches of New Mexico*, front matter.

51. Prince, *Historical Sketches of New Mexico*, 327.

52. For the program of the exposition, see above, note 36. See also "Santa Fe: Big Festival," *New York Times*, 14 June 1883; "The Opening of a Month's Festivities in Santa Fe," *Emporia (KS) Weekly News*, 5 July 1883; and "A Month's Festivities Begins," *Indiana State Sentinel* (Indianapolis), 4 July 1883.

53. Whitman's letter, dated 20 July 1883, printed in W. Whitman, "Correspondence of Walt Whitman." See also C. Wilson, *Myth of Santa Fe*, 188.

54. Vallejo's letter, as printed in Ruiz de Burton, *Conflicts of Interest*, 59. On Vallejo, see Pubols, "Fathers of the Pueblo." On race in nineteenth-century California, see Lint Sagarena, *Aztlán and Arcadia*.

55. See Hackel, "Junípero Serra across the Generations."

56. Gleeson, *History of the Catholic Church in California*.

57. For this ceremony and Casanova's efforts to restore the Carmel mission, see *Fray Junipero Serra and the Mission Church of San Carlos de Carmelo*.

58. Hughes, *California of the Padres*.

59. Forbes, *California*, 231; Hughes, *California of the Padres*, esp. 29, where "Jumpero Lerra" appears. For more on efforts to revive Serra's memory, see Kagan, "Invention of Junípero Serra and the 'Spanish Craze.'"

60. Jackson, "Junipero Serra and His Work," part 1, 11–12, and part 2, 201. Oddly enough Jackson made no mention either of Serra or the missions in her *Century of Dishonor* (1881), a scathing report on U.S. mistreatment of Native Americans written in the hope of persuading Congress to reform its Indian policy. For more on Jackson, see Phillips, *Helen Hunt Jackson*.

61. Jackson, "Junipero Serra and His Work," 203, 205, 201, respectively.

62. Hittell, *History of California*, 1:448, 2:528. Hittell can be approached through Righter, "Theodore Henry Hittell and his "Theodore H. Hittell and Hubert H. Bancroft." See also Hittell, *In Memoriam*.

63. Quotations from Thomas, *Our Centennial Memoir*.

64. Quotations from Thomas, *Our Centennial Memoir*.

65. For this campaign, see R. G. White, *Padre Junípero Serra and the Mission Church of San Carlos de Carmelo*.

66. See Regenry, "Stanfords and the Serra Statue."

67. H. Bancroft, *California Pastoral*, 43, 72, 88.

68. The best biography of Lummis is M. Thompson, *American Character*. See also Simmons, *Charles F. Lummis*.

69. Lummis, *Letters from the Southwest*, 112.

70. Lummis, *Letters from the Southwest*, 124.

71. Lummis, *Tramp across the Continent*, 113.

72. Lummis, *Spanish Pioneers*.

73. See Herbert B. Adams, *Germanic Origin of New England Towns*.

74. Blackmar, *Spanish Institutions of the Southwest*, vii.

75. Lowery, *Spanish Settlements within the Present Boundaries of the United States*, 1:vi.

76. Edward G. Bourne, "The Interpretations of American and European History," 5, 7, box 7, Edward G. Bourne Papers, Beinecke Library, Yale University. For a brief description of Bourne written by a colleague at Yale, see Rhodes, *Historical Essays*, 191–200.

77. These three works by Bourne are *The Spanish Colonial System*; *Narratives of the Career of De Soto in the Conquest of Florida*; and *Discovery, Conquest, and Early History of the Philippine Islands*.

78. Bolton, "Mission as a Frontier Institution," 42. See also his *Spanish Exploration in the Southwest, 1542–1706*.

79. For Bolton's career as a historian, see Hurtado, "Parkmanizing the Spanish Borderlands"; Hurtado, *Herbert Eugene Bolton*; and Truett, "Epics of Greater America." For Bolton's involvement in the beatification of Serra, see Sandos, "Junípero Serra's Canonization." More recent borderlands

studies include Weber, *Spanish Frontier in North America*; and Truett, *Fugitive Landscapes*, focused on the copper mining industry straddling the border between Arizona and the Mexican state of Sonora.

80. Lummis, *Spanish Pioneers*, 23–24.

81. Lummis, *Spanish Pioneers and the California Missions*, 91 (1929 ed.), 297 (1936 ed.).

82. Lummis, *Spanish Pioneers and the California Missions*, 302 (1936 ed.).

83. For this frieze, see Wolanin, *Constantino Brumidi*; and Matthew Restall, "Montezuma Surrenders in the Capitol," *Capitol Dome*, Fall 2016, http://www.e-digitaleditions.com/i/772281-fall-2016.

84. For the possible origins of Brumidi's frieze, see Wierich, *Grand Themes*, 64.

85. For more the Southwest's embrace of a romanticized "Spanish" past, see J. Chávez, *Lost Land*, 87–91; and Nieto-Philips, *Language of Blood*, 145–70.

86. Lummis to Arturo Cuyas, 7 March 1914, box 1.1.992A, Charles F. Lummis Collection, BRL.

87. Secretaría Particular de S. M. Alfonso XIII, anonymous typed report entitled *De interés nacional*, caja 15.592, expediente 2, AGPR.

88. Lummis, *Flowers of Our Lost Romance*, xiv.

3. Sunny Spain

1. Wharton, *Letters of Edith Wharton*, 325–26 (letter written at Burgos, 26 July 1914).

2. Lummis to J. L. Kobrin, 10 October 1919, box 1.1.709, Charles F. Lummis Collection, BRL.

3. For U.S. tourism to Spain during this era, see Varela-Lago, "Conquerors, Immigrants, Exiles," chap. 3. For Vega-Inclán, see Menéndez Robles, *El Marqués de la Vega-Inclán y los orígenes turismo en España*. Also useful is Moreno Garrido, *Historia del turismo en España en el siglo XX*; Afinoguénova, "Organic Nation"; and the essays in Afinoguénova and Martí-Olivella, *Spain Is (Still) Different*. I am grateful to M. Elizabeth Boone for drawing my attention these last two works.

4. Voltaire, as translated in Salvio, "Voltaire and Spain," 69.

5. T.M., "Observations Made in a Journey through Spain by a Private Gentleman," 251.

6. Gifra-Adroher, *Between History and Romance*.

7. Southey, *Poetical Works, Collected by Himself*, 2:234; Southey, *Letters Written during a Short Residence in Spain*, 126.

8. Scott as quoted in Saglia, *Poetic Castles in Spain*, 54.

9. Hugo, *Les orientales*, 15.

10. The phrase is best attributed to Dominque Dufour de Pradt, *Mémoires historiques sur la révolution d'Espagne* (168): "It is an error of geography to have assigned Spain to Europe; it belongs to Africa: blood, manners, language, the way of life and making war, in Spain everything is African" (C'est une erreur de la géographie que d'avoir attribué l'Espagne à l'Europe; elle appartient à l'Afrique: sang, mœurs, langage, manière de vivre et de combattre; en Espagne tout est africain).

11. Byron, *Selected Letters and Journals*, 25–27 (letter written at Gibraltar, 11 August 1809).

12. Byron, *Childe Harold's Pilgrimage*, canto I, lxv.

13. Byron, *Childe Harold's Pilgrimage*, canto I, xxxv.

14. W. Irving as quoted in Hoffmeister, "Exoticism," 114. See also W. Irving, *Journals and Notebooks*, 3:692–707.

15. Swinburne, *Travels through Spain, in the Years 1775 and 1776*, 1:275.

16. Chateaubriand, *Last of the Abencerrajes* (*Les aventures du dernier Abencérage*), 33.

17. Ticknor, *Life, Letters, and Journals of George Ticknor*, 1:232.

18. W. Irving, *Letters*, 2:197 (letter dated May 1826); W. Irving, *Journals and Notebooks*, 4:272 (entry for 11 July 1829).

19. W. Irving, *Alhambra* (1832), preface. For Irving and Wilkie, see Miles, "*Adnotatiunculae Leicestrienses.*"

20. W. Irving, *Alhambra* (1851), 14–15.

21. W. Irving, *Alhambra* (1851), 14–15.

22. Mackenzie's *A Year in Spain by a Young American* was reissued in 1831 and 1836. There was also a sequel: *Spain Revisited* (1836), which focused mainly on Spanish politics. Spain's troubled politics also figured in *Scenes of Spain* (1837), the work of an anonymous New Orleans author who, as noted in the preface, observed the country's transition from the "tyranny of despotism to the worse tyranny of anarchism" following his visit there in 1831. On U.S. travelers to nineteenth-century Spain, see Gifra-Adroher, *Between History and Romance*; Kagan, *Spain in America*; and Fernández-Montesinos, *Viajeras anglosajonas por España*. Other studies include Sánchez Mantero, "Viajeros y diplomáticos en el reinado de Fernando VII"; García-Montón and García-Romeral, "Viajeros americanos en Andalucía durante los siglos XIX y XX"; and Gamir Sandoval, *Los viajeros ingleses y norteamericanos en la Granada del siglo XIX*.

23. Ford, *Handbook for Travellers in Spain*, 1:304, 312.

24. Wallis, *Glimpses of Spain*, 363. The French authors mentioned were Théophile Gautier, Alexandre Dumas, and François Guizot. In making these comments, Wallis anticipated by more than fifty years those of Royall Tyler, an English author who, with reference to the same authors Wallis was criticizing, wrote, "All of them ran riot in a Spain of their own imagining." See Tyler, *Spain*, 19. See also Gautier, *Romantic in Spain*.

25. Disraeli, *Contarini Fleming*, 214, 223. Disraeli had visited Spain in 1830. For this visit, see Sultana, *Benjamin Disraeli in Spain, Malta and Albania*.

26. Longfellow, *Letters of Henry Wadsworth Longfellow*, 1:238; Longfellow, *Outre-Mer*, 226–42. Longfellow is likely to have modeled this village after the one featured in Jorge de Montemayor's sixteenth-century pastoral novel, *Diana*. For more on Longfellow's visit, see I. Whitman, *Longfellow in Spain*.

27. Borrow, *Bible in Spain*, preface.

28. Borrow, *Zincali*, 157–59.

29. Mérimée, *Carmen and Other Stories*, 20.

30. For the Carmen phenomenon, see Fanjul, *Buscando a Carmen*; and Miralles, *El descubrimiento de España*, esp. chap. 3. See also Charnon-Deutsch, *Spanish Gypsy*, and DeGuzmán, *Spain's Long Shadow*.

31. K. Field, *Ten Days in Spain*, 100, 110–11, 179, 190, 201, 222. Kate Field's book was reprinted four times.

32. Hay, *Castilian Days* (1871), 349, 371, 391, 399.

33. W. Irving, *Alhambra* (1851), 425.

34. Libro de Visitantes, Archivo de la Alhambra.

35. Allen, *Travels in Europe and the East*, 487, 493, 494.

36. Hoganson, *Consumers' Imperium*, esp. chap. 1.

37. "Travels in Sunny Spain," *Washington Post*, 7 February 1888. For Stoddard, see Taylor, *John L. Stoddard*; and Michaelene Cox, *Politics and Art of John L. Stoddard*. For the Chicago lectures, see "Stoddard Lecture Series," *Chicago Daily Tribune*, 19 January 1891. For the New York lecture, see "Stoddard's Entertainments," *New York Times*, 8 April 1883. Stoddard first lectured on Spain in New York on 29 March 1882.

38. Doré's engravings of Don Quixote, Sancho Panza, and other characters from Cervantes's famous novel first appeared in a French edition of *Don Quixote* (1863), with one of his illustrations, *La Siesta*, featuring Moorish-like gypsies and street urchins.

39. Eakins quoted in Goodrich, *Thomas Eakins*, 1:54–59. See also Foster and Leibold, *Writing about Eakins*, 60; and Boone, *Vistas de España*, 63–69.

40. For Cassatt's 1872–73 visit to Spain, see Matthews, *Cassatt and Her Circle*, 102–15. See also Boone, *Vistas de España*, 93–94.

41. For the Spanish pictures of these and other American artists, Boone, *Vistas de España*, is the essential starting point. Also see the essays in *Spanish Sojourns: Robert Henri and the Spirit of Spain*.

42. The history of *El Jaleo* is best approached through Volk, *John Singer Sargent's "El Jaleo."*

43. See "Madrid from Noon to Midnight"; E.L, "Spain, Her Ways, Her Women, and Her Wines"; "From Gibraltar to the Bidasoa," in two parts, published in 1856 and 1857; and Carter, "Street Life in Spain."

44. Bryant, Letters of William Cullen Bryant, 3:477 (Bryant to Mrs. Kirkland, 5 November 1857).

45. James Harrison, *Spain in Profile*, v, 67, 293, 295. Harrison followed this travel book with *Spain* (1881), a sweeping history of the country aimed at a general readership. It was reissued in 1895 and again in a revised edition in 1899 that included a chapter (written by the editors) on the 1898 war. It was reissued again in 1903.

46. Champney, *Three Vassar Girls Abroad*, 91.

47. Day, *From the Pyrenees to the Pillar of Hercules*, 22.

48. Downes, *Spanish Ways and By-Ways*, 14.

49. *Harper's New Monthly Magazine* 67 (August 1883): 36.

50. Parts of Lathrop's *Spanish Vistas* (1883) had previously appeared in the *Atlantic Monthly*.

51. Vincent, *Shadow of the Pyrenees*, 123.

52. Bodfish, *Through Spain on Donkey-Back*, ii, xv, xxiv.

53. S. Hale, *Family Flight through Spain*, 145.

54. E. Hale, *Seven Spanish Cities and the Way to Them*, 5, 320–21. It was also released in later editions. The closing words in that book set the stage for his adulatory *Life of Columbus*, published in 1891 and repluglished in 1893 as *The Story of Columbus*. Arnyas Leigh was a sixteenth-century English corsair who figured in the British author Charles Kingsley's historical novel *Westward Ho!*, first published in 1865.

55. "The Spanish Peninsula in Travel," *Atlantic Monthly* 52, no. 311 (September 1883): 408–11.

56. Scott's later publications included a hefty, three-volume *History of the Moorish Empire in Europe* (1904), focused primarily on Iberia, together with a translation of the medieval Spanish legal code, *Las siete partidas* (1929).

57. F. Smith, *Well-Worn Roads of Spain*, 39. The book was reprinted on several occasions.

58. H. Field, *Old Spain and New Spain*, 300. Henry Field also writes, "As soon as I crossed the frontier, I have observed with wonder and surprise that I was in a country as a free as my own" (101).

59. Nixon-Roulet, *Spaniard at Home*, v, 320.

60. For more this exhibit, see Olson, *That St. Louis Thing*, 209–10. The "Streets of Seville" arcade does not appear in Birk, *World Comes to St. Louis*.

4. Hispanism, *Hispanismo*, and the HSA

1. Hume, "United States and Spain," 5.

2. Rennert's books included *The Life of Lope de Vega, 1562–1635* (1904) and *The Spanish Stage in the Time of Lope de Vega* (1909). As for Henry Charles Lea, I refer to his *History of the Inquisition of Spain* (1906–7). Samuel Parsons Scott also translated and published *The Visigothic Code (Forum Judicum)* (1910). For Archer M. Huntington and the creation of the Hispanic Society of America, see Codding, "Archer Milton Huntington, Champion of Spain."

3. Miguel de Unamuno, "Los hispanistas norteaméricanos," Salamanca, August 1906, in Unamuno, *De patriotismo espiritual*, 58.

4. Quoted in Fernández, "'Longfellow's Law,'" 122. See also Vilar García, *El español segunda lengua en los Estados Unidos*, 63–64, 77–78.

5. For Jefferson and Spain, see Williams, *Spanish Background of American Literature*, 1:24–26. Jefferson's contacts with Spanish scientists, among them Juan Bautista Bru de Ramón, director of Madrid's Real Gabinete de Historia Natural, are discussed in López Piñero and Glick, *El megaterio de Bru y el Presidente Jefferson*.

6. For Jefferson's interest in the teaching of Spanish, see Adorno, "Washington Irving's Romantic Hispanism and Its Columbian Legacies," esp. note 10.

7. Jefferson to Randolph, 6 June 1787, in Jefferson, *Papers of Thomas Jefferson*, 11:558.

8. Jefferson, *Papers of Thomas Jefferson*, 13:358.

9. Cogswell and Bancroft, *Prospectus of a School*, 14. For Round Hill, see Bassett, "Round Hill School."

10. Edmonds, *History of the Central High School of Philadelphia*, 62, 136:

11. Handschin, *Teaching of Modern Languages in the United States*.

12. Hazard et al., *Pennsylvania Archives*, 9:728.

13. Paul Fooks, "On the Advantages of being acquainted with both the French and the Spanish languages," *Pennsylvania Gazette*, 3 July 1776. Fooks awaits a biographer. For his appointment as Pennsylvania's official interpreter, see Hazard et al., *Pennsylvania Archives*, 727–28. For his teaching, see Vilar García, *El español segunda lengua en los Estados Unidos*.

14. Furstenberg, *When the United States Spoke French*.

15. For Rocafuerte's view of Philadelphia and the city's Spanish-language printers, see Rodrigo Lazo, "La Famosa Filadelfia." For Mathew Carey, see Bradsher, *Mathew Carey*; Kaser, *Messrs. Carey & Lea and the Philadelphia Book Trade*; and Green, *Mathew Carey*. For Spanish-language newspapers in Philadelphia (and New York), see Vilar García, *El español segunda lengua en los Estados Unidos*, 79–101.

16. The names of Merino, Willis, Cova, and Rennert appear in *University of Pennsylvania: Biographical Catalogue*, xxiv, xxvi. For an introduction to Spanish-language instruction, see Vilar García, *El español segunda lengua en los Estados Unidos*.

17. For the teaching of Spanish at William and Mary, Virginia, and other U.S. colleges at the end of the eighteenth century, see Vilar García, *El español segunda lengua en los Estados Unidos*; and Castañeda, *Modern Language Instruction in American Colleges*.

18. Velázquez de la Cadena's *A Dictionary of the Spanish and English Language* (1855), became known as the "Velázquez dictionary."

19. W. Shaw, *University of Michigan—An Encyclopedic Survey*, part IV, Department of Romance Languages and Literatures, 722. The department taught one section of Spanish in 1900, five in 1914, twelve in 1916, and fifteen in 1919. Professor Benjamin P. Bourland began teaching *Don Quixote* in 1895, Spanish golden age literature after 1900, and Spanish-American literature starting in 1925.

20. For Sales, see Coester, "Francis Sales—A Forerunner." See also Doyle, "Spanish Studies in the US."

21. For Ticknor's teaching at Harvard, see Ticknor, *Syllabus of a course of lectures on the history and criticism of Spanish Literature*, available in box 3, George Ticknor Papers, Harvard University Archives. See also Doyle, *George Ticknor*; and Long, *Thomas Jefferson and George Ticknor*.

22. Williams, *Spanish Background of American Literature*, 2:162. On Elssler, see Costonis, "Personification of Desire."

23. Quoted in Doyle, "Longfellow as Professor at Harvard," 327. See also C. Johnson, *Professor Longfellow at Harvard*.

24. See Leavitt, "Teaching of Spanish in the United States"; and Coester, "Francis Sales—A Forerunner." Sales's successors included Cancio-Bello (1858), B. H. Nash (1866), Joseph Randolph Coolidge (1883), and Carlos Valerién Cusachs (1897, teaching both Spanish and Italian).

25. Lowell remained skeptical about Spain, labeling Spaniards a "semi-oriental people" ill-equipped to enter the modern world (quote from Lowell letter written from Madrid, 4 May 1879, cited in Williams, *Spanish Background of American Literature*, 2:197). For his *Don Quixote* essay, see Lowell, Democracy, 157–86.

26. See C. Johnson, *Longfellow at Harvard*; and Marshall, "Professor Longfellow at Harvard."

27. Eliot, "New Education."

28. Knapp had lived in Spain for almost a decade and knew the country, and its language, firsthand. He was also the author of several scholarly monographs by the time he joined the Yale faculty as a professor of Romance languages in 1879. He subsequently published a widely used Spanish grammar (1882) and accompanying book of readings (1883). He also edited the *Life, Writings, and Correspondence of George Borrow*.

29. A recent, and readable, account of Bingham's "discovery" is Heany, *Cradle of Gold*.

30. For these developments see Delpar, *Looking South*; and Cline, "Latin American History."

31. Bourland letter of 7 October 1949, box 42, Caroline Bourland Correspondence, Smith College Archives.

32. For the evolution of the teaching of Spanish in American higher education, see Handschin, *Modern Language Teaching*; and Nichols, "History of Spanish and Portuguese Teaching in the United States."

33. In the field of history Johns Hopkins dragged its feet. Its first appointments in the Latin American field only came in the late 1960s. I joined the faculty there, teaching Spanish history, in 1972.

34. For the official account of Spain's presence at the exposition by the responsible royal commissioner, see Depuy de Lôme, "Spain at the World's Fair." For a contemporary American account, see H. Bancroft, *Book of the Fair*, 655–62, 910–12, 971. For Spaniards critical of their country's exhibits, see Serafín Pichardo, *La ciudad blanca*; Puig y Valls, *Viaje á América 1894–95*; and Cabrera, *Cartas a Govin*. More recent literature includes C. Vallejo, "Seeing 'Spain' at the 1893 Chicago World Fair"; and Boone, "Marginalizing Spain at the World's Columbian Exposition of 1893."

35. Quoted in R. Wilson, "Infanta at the Fair." For more on Eulalia's controversial visit, see Valis, "Women's Culture in 1893"; and C. Vallejo, "Seeing 'Spain' at the 1893 Chicago World Fair." For Eulalia's own and rather
more positive view of her reception in Chicago, see Eulalia, Infanta of
Spain, *Memoirs of a Spanish Princess*.

36. The classic study on pan-Americanism is Whitaker, *Western Hemisphere
Idea*. Whitaker traces its origins to Thomas Jefferson. For more on Pan-
Americanism and instruction in Spanish, see Lozana, *An American Lan-
guage*, 193–99.

37. Arnold, *Pan-American Exposition Illustrated*, 28–30. The literature on the
architecture of the Buffalo exhibition is best approached through "Pan-
American Exposition of 1901: The Visual Landscape," University at
Buffalo Libraries, https://library.buffalo.edu/pan-am/exposition/art/.
Relevant publications include *Pan-American Exposition, Buffalo May 1 to
November 1, 1901*; K. Grant, *Rainbow City*; and J. Thompson, "Art and
Architecture of the Pan-American Exposition, Buffalo, New York, 1901."

38. Barrett, "All American." See also Barrett's "Get Ready for the Panama
Canal"; and his *Panama Canal*.

39. For this jump in enrollments, see Fernández, "Longfellow's Law."

40. New York City, *Report of the Commissioner of Education for the Year ending
in June, 1914*, 790.

41. Kolbe, *Colleges in War Time and After*, 106.

42. Huntington's comment was as follows: "It is must be remembered that at
the best in the US there are very few people indeed who call for or have
knowledge to read a Spanish book. There is great talk in our institutions
of learning regarding Spanish and the teaching of Spanish but there are
few students. It is only now that there is growing a desire for commercial
Spanish and that is little in the line of literature." Archer M. Huntington
to Marqués de Vega-Inclán, 24 April 1916, HSA.

43. For the supposed "decline" in American culture at the start of the twentieth century, see Levine, *Highbrow/Lowbrow*. Levine makes no mention of
the "rise" of Spanish-language study.

44. "Report of Dr. Sullivan," 202. This report was on the speech Price delivered in Elmira, New York, in 1915. Price, never a fan of Spanish, believed
that French and German were the two modern foreign languages students ought to learn.

45. E. Wilkins, "Italian and Spanish in American Education," 12–14.

46. Cebrián lacks a biography but may be approached through "Juan Cebrián Cervera (1848–1935), apuntes para una biografía, por L. Español Bouché," available online at Biblioteca ETSAM, http://biblioteca.aq.upm .es/informacion/cebrian.html.

47. Luquiens, "National Need for Spanish," 710; *Elementary Spanish-American Reader* (first edition, 1917).

48. Doyle, "'Tumefaction' in the Study of Spanish." For his biography, see Huntington et al., "Henry Grattan Doyle."

49. See Turrell, *Spanish-American Short Stories*.

50. See the reports on Roosevelt's schedule published in the Madrid daily, *La Mañana*, 11 June 1914.

51. "A Boom for Spanish," editorial, *Washington Times*, 11 June 1914. The editors also commented that "Spain has a habit of losing her possessions, but her language does not grow less. There are only 20,000,000 subjects of King Alfonso, but nearly three times as many persons use Spanish to convey their thoughts. On this continent, south of Texas, nearly every person of white blood speaks the language of the conquerors."

52. Schmidt-Nowara, "Spanish Origins of American Empire."

53. The classic study of hispanismo is Pike, *Hispanismo, 1898–1936*, but it needs to be supplemented by Schmidt-Nowara, "Spanish Origins of American Empire."

54. Fitz-Gerald, *Importance of Spanish to the American Citizen*, 19.

55. L. Wilkins, "Spanish as a Substitute for German for Training and Culture."

56. According to Huntington, he refused the professorship partly because he suspected that Butler wanted "to make the Hispanic Society part of Columbia." To this he added the comment, "It is strange that Butler could imagine that I would exchange a house for a chair." Archer M. Huntington Diaries, entry for 27 October [1916?], HSA.

57. F. de Onís, "El Español en Los Estados Unidos," 275.

58. F. de Onís, "El Español en Los Estados Unidos," 272.

59. Archer M. Huntington to Arabella Huntington, Diaries, 1898, HSA.

60. From the original 1904 constitution of the HSA as cited in *Hispanic Society of America, Founded 1904*, 3–4. For the foundation and aims of the HSA, see Codding, "Archer Milton Huntington, Champion of Spain."

61. Archer M. Huntington to Guillermo de Osma, 9 November 1920, in Santos Quer, "La correspondencia de Archer M. Huntington con Guillermo de Osma y Javier García de Leaniz," 234.

62. Archer M. Huntington to Guillermo de Osma, 9 November 1920, in Santos Quer, "La correspondencia de Archer M. Huntington con Guillermo de Osma y Javier García de Leaniz," 234. The philanthropy of Huntington, together with that of his mother, Arabella, and cousin, Henry, is the subject of Bennett, *Art of Wealth*. Bordering on the hagiographic, this handsome volume is much better on Henry than Archer.

63. Archer M. Huntington to Arthur Hadley, December [n.d.] 1902, Archer M. Huntington Correspondence 1902, HSA.

64. "Our Mission," Smithsonian Institution, https://www.si.edu/about/mission.

65. Arabella's dinner party is described in "Giving Spanish Dinners," *Los Angeles Herald*, 21 November 1899.

66. Biographies of Collis P. Huntington are plentiful. The most accessible is Lavender, *Great Persuader*. For his art collecting, see Bennett, *Art of Wealth*.

67. Archer M. Huntington Diaries, HSA.

68. Archer M. Huntington Diaries, June 1920, HSA.

69. Archer M. Huntington Diaries, June 1882, HSA.

70. Archer M. Huntington Diaries, August 1882, HSA.

71. Archer M. Huntington Diaries, July 1884, HSA.

72. Archer M. Huntington Diaries, entry for 12 July 1884, HSA.

73. Archer M. Huntington Diaries, July 1886, HSA.

74. Archer M. Huntington Diaries, 1886, HSA.

75. Archer M. Huntington Diaries, 1889, HSA.

76. Archer M. Huntington Diaries, 1890, HSA.

77. Archer M. Huntington Diaries, 1890, HSA.

78. Archer M. Huntington Diaries, 1891, HSA. For Jesup, see W. Brown, *Morris Ketchum Jesup*."

79. Archer M. Huntington Diaries, 1891, HSA.

80. "Carmencita's Rival," *Chicago Daily Tribune*, 23 August 1890, citing a description previously published in the *New York World*.

81. For Otero's performances in 1890, see Lewis, *La Belle Otero*. See also Castle, *La Belle Otero*.

82. Archer M. Huntington Diaries, 1891, HSA.

83. Archer M. Huntington Diaries, 1891, HSA.

84. Knapp seemed an ideal choice. He had experience living in the country. He was also prepared to leave Yale and agreed to accompany Huntington to Spain just prior to accepting a professorship at the University of Chicago.

85. Archer M. Huntington Diaries, 1892, entry for 9 February, HSA. Huntington also worried about his "good American eyeglasses," even asking himself, "Will they distort? National eyeglasses surely do sometimes change the world from mystery to muddledom, do they not?" (entry for 1 March 1892).

86. Archer M. Huntington Diaries, 1892, entry for 4 July 1892, HSA.

87. Archer M. Huntington Diaries, 1892, July, HSA.

88. Archer M. Huntington Diaries, 1892, August, HSA.

89. Archer M. Huntington Diaries, 1892, July and August, HSA.

90. Archer M. Huntington Diaries, 1892, December, HSA.

91. Archer M. Huntington, *Note-Book in Northern Spain*, 5, 3. In a letter to Arabella he describes the book as "a bit helter-skelter, as it is practically nothing more than a number of letters to you fitted together, and expurgated." Archer M. Huntington Diaries, December 1896, HSA.

92. Archer M. Huntington, *Note-Book in Northern Spain*, 1.

93. The literature, both in English and in Spanish, on the Generation of 1898 is vast. For English readers, good starting points include Ramsden, *1898 Movement in Spain*; D. Shaw, *Generation of 1898 in Spain*; and the essays in Joseph Harrison and Hoyle, *Spain's 1898 Crisis*.

94. Archer M. Huntington Diaries, July 1898, HSA.

95. Archer M. Huntington Diaries, 1893, HSA.

96. Archer M. Huntington to Lathrop, 14 April 1902, Francis Lathrop Correspondence, HSA.

97. Archer M. Huntington Diaries, 1894, HSA.

98. Archer M. Huntington Diaries, 1897, HSA.

99. Archer M. Huntington Diaries, 1896, 1898, HSA. For an overview of the diversity of the HSA's collection, see the valuable essays in *Perspectivas y Reflexiones sobre el Coleccionismo de Archer Milton Huntington (1870–1955)*, which is a special issue of *Cuadernos de Arte e Iconografía*. See also the various essays included in the exhibition catalog *Tesoros de la Hispanic Society of America*.

100. Archer M. Huntington Diaries, 1898, HSA. For more on Bonsor's and Engel's relations with Huntington, see González Pradilla, "Archer Milton Huntington y la arqueología italicense." See also Maier Allende, *Epistolario de Jorge Bonsor, 1866–1930*.

101. Archer M. Huntington Diaries, 1898), HSA.

102. Archer M. Huntington Diaries, 1898, HSA.

103. "A.M. Huntington's View," *New York Herald*, 6 April 1896, as cited in Fernández Lorenzo, "Archer M. Huntington," 31.

104. Archer M. Huntington Diaries, 1898, HSA.

105. Archer M. Huntington Diaries, 1897, HSA. For a list of these facsimiles, see *Hispanic Society of America*.

106. Archer M. Huntington Diaries, 1902, entry for January 14, HSA.

107. Menéndez y Pelayo, *Epistolario de Menéndez y Pelayo y Rodríguez Marín*, 222 (letter dated 22 October 1902). For more on Menéndez y Pelayo and Huntington, see Kagan, *Marcelino Menéndez y Pelayo y el hispanismo norteamericano*.

108. Archer M. Huntington Diaries, 1902, HSA.

109. Archer M. Huntington to Baron de Vega de la Hoz, 17 November 1905, Archer M. Huntington Correspondence 1905, HSA.

110. Archer M. Huntington to Arabella Huntington, 25 and 27 November 1905, Archer M. Huntington Correspondence 1905, HSA.

111. Archer M. Huntington Diaries, 1906, entry for 13 June, HSA.

112. Archer M. Huntington Diaries, entry for 4 January 1904, HSA.

113. Archer M. Huntington Diaries, 1898, HSA.

114. Lathrop to Archer M. Huntington, 5 May 1901, 26 March 1902, Francis Lathrop Correspondence, HSA. The Art Institute of Chicago purchased El Greco's *Assumption of the Virgin* in 1906, the same year in which London's National Gallery, using a special fund created by Britain's national government to prevent the sale of the country's art treasures to wealthy foreign buyers, acquired the Rokeby Venus.

115. Quoted in Codding, "Legacy of Spanish Art for America," 316.

116. Archer M. Huntington Diaries, 1916, HSA. On Huntington's "collecting," see Codding, "Legacy of Spanish Art for America," 307–27; Bennett, *Art of Wealth*; and M. Davis, "Collecting Hispania."

117. Archer M. Huntington Diaries, 1910, HSA. Huntington reiterated this policy to the Spanish king, Alfonso XIII, and his queen in 1912. On Monday, 17 June 1912, Huntington wrote in his diary, "We lunched at the Palace today, and the King brought up the question of my purchase of Spanish Art. I explained to him, although I am sure he already knew it, that I only purchased books in Spain, as I felt that Spanish paintings should remain where they were. So many had drifted abroad that it was perfectly easy for me to obtain all the necessary types without robbing Spain. The Queen seemed quite pleased with the idea." Archer M. Huntington Diaries, 1912, HSA.

118. In 1912, Benjamin Chew, the photographer Huntington had engaged to take pictures in Peru and other parts of Latin America, purchased on

behalf of the Hispanic Society a set of a seventeenth-century choir stalls previously in Lima's Convento de San Francisco. See Benjamin Chew Correspondence, HSA.

119. See Lenaghan, "Tombs from San Francisco in Cuéllar." This article does little to clarify the circumstances surrounding Harris's acquisition of the sculptures or their subsequent sale to Huntington.

120. "Another Fine Museum Added to the City's List," *New York Times*, 19 January 1908.

121. "Another Fine Museum Added to the City's List," *New York Times*, 19 January 1908.

122. Archer M. Huntington Diaries, entry for 6 December 1920, HSA.

123. The purpose of the HSA's museum is as follows: "While the building of the Hispanic Society actually includes, in the strict sense, a museum, this title as usually and broadly understood is [in] a measure pretentious. Nor was it the original intention that it should ever be strictly applies. The building is simply the home of the Hispanic Society, and the small collection of objects was included solely for the convenience of the students and members." *Hispanic Society of America*, 8.

124. Archer M. Huntington to Arabella Huntington, 6 December 1920, Archer M. Huntington Diaries, 1920, HSA.

125. He then added, "You will be interested to know that the staff is gradually taking shape, and some day I hope to get each one interested in a single subject, so that they may become expert in each case along a definite line." Archer M. Huntington to Arabella Huntington, 6 December 1920, Archer M. Huntington Diaries, 1920, HSA.

126. Archer M. Huntington Diaries, 1918, HSA.

127. King to Archer M. Huntington, 3 January 1923, cited in Mann, "Hark the Herald Angels Sing," 113.

128. For the Bynes, see Rodríguez Thiessen, "Byne and Stapley."

129. Huntington note, 4 January 1919, quoted in Thiessen, "Byne and Stapley."

130. Archer M. Huntington to Arthur Byne, 16 April 1919, 30 May 1920, Byne Correspondence, HSA.

131. Arthur Byne to Archer M. Huntington, 4 January 1921, Byne Correspondence, HSA.

132. Archer M. Huntington, letter dated 3 February 1916 and addressed to "Dear Frank," Archer M. Huntington Diaries, 1916, HSA.

133. *Sorolla y la Hispanic Society*, 378. Two years later Huntington offered Sorolla the opportunity to decorate the interior of the Hispanic Society with a series of large-scale paintings depicting great moments in the history of Spain. Sorolla refused on the grounds that history painting was not to his taste, and the two soon agreed on a series of landscapes of the provinces, featuring peasants in regional dress, traditional dances and pastimes, and other picturesque aspects of each region. Sorolla completed these paintings in 1920, but for various reasons they did not go on public display at the Hispanic Society until January 1926. They can still be seen there.

134. Tyrell, "Spanish Revival."

5. Collectors and Collecting

1. The first epigraph is from Archer M. Huntington Diaries, 1889, HSA.

2. Berenson, *Letters of Bernard Berenson and Isabella Stewart Gardner*, 69.

3. Velázquez, 1904, Curatorial Files, Museum of Fine Arts, Boston.

4. For these prices, see "Velasquez [*sic*] Works to Go to B. Altman," *New York Times*, 20 March 1912.

5. Hoganson, *Consumers' Imperium*.

6. Henry James to Thomas Sargent Perry, 20 September 1867, in H. James, *Complete Letters of Henry James*, 1:179.

7. H. James, *Roderick Hudson*, 1:8–9.

8. N. Harris, *Cultural Excursions*, 137.

9. Veblen, *Theory of the Leisure Class*.

10. Americans' growing interest in European Old Master pictures is explored in Santori, *Melancholy of Masterpieces*.

11. For Soult and more generally the European appetite for Spanish art in the age of Napoleon, see Santos García, *Viajeros, eruditos, y artistas*.

12. See "Importation of Spanish Merino Sheep," 338, which reproduces Sales's letter, written at Cambridge (Massachusetts) and dated 9 October 1845. I first encountered this letter in Alcolea Albero, "El anticuario y marchante Francesc Guiu i Gabalda," 181. (I am grateful to Prof. Fernando Marías for bringing this article to my attention.) If Sales is correct in his information about how this picture reached the United States, it is a datum that previous scholars who have written about this picture (now lost) have missed. As for the person responsible for donating it to the Athenæum, according to Hirayama, *"With Éclat,"* 180n48, it is listed as a gift of William Foster rather than Sales.

13. The "most contemptible of mortals" comment is from Henry Adams, *History of the United States*, 1:348. Meade's *Roman Charity* (wrongly identified as *Magdalen*) appears in *A Catalogue of Paintings, Statues, Prints, etc. Exhibiting at the Pennsylvania Academy of the Fine Arts* (1818), 23, item no. 46. For Meade, whose biography remains to be written, see Stratton, *Spain, Espagne, Spanien*; and Boone, *Vistas de España*, 40, although neither study refers to his imprisonment in Spain. For this incident, see Avezuela Calleja, "El Tratado de la Florida"; and Villalba, *Silver Teacup*, 63–80. As for where and how Meade acquired the picture, see Rose de Viejo, "Desde palacio madrileño de Godoy al mundo entero." She argues that in 1807 Godoy gave the Murillo to Tomás López Enguídanos, who subsequently took it to Valencia and sold it to an English merchant named Orcho, whom she identifies as Obadiah Rich, an American merchant then in Valencia. No mention is made of how the picture got to Meade. For more on Meade, see Carrasco González, "Richard Meade," 2:101–14; and her "Presencia de Comerciantes Estadounidenses en España."

14. "Exhibition of Paintings, Collected in Spain, by the Late Richard W. Meade," *New-York Mirror*, 17 September 1831.

15. "Murillo the Artist," 81.

16. *Catalogue of the Very Valuable and Well Known Collection of Paintings.*

17. W. Johnston, *William and Henry Walters*, 12, 238. The Murillo in question turned out to be a copy. For other Murillos in the United States, see Stratton-Pruitt, "Early Appreciation of Murillo"; and Cano and Ybarra, "Early Collecting of Bartolomé Esteban Murillo's Paintings in the United States (1800–1925)."

18. After Bryan's death, his pictures entered the collection of the New-York Historical Society. For his collection and some details of his life, see R. White, *Companion to the Bryan Gallery of Christian Art*; New-York Historical Society, *Catalogue of the Museum and Gallery of Art of the New-York Historical Society*; J. Sitwell, "Thomas J. Bryan—the First Art Collector and Connoisseur in New York City"; and Schaeffer, "Private Collecting and the Public Good"; and his "Note on the Catalogues of the Collections from the New-York Historical Society."

19. "A Great Art Gallery Founded: Louis Durr's Collection of Paintings to Entertain and Instruct the Public," *New York Times*, 4 April 1880. For his collection, see New-York Historical Society, *Catalogue of the Museum and Gallery of Art of the New-York Historical Society*, which includes a short sketch of Durr's life. Bryan's collection of pictures had been deposited at

the society a few years earlier. For more on early collectors of Murillo, see Stratton, "Murillo in America."

20. The arrival of Aspinwall's "Murillo" in New York merited headlines. See "Mr. Aspinwall's Murillo," *New York Times*, 4 January 1858; and "Mr. Aspinwall's Murillo," *Harper's Weekly*, 30 January 1858, 77. With the exception of the *Immaculate Conception* attributed to Murillo and now in Detroit, Aspinwall bequeathed the bulk of his collection to his son-in-law, James Renwick. In 1895 Renwick gave his collection to the Metropolitan Museum of Art, but the authenticity of most of its Old Master pictures was challenged soon after this gift was announced. Relevant articles include "Gifts to the Museum," *New York Times*, 2 July 1895; and "A Delicate Position," *New York Times*, 5 July 1895.

21. "The Stolen Murillo," *New York Times*, 13 January 1875, 28 January 1875. The story of this theft and the painting's recovery became something of a legend. See the October 1900 monograph *Murillo* (part of the Masters in Art series of illustrated monographs); "St. Anthony of Padua and the Infant Jesus," *Lotus Magazine*, January 1915, 198–206; and "Art Theft History: 1874, Murillo's 'Vision of St. Anthony,'" 14 April 2009, Art Theft Central, http://archive.li/OI1hp.

22. "The Fine Arts in America," *New York Times*, 22 October 1877.

23. C. Curtis, *Velázquez and Murillo*, xxii.

24. "Lost Picture." For a fascinating account of the history of Snare's "Velázquez," see Cumming, *Vanishing Man*. According to one estimate, there were only eight "genuine" Murillos in the United States before 1890. See Stratton, "Murillo in America." For contemporary listings, see C. Curtis, *Velázquez and Murillo*; and *The Collector*, 15 November 1891.

25. For the Manchester exhibition and more on Spanish art in nineteenth-century Britain, see Glendinning and Macartney, *Spanish Art in Britain and Ireland, 1750–1920*. For Hawthorne's comments, see his entries for 16 and 20 August 1857 in *Passages from the English Note Books*, https://ia601406.us.archive.org/28/items/passagesfromthee07878gut/engn310.txt. For a general introduction to temporary art exhibitions such as the one in Manchester, see Haskell, *Ephemeral Museum*.

26. See Baticle, "Galerie Espagnole of Louis-Philippe," together with Roberts, *Memorials of Christie's*, 1:62–66.

27. Bryant, *Letters of a Traveler*, 134.

28. W. Irving, *Journals and Notebooks*, 4:19.

29. W. Irving, *Journals and Notebooks*, 4:20. In Madrid, Irving is referring
    to Murillo's *St. Elizabeth of Hungary Tending the Sick* (which remains in
    Madrid's Real Academia de Bellas Artes de San Fernando [Royal Acad-
    emy of Fine Arts]) and *The Patrician Juan and His Wife Reveal His Dream
    to Pope Liberius* (Prado). It should be noted that Irving erred in thinking
    the dream referred to the founding of St. Peter's. The church in question
    was rather that of Santa Maria Maggiore in Rome. See also Miles, *"Adno-
    tatiunculae Leicestrienses."*
30. W. Irving, *Letters*, 2:264.
31. Prior to his appointment in Madrid in 1823, Rich became U.S. consul in Valen-
    cia in 1816. He had worked previously as a merchant in that city and possibly
    was the source of Murillo picture acquired by Meade. See note 13 above.
32. For Burke's aesthetic ideas, see Burke, *Philosophical Enquiry into the Origin
    of Our Ideas of the Sublime and Beautiful*; and, more broadly, Hipple, *Beau-
    tiful, the Sublime, and the Picturesque*; and Cranston, *Romantic Movement*.
33. [A. Everett], "Collection of the Pictures Exhibited at the Fourth Exhibi-
    tion in the Gallery of the Boston Athenaeum," 320.
34. Caroline Cushing, *Letters Descriptive of Public Monuments*, 2:67. For her
    reactions to Spain, see Gifra-Adroher, "Caroline Cushing's Letters from
    Spain Reconsidered"; and Kagan, "From Noah to Moses."
35. Mackenzie, *Spain Revisited*, 225. The Prado's "comfortable chairs and
    benches," together with its "heated galleries" and "order and stillness,"
    also merited praise from Frances Calderón de la Barca, a Bostonian who
    had married a Spanish diplomat. Echoing Ford, she also referred to the
    Prado as "the finest gallery of paintings in the world." Calderón de la
    Barca, *Attaché in Madrid*, 150–51.
36. For more on Stirling-Maxwell, see E. Harris, "Sir William Stirling Maxwell
    and the History of Spanish Art"; Macartney, "Sir William Stirling-Maxwell";
    Macartney, "La Colección Stirling Maxwell en Pollok House"; and Glendin-
    ning and Macartney, *Spanish Art in Britain and Ireland, 1750–1920*.
37. For Manet's and other signatures, see Libros de Visitas, 28–30, 70–76,
    Archivo del Museo del Prado. For the influence of Velázquez on Manet,
    see the essays in Tinterow and Lacambre, *Manet/Velázquez*.
38. Bryant, *Letters of William Cullen Bryant*, 3:481–87.
39. Other post–Civil War visitors included Charles B. Curtis (1827–95),
    later to publish an important guide to the oeuvre of both Murillo and
    Velázquez (he was there on 2 December 1867), and William Knapp, Hun-
    tington's future tutor (he signed the registers on 24 December 1867).

40. For more on the Americans who visited the Prado during this era, see Kagan, "Yankees in the Prado."

41. E.L., "Spain, Her Ways, Her Women, and Her Wines," 292–300. E.L.'s account echoes the introduction to Stirling-Maxwell's *Annals* where Spanish art is characterized by its "severity, decency, and deeply religious tone."

42. Hay, *Castilian Days* (1871), 130.

43. Baxley, *Spain*, 2:262, 295, 311.

44. For Ruskin's aesthetic ideas and their influence in the United States, see R. Stein, *John Ruskin and Aesthetic Thought in America*.

45. Jarves, *Art-Idea*, 296; Jarves, *Art Thoughts*, 74, 75, 177.

46. Jarves, *Art Thoughts*, 179. For a description of the Jarves collection in 1868 and essentially the one bequeathed to Yale, see Gilman, "Jarves Collection in the Yale School of the Fine Arts." See also Sizer, "James Jackson Jarves," for details on his life.

47. "Cook's Tourist in Spain," 47–48.

48. James, "Duke of Montpensier's Pictures," 80, 82–85.

49. James, "Duke of Montpensier's Pictures," 86–87. For more on the Montpensier exhibit, see "The Montpensier Pictures," *Boston Evening Transcript*, 21 September 1874; and Hirayama, *"With Éclat,"* 124–25.

50. Henry Adams, *Letters of Henry Adams*, 4:75 (letter of 12 December 1894).

51. Bargellini, "La colección de pintura colonial de Robert Lamborn en el Philadelphia Museum of Art."

52. *Charter of the Metropolitan Museum of Art, State of New York, Laws of 1870*, chap. 197, passed 13 April 1870 and amended L.1898, ch. 34; L. 1908, chap. 219.

53. Perkins, "American Art Museums," 8. Perkins, a lecturer in art history at Harvard, wrote primarily about Italian art of the Middle Ages and Renaissance.

54. Lamborn, *Mexican Paintings and Painters*, 6, 21. For more on the reluctance of the Met's directors to allocate a space in the museum's collections for Mexican colonial art, see Kasl, "An American Museum."

55. Bouton, "Mexican Painters and Painting," 262.

56. Lamborn to Dalton Dorr, 9 December 1989, Letter Book 9, 125, Philadelphia Museum of Art. For Lamborn's collecting and the history of his collection, see Bargellini, "La colección de pintura colonial de Robert Lamborn en el Philadelphia Museum of Art," together with Rishel, "The Philadelphia Story." As for the precise nature of the room in which the Lamborn collection was first displayed, ambiguity remains, as the photo-

graph depicting Dorr and Lamborn could have been deliberately staged in what was otherwise a public gallery.

57. For more on Barber and his museological concerns, see Curran, *Invention of the American Art Museum*, 183–90.

58. Charles C. Perkins, "Journal written in Spain, 1854," folios 367–467, microfilm roll 268, Archives of American Art, Smithsonian Institution.

59. Goodrich, *Thomas Eakins*, 1:54. See also Boone, *Vistas de España*, 63–69.

60. Chase quoted in Weinberg, "William Merritt Chase and the American Taste for Painting," 2.

61. William Merritt Chase, *Outlook* 95 (June 25, 1910): 442, quoted in Bolger Burke, *American Paintings in the Metropolitan Museum of Art*, 3:90.

62. For Chase and Spanish art, see Pisano, *Leading Spirit in American Art*; and Boone, *Vistas de España*, 147–58.

63. For Marquand's acquisition of works by Velázquez, see Colomer, "Competing for Velázquez," 252–55. Marquand bequeathed these pictures together with his other Old Masters to the Metropolitan Museum in 1889. In addition, as the catalog of his property after his death in 1902 indicates, he also owned works by two contemporary Spanish artists, Raimundo de Madrazo and José Villegas. For a contemporary account of Marquand's collection and his bequests to the Met, see Alexander, "Henry G. Marquand." See also Metropolitan Museum of Art, *Catalogue of Paintings*.

64. "The Durcal Picture Sale," *New York Times*, 12 April 1889. The sale was widely reported in the press. For the "race" for Old Masters, see *Chicago Tribune*, 13 April 1889. For the Dúrcal collection, see *Catalogue of Oil Paintings, Drawings, and Original Sketches by the Old Masters Belonging to his Highness, Don Pedro de Borbon, Duque de Durcal.*

65. "Queer Old Pictures," *New York Times*, 29 March 1890.

66. For this sale, see Alcolea Albero, "El anticuario y marchante Francesc Guiu i Gabalda."

67. Isabella Stewart Gardner's scrapbooks, Archives of the Isabella Stewart Gardner Museum.

68. Berenson, *Letters of Bernard Berenson and Isabella Stewart Gardner*, 339–43. For Gardner's collection, see Hendy, *Isabella Stewart Gardner Museum Catalogue of Exhibited Paintings and Drawings*. For her biography, see Tharp, *Mrs. Jack*.

69. Berenson, *Letters of Bernard Berenson and Isabella Stewart Gardner*, 386.

70. Berenson, *Letters of Bernard Berenson and Isabella Stewart Gardner*, 386 (Gardner letter of 12 February 1909).

71. Prokop, "'Here One *Feels* Existence,'" 99n7.

72. According to Stevenson, "Whether directly or indirectly, whether consciously or unconsciously, artists have decided after a century of exploration to follow the path of Velasquez. . . . The sight of Velasquez at Madrid does not make us look upon the works of Regnault, Courbet, Manet, Carolus-Duran, Monet, Henner, Whistler, Degas, Sargent and the rest as plagiary. It rather gives the man of our century confidence that he is following a path not unlike that trod to such good purpose by the great Spaniard." Stevenson, *Velasquez*, 142, 150. For more on the artists influenced by Velázquez, see Simpson, "Sargent, Velázquez, and the Critics."

73. Quoted in Weinberg, "William Merritt Chase and the American Taste for Painting," 2. See also Weinberg, "American Artists' Taste for Spanish Painting, 1860–1915."

74. New Gallery, *Exhibition of Spanish Art* [. . .]. For the review, see "Spanish Art at the New Gallery."

75. For this collection, see Widener, *Pictures of the Collection of P. A. B. Widener at Lynnewood Hall*; and Quodbach, "Last of the American Versailles" (photo of first gallery is on p. 69).

76. See Colomer, "Competing for Velázquez," 257–58. In 1905 Morgan expressed some interest in another Velázquez portrait but did not purchase it.

77. Cassatt to Louisine Havemeyer, 19 February 1903, B 179A, Louisine Havemeyer Papers, Metropolitan Museum of Art Archives.

78. Quoted in Weitzenhoffer, *The Havemeyers*, 111. See also Havemeyer, *Sixteen to Sixty*. For the Havemeyers as collectors, see *Splendid Legacy*.

79. For this exhibition, see "Art Notes: Loan Exhibition of Paintings by El Greco and Goya at Knoedler's," *New York Times*, 13 January 1905. The reporter who covered the opening of this exhibition coolly noted that "in recent years the fame of El Greco and Goya has grown with astonishing rapidity." Lenders included Henry C. Frick and Louisine Havemeyer.

80. Frick first purchased an El Greco in 1905. Four years later, on a visit to Madrid, he acquired two more, one of which, *Purification of the Temple*, still hangs in the Frick Collection. Frick's daughter Helen notes that, in the course of a visit to the studio of the Madrid dealer Aureliano de Beruete, "he [Beruete] presented me with a lovely picture and saw two Grecos which Papa bought." Helen Clay Frick, diary entry of 13 March 1909, Travel Diary 1909, Helen Clay Frick Papers, Frick Museum Archives.

81. For the Altman collection, see Metropolitan Museum of Art, *Handbook of the Benjamin Altman Collection*; Haskell, "Benjamin Altman Bequest";

and Colomer, "Competing for Velázquez," 260–62. Altman, a lifelong bachelor, ultimately left his collection to the Met. See the essays in Altman Foundation, *Life and Legacy of Benjamin Altman*.

82. "Increasing Popularity of El Greco," *New York Times*, 29 December 1912. See also Rubinstein-Bloch, *Catalogue of the Collection of George and Florence Blumenthal*. The El Grecos in the Blumenthal collection included *The Adoration of the Shepherds* (Metropolitan Museum of Art) and *St. James the Younger* and *St. Philip* (both from the Añover Collection in Madrid), and *A Cavalier of Malta*, a portrait mistakenly attributed to the Toledan artist. Also in the collection was a *Life of Virgin and Christ* by the fifteenth-century Catalan artist Jaume Huguet, as well as a *Pietà and Saints* by Fernando Gallego, another fifteenth-century artist.

83. Archer M. Huntington, Diaries 1913, HSA.

84. For the Met's decision, see Weitzenhoffer, *The Havemeyers*. For the Art Institute's decision to purchase the picture, see the curatorial file for El Greco's *Assumption of the Virgin*, Archives of the Art Institute of Chicago.

85. J. Johnson, *Catalogue of a Collection of Paintings and Some Art Objects in the Collection of John G. Johnson*. For Johnson's correspondence with Fry, see folder 1, box 4, John G. Johnson Collection, Philadelphia Museum of Art.

86. Justi's work is *Diego Velázquez and His Times*.

87. "Pictures in Sir William Van Horne's Collection," *New York Times*, 19 September 1915. See also von Loga, "Spanish Pictures of Sir William Van Horne's Collection in Montreal."

88. A. Jaccaci to William Van Horne, 22 July 1912, box 3, series 2, Van Horne Family Fonds, Art Gallery of Ontario. The inventories of Van Horne's collection available at this gallery await detailed study. See also Collard, "Sir William Van Horne as an Art Collector"; "Art at Home and Abroad," *New York Times*, 5 October 1913; Vaughan, *Life and Work of Sir William Van Horne*; and V. Knowles, *From Telegrapher to Titan*.

89. For a short biography of Deering, see W. Scott, *Memoir of Charles Deering*; and W. Scott, "Life of Charles Deering."

90. For Deering's stamp collection, see William Deering to Charles Deering, 23 May 1868, folder 6, box 1, William Deering Family Papers, Deering Library, Northwestern University.

91. Deering to Vega-Inclán, [1912?], box 54/8121, AGA.

92. *¡Otra Margarita!*, meaning another Marguerite, may have referred to the term for prostitutes in the city of Valencia, Sorolla's birthplace. It has also been suggested that the name is a reference to Goethe's tragic play *Faust*,

in which Margaret (also referred to as Gretchen), following her seduction by Faust, is repentant not only for the accidental death of her mother but also that of her newborn child.

93. For their relationship, see Domènech, "Utrillo, Deering i Maricel"; Bassegoda and Domènech, "Charles Deering and the Palacio Maricel in Sitges"; and Sánchez Sauleda, "Charles Deering, Miquel Utrillo i Ramon Casas." See also Coll Mirabent, *Charles Deering and Ramón Casas*.

94. Alcoy, *Art fugitiu*, 429.

95. "Un tesoro artístico que emigra," newspaper clipping from *Publicidad* [location unspecified], 17 July 1922, 52/8257, AGA.

96. The only inventory of Deering's collection is a posthumous one, dated 27–28 February 1927 and prepared by Robert B. Hershe, director of the Art Institute of Chicago. It lists items that Deering shipped in 1921 to his Florida home. See box II, Charles Deering Archives, Art Institute of Chicago. For Spanish paintings in Maricel, see Coll i Mirabent, "La pintura española en la colección de Charles Deering."

97. For what little is known about the sale of this altarpiece, see Coll i Mirabent, "La pintura española en la colección de Charles Deering"; Molero-Moneo, "Retablo y frontal del convento de San Juan de Quejana"; and Stratton-Pruitt, "Lionel Harris, Tomás Harris, the Spanish Art Gallery."

98. Coll i Mirabent, "La pintura española en la colección de Charles Deering," 66.

99. Zuloaga, *Correspondencia de Ignacio Zuloaga con su tío Daniel*, 484.

100. Walter Dill Scott, "Life of Charles Deering," *Northwestern University Alumni News*, March 1930, 6, in folder 1, box 2, William Deering Family Papers.

101. Vega-Inclán to Juan de Riaño, Madrid, 27 November 1922, box 54/8247, AGA. The original reads: "su estado crónico de alcohólico senil."

102. Deering to Gary, 20 April 1921, folder 4, box 2, William Deering Family Papers.

103. Socias Batet, "Nuevas fuentes documentales para la interpretación del levantamiento de la colección Deering."

104. "Exportación de piezas artísticas fuera de España de Charles Deering, 1921–1923," box 54/8247, AGA.

105. Gary to Deering, 27 December 1921, folder 2, box 2, William Deering Family Papers.

106. Sánchez Sauleda, "Charles Deering, Miquel Utrillo i Ramon Casas," 218.

107. Byne to Archer M. Huntington, 8 April 1917, quoted in Socias Batet, "Nuevas fuentes documentales para la interpretación del levantamiento de la colección Deering," 397.

108. Coll i Mirabent, "La pintura española en la colección de Charles Deering."

109. Eco, *Travels in Hyperreality*, 22. The epithet for Hearst appears in the subtitle of the book by Merino de Cáceres and Martínez Ruiz, whose title in full is *La destrucción del patrimonio artístico español: W. R. Hearst, "el gran acaparador."*

110. Levkoff, *Hearst the Collector*. See also Levkoff, "Hearst and Spain."

111. William Randolph Hearst to "Mama," Monterey, California, 1899[?], frame 29, reel 6, WRHP, Bancroft Library, UC Berkeley.

112. Quoted in Mugridge, *View from Xanadu*, 30.

113. William Randolph Hearst to Phoebe Apperson Hearst, undated letter from Portugal, 1911, frame 8, reel 7, WRHP.

114. "The Cost of Kings," in Hearst, *Selections from the Writings and Speeches of William Randolph Hearst*, 566.

115. Mugridge, *View from Xanadu*, 141–42.

116. William Randolph Hearst to Phoebe Apperson Hearst, April 1905, folder 2, box 7, WRHP.

117. Quoted in Levkoff, *Hearst the Collector*, 33. See also Coffman, *Hearst as Collector*, 16–17.

118. Hearst to Morgan, 31 December 1919, quoted in Loe, *San Simeon Revisited*, 23.

119. "Pride of Burgos," *New York Times*, 3 November 1910.

120. Bainbridge Colby [Hearst's lawyer] to Juan de Riaño [Spain's ambassador in Washington DC], 23 July 1915, box 54/1828, AGA.

121. For correspondence relating to Hearst's efforts to export the patio, see box 54/8128, AGA; and leg. H 2241, AMAE. For his declaration of "ownership" of the patio, see William Randolph Hearst to Morgan, 30 December 1919, folder 1, box 47, E: Correspondence with Client W. R. Hearst, Series 5: San Simeon Project Records, Julia Morgan Papers, KL (cited hereafter with folder and box number in Julia Morgan Papers); and Levkoff, *Hearst the Collector*, 57.

122. For Hearst's "Spanish" style, see Levkoff, *Hearst the Collector*.

123. William Randolph Hearst to Morgan, 19 December 1919, folder 5, box 47, Julia Morgan Papers, KL. Parts of the Hearst-Morgan correspondence have been digitized and are available at the Online Archive of California, http://

www.oac.cdlib.org/findaid/ark:/13030/kt9s2030pj/. Excerpts may be found in Loe, *San Simeon Revisited*; and Boutelle, *Julia Morgan, Architect*.

124. For the Morgan-Byne correspondence, see boxes 44–45, Julia Morgan Papers, KL. For the Bynes' activities as art dealers, see Rodríguez Thiessen, "Byne and Stapley"; Merino de Cáceres, "Arthur Byne, un expoliador de guante blanco"; Martínez Ruiz, *La enajenación del patrimonio en Castilla y León (1900–1936)*, 2:326–36; Merino de Cáceres and Martínez Ruiz, *La destrucción del patrimonio artístico español*; and Brotherston, *Arthur Byne's Diplomatic Legacy*.

125. Julia Morgan to William Randolph Hearst, 5 January 1920, folder 5; Julia Morgan to William Randolph Hearst, 23 May 1920, folder 6, both in box 47 Julia Morgan Papers, KL.

126. Morgan to Mildred Stapley Byne, 19 September 1921; Mildred Stapley Byne to Morgan, 1 October 1921, both in folder 2, box 44, Julia Morgan Papers, KL.

127. Arthur Byne to Morgan, 15 December 1921, folder 2, box 44, Julia Morgan Papers, KL.

128. Julia Morgan to Mildred Stapley Byne, 1 November 1921, 15 December 1921, folder 2, box 44, Julia Morgan Papers, KL.

129. Morgan to Arthur and Mildred Stapley Byne, 16 November 1921 (includes copy of a cable from William Randolph Hearst to Morgan), folder 2, box 44, Julia Morgan Papers, KL.

130. For these auctions, see Martínez Ruiz, "Entre negocios y trapicheos"; and Martínez Ruiz, "Raimundo y Luis Ruiz."

131. Morgan cables to Bynes, November 1923 (folder 4), February 1925 (folder 6), August 1925 (folder 13), all in box 44, Julia Morgan Papers, KL.

132. Morgan cables to Bynes, 25 August 1925, 9 September 1925, folder 13, box 44, Julia Morgan Papers, KL. For Hearst's purchase of the Sacramenia cloister, see Merino de Cáceres and Martínez Ruiz, *La destrucción del patrimonio artístico español*, 421–49. Also useful is Clements, "William R. Hearst's Monastery." Contemporary reports on the purchase include "Hearst Importing a Spanish Cloister," *New York Times*, 14 December 1926.

133. Morgan cable to Bynes, March 12, 1926, folder 3, box 45, Julia Morgan Papers, KL.

134. A. Byne cable to Morgan, 25 April 1929; Morgan cable to A. Byne, 29 April 1929; A. Byne cable to Archer M. Huntington, 11 May 1929, referring to cable from William Randolph Hearst to Byne, 9 May 1929; Wil-

liam Randolph Hearst cable to A. Byne, 13 May 1929, all in folder 14, box 45, Julia Morgan Papers, KL.

135. A. Byne cable to William Randolph Hearst, 27 May 1929, folder 14, box 45, Julia Morgan Papers, KL.

136. For details, see Merino de Cáceres and Martínez Ruiz, *La destrucción del patrimonio artístico español*, 506–9.

137. For the Guildhall exhibition, see Temple, *Modern Spanish Painting*.

138. For these debates, see Alvarez Lopera, "Coleccionismo, intervención estatal y mecenazgo en España"; and Bosch, *Informe del seño ante la comisión del congreso de diputados* (quotation, 24). For Spanish legislation restricting art exports, see Alvarez Lopera, *La política de bienes culturales del gobierno republicano durante la guerra civil*; Tusell, "La política de Bellas Artes durante la II Republica"; and Quirosa García, "Historia de la protección de los bienes muebles culturales."

139. Letter dated 12 October 1926, Ms. 9/7959/54/8, RAH.

140. Bynes cable to Morgan, 19 July 1931, folder 26, box 45, Julia Morgan Papers, KL.

141. A. Byne cable to Morgan, 25 August 1931, folder 26, box 45, Julia Morgan Papers, KL. For more on the purchase, dismantling, and shipment of Monte Oliva, see Merino de Cáceres and Martínez Ruiz, *La destrucción del patrimonio artístico español*, 450–74; and Morgan, *Julia Morgan Architectural History Project*, 333–36.

142. Hearst, *Selections from the Writings and Speeches of William Randolph Hearst*, 681.

143. William Randolph Hearst to Phoebe Apperson Hearst, undated letter from Portugal, 1911, frame 8, reel 7, WRHP.

6. "Castles in Spain Made Real"

1. Cram, "Renaissance in Spain," 289.

2. Cram, *Gothic Quest*, 58. See also his comments on the virtues of the Gothic in his autobiography, Cram, *My Life in Architecture*, 140–43.

3. For Cram's early career as an architect, see Shand-Tucci, *Boston Bohemia, 1881–1900*, and for his later years see Shand-Tucci, *Ralph Adams Cram*.

4. Cram, *My Life in Architecture*, 143. See also Cram, *Cathedral of Palma de Mallorca*.

5. Cram, *My Life in Architecture*, 143.

6. Cram, *My Life in Architecture*, 144.

7. Cram, *My Life in Architecture*, 144.

8. Cram, "Spanish Notes," 47. The next installments include his "Spanish Gothic," 125 (27 February 1924): 103–10; "Renaissance in Spain," 125 (26 March 1924): 289–96; and "Domestic Architecture in Spain," 125 (23 April 1924): 371–78. The editors reported that all copies of these issues of the journal were sold.

9. Cram, "Spanish Notes," 47.

10. Cram, "Spanish Gothic," 109 (first quote); Cram, "Domestic Architecture in Spain," 374–76 (remaining quotes).

11. The bibliography may be found at the close of Cram, "Domestic Architecture in Spain."

12. Cram's Spanish houses and buildings in Texas can be approached through Fox, *Spanish-Mediterranean Houses in Houston*; and Shand-Tucci, *Ralph Adams Cram*, 254–56.

13. Quoted in Barrick, *Texas Tech*, 19. For Spanish-style homes and buildings in Texas, see Simons and Hoyt, *Hispanic Texas*.

14. Quoted in Graham, "Flagler's Grand Hotel Alcazar," 6.

15. For a reprint of the account of this festival originally published in the *St. Augustine Evening Record* on 3 April 1885, see *El Escribano* 5, no. 2 (April 1988): 4–5. For the festival's influence on Flagler, see Martin, *Henry Flagler*, 106.

16. Chandler, *Henry Flagler*, 101.

17. For the architecture and decoration of the Ponce de León Hotel, see Graham and Keys, *Hotel Ponce de Leon*; and Keys, *Hotel Ponce de Leon*. Also useful are Graham, "Flagler's Magnificent Hotel Ponce de Leon"; Crespo, "Florida's First Spanish Renaissance Revival"; Braden, *Architecture of Leisure*; and Graham, *Mr. Flagler's St. Augustine*.

18. Quoted in Galenter, *History of American Architecture*, 199.

19. Castleden, *Early Years of the Ponce de Leon*, 13, 40–41. For Flagler's interest in Spanish culture, see Ralph, "Riviera, Our Town"; and Lefevre, "Flagler and Florida."

20. Smith noted that the design of the Villa Zorayda was in keeping with "the Spanish style of architecture." See article by Frank W. Smith, clipping from *St. Augustine Record*, 17 April 1937, folder 18, St. Augustine Historical Society. For Smith, see Nolan, *Fifty Feet in Paradise*, esp. 87–80; and Clarke, "Franklin W. Smith, St. Augustine's Concrete Pioneer."

21. "Balmy South."

22. These articles began with "Seville's Cathedral, a History."

23. Quoted in Hewett et al., *Carrère & Hastings, Architects*, 1:74.

24. "Thomas Hastings: Architect of Famous Hotels in the Old City," *St. Augustine Record*, 21 January 1924. For Flagler's interest in Spanish culture, see Ralph, "Riviera, Our Town," 498. See also Reynolds, *A Tribute*.

25. Lears, *No Place of Grace*.

26. For these changes, see Graham, "Henry Flagler's St. Augustine," 9.

27. For the program books and other materials relating to these festivals, see the folder "Festivals: Ponce de Leon Celebration," St. Augustine Historical Society. These celebrations were held in 1885, 1889, 1890, 1901, 1907–10, 1913, 1923–27, and 1929–30. For the renaming of St. Augustine's streets, see "Excerpts from a Florida Diary"; and "Henry M. Flagler," both published in *El Escribano*.

28. Mrs. G[riswold]. Van Rensselaer, "Madison Square Garden," 746. Other comments may be found in Pullen, "Madison Square Garden"; and De Kay, "Madison Square Garden."

29. Quoted in Lowe, *Stanford White's New York*, 202. For the tower and White's interest in Spanish art, see also Craven, *Stanford White*, 208–12; and Kagan, "Blame It on Washington Irving."

30. For the drawing of Giralda, see *American Architect and Building News* 18, no. 5252 (26 December 1885).

31. Holliday, *Leopold Eidlitz*, 70. For the Casino Theatre, see Tom Miller, "The Lost 1882 Casino Theatre—39th Street and Broadway," *Daytonian in Manhattan*, 3 June 2013, http://daytoninmanhattan.blogspot.pe/2013/06/the-lost-1882-casino-theatre-39th.html.

32. For more on America's Giraldas, see Kagan, "Blame It on Washington Irving."

33. California World's Fair Commission, *Final Report*, 11. The committee was not the first to link the Moorish and mission styles. That connection had already been made by Leland Stanford, who envisioned that the buildings of his new university "will be in the Moorish style of architecture . . . to preserve as a local characteristic the style of architecture given to California in the churches and the mission buildings of the early missionary fathers." Weitze, *California's Mission Revival Architecture*, 22. See also Blackmar, *Spanish Institutions of the Southwest*, 126–28, where he suggests that the design of the early Spanish buildings in the Southwest was a mixture of ancient Roman (i.e., classical) and Moorish styles.

34. For this connection, see Francaviglia, *Go East, Young Man*.

35. *California's Monthly World Fair Magazine*, quoted in Weitze, *California's Mission Revival Architecture*, 40.

36. Gill, "Home of the Future," 151.

37. G. James, *In and Out of the Missions of California*, 1.

38. G. James, *Through Ramona's Country*, 361; George Wharton James, "The Influence of the 'Mission' Style upon the Domestic, Civic & Religious Architecture of Modern California," draft of article, ca. 1906, 2–3, as cited in Moran, "Devotion of Others," 47. For the sometimes problematic relationship between James and Lummis, see Moran, "Catholicism and the Making of the U.S. Pacific." For more on James, see Kropp, *California Vieja*; and Starr, *Inventing the Dream*, chap. 2.

39. See Roth, "Company Towns in the Western United States," esp. 182–84. For Tyrone, which was built for the Phelps Dodge mining company, see Crawford, *Building the Workingman's Paradise*, 129–52.

40. "The Architectural Scheme," Pan-American Exposition of 1901, http://library.buffalo.edu/pan-am/exposition/art/plan.html.

41. *Pan-American Exposition, Buffalo, May 1 to November 1, 1901*. See also Pan-American Exposition of 1901, http://library.buffalo.edu/pan-am/exposition/art/plan.html.

42. For the exposition's architecture, see Carrère, "Architectural Scheme." For a general introduction to this and other fairs of the era, indispensable studies include Rydell, *All the World's a Fair*.

43. *Pan-American Exposition, Buffalo, May 1 to November 1, 1901*; R. Grant, "Notes on the Exposition"; J. Hawthorne, "Some Novelties at the Buffalo Fair," 485. See also J. Thompson, "Art and Architecture of the Pan-American Exposition, Buffalo, New York, 1901."

44. R. Grant, "Notes on the Exposition," 455.

45. J. Hawthorne, "Some Novelties at the Buffalo Fair," 485.

46. Quoted in Chibbaro, *Charleston Exposition*.

47. E. Brown and F. Brown, "English and Spanish Precedents in American Domestic Architecture," 247. For an overview of mission style, see Weitze, *California's Mission Revival Architecture*.

48. Quoted in Weitze, *California's Mission Revival Architecture*, 135.

49. For this celebration, see Thornton, "San Diego's First Cabrillo Celebration, 1892." Historical reenactments of events such as the Cabrillo landing were regular occurrences as cities across the entire region groped for a past around which an increasingly pluralistic citizenry might unite. For this tradition, see Glassberg, *Place of the Past in American Life*.

50. Bokovoy, *San Diego's World Fairs and Southwestern Memory*.

51. See G. Montes, "Balboa Park, 1909–1911." For Goodhue, see Oliver, *Bertram Grosvenor Goodhue*.

52. Baxter, Peabody, and Goodhue, *Spanish-Colonial Architecture in Mexico*, 4. For the fair's architecture, see Winslow, *Architecture and Gardens of the Panama-California Exposition*; Engstrand, "Inspired by Mexico"; and Engstrand and Schiff, "San Diego Invites the World."

53. "Architectural Gems of Old Spain Revived," *San Diego Union*, 1 January 1915, special section 4.

54. *San Diego Evening Tribune*, 30 September 1914, www.sandiegohistory .org/amero/notes-1914.htm.

55. Herzog, *From Aztec to High Tech*, 110–11.

56. Quoted in Lint Sagarena, *Aztlán and Arcadia*, 66.

57. Sands, *Santa Barbara*, 47.

58. Steedman and Smith's correspondence regarding the decoration and design of the Casa del Herrero can be found in the archives of the Casa del Herrero as well as in the library of the University of California, Santa Barbara; see the George W. Smith Papers in the library's Architecture and Design Collection. See also Sweeney, *Casa del Herrero*. Santa Barbara's embrace of its "Spanish" past helps to explain why one writer, in a 1921 article commenting on architectural trends in California and published in *House Beautiful*, observed that Spanish style had recently become "really popular." McCorkle, "Doorways That Hint of Sunny Spain," 306.

59. Lummis to J. L. Cebrián, 5 January 1925, item 709, folder 1, box 1, Charles F. Lummis Collection, BRL.

60. Studies of Santa Barbara's hispanicization are many. I have relied principally upon D. Gebhard, *Creation of a New Spain in America*. More recent and exceptionally well documented is E. Knowles, "Unifying Vision." For the courtyard and Groesbeck mural, see P. Gebhard and Masson, *Santa Barbara County Courthouse*.

61. D. Gebhard, *Creation of a New Spain in America*, 117–25. For a day-by-day account of the festival, see Rose, *Santa Barbara's Spanish Renaissance & Old Spanish Days Fiesta*.

62. McWilliams, *Southern California Country*, 21, and see 73–80; as well as his *North from Mexico*.

63. Lummis to the Duke of Alba, 15 April 1924, item 44, folder 1, box 1, Charles F. Lummis Collection, BRL.

64. Shelton, "As a Boy He Dreamed of Castles in Spain," 46. Merrick also referred to this trip in an article, "Millions of Capital Drawn to Miami," *New York Times*, 15 March 1925.

65. Quoted in *Miami Herald*, 30 October 1921.

66. "Castles in Spain Made Real," printed in both *Miami Metropolis*, 18 November 1921; *Miami Herald*, 20 November 1921.

67. Quoted in Patricios, "Phineas Paist and the Architecture of Coral Gables," 24.

68. *New York Times*, 3 May 1925, reprinted in Douglas, *Coral Gables: Miami Riviera*. Douglas also published *Coral Gables: America's Finest Suburb*, evidently a promotional pamphlet that Merrick had sponsored.

69. For the design and planning of Coral Gables, see Hatton, *Tropical Splendor*, 60–63.

70. Quoted in Holley, "Creator of Castles in Spain," clipping from box 1, "Magazine Articles," Mizner Collection, HSPBC. For more on his life, see Addison Mizner, unpublished autobiography, 1932, box 1, Mizner Collection, HSPBC; and his published autobiography, Mizner, *Many Mizners*; and Boyd, "Florida House."

71. Kane, "Finding Addison Mizner," 62.

72. A. Johnston, *Legendary Mizners*, 31. For a recent perceptive analysis of these albums, see Kane, "Finding Addison Mizner."

73. Quoted in Boyd, "Spanish House," 40.

74. Curl, *Mizner's Florida*.

75. Mizner, unpublished autobiography, quoted in Orr-Cahall, *Addison Mizner*, 3. See also "Wonderful Artistic Effects Achieved in Architecture of Paris Singer's Home for Convalescent Soldiers," *Palm Beach Post*, 27 October 1918.

76. A. Johnston, *Legendary Mizners*, 25.

77. Curl, *Mizner's Florida*, 132.

78. "Mizner Building a Priceless Gem," *Palm Beach Daily News*, 8 January 1925, quoted in Kane, "Finding Addison Mizner," 43. Another article, "Spanish Style Shops Going Up," *Palm Beach Times*, 14 November 1927, suggested that the Via Mizner successfully captured the "atmosphere of real Spain."

79. Alex Waugh, "Mizner Industries," 5, box 3, Alex Waugh Papers, Mizner Collection, HSPBC.

80. Alex Waugh, "Mizner Industries," 6, box 3, Alex Waugh Papers, Mizner Collection, HSPBC.

81. Amy Lyman Phillips, "Summer Construction in Palm Beach Will Transform Landscape," *Palm Beach Post*, 10 May 1923, as quoted in Kane, "Finding Addison Mizner," 43.

82. "The New South," Mizner Development Corporation advertisement in *Palm Beach Post*, 14 April 1926, Mizner Collection, HSPBC.

83. On Boca Raton, see Seebohm, *Boca Rococo*.

84. Bayer, "Bit of Old Spain Transplanted to Tampa," 37.

85. St. Petersburg's architecture may be approached through Arsenault, *St. Petersburg and the Florida Dream*; Hatton, *Tropical Splendor*; and Braden, *Architecture of Leisure*.

86. Major, *Domestic Architecture of the Early American Republic*, 89. See also Major, "Theory Relating to Spanish and Italian Houses in Florida."

87. Goodhue, introduction to *Minor Ecclesiastical, Domestic, and Garden Architecture of Southern Spain* by Whittlesey, vi, viii.

88. Soule discovered an "old Spain of evangelical religious faith, of aristocratic democracy, of austerity, and courtesy and grave self-respect." Soule, *Spanish Farm Houses*, introduction.

89. Bottomley, *Spanish Details*, xx. Also see Frazer, *William Lawrence Bottomley*.

90. A relatively late entrant in terms of Cram's bibliography was Gerstle and Gibson, *Architectural Details of Southern Spain*.

91. Sexton, *Spanish Influence on American Architecture and Decoration*, 9–10. For the Sears and Montgomery Ward home kits, see "Sears Homes of Chicagoland," 29 March 2016, http://www.sears-homes.com/2016/03/the-spanish-craze-that-swept-country.html.

92. Sexton, *Spanish Influence on American Architecture and Decoration*, 11.

93. See Moul and Tigges, "Santa Fe 1912 City Plan"; Morley, "Santa Fe Architecture"; Nusbaum, "Van Morley and the Santa Fe Style"; and Montgomery, *Spanish Redemption*, 113–20.

94. Gerould, *Aristocratic West*, 110–14.

95. Quoted in Montgomery, *Spanish Redemption*, 123. For a résumé of Hewlett's "Spain the Motherland" lecture, see *El Palacio* 6, no. 1 (8 February 1910): 63–64.

96. For these murals, see C. Wilson, *Myth of Santa Fe*, 115–16, where he attributes, possibly mistakenly, the murals to a certain J. G. Vyskel, an artist for whom no other record exists. Whether Vysekal or Vyskel, the murals await detailed study.

97. Edgar L. Hewett, "Report of Planning Board to Mayor Celo Lopez," by Santa Fe City Planning, folder 7, box 1, Fray Angélico Chavez History Library, New Mexico History Museum.

98. For Eagle's Nest, see Platt, *America's Gilded Age*, 284; and "Eagle's Nest," Vanderbilt Museum, http://www.vanderbiltmuseum.org/about -us/history/eagles-nest/.

99. "Massapequa Long Island: Shores of Seville add Touch of Spain" (ad), *Brooklyn Daily Eagle*, 14 May 1926, A9; "A Touch of Old Spain—on the South Shore of Long Island" (ad), *Brooklyn Daily Eagle*, 17 June 1928; "Waterfront Spanish Villas on Manhasset Bay" (ad), *Brooklyn Daily Eagle*, 16 September 1928, 59.

100. Christopher Gray, "When Spain Reigned on Central Park South," *New York Times*, 17 June 2006, real estate section.

101. This paragraph relies upon DeAloia, *Lost Grand Hotels of Cleveland*, 19.

102. Morley, "Santa Fe Architecture," 247. See also Fogelson, *Bourgeois Nightmares*, 66. Country Club Plaza was the centerpiece of the lushly landscaped Country Club District, designed in accordance with the then-popular "Garden City" ideal of urban planning. See Longstreth, "J. C. Nichols, the Country Club Plaza, and Notions of Modernity."

103. Worley, *J. C. Nichols and the Shaping of Kansas City*, 248. For more on this plaza, see Worley, *The Plaza*; Morton, *Country Club District of Kansas City*; Pearson, *Chronicle of J. C. Nichols*; and Larson, "La gramática de la 'Hispanidad.'"

104. Shea, *From No Man's Land to Plaza del Lago*, 54.

105. "This Home Costs $9,500; It Looks Like a Million," *Chicago Tribune*, 21 March 1926, 1 May 1927.

106. Walter Rendell Storey, "Old Spain Enters the American Home," *New York Times*, 7 March 1926. A similar article also made reference to "the vogue . . . for things Spanish. In design, nearly everybody wants a Spanish Home." Helen Herbert Foster, "Woman Designs Pretty Houses," *Brooklyn Daily Eagle*, 20 June 1926, 92.

107. Designed by Lester B. Scheide and completed in 1928, the "Spanish House" was added to the National Register of Historic Places in 1979.

7. The Spanish Blaze

1. "The 'Land of Joy' with L'Argentina," *New York Times*, 2 November 1917; "A Breath of Spain," *New York Times*, 11 November 1917. For other equally enthusiastic reviews, see Sturman, *Zarzuela*, 62.

2. Van Vechten, *Music of Spain*, 94; "The 'Land of Joy' with L'Argentina," *New York Times*, 2 November 1917. See also Bennahum, *Antonia Mercé, "La Argentina."*

3. Van Vechten, *Music of Spain*, 94–97. Van Vechten's review originally appeared as "Valverde and the *Land of Joy*," *The Bellman* 23 (3 November 1917). For a recent biography of Van Vechten, see E. White, *The Tastemaker.*

4. "Spanish Art at Ehrich Gallery," *New York Times*, 20 February 1916, Art Notes.

5. Van Vechten, *Music of Spain*, 16. For the merchandising that facilitated this "blaze" and other fashion fads, see Leach, *Land of Desire.*

6. "Sorceress Meller: Her Hands Are Like Feet," *Time*, 26 April 1926, 18.

7. For Meller, see Woods Peiró, *White Gypsies.*

8. With the exception of music and film, other aspects of the craze are examined in the essays collected in *When Spain Fascinated America.*

9. For the history of Spanish music in the United States, see L. Stein, "Before the Latin Tinge." What follows relies extensively on this indispensable work together with Llano, *Whose Spain?*

10. *New York Times*, 29 January 1916.

11. L. Stein, "Before the Latin Tinge."

12. Lummis's *Land of Poco Tiempo* (1893) was reprinted in 1897 and again in 1913.

13. Quoted in Watkins, "'He Said It with Music,'" 363.

14. Earle, "Old-Time Collector."

15. Lummis to Juan Riaño, 17 January 1924, box 1.1.3716; Lummis to David. C. Collier, 24 January 1924, box 1.1.843, both in Charles F. Lummis Collection, BRL. See also in Watkins, "'He Said It with Music.'"

16. Lummis to Blasco Ibáñez, 11 September 1923, box 1.1.2179, Charles F. Lummis Collection, BRL.

17. Lummis to Juan Riaño, 17 January 1924, 24 March 1924, box 1.1.3716, Charles F. Lummis Collection, BRL.

18. Lummis to Julián Ribera, 17 November 1924, box 1.1.3717, Charles F. Lummis Collection, BRL.

19. C.M.P., "Spanish Love Story with a Raisin in It" (review of *Spanish Love*), *Columbia Spectator* (newspaper of Columbia University), 13 October 1920. I have compiled the list of works discussed using as my guide Hischak, *TPA Song Encyclopedia*. My list may not be complete.

20. Hischak, *TPA Song Encyclopedia*, 178.

516   NOTES TO PAGES 389–400

21. For the issue of race in Griffith's *Ramona*, see Bernardi, "Voice of White-ness," 104; and Simmon, *Films of D. W. Griffith*.

22. "Ramona Shown upon the Screen," *New York Times*, 11 November 1917. For the "rage," see "Ramona Launches Old Spanish Fad Wave in New York," *Los Angeles Herald*, 5 April 1916.

23. For a review, see Mordaunt Hall, "The Screen," *New York Times*, 15 May 1928.

24. See Brégent-Heald, *Borderland Films*. For Griffith, see Noriega, "Birth of the Southwest"; and McKenna, "City That Made the Pictures Move."

25. Brégent-Heald, *Borderland Films*, 48; quoted in Brégent-Heald, *Border-land Films*, 51.

26. Quoted in Brégent-Heald, *Borderland Films*, 53.

27. For the *Times* review, see Mordaunt Hall, "The Screen: A Chip of the Old Block," *New York Times*, 16 June 1925.

28. For more on this film, see Bradley, *First Hollywood Sound Shorts*.

29. For Carmen in Hollywood, see Vilches, "El mito de Carmen en el cine de Hollywood."

30. "Pola Negri Scores in Alluring, Vivid Role at Columbia," *Washington Post*, 11 December 1923; Delgado, *Pola Negri*, 72.

31. Delgado, *Movie Roadshows*, 33; "Mary Pickford in 'Rosita,'" *Providence Sunday Tribune*, 18 November 1923; "Put 'Rosita' among Year's Best Pic-tures," *Chicago Daily Tribune*, 2 November 1923. Movie posters announc-ing the film's debut carried the line "A Spanish Romance."

32. For *Rosita*, see Eyman, *Ernst Lubitsch*, 93–94. For the recently discovered *From Far Seville*, see Martínez Fouce, *Made in Spain*, 169–70; Labanyi and Pavlovic, *Companion to Spanish Cinema*, 371; and Bradley, *First Hol-lywood Sound Shorts*, 15. For a review of Piquer's live dance performances in Chicago, see "She's from Spain," *Chicago Daily Tribune*, 3 June 1923.

33. For this criticism, see Bernadete, "Spiritual Spain—A Synthesis."

34. On *Visions of Spain*, see Bradley, *First Hollywood Sound Shorts*, 422; and Liebman, *Vitaphone Films*, 172.

35. "Coming Soon" (film preview), *Washington Post*, 23 August 1936; Frank S. Nugent, "The Screen: With Its Technicolors Flying and Its Old, Old Plot, 'Ramona' Comes to Rest at the Criterion," *New York Times*, 7 October 1936.

36. H. Ellis, *Soul of Spain*, viii.

37. "Havelock Ellis's 'Soul of Spain,'" *New York Times*, 9 May 1908.

38. May, *End of American Innocence*.

39. Santayana, "Genteel Tradition in American Philosophy." Santayana coined the term "Genteel Tradition" in a speech delivered before the Philosophical Union of the University of California, Berkeley, on 25 August 1911.

40. Lears, "From Salvation to Self-Realization"; Lears, *No Place of Grace*, chap. 1.

41. See Hemingway's *The Sun Also Rises*, epigraph; and his *A Moveable Feast*, chap. 3.

42. Although somewhat dated, the indispensable guide to this literature remains Williams, *Spanish Background of American Literature*.

43. Lea's four-volume *A History of the Inquisition of Spain* figures prominently in my current book in progress, on Henry Charles Lea and the invention of the Inquisition.

44. Quoted in Goodman and Dawson, *William Dean Howells*, 339. In a letter of 3 April 1898 to his sister Aurelia, Howells expressed his opposition to the war with the comment, "We have no right to interfere in Cuba, and we have no cause of quarrel with Spain." See M. Howells, *Life in Letters of William D. Howells*, 2:90.

45. W. Howells, *Familiar Spanish Travels*, 2.

46. W. Howells, *Years of My Youth*, 48

47. W. Howells, *Years of My Youth*, 53–54, 83. For his thoughts on Cervantes and Irving, see W. Howells, *My Literary Passions*, 17–27. For an overview of Howells's connections with Spain and its literature, see Morby, "William Dean Howells and Spain."

48. W. Howells, *My Literary Passions*, 143.

49. W. Howells, *My Literary Passions*, 245. He also writes that "there has always been a strange affinity between the Anglo-Saxon mind and the Spanish mind; the two races brought the romantic drama to its highest perfection, and both rejected the classicistic, and the same comic strain seems to run through both people, so widely differenced by origin, by language, by religion, and by polity." W. Howells, "Editor's Study," 482.

50. W. Howells, *Life in Letters*, 2:90 (letter to his sister Aurelia, 3 April 1898), 2:95 (letter to Henry James, 31 July 1898), cited in Palacio Valdés, *Joy of Captain Ribot*, v. Although Valdés refers to Howells's *Literature*, the quotation does not ultimately appear in the *Literature and Life* volume, but that volume does include Howells's essay "Spanish Prisoners of War," in which he strongly reiterated his opposition to the Spanish-American War.

51. "Editor's Note," *Harper's*, November 1915, 957. Elsewhere, with respect to Blasco Ibáñez, he observed, "He belongs to their realistic order of the

imagination, and he is easily the first of living European novelists outside of Spain, with the advantage of superior youth, freshness of invention, and force of characterization. The Russians have ceased to be actively the masters, and there is no Frenchman, Englishman, or Scandinavian who counts with Ibanez, and of course no Italian, American, and, unspeakably, no German." Quoted in Morby, "William Dean Howells and Spain," 207.

52. Brooks, *Howells*, 241.

53. W. Howells, *William Dean Howells: Selected Letters*, 370n3 (letter to Joseph A. Howells, 14 November 1911).

54. W. Howells, *Familiar Spanish Travels*, 327.

55. W. Howells, *Familiar Spanish Travels*, 327.

56. W. Howells, *William Dean Howells: Selected Letters*, 371 (letter to Henry James, 3 November 1911). For James in San Sebastián, see H. James, *Letters of Henry James*, 66 (letter to his father, 16 September 1876).

57. Quoted in Wineapple, *Sister Brother*, 148.

58. G. Stein, *Fernhurst, QED and Other Early Writings*, 68.

59. Murad, "American Images of Spain," chap. 2.

60. G. Stein, *Everybody's Autobiography*, 71. *Everybody's Autobiography* was the sequel to Stein's first autobiography, *The Autobiography of Alice B. Toklas*.

61. G. Stein, *Gertrude Stein on Picasso*, 38.

62. G. Stein, *Autobiography of Alice B. Toklas*, 141; G. Stein, *Everybody's Autobiography*, 108.

63. G. Stein, *Letters of Gertrude Stein and Carl Van Vechten*, 1:432 (letter dated Palma, 18 April 1916). In a previous letter, Stein, commenting on an article she had read in a Spanish newspaper, also told Van Vechten about "Spain's peaceful revenge for the Spanish war. How music, dress, painting and everything in Yankilandia, as they poetically call the US, is dominated by Spain" (1:432 [letter dated Palma, 10 April 1916]).

64. G. Stein, *Autobiography of Alice B. Toklas*, 145.

65. G. Stein, *Letters of Gertrude Stein and Virgil Thompson*, 10. The opera had more than four saints. In addition to Ignatius of Loyola and Francis of Assisi, there were several Stein had invented, among them Saint Plan, Saint Settlement, Saint Plot, Saint Chavez, and so on.

66. G. Stein, *Autobiography of Alice B. Toklas*, 141. *Tender Buttons*, according to Sherwood Anderson, was greeted with "shouts of laughter" when read aloud at a New York dinner party, as well as complaints that Stein was "putting something across" with a "strange freakish performance" that

served only to draw attention to herself. Anderson, preface to *Geography and Plays*, by G. Stein, 3.

67. G. Stein, *Autobiography of Alice B. Toklas*, 145.

68. Wright, *Pagan Spain*, 14, recounting a conversation in Paris with the aging Stein 1945.

69. G. Stein, *Everybody's Autobiography*, 109.

70. Dos Passos, "America and the Pursuit of Happiness," 777–78. Notes that slightly altered versions of the same conversation appeared in several of Dos Passos's later publications.

71. Dos Passos, *Fourteenth Chronicle*, 53 (letter to Rumsey Martin, 30 October 1916).

72. Dos Passos, *Travel Books and Other Writings*, 648 (letter to Rumsey Marvin, 4 December 1916).

73. Dos Passos, *Travel Books and Other Writings*, 648 (letter to Rumsey Marvin, 4 December 1916).

74. "Against American Literature," in Dos Passos, *Travel Books*, 587–88.

75. "Against American Literature," in Dos Passos, *Travel Books*, 588.

76. "Against American Literature," in Dos Passos, *Travel Books*, 588, 589.

77. Quoted in Reinitz, "Revolt, However, Brews," 58.

78. Dos Passos, "Young Spain," 475–76.

79. Dos Passos, "Young Spain," 476.

80. Dos Passos, "Young Spain."

81. Dos Passos, "Young Spain," 487.

82. Dos Passos, *Travel Books*, 774 (letter to Rumscy Marvin, 17 March 1919).

83. Dos Passos, *Travel Books*, 780 (letter to Rumsey Marvin, 20 September 1919).

84. For more on the place of Spain in Dos Passos's career, see C. Montes, *La visión de España en la obra de John Dos Passos*. For a more recent bibliography, see Juncker, "John Dos Passos in Spain."

85. "A Gesture and a Quest," in Dos Passos, *Rosinante to the Road Again*, 20.

86. "A Gesture and a Quest," in Dos Passos, *Rosinante to the Road Again*, 17.

87. "A Gesture and a Quest," in Dos Passos, *Rosinante to the Road Again*, 14–15.

88. "A Gesture and a Quest," in Dos Passos, *Rosinante to the Road Again*, 18–19.

89. Dos Passos, *Fourteenth Chronicle*, 152.

90. Hemingway, *Letters of Ernest Hemingway*, 4:534 (letter to John Dos Passos, 26 June 1931).

91. Dos Passos, *Fourteenth Chronicle*, 430–31 (letter to Hemingway, 25 May 1933).

92. "The Republic of Honest Men," in Dos Passos, *Travel Books*, 344.

93. "Death of José Robles," in Dos Passos, *Travel Books*, 623–25. The essay appeared in the *New Republic* on 19 July 1939.

94. "The Villages Are the Heart of Spain," in Dos Passos, *Travel Books*, 486.

95. "The Villages Are the Heart of Spain," in Dos Passos, *Travel Books*, 488.

96. Brooks, *Autobiography*, 280.

97. Frank, *Memoirs of Waldo Frank*, 109.

98. Frank, *Memoirs of Waldo Frank*, 110.

99. Frank, *Memoirs of Waldo Frank*, 111.

100. Frank, *Memoirs of Waldo Frank*, 128. Ogorzaly, *Waldo Frank*, offers the best introduction to Frank's relationship with both Spain and Spanish America, but see also Faber, "Learning from the Latins."

101. Frank, *Memoirs of Waldo Frank*, 128.

102. Frank, *Memoirs of Waldo Frank*, 128.

103. Frank, *Memoirs of Waldo Frank*, 132, 133.

104. Ganivet, *Idearium español*, 1. The original reads: "venimos á hallarnos a la vejez con el espíritu virgen."

105. Frank, *Virgin Spain*, 2.

106. Frank, *Virgin Spain*, 299.

107. Brooks, *Autobiography*, 280.

108. Bernadete, "Spiritual Spain," 4; Muna Lee, "Speaking of Spain: Here Is Waldo Frank," *New York Times*, 18 April 1926.

109. Dos Passos, "Spain on a Monument," 27.

110. S. Sitwell, review of *Virgin Spain*, by Waldo Frank, 64–65.

111. Hemingway, *Letters of Ernest Hemingway*, 3:41 (letter to Isidor Schneider, 23 March 1926).

112. Hemingway, *Letters of Ernest Hemingway*, 2:394 (letter to Ezra Pound, 30 September 1925).

113. Frank, *Virgin Spain*, 237.

114. Hemingway, *Death in the Afternoon*, 52.

115. Frank, *Virgin Spain*, v.

116. See Frank, "Viva España Libre," 13.

117. Frank, "Spain in War I: The People" 272; Frank, "Spain at War: Parties and Leaders"; Frank, "Spain in War III: Meaning of Spain." 327.

118. This observation also pertains to Dearborn, *Ernest Hemingway*.

119. *New York Times*, 5 November 1925.

120. Hemingway, *Dangerous Summer*, 1.

121. Hemingway, *Letters of Ernest Hemingway*, 1:312 (letter to William B. "Bud" Smith, 20 December 1921).

122. Quoted in Eby and Cirino, *Hemingway's Spain*, 1. For Hemingway's dispatches in the *Toronto Star Weekly*, see Hemingway, *By-Line*, which includes his "At Vigo, in Spain, Is Where You Catch the Silver and Blue Tuna, the King of All Fish" (18 February 1922), "Bullfighting Is Not a Sport—It Is a Tragedy" (20 October 1923), "Pamplona in July" (27 October 1923), and others.

123. "At Vigo, in Spain," in Hemingway, *By-Line*.

124. Hemingway, *Death in the Afternoon*, 1.

125. Hemingway, *Letters of Ernest Hemingway*, 2:88 (letter to James Gamble, 12 November 1923).

126. Hemingway, "Bullfighting Is Not a Sport—It Is a Tragedy" and "World's Series of Bull Fighting a Mad, Whirling Carnival," as cited in Eby and Cirino, *Hemingway's Spain*, 1.

127. Hemingway, *Letters of Ernest Hemingway*, 2:54–55 (letter to Stein and Toklas, 11 October 1923).

128. Hemingway, *Letters of Ernest Hemingway*, 2:71–72 (letter to Clarence Hemingway, 6 November 1923), 2:87–88 (letter to James Gamble, 12 November 1923).

129. Hemingway, *Letters of Ernest Hemingway*, 2:175 (letter to Harold Jenkins, 9 November 1924).

130. Hemingway, *Letters of Ernest Hemingway*, 2:175–76 (letter to Harold Jenkins, 9 November 1924).

131. Hemingway, *Letters of Ernest Hemingway*, 2:252 (letter to William B. Smith, 17 February 1925).

132. Hemingway, *Letters of Ernest Hemingway*, 3:459 (letter to Waldo Pierce, 29 November 1927).

133. Quoted in Eby and Cirino, *Hemingway's Spain*, 4.

Conclusion

1. *De interés nacional*, caja 15592, Secretaría Particular de Alfonso XIII, AGPR.

2. The history of the "Comisión nacional encargada de fomentar en España . . . las excursiones artísticas de recreo del público extranjero" and other early Spanish efforts to promote foreign tourism is examined in González Martínez, "La comisión nacional de turismo." See also the introduction to Afinoguénova and Martí-Olivella, *Spain Is (Still) Different*.

3. Levenstein, *Seductive Journey*, 129. For earlier periods, see Stowe, *Going Abroad*.

4. Vega-Inclán, *Obra encomendado a la Comisaría de Turismo*. See also Vega-Inclán, *Turismo en España*, 6. For the origins of the CRT, see Rosa Cal, "La propaganda del turismo en España"; and Afinoguénova, "Organic Nation."

5. For his biography, see Traver Tomás, *El Marqués de la Vega-Inclán*; and Campos Setién, *La aventura del Marqués de la Vega-Inclán*.

6. See Schmidt-Nowara, "Spanish Origins of American Empire." For more background, see Schmidt-Nowara, *Conquest of History*.

7. For the European rediscovery of El Greco, see Alvarez Lopera, "Construction of a Painter"; *El Greco and Modernism*; and Storm, *Discovery of El Greco*. For this phenomenon in the United States, see Kagan, "Cult of El Greco."

8. For this "mania," see Beruete to José Pijoán, 29 July 1905, Fondo Giner de los Ríos, 14/345/3, RAH.

9. Vega-Inclán to Sorolla, quoted in Menéndez Robles, "Sorolla, Benlliure y el Segundo Marqués de Vega-Inclán," 63. For Widener's El Grecos, see chapter 5; and Kagan, "Cult of El Greco." For Vega-Inclán's sales of pictures abroad, see Kagan, "El Marqués de Vega-Inclán y el patrimonio artístico español"; and Menéndez Robles, *El Marqués de la Vega-Inclán y los orígenes turismo en España*. For the rationale underpinning the Casa-Museo, see Doménech, "Vivir el Pasado."

10. Vega-Inclán, "Turismo Hispano-Americano," 9 December 1914, caja 51/4056, AGA. For more on the financing of the CRT, see Moreno Garrido, "Turismo de élite y administración turística en la época (1911–1936)."

11. Transcript of an interview with Vega-Inclán originally published in *El Norte de Castilla*, 8 December 1912, and quoted in Menéndez Robles, *El Marqués de la Vega-Inclán y los orígenes turismo en España*, 149.

12. Archer M. Huntington to Sorolla, 7 March 1912, Correspondencia de Sorolla, CS 2982, Archivo del Museo Sorolla.

13. Vega-Inclán to Presidente Consejo de Ministros, 27 July 1911, caja 51/4056, CRT, AGA.

14. Vega-Inclán to Archer M. Huntington, 12 October 1911, Vega-Inclán Correspondence, HSA, acknowledging receipt of the check.

15. Menéndez Robles, *El Marqués de la Vega-Inclán y los orígenes turismo en España*, 149.

16. Vega-Inclán, *Guía del viaje a Santiago de Compostela*. The series, El Arte de España, awaits detailed study.

17. See Menéndez Robles, *El Marqués de la Vega-Inclán y los orígenes turismo en España*, 209–11.

18. Vega-Inclán quoted in "Turismo Hispano-Americano," *El Diario Español* (Buenos Aires), 10 August 1912. I found this clipping in Secretaría Particular de S.M. Alfonso XIII, caja 15592, expediente 1, AGPR.

19. Interview in *El Norte de Castilla*, 8 December 1912, quoted in Menéndez Robles, *El Marqués de la Vega-Inclán y los orígenes turismo en España*, 149. See also Vega-Inclán, *Índice de una memoria documentada próxima a publicarse con noticias de la CRT y de las obras que ha realizado y terminado en 1915* (1915), and his *Turismo en España* (1927).

20. Vega-Inclán to Sorolla, Madrid, 10 July 1911, quoted in Menéndez Robles, *El Marqués de la Vega-Inclán y los orígenes turismo en España*, 532n52, where he refers to "la vinculación espiritual y económica entre España y los Estados Unidos."

21. Menéndez Robles, *El Marqués de la Vega-Inclán y los orígenes turismo en España*, 532.

22. "Marques de la Vega," *New York Times*, 29 December 1912.

23. Clippings and correspondence related to these courses may be found in caja 54/8122, CRT, AGA.

24. Archer M. Huntington to Vega-Inclán, 15 July 1922, Vega-Inclán Correspondence, HSA.

25. Marqués de la Vega-Inclán, *Hospederías rurales*, 16.

26. See Vazquez, *El barrio de Santa Cruz*. More generally, see Villar Movellán, *Arquitectura del regionalismo en Sevilla*.

27. Vega-Inclán, *Hospederías rurales*, 16. Menéndez Robles, *La huella del Marqués de la Vega-Inclán en Sevilla*, provides more information about Vega-Inclán's activities in Seville but without reference to his visit to the United States.

28. Vega-Inclán, *Hospederías rurales*, 12.

29. Mendez Casal, "La arquitectura española."

30. From an article published in an 1865 issue of *Harper's Monthly* and quoted in Stowe, *Going Abroad*, 3.

31. Cited in Moreno Garrido, *Historia del turismo en España en el siglo XX*, 124. The total number of tourists visiting Spain that year was approximately 360,000, of whom no fewer than 75,000 were French and 21,000 British.

32. Frank, "Pilgrimage to Mexico," 183.

33. Quoted in Delpar, *Enormous Vogue of Things*, 55. For more on the history of tacos, tamales, and other Mexican foods in the United States, see Arellano, *Taco USA*. For the Philadelphia exhibition, see Affron, *Paint the Revolution*.

34. Quoted in Delpar, *Enormous Vogue of Things*, 58.
35. As of early 2018, the program had been suspended pending a reevaluation.
36. "Local Architect Designs Building for Government: William Templeton Johnson to Create U.S. Castle in Spain," *Coronado Eagle and Journal* (vicinity of San Diego CA), 8 March 1927. Members of the commission included Thomas E. Campbell, a former governor of Arizona, and Roderick N. Matson, an influential Wyoming judge. For more on U.S. involvement in this exposition, see *Bulletin of the Pan American Union* (1928).
37. Quoted in Krop, *California Vieja*, 121. See also Schaffer, "Civic Architect for San Diego."
38. For Templeton in Spain and a brief description of his work there, see "Local Architect Returns from a Visit to Spain: William Templeton Johnson Designer of U.S. Buildings at Seville," *San Diego Union*, 26 and 28 June 1927.

Epilogue

1. Larry Rohter, "Forget the *Maine*: Spain Is Back," *New York Times*, 15 February 1998.
2. For more on the topic, see the valuable studies gathered in Sánchez Montañes and Sánchez Suárez, *Norteamérica y España*.
3. For a mini history of tapas in the United States, see Florence Fabricant, "Putting the World on a Little Plate," *New York Times*, 16 July 1997.
4. American Academy of Arts and Sciences, *State of Languages in the U.S.* The data cited refer to 2011–12 for secondary schools and 2013 for postsecondary education.
5. "Que será, será" (Whatever will be, will be) is the title of a song composed by Jay Livingston and Ray Evans and sung by Doris Day in Alfred Hitchcock's *The Man Who Knew Too Much* (1956).

Bibliography

Archival Sources

Adams Family Papers: An Electronic Archive. Massachusetts Historical Society, Boston, Massachusetts. http://www.masshist.org/digitaladams/archive/autobio/

Archives of American Art, Smithsonian Institution, Washington DC.

Archives of the Art Institute of Chicago, Chicago, Illinois.

Curatorial Files.

Deering, Charles. Archives.

Archives of the Isabella Stewart Gardner Museum, Boston, Massachusetts.

Archivo de la Alhambra, Granada, Spain.

Archivo del Ministerio de Asuntos Extranjeros, Madrid, Spain.

Archivo del Museo del Prado, Madrid, Spain.

Archivo del Museo Sorolla, Madrid, Spain.

Archivo General de la Administración, Alcalá de Henares, Spain.

Archivo General de Palacio Real, Madrid, Spain.

Bourland, Caroline. Correspondence. Smith College Archives, Northampton, Massachusetts.

Bourne, Edward G. Papers. Beinecke Library, Yale University, New Haven, Connecticut.

Curatorial Files. Museum of Fine Arts, Boston, Massachusetts.

Deering, William. Family Papers. Deering Library, Northwestern University, Evanston, Illinois.

Fray Angélico Chavez History Library, New Mexico History Museum, Santa Fe, New Mexico.

Frick, Helen Clay. Papers. Frick Museum Archives, New York.

Hearst, W. R. Papers. Bancroft Library, University of California, Berkeley.

Havemeyer, Louisine. Papers. Metropolitan Museum of Art Archives, New York.

Hispanic Society of America, New York.

Johnson, John G. Collection. Philadelphia Museum of Art, Philadelphia, Pennsylvania.

Lummis, Charles F. Collection. Braun Research Library, Southwest Museum, Los Angeles, California.

Mizner Collection. Historical Society of Palm Beach County, West Palm Beach, Florida.

Waugh, Alex. Papers.

Morgan, Julia. Papers. Kennedy Library, California Polytechnic State University, San Luis Obispo.

Real Academia de la Historia, Madrid, Spain.

Saint-Gaudens, Augustus. Papers. Rauner Library, Dartmouth College, Hanover, New Hampshire.

Smith, George W. Papers. Architecture and Design Collection, University of California, Santa Barbara, Library.

Smith, Thomas Buckingham. Papers. New-York Historical Society, New York.

St. Augustine Historical Society, St. Augustine, Florida.

Ticknor, George. Papers. Harvard University Archives, Cambridge, Massachusetts.

Van Horne Family Fonds. Art Gallery of Ontario, Toronto.

Printed Sources

Adams, Brooks. *The Law of Civilization and Decay*. New York: Macmillan, 1895.

————. *The New Empire*. New York: Macmillan, 1903.

Adams, Henry. *History of the United States during the Administrations of Thomas Jefferson and James Madison*. 2 vols. New York: Scribner's, 1909. HathiTrust Digital Library.

————. *The Letters of Henry Adams*. Edited by J. C. Levenson, Ernest Samuels, Charles Vandersee, and Viola H. Winner. 6 vols. Cambridge MA: Belknap Press of Harvard University Press, 1982–88.

Adams, Herbert B. *The Germanic Origin of New England Towns*. Baltimore: Johns Hopkins University Press, 1882.

Adams, John. *Diary and Autobiography of John Adams*. Edited by L. H. Butterfield. Cambridge MA: Belknap Press of Harvard University Press, 1961. http://www.masshist.org/digitaladams/archive

Adams, John Quincy. *Diary of John Quincy Adams*. Edited by David G. Allen, Robert J. Taylor, Marc Friedlander, and Celeste Walker. 2 vols. Cambridge MA: Belknap Press of Harvard University Press, 1981.

————. *Memoirs of John Quincy Adams*. 12 vols. Philadelphia: J. B. Lippincott, 1874–77.

————. *Writings of John Quincy Adams*. Edited by Worthington Chauncey Ford. 7 vols. New York: Macmillan, 1913–17.

Adams, Mrs. Henry. *The Letters of Mrs. Henry Adams, 1865–1883*. Edited by Ward Thoron. Boston: Little, Brown, 1936.

Adorno, Rolena. "Washington Irving's Romantic Hispanism and Its Columbian Legacies." In Kagan, *Spain in America*, 49–105.

Affron, Matthew, ed. *Paint the Revolution: Mexican Modernism, 1910–1950*. New Haven: Yale University Press, 2016.

Afinoguénova, Eugenia. "An Organic Nation: State-Run Tourism, Regionalism, and Food in Spain, 1905–1931." *Journal of Modern History* 86, no. 4 (1914): 743–79.

Afinoguénova, Eugenia, and Jaume Martí-Olivella, eds. *Spain Is (Still) Different: Tourism and Discourse in the Spanish Identity*. Lanham MD: Lexington Books, 2008.

Alcolea Albero, Fernando. "El anticuario y marchante Francesc Guiu i Gabalda (1843–ca. 1914) y el mercado norteamericano." *Locus Amoenus* 13 (2015): 167–85.

Alcoy, Rosa. *Art fugitiu: Estudis d'art medieval desplaçat*. Barcelona: University of Barcelona, 2014.

Alexander, E. A. "Henry G. Marquand." *Harper's New Monthly Magazine* 94 (March 1897): 560–71.

Allen, Harriet Trowbridge. *Travels in Europe and the East during the Years 1858–59 and 1863–64*. New Haven CT: Tuttle, Morehouse, and Taylor, 1879.

Alvarez Lopera, José. "Coleccionismo, intervención estatal y mecenazgo en España (1900–1936): Una aproximación." *Fragmentos: Revista de Arte* 11 (1987): 33–47.

————. "The Construction of a Painter: A Century of Searching and Interpreting El Greco." In Alvarez Lopera, *El Greco*, 25–56.

————, ed. *El Greco: Identity and Transformation*. Madrid: Museo Thyssen-Bornemisza, 1999.

————. *La política de bienes culturales del gobierno republicano durante la guerra civil*. Madrid: Ministerio de Cultura, 1982.

American Academy of Arts and Sciences. *The State of Languages in the U.S.: A Statistical Report*. Cambridge MA: American AAAS, n.d.

Anderson, Sherwood. Preface to *Geography and Plays*, by Gertrude Stein. 1922. Madison: University of Wisconsin Press, 1993.

Arellano, Gustavo. *Taco USA: How Mexican Food Conquered America*. New York: Scribner, 2012.

Arnold, C. D. *The Pan-American Exposition Illustrated*. Buffalo NY: C. D. Arnold, 1901.

Arsenault, Raymond. *St. Petersburg and the Florida Dream, 1888–1950*. Norfolk VA: Donning Company, 1988.

Avezuela Calleja, Manuel. "El Tratado de la Florida: Una conexión interesante; Cádiz y la familia Meade." *Revista General de Marina* 251, no. 11 (November 2006): 609–14.

Baker, George E., ed. *The Works of William Henry Seward*. 5 vols. New York: Redfield, 1853–84.

"The Balmy South: St. Augustine in the Season (Extracts from the *Florida Reporter*)." *El Escribano* 4, no. 2 (1967): 10–11.

Bancroft, Frederic, ed. *Speeches and Political Papers of Carl Schurz*. Volume 1. New York: Putnam's, 1913.

Bancroft, George. *History of the Colonization of the United States*. Abridged by the author. 2 vols. Boston: Charles C. Little and James Brown, 1841.

——. *History of the United States*. Boston: Charles C. Little and James Brown, 1844.

——. *History of the United States of America*. Rev. ed. 6 vols. New York: D. Appleton and Co., 1888.

Bancroft, Hubert Howe. *The Book of the Fair*. Chicago and San Francisco: Bancroft Company, 1893.

——. *California Pastoral*. San Francisco: San Francisco History Co., 1888.

Bargellini, Clara. "La colección de pintura colonial de Robert Lamborn en el Philadelphia Museum of Art." In *Patrocinio, colección y circulación de las artes*, edited by Gustavo Curiel, 572–93. Mexico City: UNAM, Instituto de Investigaciones Estéticas, 1997.

Barrett, John. "All American." *North American Review* 192 (August 1910): 178–87.

——. "Get Ready for the Panama Canal." *New York Times Sunday Magazine*, February 12, 1911.

——. *The Panama Canal: What It Is, What It Means*. Washington DC: Pan American Union, 1913.

Barrick, Nolan E. *Texas Tech: The Unobserved Heritage*. Lubbock: Texas Tech Press, 1985.

Bartlett, John Russell. *A Personal Narrative of Explorations and Incidents in Texas, New Mexico, California, Sonora and Chihuahua* [. . .]. 2 vols. New York: D. Appleton and Co., 1854.

Bartosik-Vélez, Elise. *The Legacy of Christopher Columbus in the Americas*. Nashville: Vanderbilt University Press, 2014.

Bassegoda, Bonaventura, and Ignasi Domènech. "Charles Deering and the Palacio Maricel in Sitges." In Reist and Colomer, *Collecting Spanish Art*, 149–73.

Bassett, John S. "The Round Hill School." *American Antiquarian Society Proceedings* 27 (1917): 18–62.

Baticle, Jeannine. "The Galerie Espagnole of Louis-Philippe." In Tinterow and Lacambre, *Manet/Velázquez*, 175–90.

Baxley, H. Willis. *Spain: Art-Remains and Art Realities*. 2 vols. New York: D. Appleton, 1875.

Baxter, Sylvester, Henry G. Peabody, and Bertram Grosvenor Goodhue. *Spanish-Colonial Architecture in Mexico*. Boston: J. B. Millet, 1901. https://archive.org/details/spanishcoloniala01baxtuoft?q=picturesque+and+enchantingly+spectacular

Bayer, Charles M. "A Bit of Old Spain Transplanted to Tampa." *Suniland Magazine* 2–3 (December 1924): 36–37, 78. http://digital.lib.usf.edu/SFS0046532/00003/pageturner?search=bayer#page/39

Bemis, Samuel Flagg. *John Quincy Adams and the Foundation of American Foreign Policy*. New York: Knopf, 1949.

Bennahum, Ninotchka Devorah. *Antonia Mercé, "La Argentina": Flamenco and the Spanish Avant Garde*. Hanover NH: published for Wesleyan University Press by the University Press of New England, 2000.

Bennett, Shelley M. *The Art of Wealth: The Huntingtons in the Gilded Age*. San Marino CA: Huntington Library, 2013.

Berenson, Bernard. *The Letters of Bernard Berenson and Isabella Stewart Gardner, 1887–1924*. Edited by Rollin van N. Hadley. Boston: Northeastern University Press, 1987.

Bernadete, M[aría] J[osé]. "Spiritual Spain—A Synthesis." *Hispania* 10 (February 1927): 1–21.

Bernardi, Daniel, ed. *The Birth of Whiteness: Race and the Emergence of U.S. Cinema*. New Brunswick NJ: Rutgers University Press, 1996.

———. "The Voice of Whiteness: D. W. Griffith's Biograph Films (1908–13)." In Bernardi, *Birth of Whiteness*, 103–28.

Billias, George Athan. "George Bancroft: Master Historian." *Proceedings of the American Antiquarian Society* 111, no. 1 (2004): 507–28.

University of Pennsylvania. Biographical Catalogue of the Matriculates of the College together with Lists of the College Faculty [. . .]. Philadelphia: Avil Printing, 1894.

Birk, Dorothy Daniels. *The World Comes to St. Louis: A Visit to the 1904 World's Fair*. St. Louis MO: Chalice Press, 1979.

Blackmar, Frank W. *Spanish Institutions of the Southwest*. Baltimore: Johns Hopkins University Press, 1891. Google Books.

Bloomfield, Max. *Bloomfield's Illustrated Historical Guide: Embracing an Account of the Antiquities of St. Augustine, Florida*. St. Augustine FL: Max Bloomfield, 1885.

Bodfish, W. Parker. *Through Spain on Donkey-Back*. Boston: D. Lothrop, 1883.

Bokovoy, Matthew F. *The San Diego World's Fairs and Southwestern Memory, 1880–1940*. Albuquerque: University of New Mexico Press, 2005.

Bolger Burke, Doreen. *American Paintings in the Metropolitan Museum of Art*. Volume 3, *A Catalogue of Works by Artists Born between 1846 and 1864*. New York: Metropolitan Museum of Art, 1980.

Bolton, Herbert E. "The Mission as a Frontier Institution." *American Historical Review* 23, no. 1 (1917): 42–61.

———. *The Spanish Borderlands: A Chronicle of Old Florida and the Southwest*. New Haven: Yale University Press, 1921.

———. *Spanish Exploration in the Southwest, 1542–1706*. New York: Charles Scribner's Sons, 1916.

Boone, M. Elizabeth. "Marginalizing Spain at the World's Columbian Exposition of 1893." *Nineteenth-Century Studies* 25 (2011): 1–13.

———. *Vistas de España: American Views of Art and Life in Spain, 1860–1914*. New Haven: Yale University Press, 2007.

Borrow, George H. *The Bible in Spain*. London: John Murray, 1841.

———. *The Zincali; or, An Account of the Gypsies in Spain*. London: John Murray, 1841.

Bosch, Pablo. *Informe del seño ante la comisión del congreso de diputados que ha de dar dictamen sobre el proyecto de ley remitido por el senado exigiendo determinadas guarantias para la exportación de obra de arte*. Madrid: Imprenta de Asilo de Huérfanos, 1906.

Botero, Rodrigo. *Ambivalent Embrace: America's Troubled Relations with Spain from the Revolutionary War to the Cold War*. New York: Praeger, 2000.

Bottomley, William Lawrence. *Spanish Details: Drawings, Photographs, and Text*. New York: William Helburn, 1924.

Bourne, Edward G. *Discovery, Conquest, and Early History of the Philippine Islands*. Cleveland: A. H. Clark Co., 1907.

———. *Narratives of the Career of De Soto in the Conquest of Florida*. New York: A. S. Barnes, 1904.

———. *The Spanish Colonial System*. New York: H. Holt, 1904.

Boutelle, Sara Holmes. *Julia Morgan, Architect*. New York: Abbeville, 1988.

Bouton, J. W. "Mexican Painters and Painting." *Literary World*, July 30, 1892, 262.

Bowen, Wayne H. *Spain and the American Civil War*. Columbia: University of Missouri Press, 2011.

Boyd, John Taylor, Jr. "The Florida House: Mr. Addison Mizner, the Architect, Recounts the Birth of the New Florida Architecture at Palm Beach in an Interview with John Taylor Boyd, Jr." *Arts and Decoration Magazine*, January 1930, 37–40, 80, 102.

―――. "The Spanish House." *Arts and Decoration Magazine* (January 1930): 37–102.

Braden, Susan R. *The Architecture of Leisure: The Florida Resort Hotels of Henry Flagler and Henry Plant*. Gainesville: University Press of Florida, 2002.

Bradley, Edwin M. *The First Hollywood Sound Shorts, 1926–1931*. Jefferson NC: McFarland & Co., 2005.

Bradsher, Earl Lockridge. *Mathew Carey: Editor, Author, Publisher*. New York: Columbia University Press, 1912.

Brauer, Kinley. "The Appointment of Carl Schurz as Minister to Spain." *Mid-America* 56 (April 1974): 75–84.

Brégent-Heald, Dominique. *Borderland Films: American Cinema, Mexico, and Canada during the Progressive Era*. Lincoln: University of Nebraska Press, 2015.

Brier, Bob. *Egyptomania: Our Three Thousand Year Obsession with the Land of the Pharaohs*. London: Palgrave Macmillan, 2013.

Brooks, Van Wyck. *An Autobiography*. New York: E. P. Dutton, 1965.

―――. *Howells: His Life and World*. New York: E. P. Dutton, 1959.

Brotherston, Jody G. *Arthur Byne's Diplomatic Legacy: The Architect, Author and Entrepreneur*. N.p.: Lope de Vega Press, 2014.

Brown, Enos, and Francis Chouteau Brown. "English and Spanish Precedents in American Domestic Architecture." *American Builders Review* (San Francisco), September 1906, 247.

Brown, William David. *Morris Ketchum Jesup: A Character Sketch*. New York: Scribner's, 1910.

Bryant, William Cullen. *Letters from Spain and other Countries in 1857 and 1858*. London: S. Low, 1859.

―――. *Letters of a Traveler: Second Series*. New York: D. Appleton, 1859.

―――. *The Letters of William Cullen Bryant*. Edited by William Cullen Bryant II and Thomas G. Voss. 6 vols. New York: Fordham University Press, 1975–92.

―――. "Letters of William Cullen Bryant from Florida." *Florida Historical Society Quarterly* 14, no. 4 (1931): 255–74.

Bulletin of the Pan American Union 62, nos. 1–12 (January–December 1928). https://archive.org/details/bulletinofpaname6228pana.

Burke, Edmund. *A Philosophical Enquiry into the Origin of Our Ideas of the Sublime and Beautiful.* Edited by Adam Phillips. 1756. Oxford: Oxford University Press, 1990.

Bushman, Claudia L. *America Discovers Columbus: How an Italian Explorer Became an American Hero.* Hanover NH: University Press of New England, 1992.

Bushman, Richard D. *The Refinement of America: Persons, Homes, Cities.* New York: Vintage Books, 1992.

Byron, George Gordon, Sixth Lord of. *Childe Harold's Pilgrimage.* London: John Murray, 1812.

———. *Selected Letters and Journals.* Edited by Leslie A. Marchand. Cambridge MA: Harvard University Press, 1982.

Cabeza de Vaca, Alvar Núñez. *The Narrative of Cabeza de Vaca.* Edited and translated by Rolena Adorno and Patrick Charles Pautz. Lincoln: University of Nebraska Press, 2003.

———. *Relation of Alvar Núñez Cabeza de Vaca.* Translated by [Thomas] Buckingham Smith. New York: n.p., 1871. https://archive.org/details/cu31924020420489

Cabrera, Raimundo. *Cartas a Govin: Impresiones de un viaje.* Havana: La Moderna, 1892.

Cal, Rosa. "La propaganda del turismo en España: Primeras organizaciones." *Historia y Comunicación Social* 2 (1997): 125–33.

Calderón de la Barca, Frances Erskine. *The Attaché in Madrid, or, Sketches of the Court of Isabella II.* New York: Appleton, 1856.

California World's Fair Commission. *Final Report of the California World's Fair Commission.* Sacramento: State Office, 1894. https://archive.org/details/finalreportcali01commgoog

Campos Setién, José María de. *La aventura del Marqués de la Vega-Inclán.* Madrid: Ambito, 2007.

Cano, Ignacio, and Casilda Ybarra. "Early Collecting of Bartolomé Esteban Murillo's Paintings in the United States (1800–1925)." In Reist and Colomer, *Collecting Spanish Art,* 297–323.

Carrasco González, María Guadalupe. "Richard Meade: Negocios y desventura de un estadounidense en Cádiz (1804–1820)." In *Comercio y cultura en la Edad Moderna,* edited by Juan José Iglesias Rodríguez, Rafael M.

Pérez Garcia, and Manuel Francisco Fernández Chaves. 2 vols. Seville: Comunicaciones de la XIII Reunión científica de la Fundación Española de Historia Moderna, 2015.

———. "La Presencia de Comerciantes Estadounidenses en España a finales del antiguo régimen: La actividad mercantil y los negocios de Richard Worsam Meade (1804–1808). Typescript essay. Library Company of Philadelphia, 2016.

Carrère, John M. "The Architectural Scheme." In *Art Handbook: Official Handbook of the Architecture, Sculpture, and Art Catalogue to the Pan-American Exposition*, 14–17. Buffalo: David Gray, 1901.

Carter, Susan. "Street Life in Spain." *Century Magazine* 39, no. 1 (1889): 396–404.

Castañeda, C. E. *Modern Language Instruction in American Colleges, 1779–1800*. Williamsburg VA: William and Mary College, 1925.

Castle, Charles. *La Belle Otero: The Last Great Courtesan*. London: Michael Joseph, 1981.

Castleden, Louis Decatur, comp. and ed. *Early Years of the Ponce de Leon: Clippings from an Old Scrap Book of those days Kept by the First Manager of this "Prince of Hotels."* [ca. 1894]. [St. Augustine FL?] St. Augustine Historical Society Library, 1958.

Catálogo general de la Exposición Histórico-Americana. Madrid: Tipógrafo Sucesores de Ribadeneira, 1892.

Catalogue of the Gallery of the New-York Historical Society. New York: Historical Society, 1915.

Catalogue of Oil Paintings, Drawings, and Original Sketches by the Old Masters Belonging to His Highness, Don Pedro de Borbón Duque de Dúrcal. New York: American Art Association, 1889.

A Catalogue of Paintings, Statues, Prints, etc. Exhibiting at the Pennsylvania Academy of the Fine Arts. Philadelphia, 1818.

Catalogue of the Very Valuable and Well Known Collection of Fine Oil Paintings known as the Meade Gallery [. . .] *March 15, 1853*. Philadelphia: M. Thomas & Sons, 1853.

Centennial Celebration: Santa Fe, New Mexico; July 4, 1876. Santa Fe NM: Williams & Shaw Printers, 1876.

Chadwick, French Ensor. *The Relations of the United States and Spain: Diplomacy*. 1909. New York: Scribner's, 1911.

Chaffin, Tom. *Fatal Glory: Narciso López and the First Clandestine U.S. War against Cuba*. Charlottesville: University Press of Virginia, 1996.

Champney, Elizabeth Williams. *Three Vassar Girls Abroad: Rambles of Three College Girls on a Vacation Trip through France and Spain for Amusement and Instruction*. Boston: Estees & Lauriet, 1883.

Chance, Jane, ed. *Woman Medievalists and the Academy*. Madison: University of Wisconsin Press, 2005.

Chancy, Frank W. *In Memoriam of L. Bradford Prince*. Santa Fe NM: Historical Society, 1923.

Chandler, David Leon. *Henry Flagler: The Astonishing Life and Times of the Visionary Robber Baron Who Founded Florida*. New York: Macmillan, 1986.

Charnon-Deutsch, Lou. *The Spanish Gypsy: The History of a European Obsession*. University Park: Pennsylvania State University Press, 2004.

Charter of the Metropolitan Museum of Art, State of New York, Laws of 1870.

Chateaubriand, François-René de. *Les aventures du dernier Abencerraje*. 1826. Translated by A. S. Kline as *The Last of the Abencerrajes*. 2011. Published online and accessed at Poetry in Translation, www.poetryintranslation.com.

Chávez, John R. *The Lost Land: The Chicano Image of the Southwest*. Albuquerque: University of New Mexico Press, 2003.

Chávez, Thomas E. *Spain and the Independence of the United States: An Intrinsic Gift*. Albuquerque: University of New Mexico Press, 2002.

Chibbaro, Anthony. *The Charleston Exposition*. Charleston SC: Arcadia, 2001.

Chodes, John J. *Destroying the Republic: Jabez Curry and the Re-education of the South*. New York: Algora, 2005.

Clarke, Susan L. "Franklin W. Smith, St. Augustine's Concrete Pioneer." Master's thesis, Cooperstown Graduate Program, 1990.

Clay, Henry. *Papers of Henry Clay*. Volume 2, *The Rising Statesman*. Edited by Jane F. Hopkins. Lexington: University of Kentucky Press, 1961.

————. *Speeches of Henry Clay*. Edited by Calvin Colton. 2 vols. New York: A. S. Barnes, 1857. https://catalog.hathitrust.org/Record/008989356

Clements, Robert M., Jr. "William R. Hearst's Monastery." *American Heritage*, April–May 1981, 51–59.

Cline, Howard F. "Latin American History: Development of Its Study and Teaching in the United States since 1898." In *Latin American History: Essays on Its Study and Teaching, 1898–1965*, edited by Howard Francis Cline. Austin: University of Texas Press, 1967.

Codding, Mitchell A. "Archer Milton Huntington, Champion of Spain." In Kagan, *Spain in America*, 142–70.

————. "A Legacy of Spanish Art for America: Archer M. Huntington and the Hispanic Society of America." In Tinterow and Lacambre, *Manet/Velázquez*, 307–27.

Coester, Alfred. "Francis Sales—A Forerunner." *Hispania* 19, no. 2 (1936): 283–302.

Coffman, Taylor. *Hearst as Collector: The First Fifty Years, 1872–1923*. Summerland CA: Coastal Heritage Press, 2003.

Cogswell, Joseph G., and George Bancroft. *Prospectus of a School to be established at Round Hill, Northampton, Massachusetts*. Cambridge MA: Hilliard & Metcalf, 1923.

Cohen, Warren. *East Asian Art and American Culture*. Baltimore: Johns Hopkins University Press, 1992.

Collard, Edgar Andrew. "Sir William Van Horne as an Art Collector." In *Montreal Yesterdays*, 49–61. Toronto: Longmans, 1962.

Collier, William. *At the Court of His Catholic Majesty*. Chicago: A. C. McClurg, 1912.

Coll i Mirabent, Isabel. "La pintura española en la colección de Charles Deering." In Socias and Dimitra Gkozgkou, *Nuevas contribuciones en torno al mundo del coleccionismo de arte hispánico en los siglos XIX y XX*, 68–88.

Coll Mirabent, Isabel. *Charles Deering and Ramón Casas· A Friendship in Art / Una amistad en el arte*. Translated by Jennifer Croft. Bilingual ed. Evanston IL: Northwestern University Press, 2012.

Colomer, José Luis. "Competing for Velázquez: New York Collectors after the Great Spanish Master." In Reist and Colomer, *Collecting Spanish Art*, 251–78.

"A Cook's Tourist in Spain." *Atlantic Monthly*, July 1884, 33–51.

Corning, A. Elwood. *Hamilton Fish*. New York: Lanmere Publishing, 1918. https://archive.org/details/hamiltonfish00corn

Cortada, James W. "Spain and the American Civil War: Relations at Mid-Century, 1855–1868." *Transactions of the American Philosophical Society* 70, no. 4 (1980): 1–121.

Costonis, Maureen Neddham. "The Personification of Desire: Fanny Elssler and American Audiences." *Dance Chronicle* 13, no. 1 (1990): 47–67.

Cox, Michaelene. *The Politics and Art of John L Stoddard*. Lanham MD: Lexington Books, 2014.

Cram, Ralph A. *The Cathedral of Palma de Mallorca: An Architectural Study*. Cambridge MA: Mediaeval Academy of America, 1932.

————. "Domestic Architecture in Spain." *American Architect and Architectural Review* 125 (April 23, 1924): 371–78.

————. *The Gothic Quest.* New York: Baker and Taylor, 1907.

————. *My Life in Architecture.* Boston: Little, Brown, 1936.

————. "The Renaissance in Spain." *American Architect and Architectural Review* 125 (March 26, 1924): 289–96.

————. "Spanish Gothic." *American Architect and Architectural Review* 125 (February 27, 1924): 103–10.

————. "Spanish Notes: An Introduction." *American Architect and Architectural Review* 125 (January 16, 1924): 47–54.

Cranston, Maurice W. *The Romantic Movement.* Oxford: Blackwell, 1994.

Craven, Wayne Frank. *Stanford White: Decorator in Opulence and Dealer in Antiquities.* New York: Columbia University Press, 2005.

Crawford, Margaret. *Building the Workingman's Paradise: The Design of American Company Towns.* London: Verso, 1995.

Crespo, Rafael A. "Florida's First Spanish Renaissance Revival." PhD diss., Harvard University, 1987.

Cumming, Laura. *The Vanishing Man: In Pursuit of Velázquez.* London: Chatto and Windus, 2016.

Curl, Donard W. *Mizner's Florida: American Resort Architecture.* Cambridge MA: Architectural History Foundation and MIT Press, 1987.

Curran, Kathleen. *The Invention of the American Art Museum.* Los Angeles: Getty Research Institute, 2016.

Curry, J[abez]. L[amar].M[onroe]. *Diplomatic Services of George William Erving.* Cambridge MA: John Wilson and Son, 1890.

Curti, Merle. "Young America." *American Historical Review* 32 (October 1926): 34–55.

Curtis, Charles B. *Velázquez and Murillo: A Descriptive and Historical Catalogue.* London: Sampson Low, Marston, Searle, and Rivington; New York: J. W. Bouton, 1883.

Curtis, William Eleroy. "The Columbus Monuments." *The Chautauquan: A Weekly Magazine* 16, no. 2 (1892): 138–46.

Cushing, Caleb. *Reminiscences of Spain: The Country, Its People, History, and Monuments.* 2 vols. Boston: Carter, Hendee and Company, and Allen and Ticknor, 1833. Google Books.

Cushing, Caroline W. *Letters Descriptive of Public Monuments, Scenery and Manners in France and Spain.* 2 vols. Newburyport MA: E. W. Allen, 1832.

Davis, Melvin Duane. "Collecting Hispania: Archer Huntington's Quest to Develop Hispanic Collections in the United States." PhD diss., University of Alabama, 2005.

Davis, William Watts Hart. *El Gringo; or, New Mexico and Her People*. New York: Harper and Brothers, 1855.

Day, Henry. *From the Pyrenees to the Pillar of Hercules: Observations on Spain, Its History and Its People*. New York: Putnam's, 1883.

DeAloia, Miguel. *The Lost Grand Hotels of Cleveland*. Cleveland OH: History Press, 2014.

Dearborn, Mary V. *Ernest Hemingway: A Biography*. New York: Knopf, 2017.

DeGuzmán, María. "Consolidating Anglo-American Imperial Identity around the Spanish-American War." In *Race and the Production of Modern American Nationalism*, edited by Reynolds J. Scott-Childress, 97–126. New York: Taylor & Francis, 1999.

——. *Spain's Lost Shadow: The Black-Legend, Off-Whiteness, and Anglo-American Empire*. Minneapolis: University of Minnesota Press, 2005.

DeKay, Charles. "The Madison Square Garden." *Harper's Weekly* 35 (July 18, 1891): 542.

Delgado, Sergio. *Pola Negri: Temptress of Silent Hollywood*. Jefferson NC: Macfarland, 2016.

Delpar, Helen. *The Enormous Vogue of Things Mexican: Cultural Relations between the United States and Mexico, 1920–1935*. Tuscaloosa: University of Alabama Press, 1992.

——. *Looking South: The Evolution of Latin Americanist Scholarship in the United States, 1850–1975*. Tuscaloosa: University of Alabama Press, 2008.

Depuy de Lôme, Enrique. "Spain at the World's Fair." *North American Review* 156 (March 1893): 332–37.

de Soto, Hernando. *Narrative of the Career of Hernando de Soto* [. . .]. Translated by Thomas Buckingham Smith. Washington DC, 1851.

The Diplomatic Correspondence of the American Revolution. Edited by Jared Sparks. 12 vols. Boston: N. Hale and Gray & Bowen, 1829. https://babel.hathitrust.org/cgi/pt?id=mdp.35112102839778;view=1up;seq=9

Disraeli, Benjamin. *Contarini Fleming*. London: David Bryce, 1853.

Domènech, Ignasi. "Utrillo, Deering i Maricel: La construcció d'una col.lecció." *Serra d'Or* 592 (2009): 76–80.

Doménech, Julia. "Vivir el Pasado: Imaginación mito-poética en las casas-museo de El Greco y Cervantes." *Anuario de Departamento de Historia y Teoría de Arte* 19 (2007): 179–88.

Donne, Barbara. "Carl Schurz, the Diplomat." *Wisconsin Magazine of History* 20, no. 3 (1937): 291–309.

Dos Passos, John. "America and the Pursuit of Happiness." *The Nation*, December 29, 1920, 777–78.

———. *The Fourteenth Chronicle: Letters and Diaries of John Dos Passos.* Edited by Townsend Ludington. Boston: Gambit, 1973.

———. *Rosinante to the Road Again.* New York: George H. Doran, 1922. Google Books.

———. "Spain on a Monument" (review of *Virgin Spain*, by Waldo Frank). *New Masses* 1, no. 3 (1926): 27.

———. *Travel Books and Other Writings 1916–1941.* New York: Library of America, 2003.

———. "Young Spain." *Seven Arts* 2, no. 4 (1917): 473–86.

Douglas, Marjory Stoneman. *Coral Gables: America's Finest Suburb.* Coral Gables FL: Parker Printing, 1925.

———. *Coral Gables: Miami Riviera.* Miami, 1925. http://dpanther.fiu.edu /dpService/dpPurlService/purl/fi07033031/00001

Downes, William Howe. *Spanish Ways and By-Ways.* Boston: Cupples, 1883.

Doyle, Henry Grattan. *George Ticknor.* Washington DC: n.p., 1937.

———. "Longfellow as Professor at Harvard: A Review of Carl L. Johnson's *Professor Longfellow at Harvard.*" *Hispania* 27, no. 3 (October 1944): 320–29.

———. "Spanish Studies in the US." *Bulletin of Spanish Studies* 2 (1925): 163–73. Reprinted, with revisions, in *Bulletin of the Pan American Union* 60 (March 1926): 223–34.

———. "'Tumefaction' in the Study of Spanish." *Hispania* 3, no. 3 (1920): 133–43.

Dufour de Pradt, Dominique. *Mémoires historiques sur la révolution d'Espagne.* Paris: n.p., 1816. Google Books.

Earle, Henry Edmond. "An Old-Time Collector: Reminiscences of Charles F. Lummis." *California Folklore Quarterly* 1, no. 2 (1942): 179–83.

Eby, Carl P., and Mark Cirino, eds. *Hemingway's Spain: Imagining the Spanish World.* Kent OH: Kent State University Press, 2016.

Eco, Umberto. *Travels in Hyperreality: Essays.* New York: Mariner Books, 1990.

Edmonds, Franklin Spencer. *History of the Central High School of Philadelphia.* Philadelphia: Lippincott, 1902.

E.L. "Spain, Her Ways, Her Women, and Her Wines." *American Review* 9 (March 1850): 292–300.

El Greco and Modernism. Madrid: Museo del Prado, 2014.

Eliot, Charles W. "The New Education." *Atlantic Monthly* 23 (February 1869): 203–21, and 23 (March 1869): 358–67.

Ellis, Bruce T. "Santa Fe's Tertio-Millennial Exhibition." *El Palacio* 65, no. 4 (1958): 121–36.

Ellis, Havelock. *The Soul of Spain*. Boston: Houghton Mifflin, 1908.

Engstrand, Iris H. W. "Inspired by Mexico: Architect Bertram Goodhue Introduces Spanish Colonial Architecture into Balboa Park." *Journal of San Diego History* 58 (Winter–Spring 2012): 57–70.

Engstrand, Iris H. W., and Matthew Schiff. "San Diego Invites the World: A Pictorial Essay." *Journal of San Diego History* 61, no. 2 (2015): 167–80.

Español Bouché, Luis. *Leyendas negras: Vida y obra de Julián Juderías*. Valladolid: Junta de Castilla y León, 2007.

Ettinger, Amos. *The Mission to Spain of Pierre Soulé, 1853–1855: A Study in the Cuban Diplomacy of the United States*. New Haven: Yale University Press, 1932.

Eulalia, Infanta of Spain. *Memoirs of a Spanish Princess: H.R.H. Infanta Eulalia*. Translated by Phyllis Marks Mégroz. New York: Norton, 1937.

[Everett, Alexander Hill]. "Collection of the Pictures Exhibited at the Fourth Exhibition in the Gallery of the Boston Athenaeum, Boston, 1830." *North American Review* 31 (1830): 309–37.

Everett, Edward. *Orations and Speeches on Various Occasions*. Volume 3. Boston: Little, Brown, 1859.

"Excerpts from a Florida Diary." *El Escribano* 2, no. 1 (1965): 6–10.

Eyal, Yonatan. *The Young America Movement and the Transformation of the Democratic Party, 1828–1861*. Cambridge: Cambridge University Press, 2007.

Eyman, Scott. *Ernst Lubitsch: Laughter in Paradise*. Baltimore: Johns Hopkins University Press, 2000.

Faber, Sebastian. "Learning from the Latins: Waldo Frank's Progressive Pan-Americanism." *New Centennial Review* 3, no. 1 (2003): 257–95.

Fairbanks, George R. *The Early History of Florida: An Introductory Lecture*. St. Augustine FL: St. Augustine Historical Society, 1857.

———. *The History and Antiquities of the City of St Augustine, Florida*. New York: C. B. Norton, 1858.

———. *History of Florida*. Philadelphia: J. B. Lippincott, 1871.

Fanjul, Serafín. *Buscando a Carmen*. Madrid: Siglo XXI, 2012.

Fell, Sister Marie Léonore. *The Foundations of Nativism in American Textbooks, 1783–1860*. Washington DC: Catholic University of America Press, 1941.

Fernández, James D. "'Longfellow's Law': The Place of Latin America and Spain in U.S. Hispanism, circa 1915." In Kagan, *Spain in America*, 122–41.

Fernández, James D., and Luis Argeo. *Invisible Immigrants: Spaniards in the United States (1868–1945)*. New York: Whitestoneridge Productions, 2015.

Fernández Lorenzo, Patricia. "Archer M. Huntington: Una amistad épica con Alfonso XII." Trabajo de investigación. Doctorado en Historia Contemporánea. Madrid: Universidad Complutense de Madrid, 2009.

Fernández-Montesinos, Alberto Egea, coord. *Viajeras anglosajonas por España: Una antología*. Seville: Centro de Estudios Andaluces, 2009.

Field, Henry M. *Old Spain and New Spain*. 2nd ed. New York: Charles Scribner's, 1889.

Field, Kate. *Ten Days in Spain*. Boston: James R. Osgood, 1875.

Field, Maunsell B. *Memories of Many Men and Some Women*. New York: Harper and Brothers, 1874.

Fillmore, Millard. *Millard Fillmore Papers*. Volume 1. Edited by Frank H. Severance. Buffalo NY: Buffalo Historical Society, 1907.

Fitzgerald, Francis. *America Revisited: History Schoolbooks in the Twentieth Century*. Boston: Little, Brown, 1972.

Fitz-Gerald, John D. *Importance of Spanish to the American Citizen*. Chicago: Benjamin H. Sanborn, 1918. https://babel.hathitrust.org/cgi/pt?id=ucl.$b256712;view=1up;seq=3

Fogelson, Robert. *Bourgeois Nightmares: Suburbia, 1870–1930*. New Haven: Yale University Press, 2005.

Forbes, Alexander. *California: A History of Upper and Lower California from their first discovery to the present time, comprising an account of the climate, soil, natural productions, agriculture, commerce &c*. London: Smith Elder and Co., 1837. Google Books.

Ford, Richard. *Handbook for Travellers in Spain*. London: John Murray, 1845. Facsimile ed. 3 vols. Carbondale: Southern Illinois University Press, 1966.

Foster, Kathleen A., and Cheryl Leibold. *Writing about Eakins*. Philadelphia: University of Pennsylvania Press, 1989.

Fox, Stephen. *Spanish-Mediterranean Houses in Houston*. Houston: Rice Design Alliance, 1992.

Francaviglia, Richard V. *Go East, Young Man: Imagining the American West as the Orient*. Logan: Utah State University Press, 2011.

Frank, Waldo. *Memoirs of Waldo Frank*. Edited by Alan Trachtenberg. Amherst: University of Massachusetts Press, 1973.

———. "Pilgrimage to Mexico." *New Republic* 67 (July 1, 1931): 183-84.

———. "Spain in War I: The People." *New Republic* 95 (July 13, 1938): 269–72.

———. "Spain at War II: Parties and Leaders." *New Republic* 95 (July 20, 1938): 298–301.

———. "Spain in War III: Meaning of Spain." *New Republic* 95 (July 27, 1938): 325–27.

———. *Virgin Spain: Scenes from the Spiritual Drama of a Great People*. New York: Boni & Liveright, 1926. HathiTrust Digital Library.

———. "Viva España Libre." *New Masses* 20, no. 8 (August 18, 1936): 12–13.

Fray Junipero Serra and the Mission Church of San Carlos de Carmelo. San Francisco: P. F. Dougherty, 1884.

Frazer, Susan H. *William Lawrence Bottomley*. New York: Acanthus Press, 2007.

French, Gregg M. "The Foundations of Empire Building: Spain's Legacy and the American Imperial Identity, 1776–1921." PhD diss., University of Western Ontario, 2017.

"From Gibraltar to the Bidasoa." *Frank Leslie's Family Magazine* 1, no. 3 (1856): 193–212; and 21, no. 1 (1857): 16–30.

Fryd, Vivien Green. *Art and Empire: The Politics of Ethnicity in the United States Capitol, 1815–1860*. Athens OH: U.S. Capitol Historical Society and Ohio University Press, 2001.

Furstenberg, François. *When the United States Spoke French: Five Refugees Who Shaped the Nation*. New York: Penguin, 2015.

Galenter, Mark. *A History of American Architecture: Buildings in Their Cultural Context*. Hanover NH: University Press of New England, 1999.

Gamir Sandoval, Alfonso. *Los viajeros ingleses y norteamericanos en la Granada del siglo XIX*. Granada: Universidad de Granada, 1954.

Ganivet, Ángel. *Idearium español*. 2nd ed. Madrid: Vitoriano Suárez, 1905.

García Carcel, Ricardo. *La leyenda negra: Historia y opinión*. Madrid: Alianza, 1992.

García-Montón, Maribel, and Carlos García-Romeral. "Viajeros americanos en Andalucía durante los siglos XIX y XX." *Revista Complutense de Historia de América* (Madrid) 26 (2000): 261–80.

Gautier, Théophile. *A Romantic in Spain: Théophile Gautier*. Translated by Catherine Alison Philips. New York: Interlink, 2001.

Gebhard, David. *The Creation of a New Spain in America*. Santa Barbara CA: University Art Museum, 1982.

Gebhard, Patricia, and Kathryn Masson. *The Santa Barbara County Courthouse*. McKinleyville CA: Daniel and Daniel, 2002.

Gerould, Katharine Fullerton. *The Aristocratic West*. New York: Harper and Bros., 1925.

Gerstle, Mack, and Thomas Gibson. *Architectural Details of Southern Spain: One Hundred Measured Drawings, One Hundred Thirteen Photographs.* New York: W. Helburn, 1928.

Gifra-Adroher, Pere. *Between History and Romance: Travel Writing on Spain in the Early Nineteenth-Century United States.* Madison and Teaneck NJ: Fairleigh Dickinson University Press, 2000.

————. "Caroline Cushing's Letters from Spain Reconsidered." In *Actas del XII Congreso Internacional de A.E.D.E.A.N.*, 509–13. Seville: Universidad de Sevilla, 1999.

Gill, Irving. "The Home of the Future: The New Architecture of the West; Small Homes for a Great Country." *The Craftsman* 30, no. 2 (May 1916): 140–51. Google Books.

Gilman, Daniel C. "The Jarves Collection in the Yale School of the Fine Arts." *New Englander and Yale Review* 27 (1868): 175–80.

Glassberg, David. *The Place of the Past in American Life.* Amherst: University of Massachusetts Press, 2001.

Gleeson, William. *History of the Catholic Church in California.* San Francisco: A. L. Bancroft, 1872.

Glendinning, Nigel, and Hilary Macartney, eds. *Spanish Art in Britain and Ireland, 1750–1920.* London: Tamesis, 2010.

Godard, Abbé Léon. *L'Espagne, mœurs et paysages, histoire et monuments.* Tours, France: A. Mame, 1862.

Goldenberg, Bonnie. *From Liberation to Conquest: The Visual and Popular Cultures of the Spanish American War.* Amherst: University of Massachusetts Press, 2011.

————. "Imperial Culture and National Conscience: The Role of the Press in the United States and Spain during the Crisis of 1898." *Bulletin of Hispanic Studies* 77, no. 3 (2000): 169–91.

Gomez, R. A. "Spanish Immigration in the U.S." *The Americas* 19 (July 1962): 69–77.

González, C. W. *Pinnick Kinnick Hill: An American Story.* Edited by Mark Brazaitis. With a preface by Suronda González. Morgantown: West Virginia University Press, 2003.

González Martínez, Juan Carlos. "La comisión nacional de turismo y las primeras iniciativas para el fomento de turismo: La industria de los forasteros (1905–1911)." *Estudios turísticos* 163–64 (2005): 17–30.

González Pradilla, José María. "Archer Milton Huntington y la arqueología italicense al fines del siglo XIX." *HABIS* 33 (2002): 487–99.

Goodhue, Bertram Grosvenor. Introduction to *The Minor Ecclesiastical, Domestic, and Garden Architecture of Southern Spain*, by Austin Whittlesey. New York: Architectural Book Publishing, 1917. https://archive.org/details/cu31924015349693

Goodman, Susan, and Carl Dawson. *William Dean Howells: A Writer's Life*. Berkeley: University of California Press, 2005.

Goodrich, Lloyd. *Thomas Eakins*. 2 vols. Cambridge MA: published for the National Gallery of Art by Harvard University Press, 1982.

Gould, Lewis L. *The Spanish-American War and President McKinley*. Lawrence: University Press of Kansas, 1982.

Graham, Thomas. "Flagler's Grand Hotel Alcazar." *El Escribano* 26 (1989): 1–32.

——. "Flagler's Magnificent Hotel Ponce de Leon." *Florida Historical Quarterly* 54 (July 1975).

——. "Henry Flagler's St. Augustine." *El Escribano* 40 (2003): 1–24.

——. *Mr. Flagler's St. Augustine*. Gainesville: University Press of Florida, 2014.

Graham, Thomas, and Leslee F. Keys. *Hotel Ponce de Leon: The Architecture and Decoration*. St. Augustine FL: Flagler College, 2013.

Grant, Kerry L. *The Rainbow City: Celebrating Light, Color and Architecture at the Pan-American Exposition, Buffalo 1901*. Buffalo NY: Canisius College Press, 2001.

Grant, Robert. "Notes on the Exposition." *Cosmopolitan* 31 (September 1901): 451–66.

Grant, Ulysses S. *The Papers of Ulysses S. Grant*. Edited by John Y. Simon (vols. 1–31) and John F. Marszalek (vol. 32). 32 vols. Carbondale: Southern Illinois University Press, 1967–2012.

Green, James N. *Mathew Carey: Publisher and Patriot*. Philadelphia: Library Company, 1985.

Groseclose, Barbara. *Emanuel Leutze, 1816–1868: Freedom Is the Only King*. Washington DC: Smithsonian Institution Press, 1976.

Hackel, Steven W. "Junipero Serra across the Generations." In *A Companion to California History*, edited by William Deverell and David Igler, 99–115. New York: John Wiley and Sons, 2013.

Hague, Eleanor. *Spanish American Folk Songs*. Lancaster PA: American Folklore Society, 1917.

Hale, Edward Everett. *Seven Spanish Cities and the Way to Them*. Boston: Little, Brown, 1883.

Hale, Edward Everett, and Susan Hale. *The Story of Spain*. New York: Put-
    nam's, 1886.

Hale, Susan. *Family Flight through Spain*. Boston: D. Lothrop, 1883.

Hall, John M. "Around the Study Lamp." *Bay View Magazine* 6, no. 1 (1898):
    36; 6, no. 2 (1898): 76; 6, no. 3 (1899): 125; and 6, no. 5 (1899): 206, 208.

Handlin, Lilian. *George Bancroft: The Intellectual as Democrat*. New York:
    Harper Collins, 1984.

Handschin, Charles H. *Modern Language Teaching*. Yonkers NY: World
    Book, 1940.

————. *The Teaching of Modern Languages in the United States*. Washington
    DC: U.S. Bureau of Education, 1913.

Harris, Enriqueta. "Sir William Stirling Maxwell and the History of Spanish
    Art." *Apollo* 79, no. 23 (1964): 73–77.

Harris, Neil. *Cultural Excursions*. Chicago: University of Chicago Press, 1990.

Harrison, James Albert. *Spain in Profile: A Summer among the Aloes and
    Olives*. Boston: Houghton, Osgood, 1879.

Harrison, Joseph, and Alan Hoyle, eds. *Spain's 1898 Crisis: Regeneration-
    ism, Modernism, Postcolonialism*. Manchester: University of Manchester
    Press, 2000.

Haskell, Francis. "The Benjamin Altman Bequest." *Metropolitan Museum of
    Art Journal* 3 (1970): 259–80.

————. *The Ephemeral Museum: Old Master Painting and the Rise of the Art
    Exhibition*. New Haven: Yale University Press, 2000.

Hatton, Hap. *Tropical Splendor: An Architectural History of Florida*. New York:
    Knopf, 1987.

Hauben, Paul J. "White Legend against Black: Nationalism and Enlighten-
    ment in a Spanish Context." *The Americas* 34, no. 1 (1977): 1–19.

Havemeyer, Louisine W. *Sixteen to Sixty: Memoirs of a Collector*. New York:
    privately printed for the family of Mrs. H. O. Havemeyer and the Metro-
    politan Museum of Art, 1961.

Hawthorne, Julian. "Some Novelties at the Buffalo Fair." *The Cosmopolitan* 31,
    no. 5 (September 1901): 463–92.

Hawthorne, Nathaniel. *Passages from the English Note Books*. 2 vols. Bos-
    ton: Houghton Mifflin, 1897. https://ia601406.us.archive.org/28/items
    /passagesfromthee07878gut/engn310.txt

Hay, John. *Castilian Days*. Boston: Houghton Mifflin, 1871; revised edition, 1903.

————. *Spain*. N.p.: D. Lothrop, 1881.

Hazard, Samuel, et al. *Pennsylvania Archives*. Philadelphia: J. Severns & Co., 1896.

Heany, Christopher. *Cradle of Gold: The Story of Hiram Bingham, a Real-Life Indiana Jones, and the Search for Machu Picchu*. New York: St. Martin's, 2011.

Hearst, William Randolph. *Selections from the Writings and Speeches of William Randolph Hearst*. San Francisco: privately printed, 1949.

Hemingway, Ernest. *By-Line: Ernest Hemingway; Selected Articles and Dispatches of Four Decades*. Edited by William White. 1967. New York: Scribner's, 2002. Kindle edition.

———. *The Dangerous Summer*. New York: Scribner's, 1985.

———. *Death in the Afternoon*. New York: Scribner's, 1932.

———. *Letters of Ernest Hemingway*. Volume 1, *1907–1922*. Edited by Sandra Spanier and Robert W. Trogdon. Cambridge: Cambridge University Press, 2011.

———. *Letters of Ernest Hemingway*. Volume 2, *1923–1925*. Edited by Sandra Spanier, Albert J. DeFazio III, and Robert W. Trogdon. Cambridge: Cambridge University Press, 2013.

———. *Letters of Ernest Hemingway*. Volume 3, *1926–1929*. Edited by Rena Sanderson, Sandra Spanier, and Robert W. Trogdon. Cambridge: Cambridge University Press, 2015.

———. *Letters of Ernest Hemingway*. Volume 4, *1929–1931*. Edited by Sandra Spanier and Miriam B. Mandel. Cambridge: Cambridge University Press, 2017.

———. *A Moveable Feast*. New York: Scribner's, 1964.

———. *The Sun Also Rises*. New York: Scribner's, 1926.

Hendy, Philip. *The Isabella Stewart Gardner Museum Catalogue of Exhibited Paintings and Drawings*. Boston: Marymount Press, 1931.

"Henry M. Flagler: Florida's Foremost Developer." *El Escribano* 40 (2003): 9.

Herzog, Lawrence A. *From Aztec to High Tech: Architecture and Landscape across the Mexican–United States Border*. Baltimore: Johns Hopkins University Press, 1999.

Hewett, Mark Alan, Kate Lemos, William Morrison, and Charles D. Wilson. *Carrère & Hastings, Architects*. New York: Acanthus Press, 2006.

Hipple, John W. *The Beautiful, the Sublime, and the Picturesque in Eighteenth-Century British Aesthetic Theory*. Carbondale: Southern Illinois University Press, 1957.

Hirayama, Hina. *"With Éclat": The Boston Athenaeum and the Origin of the Museum of Fine Arts, Boston*. Boston: University Press of New England, 2013.

Hischak, Thomas S. *The TPA Song Encyclopedia*. Westport CT: Greenwood Press, 2002.

Hispanic Society of America, Founded 1904. New York: Hispanic Society of America, 1909. Google Books.

Hittell, Theodore H. *History of California.* 4 vols. San Francisco: N. J. Stone, 1898.

————. *In Memoriam: Theodore Henry Hittell, Born April 5, 1830, Died February 23, 1917.* San Francisco: The Academy, 1918.

Hoffmeister, Gerhart. "Exoticism: Granada's Alhambra in European Romanticism." In *European Romanticism: Literary Cross-Currents, Modes and Models,* edited by Gerhart Hoffmeister, 113–26. Detroit: Wayne State University Press, 1990.

Hoganson, Kristin L. *Consumers' Imperium: The Global Production of American Domesticity, 1865–1920.* Chapel Hill: University of North Carolina Press, 2007.

Hollander, Gail M. *Raising Cane in the 'Glades: The Global Sugar Trade and the Transformation of Florida.* Chicago: University of Chicago Press, 2008.

Holley, Lillian Harlow. "A Creator of Castles in Spain." *Hollywood Magazine* 1, no. 11 (September 1925): 33–43.

Holliday, Kathryn E. *Leopold Eidlitz: Architecture and Idealism in the Gilded Age.* New York: Norton, 2008.

Holston, Kim R. *Movie Roadshows: A History of Reserved-Seating Limited Showings, 1911–1973.* Jefferson NC: McFarland, 2012.

Howells, Mildred, ed. *Life in Letters of William D. Howells.* 2 vols. Garden City NY: Doubleday, 1928.

Howells, William Dean. "Editor's Note." *Harper's New Monthly Magazine* 131 (November 1915): 957–65.

————. "Editor's Study." *Harper's New Monthly Magazine* 76, no. 451 (December 1887): 476–82.

————. *Familiar Spanish Travels.* New York: Harper and Bros., 1913.

————. *My Literary Passions.* New York: Harper and Bros., 1895.

————. *William Dean Howells: Selected Letters.* Volume 5, edited by William C. Fischer with Christopher K. Lohmann. Boston: Twayne, 1983.

————. *Years of My Youth.* New York: Harper and Bros., 1916.

Hughes, Elizabeth. *The California of the Padres, or, Footprints of Ancient Communism.* San Francisco: I. N. Choynski, 1875. Google Books.

Hugo, Victor. *Les orientales.* 1829. Brussels, 1882.

Hume, Martin. "The United States and Spain." *International Conciliation* 23 (October 1909): 3–9.

Hunt, Aurora. *Kirby Benedict: A Frontier Federal Judge.* Glendale CA: Arthur H. Clark and Co., 1961.

Huntington, Archer M. *A Note-Book in Northern Spain*. New York: Putnam's, 1898. Google Books.

Huntington, Archer M., et al. "Henry Grattan Doyle." *Hispania* 33, no. 1 (1950): 5–15.

Hurtado, Albert H. *Herbert Eugene Bolton: Historian of the American Borderlands*. Berkeley: University of California Press, 2012.

———. "Parkmanizing the Spanish Borderlands: Bolton, Turner and the Historians' World." *Western Historical Quarterly* 26 (Summer 1995): 149–67.

Hutchinson, Elizabeth. *The Indian Craze: Primitivism, Modernism, and Transculturation in American Art, 1890–1915*. Durham: Duke University Press, 2008.

Important Old Master Paintings: The Property of the New-York Historical Society. New York: Sotheby's, 1995.

"The Importation of Spanish Merino Sheep." *The Cultivator* (Albany NY), 2 (1845): 338.

Ingersoll, Ernest. "La Villa Real de Santa Fe." *Harper's New Monthly Magazine* 60, no. 359 (1880): 667–82.

Irving, Theodore. *The Conquest of Florida by Hernando de Soto*. Philadelphia: Carey, Lea and Blanchard, 1835.

Irving, Washington. *Alhambra*. Rev. and expanded ed. New York: G. P. Putman's Sons, 1851.

———. *The Alhambra: A Series of Tales and Sketches of the Moors and Spaniards*. Philadelphia: Lea and Carey, 1832.

———. *Journals and Notebooks*. Volume 3, *1818–1827*. Edited by Walter A. Reichart. Madison: University of Wisconsin Press, 1970.

———. *Journals and Notebooks*. Volume 4, *1826–1829*. Edited by Wayne R. Kime and Andrew B. Myers. Boston: Twayne, 1984.

———. *Letters*. Volume 2, *1823–1838*. Edited by Ralph M. Aderman, Herbert L. Kleinfield, and Jenifer S. Banks. Boston: Twayne, 1979.

———. *Letters*. Volume 3, *1839–1845*. Edited by Ralph M. Aderman, Herbert L. Kleinfield, and Jenifer S. Banks. Boston: Twayne, 1982.

Jackson, Helen Hunt. *Century of Dishonor*. New York: Harpers, 1881.

———. "Junipero Serra and His Work [parts 1 and 2]." *Century Magazine* 26 (May 1883): 3–19; and (June 1883): 199–216.

Jaksic, Ivan. *The Hispanic World and American Intellectual Life, 1820–1880*. New York: Palgrave-Macmillan, 2007.

James, George Wharton. *In and out of the Missions of California*. Boston: Little, Brown, 1905.

———. *Through Ramona's Country*. Boston: Little, Brown, 1909.

James, Henry. *The Complete Letters of Henry James*. Volume 1. Edited by
Pierre A. Walker and Greg W. Zacharias. Lincoln: University of
Nebraska Press, 2006.

————. "The Duke of Montpensier's Pictures in Boston." *Atlantic Monthly*,
November 1874, reprinted in *The Painter's Eye: Henry James Notes and
Essays on the Pictorial Arts*, edited by John L. Sweeny, 79–87. Madison:
University of Wisconsin Press, 1989.

————. *The Letters of Henry James*. Volume 2, *1875–1883*. Edited by Leon
Edel. Cambridge MA: Harvard University Press, 1975.

————. *Roderick Hudson*. London: Macmillan & Co. 1879. HathiTrust Digital Library.

Jarves, James Jackson. *The Art-Idea*. Edited by Benjamin Rowland Jr. 1864.
Cambridge MA: Harvard University Press, 1960.

————. *Art Thoughts: The Experiences and Observations of an American Amateur in Europe*. New York: Hurd and Houghton, 1871.

Jay, John. *Correspondence and Public Papers of John Jay*. Edited by Henry P.
Johnston. 4 vols. New York: Putnam's, 1893.

————. *Diplomatic Correspondence of the United States*. Washington DC: Blair
& Rives, 1837. Google Books.

Jay, John, and Sarah Livingston Jay. *Selected Letters of John Jay and Sarah Livingston Jay*. Edited by Landa M. Freeman, Louise V. North, and Janet M.
Wedge. Jefferson City MO: Macfarland, 2005.

Jefferson, Thomas. *Catalogue of the Library of Thomas Jefferson*. Compiled
with annotations by E. Millicent Sowerby. 5 vols. Washington DC: Library
of Congress, 1952–59. HathiTrust Digital Library.

————. *Papers of Thomas Jefferson*. Edited by Julian P. Boyd. Multiple vols.
Princeton: Princeton University Press, 1950–2008.

Johnson, Carl L. *Professor Longfellow at Harvard*. Eugene: University of Oregon Press, 1944.

Johnson, John G. *Catalogue of a Collection of Paintings and Some Art Objects in
the Collection of John G. Johnson*. Philadelphia, 1913–14.

Johnston, Alva. *The Legendary Mizners*. Farrar, Straus, and Young, 1953.

Johnston, W. R. "W. H. Stewart, the American Patron of Mariano Fortuny."
Gazette des Beaux-Arts 67 (March 1971): 183–87.

————. *William and Henry Walters: The Reticent Collectors*. Baltimore: Johns
Hopkins University Press in association with Walters Art Gallery, 1999.

Juderías, Julián F. *La leyenda negra y la verdad histórica*. Madrid: Revista de
Archivos, 1914.

Juncker, Clara. "John Dos Passos in Spain." *Miscelánea: A Journal of English and American Studies* 42 (2010): 91–103.

Justi, Carl. *Diego Velázquez and His Times*. Translated by A. H. Keane. London: H. Grevel, 1889.

Kagan, Richard L. "The Accidental Traveler: John Adam's [*sic*] Journey through Northern Spain, 1779–1780." *Espacio, Tiempo, Forma: Serie 4, Historia Moderna* 28 (2015): 117–32.

—————. "Blame It on Washington Irving: New York's Discovery of the Art and Architecture of Spain." In *Nueva York: 1613–1945*, edited by Edward Sullivan, 155–71. New York: New-York Historical Society and Scala, 2010.

—————. "The Cult of El Greco: 'El Grecophilitis' in Philadelphia." In *El Greco Comes to America: The Discovery of a Modern Old Master*. Madrid and New York: Centro de Estudios Europas Hispánicos, for the Frick Collection, 2018.

—————. "El Marqués de Vega-Inclán y el patrimonio artístico español: ¿Protector o expoliador?" In Socias and Gkozgkou, *Nuevas contribuciones en torno al mundo del coleccionismo de arte hispánico en los siglos XIX y XX*, 193–203.

—————. "From Noah to Moses: The Genesis of Historical Scholarship on Spain in the United States." In Kagan, *Spain in America*, 21–48.

—————. "The Invention of Junípero Serra and the 'Spanish Craze.'" In *The Worlds of Junípero Serra: Historical Contexts and Cultural Representations*, edited by Steven W. Hackel, 227–56. Oakland: University of California Press, 2018.

—————. *Marcelino Menéndez y Pelayo y el hispanismo norteamericano*. Santander: Real Sociedad Menéndez Pelayo, 2013.

—————. "Prescott's Paradigm: American Historical Writing and the Decline of Spain." *American Historical Review* 101 (April 1996): 423–46.

—————. "The Secrets of Simancas." In *Hacer historia desde Simancas: Homenaje a José Luis Rodríguez de Diego*, edited by Alberto Marcos Martín, 439–44. Valladolid: Junta de Castilla y León, 2011.

—————, ed. *Spain in America: The Origins of Hispanism in the United States*. Urbana: University of Illinois Press, 2002.

—————. "Yankees in the Prado: A Historiographical Overview." *Boletín del Museo del Prado* 25, no. 43 (2007): 32–45.

Kane, Suzanne B. "Finding Addison Mizner: His Scrapbook Testimony." Master's thesis, University of Nebraska, 2014.

Kaser, Donald. *Messrs. Carey & Lea and the Philadelphia Book Trade*. Philadelphia: University of Pennsylvania Press, 1957.

Kasl, Ronda. "An American Museum: Representing the Arts of Mexico at the Metropolitan Museum of Art." In Sullivan, *The Americas Revealed*, 78–91.

Keys, Leslee F. *Hotel Ponce de Leon: The Rise, Fall, and Rebirth of Flagler's Gilded Age Palace*. Gainesville: University Press of Florida, 2015.

Keneally, Thomas. *American Scoundrel: The Life of the Notorious Civil War General Dan Sickles*. New York: Doubleday, 2002.

Kibble, Lawrence H. "James Russell Lowell's Residence in Spain." *Hispania* 46, no. 2 (1950): 190–94.

Knapp, William I. *Grammar of the Modern Spanish Language* [. . .]. [Boston]: Ginn, Heath, & Co., 1882.

———. *Life, Writings, and Correspondence of George Borrow*. New York: Putnam's, 1899.

———. *Modern Spanish Readings* [. . .]. Boston: Ginn, Heath & Co., 1883.

Knowles, Ellen. "A Unifying Vision: Improvement, Imagination and Bernhard Hoffmann in Stockbridge (New England) and Santa Barbara (New Spain)." Master's thesis, University of Southern California, 2011. http://digitallibrary.usc.edu/cdm/ref/collection/p15799coll3/id/197183

Knowles, Valerie. *From Telegrapher to Titan: Life and Work of William Van Horne*. Toronto: University of Toronto Press, 2004.

Koerner, Gustav. *Memoirs of Gustave Koerner, 1809–1896: Life-Sketches Written at the Suggestion of His Children*. Edited by Thomas J. McCormack. Cedar Rapids IA: Torch Press, 1909.

Kolbe, Parke Rexford. *The Colleges in War Time and After*. New York: Appleton, 1919.

Kramer, Paul. *The Blood of Government: Race, Empire, the United States, and the Philippines*. Chapel Hill: University of North Carolina Press, 2006.

Kropp, Phoebe S. *California Vieja: Culture and Memory in a Modern American Place*. Berkeley: University of California Press, 2006.

Labanyi, Jo, and Tatjana Pavlovic, eds. *A Companion to Spanish Cinema*. Chichester: Wiley-Blackwell, 2013.

Lamborn, Robert H. *Mexican Paintings and Painters*. New York: privately printed for the author by Allen, Lane & Scott, 1891.

Lancaster, Clay. *The Japanese Influence in America*. New York: Walton H. Rawls, 1963.

Larson, Susan. "La gramática de la 'Hispanidad': Retórica del imperio y arquitectura historicista en los discursos públicos de J. C. Nichols." *Bulletin d'Histoire Contemporaine de l'Espagne* 53 (2018): 43–53.

Lathrop, George Parsons. *Spanish Vistas*. New York: Harper & Bros., 1883.

Latimer, Elizabeth Wormeley. *Spain in the Nineteenth Century*. Chicago: A. C. McClurg, 1897.

Lavender, David. *The Great Persuader: The Biography of Collis P. Huntington*. Niwot: University Press of Colorado, 1998.

Lazo, Rodrigo. "La Famosa Filadelfia: The Hemispheric American City." In *Hemispheric American Studies*, edited by Caroline Field Levander and Robert S. Levine, 57–75. New Brunswick NJ: Rutgers University Press, 2008.

Lea, Henry Charles. "The Decadence of Spain." *Atlantic Monthly* 82 (July 1898): 36–46.

———. *A History of the Inquisition of Spain*. 4 vols. New York: Macmillan, 1906–7.

Leach, William. *Land of Desire: Merchants, Power and the Rise of a New American Culture*. New York: Vintage, 1993.

Lears, T. J. Jackson. "From Salvation to Self-Realization: Advertising and the Therapeutic Roots of the Consumer Culture, 1880–1930." In *The Culture of Consumption: Critical Essays in American History, 1880–1980*, edited by Richard Wightman Fox and T. J. Jackson Lears, 1–38. New York: Pantheon, 1988.

———. *No Place of Grace: Anti-Modernism and the Transformation of American Culture, 1880–1920*. New York: Pantheon Books, 1981.

Leavitt, Sturgis E. "The Teaching of Spanish in the United States." *Hispania* 44, no. 4 (1961): 591–625.

Lefevre, Edwin. "Flagler and Florida." *Everybody's Magazine* 22 (February 1910): 168–88.

Lenaghan, Patrick. "The Tombs from San Francisco in Cuéllar: Sacred Images in Digital Reconstructions." *Hispanic Research Journal* 16, no. 5 (2015): 379–402.

Levenstein, Harry. *Seductive Journey: American Tourists in France from Jefferson to the Jazz Age*. Chicago: University of Chicago Press, 1998.

Levine, Lawrence W. *Highbrow/Lowbrow: The Emergence of Cultural Hierarchy in America*. Cambridge MA: Harvard University Press, 1988.

Levkoff, Mary L. "Hearst and Spain." In Reist and Colomer, *Collecting Spanish Art*, 175–202.

———. *Hearst the Collector*. New York: Harry N. Abrams and Los Angeles County Museum of Art, 2008.

Lewis, Arthur H. *La Belle Otero*. New York: Trident Press, 1967.

Liebman, Roy. *Vitaphone Films: A Catalogue of Features and Shorts*. Jefferson NC: MacFarland, 2003.

Linderman, Gerald F. *Mirror of War: American Society and the Spanish-American War*. Ann Arbor: University of Michigan Press, 1974.

Lint Sagarena, Roberto Ramón. *Aztlán and Arcadia: Race, Ethnicity, and the Creation of Place*. New York: New York University Press, 2014.

Llano, Samuel. *Whose Spain? Negotiating "Spanish Music" in Paris, 1908–1929*. Oxford: Oxford University Press, 2013.

Loe, Nancy, ed. *San Simeon Revisited: The Correspondence between Architect Julia Morgan and William Randolph Hearst*. San Luis Obispo: Library Associates of California Polytechnic State University, 1987.

Loga, Valerian von. "The Spanish Pictures of Sir William Van Horne's Collection in Montreal." *Art in America* 1 (1913): 92–104.

Long, Orie W. *Thomas Jefferson and George Ticknor: A Chapter in American Scholarship*. Williamstown MA: McClelland Press, 1933

Longfellow, Henry Wadsworth. *Letters of Henry Wadsworth Longfellow*. Edited by Andrew Hilen. 6 vols. Cambridge MA: Harvard University Press, 1966–82.

———. *Outre-Mer: Pilgrimage beyond the Sea*. 2nd ed. Boston: Ticknor & Fields, 1846.

Longstreth, Richard. "J. C. Nichols, the Country Club Plaza, and Notions of Modernity." *Harvard Architecture Review* 5 (1986): 120–35.

———. *On the Edge of the World: Four Architects in San Francisco at the Turn of the Century*. Berkeley: University of California Press, 1998.

López Piñero, José María, and Thomas F. Glick. *El megaterio de Bru y el Presidente Jefferson: Relación insospechada en los albores de la paleontología*. Valencia: Universitat de Valencia, 1993.

Lorenzo, Henry J. "Black Warrior Affair." *American Historical Review* 12, no. 2 (1907): 280–98.

"The Lost Picture." *American Phrenological Journal* 23, no. 6 (1856): 131.

Lowe, David Garard. *Stanford White's New York*. New York: Watson-Guptill, 1999.

Lowell, James Russell. *Democracy, and other Addresses*. Boston: Houghton Mifflin, 1887.

———. *Impressions of Spain*. Edited by Joseph E. Gilder. Boston: Houghton Mifflin, 1899.

———. *Letters of James Russell Lowell*. Edited by Charles Eliot Norton. 16 vols. Cambridge: Riverside Press, 1904.

Lowery, Woodbury. *Spanish Settlements within the Present Boundaries of the United States*. Volume 1, 1513–1561. New York: Putnam's, 1905.

Lozano, Rosina. *An American Language: The History of Spanish in the United States*. Los Angeles: University of California Press, 2018.

Lummis, Charles F. *Flowers of Our Lost Romance*. Boston: Houghton Mifflin, 1929.

——. *The Land of Poco Tiempo*. New York: Scribner's, 1893.

——. *Letters from the Southwest: September 20, 1885 to March 14, 1885*. Edited by James W. Byrkit. Tucson: University of Arizona Press, 1989.

——. *A New Mexico David and Other Stories & Sketches of the Southwest*. New York: Scribner's, 1891.

——. "The Spanish American Face." *Land of Sunshine* 2, no. 2 (1895): 21–23.

——. *The Spanish Pioneers*. Chicago: A. C. McClurg, 1893.

——. *The Spanish Pioneers and the California Missions*. Chicago: A. C. McClurg, 1929. New and enlarged ed. Chicago: A. C. McClurg, 1936.

——. *Spanish Songs of Old California, Collected and Translated by Charles F. Lummis*. San Francisco: Scholz, Erickson & Co., 1923.

——. *A Tramp across the Continent*. 1892. Lincoln: University of Nebraska Press, 1982.

Luquiens, Frederick Bliss. *Elementary Spanish-American Reader*. New York: Macmillan, 1917.

——. "The National Need for Spanish." *Yale Review* 4 (July 1915): 699–711.

Lynch, Arthur J. *George Rainsford Fairbanks: A Man of Many Facets*. Los Altos CA: Shambles Press, 1999.

Macartney, Hilary. "La Colección Stirling Maxwell en Pollok House, Glasgow." *Goya: Revista de Arte* 291 (2002): 345–56.

——. "Sir William Stirling Maxwell: Scholar of Spanish Art." *Espacio Tiempo y Forma*, serie VII, *Historia del Arte* 12 (1999).

Mackenzie, Alexander Slidell. *Spain Revisited*. New York: Harpers & Bros., 1836.

——. *A Year in Spain by a Young American*. Boston: Hilliard, Gray, Little & Wilkins, 1829.

Madison, James. *The Papers of James Madison Digital Edition*. Edited by J. C. A. Stagg. Charlottesville: University of Virginia Press, 2010–17. http://rotunda.upress.virginia.edu/founders/JSMN.html

"Madrid from Noon to Midnight." *Putnam's Magazine*, April 1870.

Maier Allende, José. *Epistolario de Jorge Bonsor, 1866–1930*. Madrid: Real Academia de la Historia, 1999.

Major, Howard. *The Domestic Architecture of the Early American Republic: The Greek Revival*. Philadelphia: J. B. Lippincott, 1926.

——. "A Theory Relating to Spanish and Italian Houses in Florida." *Architectural Forum* 25 (August 1926): 97–120.

Maltby, William S. *The Black Legend in England*. Durham: Duke University Press, 1971.

Mann, Janice. "Hark the Herald Angels Sing: Here's to Georgiana Goddard King (1871–1939)." In *Women Medievalists and the Academy*, edited by Jane Chance, 111–26. Madison: University of Wisconsin Press, 2005.

Manning, William Ray, ed. *Diplomatic Correspondence of the United States: Inter-American Affairs, 1831–1806*. 12 vols. Washington DC: Carnegie Endowment, 1932–39.

Marshall, Dwight C. "Professor Longfellow at Harvard." *Bulletin of Spanish Studies* 21 (1944): 227–30.

Martí, José. "Our America." *Martí, the Diplomat*. http://writing.upenn.edu/library/Marti_Jose_Our-America.html

Martin, Sidney. *Henry Flagler: Visionary of the Gilded Age*. 1949. Lake Buena Vista FL: Tailored Tours, 1998.

Martínez, Silvia, and Hector Fouce, eds. *Made in Spain: Studies in Popular Music*. New York: Routledge, 2013.

Martínez Ruiz, M. J. "Entre negocios y trapicheos: Anticuarios, marchantes, y autoridades eclesiásticas en las primeras décadas del siglo XX; El caso singular de Raimundo Ruiz." In Pérez Mulet and Immaculada Socias Batet, *La dispersión de objetos de arte fuera de España en los siglos XIX y XX*, 151–90.

———. *La enajenación del patrimonio en Castilla y León (1900–1936)*. 2 vols. Valladolid: Junta de Castilla y León, 2008.

———. "Raimundo y Luis Ruiz: Pioneros del mercado de antigüedades españolas en los EE.UU." *Berceo* 161 (2011): 49–87.

Materassi, Mario, and Maria Irene Ramalho Sousa Santos, eds. *American Columbiad: Discovering America, Inventing the United States*. Amsterdam: UV University Press, 1996.

Matthews, Nancy Mowll, ed. *Cassatt and Her Circle: Selected Letters*. New York: Abbeville, 1984.

Mauzy, Wayne. "The Tertio-Millennial Exposition." *El Palacio* 37 (1934): 185–99.

May, Henry F. *The End of American Innocence: A Study of the First Years of Our Own Time, 1912–1917*. New York: Knopf, 1959.

McCadden, Helen M. "Juan de Miralles and the American Revolution." *The Americas* 29, no. 3 (1973): 259–375.

McCorkle, Julia Norton. "Doorways That Hint of Sunny Spain." *House Beautiful* 44 (April 1921): 306–7, 338. Google Books.

McKenna, Denise M. "The City That Made the Pictures Move: Gender, Labor, and the Film Industry in Los Angeles, 1908–1917." PhD diss., New York University, 2008.

McWilliams, Carey. *North from Mexico*. Philadelphia: J. B. Lippincott, 1949.

————. *South California Country: An Island on the Land*. New York: Duell, Sloane & Pearce, 1946.

McCarthy, Charles H. *Columbus and His Predecessors*. Philadelphia: John Joseph McVey, 1912.

Mendez Casal, Antonio. "La arquitectura española en California." *La Raza: Revista de España y América* 143–44 (November–December 1930): 66–73.

Menéndez y Pelayo, Marcelino. *Epistolario de Menéndez y Pelayo y Rodríguez Marín*. Madrid: C. Bermejo, 1935.

Menéndez Robles, María Luisa. *El Marqués de la Vega-Inclán y los orígenes turismo en España*. Madrid: Ministerio de Ciencia y Tecnología, 2007.

————. *La huella del Marqués de la Vega-Inclán en Sevilla*. Seville: Arte Hispalense, 2008.

————. "Sorolla, Benlliure y el Segundo Maraués de Vega-Inclán: Interrelaciones amistosas y artísticas." In *Mariano Benlliure y Joaquín Sorolla: Centenario de un homenaje*, 56–75. Valencia: Museu de Belles Arts de Valencia, 2000.

Mérimée, Prosper. *Carmen and Other Stories*. 1846. Translated by Nicolas Jotcham. Oxford: Oxford University Press, 1988.

Merino de Cáceres, José. "Arthur Byne, un expoliador de guante blanco." In Pérez Mulet and Immaculada Socias Batet, *La dispersión de objetos de arte fuera de España en los siglos XIX y XX*, 241–72.

Merino de Cáceres, José Miguel, and María José Martínez Ruiz. *La destrucción del patrimonio artístico español: W. R. Hearst, "El gran acaparador."* Madrid: Catedra, 2012.

Metropolitan Museum of Art. *Catalogue of Paintings*. New York, 1914.

————. *Handbook of the Benjamin Altman Collection*. New York: Metropolitan Museum of Art, 1914.

Miles, Hamish. "*Adnotatiunculae Leicestrienses*: Wilkie and Washington Irving in Spain." *Scottish Historical Review* 12 (1969): 21–28.

Miralles, Xavier Andreu. *El descubrimiento de España: Mito romántico e identidad nacional*. Madrid: Taurus, 2016.

Mizner, Addison. *The Many Mizners*. New York: Sears, 1932.

Molero-Moneo, Merisa. "Retablo y frontal del convento de San Juan de Quejana, en Alava." *Locus Amoenus* 5 (2000–2001): 33–51.

Monroe, James. *The Writings of James Monroe*. Edited by Stanislaus Murray Hamilton. 7 vols. New York: Putnam's, 1903.

Montero, José Antonio. *El despertar de la gran potencia: Las relaciones entre España y los Estados Unidos, 1898–1930*. Madrid: Biblioteca Nueva, 2011.

Montes, Catalina. *La visión de España en la obra de John Dos Passos*. Salamanca: Almar, 1980.

Montes, Gregory. "Balboa Park, 1909–1911: The Rise and Fall of the Olmsted Plan." *Journal of San Diego History* 28, no. 1 (1982). https://www .sandiegohistory.org/journal/1982/january/balboapark/

Montgomery, Charles. *The Spanish Redemption: Heritage, Power and Loss on New Mexico's Upper Rio Grande*. Berkeley: University of California Press, 2002.

Montoya, Maria E. "L. Bradford Prince: The Education of a Gilded Age Politician." *New Mexico Historical Review* 66 (April 1991): 179–201.

Moors, Preston. "Pierre Soulé: Southern Expansionist and Promoter." *Journal of Southern History* 21, no. 2 (1955): 203–23.

Moran, Katherine. "Catholicism and the Making of the U.S. Pacific." *Journal of the Gilded and Progressive Era* 12, no. 4 (2013): 434–74.

———. "The Devotion of Others: Secular American Attractions to Catholicism, 1870–1930." PhD diss., Johns Hopkins University, 2009.

Morby, Edwin S. "William Dean Howells and Spain." *Hispanic Review* 14, no. 3 (1946): 187–212.

Moreno Garrido, Ana. "Turismo de élite y administración turística en la época (1911–1936)." *Estudios turísticos* 163–64 (2005): 31–54.

———. *Historia del turismo en España en el siglo XX*. Madrid: Editorial Sintesis, 2007.

Morgan, Julia. *The Julia Morgan Architectural History Project I*. Berkeley: Bancroft Library, University of California, 1976.

———. *San Simeon Revisited: The Correspondence between Julia Morgan and William Randolph Hearst*. Edited by Nancy E. Loe. San Luis Obispo: Library Associates of California Polytechnic State University, 1987.

Morley, Sylvanus Griswold. "Santa Fe Architecture." *Old Santa Fe Quarterly Magazine*, January 1915, 273–302.

Morleyana: A Collection of Writings in Memoriam of Sylvanus Griswold Morley 1883–1948. Santa Fe: School of American Research and Museum of New Mexico, 1950.

Morse, Jedidiah. *The American Universal Geography*. 3rd ed. 2 vols. Boston, 1796. http://onlinebooks.library.upenn.edu

————. *Geography Made Easy.* 5th ed. Boston, 1796.

Morton, LeDane. *The Country Club District of Kansas City.* Charleston SC: History Press, 2015.

Motley, John Lothrop. *Rise of the Dutch Republic: A History.* 3 vols. New York: Harper & Bros., 1856. HathiTrust Digital Library.

Moul, Harry, and Linda Tigges. "The Santa Fe 1912 City Plan." *New Mexico Historical Review* 71, no. 1 (1996): 135–56.

Mugridge, Ian. *The View from Xanadu: William Randolph Hearst and US Foreign Policy.* Montreal: McGill-Queen's University Press, 1995.

Murad, David. "American Images of Spain, 1905–1936: Stein, Dos Passos, Hemingway." PhD diss., Kent State University, 2013.

Murillo, Bartolomé Esteba. *Bartolomé Esteban Murillo: Paintings from American Collections.* New York: H. N. Abrams, 1902.

Murillo. Volume 1, part 10, of the Masters in Art series of illustrated monographs. Boston: Bates & Guild, 1900.

"Murillo the Artist: Extraordinary Auction-Scene." *The National Magazine: Devoted to Literature, Art and Religion* 1, no. 1 (May 1852): 79–81.

New Gallery [London]. *Exhibition of Spanish Art* [. . .]. London, 1895.

New York City. *Report of the Commissioner of Education for the Year ending in June, 1914.* New York, 1914.

New-York Historical Society. *Catalogue of the Museum and Gallery of Art of the New-York Historical Society.* New York, 1903.

Nichols, Madaline Wallis. "The History of Spanish and Portuguese Teaching in the United States." In *A Handbook on the Teaching of Spanish and Portuguese,* edited by Henry G. Doyle, 97–146. Boston: D. C. Heath and Company, 1945.

Nieto-Phillips, J. M. *The Language of Blood: The Making of Spanish-American Identity in New Mexico, 1880s–1930s.* Albuquerque: University of New Mexico Press, 2004.

————. "When Tourists Came, the Mestizos Went Away: Hispanophilia and the Racial Whitening of New Mexico, 1880s–1940s." In Schmidt-Nowara and Nieto-Phillips, *Interpreting Spanish Colonialism,* 187–212.

Nixon-Roulet, Mary F. *The Spaniard at Home.* Chicago: A. C. McClurg, 1910.

Nolan, David. *Fifty Feet in Paradise: The Booming of Florida.* New York: Harcourt Brace, 1984.

Noriega, Chon A. "Birth of the Southwest: Social Protest, Tourism and D. W. Griffith's *Ramona.*" In Bernardi, *Birth of Whiteness,* 204–26.

Nusbaum, Jesse L. "Van Morley and the Santa Fe Style." In *Morleyana,* 162–73.

Official Reports of the Territory of New Mexico for the Years 1882 and 1883. Santa Fe, 1884.

Ogorzaly, Michael A. *Waldo Frank: Prophet of Hispanic Regeneration*. Lewisburg PA: Bucknell University Press, 1994.

Oliver, Richard. *Bertram Grosvenor Goodhue*. Cambridge MA: MIT Press, 1983.

Olson, Bruce R. *That St. Louis Thing*. Volume 1, *An American Story of Roots, Rhythm, and Race*. N.p.: Lulu Publishing, 2016.

Onís, Federico de. "El Español en Los Estados Unidos." *Hispania* 3, no. 5 (1920): 265–86.

Onís, Luis de. Letter to the Secretary of State [. . .], 30 December 1815, as reproduced in *Message from the President of the United States*, 26 January 1816. Washington DC: William A. Davis, 1816.

————. *Memoir upon the negotiations between Spain and the United States, which led to the Treaty of 1819. With a statistical notice of that country* [. . .]. Translated by Tobias Watkins. Baltimore: F. Lucas Jr., 1821.

————. *Memoria sobre las negociaciones entre España y los Estados Unidos de América, que dieron motivo al tratado de 1819* [. . .] Rev. ed. [Mexico?]: C. Martín Rivera, 1826.

Orr-Cahall, Christina. *Addison Mizner: Architect of Dreams and Realities (1872– 1933)*. West Palm Beach FL: Norton Gallery and School of Art, 1977.

Palacio Valdés, Armando. *The Joy of Captain Ribot*. New York: Brentano's, 1900.

Pan-American Exposition, Buffalo, May 1 to November 1, 1901: Its Purpose and Plan. [Buffalo NY]: Courier, 1901.

Paredes, Raymund A. "The Mexican Image in American Travel Literature, 1831–1869." *New Mexico Historical Review* 52, no. 1 (1977): 5–29.

Parkman, Francis, Jr. *Pioneers of France in the New World*. Boston: Little, Brown, 1865.

Patricios, Nicholas N. "Phineas Paist and the Architecture of Coral Gables." *Tequesta* 64 (2004): 4–27.

Pearson, Robert, and Brad Pearson. *The J. C. Nichols Chronicle: The Authorized Story of the Man, His Company, and His Legacy, 1880–1984*. Lawrence: University Press of Kansas, 1994.

Pelzer, Louis. *Augustus C. Dodge: A Study in American Politics*. Iowa City: State Historical Society, 1909. Archive.org.

Perez, Louis A., Jr. *The War of 1898*. Chapel Hill: University of North Carolina Press, 1898.

Pérez Mulet, Fernando, and Immaculada Socias Batet, eds. *La dispersión de objetos de arte fuera de España en los siglos XIX y XX*. Barcelona: Universitat de Barcelona, 2011.

Perkins, Charles C. "American Art Museums." *North American Review* 111, no. 228 (July 1870): 1–29. HathiTrust Digital Library.

Perspectivas y Reflexiones sobre el Coleccionismo de Archer Milton Huntington (1870–1955). Special issue of *Cuadernos de Arte e Iconografía* 24, no. 47 (2015).

Pettigrew, James Johnston. *Notes on Spain and the Spaniards, in the Summer of 1859, with a Glance at Sardinia*. 1861. New edition with an introduction by Clyde N. Wilson. Columbia: University of South Carolina Press, 2010.

Phillips, Kate. *Helen Hunt Jackson: A Literary Life*. Berkeley: University of California Press, 2003.

Pike, Fredrick B. *Hispanismo, 1898–1936: Spanish Conservatives and Liberals and Their Relations with Spanish America*. Notre Dame IN: University of Notre Dame Press, 1971.

Pisano, Ronald G. *A Leading Spirit in American Art: William Merritt Chase, 1849–1916*. Seattle: Henry Art Gallery, University of Washington, 1983.

Platt, Frederick. *America's Gilded Age: Its Architecture and Decoration*. New York: A. S. Barnes, 1972.

Polt, John H. R. *Gaspar Melchor de Jovellanos*. New York: Twayne, 1970.

Porter, A. Kingsley. *Romanesque Sculpture of the Pilgrimage Roads*. 2 vols. Boston: Marshall Jones, 1923.

Powell, Philip Wayne. *Tree of Hate: Propaganda and Policies Affecting United States Relations with the Hispanic World*. 2nd ed. Albuquerque: University of New Mexico Press, 2008.

Prescott, William H. *Historical Sketches of New Mexico*. New York: Leggatt Brothers, 1883.

———. *History of the Conquest of Mexico*. 3 vols. 1843. Philadelphia: Lippincott, 1905.

———. *History of the Reign of Ferdinand and Isabella*. Boston: American Stationery Co., 1837.

Prokop, Ellen. "'Here One *Feels* Existence': Isabella Stewart Gardner's Spanish Cloister." In Reist and Colomer, *Collecting Spanish Art*, 97–123.

Pubols, Louise. "Fathers of the Pueblo: Patriarchy and Power in Mexican California, 1800–1880." In Truett and Young, *Continental Crossroads*, 67–93.

Puig y Valls, Rafael. *Viaje á América 1894–95: Exposición Universal* [. . .]. Barcelona: Luis Taso, 1894.

Pullen, Clarence. "Madison Square Garden." *Harper's Weekly* 34 (September 13, 1890): 718.

Quirosa García, Victoria. "Historia de la protección de los bienes muebles culturales [. . .]." *Artigrama* 21 (2006): 697–709.

Quodbach, Esmée. "The Last of the American Versailles: The Widener Collection at Lynnewood Hall." *Simiolus: The Netherlands Quarterly for the History of Art* 29, nos. 1–2 (2002): 42–96.

Ralph, Julian. "Riviera, Our Town." *Harper's New Monthly Magazine* 86, no. 514 (1893): 489–510.

Ramsden, Herbert. *The 1898 Movement in Spain*. Manchester: University of Manchester Press, 1974.

Regenry, Dorothy. "The Stanfords and the Serra Statue: Presidio Monterrey." *Sand and Tile* 13, no. 2 (1989): 1–12.

Reinitz, Neale. "Revolt, However, Brews: An Unpublished Dos Passos Letter." *English Language Notes* 32, no. 2 (1994): 53–68.

Reist, Inge, and José Luis Colomer, eds. *Collecting Spanish Art: Spain's Golden Age and America's Gilded Age*. New York: Frick Collection in association with Centro de Estudios Europa Hispánica, Madrid, and Center for Spain in America, New York, 2012.

Remini, Robert V. *Henry Clay, Statesman for the Union*. New York: Norton, 1991.

Rennert, Hugo A. *The Life of Lope de Vega, 1562–1635*. New York: B. Blom, 1904.

————. *The Spanish Stage in the Time of Lope de Vega*. New York: Hispanic Society of America, 1909.

"Report of Dr. Sullivan." *Hispania* 9, no. 3 (1926): 202–4.

Reynolds, Charles. *A Tribute: The Architecture of the Hotel Ponce de León in Relation to the History of St. Augustine*. N.p., 1890.

Rhodes, James F. *Historical Essays*. New York: Macmillan, 1909.

Ribes, Vicente. "Nuevos datos biográficos sobre Juan de Miralles." *Revista de Historia Moderna* 16 (1997): 363–74.

Righter Robert W. "Theodore Henry Hittell." *Southern California Quarterly* 48, no. 3 (1966): 289–306.

————. "Theodore H. Hittell and Hubert H. Bancroft: Two Western Historians." *California Historical Quarterly* 50, no. 2 (1971): 101–10.

Río, Ángel del. *La misión de Don Luis de Onís en los Estados Unidos (1809–1819)*. Barcelona: Editorial Novagrafik, 1981.

Rishel, Joseph. "The Philadelphia Story." In Sullivan, *The Americas Revealed*, 56–65.

Ritch, William G. *Aztlan: The History, Resources and Attractions of New Mexico*. 6th ed. Boston: D. Lothrop, 1865.

———. *Inaugural Address: Historical Society of New Mexico*. Santa Fe: New Mexican Book and Printing, 1881.

Roberts, W. *Memorials of Christie's: A Record of Art Sales from 1766 to 1896*. London: George Bell and Sons, 1897.

Robertson, Ian. *Richard Ford, 1796–1858: Hispanophile, Connoisseur and Critic*. London: Michael Russell, 2004.

Rodríguez Thiessen, Victoria. "Byne and Stapley: Scholars, Dealers and Collectors of Spanish Decorative Arts." Master's thesis, Cooper-Hewitt National Design Museum and Parsons School of Design, 1998.

Romera-Navarro, Miguel. *El hispanismo en Norte-América*. Madrid: Renacimiento, 1917.

Roosevelt, Theodore. *The Winning of the West*. 4 vols. New York: G. P. Putnam's Sons, 1889–96.

Rose, Stella Haverland. *Santa Barbara's Spanish Renaissance & Old Spanish Days Fiesta*. Santa Barbara CA: Schauer Printing, 1974.

Rose de Viejo, Isadora. "Desde palacio madrileño de Godoy al mundo entero." In *El arte español fuera de España*, edited by Miguel Cabañas Bravo, 317–31. Madrid: CSIC, 2003.

Roth, Leland M. "Company Towns in the Western United States." In *The Company Town: Architecture and Society in the Early Industrial Age*, edited by John S. Garner, 173–206. New York: Oxford University Press, 1992.

Rubinstein-Bloch, Stella, ed. *Catalogue of the Collection of George and Florence Blumenthal*. 4 vols. Paris: Editions Albery Lévy, 1926.

Ruiz de Burton, María Amparo. *Conflicts of Interest: The Letters of María Amparo Ruiz de Burton*. Edited by Rosaura Sánchez and Beatrice Pita. Houston: Arte Público Press, 2001.

Rydell, Robert W. *All the World's a Fair: Visions of Empire at American International Expositions, 1876–1916*. Chicago: University of Chicago Press, 1987.

Saglia, Diego. *Poetic Castles in Spain: British Romanticism and Figurations of Iberia*. Amsterdam: Rodopi, 2000.

Salvio, Alfonso de. "Voltaire and Spain." *Hispania* 7, no. 2 (1924): 69–110.

Sanchez, Joseph P. *The Spanish Black Legend: Origins of Anti-Hispanic Stereotypes*. Albuquerque: National Park Service Spanish Colonial Research Center, 1990.

Sanchez, Mark G. "Anti-Spanish Sentiment in English Literary and Political Writing, 1553–1603." PhD diss., University of Leeds, 2004. http://etheses.whiterose.ac.uk/392/1/uk_bl_ethos_414874.pdf

Sánchez Mantero, Rafael. "La misión de John Jay en España (1776–1782)." *Anuario de Estudios Americanos* 24 (1967): 1389–1431.

————. "Viajeros y diplomáticos en el reinado de Fernando VII: El descubrimiento de España por los americanos." *Ayer: Revista de Historia Contemporánea* (Madrid), 41 (2001): 141–60.

Sánchez Mantero, Rafael, L. Álvarez Rey, and J. M. Macarro Vera, eds. *La imagen de España en América, 1898–1931.* Seville: CSIC, 1994.

Sánchez Montañes, Emma, and María Eugenia Sánchez Suárez, eds. *Norteamérica y España: Percepciones y relaciones históricas: Una aproximación interdisciplinar.* Madrid: Sepha, 2010.

Sánchez Padilla, Andrés. "Entre la modernidad y el absolutismo: La percepción de España en la diplomacia norteamericana (1868–1898)." *Historia y Política*, July–December 2016, 163–90.

Sánchez Sauleda, Sebastià. "Charles Deering, Miquel Utrillo i Ramon Casas: Una amistat per a una col.lecció." Màster d'Estudis Avançats en Història de l'art, University of Barcelona, 2009.

Sandos, James A. "Junípero Serra's Canonization and the Historical Record." *American Historical Review* 93, no. 5 (1988): 1253–69.

Sands, Frank. *Santa Barbara at a Glance.* Santa Barbara CA: n.p., 1895.

Santayana, George. "The Genteel Tradition in American Philosophy." In *The Genteel Tradition: Nine Essays by George Santayana*, edited by Douglas L. Wilson, 37–64. Lincoln: University of Nebraska Press, 1998.

Santori, Flaminia G. *The Melancholy of Masterpieces: Old Master Paintings in America, 1900–1914.* Milan: 5 Continents, 2003.

Santos García, María de los. *Viajeros, eruditos, y artistas: Los europeos ante la pintura española del Siglo de Oro.* Madrid: Alianza, 1991.

Santos Quer, María Angeles. "La correspondencia de Archer M. Huntington con Guillermo de Osma y Javier García de Leaniz." *Cuadernos de Arte e Iconografía* 24, no. 47 (2015): 209–93.

Saulnier, Eric Scott. "'You could there write the fates of nations': The Ideology of George Bancroft's History of the United States during the Age of Jackson." PhD diss., UCLA, 2010.

Scenes of Spain. New York: George Dearborn, 1837.

Schaeffer, Scott. "Private Collecting and the Public Good," and "A Note on the Catalogues of the Collections from the New-York Historical Society." In *Important Old Master Paintings: The Property of the New-York His-torical Society*. New York: Sotheby's, 1995.

Schafer, Joseph, ed. *Intimate Letters of Carl Schurz*. Madison: State Historical Society of Wisconsin, 1928.

Schaffer, Sarah. "A Civic Architect for San Diego: The Work of William Templeton Johnson." *Journal of San Diego History* 45, no. 3 (1999): 166–87.

Schmidt, Benjamin. *Innocence Abroad: The Dutch Imagination and the New World, 1570–1670*. Cambridge: Cambridge University Press 2001.

Schmidt-Nowara, Christopher. "The Broken Image: The Spanish Empire in the United States after 1898." In *Endless Empire: Spain's Retreat, Europe's Eclipse, America's Decline*, edited by Alfred McCoy, Josep M. Fradera, and Stephen Jacobson, 160–66. Madison: University of Wisconsin Press, 2012.

———. *The Conquest of History: Spanish Colonialism and National Histories in the Nineteenth Century*. Pittsburgh: University of Pittsburgh Press, 2006.

———. "Spanish Origins of American Empire: Hispanism, History, and Commemoration, 1898–1915." *International History Review* 30, no. 1 (2008): 32–51.

Schmidt-Nowara, and John M. Nieto-Phillips, eds. *Interpreting Spanish Colonialism: Empire, Nations, and Legends*. Albuquerque: University of New Mexico Press, 2005.

Schoonover, Thomas. *Uncle Sam's War of 1898 and the Origins of Globalization*. Lexington: University Press of Kentucky, 2003.

Scott, Annette. *Holland Mania: A Dutch Period in American Art and Culture*. New York: Overlook Press, 1998.

Scott, Samuel Parsons. *History of the Moorish Empire in Europe*. 3 vols. Philadelphia: J. B. Lippincott, 1904.

———. *Through Spain: A Narrative of Travel and Adventure in the Peninsula*. Philadelphia: Lippincott, 1886.

———. *The Visigothic Code (Forum Judicum)*. Boston: Boston Book Co., 1910.

Scott, Walter Dill. "Life of Charles Deering." *Northwestern University Alumni News*, March 1930, 5–7.

———. *Memoir of Charles Deering*. Boston: New England Historic Genealogical Society, 1927.

Seebohm Caroline. *Boca Rococo: How Addison Mizner Invented Florida's Gold Coast*. New York: Clarkson Potter, 2001.

Serafín Pichardo, Manuel. *La ciudad blanca: Crónicas de la Exposición Columbiana de Chicago*. Havana: Biblioteca El Fígaro, 1894.

"Seville's Cathedral, a History." *American Architect and Building News* 17, no. 473 (January 17, 1885): 34.

Sewall, Rufus King. *Sketches of St. Augustine with a view to its history and advantages as a resort for invalids*. New York: Putnam's, 1848.

Sexton, Randolph Williams. *Spanish Influence on American Architecture and Decoration*. New York: Brentano's, 1927.

Shand-Tucci, Douglass. *Boston Bohemia, 1881–1900: Ralph Adams Cram; Life and Architecture*. Amherst: University of Massachusetts Press, 1995.

———. *Ralph Adams Cram: An Architect's Four Quests*. Amherst: University of Massachusetts Press, 2005.

Shaw, Donald L. *Generation of 1898 in Spain*. London: E. Benn, 1974.

Shaw, Wilfred B., ed. *University of Michigan—An Encyclopedic Survey*. 7 vols. Ann Arbor: University of Michigan Press, 1941. https://quod.lib.umich .edu/u/umsurvey/

Shea, Robert. *From No Man's Land to Plaza del Lago*. Chicago: American References, 1987.

Shelton, S. M. "As a Boy He Dreamed of Castles in Spain." *Suniland* 1, no. 2 (November 1924): 46.

Simmon, Scott. *The Films of D. W. Griffith*. New York: Cambridge University Press, 1993.

Simmons, Marc. *Charles F. Lummis: Author and Adventurer*. Santa Fe NM: Sunstone Press, 2008.

Simons, Helen, and Cathryn Ann Hoyt, eds. *Hispanic Texas: A Historical Guide*. Austin: University of Texas Press, 1992.

Simpson, Marc. "Sargent, Velázquez, and the Critics." *Apollo* 148 (September 1998): 3.

Sitwell, John E. "Thomas J. Bryan—the First Art Collector and Connoisseur in New York City." *New-York Historical Society Quarterly Bulletin* 1 (January 1918): 105–13.

Sitwell, Sacherverell. Review of *Virgin Spain*, by Waldo Frank. *Dial* 82 (January 1927): 64–65.

Sizer, Theodore. "James Jackson Jarves—A Forgotten New Englander." *New England Quarterly* 6, no. 2 (June 1933): 328–52.

Smith, Francis Hopkinson. *Well-Worn Roads of Spain, Holland, and Italy travelled by a painter in search of the picturesque*. Boston: Houghton Mifflin, 1886.

Smith, Joseph. *The Spanish-American War: Conflict in the Caribbean and the Pacific, 1895–1902*. London: Longman, 1994.

Socias, Immaculada, and Dimitra Gkozgkou, eds. *Nuevas contribuciones en torno al mundo del coleccionismo de arte hispánico en los siglos XIX y XX.* Gijón: Ediciones Trea, 2013.

Socias Batet, Immaculada. "Nuevas fuentes documentales para la interpretación del levantamiento de la colección Deering de Sitges en 1921." In Socias and Gkozgkou, *Nuevas contribuciones en torno al mundo del coleccionismo de arte hispánico en los siglos XIX y XX,* 395–406.

Sorolla y la Hispanic Society. Madrid: Museo Thyssen-Bornemisza, 1998.

Soule, Winsor. *Spanish Farm Houses and Minor Public Buildings.* New York: Architectural Book Publishers, 1924. https://archive.org/stream /SpanishFarmHousesAndMinorPublicBuildings/Spanish-Farm-Houses -and-Minor-Public-Buildings_djvu.txt

Southey, Robert. *Letters Written during a Short Residence in Spain.* 2nd ed. Bristol: Biggs & Cottle, 1799.

———. *The Poetical Works, Collected by Himself.* 10 vols. London: Longman, 1837–38.

"Spaniards in the United States." *Literary Digest,* March 22, 1919, 40–41.

"Spanish Art at the New Gallery." *American Architect and Building News* 51, no. 1056 (March 21, 1896): 131–32.

"The Spanish Peninsula in Travel." *Atlantic Monthly* 52, no. 311 (September 1883): 408–11.

Spanish Sojourns: Robert Henri and the Spirit of Spain. Savannah GA: Telfair Books, 2014.

Sparks, Jared. *Life of Jean Ribault.* Boston: Charles C. Little and James Brown, 1845.

Splendid Legacy: The Havemeyer Collection. New York: Metropolitan Museum of Art, 1993.

Stagg, J. C. A. *Mr. Madison's War: Politics, Diplomacy and Warfare in the Early American Republic, 1783–1830.* Princeton: Princeton University Press, 1983.

Starr, Kevin. *Inventing the Dream: California through the Progressive Era.* New York: Oxford University Press, 1985.

Stein, Gertrude. *The Autobiography of Alice B. Toklas.* New York: Harcourt Brace, 1933. https://ebooks.adelaide.edu.au/s/stein/gertrude/toklas/index.html

———. *Everybody's Autobiography.* New York: Random House, 1937.

———. *Fernhurst, QED and Other Early Writings.* New York: Liveright, 1996.

———. *Geography and Plays.* 1922. Madison: University of Wisconsin Press, 1993.

———. *Gertrude Stein on Picasso.* New York: Norton, 1970.

————. *The Letters of Gertrude Stein and Carl Van Vechten, 1913–1946.* 2 vols. Edited by Edward Burns. New York: Columbia University Press, 2013.

————. *The Letters of Gertrude Stein and Virgil Thompson.* Edited by Susan Holbrook and Thomas Dilworth. Oxford: Oxford University Press, 2010.

Stein, Louise K. "Before the Latin Tinge: Spanish Music and the 'Spanish Idiom' in the United States, 1778–1940." In Kagan, *Spain in America*, 193–245.

Stein, Roger B. *John Ruskin and Aesthetic Thought in America, 1840–1900.* Cambridge: Cambridge University Press, 1967.

Stensvaag, James. "Clio on the Frontier: The Intellectual Evolution of the Historical Society of New Mexico, 1855–1929." *New Mexico Historical Review* 55, no. 4 (1980): 293–308.

Stevenson, R[obert] A[lan] M[owbray]. *Velasquez.* Revised and annotated by Theodore Crombie. 1895. London: G. Bell and Sons, 1962.

Stirling-Maxwell, William. *Annals of the Artists of Spain.* 3 vols. London: J. Ollivier, 1848.

Storm, Eric. *Discovery of El Greco.* Sussex: Sussex Academic Press, 2016.

Stowe, William W. *Going Abroad: European Travel in Nineteenth-Century American Culture.* Princeton: Princeton University Press, 1994.

Strahan, Edward. *The Masterpieces of the Centennial International Exhibition Illustrated.* Volume 1, *Fine Art.* Philadelphia: Gebbie & Barrie, 1876.

Stratton, Suzanne L. "Murillo in America." In *Bartolomé Esteban Murillo: Paintings from American Collections.* New York: H. N. Abrams, 1902.

————, ed. *Spain, Espagne, Spanien: Foreign Artists Discover Spain.* New York: Equitable Gallery, 1993.

Stratton-Pruitt, Suzanne L. "An Early Appreciation of Murillo." In Reist and Colomer, *Collecting Spanish Art*, 279–95.

————. "Lionel Harris, Tomás Harris, the Spanish Art Gallery (London), and North American Collections." In Pérez Mulet and Socias Batet, *La dispersión de objetos de arte fuera de España en los siglos XIX y XX*, 303–11.

Strong, George Templeton. *Diary of George Templeton Strong.* Edited by Allan Nevins and Milton P. Thomas. 4 vols. New York: Macmillan, 1952.

Stuart, Henri L. *William H. Powell's Historical Picture of the Discovery of the Mississippi by De Soto, A.D. 1541.* New York: Baker Godwin, 1853.

Sturman, Janet Lynn. *Zarzuela: Spanish Operetta, American Stage.* Urbana: University of Illinois Press, 2000.

Sullivan, Edward, ed. *The Americas Revealed: Collecting Colonial and Modern Latin American Art in the United States.* New York: Frick Collection-Penn State University Press, 2018.

Sultana, Donald. *Benjamin Disraeli in Spain, Malta and Albania*. London: Boydell and Brewer, 1976.

Sutherland, Donald. "A Viscous Thought: Henry Adams and American Character." *Biography* 12, no. 3 (1989): 227–50.

Sweeney, Robert L. *Casa del Herrero: The Romance of Spanish Colonial*. New York: Rizzoli, 2009.

Swinburne, Henry. *Travels through Spain, in the Years 1775 and 1776*. 2 vols. London: P. Elmsly, 1779.

Tafton, Scott. *Egypt Land: Race and Nineteenth-Century American Egyptomania*. Durham: Duke University Press, 2004.

Tatlock, Lynne, and Matt Erlin, eds. *German Culture in Nineteenth-Century America: Reception, Adoption, Transformation*. Rochester NY: Camden House, 2005.

Taylor, Daniel Crane. *John L. Stoddard: Traveller, Lecturer, Litterateur*. New York: P. J. Kennedy & Sons, 1935.

Temple, Alfred George. *Modern Spanish Painting*. London: L. Arnold Fairbairns, 1908.

Tesoros de la Hispanic Society of America. Madrid: Museo Nacional del Prado and Hispanic Society of America, 2017.

Tharp, Louise Hall. *Mrs. Jack: A Biography of Isabella Stewart Gardner*. New York: Congdon and Weed, 1965.

Thomas, Patrick J. *Our Centennial Memoir: Founding of the Missions, San Francisco de Assis in Its Hundredth Year* [. . .]. San Francisco: P. J. Thomas, 1877.

Thompson, Joann. "The Art and Architecture of the Pan-American Exposition, Buffalo, New York, 1901." PhD diss., Rutgers University, 1980.

Thompson, Mark. *American Character: The Curious Life of Charles Fletcher Lummis and the Rediscovery of the Southwest*. New York: Arcade Press, 2001.

Thornton, Sally Bullard. "San Diego's First Cabrillo Celebration, 1892." *Journal of San Diego History* 30, no. 3 (1984): 167–80.

Ticknor, George. *Life, Letters, and Journals of George Ticknor*. Volume 1. Edited by George Stillman Hillard. Boston: Houghton Mifflin, 1876.

————. *Syllabus of a course of lectures on the history and criticism of Spanish Literature*. Cambridge [MA]: [Harvard] University Press, 1823.

Tilton, Robert S. *Pocahontas: The Evolution of an American Narrative*. Cambridge: Cambridge University Press, 1994.

Tinterow, Gary, and Geneviève Lacambre, eds. *Manet/Velázquez: The French Taste for Spanish Painting*. New York: Metropolitan Museum of Art; New Haven: Yale University Press, 2003.

T.M. "Observations Made in a Journey through Spain by a Private Gentle-
    man." *London Magazine* 47 (1778): 249–53, 292–95.

"The Trait of the Spanish Character." *North American Review* 5 (1817): 30.

Trask, David F. *The War with Spain in 1898*. New York: Macmillan, 1981.

Traver Tomás, Vicente. *El Marqués de la Vega-Inclán*. Castellon: Fundaciones
    Vega-Inclán, 1966.

Truett, Samuel. "Epics of Greater America: Herbert Eugene Bolton's Quest
    for a Transnational American History." In Schmidt-Nowara and Nieto-
    Phillips, *Interpreting Spanish Colonialism*, 213–47.

———. *Fugitive Landscapes: The Forgotten History of the US-Mexican Border-
    lands*. New Haven: Yale University Press, 2006.

Truett, Samuel, and Elliott Young, eds. *Continental Crossroads: Remapping
    U.S.-Mexican Borderlands History*. Durham: Duke University Press: 2004.

Truettner, William H. "The Art of History: American Exploration and Dis-
    covery Scenes, 1840–1860." *American Art Journal* 14, no. 1 (1982): 4–31.

Turrell, Charles Alfred. *Spanish-American Short Stories*. Boston: Allyn and
    Bacon, 1920.

Tusell, Javier. "La política de Bellas Artes durante la II Republica." *Revista de
    Occidente* 17 (October 1982): 51–67.

Tyler, Royall. *Spain: A Study of Her Life and Arts*. New York: M. Kennerly, 1909.

Tyrell, Henry. "The Spanish Revival." *Word Magazine*, March 25, 1907.

Unamuno, Miguel de. *De patriotismo espiritual: Artículos de "La Nación" de
    Buenos Aires, 1901–1914*. Edited by Victor Ouimette. Salamanca: Edi-
    ciones Universidad, 1997.

Valis, Noel. "Women's Culture in 1893: Spanish Nationalism and the Chicago
    World's Fair." *Letras Peninsulares* 13, nos. 2–3 (2000–2001): 633–64.

Vallejo, Catherine. "Seeing 'Spain' at the 1893 Chicago World Fair." In *Spec-
    tacle and Topophilia: Reading Early Modern and Post Modern Hispanic
    Cultures*, edited by David R. Castillo and Bradley J. Nelson, 155–72.
    Nashville: Vanderbilt University Press, 2012.

Vallejo, Guadalupe. "Ranch and Mission Days in Alta California." *Century
    Magazine*, December 1890, 183–92.

Van Rensselaer, Mrs. G[riswold]. "Madison Square Garden." *Century Maga-
    zine* 47, no. 5 (March 1894): 732–47.

Van Tyne, Lindsey. "Translated Conquests: Spanish New World History in
    U.S. Literature, 1823–1854." PhD diss., Columbia University, 2015.

Van Vechten, Carl. *Music of Spain*. New York: Knopf, 1918. Google Books.

Varela-Lago, Ana María. "Conquerors, Immigrants, Exiles: The Spanish Diaspora in the United States (1848–1948)." PhD diss., University of California, San Diego, 2008.

Vaughan, Walter. *The Life and Work of Sir William Van Horne*. New York: Century Press, 1920.

Vazquez, José Andrés. *El barrio de Santa Cruz*. Madrid: n.p., 1920.

Veblen, Thorstein. *Theory of the Leisure Class*. New York: Macmillan, 1899.

Vega-Inclán, Marqués de la. *Guía del viaje a Santiago de Compostela*. Madrid: Real Academia de la Historia, 1927.

———. *Hospederías rurales: Hospederías y alojamientos populares*. Madrid, 1925.

———. *Índice de una memoria documentada próxima a publicarse con noticias de la CRT y de las obras que ha realizado y terminado en 1915*. Madrid: Comisaría Regia de Turismo, 1917.

———. *Obra encomendado a la Comisaría de Turismo*. Madrid: Comisaría Regia de Turismo, 1917.

———. *Turismo en España*. Madrid and Barcelona: Comisaría Regia del Turismo, 1927.

Velázquez de la Cadena, Mariano. *A Dictionary of the Spanish and English Language*. New York, 1855.

Verus [Luis de Onís]. *The passage of the President's Message which deals with the forcible occupation of Western Florida [. . .]*. Philadelphia, [1810?].

———. *Observations on the existing differences between the government of Spain and the United States*. Philadelphia: n.p., 1817.

Vignoles, Charles. *Observations upon the Floridas*. New York: E. Bliss and E. White, 1823.

Vilar García, Mar. *El español segunda lengua en los Estados Unidos*. Murcia: Universidad de Murcia, 2000.

Vilches, Gloria T. "El mito de Carmen en el cine de Hollywood." *Archivos de la Filmoteca* 51 (2005): 10–15.

Villalba, Louis. *The Silver Teacup: Tales of Cádiz*. N.p.: n.p., 2012.

Villar Movellán, Alberto. *Arquitectura del regionalismo en Sevilla (1900–1935)*. Seville: Diputación Provincial de Sevilla, 1979.

Vincent, Marvin Richardson. *Shadow of the Pyrenees*. New York: Scribner's, 1883.

Volk, Mary Crawford. *John Singer Sargent's "El Jaleo."* Washington DC: National Gallery of Art, 1992.

Wallis, Severn T. *Glimpses of Spain: Notes of an Unfinished Tour in 1847*. New York: Harper & Bros., 1849.

Watkins, Francis E. "'He Said It with Music': Spanish-California Folk Songs Recorded by Charles F. Lummis." *California Folklore Quarterly* 1, no. 4 (1942): 359–67.

Weber, David J. *The Spanish Frontier in North America*. New Haven: Yale University Press, 1992.

Weinberg, H. Barbara. "American Artists' Taste for Spanish Painting, 1860–1915." In Tinterow and Lacambre, *Manet/Velázquez*, 259–305.

———. "William Merritt Chase and the American Taste for Painting." *Magazine Antiques* 163, no. 4 (2003): 92–101.

Weitze, Karen. *California's Mission Revival Architecture*. Los Angeles: Hennessey & Ingalls, 1984.

Weitzenhoffer, Frances. *The Havemeyers: Impressionism Comes to America*. New York: H. N. Abrams, 1986.

Wharton, Edith. *The Letters of Edith Wharton*. Edited by R. W. B. Lewis and Nancy Lewis. New York: Scribner's, 1988.

When Spain Fascinated America. Madrid: Fundación Zuloaga, 2010.

Whitaker, Arthur P. *The Western Hemisphere Idea: Its Rise and Decline*. Ithaca: Cornell University Press, 1954.

White, Edward. *The Tastemaker: Carl Van Vechten and the Birth of Modern America*. New York: Farrar, Straus and Giroux, 2014.

White, Richard Edward. *Padre Junípero Serra and the Mission Church of San Carlos de Carmelo*. San Francisco: P. E. Dougherty & Co., printers, 1884.

White, Richard G. *Companion to the Bryan Gallery of Christian Art*. New York: Baker, Godwein & Co., 1853.

Whitman, Iris L. *Longfellow in Spain*. New York: Instituto de las Españas, 1917.

Whitman, Walt. "The Correspondence of Walt Whitman: A Third Supplement with Addenda to the Calendar of Letters Written to Whitman." Edited by Ted Genoways. *Walt Whitman Quarterly Review* 18, no. 1 (2000): 31–33.

Whittlesey, Austin. *The Minor Ecclesiastical, Domestic, and Garden Architecture of Southern Spain*. Introduction by Bertram Grosvenor Goodhue. New York: Architectural Book Publishing, 1917.

———. *Renaissance Architecture of Central and Northern Spain*. New York: Architectural Book Publishing, 1920.

Widener, P. A. B. *Pictures of the Collection of P. A. B. Widener at Lynnewood Hall*. 3 vols. Elkins Park PA: privately printed, 1916.

Wierich, Jochen. *Grand Themes: Emanuel Leutze, "Washington Crossing the Delaware," and American History Painting*. University Park: Pennsylvania State University Press, 2011.

Wilkins, Ernest Hackett. "Italian and Spanish in American Education." *Bulletin of the New England Chapter of the Modern Language Association* 9 (1919): 12–14.

Wilkins, Lawrence A. "Spanish as a Substitute for German for Training and Culture." *Hispania* 1, no. 4 (1918): 205–21.

Williams, Stanley T. *The Spanish Background of American Literature*. 2 vols. New Haven: Yale University Press, 1955.

Wills, Gary. *Henry Adams and the Making of America*. Boston: Houghton Mifflin, 2007. Kindle edition.

Wilmer, Lambert W. *The Life, Travels, and Adventures of Ferdinand de Soto, Discoverer of the Mississippi*. Philadelphia: J. T. Lloyd, 1859.

Wilson, Chris. *Myth of Santa Fe: Creating a Modern Regional Tradition*. Albuquerque: University of New Mexico Press, 1997.

Wilson, Robert E. "The Infanta at the Fair." *Journal of the Illinois State Historical Society* 59, no. 3 (1966): 252–73.

Wineapple, Brenda. *Sister Brother: Gertrude and Leo Stein*. New York: Putnam's, 1996.

Winslow, Carleton, Jr. *Architecture and Gardens of the Panama-California Exposition: A Pictorial Survey of the Aesthetic Features of the Panama Californian International Exposition*. San Francisco: Paul Elder and Company, 1916.

Wisan, Joseph. *The Cuban Crisis as Reflected in the New York Press (1895–1898)*. New York: Columbia University Press, 1934.

Wolanin, Barbara A. *Constantino Brumidi: Artist of the Capitol*. Washington DC: U.S. Government Printing Office, 1998.

Wolicki, Dale Patrick, and Rosemary Thornton. *Montgomery Ward's Mail Order Homes*. Norfolk VA: Gentle Beam Publications, 2010.

Woods Peiró, Eva. *White Gypsies: Race and Stardom in Spanish Musicals*. Minneapolis: University of Minnesota Press, 2012.

Worley, William C. *J. C. Nichols and the Shaping of Kansas City*. Columbia: University of Missouri Press, 1990.

————. *The Plaza: First and Always*. Lenexa KS: Addax Publishing, 1997.

Wright, Richard. *Pagan Spain*. London: Bodley Head, 1960.

Yela Utrilla, Juan Francisco. *España ante la Independencia de los Estados Unidos*. Madrid: Ediciones Istmo, 1988.

Yoshihara, Mari. *Embracing the East: White Women and American Orientalism*. New York: Oxford University Press, 2003

Zuloaga, Ignacio. *Correspondencia de Ignacio Zuloaga con su tío Daniel*. Edited by Mariano Gómez de Caso Estrada. Segovia: Diputación Provincial, 2002.

Index

Page numbers in italic indicate illustrations.

Abengoa (Spanish energy firm), 461–62

Adams, Brooks, 71

Adams, Clover, 30, 34

Adams, Henry, *30*; antimodernism of, 398–99; on commerce treaty, 41; history of U.S. by, 27–29; impressions of Spain, 30–32, 35, 37, 71, 115, 131, 165; on Manuel de Godoy, 237, 497n13; on Mexican art, 252; at Prado Museum, 246

Adams, Herbert Baxter, 127

Adams, John, 20, 32–34, 65, 134

Adams, John Quincy, 32–34, *43*, 48–50, 52, 57, 89, 194, 237

Africa, 136, 193, 379, 484n10

African Americans, 384, 407

Agnew's (art dealer), 267

Agroman (Spanish engineering firm), 462

Ajo AZ, 326

al-Andalus, 318, 408

Alaska, 462

Alba, Duke of, 81

Albéniz, Isaac, 376, 378, 416

Alcalá de Henares, 310, 466

Alemany, Joseph Sadoc, 120, 121

Alexander VI, Pope, 128

Alfaro Siqueiros, David, 455

Alfonso XII, King, 65, 160

Alfonso XIII, King: declaration of holiday, 443; family of, 259; history of, 163; honoring of, 75; and Huntington collection, 494n117; and Marqués de Vega-Inclán's trip to U.S., 449, 450; on Miranda patio sale, 289, 300; regent of, 165; and Spanish tourism, 441, 442; support of El Greco museum, 446; Theodore Roosevelt with, 81, 191

Algeciras, 425, 433

Alhambra: architecture of, 19, 314, 322, 347; Court of the Lions in, 141, *151*, 167; descriptions of, 138–42; as emblem of Spain, 22, 318, 362; Gertrude Stein at, 408; Harry Humphrey Moore at, 156; illustrations of, *plate 2*, 10, *149*, 153; I. S. Gardner at, 261; last Muslim ruler in, 358; namesake buildings in U.S., 344, 371; replica of, 167; restoration of, 447; Thomas Buckingham Smith at, 99; Thomas

Alhambra (*continued*)
     Hastings at, 316; tourism at, 148–
     52, 162; Washington Irving at, 8,
     140–41, 148. *See also* Moors; Mus-
     lim monuments
Allen, Harriet Trowbridge, 152, 159
Allen, Woody, 467
Almodóvar, Pedro, 467
Almorox, 416
Altamira, Rafael, 399
Altman, Benjamin, 233, 269, 450
Ameche, Don, 398
Amelia Island, 46
*American Architect and Architectural
     Review*, 308–9
American Architect and Building News,
     266, 316
American Art Association, 259, 260
American Art-Union, 98
American Association of Teachers of
     Spanish (AATS), 190–91, 194, 204
American Ethnological Society, 105
American Folklore Society, 382
American Museum of Natural His-
     tory (New York), 204
American Philosophical Society, 175
Andalucia: A. M. Huntington in, 206;
     architectural style of, 337, 452;
     artistic renderings of, 10; Augus-
     tus Saint-Gaudens in, 3; Christo-
     pher Columbus in, 163; Gertrude
     Stein in, 408; Henry Adams in,
     31; John Dos Passos in, 414; Lord
     Byron in, 137; Samuel Colman
     in, 155; Thomas Hastings in, 316;
     travel literature about, 162, 164;
     Washington Irving in, 8, 19, 22,
     140; W. R. Hearst in, 288

Andersen, Hans Christian, 246
Anderson, Sherwood, 518n66
antiques: Addison Mizner's dealings
     in, 345, 347–49; Bynes' dealings
     in, 291–95, 301; at Grand Central
     Palace, 344; Hearst collection of,
     284, 285, 288, 290, 292–94; pop-
     ularity of Spanish-style, 365–66.
     See also art
Apache Indians, 125
Arabic language, 202
Arabs, 220, 221
Aragon, 3, 211, 472n24
Aranda de Duero, 209
Araquistáin, Luis, 424, 425
Archaeological Institute of Amer-
     ica, 380
archeology, 183, 198, 213–15, 221, 253
architecture: arts and crafts style, 355;
     in Florida, 13, 310, 340–44, 350; of
     Gilded Age, 12; Gothic style, 305,
     306, 309, 318, 327–28, 332, 347,
     367, 369; of Hearst homes, 21,
     288, 290–98; of hospederías, 452;
     at HSA, 225–26, 291; of Milwaukee
     Art Museum, 467; mission style,
     24, 323–32, 337, 346, 349, 351, 357,
     369, 509n33; mixed Spanish style,
     321, 323–36, 339, 342, 344–47, 351,
     355–57, 359, 362–68; in New Mex-
     ico, 107–9, 326, 327, 355–58; plat-
     eresque style, 288, 290, 304, 305,
     307, 309, 347; popularity of Span-
     ish, 13–14, 23–25, 132, 229, 304,
     308–10, 369; Renaissance style,
     305, 306, 318, 328, 330, 331, 347;
     Spanish colonial/revival styles,
     plate 6, 13, 19, 331, 333, 335, 336,

350–52, 362, 369; of Spanish-style homes, 351–55, *353*, 360, 365–67; in St. Augustine, 90, 312–14; at U.S. expositions, 328–30, 458, *460 fig. 88, 460 fig. 89*; W. R. Hearst's interest in Spanish, 284, 288–90, 300, 302, 303

Arcos, Duke of, 75, 77, 127

Argentina, 18, 41, 192, 378, 423, 430, 448, 449

La Argentina (flamenco dancer), 371–72, 410

Arizona, 326, 327

art: American attitudes toward Spanish, 157, 158, 241, 247–61, 264–66, 268, 286, 287, 429, 444, 467; authenticity of, 263, 266, 272, 274, 498n20, 498n24; at Centennial Exposition, 64–65; collections of Spanish, 204, 213, 217–21, 229, 231–35, 269, 270, 294–95, 449–50, 494n117; export from Spain, 267, 268, 282, 284, 288–90, 292, 294, 298–301; at Grand Central Palace, 344; at HSA, 197, 223; at Ibero-American International Exposition, 459; influence of Spanish, 10, 12, 23, 244–45, 372, 416, 443, 467; Marqués de Vega-Inclán's dealings in, 197, 443–46, 449; in Mexico, 15, 252–56, 455; of Old Masters, 158, 199–200, 219, 231–38, 241, 256, 259, 260, 266, 268, 269, 273–77; study of Spanish, 463, 464; of Sunny Spain, 153–59, 164; Theodore Roosevelt on Spanish, 81–82; in U.S. capitol, 96, 130–31. *See also* antiques

Art Institute of Chicago, 270, 276, 280, 283, 494n114, 504n96

Arzak (restaurant), 466

Aspinwall, William H., 239, 498n20

Astor, John Jacob, III, 239, 246

Atchison, Topeka, and Santa Fe Railway, 327

Atlantic Monthly, 72, 87, 147, 182, 251, 402

Audubon, John James, 197

Austin, Gene, 388

Avangrid (Spanish energy firm), 461

Avery, Samuel, 221

Avery's (art dealer), 217

Ávila, 11, 412

Avilés, Pedro Menéndez de, 91, 100, 103

Ayala altarpiece, 277–80, *279*, 282, 283

Azaña, Manuel, 420

Azorín (José Martínez Ruiz), 424

Aztecs, 92

Badajoz, Spain, 424

Baedeker: *Handbook for Travellers to Spain and Portugal*, 303

Bailey, Francis, 175

Bakersfield CA, 326

Balearic Islands, 159

Baltimore, 53, 83, 236, 360, 369, 466

Banco Santander, 461

Bancroft, George, 90, 95, 98, 100, 101, 126, 173

Bancroft, Hubert Howe, 121–23, 392

Bandelier, Adolph, 17, 125

Bara, Theda, 378

Barber, Edwin Atlee, 254–56

Barça (FC Barcelona), 467

Barcelona: A. M. Huntington in, 207; architecture in, 307; art from, 280; art museums in, 282; Charles Deering in, 275; clothing company in, 461; corduroy from, *124*; Gertrude Stein in, 410; image of, 167; Olympics in, 465; Pedralbes Museum in, 282; Picasso in, 463; political unrest in, 287; steamship route to, 1; tourist agency in, 441

Bard, John, 39

Bardem, Javier, 467

Bargellini, Clara, 252

Baroja, Pío, 416, 418, 425

Barrett, John, 187

Barrientos, María, 377

Barringer, Daniel, 54

Barry, Charles, 328

Bartlett, John Russell, 105

Basque Country: altarpiece from, 277, 280; art from, 228; cuisine of, 466; Henry James in, 251; John Dos Passos in, 417; literature about, 162, 427; threat of rebellion in, 59; Waldo Frank in, 424

Basquette, Lina, 397

Baton Rouge LA, 44

Battle Creek MI, 327

Baxley, H. (Henry) Willis, 248–49

Baxter, Sylvester, 333

Bay View Association, 72–73

Beaumarchais, 143

Beckwith, J. Carroll, 157

Bécquer, Gustavo Adolfo, 210

Belgium, 60, 475n72

Bellini, Carlos, 177

Belmont family, 205

Benedict, Kirby, 105

Benton, Arthur B., 326, *327*, 337

Berenson, Bernard, 231–33, 261–63, 272

Berlin, 242, 301; Gemäldegalerie in, 199

Berlin, Irving, 384

Bermejo, Bartolomé, 263

Bernadete, M. J., 427

Bernis, Alberto, 202

Berruguete, Pedro de, 307

Beruete, Aureliano de, 273, 502n80

Biarritz, 251

Biedma, Luis Hernández de, 97

Bierstadt, Albert, 200

Bilbao, 39

Bindley, John, 341

Bingham, Hiram, III, 183, 198

Biograph studio, 388, 390

Birth of a Nation (film), 388, 389

Bismark ND, 327

Bizet, Georges, 6, 22, 146, 153, 374, 376

Black Legend: and Charles Lummis, 125, 126; in Cuba, 69, 70; definition of, 8–9; in discovery histories, 91, 98; dispelling of, 123, 131, 446; Henry Adams's agreement with, 32, 34; and Spanish art, 248; in U.S., 21, 22, 28, 78, 132, 135, 457, 462

Blackmar, Frank W., 126–27, 128

Black Warrior (ship), 59, 63

Blaetterman, George, 177

Blanton Museum of Art, 198

Blasco Ibáñez, Vicente, 14–15, 395, 404, 406, 416, 418, 517n51

Blood and Sand (film), *396*

Bloomington IL, 73

Blumenthal, George, 269, 270, *271*, 503n82

Boabdil, 358

Boca Raton FL, 344, 349–50, 360

Bode, Wilhelm von, 273

Bodfish, W. Parker, 162

Bokovoy, Matthew, 332

Boldini, Giovanni, 275

Bolívar, Simón, 454

Bolshevik Revolution, 400

Bolton, Herbert E., 128–29

Bonaparte, Joseph, 42

Bonnat, Léon, 155, 157

Bonnie Blue flag, 44

Bonsor, George Edward, 214

Boone, Daniel, 96

Boone, M. Elizabeth, 153–55

Borbón, Eulalia de, 184–86, *185*

Borbón, María Cristina de, 219

Borbón y Braganza, Pedro Alcántara
    de, Duke of Dúrcal, 259

Borrow, George, 144–46, 201–3, 212

Bosch, Pau, 272

Bosch y Barrau, Pablo, 209

Boston: American tourists from,
    246; art in, 12, 23, 158, 228, 236,
    242, 244, 250–51; *Carmen* in, 146;
    Columbus monument in, 83;
    entertainment in, 376; Marqués de
    Vega-Inclán in, 450; museum col-
    lections in, 293; *Ramona* screen-
    ing in, 390; Spanish influence
    in, 366; sympathy for Spain in,
    472n24

Boston Athenaeum, 236, 241, 244,
    250–51, 496n12

Boston Symphony Orchestra, 376

Bosworth, Hobart, 392

Bottomley, William Lawrence, 352

Bourland, Benjamin P., 488n19

Bourland, Caroline, 183

Bourne, Edward G., 128, 183, 482n60

Boussod, Valadon & Cie., 267

Bouton, J. W., 254

Bowdoin College, 179

Brégant-Heald, Dominique, 392

Brenon, Herbert, 395

British Museum, 199

Brooklyn Daily Eagle, 360, *361*

Brooklyn NY, 360

Brooks, Mel, 465

Brooks, Van Wyck, 423, 427

Brown, Arthur Page, 13, 24, *323*,
    323–25, *324*

Brown, Enos, 331

Brown, Frank Chouteau, 331

Brown University, 464

Bru de Ramón, Juan Bautista, 487n5

Brumidi, Constantino, 130–31; *The
    Burial of Hernando de Soto*, *131*

Brunetti, José Ambrosio. *See* Arcos,
    Duke of

Bryan, Thomas J., 238, 241, 497n18;
    Gallery of Christian Art of, 238, 241

Bryan, William Jennings, 341

Bryant, William Cullen, 90, 159, 242,
    246, 247

Bryn Mawr College, 223, 368–69, 408

Bryn Mawr PA, 367, *368*, 457

Buchanan, James, 54, 57, 60

Buenos Aires, 85, 374, 448, 458

Buffalo NY, 12, 24, 187, 228, 322. *See
    also* Pan-American Exposition

bullfights: Americans' attitudes
    toward, 3, 160, 407; art featur-
    ing, 246; design of arenas for,
    328; Ernest Hemingway's interest
    in, 11, 410, 418, 429, 432, 434–37,
    436, 439; in films, 395, 397;

bullfights (*continued*)

Gertrude Stein's opinion of, 410, 413; Henry James's attendance at, 251; I. S. Gardner's attendance at, 260; John Dos Passos's opinion of, 417; John Jay's opinion of, 39; literature about, 15, 404, 419, 432; at Louisiana Purchase exposition, 167; photos of, 211; tourist lectures on, 153; Waldo Frank's impression of, 427–29; W. D. Howells's attendance at, 406

Bureau of International Affairs. *See* Pan-American Union

Bureau of the American Republics, 478n1. *See also* Pan-American Union

Burgos, 3, 207, 260, 307, 345, 348; Casa de Miranda in, 288–90, 300

Burguete, 435

Burke, Edmund, 244

Burnham, Daniel H., *84*, 85

Bushman, Richard, 4

Butler, Margaret Coates, 237

Butler, Nicholas M., 194, 491n56

Byne, Arthur, *294*; background of, 290–91; death of, 293, 302; and Deering collection, 283; and Hearst collection, 291–98, 300–302; at HSA, 225–26, 291; publications by, 225, 292, 309, 329, 351

Byne, Mildred Stapley, 225–26, 290–98, 301, 302, 309, 329, 351

Byron, Lord, 137

Cabeza de Vaca, Álvar Núñez, 93–95, 98, 468, 479n20

Cabrera, Miguel de, 253

Cabrillo, Juan Rodríguez, *plate 7*, 332, 339, 510n49

Cadena, Mariano Velázquez de la, 177

Cádiz, 1, 42, 137, 176, 236–37, 259

Calatrava, Santiago, 467

Calderón de la Barca, Ángel, 54, 58

Calderón de la Barca, Frances, 499n35

Calderón de la Barca, Pedro, 137, 182, 489n25

California: Addison Mizner in, 344, 345; films set in, 389–93; furnishings in, 349; Gertrude Stein in, 409; Hearst collection in, 284, 285, 288; Huntingtons in, 203; immigrants in, 18; language education in, 173; lodging in, 452, 459; maps of, 459; mining entrepreneur in, 190; music in, 379–84; racial distinctions in, 115–16, 336, 339–40, 364, 454; Serra holiday in, 120; similarity to Spain, 408, 450; Spanish history in, 104, 115–32, 178, 186, 235–36, 290, 324–26, 478n4; Spanish influence in, 6, 9, 13, 17, 21–22, 79, 86, 132, 323–27, *327*, 331, 335–36, 351, 355, 367, 389, 390, 392, *453*, 457, 462, 509n33, 511n58; tourism in, 123, 130, 339–40; Zorro in, 19

Cambridge University, 408, 463

Camino de Santiago, 447

Campbell, Thomas E., 524n36

Camper (footwear company), 461

Cancio-Bello, Santiago, 182

Cano, Alonso, 241

Cánovas de Castillo, Antonio, 165

Capriccio espagnol (Rimsky-Korsakov), 377

Carewe, Edwin, 390

Carey, James, 176

Carey, Mathew, 176

Carey and Son, 176

Caribbean, 11, 40, 456

Carlists, 59

Carmen (Bizet), 6, 22, 146, 153, 374, 376, 378

Carmen (gypsy), 6, 22, 146, 186

Carmen (Mérimée), 145–46, 395, 419

La Carmencita (flamenco dancer), 6, 7, 204, 321, 372, 393, 419, 448

Carmichael, William, 55

Carmona, 214

Carolus-Durand, C. A. E., 157, 242

Carreño de Miranda, Juan, 259

Carrère, John M., 328–30

Carter, Susan, 158

Caruso, Enrico, 378

Casa Botín (restaurant), 437

Casals, Pablo, 377

Casa-Museo de El Greco, 191, 197, 279, 282, 349, 362, 444, *445*, 446

Casanova, Rev. Angelo D., 117, 121

Casas, Fray Bartolomé de Las, 9

Casas, Ramon, 275–77, 280, 283

Casa Yrujo, Marqués de, 176

Case, Anna, 397

Cassatt, Mary, 10, 156–57, 258, 267–68, 273

Castelar, Emilio, 147, 165

Castile, 8, 209, 210–11, 344, 362, 447

Catalonia, 159, 276, 282, 307, 349, 409, 467; Generalitat of, 468

Cather, Willa, 108

Catholic Church: American attitudes toward, 135; art of, 32–33, 249–52, 299–301; and censorship, 464; and Mexicans, 105, 106; and promotion of Fr. Serra, 116–21; propaganda against, 8–9; and Spanish government, 28, 33–34, 43; and Spanish national character, 307; in St. Augustine, 89–90. *See also* Christianity; Knights of Columbus

Ceán Bermúdez, Juan Agustín, 245

Cebrián, Juan Carlos, 190

Celma, Juan Baptista, 298

Centennial Exposition (Philadelphia), 15, 64–65

Centerport, Long Island, 359; Eagle's Nest home in, *359*

Central America, 1, 129, 187, 341, 461

Century Magazine, 118, 158, 321

Cervantes, Miguel de: influence of, 136, 137, 308, 403, 406, 407, 416, 427, 468; museum devoted to, 197, 447, 449; study of, 181, 182, 489n25. See also *Don Quixote* (Cervantes)

Cesnola, Luigi (Louis) Palma di, 253–54

Cézanne, Paul, 443

Chabrier, Emmanuel, 376–77

Chadwick, French Ensor, 35–36, 41, 74–75

Champney, "Lizzie" Williams, 160

Chaplin, Charlie, 378

Chapman, John, 96

Charles III, King, 37–39

Charles IV, King, 27, 28, 44

Charles V, King, 163, 448

Charleston SC, 52, 331

Chase, Pearl, 337

Chase, William Merritt, 3, 10, 157, 158, 258, 273, 291, 321, 419

Chateaubriand, François René de, *The Last of the Abencerrajes*, 138, 141

Chatfield-Taylor, Hobart, 165

Chautauqua movement, 73

Chávez, Amado, 125, 126, 448

Chew, Benjamin, 198, 494–95n118

Chicago: architecture in, 24, 183, 322, *324*, 325, *341*, 364, 365; art in, 12, 13, 251; Carmencita in, 6; Columbus monument in, 83; Cubans in, 68; Diana sculpture in, 320; Eulalia de Borbón in, 184–86; Marqués de Vega-Inclán in, 449; *Ramona* screening in, 390; skyscrapers in, 318; Spanish-themed entertainment in, 372, 376, 377, 397; speeches about Spain in, 79; tourist lecture in, 153; veterans tribute in, 77. *See also* Illinois; World's Columbian Exposition

Chicago Daily Tribune, 374

Chicago Symphony Orchestra, 377

Chicago Tribune, 70, 186, 365

Chicote (Madrid bar), 432

Chile, 454

China, 6, 12, 235

Christianity, 8, 247–51, 306, 318. *See also* Catholic Church; Spain: civilization and evangelization by

Christie's auction house, 242

Churriguera, José de, 307, 333

El Cid, 206, 207, 457–58

cinema: borderland-themed, 390–95; censorship of Spanish, 464; influence of Spanish, 4, *plate 8*, 15, 24–25, 374, 388–98, 467; innovations in, 393, 397, 398; music for, 388; portrayals of Spaniards and Mexicans in, 392–93; about Spain, 431; Spanish missions in, 392, 393; of Spanish opera, 378.

Cintra (Spanish firm), 462

Clark, Edwin H., 364

Clark, William George, 159

Clay, Henry, 48, 49, 473n44

Cleveland, Grover, 70

Cleveland OH, 293, 322, 390; Alcazar hotel in, 360–62

Clune, W. H., 389–90

Coconut Grove FL, 341

Codding, Mitchell, 218

Coello, Claudio, 288

Cogswell, Joseph Green, 173

Cohan, George M., 384

Cold War, 432, 465

College of William and Mary, 172, 177

Collier, William, 76

Colman, Samuel, 10, 153–55, 157, 321; *Hill of the Alhambra*, 155, *plate 2*

Colnaghi Gallery, 221, 233

Colorado, 106, 423

Columbian Quincentenary, 466

Columbia University, 177, 183, 194, 462–63, 491n56

Columbus, Christopher: attitudes toward, 466–67; biographies of, 7–8, 96, 163, 486n54; casket of, 260; commemoration of, 6, 83–87, 96, 193, 206, 478n1; at monastery, 184; U.S. postage stamps honoring, 284; in Waldo Frank's book, 427; Walt Whitman's interest in, 9

Columbus, Ferdinand, 163

Columbus Day, 83, 443, 467

Combs, John W., 121, *122*

commerce. *See* trade

Compañía Transatlántica, 1
Coney Island, 322
Connecticut, 83, 367
conquistadors: artistic renderings of, 325; attitudes toward, 21, 129, 131, 466; in New Mexico, 104, 110, 111, 357; in parade, 103
Continental Congress, 32, 36, 39, 174
Coolidge, Calvin, 454
Coolidge, Charles A., 324–25, 458
Coolidge, Thomas Jefferson, 158, 264
Cooper, James Fenimore, 401
Coral Gables Development Commission, 457
Coral Gables FL, 340–44, 359–60, 512n68; marketing of, 342, 343, 344
Córdoba, 3, 65, 153, 155, 164, 261, 448
Coronado, Francisco Vázquez de, 103–4
Cortés, Hernán, 93, 98, 325, 379
Cortissoz, Royal, 264–66
cosmopolitanism: American attitudes toward, 234, 398–99, 423; and architecture, 331; of Hearst collection, 285; Spanish attitudes toward, 210, 417, 426, 427, 431
Cossío, Manuel B., 273, 429, 443–44
Courbet, Gustave, 264
Cova, León de la, 177
Cram, Goodhue, and Ferguson, Architects, 332
Cram, Ralph A., 305–10, 332, 352
Creoles, 68
Crisp, Donald, 389, 393
Crosby, Bing, 385
Cruz, Penelope, 467
Cruz, San Juan de la, 308
Cruz, Sor Juana Inés de la, 252

Cuba: architectural style in, 365, 367; civil war in, 165, 215; cuisine of, 466; Ernest Hemingway in, 437–39; filibusteros in, 53–54, 57–59, 63, 246; Florida residents to, 89; immigrants from, 18; independence movement in, 68–69; political publications in, 176; slavery in, 53, 62–64, 68; Spanish-American War in, 1, 20, 66, 135, 476n89; Spanish language in, 461; Spanish ownership of, 49, 50, 57–60, 62, 167; trade in, 40; uprisings in, 35, 62–64, 67–68; U.S. involvement in, 68–69, 170, 186, 285, 404, 454
Cuéllar, 221, 272
Cuenca, 412
Cuernavaca, 456
Cugat, Xavier, 388
cultural transfer, 16–18, 25, 470n19
Cummings, E. E., 418
Curry, Jabez L. M., 75–76
The Curse of Capistrano (McCulley), 393
Curtis, Charles B., 272, 499n39
Curtis, William, 478n1
Cushing, Caleb, 63, 148, 244
Cushing, Caroline, 148, 244–45
Cushing, Frank Hamilton, 17
Cutler FL, 281, 283
Cyprus, 253

Dallas TX, 467; Julia Ideson Library in, 310
Dana, Charles, 68
dance: at expositions and festivals, 167, 335, 339, 448; in films, 397; Gertrude Stein at performances of, 410, 412; in literature, 162, 419;

dance (*continued*)
  music for, 378; paintings of, 157,
    264; play inspired by, 179, *180*;
    Spanish style of, 6, *7*, 15, 144,
    204–5, 229, 371–79, 385
Dante, 181–82
Darley, Felix O. C., 148, *149*
Davies, Marion, 297
Davis, William Watts Hart, 105, 108,
    111, 115
Day, Henry, 160
Deering, Charles, 13, 274–84, 301,
    449–50, 504n96; art collection of,
    276–80, 282–83; castle in Tamarit,
    Spain; residence in Sitges, Spain,
    277–82, *278*, *279*, 284, 301
Deering, James, 282
Deering, Marion Whipple, 281
Deering-McCormick family collec-
    tion, 283
De Forest, Lee, 397
De Forest Phonofilm Company, 15
Degas, Edgar, 264, 267
De La Plaza and Juanita with Their
    Spanish Serenaders, 388
Delk, Edward Buehler, 362–63, *363*
Delpar, Helen, 454
DeMille, Cecil, 378, 392
Dénia, 418
Desigual (Spanish clothing firm), 461
Detroit Institute of Art, 239, 498n20
Detroit MI, 390
Dewey, George, 77, 215
Día de la Raza, 193, 443, 448
Díaz, Porfirio, 203, 449
Disraeli, Benjamin, 143
Dodge, Augustus C., 61–62, 76, 97, 99
Dolores Mission, 119–20

Doloretes (flamenco dancer), 372, 419
Doménech, Rafael, *445*, 447
Don César de Bazan (film), 395
Donizetti, Gaetano, 377, 381
Don Q, Son of Zorro (film), 19, 393, *394*
Don Q's Love Story (Hesketh-
    Prichard), 393
Don Quixote, 113, 136, 368, 485n38
Don Quixote (Cervantes): A. M.
    Huntington's reading of, 206;
    influence of, 136, 403, 406, 416–
    18, 425, 485n38; study of, 181,
    488n19, 489n25; Thomas Jeffer-
    son's reading of, 172. *See also*
    Cervantes, Miguel de
Doré, Gustave, 153, 485n38
d'Orléans, Antoine Marie, Duke of
    Montpensier, 250–52
Dorr, Dalton, 254, *255*
Dos Passos, John: essays and reviews
    by, 415–18, 420, 421; influence of,
    309; as Lost Generation writer,
    401; in Mexico, 455; *Rosinante to
    the Road Again*, 309, 418–19; and
    Spanish civil war, 457; Spanish
    fever of, 11, 25, 374, 413–23, 435;
    and Waldo Frank, 426, 428, 430
Dos Passos, Katherine, 420, 455
Douglas, Marjory Stoneman, 512n68
Downes, William Howe, 160–62
Doyle, Henry Grattan, 191
Dreamland amusement park (Coney
    Island NY), 322
Dresden, Germany, 242
Drexel, Joseph W., 259
Drexel, Lucy Wharton, 259
Dufour, Dominique, 484n10
Dulwich Picture Gallery, 241

Dumas, Alexandre, 136, 143, 485n24
Durand-Ruel, Paul, 272, 280
Dúrcal, Duke of, 287
Durchslag (developer), 365
Durr, Louis, 238–39, 497n19
Duval, Arabella Yarrington. *See*
    Huntington, Arabella
DuVal, William P., 11
Duveen, Joseph, 221, 272
Duveneck, Frank, 157
Dwinelle, John W., 120

Eakins, Thomas, 10, 155, 156, *156*, 258
Earle, Henry Edmond, 381
Eastern Europe, 18, 465
Eco, Umberto, 284
École des Beaux-Arts (Paris), 3
economy: and crazes, 16; of Cuba,
    68; during Roaring Twenties,
    358–59; of Spain and U.S., 34, 50,
    66, 287, 322, 449, 461–62, 467–68.
    See also Great Depression; trade
Ecuador, 125, 176
Edinburgh, Scotland, 159
Edison, Thomas Alva, 6, *7*, 393, 395;
    Black Maria Studio of, *7*, 393
Edison Home Phonograph, 380
education: through art museums,
    253; exchange programs, 76–77;
    at Ibero-American International
    Exposition, 459; about Spain, 73,
    169–70, 462–63. *See also* litera-
    ture: education in Spanish; Span-
    ish language: education in
Eguiara y Eguren, Juan José, 217
Eguílaz, Leopold, 30
Egypt, 6, 15, 17, 144, 221, 252

Ehrich Galleries (New York), 221,
    263, 268, 272, 449
Eichenbaum, Edward, *341*
Eidlitz, Leopold, 19, 322
Eisenhower, Dwight W., 432, 465
E.L., 247, 500n41
El Bulli (restaurant), 466
El Celler de Can Roca (restaurant), 466
El Ferrol, 32
Eliot, Charles William, 182
Eliot, George, 146
Elizabeth I, Queen of England, 35
El Jaleo (restaurant), 466
Elkins Park PA, 267
Elliott, John H., 463
Ellis, Havelock, 399–400, 426
Elssler, Fanny, 179, *180*
Engel, Arthur, 214
Erving, George, 48
Escorial monastery, 3, 65, 81, 147,
    191, 243, 261
Espartero, Bartolomé, 59–60
estilo de ida y vuelta, 25, 453
Etting, Ruth, 388
European Union, 465
Everett, Alexander Hill, 7, 55, 244
Everett, Edward Hill, 101, 162
Everglades, 92
Ezdorf, Robert von, 367

Fairbanks, Douglas, Sr., 19, 393
Fairbanks, George Rainsford, 99–
    101, 103, 129
Falla, Manuel de, 378, 416
Farrar, Geraldine, 378
Farwell, Arthur, 381, 384
Far West, 380
fashion, 4, 374, 376, 389, 395, 397, 461

Fasquelle, Louis, 178
Feliu i Codina, José, 395
Ferdinand II, King, 83, 206, 357
Ferdinand VII, King, 42, 45, 50, 237, 358
Fernández, James D., 170
Fernández de Navarrete, Manuel, 469n8
Fernandina FL, 103
Field, Henry M., 163–65, 487n57
Field, Kate, 147
FIFA World Cup, 467
filibusteros, 53–54, 57–59, 63, 246, 474n54
Fillmore, Millard, 53, 246, 474n54
Fink, Denman, 342
Fink, H. George, 342
Fish, Hamilton, 63
Fisher, Fred, 385
Fiske, Eugene A., 109–10
Fitz-Gerald, John D., 193
Flagler, Henry, 13, 23, 103, 310–14, 316, 317
Flagler College, 312
flamenco. See dance
Florence, Edna, 362
Florence, Italy, 159, 272
Florida: architecture and furnishings in, 13, 310, 340–51, 355, 367; boundary of, 28; Cubans in, 68; Deering estate in, 281, 282, 504n96; Hearst collection in, 284; Historical Society, 99; hotels in, 13; immigrants in, 18; Spain-U.S. disputes in, 20, 35, 36, 41, 43–46, 135, 473n36; Spanish craze in, 6, 17, 21, 457; Spanish history in, 86, 88–103, 129, 186, 310–12, 351; tourism in, 101–3; as U.S.

territory, 11, 43, 49, 173. See also Coral Gables FL; Miami; Palm Beach FL; St. Augustine FL; St. Petersburg FL
Floridablanca, Count of. See Jovellanos, Gaspar Melchor de
Foerderer, Ethel, 367–69
Foerderer, Percival E., 367–69
Fogg Museum, 301
food: criticism of Anglo-American, 48; description of Spanish, 33, 39, 159, 303; influence of Spanish, 4, 14, 374, 461, 466; popularity of Mexican, 15, 455; at tourist exhibition, 448
Fooks, Paul, 174–75, 177
Forbes, Alexander, 117
Ford, Jeremiah D. M., 184
Ford, Richard, 92, 142, 159
Ford Foundation, 463
Forest Hills NY, 340
Fort Caroline FL, 100
Fortuny, Mariano, 12, 64
Foster, Thomas, 236
Four Horsemen of the Apocalypse (film), 15, 395, 404. See also Blasco Ibáñez, Vicente
Fox Studios, 378
France: A. M. Huntington in, 215; archbishop from, 108; architecture in, 328; art in, 200, 242, 256, 266, 443; border with Spain, 464; and control of New Orleans, 31; in Florida, 89, 91, 100; Gertrude Stein in, 407; impressions of Spain in, 3, 143, 485n24; influence on American culture, 4, 12, 132; John Adams to, 32; and Kansas

City MO, 363; literature in, 403, 429; Picasso in, 463; Pierre Soulé in, 58, 475n72; Spanish cultural journal in, 197; Spanish resistance to, 472n24; tourists from, 148–50, 441, 448; U.S. territory from, 43

Franciscans: in California, 21–22, 116, 118, 126, 129, 325, 326, 332, 336, 337, 392; design of missions of, 324; in festival parade, 113; portrayal in film, 389; and Spanish music, 379; tomb statues of, 221; at world's fair, 184

Franco, Francisco: American attitudes toward, 135, 421, 431–32; death of, 457, 462, 465; living conditions under, 430, 464, 465; victory of, 423, 439, 457, 462

Frank, Waldo, 11, 25, 423–31, 455, 457

Frankfurt, 218

Franklin, Benjamin, 36, 39, 174, 175

French language: American attitudes toward, 14; education in, 172–75, 177–82, 187–90, 202, 401, 468, 490n44; literature in, 141, 190; Spain-U.S. negotiations in, 39

Frick, Helen Clay, 502n80

Frick, Henry Clay, plate 5, 221, 233, 268, 269, 273, 300, 502n80

Fry, Roger, 272

Fuenterrabía, 32

Fulton, Jack, 385

Furstenberg, François, 175

Galicia, 432, 433, 435, 437

Gallego, Fernando, 279, 503n82

El Gallo (matador), 434–35

Galveston TX, 93

Gamble, James, 435

Ganivet, Ángel, 307–9, 399, 400, 424, 426, 443

García, Fernando, 239–41

García Izcabalceta, Joaquín, 95

Garcilaso de la Vega, Inca, 91, 95, 97

Gardner, Isabella Stewart, 23, 158, 231–32, 260–64, 265

Gardoquí, Diego María de, 39, 40, 55

Gary, Elbert, 281

Gautier, Théophile, 143, 246, 485n24

gazpacho, 159. See also food

Gebhard, D., 511n60

Generation of '98, 192, 210, 287, 399, 400, 425

Genovar, Francis B., 103

Genteel Tradition, 400, 402, 407, 517n39

George Washington University, 191

Georgia, 28, 46, 101, 367

German language: American attitudes toward, 14; education in, 125, 173, 177–79, 181, 182, 187, 188, 401, 490n44

Germany: art experts in, 218, 273; education about, 6, 73, 184; influence on American culture, 4; museums in, 222; Spanish art in, 242; and U.S. history, 127, 187–88

Gérôme, Jean-Léon, 155, 156, 157, 242

Gerona, 307, 347

Geronimo, 125

Gerould, Katharine Fullerton, 355–56

Gershwin, George, 385

Gibraltar, 215, 433

Gibson, Charles Dana, 66–67, 67, 71–72, 75

Gifra-Adroher, Pere, 135

Gilbert, L. Wolfe, 385

Gilded Age: art collecting during, 204, 234, 235, 285; Met museum during, 253; Spanish influence during, 4, 12, 24, 152, 401

Gil de Hontañón, Rodrigo, 310

Gill, Irving, 325–26

Gillespie, James Waldron, 333

Giralda, 13, 318, 321, 325; replicas of, 24, *323*, 325, *329*, 330, 344, 349, 363–64

The Girl from Madrid (vaudeville show), 167

Girona, 466

Gisbert, Antonio, 65

gitanos. *See* gypsies

Glasgow, Scotland, 245

Gleason, Adda, 389

Gleeson, William, 116

Godard, Abbé Léon, 153

Godoy, Manuel de, 28–29, 41, 237, 497n13

Goes, Hugo van der, 301

Goethe, Johann Wolfgang, 181

Gogorza, Emilio de, 385

Goldenberg, Bonnie, 70–71

Gómez, Máximo, 70

Goodhue, Bertram Grosvenor, 24, 326–27, 351–52, 458; buildings in San Diego, 332–35, *334*, 337, 351–52, 458; El Fueridis, 332–33

Good Neighbor policy, 15, 17, 198, 388, 454

Gourgue, Domingue de, 100

Goya, Francisco José de: in art guide, 447; authenticity of paintings by, 266, 272; collections of, 191, 220, 231, 267, 268, 269, 272, 277, 280,

444–46, 449, 502n79; influence of, 10, 23, 374, 377, 416, 429

Grady, Henry W., 349

Granada: architecture and furnishings in, 292, 300, 314, 348; Augustus Saint-Gaudens in, 3; buildings named after, *341*, 344, 350; bullfights in, 434; Gertrude Stein in, 408, 412; Henry Adams in, 30, 31; hotels in, 451; Muslim history in, 138, 357, 358; name of, 141; paintings of, 153; parks in, 317; Richard Ford in, 142; Samuel Colman in, 155; Thomas Buckingham Smith in, 99; tourism in, 148, 150, 153, 164; U. S. Grant in, 65; Washington Irving in, 8, 137, 140; W. D. Howells in, 406

Granados, Enrique, 376, 378, 416; *Goyescas* by, 377

Grant, Robert, 330

Grant, U. S., 63–66, 150

Great Britain: architecture in, 327–28; Bible Society in, 144; and control of New Orleans, 31; in Florida, 89, 101, 312; hispanophilia in, 3; Huntingtons in, 201, 212; influence on American culture, 4, 6, 12; museums in, 199; Spanish art in, 153, 241, 266, 494n114; Teutonic influence in, 127; tourists from, 148–50, 159, 448; U.S. treaty with, 32; in war of 1812, 45

Great Depression, 134, 298, 367, 454, 455, 462. *See also* economy

El Greco, *Adoration of the Magi*, 263; authenticity of paintings by, 266, 272, 273; *Burial of the*

Count of Orgaz, 261, 267; collections of, *plate 5*, 219, 220, 231, 259, 266–69, 272, 277, 279, 280, 494n114, 502nn79–80, 503n82; *Crucifixion*, 257; exhibition of, 241–42; influence of, 10, 23, 258, 267, 307, 416, 427, 429; legality of sales of, 300; monument to, 277; museum devoted to, 81, 197, 443–46; at Pennsylvania art museum, 256, 270; *View of Toledo*, 268. *See also* Casa-Museo de El Greco

Greene, Jack P., 463

Gregg, Josiah, 104

Griffith, D. W., 388–92, 395

gringos, 105, 382, 390

Groesbeck, Daniel Sayre, *plate 7*, 339

Guadalajara (Mexico), 252

Guatemala, 125, 344

Guiu i Gabalda, Francesc, 260, 272

Guizot, François, 485n24

Guzman, Roberto, 397

gypsies: in Basque Country, 162; dance of, 374, 385; descriptions of, 144–46, 201; in films, 397; illustrations of, 153, 155–56, 158, 264; influence on A. M. Huntington, 204; at Louisiana Purchase exposition, 167

Gypsy Blood (film), 378, *379*

Hackel, Steven, 116

Hadley, Arthur, 198

Hague, Eleanor, 380, 382

Hakluyt, Richard, 95

Hale, George, 362

Hale, Rev. Edward Everett, 162–63, 202, 486n54

Hale, Susan, 162, 202

Hall, John M., 73, 74

Hamilton, Alexander, 176

Hanson, Ole, 336

Harding, Warren, 454

Harlem Evening School, 202

Harper's Monthly Magazine, 225, 406

Harper's New Monthly Magazine, 14, 158, 321, 404

Harper's Pictorial History of the War with Spain, 1

Harris, Lionel (art dealer), 221, 272, 280, 283; Spanish Gallery of, 221

Harrison, Benjamin, 83

Harrison, James Albert, 159–60, 486n45

Harrison County wv, 18

Hart and Burns firm, 357

Harvard University: Charles Lummis at, 123, 125; Charles Perkins at, 500n53; George Ticknor at, 138; Henry Adams at, 29; John Dos Passos at, 414; Spanish studies at, 178–79, 181–84, 489n25; tomb sculptures at, 301; W. R. Hearst at, 287

Hastings, Thomas W., 312–14, *313*, 316, 317, 325, 328

Hastings NE, 327

Hatch, Edith, 385

Havana, 35, 40, 59, 92, 176, 214, 341

Havemeyer, Henry O., 267–68

Havemeyer, Louisine, 23, 267–68

Havemeyer family, 446

Haverford PA, 360

Hawthorne, Charles W., *224*

Hawthorne, Julian, 24, 330

Hawthorne, Nathaniel, 242, 330
Hay, John, 74, 407; *Castilian Days*, 76, 147–48, 159, 248, 407
Hearst, Phoebe Apperson, 285, 287–88, 303, 326; Hacienda del Pozo de Verona, 326
Hearst, William Randolph, *294*; architects of, 225, 309, 326, 336; attitude toward Spain, 21, 22, 70, 166, 285–87, 301–4; bankruptcy of, 298, 302; collecting by, 221, 270, 284–304; image of, 284; "Ronda—A Spanish Song" by, 303; Spanish monasteries purchased by, 302, 395–97
Hearst San Simeon State Historical Monument. *See* San Simeon
Hemet CA, 390
Hemingway, Clarence, 435
Hemingway, Ernest: as ambulance driver, 417; and bullfighting, 11, 410, 418, 435–37, *436*, 439; critiques of writers, 429–30; *Death in the Afternoon*, *438*; *For Whom the Bell Tolls*, 432, 457, 462; and John Dos Passos, 417, 418, 420, 421; as Lost Generation writer, 401; as reporter in Spain, 429, 432–34; and Spanish civil war, 457; Spanish fever of, 11, 25, 374, 431–39, 462; on Spanish tourism, 454; *The Sun Also Rises*, 429, 432, 437, 439
Hemingway, Hadley, 433, 435
Hemingway, John Hadley Nicanor, 435
Hemingway, Pauline Pfeiffer, 437
Henri, Robert, 157
Hershe, Robert B., 504n96
Hershey, J. Wilmer, *338*

Hershey, Milton, 367
Hershey Hotel, *366*, 367
Hesketh-Prichard, H., 393
Hewett, Edgar Lee, 356, 357
Hiersemann, Karl W., 217
Hispania, 190, 194, 402, 427
Hispanic American Historical Review, 402
Hispanics, 115. *See also* Latin America
Hispanic Society of America (HSA): art exhibits of, 12, *226*, 227–29, 496n133; building of, 217; collections of, 197, 200, 217–21, 467, 494–95n118, 495n123; employees of, 222–26, 291, 410, 495n125; foundation of, 4, 170, 196, 203, 212–14, 221–22; gift to Seville, 457; purpose of, 23, 197, 199, 212, 222, 226–27, 495n123; and Spanish tourism, 451; supporters of, 209
hispanidad, 193, 425, 427, 430, 442, 448–49. *See also* Latin America
hispanismo, 192–93, 198, 402. *See also* Spanish studies
hispanophilia. *See* Spanish fever
History of the World: Part I (film), 465
Hitler, Adolf, 421, 457, 462
Hittell, Theodore, 118–19
Hoffmann, Bernhard, 337
Hoganson, Kristin, 4, 152
Hold, Thomas, 138
Hollywood CA, 378, 390, 392
Hondarribia. *See* Fuenterrabía
Hoover, Herbert, 454, 456
Hoppin, James M., 249
Hopwood, Avery, 385
Hot Springs AR, 367
Houghton, Joab, 108

Houston TX, 309–10
Howard, John Galen, *329*
Howden, Lord, 61
Howells, Joseph, 406
Howells, William Dean, *405*; at
   Atlantic Monthly, 87, 402; attitude
   toward Spain, 25, 72, 402–7, 415,
   517n44, 517n49, 517n50; on Span-
   ish literature, 14, 403–7, 517n51
Hudson-Fulton Celebration, 15
Hughes, Elizabeth, 117
Hugo, Victor, 136, 395
Huguet, Jaume, 503n82
Hume, Martin, 128, 169
Hunt, Myron, *327*, 335
Hunt, Sumner P., 326
Huntington, Anna Hyatt, 457
Huntington, Arabella: background
   of, 199–200; correspondence of,
   196, 203, 209, 212–14, 216, 220,
   222–23, 493n91; diary for, 200,
   201; philanthropy of, 492n62;
   purchase of Velázquez, 200, 233
Huntington, Archer Milton, *205*;
   art exhibits by, 227–28, 496n133;
   autobiography of, 200, 202, 204,
   218, 220; and Carolina Otero,
   204–6; collecting by, 207, 212–
   21, 263–64, 269–70, 272, 273,
   280, 283, 284, 446–47, 494n117;
   employees of, 222–26, 291,
   495n125; gift to Seville, 457–
   58; honored in Spain, 283–84;
   interest in Spanish culture, 4, 13,
   23, 170, 196, 199–204, 456; *Note
   Book in Northern Spain*, 209–11,
   493n11; philanthropy of, 197,
   447, 492n62; in Spain, *205*, 206–

15, 492n84, 493n85; and Spanish
   language study, 188, 190, 194,
   490n42, 491n56; on Spanish politics, 456–57; and Spanish tourism, 449, 451
Huntington, Charles Pratt, 203
Huntington, Collis P., 196, 200, 202,
   204, 218–19
Huntington, Henry E., 203–4, 326,
   492n62

Iberdrola (Spanish energy firm), 461
Ibero-American International Expo-
   sition, 457–59, *460 fig. 88*, 460
   fig. 89
Ignatius, Saint, 412, 427
Illinois, 73, 365, 366. *See also* Chicago
immigration, 16–18, 107, 455–56
"In a Little Spanish Town" (Wayne,
   Lewis, and Young), 385, *387*
Indiana, 462
Indiana University, 463
Indigenous Peoples Day, 467
Ingersoll, Ernest, 107, 108
Ingram, Rex, 395
Inman, Henry, 96
Innocent VIII, Pope, 263
Innocent X, Pope, 251
In Old California (film), 392
"In Old Madrid" (Gogorza), 385
Inquisition: American attitudes
   toward, 12, 21, 64, 71, 72, 163, 175;
   and art, 247, 308; study of, 170, 402
International Studio Corporation, 290
Irun, Spain, 251
Irving, Edgar, 148
Irving, Theodore, 91, 95

Irving, Washington, *139*; *Alhambra*, 8, 30, 140–41, 148–52, *149*, 158, 164, 274–75, 314; *Conquest of Granada*, 403; diplomacy of, 55; and Edward Everett, 162; image of Spain, 87, 158, 164, 316, 342; influence of, 401, 402, 403, 406; influences on, 137–38; *The Life and Voyages of Christopher Columbus*, 7–8, 85, 96, 140, 142; at Prado Museum, 242–43, 499n29; in Spain, 140, 155, 469n8; Spanish fever of, 7–10, 19, 22, 30, 77, 137, 142, 194, 195, 308, 457

Isabella, Queen: American attitudes toward, 163; artistic renderings of, 243, 358; history of, 426; honoring of, 83, 84, 206; and Huntington collection, 494n117; military encampment of, 357

Isabella II, Queen, 58, 60

Italian language, 176–79, 189, 190

Italica, 214, 215

Italy: architecture in, 344, 347, 367; art in, 235, 237, 238, 244, 247, 249, 250, 251, 260, 261, 270; El Greco in, 443; Ernest Hemingway in, 433, 437; export laws in, 300; immigrants from, 18; influence on American culture, 4, 12, 132; tourism in, 212; U.S. exposition pavilion in, 458; W. D. Howells's impressions of, 406

Izcabalceta, Joaquín García, 95

Jaca, 211, 277, 282

Jaccaci, August F., 274

Jackson, Andrew, 45, 46

Jackson, Helen Hunt: on Fr. Serra, 117–18, 482n60; *Ramona*, 9, 21–22, *119*, 123, 339, 388–92, 398; on Santa Barbara architecture, 336

Jackson, Roland, 415

El Jaleo de Jeres (playbill), *180*

James, George Wharton, 326

James, Henry, 11, 234–35, 250–52, 264, 404, 407

Japan, 6, 12, 15, 16

Jarves, James Jackson, 12, 249–50; *Art-Idea*, 249; *Art Thoughts*, 249

Jay, John, 36–40, *38*, 55, 76

Jefferson, Martha, 172

Jefferson, Thomas, 27, 31, 39, 42–43, 172–73, 176, 177, 487n5

Jeffrey, Harry T., 362

Jenkins, Howell Griffiths, 435

Jérez de los Caballeros, Marqués de, 215–16, 300

Jesuits, 325, 427

Jesup, Morris Ketchum, 4, 204

Jewitt, S. W., 236

Jews: A. M. Huntington's attitude toward, 220; Ernest Hemingway's attitude toward, 429; immigration of, 18; Moorish architectural style of, 19; music written by, 384; in New Mexico, 107; in Spain, 21, 144, 447, 451; synagogues of, 191

Jiménez, Juan Ramon, 425, 427

Johns Hopkins University, 126–27, 184, 408, 463–64, 489n33

John Simon Guggenheim Foundation, 456

Johnson, John G., 256, 270–73, 444

Johnson, William Templeton, 458–59, *460 fig 88*, *460 fig. 89*, 524n36

Joliet IL, 366
Jolson, Al, 374, 384–85
Jones, Isham, 385
Joselito (matador), 434
Jovellanos, Gaspar Melchor de,
    Count of Floridablanca, 37–39
Juanes, Juan de, 259, 272
Juderías, Julián, 8–9
Justi, Carl, 209, 273

Kahlo, Frida, 455
Kansas, 53, 85
Kansas City MO, 293; Country Club
    Plaza in, 362–64, *363*, 514n102
Kelly, Sir Gerald, *plate 5*
Kentucky, 41, 69, 96
Kenyon, William, 326
Key West FL, 439
Kiehnel, Richard, 342
Kimball, Francis Hatch, 322
King, Georgiana Goddard, 223, *224*,
    369, 410
King, Henry, 398
Kingsley, Charles, 486n54
Kirkland, John T., 178
Knapp, William I., 183, 206–7,
    489n28, 492n84, 499n39
Knights of Columbus, 85. *See also*
    Catholic Church
Knoedler's (art gallery), 272, 280,
    502n79
Knowles, E., 511n60
Koerner, Gustav, 61, 62

Labrador, Juan, 259
La Jolla (California) Library (Athe-
    naeum), 458

Lake Worth FL, *346*, 347
Lalo, Édouard, 376
La Mancha, 207, 406
Lamborn, Robert H., 252–56, *255*,
    333, 500n56
Lamy, Jean-Baptiste, 108
*The Land of Joy (La tierra de la
    Alegría)* (musical), 371–72, *373*
Land of Sunshine, 125, 380
Lathrop, Francis, 218–19, 270, 273, 321
Lathrop, George Parsons, *161*, 162, 321
Latimer, Emily Wormeley, 71
Latin America: art from, 220, 252;
    HSA's promotion of, 199; music in,
    371, 379, 388; race in, 35, 115, 193;
    studies of, 170–72, 182–83, 190–
    91, 425, 427, 463, 488n19, 489n33;
    U.S. policy toward, 454, 456;
    Waldo Frank's interest in, 430. *See
    also* hispanidad; South America
Latin language, 173, 182, 424
Latinos. *See* Hispanics
Lazard Frères & Co., 269
Lazarillo de Tormes, 403, 406, 427
Lea, Henry Charles, 72, 170, 402
Lears, T. J. Jackson, 317, 400–401
Lee, Muna, 428
Lehman, Philip, 269
Leigh, Arnyas, 163, 486n54
Leland Stanford Junior University,
    121, 324–25
León, Spain, 211, 261, 307, 310, 344
Leopoldina (ship), 433
Lester, C. Edwards, 58
Leutze, Emanuel, 98
Leviathan (ship), 374
Levine, Lawrence, 4, 222
Levkoff, Mary, 285

Lewis, John Frederick, 153

Lewis, Sam M., 385, *387*

Libbey, Edward, 335

Library of Congress, 172, 198

Life magazine, 66–67, *67*, 71–72

Lima, 220, 317, 494–95n118

Lincoln, Abraham, 61, 62, 74

Lincoln, Grace Spear, 367

Lippi, Filippino, 263

Lisbon, 135, 172, 261, 424

literature: on architecture, 306–9, 351–52; collections of, 197, 213, 215–17, 220, 267, 447, 494n117; education in Spanish, 170, 172, 175, 178–84, 190, 191, 402, 414, 451, 488n19, 490n42; gypsies in, 144–46; influence of Spanish, 4–11, 14, 17, 21–23, 25, 137, 194, 374, 398–439, 467; picaresque genre of, 403; publication of Spanish, 175–76; quality of Spanish, 415, 429; on Spanish missions, 326; Spanish national character in, 210, 212, 416; on travel in Spain, 159–67, 209, 424. *See also* Spanish language; Spanish studies

Liverpool, 212; Walker Art Gallery in, 201

Livingston, Robert, 37, 40

Llobet, Miguel, 377

Loga, Valerian von, 273

Logroño, 209

London: art in, 218, 233, 241, 242, 244, 250–51, 259, 263, 272, 300; entertainment in, 371, 374, 376; Huntingtons in, 203; James Buchanan in, 60; museums in, 199; New Gallery in, 266; *Sunny Spain* exhibition in, 448; Washington Irving in, 138

London Magazine, 135

Longfellow, Henry Wadsworth: *Castles in Spain*, 202; impressions of Spain, 9, 22, 143–44, 401, 485n26; influence of, 403; as language instructor, 179–81; law of, 170–72, 462, 463, 468; self-portrait of, *171*

Long Island NY, 75, 346, *359*

López, Narciso, 53–54, 57, 246, 474n54

López de Ayala, Don Pedro, 280

López de Gómara, Francisco, 93

López Enguídanos, Tomás, 237, 497n13

Los Angeles: architecture in, 297, 326, 452; chamber of commerce in, 85; Charles Lummis in, 123, 125, 130, 380; entertainment in, 376, 384, 389; Landmarks Club in, 130; Marqués de Vega-Inclán in, 450

Los Angeles *Daily Times*, 123–25

Los Angeles Times, 77

Lost Generation, 374, 401

Louisiana, 18, 27, 173. *See also* New Orleans

Louisiana Purchase, 43, 79, 173

Louisiana Purchase Exhibition (St. Louis), 79, *166 fig. 22*, *166 fig. 23*, 167

Louis-Philippe, King, 58, 238, 242, 250

Louvre, 199, 236, 242; Galerie Espagnol in, 242

The Loves of Carmen (film), 397

Loves of Carmen (poster), *plate 8*

Low Countries, 12, 15–17, 235, 238, 259, 260, 270

Lowell, James Russell, 87–88, 150, 160, 181–82, 308, 407, 413, 489n25
Lowery, Virginia, 127
Lowery, Woodbury, 127–28
Lubbock TX, 310
Lubitsch, Ernst, 378, 397
Lucas, Wilfred, 395
Lucia di Lammermoor (Donizetti), 377
Lummis, Charles F., *124*; associates of, 326; background of, 123; on California's Spanish heritage, 326, 339–40, 392; death of, 457; on El Paseo, 337; *Home of Ramona*, 119; image of Spain, 325; interest in Spain, 9–10, 22, 123–24, 129–31, 133–34, 196; Marqués de Vega-Inclán with, 450; photo album of, *119*; on racism, 132; on Spanish-American War, 215; and Spanish music, 380; *Spanish Songs of California*, 382–84, *383*; writing style of, 129, 140
Luquiens, Frederick Bliss, 183, 190
Lydig, Philip, 264

MacDonald, Ballard, 384
Machado, Antonio, 416, 418
Machu Picchu, 183
Macías Picavea, Ricardo, 399
Mackenzie, Alexander Slidell, 141, 146, 245, 401, 484n22
Madame Butterfly, 15
Madison, James, 41, 42, 44–46
Madison Square Garden, 13, 318–22, *319*
Madrazo, Raimundo de, 501n63
Madrid: American authors in, 172, 407, 408, 410, 414–16, 418, 420, 421, 426, 434, 437; A. M. Huntington in, 207, 209; architecture and furnishings in, 345, 348; art and antiques in, 147, 242–43, 245, 267–68, 280, 307, 447, 448, 502n80, 503n82; Augustus Saint-Gaudens in, 3; Bynes in, 226, 291; Centro de Estudios Históricos in, 414; D. W. Eisenhower in, 432; education in, 451; Exposición Histórico-Americano, 478n1; government in, 42, 160; Henry Adams in, *30*, 31; historical research in, 127; hotels in, 451; image of, 167; I. S. Gardner in, 260, 261; James Monroe in, 44; John Rutledge in, 172; Luis de Onís in, 50–52; Museo de Artes Decorativos in, 447; newspapers in, 14, 60, 81, 464; Palace hotel in, 451; photographs of, 64, 211; reaction to filibusteros in, 54; Ritz hotel in, 451; short stories set in, 432; Spanish life in, 142–43, 427; Theodore Roosevelt in, 191, 192; Toledo Street in, 211; tourism in, 442; U.S. diplomacy in, 36–40, 55–63, 74–76, 81, 97, 99, 147, 150, 182, 241, 243, 246–47, 475n72, 499n31; U.S. Grant in, 65; Washington Irving in, 7, 140, 469n8, 499n29
Magoon, Elias Lyman, 247
Maine (ship), 35, 75, 214
Maine (state), 179
Maine, Maurice, 326
Major, Howard, 350
Málaga, 417, 434, 463
Mallon, Mary (Typhoid Mary), 9
Mallorca (island), 14, 410, 461. *See also* Palma de Mallorca

Manchester Art Treasures Exhibition, 241–42

Manet, Édouard, 10, 242, 246, 264, 266, 267

Manhasset Bay NY, 360

Manila, 77, 215

Manrique, Jorge, 179

La Manzantinita (flamenco dancer), 372

Maracaibo, 43

Marcy, William, 57, 60, 61

Marden, Charles Carroll, 184

María Christina, Queen, 165

Marías, Javier, 467

María Teresa, Infanta, 266–69

Marichu (restaurant), 466

Mariners' Museum, 198

Marino, Felix, 177

The Mark of Zorro (film), 19, 393

Marquand, Henry G., 258–59, 261, 501n63

Marseille, 215

Marshall, George, 397

Marshall Plan, 465

Martí, José, 68

Martin, Dean, 385

Martorell, Bernat, 277

Mason, John Y., 60

Massapequa NY, Shores of Seville in, 360, 361

Massenet, Jules, 395

Matson, Roderick N., 524n36

May, Henry F., 400, 407, 415

Maybeck, Bernard, 325

Mayer, Henry "Hy," 235

Maynard, George W., 312

Mazo, Juan Bautista del, 267

McAlmon, Robert, 434

McCarthy, Charles H., 87

McCleary, James T., 85

McCormick, E. O., 451

McCulley, Johnston, 19, 393

McKim, Mead and White, 316, 346

McKim, W. Duncan, 259

McKinley, William, 74, 148, 285, 330

McWilliams, Carey, 339, 478n4

Meade, George, 236

Meade, Gordon, 237

Meade, Richard Worsam, 176, 236–38, 243–44, 497n13, 499n31

Meadows Museum (Dallas), 467

medievalism, 317, 399

Meier-Graefe, Julius, 273, 429

Meigs, Montgomery C., 131

Meiji restoration, 16

Meller, Raquel, 374–76, 375, 378

Mendez Casal, Antonio, 453

Menéndez y Pelayo, Marcelino, 216

Mercé y Luque, Antonia (La Argentina). See La Argentina

Merino de Cáceres, José, 284

Mérimée, Prosper, 22, 145–46, 419

Merrick, George, 340–41, 344, 359–60, 457, 512n68

Merriman, Roger B., 183–84, 425

Methodists, 72

Metropolitan Museum of Art (New York): George Blumenthal with, 269; holdings of, 199, 204, 239, 253, 259, 263, 267, 270, 284, 298, 498n20, 501n63, 503n82; Roger Fry with, 272; Spanish patio at, 270

A Mexican Lothario (film), 392

Mexicans: American attitudes toward, 18–19, 201, 384; in California, 115, 123, 125, 332, 339–40; in New Mexico, 103–7, 111,

481n44; portrayals of, 390–93; race of, 192

Mexico: American attitudes toward, 132, 163; American interest in, 6, 15, 16, 454–55; architecture and furnishings in, 13, 331, 333, 341, 362; art from, 252–56; Charles Lummis in, 125; history of, 34, 79, 92, 93, 127–28, 355; Huntingtons in, 200, 203; music in, 378–81; revolution in, 420, 449; Spanish language in, 461, 468; U.S. involvement in, 41, 46; Waldo Frank in, 423, 430; and water usage, 127

Mexico City, 92, 93, 95, 116, 252, 333

Miami, 296, 297, 322, 341; Vizcaya estate in, 282

Michener, James, 464–65

Michigan, 72, 327, 349, 433

Millet, Jean François, 242

Milwaukee Art Museum, 467

Minorca, 89, 90, 103, 312

Miralles, Juan de, 36

Miranda, Carmen, 388

Mission Carmel, 117, 121

missions. See architecture: mission style; cinema: Spanish missions in; Franciscans

Mission San Francisco de Asís. See Dolores Mission

Mission San Gabriel, 388, 392

Mission Santa Barbara, 389

Mission Trail, 450

Mississippi River: discovery of, plate 1, 79, 95, 96; Spain-U.S. disputes over, 20, 27–28, 35, 37, 39–41, 135

Mitchell, John Ames, 72

Mizner, Addison: advertisements of, 360; architecture and furnishings of, 13, 341, 346–50, 348, 359, 368; background of, 344–45; Cloister Inn, 367; home of, 350, 457; manufactories of, 349; El Mirasol, 347, 348; La Ronda, 367, 368, 457

Moctezuma, 92

modernization. See cosmopolitanism

Molière, Jean-Baptiste Poquelin, 181

Monet, Claude, 264

Monforte de Lemos, 301

Monroe, James, 11, 44–46, 473n36

Monroe Doctrine, 454

Monserrat, 11

Montecito CA, 332–33, 335, 359; Casa del Herrero in, plate 6, 337, 511n58

Montemayor, Jorge de, 485n26

Monterey CA, 117, 121, 122

Montgomery, Frank, 392

Montgomery Ward, 13, 353, 355

Montijo, Countess of, 146

Montpelier VT, 108

Moore, Alexander, 374

Moore, Dudley, 417

Moore, Harry Humphrey, 155, 156

Moors: architecture of, 19, 305, 314–17, 322–25, 328, 347, 352, 356, 357–59, 367, 509n33; Gertrude Stein on, 408; history of, 8, 136–38, 164; monuments of, 10. See also Alhambra; Muslim monuments; Muslims

Mooser, William, III, 338

Moran, Thomas, 314, 315

Morgan, J. P., 78, 227, 235, 267, 502n76

Morgan, Julia, 225, 288–98, 301, 302, 309, 336

Morley, Sylvanus Griswold, 356, 357

Morley, William T., 187

Morocco, 314

Morris, Robert, 40

Morristown NJ, 36

Moses, Bernard, 71, 80

Motley, John Lothrop, 16–17

Moulton, Louise Chandler, 165

Munich, 275

Murad, David, 409

Murillo, Bartolomé Esteban: in art guide, 447; collections of, 235–44, 250, 259, 266, 268, 279, 287–88, 497n13, 498n20, 499n29, 499n31; copies of art by, 238, 497n17, 498n20, 498n24; Henry James's viewing of, 251; *Jacob and Rebecca at the Well*, 236, 244, 496n12; popularity of, 12, 235–39, 242–45, 248, 300, 307; theft of, 239–41, 260, 498n21; *Vision of St. Anthony of Padua*, 239–41, *240*, 498n21

Museum of Fine Arts, Boston, 233, 253, 263, 270

Museum of New Mexico, 356

music: authenticity of Spanish, 376–78, 381; in films, 390, 397–98; influence of Spanish, 4, 24–25, 371–88, 416; instruments of Spanish, 379; at Santa Barbara festival, 339; study of Spanish style, 378–82; of Sunny Spain, 144, 153, 162

Muslim monuments, 3, 65. *See also* Alhambra; Moors

Muslims, 87, 136, 138, 164, 247, 318, 357, 425, 426. *See also* Moors

Mussolini, Benito, 421, 462

Nadal, Rafael, 467

Napoleon, 15, 27, 42, 43, 45, 173, 236, 237, 472n24

Narváez expedition, 93

The Nation, 418, 426

National Gallery (London), 199, 241, 242, 494n114

National Gallery of Art, 266

National Gallery of British Art (Tate Gallery), 199

National Intelligencer, 96

National Portrait Gallery (London), 199

National Register of Historic Places, 369

Native Americans: architectural style of, 356; and Charles Lummis, 123–25; craze associated with, 15, 17; in Florida, 89, 103; Franciscans' treatment of, 118, 123, 326; in New Mexico, 105, 106, 110–12; representations of, 339, 388–90, 398; songs of, 380, 381; Spanish treatment of, 85–86, 93, 97–101, 357, 379; U.S. government's treatment of, 482n60

Navarre, 435

Navarro, José Francisco de, 360

Nebraska, 327

Negri, Pola, 378, *379*, 397

Netherlands. *See* Low Countries

New England, 6, 21, 327, 336, 423, 461

New Hampshire, 59

New Haven CT, 83

New Jersey, *7*, 393, 450, 462

New Mexico: architecture in, 107–9, 326, 327, 355–58; Charles Lummis in, 125–26, 380; Historical Society

of, 109; racial distinctions in, 104–
7, 110, 113, 481n44; Spanish craze
in, 6; Spanish history in, 86, 103–
15, 125, 351, 355–58; tourism in,
104, 109, 358; Waldo Frank in, 423
New Orleans, 27, 28, 31, 41, 53, 54,
68, 115, 484n22
Newport News VA, 198, 200
New Republic, 415, 426
newspapers, 68, 70, 78, 165–66, 175, 464
New York: A. M. Huntington's collecting in, 221; antiques in, 293,
365; architecture and furnishings
in, 24, 294, 318, 320, 322, 346,
349, 359–60, 467; art in, 12, 13,
23, 155, 217, 227–29, 231, 237–
41, 251, 253–54, 259, 260, 263,
268–72, 280, 282, 284, 285, 287–
90, 294–95, 298, 446, 449, 450,
498n20; Casino Theatre in, 322;
Cathedral of St. John the Divine
in, 306; Central Park in, 332, 360;
Clarendon apartment building in,
285, 288; Columbus monument
in, 83; criticism of U.S. diplomat
in, 58; Daly's Theatre in, 153;
Eden Musée music hall in, 205,
206; Empire Theatre, 374–76; filibusteros in, 53; HSA in, 197, 217,
221; Gallery of Christian Art in,
238, 241; Grand Central palace
in, 344; immigrants in, 18, 68;
Jay-Gardoquí treaty in, 40–41;
Koster and Bial's Music Hall in,
393; Maxine Elliott's Theatre in,
371, *386*; New York World skyscraper in, 318; Park Theatre in,
371; publishers in, 176; Spain-U.S.
disputes in, 35; Spanish Flats in,
360; Spanish influence in, 4, 6, 10,
13, 14, 19, 344, 466; Spanish language newspaper in, 176; Spanish
studies in, 174, 187, 188, 190, 194;
Spanish-themed entertainment in,
6, 146, 204–6, 371–78, 384, 389,
390, 393, 397; steamship route
to, 1; St. Thomas Church in, 332;
Stuyvesant Institute in, 241; Temple Emanu-El in, 19, 322; tourism
in, 153, 246, 451; typhoid epidemic
in, 9; Winter Garden Theater in,
371; W. M. Chase in, 258; World
Trade Center Transportation
Hub in, 467. *See also* Long Island
NY; Madison Square Garden
New York Armory Show, 231
New York Herald, 59, 77–78, 215
New-York Historical Society, 99,
239, 497nn18–19
New York Metropolitan Opera, 15,
376–78, 397
New York Museum of Modern Art, 455
New York Post, 159
New York Sun, 68, 82
New York Times: on art collections,
235, 241, 260, 269, 270, 273; on
California as Spain, 450; on Ellis's
Soul of Spain, 400; on entertain-
ment, 371, 372, 377, 393, 398; on
HSA, 221–22; on Mexico and Mex-
icans, 106–7, 455, 456; on Miranda
patio sale, 289; on Spanish influ-
ence, 366, 461, 467; on Theodore
Roosevelt, 82; on tourism, 431; on
Virgin Spain, 428
New York University, 464

New York World's Fair (1964), 466

Nicaragua, 454

Nichols, Jesse Clyde, 362–63

Nixon-Roulet, Mary F., 165–67

Noah, Mordecai, 401

North American Review, 47, 244, 406, 426

Northampton MA, 173

North Dakota, 327

Norton, Charles Eliot, 249, 251, 328, 407

Oakland CA, 120, 409

Ohio, 123, 403

Ojai CA, 335, 337, 364

Ojeda, Emilio de, 77–79, 167

Olivares, Count-Duke of, 233, 259

Olivier, Fernande, 409

Olmsted, Frederick Law, Jr., 332

O'Neill, Charles, 478n1

Onís, Federico de, 194–95, *195*

Onís, Luis de, *43*; publications of, 43–48; reputation of, 50–52; treaty by, 20, 48–52, *51*, 89, 194, 237; in U.S., 41–43

Oregon Country, 35, 49

Orozco, José Clemente, 15, 455

Orrente, Pedro de, 272

Ortega y Gasset, José, 307–9, 399, 424–26

Ostend Manifesto, 60–61

O'Sullivan, John L., 57, 246

Otero, Carolina "La Belle" (flamenco dancer), 204–6, *208*, 372

Padilla, José, 385

paella, 466. *See also* food

Paine, Thomas Paine, 176

Paist, Phineas, 342

Palacio Valdés, Armando, 404

Palma de Mallorca, 14, 307, 310, 410, 441

Palm Beach FL, 314, 341, 344–47, 359; Everglades Club in, *346*; King Library of the Society of the Four Arts in, 345; Via Mizner in, 347

Palmer, Bertha, 184

Palo Alto CA, 324

Palomino, Acislo Antonio, 279

Palos, 163

Palos Verdes Estates (California), 336

Palóu, Francisco, 116, 118, 121. *See also* Serra, Father Junípero

Pamphili, Camillo Astalli, 219

Pamplona, 11, 418, 429, 434, 435, *436*, 437; festival of San Fermín in, 11, 418, 434, 435

Panama, 239

Panama-California Exposition (San Diego), 24, 331–35, *334*, 450, 458, 524n36

Panama Canal, 14, 23, 187–88, 332, 456

Panama-Pacific International Exposition (San Francisco), 331, 449, 450

Pan-American Exposition (Buffalo), 24, 186–87, 322, 328–30, *329*

pan-Americanism: of A. M. Huntington, 198; and architecture, 328–31; beginnings of, 6, 186–87; in California, 332, 340; and Mexican craze, 16; and Spanish studies, 23, 187–88, 190, 193–95; Theodore Roosevelt on, 192; of Waldo Frank, 430. *See also* South America

Pan-American Union, 186. *See also* Bureau of the American Republics

Panza, Sancho, 113, 136, 210, 416, 417, 485n38
Pardo Bazán, Emilia, 399, 404
Parés, Émile, 268
Paris: American artists in, 3, 155–58, 256–58; American authors in, 7, 11, 170–72, 407–10, 418, 425, 434; architecture in, 328; artists from, 10; art market in, 218, 220, 221, 233, 237, 238, 272, 274, 275, 449; entertainment in, 22, 146, 374–77; Huntingtons in, 201, 207; John Y. Mason in, 60; Marqués de Vega-Inclán in, 442, 444; museums in, 199; Spanish art in, 236, 242, 263, 264, 267, 269–70, 273, 274, 280; U.S. exposition pavilion in, 458; U.S.-Spain peace treaty in, 75
Parkman, Francis, Jr., 98, 100, 101, 126
Park Ridge IL, 365
Parma, María Luisa de, 28
Partipilo, José, 385
Pasadena CA, 326; Carnival of Roses Festival in, 339
Payne-Aldrich Tariff Act, 235, 300
Peabody, Henry Greenwood, 333
Pearce, Ronald, 359
Pennell, Joseph, 74
Pennsylvania Academy of the Fine Arts, 156, 237, 255
Pennsylvania Gazette, 174
Pennsylvania Museum of Fine Arts, 254–56, 255, 270, 550n56. See also Philadelphia Museum of Art
Pensacola, 43, 45
Perdigón, Licinio, 195
Pereda, Antonio de, 259
Pérez de Ayala, Ramon, 424

Pérez de Hita, Ginés, 137–38
Pérez Galdós, Benito, 404
Pérez Reverte, Arturo, 467
Perkins, Charles C., 253, 256–58, 500n53
Perry, Horatio J., 59, 61, 246
Perry, Matthew, 16
Peru: A. M. Huntington's collecting in, 220, 494–95n118; archeology in, 183, 198; Charles Lummis in, 125; history of, 79; parks in, 317; race in, 192; Spanish conquest of, 34
Pettigrew, James Johnston, 52, 54–55, 57, 61
Pfeiffer, Pauline. See Hemingway, Pauline Pfeiffer
Philadelphia: American tourists from, 246; architecture in, 360, 368; art in, 12, 237, 238, 267, 270; artists from, 155, 156, 157; Banco Santander in, 461; Centennial Exposition in, 15, 64–65; Mummer's Parade in, 89; museum collections in, 293; publications in, 176; reaction to Whitman poem in, 115; R. W. Meade in, 236, 237; Spanish diplomats in, 44–47, 55; Spanish studies in, 174–76; Spanish themed entertainment in, 146, 377–78; trade exhibit in, 76
Philadelphia Central High School, 174
Philadelphia Museum of Art, 322, 455. See also Pennsylvania Museum of Fine Arts
Philadelphia Public College, 174, 175. See also University of Pennsylvania
Philadelphia Tractor Company, 266

Philip II, King, 16, 35, 37, 147, 163

Philip IV, King, *plate 5*, 231–33, *232*, 238, 263

Philippines, 1, 50, 77, 80, 128, 186, 215

Phillip, John, 153

Picasso, Pablo, 231, 276, 409, 410–12, 427, 443, 463

Pickford, Mary, 388, 392, 397

Pierce, Franklin, 53, 54, 60, 61

Pinckney, Thomas, 27–28, 41

Piquer, Concha (Conchita, flamenco dancer), 15, 397

Pittsburgh PA, 310

Pius X, Pope, 326

Pizarro, Francisco, 325

Pleasanton CA, 326

Poe, Edgar Allan, 9, 160, 401

Poem of the Cid, 206, 210

politics: and crazes, 16, 456–57, 462; during economic crisis, 468; under Francisco Franco, 465; of Lost Generation writers, 401, 417, 420, 429–31; in New Mexico, 111; and pan-Americanism, 191; of Spain and U.S., 20, 214–15, 467; after Spanish-American War, 77–78; and Spanish art, 248–50, 300–302; and Spanish language publications, 176; and tourism, 165, 454; troubles in Spanish, 141, 146–48, 152, 160, 163, 164, 285–87, 484n22; of Waldo Frank, 429. *See also* art: export from Spain

Polk, James, 53, 55–57, 474n54

Polk, Willis, 345–46

Ponce de León, Juan, 88, 90, 100–103, *102*, 310, 317; Thomas Moran's painting of, 314–15

Porter, Arthur Kingsley, 309

Porter, Katherine Anne, 454–55

The Portico, 52

Portugal: architectural style of, 305; De Soto historian from, 95; history of, 128; I. S. Gardner in, 261; John Rutledge in, 172; Napoleon's intentions in, 42; Robert Southey in, 135; study of, 73; Waldo Frank in, 424; W. R. Hearst in, 288

Portuguese language, 197, 199

Post, Marjorie Merriweather, *348*

Potter, Edward C., *166*, 167

Pound, Ezra, 401, 429

Powell, William (actor), 385

Powell, William H., *plate 1*, 96, 130

Prado Museum: A. M. Huntington at, 207; El Greco exhibit at, 443; Gertrude Stein at, 408; Henry Adams at, 31; holdings of, 199, 266; I. S. Gardner at, 260; John Hay at, 147; John Singer Sargent at, 157; replica of, 448; Theodore Roosevelt at, 81–82, 191, 192; visitors at, 242–48, 250, 258, 499n35, 499n39

Prescott, Vivian, 395

Prescott, William Hickling: effect on A. M. Huntington, 202; on Hernán Cortés, 98; *History of the Conquest of Mexico*, 92–93; *History of the Reign of Ferdinand and Isabel*, 34–35, 92; impressions of Spain, 21, 34–35, 79, 130, 131, 325, 401; influence of, 163, 195, 275, 342, 402, 425; as language student, 178; and Reconquest, 247; writing of, *94*

Prettyman, Harry E., 350
Price, William R., 188, 490n44
Prince, LeBaron Bradford, 106, 110–11, 113, 481n44
Princeton NJ, 450
Princeton University, 306
Pritchard, Emilio, 150
Prokop, Ellen, 264
A Proposal from a Spanish Don (film), 395
Protestants: attitudes toward Spain, 21, 28, 144; in California, 336; in Florida, 312; and Fr. Serra, 117, 118, 120, 121; in propaganda against Catholics, 8–9; Spain, 164
Puccini, Giacomo, 15
Puebla, Dióscoro, 65
Puebla, Mexico, 252, 333
Pueblo Indians, 423
Pueblo style, 356
Puerto Rico, 20, 57, 64, 88, 170, 186, 192, 442–43, 461
Pugin, Augustus, 328
Puglia, Santiago (James) Felipe, 175–77, 236
Pulitzer, Joseph, 21, 70, 166
Purchas, Samuel, 93–95
Puritans, 118, 327, 423

Quejana, 277, 280

race. *See* hispanidad
Ramírez, José Fernando, 95
Ramona (film), 388–92, *391*, 398
Ramona (Jackson), 9, 21–22, *119*, 123, 339, 388–92, 398
"Ramona" (song), 385–88, 390

"Ramona's House" mission, 335
Ramón y Cajal, Santiago, 196
Rancho Santa Fe, 336
Randolf, Thomas Mann, 172
Raphael, 244
Rapp, Isaac H., *356*, 357
Rau, William H., *166*
Real Madrid, 467
Reinhart, Charles Stanley, 157, 160, 162; *A Mandurra Sola*, *161*
religion. *See* Catholic Church; Jews; Protestants; Spain: civilization and evangelization by
Rembrandt, 269
Rennert, Hugo A., 170, 177
Renwick, James, Jr., 239, 498n20
Repsol (Spanish energy firm), 462
Requa, Richard, 335, 336
Revelers, 385
Revue Hispanique, 197
Reyes, Alfonso, 425
Reynolds, William, 322
Riaño y Gayangos, Juan, 209, 382, 449
Ribault, Jean, 91
Ribera, Julián, 105
Ribera, Jusepe de, 241, 248, 251, 300
Rice, Lilian, 336
Rich, Obadiah, 6–7, 237, 243–44, 497n13, 499n31
Richardson, H. H., 325
Ries, Ignacio de, 259
Riggs, George Washington, 95, 98
Rimsky-Korsakov, Nikolay, 377
Río, Dolores del, *plate 8*, 388, 390, 397
Ritch, William G., 109, 110, 113
Rivera, Diego, 15, 455
Riverside CA, 335, 450; Glenwood-Mission Inn in, 326, *327*, 337

Roaring Twenties, 331, 358–59

Roberts, David, 10, 153, 321

Robertson, William, 34, 71

Robles, José, 421

Rocafuerte, Vicente, 176

Rockefeller Foundation, 463

Rodríguez, Isabel, 377

Roehrig, Frederick, 326

Rollins College, 310

Roma. *See* gypsies

Rome, 251, 443

Romera-Navarro, Miguel, 402

Ronda, Spain, 288, 290, 302–4, 434

Roosevelt, Cornelius, 150

Roosevelt, Franklin D., 15, 454, 456

Roosevelt, Kermit, 81, 191

Roosevelt, Theodore: grandfather of, 150; and Panama Canal, 187; racial thinking of, 69; relations with Spain, 75; at San Diego exposition, 335; and Spanish-American War, 74, 192, 285, 476n89; visit to Spain, 81, 191–92; *Winning of the West*, 69, 192

Root, Elihu, 85

Rosa de Lima, Santa, 252–53

Rosita (film), 397

Round Hill School, 173–74

Rousseau, Jean-Jacques, 176

Royal Academy of Fine Arts (Spain), 243, 289, 301, 499n29

Royal Academy of History (Spain), 301

Royal Academy of Sciences (Spain), 76–77

Ruiz, Raimundo and Luis, 294, 301, 365

Ruiz de Burton, María Amparo, 115

Ruiz de Padrón, Josef, 175

Rusiñol, Santiago, 275–77

Ruskin, John, 249, 251, 253, 306, 307

Russia: containment during Cold War, 432, 465; influence in Spain, 456; literature in, 14, 403, 406, 415, 517n51; revolution in, 400, 420; tourist lectures on, 6

Rutledge, John, 172

Sacramenia monastery, 295, *296, 297*. *See also* Hearst, William Randolph

Saint-Gaudens, Augustus, 1–4, *2*, 10, 16, 76, 87, 133; Statue of Diana by, 319–22, *320*

Salamanca, 194, *195*, 203, 261, 307, 310; University of, 344

Sale, Kirkpatrick, 466

Sales, Francis, 178–79, 181, 236, 496n12

San Antonio TX, 310

Sánchez, Apolinar, 280

San Clemente CA, 336, 337

San Diego CA, *plate 7*, 24, 331, 450, 452, 458; Balboa Park in, 332–33, 335

San Francisco: Arabella Huntington in, 200; architecture in, 322–23, *323*, 325; art in, 251; entertainment in, 384, 390; international exposition in, 331, 449; Marqués de Vega-Inclán in, 450; mission in, 119–20; monastery in, 302; Spanish consul in, 190; statues in, 458

Sangre y arena (Blasco Ibáñez). See *Blood and Sand* (film)

San Marcos TX, 200–201

San Marino CA, 203

San Miguel de Allende, 456

San Sebastián, 162, 407, 424, 466

San Simeon, 21, 285, 288, *289*, 290–98, 309, 336; Casa Grande in, 288, *289*, 295–98

Santa Barbara CA, *336*, 336–40, *338*, 511n58; Casa del Herrero in, *plate 6*, 337, 511n58; El Paseo in, 337; Lobero Theatre, in, 337–39; Old Spanish Days festival in, 339–40, 384

Santa Fe (Spain), 357–58

Santa Fe NM: architecture in, *354 fig. 62*, *354 fig. 63*, 355–58; Charles Lummis in, 125–26; colonial history of, 103, 108–9; Fourth of July parade in, 113; Kirby Benedict in, 105; Marqués de Vega-Inclán in, 450; Order of Coronado in, 113; Palace of the Governors in, 108, *354 fig. 62*, *354 fig. 63*, 355–56; Scottish Rite temple in, *356*, 356–58, 513n96; Tertio-Millennial Celebration in, 103, 110–14, *112*; tourism in, 104, 109, 358

Santa Fe Trail, 111, 363

Santayana, George, 400, 408, 413, 517n39

Santiago de Compostela, 32–33, 312, 437

Santiago de Cuba, 63

Santo Domingo, 62, 454

Sant Pol de Mar, 421

Sarasota FL, 239

Sargent, John Singer: and art collectors, 260, 261; on authenticity of artwork, 273; and Charles Deering, 274–75, 277; influences on, 10, 157, 258, 264, 321, 419; *El Jaleo, plate 3*, 157–58, 264;

on Spanish fever, 8; and visiting Spain, 2, 3, 260

Sargent, Paul Dudley, 236

Sartain, William, 155, 156

Saunders, Romulus, 55–57

Savage, Juanita, 397

Schaus, William (art dealer), 239–41, 260

Schmidt-Nowara, Christopher, 192, 442

Schultz, Henry A., 326

Schurz, Carl, 61, 62

Schweinfurth, A. C., 326

Scott, Joseph, 85–86, 101, 123, 131

Scott, Samuel Parsons, 164, 170, 425, 486n56

Scott, Walter, 136

Scribner's Magazine, 158

Sears Roebuck & Co., 13–14, *353*, 355

Sedelmeyer, Charles (art dealer), 221, 272, 273

Segovia, 144, 261, 295, *296*, *297*, 307

Segurola, Andrés de, 377

Selig, William, 392

Seligmann, Jacques (art dealer), 221, 272

Selig Polyscope Company, 392

Serenade (film), 395

Serra, Father Junípero, 21–22, 86, 116–21, 123, 129, 130, 340, 468, 482n60

Sert, Josep Maria, 275–77

Sesto, Duke of, 221

Seven Years' War, 89

Seville: Alcázar palace in, 447, 452; A. M. Huntington in, 196, 212–16; architecture and furnishings in, 306, 309, 318, 321–23, 344, 348, 350, 360–65; archive of the Indies in, 97, 163;

Seville (*continued*)
    art in, 155–57, 239, 241, 243, 245,
    250, 261, 307; Augustus Saint-
    Gaudens in, 3; Barrio de Santa
    Cruz in, 451–52, *453*, 454; bull-
    fights in, 434; Edward Hale in,
    163; films set in, 397; Giralda in,
    13, 24, 318, 321; gypsies in, 144–
    45; historical research in, 127;
    Hospital de la Caridad in, 243;
    Ibero-American International
    Exposition in, 457–59, *460 fig.*
    88, *460 fig. 89*; I. S. Gardner in,
    260–61, *262*; Lord Byron in, 137;
    paintings of, 153; palace in, 212;
    parks in, 317; renovations in, 447,
    451–52, *453*; Richard Ford in, 142;
    Thomas Buckingham Smith in,
    97; Torre de Oro in, 350; as tour-
    ist destination, 22, 153, 164–65,
    451–52; U. S. Consulate in, 459;
    U.S. Grant in, 65; Waldo Frank
    in, 424; Washington Irving in, 8,
    140, 243; W. D. Howells in, 406;
    world's fair in, 465
Sewall, Blanche Harding, 309–10
Sewall, Rufus King, 88–89
Seward, William Henry, 62
Sexton, Randolph Williams, 351–55
Shaw, George Bernard, 390
sheep, merino, 236
Sheffield Scientific School, 190. *See*
    also Yale University
Sheldon, Lionel Allen, 113
Shinn, Edward. *See* Strahan, Edward
Sickles, Daniel, 63
Simitière, Pierre Eugène, *38*
Singer, Paris, 346

Sitges, 276–84, *278*, *279*, 450
Sitwell, Sacheverell, 428
Slidell. *See* Mackenzie, Alexander
    Slidell
Smith, Adam, 176, 209–10
Smith, Bud, 433, 437
Smith, Francis Hopkinson, 157,
    164–65
Smith, Franklin W., 314–16
Smith, George Washington, *plate 6*,
    335, 337–39, 359, 511n58
Smith, Julia, 150
Smith, Thomas Buckingham, 92–101,
    129, 150, 350
Smith College, 183
Smithsonian Institution, 76–77, 199
Snare, John, 241
Snell, Perry, 350
Society of California Pioneers, 120
Solera (restaurant), 466
Sorolla y Bastida, Joaquín: and art
    market, 220, 446–47; birthplace
    of, 503n92; collections of, 275,
    277; correspondence of, 444; HSA
    exhibit of, *226*, 227–29, 496n133;
    ¡Otra Margarita!, 275, *276*,
    503n92; popularity of, 12, 231,
    275–76, 300, 372, 449
Soto, Hernando de: description of,
    93; monuments for, 79, *166*, 167,
    344; portrayals of, *plate 1*, 130, *131*;
    publications about, 91, 96, 97, 128,
    479n20; travels of, 95–100, 468
Soulé, Pierre, *56*, 57–61, 76, 115,
    475n72
Soule, Winsor, 309, 352
Soult, Maréchal Jean-de-Dieu, 236, 238
The Sound of Music, 464

South America: books for, 175; education about, 190–91, 198; Spanish influence in, 129, 187, 442; Spanish language in, 192; tourism in, 448; U.S. neutrality in, 41, 44. *See also* Latin America; pan-Americanism

South Carolina, 52

South Carolina Interstate and West-Indian Exposition, 331

Southern Pacific Railroad, 200, 451

Southey, Robert, 135–36

Southwest, American: explorers in, 93, 104; Franciscan missions in, 126, 129; history in, 186, 423; maps of, 459; music in, 379, 380; portrayals of, 392; "Spanish Americans" in, 18, 106, 454; Spanish influence in, 9, 13, 14, 17, 21, 24, 123, 125, 132, 324, 326, 351, 450, 457, 462, 509n33; Spanish language education in, 173

Southwest Museum (Los Angeles), 85, 125

Southwest Society (Los Angeles), 380, 381

Soviet Union. *See* Russia

Spain: castles in, 13; civilization and evangelization by, 79–80, 85–86, 92–93, 98, 101, 105, 109–10, 113, 115–21, 126, 129–31, 325, 326, 357, 358, 389; civil war in, 25, 135, 302, 398, 421–23, 430–32, 439, 456, 462; Comisería Regia del Turismo, 134, 197–98, 441–42, 446–48, 451–52; constitutional freedoms in, 65; Cortes of, 58, 60–62, 68, 147, 267, 300; diplomatic relations with U.S.,

1–2, 209; and discovery of U.S., 79, 85, 86, 95; effect of craze in, 25; fishing in, 433–35, 437; immigrants from, 18, 455–56, 470n21; interest in history and culture of, 6–11, 72–74, 88, 133, 163–64, 169–70, 182–87, 190, 193, 194, 197, 226–29, 256–58, 366, 401–2, 407–8, 423, 425, 461, 468; map of, *5*; modernization in, 211–12; national character of, 1, 3, 8, 10, 21–22, 28–36, 41, 46–47, 54, 61–72, 76, 80, 87–88, 90–91, 98, 104, 105, 114, 121–23, 135, 136, 169, 170, 184, 192, 209–12, 247, 248, 307–8, 316, 317, 399–400, 406–7, 413–19, 424–31, 435, 437, 439, 446, 457, 464–65, 468, 473n38, 484n10, 517n49; as "natural enemy," 29–31, 35, 115, 131; naval involvement in Mexico, 46; paradores in, 452; Peninsular War in, 236; photographs of, 197, 211, 225, 226, 228, 245, 260–61, *262*, 290–92, 345; romance and lifestyle of, 133–46, 152, 155–57, 160–66, 308, 316–19, 322, 325–26, 335, 339, 340, 342, 347, 349, 358–67, 381, 393–98, 409, 485n24; Simancas archive in, 7, 97; sports in, 467; tourism in, 4–6, 7, 65–66, 74, 76, 133–34, 142, 152, 159–67, 211–12, 242, 247, 431, 441–43, 446–54, 464, 467. *See also* Sturdy Spain; Sunny Spain; United States: relations with Spain

The Spaniard (film), 397

Spaniards, definition of, 18–19

"The Spaniard That Blighted My Life," 384

Spanish-American War: aftermath of, 66, 75–77, 80–81, 131, 186, 192, 286–87, 408, 518n63; American attitudes toward, 69–72, 74, 129, 148, 402–4, 517n44, 517n50; and American interest in Spain, 6, 10–11, 194; films during, 393; immigration after, 18; lead-up to, 20, 21, 28, 35, 165, 214–15, 285; literature on, 476n85; and Pan-American Exposition, 328; Spanish literature after, 399; Theodore Roosevelt in, 74, 192, 285, 476n89; veterans of, 85

The Spanish Cavalier (film), 395

Spanish craze: and antiques collecting, 294; definition of, 16; duration of, 17, 367, 378, 431, 437, 439, 455–57; and films, 389, 393, 395, 398; at HSA, 228–29; inspirations for, 132, 133, 140, 310, 372–74, 377, 388, 400; and language study, 188; and literature, 402, 418–19, 423, 431; scholarship on, 23; and U.S.-Spanish history, 87, 351. *See also* Spanish fever

Spanish Dancer (film), 395–97

The Spanish Earth (film), 421, *422*, 431

Spanish fever: description of, 3–4; geographical scope of, 19–20; origins of, 194–95. *See also* Spanish craze

Spanish Fiesta (film), 397

The Spanish Gypsy (Eliot), 146

Spanish Gypsy (film), 395

Spanish language: American attitudes toward, 14, 81, 186, 188, 192, 403; A. M. Huntington's study of, 202;

Charles Lummis's knowledge of, 125, 126; education in, 23, 132, 170–83, 187–94, 401, 414, 451, 456, 462, 468, 489n28, 490n42, 491n51; Ernest Hemingway's knowledge of, 437; Henry Adams's knowledge of, 30; HSA's promotion of, 197, 199; publications in, 175–78; spoken in U.S., 105, 461, 468, 491n51; Waldo Frank's knowledge of, 424; W. D. Howells's knowledge of, 403, 406. *See also* literature; Spanish studies

Spanish Love (film), 385, *386*

"Spanish Love" (Gershwin), 385

Spanish missions: in California, 21–22, 79, 86, 116–19, *119*, 126, 130; portrayal of, 123; in Texas, 310; in U.S. history, 121, 129, 130

Spanish Onions (film), 398

A Spanish Romeo (film), 397

Spanish studies, 14, 23, 170–84, 194–95, 209, 402, 462–64, 467. *See also* literature; Spanish language

A Spanish Wooing (film), 392

Sparks, Jared, 91, 100

Spelter WV, 18

Squier, Ephraim G., 97

Stanford, Jane, 121, *122*

Stanford, Leland, 121, 324–25, 509n33

Stanford University. *See* Leland Stanford Junior University

St. Augustine FL: architecture in, 23, 313–17, 341; Fort of San Marcos (Fort Marion) in, 89, 312; history in, 88–90, 99, 100, 358; Magnolia Hotel in, 90; Parada de los Coches y Caballos in, 103; Ponce de León Hotel in, 23, 312–17, *313*, 325, 341; San Marco hotel in, 90, 312; tourism in, 101–3, 159, 206, 317; Villa Zorayda in, 314–16

St. Augustine Historical Society, 101, 310–12

Steedman, George, 337, 511n58

Stein, Gertrude, *411*; autobiographies by, 410, 412–13; correspondence of, 434, *436*; on Lost Generation, 401; and Spanish civil war, 457; on Spanish culture, 398; Spanish fever of, 11, 14, 25, 374, 407–15, 434, 435, 518n63; style and content of works, 412, 518n65

Stein, Leo, 408

Stein, Louise, 379

Stevenson, R. A. M., 264, 502n72

Stirling-Maxwell, William, 245, 272–73, 500n41

St. Louis, 79, 167, 228, 331, 372, 376, 477n117. *See also* Louisiana Purchase Exhibition

Stoddard, Charles A., 165

Stoddard, John L., 6, 152–53, *154*

Storey, Walter Rendell, 366–67

Stotesbury, Edward T., 347

St. Petersburg FL, 350

Strahan, Edward, 64–65

Street, George E., 223

Strong, George Templeton, 54

St. Simons Island GA, 367

Stuart, Henri L., 97

Sturdy Spain, 21–23, 86, 88, 163, 184, 210, 308, 325, 435. *See also* White Legend

Sturgis, Russell, 266

Sunny Spain: American interest in, 148; architecture inspired by, 355; art of, 153–59; description of, 144; gypsies in, 145; image of, 6, 9, 22, 87, 88, 152, 186, 397; and tourism, 153, 160, 162, 165, 167. *See also* Spain: romance and lifestyle of

Swinburne, Henry, 138

Symphonie espagnole (Lalo), 376

Taft, Lorado, 83, *84*, 85

Taft, William Howard, 12, 85, 228, 335, 450

talbotypes, 245

Tampa FL, 18, 68, 93, 350

tapas, 466. *See also* food

Tarragona, archbishop of, 279

Tate Gallery. *See* National Gallery of British Art

Taylor, Bayard, 159

Taylor, I. M. "Jack," 350

Temecula, 389

Tennessee, 41

Tenochtitlan, 92

Teresa, Saint, 308, 412, 427

Terry, Paul, 398

Terrytoons, 398

Texaco, 456

Texas: architecture in, 310, 327, 355; explorers in, 93; highway management in, 462; history in, 128, 186; Huntingtons in, 200–201, 203; Marqués de Vega-Inclán in, 450; Spanish craze in, 6; Spanish sovereignty in, 49; uprising in, 45, 46

Texas Technical College, 310, *311*

"That Wonderful Kid from Madrid" (MacDonald), 384–85

Theotokopoulos, Domenikos. *See* El Greco

Thompson, Virgil, 412

The Thousand and One Nights, 136–37

Thread of Destiny (film), 392

Throckmorton, Charles Wickliffe, 204

Thurston, John M., 79

Ticknor, George: influence of, 202; as literature instructor at Harvard, 178–79, 181; at Manchester art exhibit, 242; Spanish fever of, 9, 138–39, 195, 402; on Spanish national character, 210, 247

Tiffany, Louis C., 312

Time magazine, *375*, 376

Tin Pan Alley, 384–88

Tintoretto, 263

Tio Pepe, 466

Titian, 244

Tocqueville, Alexis de, 24, 132, 143

Toklas, Alice B., 410, 434, *436*

Tokyo, 16

Toledo: altarpiece from, 266–67; architecture in, 307, 310, 345, 349, 350; art collecting in, 267; art museums in, 197, 279, 282, 443–46, *445*; Augustus Saint-Gaudens in, 3; Capilla de San José in, 266–67; descriptions of, 147; I. S. Gardner in, 261; Mozarbic liturgy in, 307; Theodore Roosevelt in, 81, 191; tourist lectures on, 153; El Tránsito synagogue in, 447; U.S. Grant in, 65; W. D. Howells in, 406; W. R. Hearst in, *294*

Tolosa, 360

Tolstoy, Leo, 403, 406

Torquemada, 426–27

Toscanini, Arturo, 378

Toulouse, France, 108

trade: disputes over, 27–28, 35; exposition on, 64, 65; of Meades, 236; and pan-Americanism, 186, 191; publications about, 176; on Santa Fe Trail, 111; and Spanish studies, 172–75, 188, 189, 191; treaties regarding, 36–37, 40, 41, 49, 75, 76. *See also* economy

Transcontinental Treaty (1821), 11, 20, 35, *43*, 49–50, *51*, 89, 194, 237

Treaty of Guadalupe Hidalgo, 104

Treaty of Paris, 89

Treaty of San Lorenzo, 27–29, 41, 55

Trinidad CO, 106

Trinity College, 92

Trumbull, John, 96

Trump, Donald, 340

Tunis, 448

Turgot, Marquis de, 58–59, 475n72

Turin, 458

Turrell, Charles Alfred, 191

Twain, Mark, 24, 72, 129, 132, 215, 407

Twentieth Century Fox, 398

Two Brothers (film), 392

Tyler, Royall, 485n24

Tyrell, Henry, 229

Tyrone NM, 326

Ulloa, Agosto, 63

Unamuno, Miguel de, 170, 194, *195*, 210, 307–9, 399, 400

Unión Iberoamericana, 448

Union Pacific Railroad, 200

United Nations, 465

United States: annexation of Puerto Rico, 442–43; *Carmen* in, 146;

civil war in, 62, 77, 99, 109, 237, 253; colonial history of, 120, 468; crazes in, 16; Cuba Libre movement in, 68, 69; cultural revolution in, 400–402, 407; focus on Latin America, 454; immigration to, 17–18, 455–56, 470n21; links to Spain, 6, 79–80, 85–87, 96, 101, 114–15, 121–23, 126–32, 163, 172, 184, 317, 339–40, 351, 357, 409–10, 413, 427, 518n63; Marqués de Vega-Inclán in, 449–51; Marshall Plan of, 465; national character of, 15, 24, 27, 29, 34–35, 47–48, 52, 66–67, 114–16, 132, 234–35, 285–87, 327–28, 331, 350, 351, 355, 398, 413–16, 423, 517n49; racial distinctions in, 18–19, 35–36, 54, 66–67, 69, 71, 73, 74, 80, 106, 113–15, 132, 192–93, 195, 199, 330, 358, 384, 400; relations with Spain, 1–2, 14, 20–23, 27–28, 32, 35, 36, 49–55, 60–66, 72–80, 132, 135, 163–66, 170–73, 192–93, 236–37, 424, 457–59, 467, 472n24; religion in, 96; revolutionary war in, 37–39; Spanish fever in, 3–4, 11–17, 19–20, 22–24, 453–54, 462, 468; tourists from, 134–35, 148–53, 159, 431, 442–43, 448–55; treatment of Native Americans, 482n60; westward expansion of, 27, 37, 57, 97, 129, 246, 380; women filmed in, 393

Universal Exposition (Paris), 458

University of Arizona, 191

University of California, 121, 128, 183, 295, 517n39

University of Chicago, 183, 189, 464, 492n84

University of Michigan, 178, 488n19

University of Pennsylvania, 174, 177, 183, 402. *See also* Philadelphia Public College

University of Texas, 128, 183, 198

University of Virginia, 172, 177

Uriarte, Hipólito de, 241

U.S. Army, 125

U.S. Bureau of Education, 174

U.S. Congress: on Adams-Onís Treaty, 49; attitude toward Spain, 78; on capitol rotunda paintings, 96; and Cuba, 53, 63, 64, 285; and education exchange programs, 76; and funding of Columbus monument, 83–85, 478n1; and funding of New Mexico capitol, 108; on seizure of *Black Warrior*, 59; on tariffs, 235; and treaties with Spain, 40–41, 75, 465; and war with Spain, 214, 215, 404

U.S.-Mexico War (1846–48), 96, 104, 130, 178

Utrillo, Miquel, 275–81, 284

Valdés, Palacio, 517n50

Valencia, 207, 237, 412, 414, 497n13, 503n92; Lonja (Merchant's Guild) in, 322, 345

"Valencia: A Song of Spain," 385

Valencia de Don Juan, Count of, 82

Valentino, Rudolph, 395

Valera, Juan, 424

Valladolid, 197, 202, 284, 406, 447, 449; cathedral of, 268, 300; grille from cathedral of, 297, *298*, 299

Vallejo, Guadalupe, 17, 448

Vallejo, Mariano G., 115–16

Valverde, Joaquín "Quinito," 371

Vanderbilt, William K., 359; Eagle's Nest home of, *359*

Vanderbilt family, 205–6

Vanderlyn, John, 65, 96

Van Dyck, Sir Anthony, 259, 268

Van Horne, William C., 273–74, 300

Van Rensselaer, Mariana Griswold, 321

Van Vechten, Carl, 25, 371–74, 377–78, 410, 419, 518n63; *Music of Spain*, 371, 378

Vargas, Diego de, 113

Vargas, Luis de, 272

Veblen, Thorstein, 235

Vega, Lope de, 175, 416

Vega-Inclán, Marqués de: art sales of, 444–46; and Charles Deering, 275, 282; museums of, 197; and Santa Cruz barrio renovation, 452; tourist commission of, 134, 198, 431, 441–54; tourist lodgings designed by, 452–53, 459; visit to U.S., 449–50

Velázquez, Diego: Americans' attitudes toward, 244, 245, 248–49; A. M. Huntington's viewing of, 207; in art guide, 447; authenticity of paintings by, 274; collections of, *plate 5*, 200, 220, 231–33, 238–41, 250, 259, 260, 263, 266–69, 272–74, 279, 287–88, 300, 502n76; Henry James's viewing of, 251; influence of, 10, 23, 155–57, 246, 258, 264–66, 307, 374, 407, 416, 427, 429, 502n72; *King Philip IV*, *plate 5*; publications about, 272–73; Theodore Roosevelt's admi-

ration of, 82, 191; *Venus with a Mirror*, 219, 494n114

Vélez Blanco, 269, *271*

Venezuela, 41, 43, 454

Venice, 344, 347, 443

Vere, Macmillan Schere de, 177

Vermeer, Jan, 259

Vermont, 108

Verus. *See* Onís, Luis de

Viardot, Louis, 245

Vich, 349

Vicky Cristina Barcelona (film), 467

Vienna, 242

Vigo, 432, 433

Villalta, Nicanor, 435

Villanueva del Pardillo, 144, 485n26

Villegas, José, 501n63

Vincent, Marvin Richardson, 162

Virginia, 198, 200, 352

Virginius (ship), 63, 64

Vitaphone shorts, 397

Voltaire, 71, 135, 427

Vysekal, E. A., 358, 513n96

Wagner, Richard, 4

Walker, John, 374

Wallace Collection, 251

Wallis, Severn Teackle, 142–43, 146, 150, 247, 485n24

Walsh, Raoul, *plate 8*, 378, 395, 397

Walters, William T., 238

Wanamaker, John, 366

Ward, Alice, 209

Warner, Charles Dudley, 129

Warren & Wetmore architects, *359*

Washington, George, 36, 93, 160, 236, 454

Washington DC: Alibi Club in, 75; Carmencita in, 6; Columbus monument in, 83–86, 478n1; Emilio de Ojeda in, 77–79; entertainment in, 372, 376; Gridiron Cub in, 78–79; Joaquin Sorolla in, 12; Joseph Scott's speech in, 123; Juan Riaño y Gayangos in, 209; Luis de Onís in, 49; Marqués de Vega-Inclán in, 449–51; restaurants in, 466; Spain's history depicted in Capitol, 65, 96, 130–31, 314; Spanish-American Athenaeum in, 450; Spanish tourist lectures in, 153

Washington Post, 153, 395, 398

Watkin, William Ward, 310, *311*

Watkins, Tobias, 52

Waugh, Alex, 347–48

"Way Down Barcelona Way" (Fisher), 385

Wayne, Mabel, 385, *387*, 388

Weeks, Mabel, 408

Weems, Mason Lock (aka Parson), 93

Weir, J. Alden, 157

Weir, Robert, 96

West Hartford CT, 367

West Indies, 236, 239

West Orange NJ, 393

West Palm Beach FL, 349

West Virginia, 18

Westward Ho! (Kingsley), 486n54

Weyler, Valeriano, 69

Wharton, Edith, 11, 133

Whistler, James, 260, 264, 275

White, Stanford, 13, 24, 318–22, 323, 346, 419

White Legend, 9, 126, 131. *See also* Sturdy Spain

Whiteman, Paul, 385

Whitman, Walt, 9, 113–15, 351

Whittlesey, Austin, 309, 351–52

Widener, Peter A. B., 266–67, 270, 273, 300, 444

The Wild Cat (film), 397

Wilkie, David, 140, 243

Wilkins, Ernest Hatch, 189–90

Wilkins, Lawrence A., 194

Wilkinson, James, 41

Willard, Belle Wyatt, 81

Willard, Joseph E., 81, 289

Willis, Augustus, 177

Willis, Charles F., 150

Willis, Nathan Parker, 150

Wills, Gary, 27

Willstach, William O., 150

Wilmer, Lambert, 98

Wilmette IL, 364–65

Wilson, Chris, 357–58

Wilson, Woodrow, 450

Wilson-Gorman Tariff Act, 68

Winslow, Carleton M., 333, 337

Winter Park FL, 310

Witmer, D. Paul, *366*, 367

Workman, Fanny Bullock, 165

World's Columbian Exposition (Chicago): architecture at, 13, 24, 85, 322–25, *324*, 331, 356–57, 458, 509n33; California State Building at, 13, 24, 323, *324*, 325, 333, *334*, 458; Diana sculpture at, 320; financing of, 83–84; interest in Spain at, 6, 79, 184; replica of La Rábida monastery at, 184, 322; Sorolla works at, 227, 275–76; Spanish ships at, 184. *See also* Chicago

World War I: and A. M. Huntington's collecting, 220; effect on
U.S. culture, 400; Gertrude Stein
during, 11, 410, 413; home for
veterans of, 346; John Dos Passos during, 417; and language
study, 132, 187–88; and literature,
14–15, 399, 401, 407, 423–31;
paintings of, 277; Spanish craze
during, 24, 371, 377; and Spanish tourism, 441, 448, 454; W. R.
Hearst on, 286
Wright, Richard, 413
Wyntoon CA, 297, 298

Yale Review, 190–91
Yale University, 177, 183, 190, 198,
206, 423, 489n28, 492n84. *See also*
Sheffield Scientific School
Young, Ammi Burnham, 108

Young, Joe, 385, *387*
Young, Loretta, 398
Young America movement, 57

Zara (Spanish clothing firm), 461
Zaragoza, 472n24
zarzuelas, 371
Zola, Émile, 403
Zorn, Anders, 275, 277
Zorro, 19
Zuloaga, Daniel, 280
Zuloaga, Ignacio, 227, 228, 275–77,
280, 300, 372, 416
Zurbarán, Francisco de: *Apparition of
Saint Peter to Saint Peter Nolasco*,
248; collections of, 231, 259, 261–
64, *262, 265*, 273–74; *Doctor of Laws
at Salamanca, plate 4*, 263; exhibi-
tions of, 242, 251, 300; influence of,
23; *Saint Romanus*, 277, 280